Lecture Notes in Artificial Intelligence 1501

Subseries of Lecture Notes in Computer Science
Edited by J. G. Carbonell and J. Siekmann

Lecture Notes in Computer Science

Edited by G. Goos, J. Hartmanis and J. van Leeuwen

T0241058

Springer
Berlin
Heidelberg
New York
Barcelona
Budapest
Hong Kong
London
Milan
Paris
Singapore
Tokyo

Michael M. Richter   Carl H. Smith
Rolf Wiehagen   Thomas Zeugmann (Eds.)

Algorithmic Learning Theory

9th International Conference, ALT'98
Otzenhausen, Germany, October 8-10, 1998
Proceedings

 Springer

Volume Editors

Michael M. Richter
Universität Kaiserslautern, AG Künstliche Intelligenz - Expertensysteme
Postfach 3049, D-67653 Kaiserslautern, Germany
E-mail: richter@informatik.uni-kl.de

Carl H. Smith
University of Maryland, Department of Computer Science
College Park, MD 20742, USA
E-mail: smith@cs.umd.edu

Rolf Wiehagen
Universität Kaiserslautern, AG Algorithmisches Lernen
Postfach 3049, D-67653 Kaiserslautern, Germany
E-mail: wiehagen@informatik.uni-kl.de

Thomas Zeugmann
Kyushu University
Graduate School of Information Science and Electrical Engineering
Department of Informatics
Kasuga 816-8580, Japan
E-mail: thomas@i.kyushu-u.ac.jp

Cataloging-in-Publication Data applied for

Die Deutsche Bibliothek - CIP-Einheitsaufnahme

Algorithmic learning theory : 9th international conference ;
proceedings / ALT '98, Otzenhausen, Germany, October 8 - 10, 1998.
Michael M. Richter ... (ed.). - Berlin ; Heidelberg ; New York ;
Barcelona ; Budapest ; Hong Kong ; London ; Milan ; Paris ;
Singapore ; Tokyo : Springer, 1998
  (Lecture notes in computer science ; Vol. 1501 : Lecture notes in
  artificial intelligence)
  ISBN 3-540-65013-X

CR Subject Classification (1991): I.2.6, I.2.3, F.4.1, I.7

ISBN 3-540-65013-X Springer-Verlag Berlin Heidelberg New York

© Springer-Verlag Berlin Heidelberg 1998
Printed in Germany

Typesetting: Camera ready by author
SPIN 10638952   06/3142 – 5 4 3 2 1 0   Printed on acid-free paper

Preface

This volume contains all the papers presented at the Ninth International Conference on Algorithmic Learning Theory (ALT'98), held at the European education centre Europäisches Bildungszentrum (ebz) Otzenhausen, Germany, October 8–10, 1998. The Conference was sponsored by the Japanese Society for Artificial Intelligence (JSAI) and the University of Kaiserslautern.

Thirty-four papers on all aspects of algorithmic learning theory and related areas were submitted, all electronically. Twenty-six papers were accepted by the program committee based on originality, quality, and relevance to the theory of machine learning. Additionally, three invited talks presented by Akira Maruoka of Tohoku University, Arun Sharma of the University of New South Wales, and Stefan Wrobel from GMD, respectively, were featured at the conference. We would like to express our sincere gratitude to our invited speakers for sharing with us their insights on new and exciting developments in their areas of research.

This conference is the ninth in a series of annual meetings established in 1990. The ALT series focuses on all areas related to algorithmic learning theory including (but not limited to): the theory of machine learning, the design and analysis of learning algorithms, computational logic of/for machine discovery, inductive inference of recursive functions and recursively enumerable languages, learning via queries, learning by artificial and biological neural networks, pattern recognition, learning by analogy, statistical learning, Bayesian/MDL estimation, inductive logic programming, robotics, application of learning to databases, and gene analyses.

The variety of approaches presented in this and the other ALT proceedings reflects the continuously growing spectrum of disciplines relevant to machine learning and its applications. The many possible aspects of learning that can be formally investigated and the diversity of viewpoints expressed in the technical contributions clearly indicate that developing models of learning is still particularly important to broaden our understanding of what learning really is, under which circumstances it can be done, what makes it feasible and complicated, respectively, and what are appropriate tools for analyzing it. This ALT conference as well as its predecessors aimed to extend and to intensify communication in the continuously growing scientific community interested in the phenomenon of learning.

Starting this year, the ALT series will further endeavor to bring both the theoretical and the experimental communities under one umbrella by organizing a satellite workshop on *applied learning theory* before or after the annual meeting. Ideally, people in theory should benefit by learning about challenging research problems which arose in practice, and people in application may benefit by getting answers to their problems from theoreticians. Putting these two activities under the unifying ALT logo prompted us to rename the ALT series into *annual conference on Algorithmic Learning Theory*.

The continuing success of these ALT meetings has been managed and supervised by its steering committee consisting of Setsuo Arikawa (Chair, Kyushu Univ., Fukuoka), Takashi Yokomori (Waseda Univ., Tokyo), Hiroshi Imai (Univ. of Tokyo), Teruyasu Nishizawa (Niigata Univ.), Akito Sakurai (JAIST, Tokyo), Taiske Sato (Tokyo Inst. Technology), Takeshi Shinohara (Kyushu Inst. Technology, Iizuka), Masayuki Numao (Tokyo Inst. Technology), and Yuji Takada (Fujitsu, Fukuoka).

ALT'98 was chaired by Michael M. Richter (University of Kaiserslautern) and co-chaired by Carl H. Smith (University of Maryland, College Park). The local arrangements chair was Edith Hüttel (University of Kaiserslautern).

We would like to express our immense gratitude to all the members of the program committee, which consisted of:

P. Bartlett (ANU, Australia)
S. Ben-David (Technion, Israel)
S. Dzeroski (Jozef Stefan Institute, Slovenia)
R. Gavaldà (Univ. de Catalunya, Spain)
L. Hellerstein (Polytechnic Univ., USA)
S. Jain (National Univ. Singapore)
S. Lange (Univ. Leipzig, Germany)
M. Li (Univ. Waterloo, Canada)
H. Motoda (Osaka Univ., Japan)
Y. Sakakibara (Tokyo Denki Univ., Japan)
K. Satoh (Hokkaido Univ., Japan)
T. Shinohara (Kyutech, Japan)
E. Ukkonen (Helsinki Univ., Finland)
R. Wiehagen (Univ. Kaiserslautern, Germany, Chair)
T. Zeugmann (Kyushu Univ., Japan, Co-Chair)

They and the subreferees they enlisted put a huge amount of work into reviewing the submissions and judging their importance and significance.

We would like to thank everybody who made this meeting possible: the authors for submitting papers, the invited speakers for accepting our invitation, the local arrangement chair Edith Hüttel, the ALT steering committee, the sponsors, IFIP Working Group 1.4, for providing a student scholarship, and Springer-Verlag. Furthermore, the program committee heartily thanks all referees who are listed on a separate page for their hard work. We also gratefully acknowledge Shinichi Shimozono's contribution in helping to produce the ALT'98 logo, and Masao Mori's assistance for setting up the ALT'98 Web pages.

Kaiserslautern   Michael M. Richter
College Park   Carl H. Smith
Kaiserslautern   Rolf Wiehagen
Fukuoka   Thomas Zeugmann
July 1998

List of Subreferees

Dana Angluin

Hiroki Arimura

Jose L. Balcazar

Carlos Domingo

Sally Goldman

Tibor Hegedüs

Koichi Hirata

Eiju Hirowatari

Hiroki Ishizaka

Roni Khardon

Jyrki Kivinen

Satoshi Kobayashi

Takeshi Koshiba

M.R.K. Krishna Rao

Phil Long

Zdravko Markov

Tetsuhiro Miyahara

Yasuhito Mukouchi

Masayuki Numao

Yoshiaki Ohkubo

Seishi Okamoto

Vijay Raghavan

Ayumi Shinohara

Frank Stephan

Noriko Sugimoto

György Turán

Dawn Wilkins

Akihiro Yamamoto

Takashi Yokomori

Table of Contents

Inductive Logic Programming

Learning Formal Languages

Inductive Inference

Inductive Logic Programming

Miscellaneous

Editors' Introduction

Learning Theory emerged roughly forty years ago, and some of the pioneering work is still influential, e.g., Gold's (1967) paper on *Language Identification in the Limit*.[1] Despite the huge amount of research invested in this area, the state of the art in modeling learning is still much less satisfactory than in other areas of theoretical computer science. For example, around 60 years ago *computability theory* emerged. Initially, many different models have been introduced, e.g., Turing machines, partial recursive functions, and Markov algorithms. Nevertheless, later on, all those models have been proved to be equivalent.

The situation in algorithmic learning theory is, however, quite different. Numerous mathematical models of learning have been proposed during the last three decades. Nevertheless, different models give vastly different results concerning the learnability and non-learnability of objects one wants to learn. Hence, finding an appropriate definition of learning which covers most aspects of learning is also part of the goals aimed at in algorithmic learning theory. Additionally, it is necessary to develop a unified theory of learning as well as techniques to translate the resulting theories into applications. On the other hand, machine learning has also found interesting and non-trivial applications but often our ability to thoroughly analyze the systems implemented does not keep up proportionally.

Moreover, nowadays the data collected in in various fields such as biology, finance, retail, astronomy, medicine are extremely rapidly growing, but our ability to discover useful knowledge from such huge data sets is still too limited. Clearly, powerful learning systems would be an enormous help in automatically extracting new interrelations, knowledge, patterns and the like from those and other *huge* collections of data. Thus, there are growing challenges to the field of machine learning and its foundations that require further efforts to develop the theories needed to provide, for example, performance guarantees, to automize the development of relevant software and the like.

Each learning model specifies the learner, the learning domain, the source of information, the hypothesis space, what background knowledge is available and how it can be used, and finally, the criterion of success. For seeing how different models can arise by specifying these parameters, we shall outline throughout this introduction different possibilities to do so. While the learner is always an algorithm, it may also be restricted in one way or another, e.g., by requiring it to be space and/or time efficient. The different learning domains considered range from learning unknown concepts, such as table, chair, car, different diseases and so on. What is then aimed at is learning a "rule" to separate positive examples from negative ones. For example, given a description of symptoms, the "rule" learned must correctly classify whether or not a particular disease is present.

In his invited lecture, Maruoka (co-authored by Takimoto) is studying structured weight-based prediction algorithms. The prediction algorithms considered

---

[1] Information and Control 10:447-474.

have a pool of experts, say $E_1, \ldots, E_N$, that at each trial, on input any member of the underlying domain, outputs either zero or one. That is, the experts perform a classification task as described above. The algorithm somehow combines these predictions and outputs its classification. Afterwards, the true classification is received, and the next trial starts. If the output made by the learner has been false, a prediction error occurred. When making a prediction error, the learner gets a penalty that is expressed by a suitably defined loss function. The learning goal consists in minimizing the loss function. The experts are assigned weights which are updated after each trial. While previous work considered the experts to be arranged on one layer only, the present paper outlines interesting ways to arrange the experts on a tree structure. As a result, the expert model can be applied to search for the best pruning in a straightforward fashion by using a dynamic programming scheme.

Learning Logic Programs and Formulae

Inductive logic programming and learning logic programs constitutes a core area of the ALT meetings, too. The basic scenario can be described as follows. The learner is generally provided background knowledge B as well as (sequences of) positive (E^+) and negative examples (E^-) (all of which can be regarded as logic programs, too). However, E^+ and E^- usually contain only ground clauses with empty body. The learning goal consists in inferring a hypothesis H (again a logic program) such that E^+ can be derived from $B \wedge H$ while $B \wedge H \wedge E^-$ is contradiction free. Again, if growing initial segments of E^+ and E^- are provided, we arrive at learning in the limit. Variations of this model include the use of membership queries to obtain E^+ and E^- and of equivalence queries (or disjointness queries) to terminate the learning process. Recently, various authors looked also at different possibilities to formulate queries, and we shall describe some of them when talking about the relevant papers in these proceedings. Alternatively, E^+ and E^- may be drawn randomly with respect to some unknown probability distribution, and the learner is required to produce with high confidence a hypothesis that has small error (both measured with respect to the underlying probability distribution).

In his invited lecture, Wrobel addresses scalability issues in inductive logic programming. This research is motivated by demands in *knowledge discovery in databases*. Very often, the databases available store the information in relational database management systems. On the other hand, most currently used knowledge discovery methods rely on propositional data analysis techniques such as decision tree learners (C4.5), or propositional rule learning methods (e.g. CN2). While these methods have the benefit of being efficient in practice, they cannot directly deal with multiple relations that are typical for relational databases. Inductive logic programming is much better suited for such purposes, but until recently it lacked the efficiency to deal with huge amount of data. Scalability turned out to be very important in this regard, and Wrobel's paper presents the progress made recently.

In their invited paper McCreath and Sharma present LIME: a system for learning relations. Their inductive logic programming system induces logic programs from ground facts. This is done via a Bayesian heuristic, where explosion of the search space is tamed by exploiting the structure of the hypothesis space. Prior probabilities are assigned by applying Occam's razor, i.e., simpler hypotheses get higher probability. Favoring the Bayesian approach leads to another peculiarity. In contrast to a variety of other approaches, LIME is *not* growing a clause one literal at a time. Instead, it builds candidate clauses from groups of literals. The clauses obtained can be efficiently combined for obtaining new clauses such that the coverage of the resulting clause is just the intersection of the coverage of the clauses it is built from. The overall result is a learning system for the fixed example size framework that is, as experiments show, particularly good when it has to learn recursive definitions in the presence of noise.

Krishna Rao and Sattar present a polynomial time learning algorithm for a rich class of logic programs, thereby considerably extending and (partially correcting) results obtained by Arimura.[2] The information source are equivalence, subsumption and request-for-hint queries. Input to a subsumption query is a clause C, and it is answered "yes" iff C is a tautology or $H^* \models C$, where H^* denotes the target concept. Otherwise, the answer is just "no." A request-for-hint query takes as input a ground clause, and answers "yes" provided C is subsumed by H^*. Otherwise, the reply is "no" and a hint, i.e., an atom along with a suitable substitution that can be refuted from target and the body of ground clause is returned. As a matter of fact, all these queries can be answered in time polynomial in the length of the target and C. The main new feature included in their article is the target class of finely-moded logic programs that allow to include *local variables*. Moreover, background knowledge previously learned is incrementally used during the learning process.

Besides ILP and the techniques developed within this framework, there is another major line of research that conceptually fits into the setting of learning logic programs, i.e., learning subclasses of concepts expressible by *elementary formal systems* (abbr. EFS). This year, Sugimoto is continuing along this line of research by extending the EFS's to linearly-moded EFS's. Again, the main new feature is the inclusion of *local variables* that turned out to be important to define translations over context-sensitive languages. The main goal is then the design of an efficient learner for such translations from input-output sentences, i.e., positive examples only. This goal is partially achieved by providing an algorithm that learns the whole class of translations definable by linearly-moded EFS's such that the number of clauses in the defining EFS's and the length of each clause are bounded by some *a priori* fixed constant. A natural generalization of this result would be bounding the length of the output sentences by a constant multiple of the input length. However, the resulting class of translations is *not* learnable from data at all.

Yamamoto provides a rigorous analysis of several learning techniques devel-

---

[2]H. Arimura, Learning acyclic first-order Horn sentences from entailment, *in* Proc. ALT'97, Lecture Notes in Artificial Intelligence 1316, pp. 432–445.

oped in the area of machine learning such as saturant generalization, bottom generalization, V^*-operation with generalization and inverse entailment. The main goal is to present a unifying framework from which all these methods can be obtained as instances. Within this framework obtained the methods are compared to one another, e.g. with respect to their inference power.

Satoh is dealing with case-based representability of Boolean function. Intuitively, a case base contains knowledge already obtained. If a new task has to be handled, i.e., one that is not in the case base, one looks for a case that is similar, where the similarity is measured by an appropriate measure. Finding good similarity measures has attracted considerable attention. Looking at a similarity measure that is based on set inclusion of different attributes in a case, Satoh establishes nice connections to the monotone theory initiated by Bshouty in 1993.

Finally, Verbeurgt addresses the problem of learning subclasses of monotone DNF. Learning DNF efficiently is for sure of major interest but apparently very hard. The learning model considered is a variant of the Valiant's PAC-learning model. In this model, examples are drawn randomly, and with high confidence, one has to find a hypothesis that has only a small error. Here, the error is measured by summing up all probabilities for elements in the symmetric difference of the target and the hypothesis output. Usually, the learner has to succeed for every underlying probability distribution. The version considered by Verbeurgt restricts the class of probability distributions to the uniform distribution. He extends previous results on read-once DNF within this model by refining the Fourier analysis methodology.

Learning Formal Languages

In this setting, the learning domain is the set of all strings over some fixed finite alphabet, and the different objects to be learned are subsets of strings. The source of information may be augmenting initial segments of sequences exhausting all strings over the underlying alphabet that are classified with respect to their containment in the target language (learning from informant), or just growing initial segments of sequences containing eventually all the strings that belong to the target language (text, or positive data). The learner has then to map finite sequences of strings into hypotheses about the target language. The investigation of scenarios in which the sequence of computed hypotheses stabilizes to a correct finite description (e.g., a grammar, an acceptor, a pattern) of the target has attracted much attention and is referred to as *learning in the limit*. Instead of requesting the learner to converge syntactically one can also consider semantical convergence, i.e., beyond some point exclusively hypotheses are output that generate the same language. The latter scenario is usually referred to as *behaviorally correct learning*. As for the present volume, there are several papers dealing with these models.

Head *et al.* study the learnability of subclasses of regular languages. While the whole class of regular languages has been known to be non-inferable from positive data, certain subclasses are. In particular, they pinpoint the common, essential properties of the previously unrelated frameworks of reversible languages and locally testable languages by defining and studying equivalence relations over the states of finite automata. If appropriately defined, both language classes emerge. The learnability result is based on Angluin's characteristic sample technique and all definable classes are shown to be learnable. Then, finally, the authors show that even the whole class of regular languages is *approximately* identifiable by using any of the defined classes as hypothesis space. That is, instead of synthesizing an acceptor correctly describing the target language, the best fit from the hypothesis space is learned.

Case and Jain consider indexed families of uniformly recursive languages, i.e., language classes that are recursively enumerable in a way such that the membership problem is uniformly decidable for all languages enumerated. Now, given as input any index (or a program) generating any such class, they address the problem of whether or not a learner, if there is any, can be algorithmically synthesized that learns the whole class even from noisy data. Noisy data are defined along the model introduced by Stephan in his ALT'95 paper. Roughly speaking, in this model correct data occur infinitely often while incorrect data are presented only finitely many times. The new restriction made is that the noisy data are computable. Then, the main positive result obtained is very strong: grammars for each indexed family can be learned from computable noisy positive data within the framework to converge semantically. And these learners can *all* be *synthesized*. Thus, there is a huge gap of what can be learned in a completely computable universe and from arbitrary positive data. In particular, these results show that additional background knowledge can considerably enhance the learning capabilities.

In a sense, Stephan and Ventsov study the same problem though in a different context, i.e., whether or not background knowledge may help in learning (here called semantical knowledge). Now, the language classes are defined via algebraic structures (e.g., monoids, ideals of a given ring, vector spaces) and the background knowledge is provided in the form of programs for the underlying algebraic operations. What is shown is that such background knowledge can improve both, the overall learning power as well as the efficiency of learners (measured in the number of mind changes to be performed). Finally, a pure algebraic notion is characterized in terms of pure learning theory. A recursive commutative ring is Noetherian iff the class of its ideals is behaviorally correct learnable from positive data.

But there are more ways to attack the problem of how additional knowledge may help. In her ALT'95 paper, Meyer has observed that in the setting of learning indexed families from positive data, probabilistic learning under monotonicity constraints is more powerful than deterministic learning. A probabilistic learner is allowed to flip a coin each time it reads a new example, and to branch its computation in dependence on the outcome of the coin flip. The monotonicity constraints formalize different versions of how to realize the *subset principle* to avoid overgeneralization, and these formalizations go in part back to Jantke's paper at the very first ALT meeting in 1990. This year, Meyer asks what knowledge is necessary to *compensate* the additional power of probabilistic learners. Now, knowledge is provided in form of oracles, and instead of flipping a coin, the deterministic learner may ask the oracle A a membership query, i.e., "$x \in A$?," where x depends on the examples received so far. For getting a flavor of the results obtained, we just mention two. First, if probabilistic learners under monotonicity constraints are requested to learn with probability ($p > 2/3$ and $p > 1/2$ in dependence on the particular type of the monotonicity constraint) then the oracle for the halting problem does suffices to compensate the power of probabilistic learning. However, these bounds are tight, i.e., if $p = 2/3$ ($p = 1/2$), then the oracle for the halting problem is too weak.

Certain classes of languages are not inferable from positive data among them the regular languages and any superset thereof. This result goes back to Gold's (1967) paper, where he showed that every language class containing at least one infinite language and all finite languages is not learnable from positive data. Thus, one may think that there are no interesting languages classes at all that can be inferred from positive data. However, this is a misleading impression. The most prominent counterexample are the pattern languages introduced by Angluin in 1980. Patterns are a very natural and convenient way to define languages. Take some constant symbols and symbols for variables. Then every finite non-null string over these symbols constitutes a pattern, e.g. ax_1bbx_1. The language generated by a pattern π is the set of all strings that can be obtained by substituting constant strings for the variables occurring in π. A pattern is said to be regular if every variable symbol occurs at most once in it.

Sato *et al.* study the learnability of the language class RP^k that can be obtained by taking the union of at most k regular pattern languages, where k is *a priori* fixed. This class has be shown to be learnable from positive data by Wright in 1989. Thus, there are characteristic samples for all these languages, i.e., for every language L there is a finite sets $S \subseteq L$ such that $S \subseteq L'$ implies $L \subseteq L'$ for every $L' \in RP^k$. These characteristic samples play an important role in the design of learning algorithms. The present paper shows that there is a simple way for getting such characteristic samples by taking all substitutions of size 1 (or 2) provided there are at least $2k + 1$ ($2k - 1$) many constants.

Sakamoto studies the versions of the consistency problem for one-variable pattern languages that may be interesting when learning from noisy data is required. The problem is, given a set of positive and negative examples, respectively, does there exist a one-variable pattern generating all positive examples and none of the negative ones. The new idea introduced is that the given strings may contain wild cards. In particular, he shows the consistency problem to be NP-complete provided the pattern must separate the set of positive and negative examples for all possible replacements of the wild cards by constant symbols.

In all the papers mentioned above, the learner has been required to behave appropriately when getting data for the languages to be learned. This also implied that some prior knowledge is provided in the form of a suitable hypothesis space. However, looking at applications such as data mining, it is well conceivable that we do not have such prior knowledge. Thus, one may just guess a hypothesis space. But then the question arises of how the learner behaves when getting data for a target that has no representation within the guessed hypothesis space. This question is meaningful as long as the hypothesis space guessed is not an acceptable programming system but rather, let's say, an indexed family. The idea that the learner must be able to refute the hypothesis space has been introduced by Mukouchi and Arikawa in their 1993 ALT paper. Subsequently, Lange and Watson (ALT'94) modified this approach by requesting that the learner must be able to refute initial segments of data sequences that do no correspond to any language in the hypothesis space. This year, Jain is continuing along this line of research. Instead of looking at indexed families as in previous work, he considers general classes $\mathcal{L}$ of recursively enumerable languages. Now, allowing the class of all computer programs as hypothesis space, one can still insist to refute all initial segments of texts (informants) that do not correspond to any language in $\mathcal{L}$. Alternatively, one may also allow the learner to either refute or identify them. Finally, one may require the learner to refute only initial segments of texts (informants) that it cannot learn. Surprisingly, the latter approach is the most powerful one, and, for learning from text, it also achieves the whole learning power of learning in the limit from positive data.

There is one more paper dealing with language learning, but is different from all the papers mentioned above in that it uses *queries* to gain information about the target objects to be learned. Therefore, we discuss it within the next section.

Learning via Queries

We can imagine the learning via queries scenario as the interaction between a teacher and a learner that can communicate using some prespecified query language. For example, when learning the concept of a chair, the learner my ask "is a sofa an example of a chair?, " or when learning a language, a query may be of the form "is w a string from the target language?" This type of question is referred to as a *membership query*. Alternatively, one can allow the learner to ask "is G a grammar for the target language?" The latter type of question is called *equivalence query*, and is easy to see how to generalize it to any learning domain. Clearly, a positive answer to an equivalence directly yields the information that the target has been learned correctly, and the learner can (and has to) stop. If the answer is negative, usually a counterexample is returned, too, i.e., an element from the symmetric difference of the target and the object described by the equivalence query. In general, whatever the query language is, now the learner is required to halt and to output a correct description for the target. Moreover, it is also easy to see that every indexed family can be learned from equivalence queries alone. However, this may require a huge amount of queries, and thus may be beyond feasibility. Therefore, within the learning via queries scenario, the query complexity is usually of major concern. What one usually wants is that the overall number of queries asked is polynomially bounded in the length of the target and the longest counterexample returned.

Melideo and Varricchio consider the learnability of unary output two-tape automata from equivalence and multiplicity queries. In order to understand what a multiplicity query is, we first have to explain what an automaton with multiplicity is. Suppose any field K, and a non-deterministic automaton that has assigned weights (i.e., elements from K) to each initial state, each final state and to each egde of the automaton. Such an automaton can be considered as computing a function that maps strings into elements of K, and a multiplicity query returns the value of this function for a given string. Now, the authors show that the behavior of a unary output two-tape automaton can be identified with the behavior of a suitably defined automaton with multiplicity. Thus, the original learning problem is reduced to that of learning the resulting automata with multiplicity. The learner provided has a query complexity that is polynomially bounded in the size of the automaton with multiplicity.

Fischlin asks whether or not learning from membership queries can be sped up by parallelizing it. Defining the depth of a query q to be the number of other queries on which q depends upon and the query depth of a learning algorithm to be the maximum query depth taken over all queries made, the problem of whether or not a query learner can be parallelized is then equivalent to asking whether or not the query depth can be reduced. Assuming the existence of cryptographic one-way functions, Fischlin proves the following strong result: for any fixed polynomial d, there is a concept class C_n that is efficiently query learnable from membership queries alone in query depth $d(n) + 1$, but C_n cannot be weakly predicted from membership and equivalence queries in depth $d(n)$.

Damaschke provides a positive result concerning the parallelizability of learning Boolean functions that depend on only a few variables. Moreover, he is not only looking at the overall number of queries but also at the resulting overall complexity of learning.

Another lower bound for the overall number of membership queries is given by Shevchenko and Zolotykh. They consider the problem of learning half-spaces over finite subsets of the n-dimensional Euclidean vector space. This is done by carefully elaborating the structure of so-called teaching sets for half-spaces, i.e., sets such that only one half-space agrees with all points in them. The lower bound obtained is close to the best known upper bound.

Ben-David and Lindenbaum (cf. EuroCOLT'95, LNAI 1208) proposed several models to adapt the idea of learning from positive data only (that has attracted so much attention in language learning) to the PAC model. Denis is continuing along this line of research. He defines an appropriate PAC model and shows that extra information concerning the underlying distribution must be provided. This information is obtained via statistical queries. A couple of concept classes are shown to be learnable within the model defined, e.g. k-DNF and k-decision lists.

Learning Recursive Functions

The area of learning recursive functions is traditionally well represented in the ALT series. The information given to the learner is usually augmenting sequences

$f(0), f(1), f(2), \ldots$ of the function f to be learned. Admissible hypothesis spaces are recursive enumerations of partial recursive functions that comprise the target class. Again, the learner has to output a sequence of hypotheses about the target function, i.e., indices or encodings of computer programs. The learning goal consists in identifying in the limit an index in the relevant enumeration such that the enumerated function correctly computes the target with respect to the correctness criterion introduced. Starting with Gold's and Putnam's pioneering work, this learning model has been widely studied. Many variations of this basic setting have been considered, and the present volume provides further specifications.

Suppose you have a learner for a class U_1 and another class U_2. Now, it would be nice to have a more powerful learner that can identify simultaneously $U_1 \cup U_2$. However, learning in the limit is not closed under union, and this fact led Apsītis et al. to investigate the following refined version of closedness under union. Assume you have classes $U_1, \ldots, U_n$ each of which is learnable in the limit. What can be said about the learnability of the union of all these classes provided that every union of at most $n - 1$ classes is learnable in the limit? Clearly, the answer may depend on n, since for $n = 2$ the answer is no as mentioned above. Therefore, more precisely, one has to ask whether or not there exists an n such that the union of all such classes is always learnable. The minimal such n is referred to as the closedness degree, and the authors determine the degree for a large number of learning types.

A natural variation of the basic scenario described above is prediction. Now, instead of outputting hypotheses about the target function, the learner can keep its guesses. Instead, the learning success is measured by its ability to predict the function values for inputs not having seen before. That is, beyond some point the learner must be able to predict correctly. Again what is meant by correctly depends on the correctness criterion considered. Example for correctness criteria comprise always correct, correct for all but a finite number (prespecified or not), a certain fraction of the inputs and so on. Case et al. consider this model for the case that the targets may *drift* over time. While similar questions have been addressed within the PAC model, this is the first paper that studies concept drift in the more general, recursion theoretic setting. Different versions are proposed and related to one another. Moreover, the authors also analyze the learnability of some natural concept classes within their models. This is a nice combination of abstract and concrete examples.

Whenever learning in the limit is concerned, one usually cannot decide whether or not the learner has already converged to its final hypothesis for the actual target. Thus, it seems only natural to demand the learner to correctly reflect all the data already seen. Learners behaving thus are said to be *consistent*. At fist glance, it may also seem useless to allow a learner to output inconsistent hypotheses. Nevertheless, consistency is a severe restriction as has been shown elsewhere. In his paper, Stein is investigating the question of how the demand to learn consistently may effect the complexity of learning. That is, assuming a function class can be learned consistently, he shows that for every recursive bound, there is class that can be learned inconsistently with polynomial update time, but every consistent learner needs an update time which is above the recursive bound given.

Case, Ott *et al.* generalize the scenario described above by looking at learning an infinite branch of a computable tree. Thus the concept class considered is the set of all computable trees that contain at least one infinite computable branch. This work derives its motivation from process-control games.

Hirowatari and Arikawa extend the classical model to learning recursive real-valued functions. These function are regarded as computable interval mappings. Both coincidences and surprising differences to the learnability of natural-valued recursive functions are shown. In particular, these differences are established with respect to recursively enumerable classes and consistent identification. This work considerably extends their results presented at ALT'97.

Bārzdiņš and Sarkans continue their work (with varying coauthors) presented at previous ALT meetings to design practically feasible inference algorithms. The new feature consists in using attribute grammars to express several kinds of additional knowledge about the objects to be learned.

We finish this section with the paper of Grieser *et al.* that looks at the learnability of recursive functions from quite a different perspective. The main problem studied is the validation of inductive learning systems. The authors propose a model for the validation task, and relate the amount of expertise necessary to validate a learning system to the amount of expertise needed for solving the learning problems considered. Within the model introduced, the ability to validate a learning system implies the ability to solve it.

Miscellaneous

Arimura *et al.* study the *data mining* problem to discover two-word association rules in large collections of unstructured texts. They present very efficient algorithms solving this task. Nice applications are outlined and the algorithms have been implemented and tested using a huge database of amino acid sequences.

Schmitt is investigating the sample complexity for neural trees. A neural tree is a feedforward neural network with at most one edge outgoing from each node. The paper relates the sample complexity to the VC dimension of classes of neural trees. The main result is a lower bound of $n \log n$ for the sample complexity of neural trees with n inputs.

Kaiserslautern, July 1998   Michael M. Richter
College Park, July 1998   Carl H. Smith
Kaiserslautern, July 1998   Rolf Wiehagen
Fukuoka, July 1998   Thomas Zeugmann

Scalability Issues in Inductive Logic Programming

Stefan Wrobel

GMD, SET.KI, Schloß Birlinghoven
53754 Sankt Augustin, Germany
stefan.wrobel@gmd.de

Abstract. Inductive Logic Programming is concerned with a difficult problem: learning in first-order representations. If stated in an unrestricted fashion, ILP's classical learning task, the inductive acquisition of first-order predictive theories from examples, is undecidable; even the more restricted practical tasks are known to be not polynomially PAC-learnable. The idea of using ILP techniques for Knowledge Discovery in Databases (KDD), or Data Mining, where very large datasets need to be analyzed, thus seems impossible at first sight. However, a number of recent advances have allowed ILP to make significant progress on the road to scalability. In this paper, we will give an illustrative overview of the basic aspects of scalability in ILP, and then described recent advances in theory, algorithms and system implementations. We will give examples from implemented algorithms and briefly introduce MIDOS, a recent first-order subgroup discovery algorithm and its scalability ingredients.

1 Introduction

Data Mining, or *Knowledge Discovery in Databases* (KDD), has recently been gaining widespread attention. In one popular definition, KDD is seen as the "non-trivial process of identifying valid, novel, potentially useful, and ultimately understandable patterns in data" [FPSS96], whereas data mining is usually seen as one step in the iterative KDD process, namely the application of (semi-automatic) analysis methods to find results. As the definition indicates, KDD focuses on the entire process of going from real-world data to useful results, i.e., including not only data mining but also tasks such as data preprocessing (selection, cleaning, transformation) and result postprocessing (evaluation, interpretation, use). KDD places a high emphasis on the understandability, novelty and usefulness of results, i.e., does not evaluate results solely on the basis of validity or accuracy. Even though not explicitly mentioned in the definition, in a KDD context it is usually assumed that real-world datasets are very large and often stored in (relational) database management systems, resulting in very high demands on the scalability of analysis methods.

When looking at the most popular data mining methods, we see that KDD currently almost exclusively relies on *propositional* data analysis techniques, i.e., algorithms that accept a single table of simple-valued data as input. Examples of such techniques for classification or prediction are decision tree learners such as C4.5 [Qui93], propositional rule learning methods such as CN2 [CN89], linear and nonlinear regression methods such as artificial neural networks [Hay98] or Bayesian methods [CL96]. None of these propositional techniques can directly deal with the multiple relations that are typical of relational databases, and some of them do not produce very explicit and understandable output. On the other hand, *first-order* techniques as developed in the field of Inductive Logic Programming (ILP, see e.g. [MDR94, Wro96, NCW97]) up to now have been perceived as too slow and plagued by scalability problems. Therefore, they are not seen as ideal candidates for KDD even though they are capable of dealing with the multiple relations of a relational database directly, produce understandable output in explicit logical form and can even use rich background knowledge.

Fortunately, recent work in the field of ILP has lead to significant progress in particular on the issue of scalability. In this paper, we present an illustrative overview of some of these advances in theory, algorithms and system implementations, focusing in particular on new task definitions and the use of sampling. In the next section, we will define the task of ILP; in section 3, we discuss the basic complexity issues entailed by this task. We then describe the classical approaches to scalability in section 4, followed by more recent approaches in section 5. As an example of scalability techniques in context, we conclude with a brief discussion of MIDOS, a recent ILP subgroup discovery algorithm (section 6).

2 The basics of Inductive Logic Programming

Let us first illustrate the most important ILP learning task by a simplified example from the domain of telecommunications described in [SMAU94]. In this domain, the goal was to replace an existing, manually created access control database with a set of verifiable access control rules in a declarative language. The database stated, for each employee, which switching systems this employee was allowed to access, but did not include the reasons why this was the case. The access rules, on the other hand, were to use the available background knowledge about the network and the employees, their affiliations and qualifications to decide about access rights in a general and explicit fashion.

In this application, the manually created access rights database can be represented by a set of first-order facts that are used as *positive examples* of the target concept may_operate:

> may_operate(bode,pabx_17).
> may_operate(meyer,pabx_15).

Here, and for the rest of the paper, we follow the convention from logic programming and Prolog (see e.g. [Llo87]) and use lowercase names for predicates, functions, and constants, whereas variable symbols always begin with an uppercase letter.

Further facts about unauthorized access are used as *negative examples* of the target concept[1]:

```
not(may_operate(bode,pabx_15)).
not(may_operate(meyer,pabx_17)).
not(may_operate(miller,pabx_15)).
```

To be able to learn from these examples, it is also necessary to represent the available *background knowledge* about the domain. Usually, this is done in the form of first-order facts and rules (clauses):

```
operator(bode).              works_for(bode,comtel).
operates(telplus,pabx_17).   subsidiary(comtel,telplus).
engineer(meyer).             works_for(meyer,nettalk).
operates(talkline,pabx_17).  subsidiary(nettalk,talkline).
accountant(miller).          works_for(miller,nettalk).
operator(X) → technical(X).
engineer(X) → technical(X).
```

From the above information, an ILP learning system can learn the rule:

```
works_for(P,C1) & operates(C2,S) & subsidiary(C1,C2)
& technical(P) → may_operate(P,S).
```

stating that all technical personnel in a subsidiary company may operate all systems managed by the parent company.

As another example, given examples of reverse, and append as background knowledge, an ILP program can find the following clause (lists written in Prolog notation):

```
reverse(B,D) & append(D,[A],C) → reverse([A | B],C)
```

More formally, we can define the basic task of ILP as follows. Assume that we are given arbitrary, but fixed languages L_B, L_E and L_H for background knowledge, examples and hypotheses. In ILP, these languages are subsets of first-order logic. In addition, we assume that we have an entailment relationship $\models$ on sets of statements from these languages. In ILP, this is usually logical entailment or a subset thereof; we require that $\models$ be reflexive ($\Gamma \models \Gamma$) and transitive ($\Gamma_1 \models \Gamma_2$ and $\Gamma_2 \models \Gamma_3$ implies $\Gamma_1 \models \Gamma_3$). We write $\Gamma \models \Box$ to denote that Γ is inconsistent. We can now formulate a precise definition of the learning from examples problem [Wro96]).

Definition 1 ILP prediction learning problem. For a background knowledge language L_B, an example language L_E, a hypothesis language L_H, and an entailment relationship $\models$, we call the following problem the *ILP prediction learning problem $ILP_P(L_B, L_E, L_H, \models)$*:
Given:

---

[1] Some learning systems allow the user to specify that all unstated examples are negative, in which case negative examples do not need to be specified explicitly.

- background knowledge B expressed in the background knowledge language L_B
- positive examples E^+ expressed in the example language L_E
- negative examples E^- expressed in the example language L_E
- such that B is consistent with E^+ and E^- ($B \cup E^+ \cup E^- \not\models \Box$),

Find:

- a learning hypothesis H expressed in the hypothesis language L_H
- such that H is complete, i.e., together with B entails ("covers") the positive examples ($H \cup B \models E^+$)
- H is correct, i.e., is consistent with the negative examples ($H \cup B \cup E^- \not\models \Box$).
- and H meets a particular *preference bias*.

The solutions to the above learning problem are by no means unique; for many problems, there will be an infinite number of solutions. Since we require $B \cup E^+ \cup E^- \not\models \Box$, there is also a trivial solution, namely $H := E^+$ (assuming $L_E \subseteq L_H$). It is the role of the *preference bias* to exclude unwanted hypotheses such as the trivial one. A common preference bias is to require H to be the *most general* complete and correct hypothesis.

Definition 2 Generality. A hypothesis H_1 is said to be *more general* than a hypothesis H_2, written $H_1 \geq_g H_2$ iff

$$H_1 \models H_2.$$

Also, in most practical applications, requiring completeness and consistency is inappropriate since usually, examples and/or background knowledge are *noisy*. Practical algorithms therefore use statistical criteria instead of strict consistency and completeness to evaluate hypotheses.

3 Basic complexity issues in ILP

The computational difficulty of the problem defined above depends on exactly how its primary components are instantiated, i.e., which languages are allowed for the specification of examples, background knowledge, and hypothesis, and which notion of explanation is used. In the most general case, full first-order logic could be used as a language, and as stated above, explanation would be identified with general logical entailment. Due to the undecidability of first-order logic, in this case it is not even decidable whether a hypothesis is a solution to the learning problem. One of the central goals of ILP is thus to find restrictions of the various components of the learning problem that on the one hand make the problem easier while on the other still allow interesting concepts to be learned.

3.1 Choice of the language

On the language side, all ILP systems in use today employ clausal first-order logic as their representation, usually concentrating on Horn clauses, i.e., clauses with one positive literal (head). Entailment in these languages is still undecidable, so many systems in addition assume *function-free* languages which are decidable and have turned out to be adequate for many practical problems. Furthermore, it is possible to automatically transform a clausal representation with function symbols into a function-free representation using a technique known as *flattening* [RP89]. However, the answer set of the transformed function-free program is equivalent to the original program with functions only under certain conditions [Sta94].

In most practical settings, one is interested in predicting membership in a single target predicate, so most systems concentrate on learning clauses for a single predicate only. Multi-clause hypotheses are typically learned by a *covering* approach, where the system first induces a single clause to cover one part of the positive examples, and then further clauses to cover the remaining examples In the following, we will concentrate on the task of learning single most general clauses, keeping in mind that multiple-clause, multiple-predicate hypotheses introduce extra complexity (see [RLD93] for multiple-clause, multiple-predicate learning).

3.2 Replacing $\models$ by θ-subsumption

Even for a Horn clause program consisting of one ground fact, one ground query and two Horn clauses with two literals, the ILP problem defined above remains undecidable (see [KD94] for an overview). Therefore, almost all approaches in ILP today have chosen to replace (semantic) logical entailment ($\models$) by (syntactic) θ-subsumption ($\geq_\theta$), defined by [Rob65] and first used for learning by Plotkin [Plo70].

θ-subsumption Let c and c' be two program clauses (in set notation). Clause c *θ-subsumes* c' ($c \geq_\theta c'$) if there exists a substitution θ, such that $c\theta \subseteq c'$. Two clauses c and d are θ-subsumption equivalent ($c \equiv_\theta d$) if $c \geq_\theta d$ and $d \geq_\theta c$. A clause is *reduced* if it is not θ-subsumption equivalent to any proper subset of itself.

An important property of θ-subsumption is that if $c \geq_\theta c'$, then $c \models c'$. The converse is not true, as shown by the following examples.

As illustrated by the last example, the incompleteness of θ-subsumption is due to clauses that can be used recursively on themselves. If these so-called self-recursive clauses are not allowed, θ-subsumption is complete with respect to $\models$ [Got87]. While there is current work in ILP on inverting implication (see e.g. the PROGOL system [Mug95]), most other algorithms currently in use are based on θ-subsumption. Checking θ-subsumption is an NP-complete problem [GJ79, p. 264], but in many cases it is possible to exploit structural properties of the

$c_1 := \mathsf{parent}(Y,X) \rightarrow \mathsf{daughter}(X,Y)$
$c_2 := \mathsf{parent}(\mathsf{ann},\mathsf{mary}) \rightarrow \mathsf{daughter}(\mathsf{mary},\mathsf{ann})$
$c_3 := \mathsf{female}(\mathsf{mary}), \mathsf{parent}(\mathsf{ann},\mathsf{mary}), \mathsf{parent}(\mathsf{tom},\mathsf{mary}) \rightarrow \mathsf{daughter}(\mathsf{mary},\mathsf{ann})$
$c_1 \geq_\theta c_2$ and $c_1 \geq_\theta c_3$, both with $\theta = \{X/mary, Y/ann\}$.

$c_4 := \mathsf{parent}(Y,X), \mathsf{parent}(U,V) \rightarrow \mathsf{daughter}(X,Y)$
$c_1 \equiv_\theta c_4$; c_1 is reduced, c_4 is not reduced.

$c_5 := \mathsf{q}(X,Y,Z) \rightarrow \mathsf{q}(Y,Z,X)$, $c_6 := \mathsf{q}(X,Y,Z) \rightarrow \mathsf{q}(Z,X,Y)$
$c_5 \not\geq_\theta c_6$ and $c_6 \not\geq_\theta c_5$, but $c_5 \models c_6$ and $c_6 \models c_5$.

Table 1. θ-subsumption examples.

data (determinacy and locality) to greatly reduce the combinatorial matching problem and runtime when compared to a blind matching approach [KL94].

Even though θ-subsumption is defined on pairs of clauses, it can still be used with background knowledge B. Assume we are given a set of atoms K such that $B \models K$. We can then transform the ILP problem specification as follows. Given unary clause examples E^+ and E^-, we are looking for a hypothesis H such that:

$$
\begin{array}{ll}
B \cup H \models E^+ & B \cup H \cup E^- \not\models \square \\
\Leftrightarrow H \models B \rightarrow P & \Leftrightarrow H \not\models B \cup E^- \rightarrow \square \\
\Leftarrow H \models K \rightarrow E^+ & \Rightarrow H \not\models K \cup E^- \rightarrow \square \\
\Leftarrow H \geq_\theta K \rightarrow e_i^+, \forall e_i^+ \in E^+ & \Rightarrow H \not\geq_\theta K \rightarrow e_i^-, \forall (\leftarrow e_i^-) \in E^-
\end{array}
$$

Just as the replacement of implication with θ-subsumption, this transformation causes the learner to miss some complete hypotheses and may cause it to output incorrect hypotheses (with respect to the original problem statement using implication). If B is not a set of atoms, K is usually taken to be some finite subset of all atomic statements entailed by B, computed by a limited-depth deduction process (e.g. saturation [RP89]).

3.3 Towards polynomial learnability

While the above restrictions ensure a decidable learning problem, they are insufficient to reach polynomial learnability. Following the popularity of Valiant's *probably approximately correct* (PAC) learning framework in the propositional learning area, significant effort was invested in ILP to examine whether polynomially PAC-learnable ILP learning tasks could be found. Indeed several authors were able to prove positive results for restricted variants of the above problem. Here are some examples all of which assume (as explained above) that the goal is to learn one or more clauses about a single target predicate, and that the available background knowledge allows any atomic query to be proved in time polynomial in the length of the atom[2].

---

[2] See [KD94] or [NCW97, ch. 18] for detailed overviews of PAC-learnability and ILP.

- function-free non-recursive clauses of at most k literals each are polynomial time PAC learnable if either all body variables occur in the head of the respective clause (*constrained* clauses) [DMR92], or background knowledge consists only of function-free ground atoms [Coh93].
- sets of at most k nonrecursive clauses are polynomial time PAC predictable if they are i, j-*determinate* [Dvz95]. This roughly means that the instantiations of head variables in the clause uniquely determine (through a chain of at most i shared variables) the instantiations of all body literals with respect to the available examples and background knowledge. If i is not restricted, the problem is no longer polynomial time PAC-learnable, neither so if we allow $1, 2$-*non*-determinate clauses (if $RP \neq PSPACE$, [Kie93]).

Unfortunately, in order to obtain these and other positive PAC-learnability results, the learning problem had to be restricted quite severely. For practical applications, it is not reasonable to assume learned clauses contain no free body variables, nor is it always possible to provide a small limit on the number k of necessary literals in the body of learned clauses. Similarly, the property of i, j-determinacy assumes that there is only one way to match a clause against examples and background knowledge which is not the case in many ILP applications. In fact, an i, j-determinate learning problem can be mapped onto a propositional learning problem that is only polynomially larger [KD94]. This means that the polynomial time PAC-learnability of i, j-determinate clauses is inherited from the propositional domain, and the problem has essentially been restricted to a propositional problem.

Nonetheless, even in this case it is a tremendous advantage in terms of useability and understandability to be able to use first-order representations: even though a propositional equivalent exists, it would be very cumbersome to construct manually. Furthermore, in problems that are not entirely determinate, it is very advantageous to construct the representation such that as many literals as possible are determinate, thus reducing the matching effort required. Further gains can be made by moving tree-structured determinate relationships into first-order terms which are handled efficiently by ILP algoritms (simply through unification or using special algorithms for terms as e.g. RIBL's tree edit distances [BHW98]).

4 Classic ingredients of scalability

Beyond theoretical learnability considerations, ILP has always constructed learning systems that, despite prohibitive theoretical results, have performed well and with acceptable runtimes in practice. This is not primarily a critique of inadequate learnability models, even though some authors have started to propose alternative learnability models like *U-learnability* which focuses on instance distributions with certain benign properties and allows more positive results to be proved [MP94]. Instead, it is the result of several practical ingredients commonly found in ILP algorithms: declarative bias, search ordering and pruning, and search heuristics.

4.1 Declarative bias

Declarative bias means that the learning system allows the user to specify a different hypothesis space for each actual instance of an ILP learning problem. Within the boundaries of high-level restrictions such as given above (e.g. restriction to function-free Horn clauses), the user can identify a subspace that is deemed appropriate to the current learning problem instance. Just how the user is to communicate his or her knowledge about the desired subspace has been an intensively studied subject. One can generally distinguish several kinds of approaches of increasing complexity:

Type and mode declarations These are the simplest form of declarative bias. A *type* declaration specifies, for each predicate and each of its argument places, which type (sort) of value is allowed. The learning system can use this information to avoid identifying variables with incompatible types, thus ruling out many useless clauses from consideration. An argument's *mode declaration* specifies whether the argument is an *input* or *output* argument. Clauses are then constructed to make sure that all input arguments of a literal are bound by preceding literals, again ruling out many uninteresting clauses. Sometimes, mode declarations are used to also specify how many instantiations of output arguments are possible given instantiated input arguments; this can be used to further optimize the search. Practically all ILP systems use type and/or mode declarations, the currently popular form of type and mode declarations was introduced for the PROGOL system [Mug95].

Schemata and templates Schemata [KW92] and templates [WO91] are clauses with designated places into which actual predicates and/or arguments can be inserted. Since the syntactic form of a schema or template is more or less fixed, the user can easily see which hypotheses will be allowed by a schema, and exert very fine-grained control over the hypothesis space. For small target hypothesis spaces and well-understood learning targets, this is a good approach. Many problems require overly large sets of templates so that a generative declarative bias language is preferable.

Generative approaches Generative approaches to declarative bias consist of programs or grammars that compute the allowed hypotheses, i.e., there does not need to be a direct correspondence between the syntax of the bias expression and the allowed hypotheses. A well-developed generative bias language is DLAB [DRD97] which allows both simple template-style specifications and complex generative expressions.

4.2 Search ordering

Within a given hypothesis space (with or without declarative bias), efficiency can be gained by exploiting the logical generality structure of the hypothesis space and using appropriate refinement operators.

Definition 3 Refinement. A (downward) *refinement operator* is a mapping

$$\rho : L_H \to 2^{L_H}$$

such that for all $H' \in \rho(H) : H \geq_g H'$.

Hypothesis search then proceeds from the most general hypothesis to more special hypotheses. If a hypothesis is found to contradict (too many) negative examples, search continues with its refinements. For this to be effective, the refinement operator should map each hypothesis to a finite set of refinements, and it should produce every hypothesis in the hypothesis space in finitely many steps when starting from the most general hypothesis[3]. This structuring of the search allows the basic forms of pruning. Whenever a hypothesis is found to exclude all (or enough) negative examples, we need not consider any of its refinements. Similarly, whenever a hypothesis is found to cover too few positive examples, it and all its refinements can be excluded from consideration.

Further optimizations are possible if an *optimal* refinement operator is used. A refinement operator is optimal if each hypothesis is produced along exactly one refinement path. Whenever hypotheses are produced along several paths, we need to keep track of visited hypotheses to avoid reexploring parts of the space that have already been visited. For optimal refinement operators, this is unnecessary, which is especially important for parallelization of search algorithms. Optimal refinement operators are used e.g. for hypothesis spaces specified using the declarative bias language DLAB [DRD97] and for the foreign link bias language of MIDOS ([Wro97], see below).

4.3 Search heuristics

Search heuristics can be used to either select a particular order of examining the search space (so that the best hypotheses are found first), or, more commonly, to greedily eliminate parts of the hypothesis space from consideration. Many of these criteria are based on the idea that when refining, it is best to continue with those refinements that best separate positive from negative examples. This idea can be mapped to various statistical criteria, one of the simplest is the *information gain* measure used in FOIL [Qui90]. If we let

$$e^+(H) := | \{e^+ \in E^+ \mid H \text{ covers } e^+\} |$$

and

$$e(H) := | \{e \in E^+ \cup E^- \mid H \text{ covers } e\} |$$

the information gain of a refinement hypothesis H' with respect to the original hypothesis H can be written as:

$$IG(H, H') := e^+(H') \cdot (-log_2(\tfrac{e^+(H)}{e(H)}) + log_2(\tfrac{e^+(H')}{e(H')}))$$

i.e., FOIL uses only the information content of positive tuples (probabilities approximated as relative frequencies) and weights the information gain so that refinements which cover many positive examples are preferred[4].

---

[3] Ideally, each refinement should also be strictly less general than its predecessor to ensure the search does not get stuck. For full clausal languages, this cannot be achieved, however, without giving up one of the first two desired properties [NCW97].

[4] The actual computation in FOIL is more complex.

5 Recent advances in practical scalability

In addition to the classic scalability ingredients described above, recently a number of alternative approaches and ideas have successfully been introduced into ILP systems. First, the use of alternative formulations of the ILP learning problem has allowed parallelizable algorithms and the use of several smaller optimizations already known in propositional learning. Second, the introduction of sampling techniques has allowed significant speedups while still maintaining asymptotically perfect accuracies[5].

5.1 Alternative ILP problem definitions

Prediction is only one of the possible interesting learning tasks. In many situations, it can be more appropriate to look for hypotheses that *describe* the existing data instead of being optimized for predicting new data. With the growing popularity of knowledge discovery, such analysis tasks have also become more popular in ILP, and several authors have proposed ILP problem definitions that can be seen as variants of a descriptive learning task (e.g. [Hel89, Fla92, DRD94]). These definitions can be generalized into the following task definition of descriptive learning in ILP, phrased using a generic *description relationship* $\models_D$ between datasets and hypotheses [WD95][6].

Definition 4 ILP description problem. For a background knowledge language L_B, a dataset language L_D, a hypothesis language L_H, an entailment relationship $\models$, and a description relationship $\models_D$, we call the following problem the *ILP description learning problem* $ILP_D(L_B, L_D, L_H, \models, \models_D)$:
Given:

- background knowledge B expressed in the background knowledge language L_B
- data D expressed in the dataset language L_D
- such that B is consistent with $D (B \cup D \not\models \Box)$

Find:

- a learning hypothesis H expressed in the hypothesis language L_H
- such that H describes B and the data D $((B, D) \models_D H)$,

Often, we also require that

- H is complete, i.e., for any other descriptive hypothesis H' in L_H, $H \models H'$,
- and H is non-redundant, i.e., for any proper subset $H' \subset H$, $H' \not\models H$.

---

[5] We do not describe preprocessing techniques like discretization or attribute selection here, since these are general techniques external to ILP algorithms. Nonetheless, their use is of course essential to scalability.

[6] We have omitted the use of *uninteresting* datasets ("negative examples"), since they are not important for our purposes here.

As described in [WD95] the properties of this learning problem depend not only on L_B, L_H, L_D and $\models$, but crucially on the choice of $\models_D$, the description relationship. One important interpretation is the one made in the so-called *learning from interpretations* or *non-monotonic* ILP setting [DRD97]. In this setting, it is assumed that L_B and L_D are such that a unique minimal Herbrand model can be assumed to exist. Then, we can define for a hypothesis H to describe a set of data D:

$(B, D) \models_{\mathcal{M}^+} H :=$ H is in true in $\mathcal{M}^+(D \cup B)$, the minimal Herbrand model of $D \cup B$.

Taking the minimal Herbrand model amounts to making the closed-world assumption, since anything not explicitly stated or inferrable is assumed to be false. This description relationship thus is appropriate especially when we can safely assume that we have complete descriptions of the objects under consideration.

From the point of view of scalability, the above is important since it entails the following property:

If $(B, D) \models_{\mathcal{M}^+} H_1$ and $(B, D) \models_{\mathcal{M}^+} H_2$, then $(B, D) \models_{\mathcal{M}^+} H_1 \cup H_2$ (compositionality or monotonicity).

This means that, in contrast to the regular ILP prediction problem, it is safe to consider each hypothesis clause separately and then join them together at the end. In the regular setting, a correct search for multi-clause hypotheses is so complex that it is usually avoided and replaced by a covering approach [RLD93]; in the nonmonotonic setting, these problems do not arise. Practically speaking, monotonicity means that parallel implementations of the search are easily possible by assigning different subareas of the hypothesis space to different processors. If an optimal refinement operator is used, this can be done with very little communication, and indeed the parallel version of CLAUDIEN, a popular learner for the nonmonotonic setting, has shown a speedup almost linear in the number of processors (for up to 16 processors, see [DRD97]).

The nonmonotonic setting can also be seen in terms of PAC-learnability if D is understood as a collection of independent subsets. This quite often is a reasonable assumption, since the data usually will be describing different objects or cases, and each data subset can collect all the information about one such object or case. The nonmonotonic description relationship is then interpreted in a local fashion:

$(B, D) \models_{\mathcal{M}^+} H :=$ for all $d \in D$, H is in true in $\mathcal{M}^+(d \cup B)$.

The minimal model of each data set is an interpretation (a particular subset of the Herbrand universe), and the set of all such interpretations can be regarded as an instance space within which the given datasets are the positive examples. In this view, it has been possible to prove that first-order clausal theories are polynomially PAC-learnable (with one-sided error from positive examples only) if they consist of clauses that are *allowed* (all head variables occur in the body) and have no more than k literals of size at most j each [DRD94].

Practically, the nonmonotonic interpretation of datasets brings about a very close relationship to propositional learning where also we are assuming complete knowledge about the observed objects. This relationship has allowed a number of important propositional learning algorithms to be upgraded to the first-order case, most notably decision tree learning, where the first-order decision tree learner TILDE [BDR98] has proven to combine good learning accuracies with excellent scalability.

5.2 Sampling

All of the approaches to scalability described above are aimed at reducing the number of hypotheses that need to be considered, or at allowing parallel and independent search for these hypotheses. Sampling approaches to scalability tackle the orthogonal problem of reducing the time it takes to check each individual hypothesis on the data. In other words, the former approaches deal with computational challenges introduced by the complexity of the data, whereas sampling deals with challenges introduced by the amount of data.

We can currently distinguish three ways in which sampling enters into ILP algorithms, namely global sampling approaches, local sampling approaches and sampling of substitutions.

Global sampling Global sampling in its simple form is probably the most popular and most heavily criticized data preprocessing technique in KDD: if the entire dataset cannot be handled by the chosen analysis method, we select a small random sample and compute the analysis result on the sample. Clearly, this is problematic since there is no guarantee that results on the sample are the same as results on the entire dataset, not only because of random fluctuations in the sample, but also because of heuristics in the analysis method that may enlarge such fluctuations.

For predictive learning tasks, these problems can be somewhat alleviated by approaches known as *windowing* [Qui93]. Windowing selects an initial subset of the examples, learns on these examples, and then checks the results on all examples. The algorithm then constructs a new sample of training examples adding in a sample from those examples that were incorrectly handled by the previous learning result. Srinivasan [Sri97] has adapted this approach for ILP in a method called *logical windowing*. This approach differs from the basic scheme described above by using individual clause deletions to arrive at the final hypothesis (a kind of covering strategy) instead of relearning an entire theory on each subsequent sample.

An alternative to windowing is *layered learning* [Mug93] which is possible if the hypothesis language allows the formulation of a hierarchy of theories where each lower level theory handles only the exceptions of the higher-level theory. In ILP, this is possible through the use of non-monotonically interpreted exception predicates that are attached to clauses (see e.g. [BM92, Wro94]). Layered learning then proceeds by first taking a small sample of data, constructing an initial theory, and then at each iteration constructing the next theory, training only on the errors of the first in a new sample that is a superset of the first. In this case, assuming we know the size of the concept class (2^n), it is possible based on lower-bound PAC results to derive optimal sizes for the successive samples to achieve exponentially decreasing error with linearly growing training sets [Mug93].

In [Sri97], the results of extensive experiments with both logical windowing and layered learning on two domains (king-rook-king end games and part-of-speech tagging) are reported. The experiments compared the runtimes and accuracies of the ILP learner PROGOL [Mug95] with the layered-learning variant of PROGOL and with a variant using a logical windowing wrapper around PROGOL. The experiments indicate that in practice, logical windowing seems to work better, delivering slightly better accuracies and shorter runtimes than layered learning. Compared to the nonsampling version of Prolog, runtimes were shorter by almost an order of magnitude, while accuracies remained comparable. These results are important especially since logical windowing can always be employed *in addition* to other optimizations like local or substitution sampling.

Local sampling Local sampling [Wro97] differs from global sampling in that sampling is done with respect to the hypothesis that is currently being considered. Whereas global sampling uses one sample for all hypotheses considered in a step, and precisely computes accuracies on the sample, local sampling uses a different-size sample for each hypothesis and selects precisely the sample size that is necessary to achieve the desired accuracy in estimating the hypothesis' properties. If, as in MIDOS [Wro97], a relative frequency is to be estimated, a (generous) upper bound on the required sample size can be computed based on elementary results from statistics. Estimating a probability amounts to repeatedly drawing samples and checking whether they have the required property, e.g. whether the current hypothesis covers the example. Repeating this experiment means we are getting a binomial distribution with underlying probability p which is the probability we are interested in. We estimate this probability by $p' := \frac{x}{s}$, where x is the number of "successes" after drawing s samples.

We then need a statement about the probability that $|p - p'|$ is smaller than a specified error threshold ϵ. From the statistics literature, we can use the so-called Chernoff bound ([AS92] foll. [AMS+96]) for this purpose. According to this bound, for any $a > 0$,

$$P(x > sp + a) < e^{-2a^2/s}$$

For the difference between estimated and actual probability, we obtain

$$P(p' > p + \epsilon) = P(x > sp + s\epsilon) < e^{-2s\epsilon^2}$$

Thus, for truly random samples, we can precisely determine which sample size is needed to stay below a desired error probability δ. In section 6 below, we will be discussing the use of this kind of sampling in an ILP subgroup discovery algorithm.

Sampling of substitutions Sampling of substitutions ("stochastic matching", [SR97]) is a recently introduced technique that is even more fine-grained than local sampling, in that it is concerned with the process of checking a hypothesis on one particular example, i.e., with the task of checking θ-subsumption. As defined above, θ-subsumption is a combinatorially expensive process, since in order to find the matching subsets of clauses, all pairs of literals with the same predicate symbol must be checked. In determinate domains, this is not a problem since there will only be one such match for each example; in highly nondeterminate domains, this can be the major problem dominating the runtime of an ILP method. Stochastic matching was introduced for one such application (mutagenesis) in which examples contain up to 40 literals for one predicate, resulting in 40^k possible matches for clauses with k such literals.

Stochastic matching simply means to consider only a fixed number of the possible matches between hypothesis literals and example literals. Clearly, as more and more matches are considered, in the limit stochastic matching approaches the standard definition of θ-subsumption. Since appropriate samples can also be constructed in polynomial time (in the number of literals and variables in the participating clause), both hypothesis construction and checking can be done in polynomial time. The stochastic matching approach was first realized and experimentally examined in the ILP learning system STILL [SR97]. The reported experimental results proved very encouraging. With sample sizes of 300 for hypothesis construction and 3 for hypothesis checking, STILL achieved accuracies comparable to those of non-sampling ILP learners while reaching runtimes that were two to three order of magnitude faster. While this extreme speedup is due to the strong nondeterminacy of the domain, smaller speedups can be expected in most domains. In addition, stochastic matching can be combined with example-based sampling approaches (however, their interactions have not been examined).

6 Ingredients in context: MIDOS

We conclude by presenting a little more detail from our recent work on MIDOS, an ILP subgroup discovery system that combines several of the scalability ingredients introduced above: novel task definition based on the descriptive learning problem, declarative bias, optimal refinement, advanced pruning based on minimal support and optimistic estimates, and local sampling for estimating frequencies.

6.1 The subgroup discovery task

The subgroup discovery task is a variant of the descriptive learning task defined above. We are interested in finding hypotheses that describe interesting subgroups of the population, where interestingness is interpreted as combination of large size (generality) and distributional unusualness. As typical example, in a medical application we are looking at, an interesting subgroup that we would like to discover could be "the subgroup of patients who once had a treatment in a small hospital are significantly more likely to suffer from complications than the reference population". For another example, here is a sample subgroup discovery result from a business application (identifying unusual club membership distributions)[7].

> Target Type is: nominal([member,non_member])
> Reference Distribution is: [66.1%, 33.9% - 1371 objects]
>
> Sex=female, ID=order.Customer ID, order.Paymt Mode=credit_card
> [69.9%, 30.1% - 478 objects] [1.53882%%]

We see that the entire population consisted of 1371 objects (i.e., customers) of which 66.1% are club members. In contrast, in the subgroup of female credit card buyers (478 customers), 69.9% are club members. This finding is assigned a quality value of 1.53882%% by MIDOS.

The requirements of subgroup discovery can be seen as soft variants of the corresponding requirements in descriptive learning, where the description relationship is defined with respect to distributional unusualness, and the generality requirement translates into preference for larger discovered groups. The setting considered makes one further assumption that is important for scalability, namely, that the k best such groups are to be discovered. The multi-relation subgroup discovery task is more precisely defined as follows.

Definition 5 Multi-relational subgroup discovery. Given

- a relational database D with relations $R = \{r_1, ..., r_m\}$
- a hypothesis language L_H (language of group descriptions)
- an evaluation function $d : h \in L_H, D \to [0, 1]$
- an integer $k > 0$

Find:

- a set $H \subseteq L_H$ of hypotheses of size at most k,
- such that for each $h \in H$, $d(h, D) > 0$
- and for any $h' \in L_H \backslash H$, $d(h', D) \leq min_{h \in H} d(h, D)$.

The evaluation function d is defined as follows, based on the evaluation measures that have been defined for propositional algorithms [Klö96].

Assume we are given a designated object relation r_o with key attributes K that is part of a database D to be examined. For the simplest case, a binary goal attribute A_g in r_o, let $T := \{t \in r_o \mid r_o[A_g] = 1\}$ denote the set of target object tuples, define $g(h) := \frac{|c(h)|}{|r_o|}$, the generality of a hypothesis, and probabilities $p_0 := \frac{|T|}{|r_o|}$ and $p(h) := \frac{|c(h) \cap T|}{|c(h)|}$. The chosen evaluation function is defined as:

---

[7] Only one group is shown. The printout does not use standard logical syntax, since the arity of predicates can be in the dozens or hundreds, and only very few arguments are typically different from "_".

$$d(h) := \begin{cases} 0 \, if \mid c(h) \mid / \mid r_o \mid > s_{min} \\ \frac{g(h)}{1-g(h)}(p(h) - p_0)^2 \, \text{otherwise} \end{cases}$$

Here, s_{min} is a user-provided minimal group size; an assumption commonly made for data mining applications ("minimal support" in association rule discovery, [AMS+96].

6.2 Scalability ingredients

MIDOS uses a relatively standard hypothesis space, describing each possible interesting group by a conjunction of linked function-free literals. In addition, the system employs a so-called *foreign link* bias inspired by the *foreign key* links available in many database systems. We interpret these links as designated shared-variable paths along which different relations can be joined together. Foreign links thus are more fine-grained than type declarations, and can be used to strongly limit the size of the hypothesis space. In addition, it is possible to easily define an optimal refinement operator for the resulting hypothesis space, so that the corresponding search optimizations can be made. MIDOS employs a top-down search from most general to most specific groups (breadth-first or best-first guided by the optimistic estimates described below). At any point, the algorithm maintains the set of k best hypotheses found so far.

Pruning during this search is based on two properties. First, since groups can only get smaller during refinement, the minimal support s_{min} can be used to cut off branches that fall below. Second, MIDOS exploits the fact that the k best existing solutions are known at any point using a technique known as *optimistic estimate pruning*. Note that the quality of considered groups can both increase or decrease as groups get smaller, depending on just how object properties are distributed. Thus, we cannot simply prune whenever the quality of a group is below all k existing solutions. However, it is possible to derive from d a function d_{max} that is guaranteed to be an upper bound on d for all refinements of a hypothesis. Thus, whenever this optimistic estimate is lower than the qualities of hypotheses found so far, we can safely prune.

Finally, in order to determine d on large datasets, MIDOS uses local sampling as described above to determine the relevant g and p values with a desired error and certainty. The primary technical problem in doing this is random sampling from $c(h)$, which (in database terminology) is defined by a project-select-join query for which uniform inclusion probabilities can be achieved only under very special circumstances [Olk93]. Fortunately, since we know the set of possible query results (the members of the object relation r_o), sampling can be performed by random sampling this relation, and then checking whether the sample has the required properties. This is efficient for hypotheses with sufficient coverage, since it can be expected that we do not need to sample the entire relation r_o to find sufficiently many instances of the hypothesis.

7 Conclusion

We have presented a short tour and overview of the complexity and scalability issues in Inductive Logic Programming (ILP). As explained, early work in ILP had concentrated on fundamental complexity aspects of the ILP prediction learning task, showing that even the commonly considered restrictions of the task (language and subsumption relationship) were insufficient to reach polynomial learnability, and that further restrictions that are often unrealistic are needed for positive theoretical results. Practical systems at the same time concentrated on scalability ingredients that are difficult to analyze theoretically: declarative bias, ordered and pruned search and heuristic search control.

Among the recently introduced techniques that influence scalability, the use of descriptive learning tasks is certainly the most fundamental, both in the learning from interpretations setting, which allows easy upgrade of powerful propositional learning techniques as well as parallel search, and in the more KDD-like reinterpretations like subgroup discovery. A more direct influence on scalability, however, is due to the newly introduced sampling techniques where orders of magnitude improvements in running times have been achieved while maintaining adequate accuracies. The challenge that is remaining lies in the theoretical analysis of these techniques. There currently is no way of estimating the loss in accuracy brought about by either of global sampling and stochastic matching, and even for local sampling, where in principle a bound is available, this local bound does not translate into a bound on predictive accuracy. These could be challenges for further theoretical developments.

Finally, one topic we have not been touching upon at all in this paper is scalability with respect to databases. Even though several ILP algorithms have been coupled to relational databases already, optimizations specific to database management systems have not been made. Similarly, there are no theoretical models that would allow to judge the computational complexity of an algorithm when used in the context of disk-based storage, where disk access patterns and resulting paging and network transfer times can totally dominate runtimes. In such a context, standard computational complexity analyses have misleading results since it is not clear what can reasonably be regarded as a constant-time operation. This, however, is not an ILP-specific problem, but affects the design of data mining algorithms in general.

References

[AMS+96] Rakesh Agrawal, Heikki Mannila, Ramakrishnan Srikant, Hannu Toivonen, and A. Inkeri Verkamo. Fast discovery of association rules. In Usama M. Fayyad, Gregory Piatetsky-Shapiro, Padhraic Smyth, and Ramasamy Uthurusamy, editors, *Advances in Knowledge Discovery and Data Mining*, chapter 12, pages 307 – 328. AAAI/MIT Press, Cambridge, USA, 1996.

[AS92] N. Alon and J. H. Spencer. *The Probabilistic Method*. John Wiley, New York, 1992.

[BDR98]   Hendrik Blockeel and Luc De Raedt. Top-down induction of first-order log-
           ical decision trees. *Artificial Intelligence*, 101(1-2):285 – 297, 1998.

[BHW98]   Uta Bohnebeck, Tamas Horvath, and Stefan Wrobel. Term comparisons
           in first-order similarity measures. In David Page, editor, *Proc. 8th Int.
           Conference on Inductive Logic Programming (ILP98)*, Madison, WI, USA,
           July 1998.

[BM92]   Michael Bain and Stephen Muggleton. Non-monotonic learning. In Stephen
           Muggleton, editor, *Inductive Logic Programming*. Academic Press, London,
           New York, 1992.

[CL96]   Bradley P. Carlin and Thomas A. Louis. *Bayes and empirical Bayes meth-
           ods for data analysis*. Chapman and Hall, London, 1996.

[CN89]   Peter Clark and Tim Niblett. The CN2 induction algorithm. *Machine
           Learning*, 3(4):261 – 283, 1989.

[Coh93]   William Cohen. Learnability of restricted logic programs. In Stephen Mug-
           gleton, editor, *Proc. Third Int. Workshop on Inductive Logic Programming
           (ILP-93)*, Technical Report IJS-DP-6707, pages 41 – 71, Ljubljana, Slovenia,
           1993. Josef Stefan Institute.

[DMR92]   S. Dvzeroski, S. Muggleton, and S. Russell. PAC-learnability of determinate
           logic programs. In *Proc. 5th Annual ACM Workshop on Computational
           Learning Theory (COLT-92)*, pages 128 – 135. ACM Press, 1992.

[DRD94]   L. De Raedt and S. Džeroski. First order jk-clausal theories are pac-
           learnable. *Artificial Intelligence*, 70:375–392, 1994.

[DRD97]   Luc De Raedt and Luc Dehaspe. Clausal discovery. *Machine Learning*.
           26:99ff., 1997.

[Dvz95]   Sašo Dvzeroski. *Numerical Constraints and Learnability in Inductive Logic
           Programming*. PhD thesis, Faculty of Electrical Engineering and Computer
           Science, University of Ljubljana, Slovenia, 1995.

[Fla92]   Peter Flach. A framework for inductive logic programming. In Stephen
           Muggleton, editor, *Inductive Logic Programming*, pages 193 – 212. Academic
           Press, London, New York, 1992.

[FPSS96]   Usama M. Fayyad, Gregory Piatetsky-Shapiro, and Padhraic Smyth. From
           data mining to knowledge discovery: An overview. In Usama M. Fayyad,
           Gregory Piatetsky-Shapiro, Padhraic Smyth, and Ramasamy Uthurusamy,
           editors, *Advances in Knowledge Discovery and Data Mining*, chapter 1,
           pages 1 – 34. AAAI/MIT Press, Cambridge, USA, 1996.

[GJ79]   Michael R. Garey and David S. Johnson. *Computers and Intractability - A
           Guide to the Theory of NP-Completeness*. Freeman, San Francisco, Cal.,
           1979.

[Got87]   G. Gottlob. Subsumption and implication. *Information Processing Letters*,
           24:109 – 111, 1987.

[Hay98]   Simon Haykin. *Neural networks*. Prentice-Hall, Englewood Cliffs, NJ, 2nd
           edition edition, 1998.

[Hel89]   Nicolas Helft. Induction as nonmonotonic inference. In *Proceedings of the
           1st International Conference on Knowledge Representation and Reasoning*,
           pages 149 – 156, San Mateo, CA, 1989. Morgan Kaufman.

[KD94]   Jörg-Uwe Kietz and Saso Dzeroski. Inductive logic programming and learn-
           ability. *SIGART Bulletin*, 5(1):22 – 32, 1994.

[Kie93]   Jörg-Uwe Kietz. Some lower bounds for the computational complexity of
           inductive logic programming. In *Proc. Sixth European Conference on Ma-*

chine Learning (ECML-93), pages 115 – 123, 1993. Also as Arbeitspapiere der GMD No. 718.

[KL94]   Jörg-Uwe Kietz and Marcus Lübbe. An efficient subsumption algorithm for inductive logic programming. In W. Cohen and H. Hirsh, editors, *Proc. Eleventh International Conference on Machine Learning (ML-94)*, pages 130 – 138, 1994. .

[Klö96]   Willi Klösgen. Explora: A multipattern and multistrategy discovery assistant. In Usama M. Fayyad, Gregory Piatetsky-Shapiro, Padhraic Smyth, and Ramasamy Uthurusamy, editors, *Advances in Knowledge Discovery and Data Mining*, chapter 10, pages 249 – 271. AAAI/MIT Press, Cambridge, USA, 1996.

[KW92]   Jörg-Uwe Kietz and Stefan Wrobel. Controlling the complexity of learning in logic through syntactic and task-oriented models. In Stephen Muggleton, editor, *Inductive Logic Programming*, chapter 16, pages 335 – 359. Academic Press, London, 1992. Presented at the Int. Workshop on Inductive Logic Programming, 1991. Also available as Arbeitspapiere der GMD No. 503 .

[Llo87]   J.W. Lloyd. *Foundations of Logic Programming*. Springer Verlag, Berlin, New York, 2nd edition, 1987.

[MDR94]   Stephen Muggleton and Luc De Raedt. Inductive logic programming: Theory and methods. *Journal of Logic Programming*, 19/20:629 – 679, 1994.

[MP94]   S. Muggleton and D. Page. A learnability model for universal representations. In Stefan Wrobel, editor, *Proc. Fourth Int. Workshop on Inductive Logic Programming (ILP-94)*, pages 139 – 160, Schloß Birlinghoven, 53754 Sankt Augustin, Germany, 1994. GMD (German Natl. Research Center for Computer Science). Order from teuber@gmd.de.

[Mug93]   Stephen Muggleton. Optimal layered learning: a pac approach to incremental sampling. In K. Jantke, S. Kobayashi, E. Tomita, and T. Yokomori, editors, *Proc. of the 4th Conference on Algorithmic Learning Theory (ALT93)*, pages 37 – 44, Berlin, New York, 1993. Springer Verlag.

[Mug95]   Stephen Muggleton. Inverse entailment and Progol. In Koichi Furukawa, Donald Michie, and Stephen Muggleton, editors, *Machine Intelligence 14*, pages 133 – 188. Oxford Univ. Press, Oxford, 1995.

[NCW97]   Shan-Hwei Nienhuys-Cheng and Ronald de Wolf. *Foundations of Inductive Logic Programming*. LNAI Tutorial 1228. Springer Verlag, Berlin, New York, 1997.

[Olk93]   Frank Olken. *Random Sampling From Databases*. PhD thesis, Univ. of California at Berkeley, 1993.

[Plo70]   Gordon D. Plotkin. A note on inductive generalization. In B. Meltzer and D. Michie, editors, *Machine Intelligence 5*, chapter 8, pages 153 – 163. Edinburgh Univ. Press, Edinburgh, 1970.

[Qui90]   J.R. Quinlan. Learning logical definitions from relations. *Machine Learning*, 5(3):239 – 266, 1990.

[Qui93]   J. Ross Quinlan. *C4.5 — programs for machine learning*. Morgan Kaufman, San Mateo, CA, 1993. Accompanying software available.

[RLD93]   L. De Raedt, N. Lavrač, and S. Džeroski. Multiple predicate learning. In *Proceedings of the 13th International Joint Conference on Artificial Intelligence*. Morgan Kaufmann, 1993.

[Rob65]   J.A. Robinson. A machine-oriented logic based on the resolution principle. *JACM*, 12(1):23–41, January 1965.

[RP89]   Céline Rouveirol and Jean François Puget. Beyond inversion of resolution. In *Proc. Sixth Intern. Workshop on Machine Learning*, pages 122 – 130, San Mateo, CA, 1989. Morgan Kaufman.

[SMAU94]   Edgar Sommer, Katharina Morik, Jean-Michel Andre, and Marc Uszynski. What online machine learning can do for knowledge acquisition — a case study. *Knowledge Acquisition*, 6:435–460, 1994.

[SR97]   Michèle Sebag and Céline Rouveirol. Tractable induction and classification in first order logic via stochastic matching. In *Proc. 15th International Joint Conference on Artificial Intelligence*, 1997.

[Sri97]   Ashwin Srinivasan. Sampling methods for the analysis of large datasets with ILP. Technical Report PRG-TR-27-97, Oxford University, Oxford, UK, 1997.

[Sta94]   Irene Stahl. Properties of inductive logic programming in function-free horn logic. In *Machine Learning: ECML-94 (Proc. Seventh European Conference on Machine Learning)*, pages 423 – 426, Berlin, New York, 1994. Springer Verlag.

[WD95]   Stefan Wrobel and Saso Dzeroski. The ilp description learning problem: Towards a general model-level definition of data mining in ilp. In K. Morik and J. Herrmann, editors, *Proc. Fachgruppentreffen Maschinelles Lernen (FGML-95)*, 44221 Dortmund, 1995. Univ. Dortmund. Research Report 580.

[WO91]   Ruediger Wirth and Paul O'Rorke. Constraints on predicate invention. In *Proc. Eighth Intern. Workshop on Machine Learning*, pages 457 – 461, San Mateo, CA, 1991. Morgan Kaufman.

[Wro94]   Stefan Wrobel. Concept formation during interactive theory revision. *Machine Learning*, 14:169–191, 1994.

[Wro96]   Stefan Wrobel. Inductive logic programming. In Gerd Brewka, editor, *Advances in Knowledge Representation and Reasoning*, chapter 5, pages 153 – 189. CSLI-Publishers, Stanford, CA, USA, 1996. Studies in Logic, Language and Information.

[Wro97]   Stefan Wrobel. An algorithm for multi-relational discovery of subgroups. In Jan Komorowski and Jan Zytkow, editors, *Proc. First European Symposion on Principles of Data Mining and Knowledge Discovery (PKDD-97)*, pages 78 – 87, Berlin, 1997. Springer Verlag. .

Learning to Win Process-Control Games Watching Game-Masters

John Case[1], Matthias Ott[2,*], Arun Sharma[3,**], and Frank Stephan[4,***]

[1] Department of CIS, University of Delaware, Newark, DE 19716, USA,
case@cis.udel.edu.
[2] Institut für Logik, Komplexität und Deduktionssysteme, Universität Karlsruhe,
76128 Karlsruhe, Germany, m_ott@ira.uka.de.
[3] School of Computer Science and Engineering, University of New South Wales,
Sydney 2052, Australia, arun@cse.unsw.edu.au.
[4] Mathematisches Institut, Universität Heidelberg, Im Neuenheimer Feld 294,
69120 Heidelberg, Germany, fstephan@math.uni-heidelberg.de.

Abstract. The present paper focuses on some interesting classes of *process-control games*, where *winning* essentially means successfully controlling the process. A *master* for one of these games is an agent who plays a winning-strategy. In this paper we investigate situations, in which even a complete model (given by a program) of a particular game does not provide enough information to synthesize — even in the limit — a winning strategy. However, if in addition to getting a program, a machine may also watch masters play winning strategies, then the machine is able to learn in the limit a winning strategy for the given game. Studied are successful learning from *arbitrary* masters and from pedagogically useful *selected* masters. It is shown that selected masters are strictly more helpful for learning than are arbitrary masters. Both for learning from arbitrary masters and for learning from selected masters, though, there are cases where one can learn programs for winning strategies from masters but not if one is required to learn a program for the master's strategy itself. Both for learning from arbitrary masters and for learning from selected masters, one can learn strictly more watching $m + 1$ masters than one can learn watching only m. Lastly a simulation result is presented where the presence of a selected master reduces the complexity from infinitely many semantic mind changes to finitely many syntactic ones.

1 Introduction

To learn to win games such as chess, besides exploring the game tree with many practice games, it is also useful, or may even be necessary, to study the games

* Supported by the Deutsche Forschungsgemeinschaft (DFG) Graduiertenkolleg "Beherrschbarkeit komplexer Systeme" (GRK 209/2-96).
** Supported by Australian Research Council Grant A49600456.
*** Supported by the Deutsche Forschungsgemeinschaft (DFG) Grant Am 60/9-1.

of master players.[1] We do not have much access to the masters' actual strategic programs mostly stored in their subconscious wetware. We have, instead, access to their game-playing *behavior*. It is also apparently useful to study the (game-playing) behavior of masters who play with very different styles. For example, it is likely better to study the behavior of *both* Kasparov and Deep Blue[2] than to study only one of them.

In machine learning, the *behavioral cloning* approach to process-control, surveyed in [1], involves using data from the behavior of master or expert human controllers, in order to make complex control learning problems feasible. For example, it has been used successfully to teach an autopilot to fly an aircraft simulator [1, 3, 12, 21, 22] and to teach a machine to operate efficiently a free-swinging shipyard crane [1, 25]. Behavioral cloning partly motivates the present paper.

For us the *masters* are players of *winning strategies* for the classes of process-control games described in Section 1.1 just below. Of course the experts behaviorally cloned in the machine learning experiments mentioned just above aren't necessarily playing exactly the same kinds of process-control games as we study herein, nor are they necessarily playing perfect, complete, winning strategies. Nonetheless, some of the parallels we describe, in the rest of this subsection, between these experimental machine learning results and our main theorems are very interesting and, we hope, instructive for the future.

In this paper we study situations in which the learnability of strategies *necessarily* depends on the fact that the learner, in addition to exploring a complete description of the game, may also watch the behaviour of master players. For pedagogical purposes, some masters may be better to watch than others. In [1, 3, 12, 21, 22] it is noted that better results were obtained using the data from some pilots rather than others. Theorem 6 in Section 2 below implies that some masters are strictly more helpful than others. Hence, we distinguish between whether we are using *arbitrary* or carefully *selected* masters.[3]

In [1, 3, 12, 21, 22] the learning program employed, C4.5 [19], did not merely learn to copy identically each pilot modeled. We show in Section 2, for both arbitrary (Theorem 3) and selected masters (Theorem 4), that there are cases where one can learn winning strategies for process-control games from masters *but not if one is required to copycat the master*. An interestingly contrasting theorem in the same section (Theorem 2) implies that, if a class of process-control games can be learned *incrementally*, i.e., after finitely many trial and error rounds, from *arbitrary* masters, then it can be incrementally learned by copycatting *selected* masters.

---

[1] In this paragraph, by *master players* we mean players who win, not players formally designated as Masters (as opposed to Grand Masters in chess, ...).

[2] In principle, in the case of Deep Blue, we could look at its actual strategic program, but, even Kasparov learned from watching Deep Blue's *behavior*.

[3] Formally, this distinction is handled definitionally by universal versus existential quantifiers over masters in positive assertions (see Definition 1 in Section 2 below).

In the learning-to-fly project [1, 3, 12, 21, 22] it was discovered that C4.5 got confused if it received data from more than one pilot at a time. Seemingly contrasting with this, in Section 3 below, we show, for both arbitrary (Theorem 8) and selected masters (Theorem 9), for each $m \geq 1$, surprisingly, one can learn strictly more watching $m + 1$ masters than one can learn watching only m.[4] Interestingly, the separation between learning from two and learning from one selected master(s) is witnessed by a class of games, which is essentially specified by the *natural* class of all trees that contain infinitely many infinite computable branches.

1.1 The Process-Control Games

In the present paper we focus on the learning of (programs for) winning strategies for two kinds of *process-control games*. The two kinds turn out to be, for all our purposes, mathematically *equivalent* [8]! The second kind is mathematically elegantly simple, so we state and prove our results in terms of it, but, although, this second kind *is* interesting in its own right, more of our motivation comes from the first kind. Again: all of our results straightforwardly carry over *mutatis mutandis* to the first kind of process-control game.

The process-control games of the first kind are called *closed computable games*. These games nicely model *reactive* process-control problems. The second are the *one-player immortality games* (synonymously: *branch games*). We describe each in turn, the first informally (with references) and the second in more detail.

To explain closed computable games, we show how to model an *archetypal* process-control problem as a closed computable game. Suppose we wish to keep the temperature t in a particular room between $t_{\min} = 18\,°C$ and $t_{\max} = 22\,°C$, inclusive, where the initial temperature is $t_0 = 20\,°C$. A temperature controller, which can sense the temperature in the room, and an *unseen* physical disturbance each act at discrete times $n = 0, 1, 2, \ldots$ on the temperature of the room as follows. At time n, the controller and the disturbance can and do choose respective actions a_n and d_n each in $\{-1, 0, 1\}$, where the resultant temperature, in degrees Celsius, at time $n + 1$, is given by $t_{n+1} = f(t_n, a_n, d_n) = t_n + a_n + d_n$. The controller sees the temperature, not the disturbance, and, from its perspective, the temperature behaves indeterministically, yet, the *controller has to do well against all possible behaviors of the temperature and disturbance*. Equivalently, the controller needs a winning strategy for the associated two-player closed computable game we describe next. Player I is the controller and Player II is the *temperature*. Of course *we* know that Player II is a mere puppet of Player I *and the unseen disturbance*, but Player I can *see* the temperature, so it is better to model Player II as the temperature. A *play* of the game is just an alternating infinite sequence $a_0 t_1 a_1 t_2 \ldots$ of controller actions and temperatures, i.e., of moves of Players I and II. Player I *wins* the play $a_0 t_1 a_1 t_2 \ldots$ iff $(\forall n)[t_{\min} \leq t_n \leq t_{\max}]$.

---

[4] In the project on teaching an autopilot, a separate attribute distinguishing one pilot from another was not used; hence, this may explain the contrast.

The *goal set* for Player I is (by definition) the set of all plays $a_0 t_1 a_1 t_2 \ldots$ where Player I wins. In topology, *closed sets* (by definition) contain their limit points. The game we have described is called *closed* since the goal set for Player I is a closed set. I.e., *if* every finite initial segment $\sigma_n = a_0 t_1 a_1 \ldots a_{n-1} t_n$ of an infinite play yields no loss for the controller (i.e., if, for each $n \geq 1$, the temperature is between $t_{\min}$ and $t_{\max}$ at times $m = 1, \ldots, n$), *then* the *limit point* $a_0 t_1 a_1 \ldots$ of the sequence $(\sigma_n)_{n \in \omega}$ is a win for the controller, i.e., is in the goal set for Player I.[5] An example *winning strategy* for Player I, the controller, is as follows:

$$a_n = \begin{cases} +1 & \text{if } t_n \leq 20 \text{ or } n = 0, \\ -1 & \text{if } t_n > 20 \text{ and } n > 0. \end{cases} \tag{1}$$

We have defined the winning strategy (1) by an informal algorithm, or program; hence, it's clearly computable. A human *master* playing strategy (1) would have stored in his/her head this or an equivalent program. Formally, the watchable *behavior* would be an enumeration of the pairs (t, a) such that t is a temperature that could be observed and a is this master's response.

Next we describe the mathematically equivalent *one player immortality games*. As an informal example, consider a robot which is placed in a (finite or infinite) environment. The robot's job is to keep exploring its environment yet not get trapped or destroyed. To help it, it has a model of its environment, from which it can generate, for example, a map showing the dangerous spots. If we model finite environments as deterministic finite automata [20], then, in these cases, the one-player immortality game can be modeled as follows: Given a finite automaton, a winning strategy is an infinite word such that the finite automaton never visits a rejecting state when run on this word.

Formally, and in general, a *one player immortality game* is (by definition) a computable tree containing at least one infinite (computable) branch. The player starts at the root, and its moves must take it successively further from the root. The winning strategies are exactly the infinite branches of the trees. The conventional, master-free, strategy learning scenario is: given an enumeration of the graph, or even a program, of the game tree, incrementally synthesize a program for following *some* such winning strategy, i.e., for traveling along some *infinite* branch. Death or entrapment is modeled, then, by the player getting stuck on a *finite* branch.

1.2 The Power of Watching Masters

As shown in [8], there are classes $\mathcal{C}$ of immortality games such that no machine can synthesize a winning strategy for every game $G \in \mathcal{C}$ *in the limit*, given an enumeration of the graph, or even a program, of G as input. However, it is reasonable that one can overcome such limitations by presenting to the machine an enumeration of a winning strategy as additional input, that is, the learner may *watch a master*. In this work we study the power of (several variants of) this new learning notion. It is *important* to note that for all our results in Sections 2 and 3,

---

[5] For more formal treatment, see [5, 8, 10, 24].

where we compare different models of learning from masters, it *does not matter* whether the game tree is presented by a program, or by an enumeration of its graph! On the other hand, this matters when one compares master learning to conventional strategy learning. This comparison is the topic of Section 4, and there, we will also discuss the effect of the two different input models on this comparison.

In order to demonstrate the additional power, which a learner may gain from watching a master, we consider the following illustrative example [16]. Let the tree T_e consist of branches $f_k = ka_0a_1 \ldots$ for every natural number $k \in \omega$, that is, T_e has an infinitely branching root such that every successor k of the root is only extended by the branch f_k. The branches f_k may be finite or infinite, depending on the e-th recursively enumerable set W_e (of an standard enumeration of all r.e. sets). More precisely, we let $0a_0 \ldots a_n$ be "on the tree" T_e iff a_m is the smallest number such that $|W_{e,a_m}| \geq m$, for $m = 0, \ldots, n$. Here, $(W_{e,n})_{n \in \omega}$ denotes a finite approximation of W_e. For $k > 0$, $k0^n$ is on the tree, iff $|W_{e,n}| < k$. It is not difficult to see, that the branch f_0 is infinite iff W_e is infinite, and that, for $k > 0$, f_k is infinite iff $|W_e| < k$. Thus, every tree T_e has an infinite branch.

Assume now, that M is a machine, which computes, for all e, from a program of T_e a sequence $i_0i_1 \ldots i_m iii \ldots$ which stabilizes on a program i for an infinite branch $f = f_k$ of T_e. Then it holds that W_e is infinite iff $k = 0$. Note that $k = f_k(0) = f(0)$ can be computed using the program i. Thus, we have a procedure which decides the index set $Inf = \{e \colon W_e \text{ infinite}\}$ in the limit, that is, Inf is Δ_1 with respect to the arithmetical hierarchy. However, as well known, Inf is Π_2-complete, which is a contradiction.

Thus, a conventional branch learning machine can not synthesize infinite branches for all T_e even if it gets a program of T_e as input (instead of just an enumeration of T_e).

Now, consider a learner, who gets a program j for T_e and who watches an enumeration $f(0)f(1) \ldots$ of an infinite branch of T_e. Clearly, having seen $f(0)$ the learner knows *that the branch extending $k = f(0)$ is infinite* and can then, using the program j of T_e, compute a program for the infinite branch f. This demonstrates that learning by watching masters may be extremely more powerful than conventional branch learning. It even allows the learner to find a branch *without* any mind changes. Moreover, the learner can even *identify* the input master, instead of just learning any infinite branch of T_e. In this work we analyze this additional power gained by watching masters, and compare several interesting variants of this learning notion.

Note that we could easily code e into the beginning of the tree T_e. Then it is still impossible to synthesize strategies for this class in the limit, however, a learner who watches a master can still be successful on this class, *even if* the learner gets only an enumeration of the graph of T_e as input. By similar reasons, all our results in Sections 2 and 3 are, as already noted, independent of the input model for the trees. Therefore, we will base our, now following, more formal treatment on the easier model, in which the learner gets a program for the game tree as input.

2 Learning from a Master

The natural numbers are denoted by ω. ω^* is the set of all *finite* sequences from ω, and ω^ω is the set of all *infinite* sequences from ω. We are using an acceptable programming system $\varphi_0, \varphi_1, \ldots$; the function computed by the e-th program within s steps is denoted by $\varphi_{e,s}$. REC is the set of all total computable functions. For strings $\sigma, \tau \in \omega^* \cup \omega^\omega$, $\sigma \preceq \tau$ means that σ is an initial segment of τ. $|a_1 \ldots a_n| = n$ denotes the length of a string $a_1 \ldots a_n \in \omega^*$. If $\sigma \in \omega^*$ and $\tau \in \omega^* \cup \omega^\omega$ then $\sigma\tau$ is the concatenation of the two strings. Let $\langle \cdot \rangle$ be a coding of ω^*, i.e., a bijective computable function $\langle \cdot \rangle : \omega^* \to \omega$, which is monotone with respect to subsequences:

$$(\forall \sigma, \tau \in \omega^*)[\sigma \text{ is a subsequence of } \tau \implies \langle \sigma \rangle \leq \langle \tau \rangle].$$

We identify finite strings with their code numbers. Total functions $f : \omega \to \omega$ are identified with the infinite string $f(0)f(1)\ldots$. We write $f[n]$ for the initial segment $f(0) \ldots f(n-1)$ of f.

$T \subseteq \omega^*$ is a *tree* if T is closed under initial segments.[6] Elements of a tree are called *nodes*. If $A \subseteq \omega^* \cup \omega^\omega$ is a set of finite and infinite strings, then the prefix closure, $\{\sigma \in \omega^* : \sigma \preceq \alpha \text{ for some } \alpha \in A\}$, is a tree. We often will define trees by specifying only such a set A. A total function $f : \omega \to \omega$ is an infinite branch of T if $f[n] \in T$ for all $n \in \omega$.

For background from inductive inference see, e.g., [14]. Remaining computability theoretic notation is from [13].

We are interested only in the class *Tree* of all computable trees which contain at least one infinite computable branch. If $f \in REC$ is an infinite computable branch of T we also say that f is *on* T. Moreover, in the context, when an f on T is given as input to a learner, such a branch is called a *master*.

In what follows, for convenience, we will say *branch* to refer only to infinite computable branches. Furthermore, also for convenience, we will sometimes speak of learning a branch when we mean learning a program for the branch.

Definition 1. *A Turing machine[7] M learns a branch from an arbitrary master for a tree $T \in$ Tree, if for all masters f on T and for all e with $\varphi_e = T$, the sequence $(M(e, f[n]))_{n \in \omega}$ converges to an infinite computable branch of T, i.e., there exists an i such that φ_i is an infinite branch on T and $M(e, f[n]) = i$ for almost all n.[8] For $C \subseteq$ Tree we write $C \in$ **ArbMa** if there exists a Turing machine M which learns branches from an arbitrary master for every $T \in C$.*

---

[6] The theory remains the same if it is based on trees over a finite alphabet, e.g., on binary trees $T \subseteq \{0,1\}^*$ [16].

[7] By a well known argument, we can assume, without loss of generality, that all learning machines considered in this paper are total [14].

[8] Note that the sequence $M(e, f[n])$ converges *syntactically* to a (program for an) infinite computable branch, i.e., our notion of learning corresponds to the version of learning in the limit, which is called **Ex**-style (or incremental) learning in the literature.

A *Turing machine M learns a branch* from a selected master *for a tree* $T \in$ *Tree, if there exists a master f on T such that for all e with $\varphi_e = T$ the sequence $(M(e, f[n]))_{n \in \omega}$ converges to a (program for an) infinite computable branch of T. For $C \subseteq$ Tree we write $C \in$* **SelectMa** *if there exists a Turing machine M which learns branches from a selected master for every $T \in C$.*

If there exists an **ArbMa**- *or* **SelectMa**-*learner which converges to a program for the input master (instead of just to a program for any infinite computable branch of T) for every tree T of a class C, we say that C is learnable from arbitrary/selected masters* **identically**. *The corresponding classes are denoted by* **ArbMaId** *and* **SelectMaId**.

The definitions directly imply **ArbMa** $\subseteq$ **SelectMa**, **ArbMaId** $\subseteq$ **ArbMa** and **SelectMaId** $\subseteq$ **SelectMa**. One can prove that these inclusions are proper. Thus, to identify a master is a proper restriction for both learning from arbitrary and learning from selected masters. This shows that the advantage in watching one master (rather than none) comes from ones creating ones own winning strategy, and not from being a copycat. This result is not as surprising for **ArbMa** since one can imagine masters who go out of their way to avoid being figured out. But for the selective version of master learning this result is much more interesting. It says that regardless of how skilled pedagogically is the selected master you are watching, if one can learn a winning strategy from him/her/it, then this is, in general, only possible by creating a new strategy which differs from that of the master.

The noninclusion **SelectMa** $\not\subseteq$ **ArbMa** shows that not all masters are equally helpful for a learner. We are even able to prove **SelectMaId** $\not\subseteq$ **ArbMa**. Thus, while watching some masters provides enough information to identify these masters, watching others may be absolutely useless. Surprisingly, the other direction of the inclusion, **ArbMa** $\subseteq$ **SelectMaId**, holds. I.e., if every master allows the learner to at least find some winning strategy, then there exists one master which can even be identified by the learner. In summary, this establishes the proper linear chain **ArbMaId** $\subset$ **ArbMa** $\subset$ **SelectMaId** $\subset$ **SelectMa**. Moreover, it holds that *Tree* $\not\in$ **SelectMa**. I.e., even if a learner can watch "a most helpful" master and is only required to output any winning strategy, it is still not possible to learn such strategies for all games, which have one.

One complexity measure of a learning task is the number of mind changes[9] which a machine needs to stabilize on a program for the target object. With respect to this complexity measure, learning without any mind changes at all provides the strongest positive results one may obtain. Zero mind change learning is also called *finite* learning in the literature. All the separation results which we give in this section are established by classes of trees so that the positive half of the separation result is witnessed by a machine which makes *no* mind changes!

---

[9] In the formal definition of *mind change* one allows the machine to output initially a special symbol "?" to indicate that it has yet not seen enough data to make up its mind for its first conjecture. So a mind change is said to happen, if $? \neq M(e, f[n]) \neq M(e, f[n+1])$.

Theorem 2. ArbMa ⊆ SelectMaId.

Proof Sketch. This simulation proof is related to the proof of Freivalds and Wiehagen that every computable function can be learned from an upper bound of any of its indices [6, 7].

Let M be an **ArbMa**-learner. Furthermore, for any given tree select that infinite branch which has among all computable infinite branches the smallest minimal index, say e. Now this branch f can be inferred as follows:

The new machine N emulates M on $f[n]$ and receives a sequence $(e_n)_{n \in \omega}$ of hypotheses which converges to an index e' of some branch of the tree. By choice, e' is greater or equal to e. At each stage, N amalgamates all programs i below e_n which are consistent with the input master f on $\{0, \ldots, n\}$ during their first n computation steps. This algorithm amalgamates in the limit all programs with indices below e' which are consistent with f and thus, identifies the master f in the limit. Hence N witnesses that the class of trees **ArbMa**-learned by M can also be **SelectMaId**-learned where the selected master is the one with the smallest index.   □

Theorem 3. ArbMa ⊄ ArbMaId. *Moreover, this noninclusion can be witnessed by a class of trees which is **ArbMa**-learnable without any mind change.*

Theorem 4. SelectMa ⊄ SelectMaId. *Moreover, this noninclusion can be witnessed by a class of trees which is **SelectMa**-learnable without any mind change.*

Proof Sketch. We will build trees T_e for all $e \in \omega$. Each tree T_e has the form $T_e = \bigcup_{i \in \omega} U_e^i$ such that $ei \preceq \sigma$ for all $\sigma \in U_e^i$, $|\sigma| \geq 2$, and each tree U_e^i contains at most one infinite computable branch f. In every tree U_e^i we will try to diagonalize against φ_e as a potential **SelectMaId**-learner for T_e. We will diagonalize against φ_e by securing that φ_e makes enough "prediction errors" on f, that is, $\varphi_e(f[n])$ is undefined or does not equal $f(n)$ for infinitely many n. Since every **SelectMaId**-learner M would yield a predictor $\lambda\sigma \in \omega^* . \varphi_{M(j,\sigma)}(|\sigma|)$ for f on $\varphi_j = U_e^i$, which is at most finitely often undefined or incorrect, this will suffice to diagonalize against all **SelectMaId**-learners. T_e will be uniformly computable from e. Since e is encoded into the master, it is therefore not necessary to give an index of T_e as input to the diagonalized machine.

Furthermore, we organize this diagonalization in such a way that it will only succeed in U_e^0 and in all trees U_e^i, for $i > 0$, such that φ_i is an infinite branch of T_e. All other trees U_e^i will be finite. This implies that for $i > 0$ every tree U_e^i contains an infinite branch iff φ_i is an infinite branch of T_e. This idea is the key to achieve $\mathcal{C} \in$ **SelectMa**, since the branch f of such an infinite tree U_e^i with $i > 0$ fulfills $f(1) = i$, that is, $f(1)$ is a program for an infinite branch of T_e. Therefore, these branches can be used as selected masters.

Construction of $T_e = \{\sigma_s^i : i, s \in \omega\}$:

Stage 0:

For all $i \in \omega$: $\sigma_0^i = \tau_0^i = ei$, $x_0^i = 2$.

Stage s+1:

1. For all $i > 0$:

   If $(\forall x < x^i_s)[\varphi_{i,s}(x) \downarrow]$ and $(\exists t \leq s)(\exists j)[\varphi_i[x^i_s] \preceq \sigma^j_t]$ then let
   $$x^i_{s+1} = x^i_s + 1.$$
   Else let
   $$x^i_{s+1} = x^i_s.$$
   {*Check whether φ_i seems to become a branch of T_e so that U^i_e may be extended in step 2.*}

2. For all i:

   If $i = 0$ or $x^i_{s+1} > x^i_s$ then

   if $(\exists \tau_i)[\tau^i_s \preceq \tau_i \preceq \sigma^i_s$ and $\varphi_{e,s}(\tau_i) \downarrow]$, then choose the smallest such τ_i and let
   $$a_i = s + 1 + \varphi_e(\tau_i),$$
   $$\sigma^i_{s+1} = \tau^i_{s+1} = \tau_i a_i.$$
   Else let
   $$a_i = s + 1,$$
   $$\sigma^i_{s+1} = \sigma^i_s a_i, \ \tau^i_{s+1} = \tau^i_s.$$
   Else let
   $$\sigma^i_{s+1} = \sigma^i_s, \ \tau^i_{s+1} = \tau^i_s.$$

End of Construction.

$\square$

Theorem 5. *Tree* $\notin$ **SelectMa**.

Theorem 6. **SelectMaId** $\not\subseteq$ **ArbMa**. *Moreover, this noninclusion can be witnessed by a class of trees which is* **SelectMaId***-learnable without any mind change.*

3 Hierarchies for Learning from Many Masters

Definition 7. *In the following we write $icb(T)$ for the number of infinite computable branches of a tree $T \in$ Tree. Note that T may have infinitely many infinite computable branches, in which case we write $icb(T) = \infty$.*

A Turing machine M learns a branch from arbitrary m masters for a tree $T \in$ Tree, if for all masters $f_1, \ldots, f_m$ on T with

$$|\{f_1, \ldots, f_m\}| \geq \min\{m, icb(T)\} \tag{2}$$

and for all e with $\varphi_e = T$ the sequence $(M(e, f_1[n], \ldots, f_m[n]))_{n \in \omega}$ converges to a (program for an) infinite computable branch of T. M learns a branch from selected m masters for a tree $T \in$ Tree, if there exist masters $f_1, \ldots, f_m$ on T such that for all e with $\varphi_e = T$ the sequence $(M(e, f_1[n], \ldots, f_m[n]))_{n \in \omega}$ converges to a (program for an) infinite computable branch of T.

The corresponding classes are denoted by **ArbMa**^{m} *and* **SelectMa**^{m}.

Requirement (2) just above *on the input masters of an* **ArbMa***-learner ensures that:*

1. If there are at least m distinct infinite branches on T, then, the m masters are pairwise distinct;
2. if the number k of distinct infinite branches on T is $< m$, then exactly k of the m masters are pairwise distinct; and,
3. hence, both $\mathbf{ArbMa}^m \subseteq \mathbf{ArbMa}^{m+1}$ and $\mathbf{SelectMa}^m \subseteq \mathbf{SelectMa}^{m+1}$.

Theorem 8. *For all $m \geq 1$: $\mathbf{ArbMa}^m \subset \mathbf{ArbMa}^{m+1}$. Moreover, the noninclusion can be witnessed by a class of trees which is $\mathbf{ArbMa}^{m+1}$-learnable without any mind change.*

The separation of $\mathbf{ArbMa}^{m+1}$ and $\mathbf{ArbMa}^m$ can also be witnessed by the natural class $\mathcal{C}_{m+1}$ of all computable binary trees from *Tree* which have at most $m+1$ (arbitrary) infinite branches. However, the $\mathbf{ArbMa}^{m+1}$ learner for $\mathcal{C}_{m+1}$ needs generally $\log(m)$ mind changes (instead of zero mind changes).

The analogous hierarchy result to Theorem 8 also holds for branch learning from *selected* masters:

Theorem 9. *For all $m \geq 1$: $\mathbf{SelectMa}^m \subset \mathbf{SelectMa}^{m+1}$.*

This result, in particular, implies that even our most powerful notion of master learning, namely, learning an arbitrary branch from several selected masters, is not strong enough to learn a branch for every tree:

Corollary 10. *For all $m \geq 1$: Tree $\not\subseteq \mathbf{SelectMa}^m$.*

Theorem 9 can be proven using a team learning result from [4]. However, interestingly, the separation of $\mathbf{SelectMa}^2$ and $\mathbf{SelectMa}^1$ is witnessed by *natural* classes of trees, in particular, by the class *TreeInf* of all trees which contain infinitely many infinite computable branches. Since such separation results, which are witnessed by natural classes, are particularly interesting for inductive inference, we present here the proof of this result instead of proving the general statement from Theorem 9.

Besides *TreeInf*, also the following natural classes witness $\mathbf{SelectMa}^2 \not\subseteq \mathbf{SelectMa}^1$ (see, e.g., [4] for definitions):

- the binary trees which contain only computable infinite branches,
- the binary trees of bounded width,
- the binary trees of bounded rank, and
- the binary trees of bounded variation.

Theorem 11. *The class TreeInf of all trees, which contain infinitely many infinite computable branches, is in $\mathbf{SelectMa}^2 - \mathbf{SelectMa}^1$.*

Proof. We first prove *TreeInf* $\in \mathbf{SelectMa}^2$. So, let an arbitrary tree $T \in$ *TreeInf* be given, and let e' be the smallest e such that φ_e is on T. Then there exists an x' such that for all $e < e'$, either $\varphi_e(x) \uparrow$ for some $x < x'$, or $\varphi_e[x'] \notin T$. Since T contains infinitely many branches, T contains an infinitely branching node, or, for every n, there exist two different branches f_1, f_2 on T with $f_1[n] = f_2[n]$. This implies that there exist an n' and two different branches f_1, f_2 on T

with $f_1[n'] = f_2[n']$, $f_1(n') \neq f_2(n')$ and $n' + f_1(n') + f_2(n') > x'$. We choose these branches f_1 and f_2 as selected masters.

Now, the machine M witnessing $TreeInf \in \mathbf{SelectMa}^2$ works as follows. On input T, f_1, f_2 the machine M waits until it finds the first n with $f_1(n) \neq f_2(n)$. Then it computes $y = n + f_1(n) + f_2(n)$. Note that $n = n'$ and $y > x'$. From now on, M outputs in stage n the smallest $e \leq n$ such that

$$(\forall x < y)[\varphi_{e,n}(x) \downarrow] \text{ and } \varphi_e[y] \in T. \tag{3}$$

If no such e exists, then M outputs 0.

By definition, there exists an $n \geq e'$ such that $e = e'$ and n satisfy (3). On the other hand, no $e < e'$ can satisfy (3) for any n. Thus, from some point on, the machine will always output e' which is a program for a branch of T. Hence, M is a correct $\mathbf{SelectMa}^2$-learner for the class $TreeInf$.

We only *sketch* the proof of the negative statement. Assume by way of contradiction that the Turing machine M witnesses $TreeInf \in \mathbf{SelectMa}$. Let η_n denote the unique string with $n = \langle \eta_n \rangle$. We will construct a tree T such that M fails to $\mathbf{SelectMa}$-learn a branch for T as follows:

Construction of $T = \bigcup_{s \in \omega} T_s$:

Stage 0: $T_0 = \emptyset$, $queue_0 = (\epsilon)$.

Stage $s+1$: Assume that $queue_s = (\sigma_0, \ldots, \sigma_q)$.
Compute $j = M(e, \sigma_0)$, where $\varphi_e = T$. {*Recursion Theorem!*}
Check whether η_s satisfies the following conditions:
(a) $\sigma_0 \prec \eta_s$,
(b) $(\forall \tau, \sigma_0 \prec \tau \prec \eta_s)[\tau \in T_s]$,
(c) $(\exists x < |\sigma_0|)[\varphi_{j,s}(x) \uparrow]$ or $(\exists x < |\eta_s|)[\varphi_{j,s}(x) \downarrow \neq \eta_s(x)]$.

If η_s satisfies (a) – (c) then
  let $T_{s+1} = T_s \cup \{\eta_s\}$;
  if $M(e, \eta_s) \neq j$ then let $queue_{s+1} = (\sigma_1, \ldots, \sigma_q, \eta_s 0, \eta_s 1)$, $\qquad$ (4)
  $\qquad$ else let $queue_{s+1} = queue_s$.
If η_s does not satisfy (a) – (c) then let $T_{s+1} = T_s$, $queue_{s+1} = queue_s$.

End of Construction.

One can show that T is actually in $TreeInf$. In order to prove that M does not $\mathbf{SelectMa}$-learn a branch of T one distinguishes the following two cases.

Case 1: There exists a stage s with $queue_s = \{\sigma_0, \ldots, \sigma_q\}$ such that σ_0 is *never* removed from the queue in any stage $t > s$. This implies that, for all masters f on T, f extends σ_0, and, furthermore, $M(e, f[n]) = M(e, \sigma_0)$ for all $n \geq |\sigma_0|$. Thus, M converges on all masters to $j = M(e, \sigma_0)$. Then, φ_j is total. However, in this case, from some point on, we will only extend branches which are inconsistent with φ_j due to condition (c). Hence, φ_j is no branch of T. Contradiction.

Case 2: Every string is eventually removed from $queue_s$. Then, by construction, M will make infinitely many mind changes on every master of T due to line (4). Thus, for every master f of T, M fails to converge to a single program on input f. Contradiction. $\qquad\qquad\square$

4 Master Learning versus Branch Learning

How is ordinary branch learning [8, 16], where the learner can only inspect the tree but has no access to a master, related to master learning? As already noted in the introduction, this comparison is, in contrast to the results of Sections 2 and 3, effected by the input model for the tree. In order to make the differences clear, we denote, for **Crit** ∈ {**ArbMaId, ArbMa, SelectMaId, SelectMa**}, the version of **Crit**, where $M(e, f[n])$ in Definition 1 is replaced with $M(T[n], f[n])$, by **Enum-Crit**.

It is well known that, in general, enumerations of graphs are far less useful then programs. Therefore, it is not so surprising that **ArbMaId** ⊈ **Enum-SelectMa**. In other words, if one is working with an enumeration of the tree, then even the most powerful master learning notion fails to capture the most restrictive master learning notion working with programs of the trees. This result, in particular, implies that **Enum-Crit** ⊂ **Crit** for all master learning criteria **Crit**.

The most powerful branch learning notion from [8] is called *weak Bc-learning*.[10] A class $C \subseteq$ *Tree* is in **BranchWBc**, if there exists a Turing machine M such that for all $T \in C$ and for almost all n, the function $\varphi_{M(T[n])}$ is an infinite computable branch of T, where the tree $T \subseteq \omega^*$ is identified with its characteristic function. Note that a **BranchWBc**-learner is allowed to make infinitely many *semantic* mind changes.

A machine *synthesizes* branches for a class $C \subseteq$ *Tree in the limit* if it computes from every index of a tree $T \in C$ a sequence of programs, which converges (syntactically) to a (program for an) infinite branch of T. The corresponding class is denoted by **SynthLim**.[11]

By using the trees from Section 1.2 one can show that no "pure branch learning class" captures any "master learning classes", demonstrating the extreme power of learning from masters:

Theorem 12. Enum-ArbMaId ⊈ (**BranchWBc** ∪ **SynthLim**).

What can we say about the other direction, that is, which master learning classes capture which branch learning classes? First, one can show, that the master learning notions which are working with enumerations of trees are too restrictive:

Theorem 13.
BranchWBc ⊈ **Enum-SelectMa** *and* **SynthLim** ⊈ **Enum-SelectMa**.

However, by definition, **SynthLim** is a subset of **ArbMa**. One can show that this inclusion is proper. Hence, we have **SynthLim** ⊂ **ArbMa** ⊂ **SelectMaId** ⊂ **SelectMa**. The classes **SynthLim** and **BranchWBc** are incomparable [8], that is, there are classes in **BranchWBc** for which one cannot synthesize branches in the limit. Thus, it is interesting to see whether one of the three master learning

---

[10] The criterion is not very restrictive (weak), but, then, many things can be learned with respect to it, so, from that perspective, it is powerful.

[11] **SynthLim** is equivalent to the learning criterion called **Uni**[K] in [8, 16].

notions extending **SynthLim** are powerful enough to capture **BranchWBc**. It turns out that while **ArbMa** is still too restrictive to cover **BranchWBc**, the power of a **SelectMaId**-learner suffices. Thus, if a learner gets the index of the tree and can watch *the right* master, then the learner can improve its weak performance of infinitely many semantic mind changes to the very strong syntactic convergence to the master in the limit. The next and the last theorem of the paper formalizes this positive mind change complexity reduction result, which has an interesting simulation proof:

Theorem 14. **BranchWBc** $\subseteq$ **SelectMaId**.

Proof. Let $\mathcal{C}$ be in **BranchWBc**. Given an index of a tree $T \in \mathcal{C}$, the set E of all programs output by the learner is uniformly enumerable and depends only on the graph of T and not on the index of T. The indices in E define the following subtree $T' \subseteq T$:

$$\sigma \in T' \Leftrightarrow \sigma \in T \wedge (\exists e \in E) (\forall x \in dom(\sigma)) [\varphi_e(x) \downarrow = \sigma(x)].$$

T' is enumerable but may not be computable. Furthermore, for all indices of T, the strings in T' are enumerated in the same order. In addition, T' has only finitely many finite branches, which cannot be extended to infinite branches, that is, almost all nodes of T' lie on an infinite branch of T'. So, knowing the enumeration of T', it is possible to extend almost every node σ of T' to an infinite branch of T'. This branch u_σ is defined inductively after initializing it with σ. Let now n be the first value not yet defined, then let

$$u_\sigma(n) = \begin{cases} a & \text{if } a \text{ is the first number such that } u_\sigma(0)u_\sigma(1)\ldots u_\sigma(n-1)\,a \\ & \text{is enumerated into } T'; \\ \uparrow & \text{otherwise, if there is no such } a. \end{cases}$$

Every function u_σ is either an infinite branch of T' or is a finite branch which cannot be extended and differs from all infinite branches of T' at some value. So, the following two propositions hold:

$$\tau \prec \sigma \text{ and } u_\tau[n] \preceq u_\sigma \implies u_\tau(n) \downarrow \tag{5}$$

$$\sigma \preceq \tau \preceq u_\sigma \implies u_\sigma = u_\tau \tag{6}$$

Since the **BranchWBc**-learner produces at least one infinite branch, T' has at least one infinite branch. Moreover, if σ is a node of T' which is longer than every finite branch, then the function u_σ is infinite. Taking the master $f = u_\sigma$, the following algorithm learns this branch. The learner starts with u_λ. Whenever for the current τ an argument n is found with $u_\tau(n) \downarrow \neq f(n)$ then τ is extended to $f(0)f(1)\ldots f(n)$ and a mind change to this new u_τ is made. After finitely many mind changes, $u_\tau = u_\sigma$ and the **SelectMaId**-learner succeeds. $\square$

5   Future Work

As already mentioned in the introduction, the experts, which have been observed in the behavioral cloning experiments, are not playing necessarily winning strategies. Also master chess players do not win every play: instead of being classified into winners and losers, real players are ranked, more or less continuously, from bad to very good players. In the present basic study of watching masters we abstracted from this fact. But in future work it would be interesting to study learning from imperfect masters. At first instance, the crucial question for this research is, how to model imperfect masters. For example, one may consider masters which are playing finite variants of winning strategies. Or one may assume, that one of m input masters, or a majority of them, knows the best move in each situation. Moreover, for imperfect masters the problem of on-line learning is no longer trivial [8]! It would be interesting to investigate probabilistic learning from imperfect masters. The performance of an on-line learner can be measured by the number of lost plays, until it is eventually playing perfectly. Is there a connection between the quality of the input masters and the number of plays which an on-line learner loses?

The one-player immortality games given by a deterministic finite automaton, as described in Section 1.1, are just a special case of the well known two-player finite-state games [2, 11, 24]. In such games there always exist winning strategies which can be executed by a finite automaton. In [15] it is investigated whether one can *efficiently* learn strategies for one- and two-player *closed* finite-state games from membership and play queries, where membership queries involve asking whether a certain position is already a loss, and play queries involve asking whether a certain finite automaton implements a winning strategy. It would be interesting to apply the master learning concept to this situation. Can the time and query complexity of a learner be improved if the learner can ask queries about a winning automaton?

In Section 3 we have stated natural examples witnessing the separation of $\mathbf{ArbMa}^{m+1}$ and $\mathbf{ArbMa}^m$, and of $\mathbf{SelectMa}^2$ and $\mathbf{SelectMa}^1$. It would be interesting to look whether further natural examples separate some other levels of the $\mathbf{SelectMa}^m$ hierarchy.

References

1. M. Bain and C. Sammut. A framework for behavioural cloning. In K. F. S. Muggleton and D. Michie, editors, *Machine Intelligence 15*. Oxford University Press, 1996.

2. J. R. Büchi and L. H. Landweber. Solving sequential conditions by finite-state strategies. *Transactions of the American Mathematical Society*, 138:295–311, 1969.

3. D. K. C. Sammut, S. Hurst and D. Michie. Learning to fly. In D. Sleeman and P. Edwards, editors, *Proceedings of the Ninth International Conference on Machine Learning*. Morgan Kaufmann, 1992.

4. J. Case, S. Kaufmann, E. Kinber, and M. Kummer. Learning recursive functions from approximations. *Journal of Computer and System Sciences*, 55:183–196, 1997.

5. D. Cenzer and J. Remmel. Recursively presented games and strategies. *Mathematical Social Sciences*, 24:117–139, 1992.

6. R. V. Freivalds and R. Wiehagen. Inductive inference with additional information. *Elektronische Informationsverarbeitung und Kybernetik*, 15:179–185, 1979.

7. S. Jain and A. Sharma. Learning with the knowledge of an upper bound on program size. *Information and Computation*, 102(1):118-166, Jan. 1993.

8. M. Kummer and M. Ott. Learning branches and learning to win closed games. In *Proceedings of Ninth Annual Conference on Computational Learning Theory*, pages 280-291, New York, 1996. ACM.

9. M. Kummer and F. Stephan. On the structure of degrees of inferability. *Journal of Computer and System Sciences*, 52(2):214-238, Apr. 1996.

10. O. Maler, A. Pnueli, and J. Sifakis. On the synthesis of discrete controllers for timed systems. In *Proceedings of the Annual Symposium on the Theoretical Aspects of Computer Science*, volume 900 of *LNCS*, pages 229-242. Springer-Verlag, 1995.

11. R. McNaughton. Infinite games played on finite graphs. *Annals of Pure and Applied Logic*, 65:149-184, 1993.

12. D. Michie and C. Sammut. Machine learning from real-time input-output behaviour. In *Proceedings of the International Conference on Design to Manufacture in Modern Industry*, pages 363-369, 1993.

13. P. Odifreddi. *Classical Recursion Theory*. North-Holland, Amsterdam, 1989.

14. D. Osherson, M. Stob, and S. Weinstein. *Systems that Learn*. MIT Press, Cambridge, Massachusetts, 1986.

15. M. Ott and F. Stephan. The complexity of learning branches and strategies from queries. In *Proceedings of the Eighth Annual International Symposium on Algorithms and Computation*, volume 1350 of *LNCS*, pages 283-292. Springer, 1997.

16. M. Ott and F. Stephan. Structural measures for games and process control in the branch learning model. In S. Ben-David, editor, *Proceedings of the Third European Conference on Computational Learning Theory*, volume 1208 of *LNAI*, pages 94--108. Springer, 1997.

17. L. Pitt. Probabilistic inductive inference. *Journal of the ACM*, 36:383-433, 1989.

18. L. Pitt and C. Smith. Probability and plurality for aggregations of learning machines. *Information and Computation*, 77:77-92, 1988.

19. J. Quinlan. *C4.5: Programs for Machine Learning*. Morgan Kaufmann Publishers, San Mateo, CA, 1992.

20. R. L. Rivest and R. E. Schapire. Inference of finite automata using homing sequences. *Information and Computation*, 103(2):299-347, Apr. 1993.

21. C. Sammut. Acquiring expert knowledge by learning from recorded behaviours. In *Japanese Knowledge Acquisition Workshop*, 1992.

22. C. Sammut. Automatic construction of reactive control systems using symbolic machine learning. *Knowledge Engineering Review*, 11(1):27-42, 1996.

23. C. Smith. The power of pluralism for automatic program synthesis. *Journal of the ACM*, 29:1144-1165, 1982.

24. W. Thomas. On the synthesis of strategies in infinite games. In *Proceedings of the Annual Symposium on the Theoretical Aspects of Computer Science*, volume 900 of *LNCS*, pages 1-13. Springer-Verlag, 1995.

25. T. Urbančič and I. Bratko. Reconstructing human skill with machine learning. In A. Cohn, editor, *Proceedings of the Eleventh European Conference on Artificial Intelligence*. John Wiley & Sons, 1994.

Closedness Properties in EX-Identification of Recursive Functions *

Kalvis Apsītis[1], Rūsiņš Freivalds[2], Raimonds Simanovskis[2], and Juris Smotrovs[2]

[1] Department of Computer Science, University of Maryland, College Park, MD 20742 USA, e-mail: kalvis@cs.umd.edu
[2] Institute of Mathematics and Computer Science, University of Latvia, Raiņa bulv. 29, Rīga, LV-1459, Latvia, e-mail: rusins@cclu.lv, raymond@alise.lv, smotrovs@cclu.lv

Abstract. In this paper we investigate in which cases unions of identifiable classes of recursive functions are also necessarily identifiable. We consider identification in the limit with bounds on mindchanges and anomalies. Though not closed under the set union, these identification types still have features resembling closedness. For each of them we find such n that

1) if every union of $n-1$ classes out of $U_1, \ldots, U_n$ is identifiable, so is the union of all n classes;

2) there are such classes $U_1, \ldots, U_{n-1}$ that every union of $n-2$ classes out of them is identifiable, while the union of $n-1$ classes is not.

We show that by finding these n we can distinguish which requirements put on the identifiability of unions of classes are satisfiable and which are not. We also show how our problem is connected with team learning.

1 Introduction

This paper considers a problem in inductive inference of recursive functions. E. M. Gold in [11] introduced the paradigm of identification in the limit: the identification strategy receives data on the object to be learned (a language, for instance) in the input, and produces an infinite sequence of hypotheses (characterzining this object) that must stabilize on some correct final value. In this paper we will concentrate on identification of total recursive functions. Many modifications to the Gold's model of learning have been proposed, such as *prediction* [3], *behaviourally correct* [4], *probabilistic* [7], and *consistent identification* [18], *co-learning* [9], *identification of minimal Gödel numbers* [8].

Each such modification introduces a new identification type. One of the first questions that arises after introducing a new identification type is: "Is it closed under the operation of set union?" I. e., is the class of functions $U_1 \cup U_2$ identifiable if classes U_1 and U_2 are identifiable? This problem is solved for most if not for all of the known identification types. The first such result was proved by

---

* Supported by [1] NSF Grant 9301339 and [2] Latvia Science Council Grant 96.0282.

E. M. Gold: he showed that there are two languages that are identifiable in the limit, while their union is not [11]. A similar result for the case of total recursive functions was obtained independently by J. Bārzdiņš in [4] and by L. Blum and M. Blum in [5].

After these results it seemed natural that, whatever requirements we put on the identifiability of classes and their unions, there are such classes that satisfy these requirements. However, in [1] it was shown that there are unsatisfiable requirements as well. It turned out that EX nonetheless has a property much resembling closedness: if all the unions of classes $U_1 \cup U_2$, $U_1 \cup U_3$ and $U_2 \cup U_3$ are identifiable, then $U_1 \cup U_2 \cup U_3$ is identifiable, too. We can formalize this property as follows: we consider an identification type to be n-closed if for every n classes of recursive functions, if all the unions of $n-1$ of these classes are identifiable, so is the union of all n classes. It turns out that to distinguish between satisfiable and unsatisfiable sets of requirements we have to find the least n for which the identification type is n-closed. In [1] this problem was solved for some cases of identification in the limit modified by bounds on the number of anomalies (see [5] and [6]) and on the number of mindchanges (see [10] and [6]).

The purpose of this paper is to show the complete picture of n-closedness of identification in the limit with bounds on mindchanges and anomalies (these are the most often considered modifications of identification in the limit) and to solve the problem of satisfiability of requirements.

Papers [2, 16] deal with a similar problem in language learning and team learning.

After the preliminaries in Sect. 2, we define n-closedness and point to its connection with team learning in Sect. 3. In Sect. 4 we show how the satisfiability of requirements problem depends on n-closedness properties. In Sect. 5 we solve the n-closedness problem for the considered identification types. Sect. 6 contains summary of the results.

2 Preliminaries

Any recursion theoretic notation not explained below is from [14]. $\mathbb{N}$ denotes the set of natural numbers, $\{0, 1, 2, \ldots\}$. $*$ denotes "an arbitrary finite (natural) number." In inequalities $(\forall n \in \mathbb{N})[n < * < \infty]$. $\langle \cdot, \ldots, \cdot \rangle$ denotes a computable one-to-one numbering of all the tuples of natural numbers.

Let $\mathcal{R}$ denote the set of total recursive functions of one argument and $\mathcal{P}$ the set of partial recursive functions of one argument. If $f(x)$ is undefined, we write $f(x) \uparrow$. By $f(x) \downarrow = y$ we mean that $f(x)$ is defined and equal to y, $f(x) \downarrow$ means that $f(x)$ is defined. If $f, g \in \mathcal{P}, a \in \mathbb{N} \cup \{*\}$, then $f =^a g$ means that $\text{card}(\{x \in \mathbb{N} \mid f(x) \neq g(x)\}) \leq a$. These a points of difference are called *anomalies*. If $f \in \mathcal{R}$, $f^{[n]}$ denotes $\langle f(0), f(1), \ldots, f(n) \rangle$.

We fix a Gödel numbering of partial recursive functions (cf. [14]) and denote it by φ.

An identification strategy F is an arbitrary partial recursive function. It receives as input $f^{[n]}$ — the initial segment of the target function $f \in \mathcal{R}$. We will refer to its output $F(f^{[n]})$ as *a hypothesis* on the function f. *A mindchange* is an event when $F(f^{[n]})$ and $F(f^{[n+1]})$ are both defined and different.

Definition 1. [11, 5, 10, 6] *Let $a, b \in \mathbb{N} \cup \{*\}$. A strategy F EX_b^a-identifies a function $f \in \mathcal{R}$ ($f \in EX_b^a(F)$) iff:*

1. $(\exists N)[(\forall n < N)[F(f^{[n]}) \uparrow] \wedge (\forall n \geq N)[F(f^{[n]}) \downarrow]]$;
2. $(\exists h)[(\forall^\infty n)[F(f^{[n]}) \downarrow = h] \wedge \varphi_h =^a f]$;
3. *the number of mindchanges made by F on f does not exceed b.*

Definition 2. [11, 5, 10, 6] *A class $U \subseteq \mathcal{R}$ is EX_b^a-identifiable ($U \in EX_b^a$) iff $(\exists F \in P)[U \subseteq EX_b^a(F)]$.*

The following relationship has been established between these identification types.

Theorem 1. [6] $(\forall a, b, c, d \in \mathbb{N} \cup \{*\})[EX_b^a \subseteq EX_d^c \Leftrightarrow a \leq c \wedge b \leq d]$.

In general, we define *an identification type* by the following scheme.

1. $\mathcal{I}$-identification is defined as a mapping $\mathcal{M} \to P(\mathcal{R})$, where $\mathcal{M}$ is the set of the subjects performing identification (in this paper, the set of strategies), and $P(\mathcal{R})$ is the set of all the subsets of $\mathcal{R}$; $\mathcal{I}(M)$ is the set of all the functions identified by $M \in \mathcal{M}$;
2. a class of functions $U \subseteq \mathcal{R}$ is considered $\mathcal{I}$-identifiable iff $(\exists M \in \mathcal{M})[U \subseteq \mathcal{I}(M)]$;
3. the identification type is characterized by the set $\mathcal{I} = \{U \subseteq \mathcal{R} \mid U \text{ is } \mathcal{I}\text{-identifiable}\}$.

3 n-closedness

Here we define n-closedness and list some of its properties.

Definition 3. *An identification type $\mathcal{I}_1$ is n-closed in $\mathcal{I}_2$ ($n \geq 1$) iff*

$$(\forall U_1, \ldots, U_n \in \mathcal{I}_1)[(\forall i \mid 1 \leq i \leq n)[\bigcup_{j=1, j \neq i}^{n} U_j \in \mathcal{I}_1] \Rightarrow \bigcup_{j=1}^{n} U_j \in \mathcal{I}_2].$$

Definition 4. [16] *An identification type $\mathcal{I}$ is n-closed ($n \geq 1$) iff $\mathcal{I}$ is n-closed in $\mathcal{I}$.*

So "2-closed" is the same as "closed." The following propositions can be easily proved by set-theoretical considerations.

Proposition 1. *If $\mathcal{I}_1$ is n-closed in $\mathcal{I}_2$, then $\mathcal{I}_1 \subseteq \mathcal{I}_2$.*

Proposition 2. *If $\mathcal{I}_2$ is n-closed in $\mathcal{I}_3$, $\mathcal{I}_1 \subseteq \mathcal{I}_2$ and $\mathcal{I}_3 \subseteq \mathcal{I}_4$, then $\mathcal{I}_1$ is n-closed in $\mathcal{I}_4$.*

Proposition 3. *Let $\mathcal{I}_1$ be n-closed in $\mathcal{I}_2$. Then $\mathcal{I}_1$ is m-closed in $\mathcal{I}_2$ for all $m \geq n$.*

Proof. Suppose $\mathcal{I}_1$ is n-closed in $\mathcal{I}_2$, $m \geq n$. Suppose sets $U_1, \ldots, U_m \in \mathcal{I}_1$ satisfy the property $(\forall i \mid 1 \leq i \leq m)[\bigcup_{j=1, j \neq i}^{m} U_j \in \mathcal{I}_1]$. Define $V_1 = U_1, \ldots, V_{n-1} = U_{n-1}, V_n = \bigcup_{j=n}^{m} U_j$. We have $V_n \in \mathcal{I}_1$ because $V_n \subseteq \bigcup_{j=2}^{m} U_j \in \mathcal{I}_1$, and $\bigcup_{j=1}^{n-1} V_j \in \mathcal{I}_1$ because $\bigcup_{j=1}^{n-1} V_j \subseteq \bigcup_{j=1}^{m-1} U_j \in \mathcal{I}_1$. Thus,

$$(\forall i \mid 1 \leq i \leq n)[\bigcup_{j=1, j \neq i}^{n} V_j \in \mathcal{I}_1].$$

Since $\mathcal{I}_1$ is n-closed in $\mathcal{I}_2$, $\bigcup_{j=1}^{n} V_j = \bigcup_{j=1}^{m} U_j \in \mathcal{I}_2$.

The proposition shows that to characterize the n-closedness properties of $\mathcal{I}_1$ in $\mathcal{I}_2$ we need to find the minimal n for which $\mathcal{I}_1$ is n-closed in $\mathcal{I}_2$.

Definition 5. *We say that n is the closedness degree of $\mathcal{I}_1$ in a superset $\mathcal{I}_2$ ($n = \operatorname{csdeg}(\mathcal{I}_1, \mathcal{I}_2)$) iff n is the smallest number such that $\mathcal{I}_1$ is n-closed in $\mathcal{I}_2$. If such n does not exist, we define $\operatorname{csdeg}(\mathcal{I}_1, \mathcal{I}_2) = \infty$.*
We will call $\operatorname{cdeg}(\mathcal{I}) = \operatorname{csdeg}(\mathcal{I}, \mathcal{I})$ the closedness degree of $\mathcal{I}$.

From Proposition 2 and Theorem 1 we get:

Proposition 4. *If $a_1 \leq a_2$, $b_1 \leq b_2$, $c_1 \leq c_2$ un $d_1 \leq d_2$, then*

$$\operatorname{csdeg}(\operatorname{EX}_{b_2}^{a_2}, \operatorname{EX}_{d_1}^{c_1}) \geq \operatorname{csdeg}(\operatorname{EX}_{b_1}^{a_1}, \operatorname{EX}_{d_2}^{c_2}).$$

It turns out that the problem of finding the closedness degree is equivalent to a problem in team learning. According to this model, many strategies participate in the identification, and we require only a certain amount of them to be successful. Team learning was suggested by Case and first investigated by Smith [15]. The general definition is due to [12].

Definition 6. *Let $\mathcal{I}$ be an identification type. $U \subseteq \mathcal{R}$ is $\mathcal{I}$-identifiable by a team "k out of l" (we write $U \in [k, l]\mathcal{I}$, $1 \leq k \leq l$) iff there is a "team" of l strategies such that every function from U is $\mathcal{I}$-identified by at least k of these strategies.*

Proposition 5. *$\mathcal{I}_1$ is n-closed in $\mathcal{I}_2$ iff $[n-1, n]\mathcal{I}_1 \subseteq \mathcal{I}_2$.*

Proof. Suppose $\mathcal{I}_1$ is n-closed in $\mathcal{I}_2$. Let $U \in [n-1, n]\mathcal{I}_1$, and let $F_1, \ldots, F_n$ be the team that $[n-1, n]\mathcal{I}_1$-identifies U. We define $U_i = \{f \in U \mid (\forall j \neq i)[f \in \mathcal{I}_1(F_j)]\}$. Clearly, $(\forall j \mid 1 \leq j \leq n)[\bigcup_{i=1, i \neq j}^{n} U_i \subseteq \mathcal{I}_1(F_j)]$. Since $\mathcal{I}_1$ is n-closed in $\mathcal{I}_2$, $\bigcup_{i=1}^{n} U_i = U \in \mathcal{I}_2$.

Now, suppose $[n-1, n]\mathcal{I}_1 \subseteq \mathcal{I}_2$. Let $U_1, \ldots, U_n$ be such sets that $(\forall j \mid 1 \leq j \leq n)[\bigcup_{i=1, i \neq j}^{n} U_i \in \mathcal{I}_1]$. Let F_j be the strategy that identifies $\bigcup_{i=1, i \neq j}^{n} U_i$. Then the team $F_1, \ldots, F_n$ $[n-1, n]\mathcal{I}_1$-identifies $\bigcup_{i=1}^{n} U_i$. So $\bigcup_{i=1}^{n} U_i \in \mathcal{I}_2$. Therefore, $\mathcal{I}_1$ is n-closed in $\mathcal{I}_2$.

Corollary 1. $\operatorname{cdeg}(\mathcal{I}) = n$ iff n is the minimal number for which $[n-1, n]\mathcal{I} = \mathcal{I}$. $\operatorname{cdeg}(\mathcal{I}) = \infty$ iff for all $n \in \mathbb{N}: \mathcal{I} \subset [n-1, n]\mathcal{I}$.

Corollary 2. $\operatorname{csdeg}(\mathcal{I}_1, \mathcal{I}_2) = n$ iff n is the minimal number for which $[n-1, n]\mathcal{I}_1 \subseteq \mathcal{I}_2$. Otherwise $\operatorname{csdeg}(\mathcal{I}_1, \mathcal{I}_2) = \infty$.

4 Satisfiability of Requirements

Suppose we have a set of requirements on the EX_b^a-identifiability of every union of some classes out of $U_1, U_2, \ldots, U_k \subseteq \mathcal{R}$. We want to find a simple criterion for distinguishing if this set of requirements is satisfiable.

A convenient way for expressing such requirements is to use the Boolean functions. We will write Boolean vectors in boldface and their components in italics with indices. A vector $\mathbf{x} \in \{0,1\}^k$ corresponds to the union $\bigcup_{x_i=1} U_i$. Let $f : \{0,1\}^k \to \{0,1\}$. If $f(\mathbf{x}) = 0$, we demand that the corresponding union is identifiable. If $f(\mathbf{x}) = 1$, the corresponding union must be unidentifiable.

Definition 7. Let $a, b \in \mathbb{N} \cup \{*\}$. A Boolean function $f : \{0,1\}^k \to \{0,1\}$ is EX_b^a-satisfiable iff $(\exists U_1, \ldots, U_k \subseteq \mathcal{R})(\forall \mathbf{x} \in \{0,1\}^k)[\bigcup_{x_i=1} U_i \in EX_b^a \Leftrightarrow f(\mathbf{x}) = 0]$.

Which of the properties of EX_b^a are relevant for the satisfiability of Boolean functions? Two properties are immediate: EX_b^a contains the empty set and together with a set EX_b^a contains all its subsets. [1] showed that another property is relevant: the closedness degree. The following definition combines these three restrictions.

Definition 8. [1,2] A Boolean function $f : \{0,1\}^k \to \{0,1\}$ is n-convolutional iff

1. $f(\mathbf{0}) = 0$;
2. $(\forall \mathbf{x}, \mathbf{y} \in \{0,1\}^k)[\mathbf{x} \leq \mathbf{y} \Rightarrow f(\mathbf{x}) \leq f(\mathbf{y})]$ (monotonicity);
3. $(\forall \mathbf{x} \in \{0,1\}^k)(\forall i_1, \ldots, i_n \mid 1 \leq i_1 < \ldots < i_n \leq k \wedge x_{i_1} = \ldots = x_{i_n} = 1)[(\forall r \mid 1 \leq r \leq n)[f(x_1, \ldots, x_{i_r-1}, 0, x_{i_r+1}, \ldots, x_k) = 0] \Rightarrow f(\mathbf{x}) = 0]$.

The next result shows that the n-convolutionality is the criterion that we desire.

Theorem 2. Let $a, b \in \mathbb{N} \cup \{*\}$. If $\mathrm{cdeg}(EX_b^a) = n \in \mathbb{N}$, then a Boolean function is EX_b^a-satisfiable iff it is n-convolutional.

If $\mathrm{cdeg}(EX_b^a) = \infty$, then a Boolean function f is EX_b^a-satisfiable iff $f(\mathbf{0}) = 0$ and f is monotone.

Proof. At first we prove the necessarity. Suppose a function $f : \{0,1\}^k \to \{0,1\}$ is EX_b^a-satisfiable. Let $U_1, \ldots, U_k$ be the classes that satisfy the requirements. Then, because of the mentioned properties of EX_b^a, $f(\mathbf{0}) = 0$ and f is monotone. Suppose $\mathrm{cdeg}(EX_b^a) = n \in \mathbb{N}$. Let $\mathbf{x}$ be an arbitrary vector from $\{0,1\}^k$. Let $i_1, \ldots, i_n$ be such that $1 \leq i_1 < \ldots < i_n \leq k$ and $x_{i_1} = \ldots = x_{i_n} = 1$. We define $\mathbf{y}^j, 1 \leq j \leq n$, to be such vectors that

1. $y_{i_j}^j = 1$,
2. $y_{i_r}^j = 0$ for $r \neq j, 1 \leq r \leq n$,
3. $y_s^j = x_s$ for $s \in \{1, \ldots, k\} - \{i_1, \ldots, i_n\}$.

Let V_j be the union of $U_1, \ldots, U_k$ corresponding to the vector $\mathbf{y}^j$. Then the vectors $(x_1, \ldots, x_{i_r-1}, 0, x_{i_r+1}, \ldots, x_k)$, $1 \leq r \leq n$, correspond to the unions of $n - 1$ classes out of $V_1, \ldots, V_n$. If these are EX_b^a-identifiable, so is $\bigcup_{j=1}^n V_j$, because EX_b^a is n-closed. Since $\bigcup_{j=1}^n V_j$ corresponds to the vector $\mathbf{x}$, we have proved that f is n-convolutional.

Now, sufficiency.

Definition 9. *A vector* $\mathbf{x}$ *is* a minimal 1-vector *for a Boolean function f iff*

1. $f(\mathbf{x}) = 1$ *and*
2. $(\forall \mathbf{y} < \mathbf{x})[f(\mathbf{y}) = 0]$.

Let $\mathbf{x}^j$, $1 \leq j \leq t$, be all the minimal 1-vectors for f. Let n_j be the number of components in $\mathbf{x}^j$ that are equal to 1. Suppose that $\mathrm{cdeg}(\mathrm{EX}_b^a) = n \in \mathbb{N}$ and f is n-convolutional. According to point 3 in the definition of n-convolutionality, $n_j < n$ for every $j \in \{1, \ldots, t\}$. Suppose $\mathrm{cdeg}(\mathrm{EX}_b^a) = \infty$, $f(\mathbf{0}) = 0$ and f is monotone. Then, trivially, every $n_j < \infty$.

So, in both cases EX_b^a is not n_j-closed, $j \in \{1, \ldots, t\}$, and there are such classes $U_1^j, \ldots, U_{n_j}^j$ that every union of $n_j - 1$ out of them is identifiable, while $\bigcup_{i=1}^{n_j} U_i^j$ is not.

Now we construct the classes $U_1, \ldots, U_k$ that satisfy the requirements given by f. Suppose $x_i^j = 1$ for some $1 \leq i \leq k$ and $1 \leq j \leq t$, and suppose x_i^j is the p-th component of $\mathbf{x}^j$ that is equal to 1. Then for every function $f \in U_p^j$ we put the function

$$f'(x) = \begin{cases} j, & x = 0 \\ f(x - 1), & x > 0 \end{cases}$$

in U_i. The class U_i contains all the functions generated by this rule for different values of j and no more.

Suppose $f(\mathbf{x}) = 1$. Then for some j, $\mathbf{x}^j \leq \mathbf{x}$, and the corresponding union contains the functions f' we constructed from every function $f \in \bigcup_{i=1}^{n_j} U_i^j \notin \mathrm{EX}_b^a$, so it is unidentifiable.

Suppose $f(\mathbf{x}) = 0$. We construct a strategy F that identifies the corresponding union. F reads $f'(0) = j$ in the input. According to the monotonicity, there is such s that $x_s = 0$ and $x_s^j = 1$. Suppose x_s^j is the p-th component equal to 1 in $\mathbf{x}^j$. Then, extracting $f(x) = f'(x + 1)$ from the input, we get a function f that belongs to $\bigcup_{i=1, i \neq p}^{n_j} U_i^j$ that is EX_b^a-identifiable. So F can use the strategy that identifies this class. $\square$

Now, to solve the satisfiability problem for EX_b^a, we have only to find the closedness degrees of EX_b^a.

5 Closedness Degrees

In this section we find the $\mathrm{cdeg}(\mathrm{EX}_b^a)$ values.

The first result in the whole area of the closedness of identification types for total recursive functions was the next theorem.

Theorem 3. [4,5] *There are such classes* $U_1, U_2 \subseteq \mathcal{R}$ *that* $U_1 \in \mathrm{EX}$, $U_2 \in \mathrm{EX}$, *and* $U_1 \cup U_2 \notin \mathrm{EX}^*$.

So, $\mathrm{csdeg}(\mathrm{EX}, \mathrm{EX}^*) > 2$. Then, in team learning, the following result was obtained.

Theorem 4. [13] $(\forall a \in \mathbb{N} \cup \{*\})[[2,3]\mathrm{EX}^a \subseteq \mathrm{EX}^a]$.

Using Proposition 4 and Corollaries 1 and 2 we get:

Theorem 5. $(\forall a \in \mathbb{N} \cup \{*\})[\mathrm{cdeg}(\mathrm{EX}^a) = 3]$.

Now we will consider the identification types EX_b and EX_b^*, $b \in \mathbb{N}$. Theorem 6 is a generalization of Theorem 4.2 in [1].

Theorem 6. $(\forall b \in \mathbb{N})(\forall a, a' \in \mathbb{N} \cup \{*\} \mid a' \geq 2^{b+1}a)[\mathrm{csdeg}(\mathrm{EX}_b^a, \mathrm{EX}_b^{a'}) \leq 2^{b+2}]$.

The proof of the theorem is based on a lemma.

Lemma 1. *For all* $b \in \mathbb{N}$, $a, a' \in \mathbb{N} \cup \{*\}$, *such that* $a' \geq 2^{b+1}a$, *there is an algorithm that can* $\mathrm{EX}_b^{a'}$*-identify any function* $f \in \mathcal{R}$ *knowing (receiving as parameters) algorithms of* $2^{b+2} - 1$ *strategies such that each of them produces at least one hypothesis on* f *and at least* $2^{b+2} - 2$ *of them* EX_b^a*-identify* f.

Proof. Let strategies $F_1, F_2, \ldots, F_{2^{b+2}-1}$ and a function f satisfy the conditions. The algorithm F redirects its input to the strategies F_i until they output hypotheses h_i, $i = 1, 2, \ldots, 2^{b+2} - 1$. Then F produces a hypothesis h such that $\varphi_h(x) = y$ iff at least 2^{b+1} of the values $\varphi_{h_i}(x)$, $i = 1, 2, \ldots, 2^{b+2} - 1$, are y.

In case $b > 0$, F waits for $2^{b+1} - 1$ of the strategies F_i to make a mindchange. Suppose it happens. Then, to EX_b-identify f, these strategies can make no more than $b - 1$ mindchanges from now on. So F selects these $2^{b+1} - 1$ strategies, disregards their hypotheses made before the mindchange and applies to them the algorithm corresponding to the case of EX_{b-1}-identification. This algorithm identifies f with no more than b additional hypotheses and with no more than $2^b a$ anomalies, so $f \in \mathrm{EX}_b^{a'}(F)$.

Suppose no more than $2^{b+1} - 2$ strategies make a mindchange or $b = 0$. Then among h_i there are no more than $2^{b+1} - 1$ hypotheses with more than a anomalies, so φ_h can have an anomaly only at the points where at least one of the remaining 2^{b+1} hypotheses have an anomaly, that is at no more than $2^{b+1}a$ points.

Proof of Theorem 6. It is sufficient to prove that EX_b^a is 2^{b+2}-closed in $\mathrm{EX}_b^{a'}$. Let $U_1, U_2, \ldots, U_{2^{b+2}} \subseteq \mathcal{R}$ be such classes that all the unions of $2^{b+2} - 1$ classes out of them are EX_b^a-identifiable. Let $F_1, F_2, \ldots, F_{2^{b+2}}$ be the strategies that identify these unions. We will construct a strategy F that $\mathrm{EX}_b^{a'}$-identifies $\bigcup_{j=1}^{2^{b+2}} U_j$.

The strategy F redirects its input to the strategies F_i until $2^{b+2} - 1$ of them output a hypothesis. Such an event happens because every function $f \in \bigcup_{j=1}^{2^{b+2}} U_j$ belongs to $2^{b+2} - 1$ of the unions of $2^{b+2} - 1$ classes, thus at most one of the strategies F_i does not identify f.

Then F selects these $2^{b+2} - 1$ strategies, applies the algorithm from the previous lemma and identifies the input function. □

The next theorem is a generalization of Theorems 3.1 and 4.1 from [1].

Theorem 7. $(\forall b \in \mathbb{N})[\mathrm{csdeg}(\mathrm{EX}_b, \mathrm{EX}_b^*) > 2^{b+2} - 1]$.

We will use the idea whose origin is the concept of "self-describing" functions used in [4, Theorem 2]. We will use functions that output instructions for EX_b^a-identification of themselves. Even more, they will output many arrays of such instructions. The instructions will be of three kinds.

1. An elementary instruction $\langle 1, j, i, n \rangle$, $i, j \geq 1$. Informally, it proposes n as the i-th hypothesis in the j-th array of instructions.
2. A compound instruction $\langle 2, y_1, \ldots, y_p \rangle$, where y_i are elementary instructions. In this way many elementary instructions can be incorporated in one value output by a function.
3. A split instruction. It consists of two values, $\langle 3, i, y_1, y_2 \rangle$ and $\langle 4, i, y_3, y_4 \rangle$, where $y_1 - y_2 + y_3 - y_4$ is an elementary or a compound instruction, and i is a unique identifier for this pair of values. In this way an instruction can be split into two parts so that by changing any of these parts we can obtain a different instruction.

Among the values $f(x)$ there must be exactly one value of kind $\langle 3, i, \cdot \rangle$ and exactly one value $\langle 4, i, \cdot \rangle$ to get a split instruction with identifier i. Naturally, other kinds of instructions can be designed to prove similar results for identification types not considered in this work.

Let $\mathrm{Instr}(f)$ be the set of elementary instructions output by f, including those that are contained in the compound and the split instructions.

Definition 10. We will say that a function $f \in \mathcal{R}$ is a j-instructor with respect to the EX_b^a-identification $(a, b \in \mathbb{N} \cup \{*\})$ iff there is an instruction $\langle 1, j, c, n \rangle \in \mathrm{Instr}(f)$ such that $\varphi_n =^a f$, $c \leq b + 1$ and, if $\langle 1, j, c', n' \rangle \in \mathrm{Instr}(f)$ for some c' and n', then $c' < c$ or $n' = n$.

Let us denote the class of j-instructors with respect to EX_b^a by $I_j^{\mathrm{EX}_b^a}$. It is easy to see that $I_j^{\mathrm{EX}_b^a} \in \mathrm{EX}_b^a$.

Proof of Theorem 7. Let us denote $k = 2^{b+2} - 1$. Define $U_i = (\bigcap_{j \neq i} I_j^{\mathrm{EX}_b})$, where $i, j \in [1, k]$. Then $\bigcup_{i \neq j} U_i \subseteq I_j^{\mathrm{EX}_b} \in \mathrm{EX}_b$.

We will prove that $\bigcup_{j=1}^k U_j \notin \mathrm{EX}_b^*$. Suppose there is a strategy F that identifies this union. The multiple recursion theorem (see [17]) lets us construct functions that use each others Gödel numbers as parameters. We construct functions φ_{n_i} one of which will be the function from $\bigcup_{i=1}^k U_i$ not identified by F.

The algorithm below uses a procedure new(x). It lets $x \leftarrow n_c$, and then $c \leftarrow c + 1$, where c is a counter in the algorithm. The algorithm describing φ_{n_i} is as follows.

- *Stage 0.*
  Let $c = 1$, $j = 0$, $p = k$, $D = \{p\}$.
  Execute new(s_i) for $1 \leq i \leq p-1$. Output values as shown in the next table.

	0	...	$p-2$	...
$\varphi_{s_1}, \ldots, \varphi_{s_{p-1}}$	$\langle 1,1,1,s_1 \rangle$	...	$\langle 1, p-1, 1, s_{p-1} \rangle$	$\langle \rangle$

The leftmost column contains the functions defined, other columns show values output at the corresponding inputs. The rightmost column means that these values are output up to infinity unless the algorithm goes to the next stage.

Let the variable y throughout this algorithm indicate the maximal value of argument at which the values have been output at the moment. We simulate the strategy F on the initial segments of φ_{s_1}. If a hypothesis is output on $\varphi_{s_1}^{[x]}$ for some x, we let $h = F(\varphi_{s_1}^{[x]})$, $x_0 = \max(x,y) + 1$; we output $\langle \rangle$ up to $x_0 - 1$, if needed, and go to stage 1.

- *Stage m ($1 \leq m \leq b + 1$).*
  Let $r = \operatorname{card}(D)$, $l = (p-1)/2$.
  Let $d_1, \ldots, d_r$ be the elements of D. Execute new(t), new(u_i) for $1 \leq i \leq l-1$, new(t'), new(v_i) for $1 \leq i \leq l-1$. Output values as shown in the next table.

	x_0	...	$x_0 + r - 1$	
$\varphi_{s_1}, \ldots, \varphi_{s_l}, \varphi_t, \varphi_{u_1}, \ldots, \varphi_{u_{l-1}}$	$\langle 1, d_1, m, t \rangle$	...	$\langle 1, d_r, m, t \rangle$	
$\varphi_{s_{l+1}}, \ldots, \varphi_{s_{p-1}}, \varphi_{t'}, \varphi_{u_1}, \ldots, \varphi_{u_{l-1}}$	$\langle 1, d_1, m, t' \rangle$	...	$\langle 1, d_r, m, t' \rangle$	
	$x_0 + r$		...	
$\varphi_{s_1}, \ldots, \varphi_{s_l}, \varphi_t, \varphi_{u_1}, \ldots, \varphi_{u_{l-1}}$	$\langle 1, j+l+1, m+1, u_1 \rangle$	...		
$\varphi_{s_{l+1}}, \ldots, \varphi_{s_{p-1}}, \varphi_{t'}, \varphi_{u_1}, \ldots, \varphi_{u_{l-1}}$	$\langle 1, j+1, m+1, v_1 \rangle$		...	
	$x_0 + r + l - 2$		...	
$\varphi_{s_1}, \ldots, \varphi_{s_l}, \varphi_t, \varphi_{u_1}, \ldots, \varphi_{u_{l-1}}$	$\langle 1, j+2l-1, m+1, u_{l-1} \rangle$	$\langle \rangle$		
$\varphi_{s_{l+1}}, \ldots, \varphi_{s_{p-1}}, \varphi_{t'}, \varphi_{u_1}, \ldots, \varphi_{u_{l-1}}$	$\langle 1, j+l-1, m+1, v_{l-1} \rangle$	$\langle 0 \rangle$		

If $m = b + 1$, the algorithm remains in this stage forever.

If $m < b + 1$, we simulate F on functions φ_{s_1} and $\varphi_{s_{l+1}}$.

If F changes the current hypothesis h on $\varphi_{s_1}^{[x]}$ for some x, we let $h = F(\varphi_{s_1}^{[x]})$, $x_0 = \max(x,y) + 1$, output $\langle \rangle$ up to $x_0 - 1$, add $j+1, \ldots, j+l, j+p-1$ to D, let $s_i = u_i$ for $1 \leq i \leq l-1$, $j = j+l$, $p = l$ and go to stage $m+1$.

If F changes the current hypothesis h on $\varphi_{s_{l+1}}^{[x]}$ for some x, we let $h = F(\varphi_{s_{l+1}}^{[x]})$, $x_0 = \max(x,y) + 1$, output $\langle 0 \rangle$ up to $x_0 - 1$, add $j+l, \ldots, j+p-1$ to D, let $s_i = v_i$ for $1 \leq i \leq l-1$, $p = l$ and go to stage $m+1$.

Let us explain the meanings of variables at the start of stage m. s_i are Gödel numbers that have been proposed as the m-th hypotheses in the instructions.

The indices of these instructions begin with $j+1$ and their amount is $p-1 = 2^{b+3-m} - 2$. D contains the indices of the arrays of instructions for which the m-th hypothesis has not been proposed yet.

At stage m two alternatives represented by φ_{s_l} and $\varphi_{s_{l+1}}$ are proposed for F. Since they differ at infinitely many points, the last hypothesis h cannot be EX_b^*-correct for both of them. If F does not make a mindchange on any of the two alternatives, the algorithm remains at stage m forever, $\varphi_{s_l}, \varphi_{s_{l+1}} \in \bigcup_{i=1}^k U_i$ and at least one of these two functions is not EX_b^*-identified by F. If F makes a mindchange on one of these alternatives, the algorithm switches to stage $m+1$, choosing this alternative for further consideration. At stage $b+1$ F cannot output a new hypothesis since it already has made b mindchanges. So F does not identify the union. Contradiction. $\qquad\square$

Corollary 3. $(\forall b \in \mathbb{N})[\mathrm{cdeg}(\mathrm{EX}_b) = \mathrm{cdeg}(\mathrm{EX}_b^*) = 2^{b+2}]$.

Lastly, we consider the case of EX_b^a-identification, where $a,b \in \mathbb{N}$, $a > 0$. The results turn out to be rather surprising. For $a = 1$, the closedness degree is finite and still grows exponentially relative to b, while for $a \geq 2$ the closedness degree is ∞.

Theorem 8. $(\forall b \in \mathbb{N})[\mathrm{cdeg}(\mathrm{EX}_b^1) > \frac{7 \cdot 6^{b+1} - 2}{5}]$.

Proof. Let us denote $k = \frac{7 \cdot 6^{b+1} - 2}{5}$.

We define $U_i = (\bigcap_{j=1, j\neq i}^k I_j^{\mathrm{EX}_b^1})$, $1 \leq i \leq k$. Then $\bigcup_{i=1, i\neq j}^k U_i \subseteq I_j^{\mathrm{EX}_b^1} \in \mathrm{EX}_b^1$, $1 \leq j \leq k$.

We will prove that $\bigcup_{i=1}^k U_i \notin \mathrm{EX}_b^1$. Suppose F is a strategy identifying this union. We define functions φ_{n_i} described by the following algorithm.

- *Stage 0.*
  Let $c = 1$, $j = 0$, $p = (7 \cdot 6^{b+1} - 2)/5$, $D = \{p\}$. Execute new(s_i) for $1 \leq i \leq p-1$. Output values as shown in the next table.

	0	$\cdots$	$p-2$	$\cdots$
$\varphi_{s_1}, \ldots, \varphi_{s_{p-1}}$	$\langle 1,1,1,s_1 \rangle$	$\cdots$	$\langle 1, p-1, 1, s_{p-1} \rangle$	$\langle \rangle$
f_0	$\langle 1,1,1,s_1 \rangle$	$\cdots$	$\langle 1, p-1, 1, s_{p-1} \rangle$	$\langle \rangle$

  The function under the last horizontal line (f_0 in this case) is the function not identified by F in case the algorithm remains in this stage.
  Let the variable y throughout this algorithm indicate the maximal value of argument at which the values have been output at the moment. We simulate the strategy F on the initial segments of f_0. If a hypothesis is output on $f_0^{[x]}$, we let $h = F(f_0^{[x]})$, $x_0 = \max(x, y) + 1$; we output $\langle \rangle$ up to $x_0 - 1$, if needed, and go to stage 1.
- *Stage m ($1 \leq m \leq b+1$).*
  Let $r = \mathrm{card}(D)$. Let $d_1, \ldots, d_r$ be the elements of D. Execute new(t_i) for $1 \leq i \leq r$. Go to substage 1.

- *Substage 1.*

Let $u = (p-2)/2$, $y_1 = \langle 3, 2m-1, 0, 0 \rangle$, $z_2 = \langle 2, \langle 1, d_1, m, t_1 \rangle, \ldots, \langle 1, d_r, m, t_r \rangle \rangle$, $y_2 = \langle 4, 2m-1, z_2, 0 \rangle$. Output values as shown in the next table.

	x_0	x_0+1	$\ldots$
$\varphi_{s_1}, \ldots, \varphi_{s_u}$	?	y_2	$\langle\rangle$
$\varphi_{s_{u+1}}, \ldots, \varphi_{s_{p-2}}$	y_1	?	$\langle\rangle$
$\varphi_{s_{p-1}}$	?	?	$\langle\rangle$
$\varphi_{t_1}, \ldots, \varphi_{t_r}$	y_1	y_2	$\langle\rangle$
f_{7m-6}	y_1	y_2	$\langle\rangle$

The question marks mean that the values are not output at these points as yet. We compute $\varphi_h(x_0)$, $\varphi_h(x_0+1)$ and the outputs of F on f_{7m-6}. If $m < b+1$ and F changes its current hypothesis on $f_{7m-6}^{[x]}$ for some x, we assign h the new hypothesis value, replace question marks with the corresponding values of f_{7m-6}, let $x_0 = max(x,y) + 1$, output $\langle\rangle$ up to $x_0 - 1$, add $j + (p-2)/6 + 1, \ldots, j + p - 1$ to D, let $p = (p-2)/6$ and go to stage $m+1$.

If $\varphi_h(x_0) = y_1$, let $x_1 = y+1$, and go to substage 2.

If $\varphi_h(x_0+1) = y_2$, let $x_1 = y+1$, and go to substage 5.

- *Substage 2.*

Let $v = (p-2) \cdot 2/3$, $w = (p-2) \cdot 5/6$. Execute new(s_i') for $w+1 \leq i \leq p-3$. Let $y_3 = \langle 3, 2m, 0, 0 \rangle$, $z_4 = \langle 2, \langle 1, j+w+1, m+1, s_{w+1}' \rangle, \ldots, \langle 1, j+p-3, m+1, s_{p-3}' \rangle \rangle$, $y_4 = \langle 4, 2m, z_4, 0 \rangle$. Output values as shown in the next table.

	x_0	x_0+1	$\ldots$	x_1	x_1+1	$\ldots$
$\varphi_{s_1}, \ldots, \varphi_{s_u}, \varphi_{s_{p-1}}$	?	y_2	$\langle\rangle$	y_3	y_4	$\langle\rangle$
$\varphi_{s_{u+1}}, \ldots, \varphi_{s_v}$	y_1	y_2	$\langle\rangle$	?	y_4	$\langle\rangle$
$\varphi_{s_{v+1}}, \ldots, \varphi_{s_w}$	y_1	y_2	$\langle\rangle$	y_3	?	$\langle\rangle$
$\varphi_{s_{w+1}}, \ldots, \varphi_{s_{p-2}}$	y_1	y_2	$\langle\rangle$	?	?	$\langle\rangle$
$\varphi_{t_1}, \ldots, \varphi_{t_r}$	y_1	y_2	$\langle\rangle$	y_3	y_4	$\langle\rangle$
$\varphi_{s_{w+1}'}, \ldots, \varphi_{s_{p-3}'}$	y_1	y_2	$\langle\rangle$	y_3	y_4	$\langle\rangle$
f_{7m-5}	y_1	y_2	$\langle\rangle$	y_3	y_4	$\langle\rangle$

We compute $\varphi_h(x_1)$, $\varphi_h(x_1+1)$ and the outputs of F on f_{7m-5}. If $m < b+1$ and F outputs a new hypothesis on $f_{7m-5}^{[x]}$ for some x, we assign h the new hypothesis value, let $x_0 = max(x,y) + 1$, output $\langle\rangle$ up to $x_0 - 1$, add $j+1, \ldots, j+w, j+p-2$ and $j+p-1$ to D, let $s_i = s_{w+i}'$ for $1 \leq i \leq (p-2)/6 - 1$, let $j = j+w$, $p = (p-2)/6$ and go to stage $m+1$.

If $\varphi_h(x_1) = y_3$, go to substage 3.

If $\varphi_h(x_1+1) = y_4$, go to substage 4.

- *Substage 3.*

Execute new(t_i) for $1 \leq i \leq r$, new(s_i') for $v+1 \leq i \leq w-1$. Let $y_5 = \langle 3, 2m-1, \langle 2, \langle 1, d_1, m, t_1 \rangle, \ldots, \langle 1, d_r, m, t_r \rangle \rangle, z_2 \rangle$, $y_6 = \langle 3, 2m, \langle 2, \langle 1, j+v+1, m+1, s_{v+1}' \rangle, \ldots, \langle 1, j+w-1, m+1, s_{w-1}' \rangle \rangle, z_4 \rangle$. Output values as shown in the next table.

	x_0	x_0+1	...	x_1	x_1+1	...
$\varphi_{s_1},\dots,\varphi_{s_u},\varphi_{s_{p-1}}$	y_5	y_2	$\langle\rangle$	y_3	y_4	$\langle\rangle$
$\varphi_{s_u+1},\dots,\varphi_{s_v}$	y_1	y_2	$\langle\rangle$	y_6	y_4	$\langle\rangle$
$\varphi_{s_v+1},\dots,\varphi_{s_w}$	y_1	y_2	$\langle\rangle$	y_3	$?$	$\langle\rangle$
$\varphi_{s_w+1},\dots,\varphi_{s_{p-2}}$	y_1	y_2	$\langle\rangle$	y_6	y_4	$\langle\rangle$
$\varphi_{t_1},\dots,\varphi_{t_r}$	y_5	y_2	$\langle\rangle$	y_6	y_4	$\langle\rangle$
$\varphi_{s'_{v+1}},\dots,\varphi_{s'_{w-1}}$	y_5	y_2	$\langle\rangle$	y_6	y_4	$\langle\rangle$
f_{7m-4}	y_5	y_2	$\langle\rangle$	y_6	y_4	$\langle\rangle$

Compute outputs of F on f_{7m-4}. If $m < b+1$ and F outputs a new hypothesis on $f^{[x]}_{7m-4}$ for some x, we assign h the new hypothesis value, let $x_0 = max(x,y) + 1$, output $\langle\rangle$ up to $x_0 - 1$, add $j + 1,\dots,j + v$, $j + w,\dots,j + p - 1$ to D, let $s_i = s_{v+i}$ for $1 \leq i \leq (p - 2)/6 - 1$, let $j = j + v$, $p = (p - 2)/6$ and go to stage $m + 1$.

- *Substage 4* is similar to substage 3.
- *Substages 5, 6, 7* are similar to substages 2, 3, 4, respectively.

End of stage m.

j in the algorithm is used as a base index for the arrays that have output their m-th hypotheses (s_i) before stage m was started. Note that the values are output so that the corresponding function f_i is a q-instructor for all $q \in \{1,\dots,k\}$ except one, so $f_i \in \bigcup_{j=1}^{k} U_j$. Note also that there is no way out of the substages 3, 4, 6 and 7 of stage $b + 1$. So the algorithm remains forever in some substage (or stage 0), and, as is easy to see, the current hypothesis of F have at least two anomalies in comparison with the function f_i, corresponding to this substage (mindchanges after the b-th mindchange made by F are ignored). $\square$

Theorem 9. $(\forall b \in \mathbb{N})[\mathrm{cdeg}(\mathrm{EX}_b^1) \leq \frac{7\cdot 6^{b+1}+3}{5}]$.

Sketch of proof. Denote $k = \frac{7\cdot 6^{b+1}+3}{5}$, $l = \frac{7\cdot 6^b+3}{5}$.

Consider classes $U_1,\dots,U_k$ such that the unions of $k - 1$ classes out of them are EX_b^1-identified by strategies $F_1,\dots,F_k$. We will construct such strategy F that will identify $\bigcup_{j=1}^{k} U_j$ using $F_1,\dots,F_k$ as subroutines.

Denote the input function by f. Strategy F simulates the strategies $F_1, \dots, F_k$ on f. F waits until $k - 1$ strategies make their first hypotheses. Suppose the strategies are $F_1,\dots,F_{k-1}$, and their hypotheses are $h_1,\dots,h_{k-1}$. Then F outputs its own first hypothesis h based on these strategies and their hypotheses.

Suppose $b > 0$ and $l-1$ out of these $k-1$ strategies output another hypothesis. Then F outputs its second hypothesis, based on these $l - 1$ strategies together with their hypotheses, and we have reduced our problem to the case of EX_{b-1}^1-identification.

So it is enough to prove that, if no more than $l - 2$ strategies make another hypothesis, or $b = 0$, then hypothesis h is correct.

In this case there is at most one strategy among $F_1, \ldots, F_{k-1}$ that does not identify f and at most $l - 2$ strategies that identify f, but output another hypothesis. So no more than $l - 1$ hypotheses among $h_1, \ldots, h_{k-1}$ are wrong.

Now we describe the algorithm for φ_h. It computes the following infinite table and the hypotheses made by F_i on all possible initial segments.

	0	$\cdots$	n	$\cdots$
φ_{h_1}	$\varphi_{h_1}(0)$	$\cdots$	$\varphi_{h_1}(n)$	$\cdots$
$\cdots$	$\cdots$	$\cdots$	$\cdots$	$\cdots$
$\varphi_{h_{k-1}}$	$\varphi_{h_{k-1}}(0)$	$\cdots$	$\varphi_{h_{k-1}}(n)$	$\cdots$

Let the weight of a value in a column be the number of occurrences of this value in the column. We will say that values u and v in different columns are p-coordinated iff there are p rows that have u and v in the corresponding columns.

The aim is to find a consistent interpretation of the table, that is, such initial subtable, such $l_0 \leq l$ and such initial segment $g^{[n]}$ that $l_0 - 2$ of strategies $F_1, \ldots, F_{k-1}$ output the second hypothesis on a subsegment of $g^{[n]}$ and there are at least $k - l_0$ rows in the subtable that have no more than one anomaly in comparison with $g^{[n]}$. Such interpretations will be found for all but finitely many n, because the initial segments of f give consistent interpretations starting with the segment on which the last of the second hypotheses is output.

When an interpretation is found, φ_h outputs values (those that are not already output) according to the following rules.

1. Value u is output if its weight is at least $\frac{k-1}{2}$ and it is l-coordinated with all the values already output.
2. Value u is output if its weight is at least $\lfloor \frac{k-l_0+1}{2} \rfloor$, it is equal to the corresponding value of g and it is l-coordinated with all the values already output.
3. Value u_1 is output at point x_1 if it is l-coordinated with all the values already output and there is a column x_2 such that:
   (a) at point x_2 a value u_2 with weight at least $\frac{k-l}{2}$ has been output;
   (b) there is another value $v_2 \neq u_2$ in column x_2 such that the number of rows that have not u_1 at x_1 and have not v_2 at x_2 does not exceed $l - 1$.
4. Suppose there are at least $2l - 1$ rows that have a guaranteed anomaly in a fixed finite set of columns, and we can output values in these columns making no more than one error. In such situation the algorithm outputs these values, and in further outputs a value iff it is in at least l of these $2l - 1$ rows (any output according to the previous rules is terminated).

The proof of the correctness of the algorithm is rather long and technical, so we omit it here. $\quad\quad\quad\quad\quad\quad\quad\quad\quad\quad\quad\quad\quad\quad\quad\quad\quad\quad\quad\quad\quad\quad\quad\quad\quad\quad\square$

Corollary 4. $(\forall b \in \mathbb{N})[\mathrm{cdeg}(\mathrm{EX}_b^1) = \frac{7 \cdot 6^{b+1} + 3}{5}]$.

Theorem 10. $(\forall a \in \mathbb{N} \mid a > 1)(\forall b \in \mathbb{N})[\mathrm{cdeg}(\mathrm{EX}_b^a) = \infty]$.

The method of proof is similar to the one used in Theorems 7 and 8; we omit it here.

6 Conclusion

The next table summarizes the obtained closedness degrees.

$EX_b^{a\rightarrow}$	0	1	2	...	*
0	4	9	∞	∞	4
1	8	51	∞	∞	8
2	16	303	∞	∞	16
...	...	...	∞	∞	...
n	2^{n+2}	$\frac{7\cdot 6^{n+1}+3}{5}$	∞	∞	2^{n+2}
...	...	...	∞	∞	...
*	3	3	3	3	3

More interesting than finding the closedness degrees for other identification types (such as BC^a, $CONS^a$, $[k,l]EX_b^a$, etc) is the question: for which identification types the cdeg is finite? How does the cdeg value affect the hierarchy of success ratios k/l that yield classes $[k,l]EX_b^a$ that are different in their learning power? And what is this hierarchy in the cases when cdeg is infinite? It seems that this hierarchy is not well ordered, unlike the cases that have been investigated at the moment. Since n-closedness uncovers structural aspects of the identification types, we feel that a further research in this direction is needed.

7 Acknowledgements

The authors wish to thank the anonymous referees for valuable comments.

References

1. K. Apsītis, R. Freivalds, M. Kriķis, R. Simanovskis, J. Smotrovs. Unions of identifiable classes of total recursive functions. In K. Jantke, editor, *Analogical and Inductive Inference. Lecture Notes in Artificial Intelligence*, vol. 642, pp. 99–107. Springer-Verlag, 1992.
2. K. Apsītis, R. Freivalds, R. Simanovskis, J. Smotrovs. Unions of identifiable families of languages. In L. Miclet, C. de la Higuera, editors, *Grammatical Inference: Learning Syntax from Sentences. Lecture Notes in Artificial Intelligence*, vol. 1147, pp. 48–58. Springer-Verlag, 1996.
3. J. Bārzdiņš. Prognostication of automata and functions, pp. 81–84, Elsevier-North Holland, 1972.
4. J. Bārzdiņš. Two theorems on the limiting synthesis of functions. In J. Bārzdiņš, editor, *Theory of Algorithms and Programs*, vol. 1, pp. 82–88. Latvian State University, Rīga, 1974. (In Russian.)
5. L. Blum and M. Blum. Toward a mathematical theory of inductive inference. *Information and Control*, vol. 28, pp. 125–155, 1975.
6. J. Case and C. Smith. Comparison of identification criteria for machine inductive inference. *Theoretical Computer Science*, vol. 25 (2), pp. 193–220, 1983.
7. R. Freivalds. Functions computable in the limit by probabilistic machines. *Lecture Notes in Computer Science*, vol. 28, pp. 77–87, 1975.

8. R. Freivalds. Minimal Gödel numbers and their identification in the limit. *Lecture Notes in Computer Science*, vol. 32, pp. 219–225, Springer-Verlag, 1975.

9. R. Freivalds, M. Karpinski, and C. H. Smith. Co-learning of total recursive functions. *Proceedings of the 7th Annual ACM Workshop on Computational Learning Theory*, pp. 190–197, ACM Press, New York, 1994.

10. R. Freivalds and R. Wiehagen. Inductive inference with additional information. *Elektronische Informationsverabeitung und Kybernetik*, vol. 15 (4), pp. 179–184, 1979.

11. E. M. Gold. Language identification in the limit. *Information and Control*, vol. 10, pp. 447–474, 1967.

12. D. Osherson, M. Stob, and S. Weinstein. Aggregating inductive expertise. *Information and Control*, vol. 70, pp. 69–95, 1986.

13. L. Pitt and C. Smith. Probability and plurality for aggregations of learning machines. *Information and Computation*, vol. 77, pp. 77–92, 1988.

14. H. Rogers, Jr. *Theory of Recursive Functions and Effective Computability.* McGraw-Hill, New York, 1967.

15. C. H. Smith. The power of pluralism for automatic program synthesis. *Journal of the ACM*, vol. 29 (4), pp. 1144–1165, 1982.

16. J. Smotrovs. Closedness properties in team learning of recursive functions. In S. Ben-David, editor, *Computational Learning Theory. Lecture Notes in Artificial Intelligence*, vol. 1208, pp. 79–93. Springer-Verlag, 1997.

17. R. Smullyan. *Theory of Formal Systems. Annals of Mathematical Studies*, vol. 47, Princeton, 1961.

18. R. Wiehagen. Limes-Erkennung Funktionen durch spezielle Strategien. *Journal of Information Processing and Cybernetics*, vol. 12, pp. 93–99, 1976.

Lower Bounds for the Complexity of Learning Half-Spaces with Membership Queries

Valery N. Shevchenko and Nikolai Yu. Zolotykh

Nizhny Novgorod State University, Gagarin ave. 23,
Nizhny Novgorod 603600, Russia

Abstract. Exact learning of half-spaces over finite subsets of $\mathbb{R}^n$ from membership queries is considered. We describe the minimum set of labelled examples separating the target concept from all the other ones of the concept class under consideration. For a domain consisting of all integer points of some polytope we give non-trivial lower bounds on the complexity of exact identification of half-spaces. These bounds are near to known upper bounds.

1 Introduction

We consider the complexity of exact identification of half-spaces over the domain M that is an arbitrary finite subset of $\mathbb{R}^n$ (n is fixed). We are interested in the model of learning with membership queries.

The main result of this paper is Theorem 2 describing the structure of the teaching set T of a half-space c, i.e. a subset of M such that no other half-space agrees with c on the whole T.

The mentioned theorem is used to obtain the lower bound for the complexity of identification of half-spaces over the domain $\{0, 1, \ldots, k - 1\}^n$. We show that $\mathrm{MEMB}(\mathrm{HS}_k^n) = \Omega(\log^{n-2} k)$. For $n \geq 3$ this significantly improves $\Omega(\log k)$ lower bound [10] on the considered quantity. The presented result can be compared with the following upper bound. From results of M. Yu. Moshkov in the test theory [11] it follows that

$$\mathrm{MEMB}(\mathrm{HS}_k^n) = O\left(\frac{\log^n k}{\log \log k}\right)$$

(see [8]). We remark that for any fixed n there is a learning algorithm that requires $O(\log^n k)$ membership queries and polynomial in $\log k$ running time. This algorithm was proposed in [20, 21, 8] .

When M is the set of all integer points of some polytope we give a lower bound for the complexity $\mathrm{MEMB}(\mathrm{HS}(M))$. We show that for any fixed n and $l > n$ and for any γ there is a polytope $P \subset \mathbb{R}^n$ described by a system of l linear inequalities with integer coefficients by absolute value not exceeding γ such that $\mathrm{MEMB}(\mathrm{HS}(P \cap \mathbb{R}^n)) = \Omega(l^{\lfloor n/2 \rfloor} \log^{n-1} \gamma)$. We remark that this bound is near to an upper bound obtained in the threshold function deciphering formalism: an algorithm that learns a half-space over $P \cap \mathbb{Z}^n$ in time bounded polynomially in l and $\log \gamma$ using $O(l^{\lfloor n/2 \rfloor} \log^n \gamma)$ membership queries was proposed in [16] (n is fixed).

Some other related results see in Sect. 6.

2 Preliminaries

Let M is an arbitrary finite non–empty subset of $\mathbb{R}^n$. M is considered as an *instance space*. A *concept* over M is a subset of M. A *concept class* is some non-empty collection of concepts over M. The concept $c \subseteq M$ is called a *half-space* over M if there exist real numbers $a_0, a_1, \ldots, a_n$ such that

$$c = \left\{ x \in M \mid \sum_{j=1}^{n} x_j a_j \leq a_0 \right\} . \tag{1}$$

The inequality in (1) is called a *threshold inequality* for c. Denote by $\mathrm{HS}(M)$ the set of all half-spaces over M. Define $\mathrm{HS}_k^n = \mathrm{HS}(E_k^n)$ where $E_k = \{0, 1, \ldots, k-1\}$. Each half-space over M is a concept. The class $\mathrm{HS}(M)$ is a concept class.

We consider the model of *exact learning* [1, 10] with *membership queries*. The goal of the learner is to identify an unknown target concept c chosen from a known concept class C, making membership queries ("Is $x \in c$?" for some $x \in M$) and receiving yes/no answers. The complexity of a learning algorithm for C is the maximum number of queries it makes, over all possible target concepts $c \in C$. The complexity $\mathrm{MEMB}(C)$ of a concept class C is the minimum learning complexity, over all learning algorithms for this class. A set $T \subseteq M$ is said to be a *teaching set* for a concept $c \in C$ with respect to the class C if no other concept from C agrees with c on the whole T. If a teaching set is of minimum cardinality, over all teaching sets for a concept c, then we call it *minimum teaching set* for c. Denote by $\mathrm{TD}(c, C)$ the cardinality of a minimum teaching set for a concept c. $\mathrm{TD}(C)$ is maximum $\mathrm{TD}(c, C)$ over all concepts c in C. $\mathrm{TD}(C)$ is called *teaching dimension* for the class C. It is clear that $\mathrm{MEMB}(C) \geq \mathrm{TD}(C)$ (cf. [9]).

Let $\mathrm{Conv}(X)$ be the convex hull of $X \subseteq \mathbb{R}^n$; $\mathrm{Affdim}(X)$ is the affine dimension of X. For a concept $c \subseteq M$ denote by $N_0(c)$ (resp. $N_1(c)$) the set of vertices of $\mathrm{Conv}(c)$ (resp. $\mathrm{Conv}(M \setminus c)$). Denote $P_\nu(c) = \mathrm{Conv}\, N_\nu(c)$ ($\nu = 0, 1$).

3 Auxiliary Results

We first remark that a concept c over the domain M belongs to $\mathrm{HS}(M)$ if and only if $P_0(c) \cap P_1(c) = \emptyset$. Indeed, the necessity is evident and the sufficiency follows from the Separating Hyperplane Theorem (see [5]).

Associated with each half-space c over M is the cone $K(c)$ of separating functionals $a = (a_0, a_1, \ldots, a_n, a_{n+1})$ in an $(n+2)$-dimensional vector space [13,

15]; $K(c)$ is described by the conditions

$$
\begin{cases}
\sum_{j=1}^{n} a_j x_j \leq a_0 & \text{for each } x \in c \ , \\
\sum_{j=1}^{n} a_j x_j \geq a_0 + a_{n+1} & \text{for each } x \in M \setminus c \ , \\
a_{n+1} \geq 0 \ .
\end{cases}
\tag{2}
$$

Any solution $(a_0, \ldots, a_{n+1})$ of this system, with $a_{n+1} > 0$, defines a threshold inequality for c. The opposite is also true: the coefficients $(a_0, \ldots, a_n)$ of any threshold inequality of c satisfy the system (2) for some positive value of a_{n+1}.

For any $T_0 \subseteq c$, $T_1 \subseteq M \setminus c$ we consider the next subsystem of (2):

$$
\begin{cases}
\sum_{j=1}^{n} a_j x_j \leq a_0 & \text{for each } x \in T_0 \ , \\
\sum_{j=1}^{n} a_j x_j \geq a_0 + a_{n+1} & \text{for each } x \in T_1 \ , \\
a_{n+1} \geq 0 \ .
\end{cases}
\tag{3}
$$

Denote by $K(T_0, T_1)$ the cone consisting of its solutions. The set

$$
K^*(T_0, T_1) = \left\{ \sum_{x \in T_0} \lambda_x \begin{pmatrix} 1 \\ -x \\ 0 \end{pmatrix} + \sum_{x \in T_1} \lambda_x \begin{pmatrix} -1 \\ x \\ -1 \end{pmatrix} + \nu \begin{pmatrix} 0 \\ 0 \\ 1 \end{pmatrix} \mid \lambda_x \geq 0, \nu \geq 0 \right\}
$$

is a cone, dual to $K(T_0, T_1)$. A cone is said to be *pointed* if it does not contain non-zero subspaces.

Lemma 1. *For any $T_0 \subseteq c$, $T_1 \subseteq M \setminus c$ the cone $K^*(T_0, T_1)$ is pointed.*

Proof. Since $0 \in K(T_0, T_1)$, for some non-negative ν and λ_x $(x \in T_0 \cup T_1)$ we have that $0 = \sum_{x \in T_0} \lambda_x \cdot (1, -x, 0) + \sum_{x \in T_1} \lambda_x \cdot (-1, x, -1) + \nu \cdot (0, 0, 1)$; consequently, $\sum_{x \in T_0} \lambda_x = \sum_{x \in T_1} \lambda_x = \nu$. If $\nu = 0$ then for any $x \in T_0 \cup T_1$ it holds that $\lambda_x = 0$, hence $K^*(T_0, T_1)$ is a pointed cone. If $\nu \neq 0$ then the point $y = \frac{1}{\nu} \sum_{x \in T_0} \lambda_x x = \frac{1}{\nu} \sum_{x \in T_1} \lambda_x x$, evidently, belongs to $P_0 \cap P_1$ that is impossible. $\square$

Lemma 2. *For any $c \in \mathrm{HS}(M)$ the dimension of $K(c)$ is $n + 2$.*

Proof. It is known [5] that the cone K has the full dimension if and only if the dual cone K^* is pointed. Since $K(c) = K(c, M \setminus c))$, the assertion follows from Lemma 1. $\square$

Lemma 3. *If $\mathrm{Affdim}\, M = n$ then for any $c \in \mathrm{HS}(M)$ the cone $K(c)$ is pointed.*

Proof. It is sufficient to verify that if $a = (a_0, a_1, \ldots, a_n, a_{n+1}) \in K(c)$ and $-a \in K(c)$ then $a = 0$. From the system (2) we get that in this case $a_{n+1} = 0$ and, consequently,

$$M \subseteq \left\{ x = (x_1, x_2, \ldots, x_n) \mid \sum_{j=1}^{n} a_j x_j = a_0 \right\} .$$

Since the dimension of M is n, all a_i $(i = 0, \ldots, n)$ are zeroes. $\qquad\square$

Now the following is a consequence of the theory of linear inequalities [5, 12].

Lemma 4. *If* Affdim $M = n$ *then for every* $c \in \mathrm{HS}(M)$

1) the cone $K(c)$ *has a unique up to positive factors generating system (the system of extreme rays)*

$$\{\widetilde{b^{(i)}} = (b_0^{(i)}, b_1^{(i)}, \ldots, b_n^{(i)}, b_{n+1}^{(i)}), \ i = 1, \ldots, s\} \ ; \tag{4}$$

2) there are unique sets $T_0(c) \subseteq c$, $T_1(c) \subseteq M \setminus c$ *such that (2) is equivalent to the system*

$$\begin{cases} \sum_{j=1}^{n} a_j x_j \leq a_0 & \text{for each } (x_1, \ldots, x_n) \in T_0(c) \ , \\ \sum_{j=1}^{n} a_j x_j \geq a_0 + a_{n+1} & \text{for each } (x_1, \ldots, x_n) \in T_1(c) \ , \\ a_{n+1} \geq 0 \end{cases} \tag{5}$$

and no subsystem of (5) is equivalent to the system (2);

3) for any $x = (x_1, \ldots, x_n) \in T_0(c)$ *there is a subset* $I \subseteq \{1, \ldots, s\}$ *such that* $|I| = n + 1$, *the system* $\{\widetilde{b^{(i)}}, i \in I\}$ *is linearly independent and*

$$\sum_{j=1}^{n} b_j^{(i)} x_j = b_0^{(i)} \ (i \in I), \quad \sum_{i \in I} b_{n+1}^{(i)} > 0 \ ; \tag{6}$$

4) for any $x = (x_1, \ldots, x_n) \in T_1(c)$ *there is a subset* $I \subseteq \{1, \ldots, s\}$ *such that* $|I| = n + 1$, *the system* $\{\widetilde{b^{(i)}}, i \in I\}$ *is linearly independent and*

$$\sum_{j=1}^{n} b_j^{(i)} x_j = b_0^{(i)} + b_{n+1}^{(i)} \ (i \in I), \quad \sum_{i \in I} b_{n+1}^{(i)} > 0 \ .$$

$\qquad\square$

There is the standard method to reduce the problem with Affdim $M < n$ to the case of full dimension. Let $M \subseteq \mathbb{Q}^n$. Denote by Aff M the affine hull of M. Suppose that Aff $M = \{x \in \mathbb{R}^n \mid Ax = b\}$ for some $A \in \mathbb{Z}^{m \times n}$. Let D be a Smith's normal diagonal matrix for A, the matrices P and Q are unimodular matrices such that $PAQ = D$. Without loss of generality we can take, $D = (I_m, 0)$

where I_m is an identity $m \times m$ matrix, 0 is a zero $n \times (n - m)$ matrix. Perform the change of variables $x = Qy$ mapping $\mathbb{Z}^n$ into $\mathbb{Z}^n$. We have that $PAx = Dy$, that is, Aff M is described by the conditions $y' = Pb$ where $y' = (y_1, \ldots, y_m)$. Thus, rewriting remaining conditions in variables $y'' = (y_{m+1}, \ldots, y_n)$ we get the problem in $\mathbb{R}^{n-m}$ with Affdim $M = n - m$. We remark that there exist P, Q such that the maximal by absolute value coefficient in the new problem does not exceed some polynomial in the maximal coefficient of the old problem (see, for example, [12]).

4 Caracterization of Teaching Sets of Half-Spaces

Theorem 1. *Let* $T_0 \subseteq c$, $T_1 \subseteq M \setminus c$. $T = T_0 \cup T_1$ *is a teaching set for a half-space* c *if and only if (3) is equivalent to (2).*

Proof. The sufficiency of the conditions is evident. We prove their necessity. Assume that there is the solution $b = (b_0, b_1, \ldots, b_n, b_{n+1})$ of (3) that does not belong to $K(c)$. By Lemma 2, we can suppose that $b_{n+1} > 0$. The threshold inequality $\sum\limits_{j=1}^{n} b_j x_j \leq b_0$ defines some concept $g \in HS(M)$. We have that $b \notin K(c)$, thus $g \neq c$. But g agrees with c on T. Hence T is not a teaching set. □

This theorem leads to

Corollary 1. *Let* $T_0 \subseteq c$, $T_1 \subseteq M \setminus c$, *then for any* $c \in HS(M)$ *the set* $T = T_0 \cup T_1$ *is a minimum teaching set if and only if* $T_\nu = T_\nu(c)$ $(\nu = 0, 1)$. □

We note that the 2nd assertion of Lemma 4 is true for any $M \subseteq \mathbb{R}^n$, also when Affdim $M < n$. By Corollary 1, we now get

Corollary 2. *For any* $c \in HS(M)$ *there is a unique minimum teaching set. It is contained in every teaching set of* c. □

Denote by $T(c) = T_0(c) \bigcup T_1(c)$ the minimum teaching set for c.

Corollary 3. *(Cf. [14, 7]) For any* $c \in HS(M)$ *it holds that* $T(c) \subseteq N_0(c) \cup N_1(c)$.

Proof. It is obvious that for $T_\nu = N_\nu(c)$ the system (3) is equivalent to the system (2). The assertion of the corollary follows now from Theorem 1. □

Let Affdim $M = n$ and $c \in HS(M)$. Without loss of generality we can assume that in (4) it holds that $b_{n+1}^{(i)} > 0$ for any $i = 1, \ldots, \mu$ and $b_{n+1}^{(i)} = 0$ for any $i = \mu + 1, \ldots, s$. Let $a = (a_1, \ldots a_n)$,

$$M_0(c, a) = \left\{ (y_1, \ldots, y_n) \in M \mid \sum_{j=1}^{n} a_j y_j = \max_{x \in c} \sum_{j=1}^{n} a_j x_j \right\},$$

$$M_1(c,a) = \left\{ (y_1,\ldots,y_n) \in M \mid \sum_{j=1}^{n} a_j y_j = \min_{x \in M \setminus c} \sum_{j=1}^{n} a_j x_j \right\}.$$

Denote by $N_\nu(c,a)$ the set of vertices of the convex hull of $M_\nu(c,a)$.

Theorem 2. *If Affdim $M = n$ then for any $c \in HS(M)$ it holds that*

$$T(c) = \bigcup_{i=1}^{\mu} \left(N_0(c,\widetilde{b^{(i)}}) \cup N_1(c,\widetilde{b^{(i)}}) \right) = \bigcup_{a} (N_0(c,a) \cup N_1(c,a)) ,$$

in the right-hand side the union is over all $a = (a_1,\ldots,a_n) \in \mathbb{R}^n$ such that the inequality

$$\sum_{j=1}^{n} a_j x_j \leq \max_{x \in c} \sum_{j=1}^{n} a_j x_j$$

is a threshold inequality for c.

Proof. First we prove the inclusion $T(c) \subseteq \bigcup_{i=1}^{\mu} \left(N_0(c,\widetilde{b^{(i)}}) \cup N_1(c,\widetilde{b^{(i)}}) \right)$. Let $y = (y_1,\ldots y_n) \in T_0(c)$. By the 3rd assertion of Lemma 4, there is $i \in \{1,\ldots,\mu\}$ such that $\sum_{j=1}^{n} b_j^{(i)} y_j = b_0^{(i)}$. Since $b_{n+1}^{(i)} > 0$, the coefficients $b_j^{(i)}$ $(j = 0,1,\ldots,n)$ are the coefficients of a threshold inequality for c and $\max_{x \in c} \sum_{j=1}^{n} x_j b_j^{(i)} = b_0^{(i)}$. It follows from this that $y \in M_0(c,\widetilde{b^{(i)}})$. Assume that $y \notin N_0(c,\widetilde{b^{(i)}})$, i.e. $y = \sum_{q=1}^{p} \alpha_q y^{(q)}$ for some $p > 1$, $\alpha_q > 0$, $\sum_{q=1}^{p} \alpha_q = 1$, $y \neq y^{(q)} \in M_0(c,\widetilde{b^{(i)}})$ $(q = 1,\ldots,p)$. Then $y \notin N_0(c)$ and, by Corollary 3, $y \notin T_0(c)$. This contradiction shows that $y \in N_0(c,\widetilde{b^{(i)}})$. The case $y \in T_1(c)$ is proved similarly by the 4th assertion of Lemma 4.

We now prove that $\bigcup_{a} (N_0(c,a) \cup N_1(c,a)) \subseteq T(c)$. Let $a = (a_1,\ldots,a_n) \in \mathbb{R}^n$ and $a_0 = \max_{x \in c} \sum_{j=1}^{n} a_j x_j$; $\sum_{j=1}^{n} a_j x_j \leq a_0$ is a threshold inequality for c. For any point $z \in N_0(c,a)$ we consider a concept $g = c \setminus \{z\}$. Let us prove that $g \in HS(M)$. Assume the contrary, then $P_0(g) \cap P_1(g) \neq \emptyset$. This means that there are points $x^{(1)},\ldots,x^{(p)}$ in g, points $y^{(0)},\ldots,y^{(q)}$ in $M \setminus g$, and positive numbers $\alpha_1,\ldots\alpha_p, \beta_0,\ldots\beta_q$ such that

$$x = (x_1,\ldots,x_n) = \sum_{r=1}^{p} \alpha_r x^{(r)} = \sum_{t=0}^{q} \beta_t y^{(t)} , \tag{7}$$

$\sum_{r=1}^{p} \alpha_r = 1$, $\sum_{t=0}^{q} \beta_t = 1$ where $x \in P_0(g) \cap P_1(g)$. It is clear that among $y^{(0)},\ldots,y^{(q)}$ there is a point z, since otherwise we obtain that $P_0(c) \cap P_1(c) \neq \emptyset$, that is

impossible, because it holds that $c \in HS(M)$. Let $z = y^{(0)}$. We have that
$$\sum_{j=1}^{n} a_j x_j = \sum_{r=1}^{p} \alpha_r \sum_{j=1}^{n} a_j x_j^{(r)} = \sum_{t=1}^{q} \beta_t \sum_{j=1}^{n} a_j y_j^{(t)} + \beta_0 \sum_{j=1}^{n} a_j z_j.$$ In the last formula
the central part does not exceed a_0; in the right-hand side the first addend is
greater than a_0, and the second one is equal to a_0. For the equality it is necessary
that $q = 0$ and $\sum_{j=1}^{n} a_j x_j^{(r)} = a_0$ $(r = 1, \ldots, p)$. Thus, $\beta_0 = 1$, $z = x$. From (7) we
now obtain that $z \notin N_0(c, a)$, that contradicts the condition. Hence $g \in HS(M)$.
Since c and g differ only at one point, we have that $z \in T(c)$.

Suppose now that $a = (a_1, \ldots, a_n) \in \mathbb{R}^n$, $a_0 = \min_{x \in M \setminus c} \sum_{j=1}^{n} a_j x_j$. The inequality $\sum_{j=1}^{n} a_j x_j \geq a_0$ is true for any point in $M \setminus c$ and it is false for any point in c.
For each $z \in N_1(c, a)$ we define a concept $g = c \cup \{z\}$. The further proof is the
same one described above.

It is obvious that $\bigcup_{i=1}^{\mu} \left(N_0(c, \widetilde{b^{(i)}}) \cup N_1(c, \widetilde{b^{(i)}}) \right) \subseteq \bigcup_{a} (N_0(c, a) \cup N_1(c, a))$. The
last inclusion finishes the proof of the theorem. □

The example $x \in M$ is called *essential* for a concept $c \in HS(M)$ if there is
$g \in HS(M)$ such that c and g agree on $M \setminus \{x\}$ and don't agree at the point x.
From the last part of Theorem 2 it follows that $T(c)$ is exactly the set of essential
examples for c. For the case of Boolean domain E_2^n this is a well-known result
(see [2] and related papers referenced in [2]).

As an example of Theorem 2, consider the concept $c \in HS(E_9^3)$ defined by
the threshold inequality $20x_1 + 28x_2 + 35x_3 \leq 140$. Rewrite the system (5) as
$Qa \geq 0$ where $a = (a_0, \ldots, a_{n+1})^T$ is a column of variables and Q is a matrix
formed from the coordinates of the points of $T(c)$. Let B be a matrix formed
from the entries of the vectors $\widetilde{b^{(i)}}$, $S = QB$, I is an identity matrix. The matrix

$$\begin{pmatrix} E & B \\ \hline Q & S \end{pmatrix}$$

is represented in Table 4. We have that $\mu = 3$,

$$N_0(c, \widetilde{b^{(1)}}) = \{p^{(1)}, p^{(3)}\}, \quad N_1(c, \widetilde{b^{(1)}}) = \{q^{(1)}, q^{(2)}\},$$

$$N_0(c, \widetilde{b^{(2)}}) = \{p^{(1)}, p^{(2)}\}, \quad N_1(c, \widetilde{b^{(2)}}) = \{q^{(1)}, q^{(3)}\},$$

$$N_0(c, \widetilde{b^{(3)}}) = \{p^{(1)}, p^{(2)}, p^{(3)}\}, \quad N_3(c, \widetilde{b^{(1)}}) = \{q^{(1)}\}$$

where $p^{(1)} = (7, 0, 0)$, $p^{(2)} = (0, 5, 0)$, $p^{(3)} = (0, 0, 4)$, $q^{(1)} = (4, 1, 1)$, $q^{(2)} = (3, 3, 0)$, $q^{(3)} = (2, 0, 3)$, $\widetilde{b^{(1)}} = (56, 8, 11, 14, 1)$, $\widetilde{b^{(2)}} = (70, 10, 14, 17, 1)$, $\widetilde{b^{(3)}} = (140, 20, 28, 35, 140)$. By Theorem 2, $T_\nu(c) = \bigcup_{i=1}^{3} N_\nu(c, \widetilde{b^{(i)}})$ $(\nu = 0, 1)$. For the
considered example in the union it suffices to retain solely 2 members. Indeed,
$T_0(c) = N_0(c, \widetilde{b^{(3)}}) = N_0(c, \widetilde{b^{(1)}}) \cup N_0(c, \widetilde{b^{(2)}})$, $T_1(c) = N_1(c, \widetilde{b^{(1)}}) \cup N_1(c, \widetilde{b^{(2)}})$.

Table 1. Example of Theorem 2

1	0	0	0	0	56	70	140	140	105	84	80	50	36	21
0	1	0	0	0	8	10	20	20	15	12	11	7	5	3
0	0	1	0	0	11	14	28	28	21	16	16	10	7	4
0	0	0	1	0	14	17	35	35	25	21	20	12	9	5
0	0	0	0	1	1	1	3	0	0	0	0	0	0	0
1	-7	0	0	0	0	0	0	0	0	0	3	1	1	0
1	0	-5	0	0	1	0	0	0	0	4	0	0	1	1
1	0	0	-4	0	0	2	0	0	5	0	0	2	0	1
-1	4	1	1	-1	0	0	0	3	1	1	0	0	0	0
-1	3	3	0	-1	0	1	1	4	3	0	1	1	0	0
-1	2	0	3	-1	1	0	2	5	0	3	2	0	1	0
0	0	0	0	1	1	1	3	0	0	0	0	0	0	0

5 Bounds for the Teaching Dimension of Half-Spaces

Denote by N the set of vertices of the polytope $\mathrm{Conv}\,M$.

Lemma 5. *If $c = M$ or $c = \emptyset$ then it holds that $T(c) = N$.*

Proof. Assume that for $c = M$ there is a point $x \in N \setminus T(c)$. Consider the concept $g = M \setminus \{x\}$. Since $x \in N$, it is clear that $g \in \mathrm{HS}(M)$ and, consequently, $x \in T(c)$. We have proved that $N \subseteq T(c)$. The opposite inclusion follows from Corollary 3. For $c = \emptyset$ the lemma can be proved by analogy. □

¿From Lemma 5 it follows that $\mathrm{TD}(\mathrm{HS}_k^n) \geq 2^n$. Indeed, assume that $c = E_k^n$. By Lemma 5 we have that $\mathrm{TD}(c) = 2^n$, hence $\mathrm{TD}(\mathrm{HS}_k^n) \geq 2^n$. Thus, no polynomial in n algorithm for learning half-spaces over E_k^n from membership queries exists. This was originally proved in [14].

Let P be a polytope in $\mathbb{R}^n$ that can be described as an integer system of l linear inequalities with integer coefficients whose absolute values do not exceed γ. Denote by $\mathcal{P}(n, l, \gamma)$ the class of all such polytopes. For the class $\mathrm{HS}(M)$ with $M = P \cap \mathbb{Z}^n$ and $P \in \mathcal{P}(n, l, \gamma)$ we have

Theorem 3. *For every natural $n \geq 2$ and $l > n$ there is γ_0 such that for every $\gamma \geq \gamma_0$ there exists a polytope $P \in \mathcal{P}(n, l, \gamma)$ such that*

$$\mathrm{MEMB}(\mathrm{HS}(M)) \geq \mathrm{TD}(\mathrm{HS}(M)) \geq D_n l^{\lfloor n/2 \rfloor} \log^{n-1} \gamma$$

where $M = P \cap \mathbb{Z}^n$ and D_n is some positive quantity depending only on n.

Proof. It was proved in [6] (cf. [3]) that for any fixed $n \geq 2$ and $l > n$, for any sufficiently large γ there exists a polytope $P \in \mathcal{P}(n, l, \gamma)$ such that the number of vertices of $\mathrm{Conv}\,(P \cap \mathbb{Z}^n)$ is not less than $D_n l^{\lfloor n/2 \rfloor} \log^{n-1} \gamma$. The assertion to be proved follows now from Lemma 5. □

Return to the class HS_k^n. Denote by $N(a_0, a_1, \ldots, a_n)$ the set of all vertices of a convex hull of solutions of the following system:

$$\begin{cases} \sum_{j=1}^{n} a_j x_j = a_0 \ ; \\ x_j \geq 0; \ x_j \in \mathbb{Z} \ (j = 1, \ldots, n) \ . \end{cases}$$

In [18] S. I. Veselov got a lower bound for the mean quantity of $|N(a_0, a_1, \ldots, a_n)|$ (see Sect. 3.5 of [15]). This leads to

Lemma 6. *For every* $n \geq 2$, $k \geq 2$ *there are positive numbers* $a_0, a_1, \ldots, a_n$ *such that* $a_i \leq k - 1$ $(i = 0, 1, \ldots, n)$ *and*

$$|N(a_0, a_1, \ldots, a_n)| \geq C_n \log^{n-2} k$$

where C_n *is some positive quantity depending only on* n. $\square$

Theorem 4. *For every* $n \geq 2$ *and* $k \geq 2$

$$C_n \log^{n-2} k \leq \mathrm{TD}(\mathrm{HS}_k^n) \leq C'_n \log^{n-1} k$$

where C_n *and* C'_n *are some quantities depending only on* n.

Proof. The lower bound was announced (without a proof) in [17]. To obtain it we construct a concept c in the following manner. Consider $a_0, a_1, \ldots, a_n$ in the assertion of Lemma 6 as the coefficients of a threshold inequality of c. Since $1 \leq a_i \leq k - 1$, we have that $N(a_0, \ldots, a_n) \subseteq E_k^n$. From Theorem 2 it follows that $T(c) \supseteq N(a_0, \ldots, a_n)$, hence, $\mathrm{TD}(c, \mathrm{HS}_k^n) \geq C_n \log^{n-2} k$, consequently, $\mathrm{TD}(\mathrm{HS}_k^n) \geq C_n \log^{n-2} k$.

The upper bound was proved by T. Hegedüs [7] on the base of [13]. It is clear that for $T_\nu = N_\nu(c)$ the system (2) is equivalent to the system (3), hence $T(c) \subseteq N_0(c) \bigcup N_1(c)$; it is known [7] that $|N_0(c)| + |N_1(c)| \leq C'_n \log^{n-1} k$ where C'_n is some quantity depending only on n. Thus for any concept $c \in \mathrm{HS}_n^k$ the inequality $\mathrm{TD}(c) \leq C'_n \log^{n-1} k$ holds. $\square$

The lower bound in Theorem 4 gives us that $\mathrm{MEMB}(\mathrm{HS}_k^n) \geq C_n \log^{n-2} k$.

6 Related Results and Open Problems

In proving the lower bound for the teaching dimension of half-spaces over E_k^n we used the fact that the quantity μ in Theorem 2 is at least 1. An open problem remains: it would be helpful to estimate from *above* the quantity μ (we remark that for $n \geq 3$ there are examples with $\mu = 2, 3$). In this way one could apparently decrease the upper bound on $\mathrm{TD}(\mathrm{HS}_k^n)$. For instance, it is known from [17] that $\mathrm{TD}(\mathrm{HS}_k^2) = 4$. This result is of considerable interest because (as it was shown in [4, 19]) $\mathrm{MEMB}(\mathrm{HS}_k^2) = \Theta(\log k)$.

References

1. Angluin, D.: Queries and concept learning. Machine Learning (2) (1988) 319–342
2. Anthony, M., Brightwell, G., Shawe-Taylor, J.: On specifying Boolean functions by labelled examples. Discrete Applied Mathematics **61** (1) (1995) 1–25
3. Bárány, I., Howe, R., Lovász, L.: On integer points in polyhedra: a lower bound. Combinatorica (12) (1992) 135–142
4. Bultman, W. J., Maass, W.: Fast identification of geometric objects with membership queries. Information and Computation **118** (1) (1995) 48–64
5. Chernikov, S. N.: Linear Inequalities. "Nauka" Moscow (1968). German transl.: VEB Deutscher Verlag Wiss. Berlin (1971)
6. Chirkov, A. Yu.: On lower bound of the number of vertices of a convex hull of integer and partially integer points of a polyhedron. Proceedings of the First International Conference "Mathematical Algorithms". NNSU Publishers Nizhny Novgorod (1995) 128–134 (Russian)
7. Hegedüs, T.: Geometrical concept learning and convex polytopes. Proceedings of the 7th Annual ACM Conference on Computational Learning Theory (COLT'94). ACM Press New York (1994) 228–236
8. Hegedüs, T.: Generalized teaching dimensions and the query complexity of learning. Proceedings of the 8th Annual ACM Conference on Computational Learning Theory (COLT'95). ACM Press New York (1995) 108–117
9. Korobkov, V. K.: On monotone functions of logic algebra. Cybernetics Problems. "Nauka" Moscow **13** (1965) 5–28 (Russian)
10. Maass, W, Turán, Gy.: Lower bound methods and separation results for on-line learning models. Machine Learning (9) (1992) 107–145
11. Moshkov, M. Yu.: Conditional tests. Cybernetics Problems. "Nauka" Moscow **40** (1983) 131–170 (Russian)
12. Schrijver, A.: Theory of Linear and Integer Programming. Wiley-Interscience New York (1986)
13. Shevchenko, V. N.: On some functions of many-valued logic connected with integer programming. Methods of Discrete Analysis in the Theory of Graphs and Circuits. Novosibirsk **42** (1985) 99–102 (Russian)
14. Shevchenko, V. N.: Deciphering of a threshold function of many-valued logic. Combinatorial-Algebraic Methods in Applied Mathematics. Gorky (1987) 155–163 (Russian)
15. Shevchenko, V. N.: Qualitative Topics in Integer Linear Programming. "Fizmatlit" Moscow (1995). English transl.: AMS Providence Rhode Island (1997)
16. Shevchenko, V. N., Zolotykh, N. Yu.: Decoding of threshold functions defined on the integer points of a polytope. Pattern Recognition and Image Analysis. MAIK/Interperiodica Publishing Moscow **7** (2) (1997) 235–240
17. Shevchenko, V. N., Zolotykh, N. Yu.: On complexity of deciphering threshold functions of k-valued logic. Russian Math. Dokl. (Doklady Rossiiskoi Akademii Nauk) (to appear)
18. Veselov, S. I.: A lower bound for the mean number of irreducible and extreme points in two discrete programming problems. Manuscript No. 619–84, deposited at VINITI Moscow (1984) (Russian).
19. Zolotykh, N. Yu.: An algorithm of deciphering a threshold function of k-valued logic in the plane with the number of calls to the oracle $O(\log k)$. Proceedings of the First International Conference "Mathematical Algorithms". NNSU Publishers Nizhny Novgorod (1995) 21–26 (Russian)

20. Zolotykh, N. Yu., Shevchenko, V. N.: On complexity of deciphering threshold functions. Discrete Analysis and Operations Research. Novosibirsk **2** (1) (1995) 72–73 (Russian)
21. Zolotykh, N. Yu., Shevchenko, V. N.: Deciphering threshold functions of k-valued logic. Discrete Analysis and Operations Research. Novosibirsk **2** (3) (1995) 18–23. English transl.: Korshunov, A. D. (ed.): Operations Research and Discrete Analysis. Kluwer Ac. Publ. Netherlands (1997) 321–326

Cryptographic Limitations on Parallelizing Membership and Equivalence Queries with Applications to Random Self-Reductions

Marc Fischlin

Fachbereich Mathematik (AG 7.2)/Informatik
Johann Wolfgang Goethe-Universität Frankfurt am Main
Postfach 111932
60054 Frankfurt/Main, Germany
marc@mi.informatik.uni-frankfurt.de
http://www.mi.informatik.uni-frankfurt.de/

Abstract. We assume wlog. that every learning algorithm with membership and equivalence queries proceeds in rounds. In each round it puts in parallel a polynomial number of queries and after receiving the answers, it performs internal computations before starting the next round. The query depth is defined by the number of rounds. In this paper we show that, assuming the existence of cryptographic one-way functions, for any fixed polynomial $d(n)$ there exists a concept class that is efficiently and exactly learnable with membership queries in query depth $d(n) + 1$, but cannot be weakly predicted with membership and equivalence queries in depth $d(n)$. Hence, concerning the query depth, efficient learning algorithms for this concept class cannot be parallelized at all. We also discuss some applications to random self-reductions and coherent sets.

1 Introduction

A fundamental problem in computer science is the question if and how sequential algorithms can be parallelized. This is an intrinsic problem in computational learning theory, too. Parallelizing PAC algorithms [27] is only a matter of parallelizing the internal computations, because a sufficient number of random examples can be generated in a single concurrent step [12, 28, 11]. For learning algorithms with membership and equivalence queries [1, 2] this problem is closely related to the "grade of adaptiveness" of the queries. A quantitative formalization is via the query depth of a learning algorithm: We assume wlog. that the learning algorithm proceeds in rounds. In each round it is allowed to put in parallel a polynomial number of membership and equivalence queries. After receiving the answers, it performs some internal computation and then starts the next round. The query depth (as a function of some complexity parameter n) is the maximal number of rounds, where the maximum is taken over all target concepts of complexity n. Bshouty and Cleve [10, 9] prove that exact learning with membership and equivalence queries e.g. of read-once Boolean functions and monotone DNF formulas in n variables requires a query depth of $\Omega(n/\log n)$. Balcázar, Diaz, Gavaldà and Watanabe [4] show that DFA with n states can be learned exactly with membership and equivalence queries in depth $\mathcal{O}(n/\log n)$. Moreover, they prove that this bound is optimal as there cannot exist a learning algorithm that learns DFA exactly in query depth $o(n/\log n)$. These negative results are not tight in the sense that it remains open if there is a concept class where allowing one additional level of query depth helps. Also, these lower bounds are sublinear and hold for exact learning exclusively. In this paper, we show that for any given polynomial $d(n)$ there is a concept class such that the class cannot be weakly predicted with membership and equivalence queries in query depth $d(n)$, though there exists a polynomial-time algorithm that learns every target concept in query depth $d(n) + 1$ exactly with membership queries. We emphasize that, adding a single "level of adaptiveness", we can learn this class exactly, while any learning algorithm with depth $d(n)$ miserably fails, i.e., cannot satisfy a potentially weaker requirement than PAC-learnability (with queries). While our impossibility result as well as the lower bound of [4] only holds for polynomial-time algorithms, the result of Bshouty and Cleve is also valid for computationally unbounded parallel learners — as long as the number of queries is polynomially bounded.

The intractability of our concept class is based on a cryptographic assumption, namely the existence of one-way functions. These are functions that are easy to evaluate but hard to invert on a random value. Despite complexity based impossibility results (see for example [23]) several negative results for learning algorithms have been based on cryptographic primitives. Angluin and Kharitonov [3] use one-way functions to show that membership queries do not add any power to PAC-algorithms when learning DNF formulas. Similarly, Kearns and Valiant [20] and Kharitonov [21] show that polynomial-size Boolean formulas are not efficiently PAC-learnable with membership queries if one-way functions exist. Rivest and Yi [25] present a concept class based on the existence of one-way functions where self-directed learning is inferior to teacher-directed learning. We exploit their idea to define our concept class using so-called collections of pseudorandom functions: Informally, a collection of pseudorandom functions is a sequence $(F_n)_{n \in \mathbb{N}}$ of function sets $F_n \subset \{g : \{0,1\}^n \to \{0,1\}^n\}$. Each set F_n contains 2^n functions, where every function in F_n is identified by a key $k \in \{0,1\}^n$. While most of the functions in the set of all 2^{n2^n} functions $g : \{0,1\}^n \to \{0,1\}^n$ must have exponential description size, F_n only contains a very small fraction of these functions and therefore supports short identifiers. Yet, F_n preserves the randomness property, that is, if we uniformly choose a key $k \in \{0,1\}^n$ then the function described by this key "looks" like a uniformly chosen function from the set $\{g : \{0,1\}^n \to \{0,1\}^n\}$. It is well-known that collections of pseudorandom functions exist if and only if one-way functions exist. Given any collection of pseudorandom functions we define the concepts of complexity n by the keys of F_n and such that a particular query sequence of depth $d(n) + 1$ yields the key of the function resp. the name of the target concept. Hence, we can easily learn the target concept in depth $d(n) + 1$. Conversely, there cannot exist any probabilistic polynomial-time algorithm that, after experimenting using membership and equivalence queries in query depth $d(n)$, classifies a random example correctly with probability at least $1/2 + 1/p(n)$ for an arbitrary positive polynomial $p(n)$ and all but finite $n \in \mathbb{N}$. Otherwise we derive a constradiction to the pseudo-randomness of the underlying collection.

We apply our result on the non-parallelizability of the queries to random self-reductions [8]. Informally, a language $\mathcal{L}$ is self-reducible [26] if, for any x, we can compute the characteristic function $\chi_\mathcal{L}$ of $\mathcal{L}$ at x from values $\chi_\mathcal{L}(y_1), \dots, \chi_\mathcal{L}(y_m)$, where $|y_1|, \dots, |y_m| < |x|$. Put differently, $\mathcal{L}$ is self-reducible if membership can be decided by querying the oracle $\chi_\mathcal{L}$ for smaller elements. A classic example of a self-reducible language is SAT. An interesting special case of self-reductions are random self-reductions, where each query y_i is a random value distributed independently of x (but not necessarily independently of the other queries). Unlike self-reductions, random self-reductions do not require that the queries are smaller elements. The query depth of a random self-reduction is defined analogously to the query depth of a learning algorithm. Feigenbaum et al. [15] show that adaptive (more specifically, query depth $|x|$) random self-reductions are more powerful than nonadaptive ones. Combining our result with [15] we establish the following hierarchy: Let $\beta(n)$ be an unbounded, nondecreasing function $\beta(n)$ such that $n^{\beta(n)}$ is time-constructible (e.g., $\beta(n) = \log^* n$) and let $d(n)$ be a fixed polynomial. If one-way functions exist, there is a language in $\mathrm{DSPACE}(n^{\beta(n)})$ such that there is a random self-reduction with query depth $d(n) + 1$, while every length-preserving random self-reduction of depth $d(n)$ fails. We show that similar results can be derived for coherent sets.

The paper is organized as follows. In Section 2 we introduce notations and definitions of learning theory, cryptography and random self-reductions and coherence. In Section 3 we define our concept class and prove the positive resp. negative result about learnability. Finally, in Section 4, we apply this result to random self-reductions as well as coherent sets.

2 Preliminaries

We introduce some basic notations. For a finite set S let $y \in_R S$ denote a uniformly chosen element y from S. We write $\pi_j(y) \in \{0, 1\}$ for the projection onto the j-th bit of $y \in \{0, 1\}^n$, where n is understood from the context and $j \in \{1, \dots, n\}$. For notational convenience, we irrationally switch between natural numbers and their binary representations.

2.1 Computional Learning Theory

We briefly recall notations and definitions of learning theory. Let $X = (X_n)_{n \in \mathbb{N}}$ denote the *domain*, where $X_n \subseteq \{0, 1\}^{p(n)}$ for some polynomial $p(n)$. For $k \in \{0, 1\}^n$, a *concept* c_k is a subset of X_n. We call k the *name* of c_k. Let $\mathcal{C}_n = \{c_k \mid k \in \{0, 1\}^n\}$ and define the *concept class* by $\mathcal{C} = (\mathcal{C}_n)_{n \in \mathbb{N}}$. We usually view c_k as a Boolean function; that is, $c_k(x) = 1$ if $x \in c_k$ and $c_k(x) = 0$ otherwise.

Let $\mathcal{D} = (\mathcal{D}_n)_{n \in \mathbb{N}}$ be a sequence of distributions $\mathcal{D}_n$ on X_n. We say that $\mathcal{D}$ is *efficiently sampleable* if there is a probabilistic polynomial-time algorithm such that for input 1^n the output of the algorithm is identically distributed to $\mathcal{D}_n$.

Following Kharitonov [21] we define a prediction with membership and equivalence queries algorithm (pwme-algorithm). Let C be a concept class and $\mathcal{D}$ be an efficiently sampleable distribution. The error parameter function $\epsilon : \mathbb{N} \to \mathbb{Q}^+$ determines the accuracy of the learning algorithm. A pwme-algorithm L is a probabilistic algorithm that gets inputs n and $\epsilon(n)$ and, after a target concept $c_k \in C$ has been chosen, may make in addition to internal computations

- membership queries, i.e., query the oracle c_k for arbitrary $x \in X_n$
- equivalence queries, i.e., give $k' \in \{0,1\}^n$ to the oracle and receive the answer "yes" if $c_k = c_{k'}$ resp. a counterexample $x \in X_n$ with $c_k(x) \neq c_{k'}(x)$
- exactly one challenge query, where an example $z \in X_n$ is randomly generated according to the distribution $\mathcal{D}_n$ and returned to L. L is then supposed to make a guess for $c_k(z)$

We say that L *successfully predicts* C with respect to $\mathcal{D}$ and ϵ iff, for all $n \in \mathbb{N}$ and $c_k \in C_n$, the probability that L's guess is correct, i.e., equals $c_k(z)$, is at least $1 - \epsilon(n)$. We call C *efficiently predictable* with respect to $\mathcal{D}$ and ϵ iff there is a pwme-alogithm L that successfully predicts C with respect to $\mathcal{D}$ and ϵ and runs in polynomial time in n and $1/\epsilon(n)$. We say that C is *weakly predictable* with respect to $\mathcal{D}$ iff it is efficiently predictable with respect to $\mathcal{D}$ and $\epsilon(n) = 1/2 - 1/p(n)$ for some polynomial $p : \mathbb{N} \to \mathbb{Q}^+$ and all but finitely many $n \in \mathbb{N}$. We call a pwme-algorithm L a pwm-algorithm if L is not allowed equivalence queries.

Note that C and $\mathcal{D}$ are fixed and therefore known by L. Note also that L cannot receive randomly generated examples (as in case of PAC algorithms), because we only consider efficiently sampleable distributions. Thus, L can generate an example by itself and then put a membership query for this example. Moreover, we remark that unpredictability implies impossibility of PAC-learnability with queries (see the discussion in [21]).

Next, we define the query depth of a pwme-algorithm. We assume wlog. that any pwme-algorithm L proceeds in rounds. At the beginning of each round, L puts in parallel membership and equivalence queries and receives the answers. Then it performs internal computations and starts the next round. After finishing the last round, it is allowed additional computations and finally gives its output. The pwme-algorithm has query depth $d(n)$ if it takes at most $d(n)$ rounds for inputs $n, \epsilon(n)$ and all target concepts of complexity n. A concept class C is *weakly predictable in query depth* $d(n)$ with respect to $\mathcal{D}$ if it is weakly predictable by a pwme-algorithm with query depth $d(n)$.

As for the positive result on the learnability of our concept class, we say that a concept class C is *exactly learnable in polynomial-time with membership queries* iff there exists a polynomial-time algorithm L such that for all $n \in \mathbb{N}$ and $c_k \in C_n$, algorithm L with oracle access to c_k outputs a name $k' \in \{0,1\}^n$ such that $c_k = c_{k'}$. The query depth of such an algorithm is defined analogously to the depth of the pwme-algorithm. If this depth is bounded by $d(n)$, we call C *exactly learnable with membership queries in query depth* $d(n)$.

2.2 Cryptography

In this section we introduce the cryptographic background. A function $\delta : \mathbb{N} \to \mathbb{R}^+$ is called *negligible* iff it vanishes faster than any polynomial fraction, i.e., iff for any polynomial $p : \mathbb{N} \to \mathbb{R}^+$ there exists $n_0 \in \mathbb{N}$ such that $\delta(n) < 1/p(n)$ for all $n \geq n_0$. For instance, $\delta(n) = 2^{-n}$ is negligible. For the rest of the paper, we abbreviate "there exists n_0 such that ... for all $n \geq n_0$" by "for all sufficiently large n". In the sequel we use the following facts about negligble functions: Let $f(n) \geq 1/p_0(n)$ for some positive polynomial p_0 and infinitely many n and let $\delta(n)$ be a negligible function; then $f(n) - \delta(n) \geq 1/2p_0(n)$ for infinitely many n. Additionally, it is easy to see that $p(n) \cdot \delta(n)$ is negligible for any positive polynomial $p(n)$ if and only if $\delta(n)$ is negligible.

A collection $F = (F_n)_{n \in \mathbb{N}}$ of functions is a sequence of functions $F_n : \{0,1\}^n \times \{0,1\}^n \to \{0,1\}^n$. The first argument is called the key and usually denoted by $k \in \{0,1\}^n$. If it is fixed and n is understood, we write $F_k(\cdot)$ for the function $F_n(k, \cdot)$. For a definition of pseudorandomness we consider the following experiment. Let D be a probabilistic polynomial-time algorithm. At the beginning, a random key $k \in_R \{0,1\}^n$ is chosen and kept secret from D. D is given 1^n (n in unary) as input and is allowed to adaptively query the oracle $F_k(\cdot)$ for values of its choice. Then D outputs a challenge $y \in \{0,1\}^n$ such that y has not been queried previously and D is disconnected from the oracle. A bit $b \in_R \{0,1\}$ is chosen at random as well as a random string $r \in_R \{0,1\}^n$ and P is given (Q_0, Q_1) where $Q_b = F_k(y)$ and $Q_{1-b} = r$. That is, D receives the value of F_k at y and a random string in random order. Finally, algorithm D is supposed to output a guess $g \in \{0,1\}$ for b. The distinguishing advantage of D is the probability (over the choice of k and the coin tosses of D) that D's guess is correct minus the pure guessing probability: $\mathsf{Adv}_D^F = |\mathrm{Prob}\,[b = g] - 1/2|$. Note that Adv_D^F is a function of $n \in \mathbb{N}$, the input of D. Roughly speaking, F is pseudorandom if any distinguisher D cannot predict b essentially better than with probability $1/2$ for sufficiently large n.

Definition 1 (Collection of Pseudorandom Functions). *A collection $F = (F_n)_{n \in \mathbb{N}}$ of functions $F_n : \{0,1\}^n \times \{0,1\}^n \to \{0,1\}^n$ is called a collection of pseudorandom functions iff*

- *there exists a polynomial-time algorithm $\mathcal{F}$ such that $\mathcal{F}(k, x) = F_n(k, x)$ for any $k, x \in \{0,1\}^n$ and all $n \in \mathbb{N}$*
- *the distinguishing advantage $\mathsf{Adv}_D^F(n)$ of any probabilistic polynomial-time algorithm D is negligible*

We remark that the second property is different from, yet equivalent to [16] the definition usually used in literature. Also note that the first property means that $(F_n)_{n \in \mathbb{N}}$ is computable in polynomial time in n. It is well-known that collections of pseudorandom functions exists if and only if one-way functions exist [16, 17]. One-way functions are believed to be the weakest assumption for non-trivial cryptography [19, 22].

In the sequel we will use the following fact about pseudorandom functions. Consider the variation of the experiment above, where D, after querying the oracle $F_k(\cdot)$, outputs a pair (y, z) such that y has not been passed to the oracle yet. The prediction probability of D (as a function of n) is the probability that $F_k(y) = z$. That is, the prediction probability denotes the probability that D can predict the function value at y without having seen it. It is not hard to show that for a collection of pseudorandom functions the prediction probability of any probabilistic polynomial-time algorithm D is negligible. This comes from the fact that if one can predict the value than it is also easy to distinguish it from a random string.

2.3   Randomly Self-Reducible and Coherent Sets

In this section we introduce the notions of random-self-reductions [8] and coherent sets [29]. The definition of the query depth of the corresponding primitive is a straightforward extension of the definition for learning algorithms. The following is taken from [15]:

Definition 2 (Random-Self-Reduction). *A function $f : \{0,1\}^* \to \{0,1\}^*$ is called nonadaptively $k(n)$-random-self-reducible if there exist polynomial-time algorithms ϕ, σ and a polynomial $p(n)$ such that for all x we have*

$$f(x) = \phi\Big(x, r, f\big(\sigma(1, x, r)\big), \dots, f\big(\sigma(k(|x|), x, r)\big)\Big)$$

with probability at least $2/3$ over the choice of $r \in_R \{0,1\}^{p(|x|)}$. Additionally, for all $x, y \in \{0,1\}^n$ the random variables $\sigma(i, x)$ and $\sigma(i, y)$ are identically distributed.

From the definition it immediately follows that a single value $\sigma(i, x, r)$ does not yield any information about x. Yet, $\sigma(i, x)$ and $\sigma(j, x)$ are dependent in general and may therefore reveal x. More generally, we consider *adaptive* random self-reductions where $\sigma(i, x, r)$ may also depend on the previous answers $f(\sigma(1, x, r)), \dots, f(\sigma(i - 1, x, r))$ for $i = 1, \dots, k(|x|)$. It is easy to see that the error probability $1/3$ can be decreased to $2^{-q(n)}$ for any polynomial $q(n)$ by standard techniques for both adaptive and nonadaptive reductions. In particular, lowering the error probability by majority decision preserves the query depth. We remark that the notion of the query depth of random self-reductions has been mentioned implicitly in [14] though, to best of our knowledge, it has not been investigated further — except for the extreme cases of adaptive and nonadaptive reductions.

A random self-reduction is *oblivious* if the queries $\sigma(1, x, r), \dots, \sigma(k(|x|), x, r)$ do not depend on x, i.e., $\sigma(i, x, r) = \sigma(i, r)$ for $i = 1, \dots, k(|x|)$. It is called *deterministic* if the queries do not depend on r. In contrast to "ordinary" self-reductions we do not restrict the queries $\sigma(i, x, r)$ to be smaller than the input, but allow queries with arbitrary length. We say that a random self-reduction is *length-preserving* if $|\sigma(i, x, r)| = |x|$ for all i, r. It is called *length-monotone* if $|\sigma(i, x, r)| \le |x|$. We say that a set $\mathcal{L}$ is randomly self-reducible if $\chi_\mathcal{L}$ is.

Closely related to random self-reducible sets are so-called coherent sets. Informally, these are sets $\mathcal{L}$ where membership of any input x can be efficiently decided with help of the oracle $\chi_{\mathcal{L}\setminus\{x\}}$. More formally, let $f : \{0,1\}^* \to \{0,1\}$ be a Boolean function. An *examiner* for f is a probabilistic polynomial-time oracle Turing machine E that, on input x, never queries the oracle f for x. Let $E^f(x)$ denote the random variable that describes the output.

Definition 3 (Coherent Set). *A set $\mathcal{L}$ is called coherent if there exists an examiner E such that $E^{\chi_{\mathcal{L}}}(x) = \chi_{\mathcal{L}}(x)$ with probability at least $2/3$.*

Again, the error probability can be decreased to $2^{-q(n)}$ while preserving the query depth. We say that $\mathcal{L}$ is *deterministic coherent* if E is (deterministic) polynomial-time. $\mathcal{L}$ is called *weakly coherent* if E is a polynomial-size circuit family. In this case, we say that E is a *weak examiner*. If $\mathcal{L}$ is not coherent it is called *incoherent*.

It is easy to see (for example [6]) that for every language $\mathcal{L}$ the set $\mathcal{L} \oplus \mathcal{L} = \{0x \mid x \in \mathcal{L}\} \cup \{1x \mid x \in \mathcal{L}\}$ is coherent. Additionally, Beigel and Feigenbaum [6] show that every randomly self-reducible set is also weakly coherent. The converse is unlikely to hold, as every NP-complete set is coherent but, unless the polynomial hierarchy collapses at the third level, is not randomly self-reducible in query depth $\mathcal{O}(\log n)$. See [14] for details.

3 Limitations on Parallelizing Queries

First, we define our concept class based on any collection of pseudorandom functions. Then we show that this class cannot be predicted with membership queries in depth $d(n)$, though it can be learned exactly in depth $d(n)+1$. Finally, we discuss that prediction remains hard even if we add equivalence queries.

Let $F = (F_n)_{n\in\mathbb{N}}$ be a collection of pseudorandom functions and let $d(n)$ be a fixed polynomial. For a function $F_k(\cdot) = F_n(k, \cdot)$ and $i = 0, \ldots, d(n)$ define

$$y_k^{(i)} = \begin{cases} 0^n & \text{if } i = 0 \\ F_k\big(y_k^{(i-1)}\big) & \text{else} \end{cases}$$

That is, $y_k^{(i)}$ is obtained by iterating i-times $F_k(\cdot)$ at 0^n. For each $k \in \{0,1\}^n$ alter $F_k(\cdot)$ to a function $F_k^*(\cdot)$ by setting

$$F_k^*(x) = \begin{cases} k & \text{if } x = y_k^{(d(n))} \\ F_k(x) & \text{else} \end{cases}$$

Thus, the only difference between F_k^* and F_k is that F_k^* reveals the key if it is evaluated at $y_k^{(d(n))} = F_k(\cdots F_k(0^n))$. Define the concept class $\mathcal{C} = (\mathcal{C}_n)_{n\in\mathbb{N}}$ by $\mathcal{C}_n = \{c_k \mid k \in \{0,1\}^n\}$, where

$$c_k = \left\{ (x,j) \in \{0,1\}^{n+\lceil \log n \rceil} \,\middle|\, \pi_j(F_k^*(x)) = 1 \right\}$$

Recall that $\pi_j(F_k^*(x))$ is the projection of $F_k^*(x)$ onto bit j. The distribution $\mathcal{D}_n$ on $\{0,1\}^{n+\lceil \log n \rceil}$ is described by picking $x \in_R \{0,1\}^n$ and $j \in_R \{1,\ldots,n\}$ independently. Obviously, $\mathcal{D}$ is efficiently sampleable.

Lemma 1. *The concept class C is exactly learnable with membership queries in query depth $d(n) + 1$.*

Proof. Let c_k be the target concept. In each round $i = 1, \ldots, d(n) + 1$ query in parallel the oracle c_k for $\left(y_k^{(i-1)}, 1\right), \ldots, \left(y_k^{(i-1)}, n\right)$. Clearly, we can reconstruct $y_k^{(i)}$ from the answers. Therefore, we finally obtain $F_k^*\left(y_k^{(d(n))}\right) = k$. $\qquad\square$

Lemma 2. *C is not weakly predictable with membership queries in query depth $d(n)$ with respect to $\mathcal{D}$.*

The outline of the proof is as follows. If C was weakly predictable then this would also hold if we choose the target concept at random, namely select $k \in_R \{0, 1\}$ and let c_k be the target concept. Since the query depth of the learning algorithm is bounded by $d(n)$, it cannot query for $y_k^{(d(n))}$ and therefore obtain the key k, unless it can guess at least one of the values $y_k^{(1)}, \ldots, y_k^{(d(n))}$ (which, as we will see, are distinct with high probability). But this would contradict the unpredictability of the pseudorandom function. Hence, as the learning algorithm cannot obtain the key, predicting a random example is almost as hard as distinguishing between the value of the pseudorandom function from a random string. The formal proof is deligated to Appendix A. We obtain:

Theorem 1. *If one-way functions exists, then there is a concept class that is not weakly predictable with membership queries in query depth $d(n)$, but can be learned exactly with membership queries in query depth $d(n) + 1$ for any fixed polynomial $d(n)$.*

It remains to show that adding equivalence queries does not help learning in query depth $d(n)$. The idea is similar to Angluin's well-known technique [1] replacing an equivalence query by a polynomial number of parallel membership queries. In our case this is even much simpler than in general. Assume that L puts an equivalence query for $k' \in \{0, 1\}^n$. Then, for a randomly chosen $x \in_R \{0, 1\}^n$, we have $F_k(x) \neq F_{k'}(x)$ with probability at least $1 - 1/q(n) \geq 1/2$ for every polynomial q and sufficiently large n. Otherwise we could use L to construct a successful predictor for pseudorandom functions, because guessing the key is even harder than predicting a single value. Thus, with probability at least $1/2n$ it holds $\pi_j(F_k(x)) \neq \pi_j(F_{k'}(x))$ for $j \in_R \{1, \ldots, n\}$. If we execute $2n^2$ such membership queries in parallel then with probability at least $1 - e^{-n}$ we find a counterexample. Summing over all (at most polynomial) equivalence queries we find counterexamples for all queries with probability at least $1 - \text{poly}(n) \cdot e^{-n}$. Hence, this simulation only fails with negligible probability and we can therefore apply the argument of the previous theorem.

Theorem 2. *If one-way functions exists, then there is a concept class that is not weakly predictable with membership and equivalence queries in query depth $d(n)$, but can be learned exactly with membership queries in query depth $d(n) + 1$ for any fixed polynomial $d(n)$.*

4 Applications to Random Self-Reductions and Coherent Sets

Feigenbaum, Fortnow et al. [15] present a set $\mathcal{L}$ in DSPACE($n^{\beta(n)}$) for any unbounded, nondecreasing function $\beta(n)$ (with $n^{\beta(n)}$ time-constructible) such that $\mathcal{L}$ is adaptively randomly self-reducible, while nonadaptive random self-reductions do not exist. This results holds unconditionally. Assuming NEEE $\not\subseteq$ BPEEE, they show that there exist such sets in NP. This assumption has been reduced to NE $\not\subseteq$ BPE by Hemaspaandra, Naik, Ogihara and Selman [18]. Combining the idea of Feigenbaum et al. [15] with our result for learning algorithms we obtain the following:

Proposition 1. *Let $\beta(n)$ be an unbounded, nondecreasing function such that $n^{\beta(n)}$ is time-constructible and $n^{\beta(n)} \cdot 2^{-n}$ is negligible. Let $d(n)$ be a fixed polynomial. If one-way functions exists, there is a language $\mathcal{L}$ in DSPACE($n^{\beta(n)}$) such that there is no length-preserving random self-reduction of query depth $d(n)$ for $\mathcal{L}$, though there is a deterministic, obliviously, length-preserving random self-reduction of query depth $d(n) + 1$.*

We remark that $n^{\beta(n)} \cdot 2^{-n}$ is negligible if, for instance, $\beta(n) \cdot \log n < n/2$ for sufficiently large n. This is true for $\beta(n) = \log^* n$.

Proof. The proof is similar to the proof given in [15]. We view a random self-reduction given by algorithms σ and ϕ as a single Turing machine M. The choice of $\beta(n)$ ensures that $n^{\beta(n)} > p(n)$ for any polynomial $p(n)$. We can therefore diagonalize against the length-preserving random self-reductions $M_1, M_2, \ldots$ of query depth $d(n)$. The language $\mathcal{L}$ consists of tuples (x, j) such that $\pi_j(F_k^*(x)) = 1$ for an appropriate key $k \in \{0, 1\}^n$.

M_i's running time and therefore the number of queries is bounded above by $n^{\beta(n)}$. Any query $\sigma(j, x)$ of M_i is distributed independently of x. If we choose a random input $(x, j) \in_R \{0, 1\}^{n + \lceil \log n \rceil}$ and let M_i run on that input, then with probability at most $n^{\beta(n)} \cdot 2^{-n}$ the value (x, j) appears among the queries. By assumption, $n^{\beta(n)} \cdot 2^{-n}$ is negligible. Hence, given that M_i does not query the input, we can turn M_i (that decides membership correctly with probability at least $2/3$) into a successful distinguisher for the underlying pseudorandom function. From this we derive that every length-preserving random self-reduction fails with probability more than $1/3$ for all sufficiently large n. We conclude that we can determine in space $\mathcal{O}(n^{\beta(n)})$ a key k and a tuple (x, j) such that M_i fails to predict $\pi_j(F_k^*(x))$ with probability more than $1/3$. Add all (x, j) with $\pi_j(F_k^*(x)) = 1$ to $\mathcal{L}$.

The fact that this language is obliviously, randomly self-reducible is straightforward as we can determine the key k in depth $d(n) + 1$. Then we can easily decide whether the input (x, j) is in $\mathcal{L}$ by computing $\pi_j(F_k^*(x))$. □

Assuming that even for polynomial-size circuit families D (instead of probabilistic polynomial-time distinguishers) the collection of pseudorandom functions remains pseudorandom, we can extend our result to length-monotone random-self-reductions. We remark that security against nonuniform distinguishers is also a widely accepted assumption in cryptography.

Corollary 1. *Let $\beta(n)$ be an unbounded, nondecreasing function and assume that $n^{\beta(n)}$ is time-constructible and that $n^{\beta(n)} \cdot 2^{-n}$ is negligible. Let $d(n)$ be a fixed polynomial. If one-way functions exists that are secure against nonuniform adversaries, there is a language $\mathcal{L}$ in $DSPACE(n^{\beta(n)})$ such that there is no length-monotone random self-reduction of query depth $d(n)$ for $\mathcal{L}$, though there is a deterministic, obliviously, length-preserving random self-reduction of query depth $d(n) + 1$.*

Proof. The proof is a straightforward extension of the proof of Proposition 1. Again, if there was a length-monotone random self-reduction we could construct a polynomial-size circuit family with distinguishing advantage that is not negligible. To answer queries that have smaller length we give the circuit that simulates the random self-reduction for inputs of length $n + \lceil \log n \rceil$ the first $n-1$ keys determined by $\mathcal{L}$ for complexity parameters $1, \ldots, n-1$ as nonuniform advice. □

Beigel and Feigenbaum [6] prove that every randomly self-reducible language is weakly coherent. Analyzing their proof it is easy to see that their transformation of a random self-reduction to a weak examiner preserve the query depth.

Corollary 2. *Let $\beta(n)$ be an unbounded, nondecreasing function. Assume that $n^\beta(n)$ is time-constructible and that $n^{\beta(n)} \cdot 2^{-n}$ is negligible. Let $d(n)$ be a fixed polynomial. If one-way functions exists, there is a language $\mathcal{L}$ in $DSPACE(n^{\beta(n)})$ that is incoherent for length-preserving examiners of query depth $d(n)$, though there exists a weak, length-preserving examiner of query depth $d(n) + 1$.*

Again, this conclusion can be extended to length-monotone examiners. Unfortunately, we do not know whether the positive result of Corollary 2 also holds for probabilistic polynomial-time examiners instead of weak examiners. But we achieve this using a somewhat stronger assumption, namely the existence one-way permutations:

Proposition 2. *Let $\beta(n)$ be an unbounded, nondecreasing function and assume that $n^\beta(n)$ is time-constructible and that $n^{\beta(n)} \cdot 2^{-n}$ is negligible. Let $d(n)$ be a fixed polynomial. If one-way permutations exists, there is a language $\mathcal{L}$ in $DSPACE(n^{\beta(n)})$ that is incoherent for length-preserving examiners of query depth $d(n)$, though there is a deterministic, length-preserving examiner of query depth $d(n) + 1$.*

Proof. Given a one-way permutation we can construct a collection of pseudo-random functions such that $F_n(k, 1^n) \neq F_n(k', 1^n)$ for $k \neq k'$; see [13]. Similar to the proof of Claim 1 on Page 84 we conclude that $y_k^{(1)}, \ldots, y_k^{(d(n))} \neq 1^n$ for all but a negligible fraction of the keys $k \in \{0, 1\}^n$. Hence, the impossibility result remains valid if we restrict ourself to such keys. Now it also suffices to show the positive result for those keys. Assume that the examiner E is given (x, j) as input. If $x \notin \{y_k^{(0)}, \ldots, y_k^{(d(n))}\}$ then E can compute k in depth $d(n) + 1$ without querying for (x, j) and decide whether $(x, j) \in \mathcal{L}$ by computing $\pi_j(F_k^*(x))$ in polynomial time. Suppose that $x = y_k^{(i)}$ for some i. Then the examiner cannot query for $(y_k^{(i)}, j)$. Fortunately, there are only two possibilities, namely $(x, j) \in \mathcal{L}$ or $(x, j) \notin \mathcal{L}$. E tries both possibilities in parallel and also asks for $F_k(1^n)$ in a single concurrent step. This is possible as 1^n is different from $y_k^{(0)}, \dots, y_k^{(d(n))}$ by assumption about k. Thus E derives two keys k_0 and k_1 and the value $F_k(1^n)$ in query depth $d(n) + 1$. It determines the correct key by computing $F_{k_0}(1^n)$ and $F_{k_1}(1^n)$ in polynomial time and comparing it to the value obtained for $F_k(1^n)$. Given the key k the examiner can decide whether $(x, j) \in \mathcal{L}$. $\square$

Assuming one-way permutations that are secure against nonuniform adversaries we can extend the negative result to length-monotone examiners.

Acknowledgements

We thank the anonymous referees of ALT'98 for valuable and comprehensive comments.

References

1. D.ANGLUIN: Learning Regular Sets from Queries and Counterexamples, *Information and Computation, vol. 75, pp. 87-106, 1987.*
2. D.ANGLUIN: Queries and Concept Learning, *Machine Learning, vol. 2, pp. 319-342, 1988.*
3. D.ANGLUIN, M.KHARITONOV: When Won't Membership Queries Help?, *23rd ACM Symposium on Theory of Computing, pp. 444-454, 1991.*
4. J.BALCÁZAR, J.DÍAZ, R.GAVALDÀ, O.WATANABE: An Optimal Parallel Algorithm for Learning DFA, *7th ACM Conference on Computational Learning Theory, 1994.*
5. R.BEIGEL, J.FEIGENBAUM: Improved Bounds on Coherence and Checkability, *Yale University Technical Report, YALEU/DCS/TR-819, 1990.*
6. R.BEIGEL, J.FEIGENBAUM: On Being Incoherent Without Being very Hard, *Computational Complexity, vol. 2, pp. 1-17, 1992.*
7. M.BELLARE, S.GOLDWASSER: The Complexity of Decision Versus Search, *SIAM Journal on Computing, vol. 23, no. 1, 1994.*
8. M.BLUM, S.MICALI: How to Generate Cryptographically Strong Sequences of Pseudorandom Bits, *SIAM Journal on Computation, vol. 13, pp. 850-864, 1984.*
9. N.BSHOUTY: Exact Learning of Formulas in Parallel, *Machine Learning, vol. 26, pp. 25-42, 1997.*
10. N.BSHOUTY, R.CLEVE: On the Exact Learning of Formulas in Parallel, *33rd IEEE Symposium on the Foundations of Computer Science, pp. 513-522, 1992.*
11. N.BSHOUTY, S.GOLDMAN, H.MATHIAS: Noise-Tolerant Parallel Learning of Geometric Concepts, *8th ACM Conference on Computational Learning Theory, 1995.*
12. B.BERGER, J.ROMPEL, P.SHOR: Efficient NC Algorithms for Set Cover with Application to Learning and Geometry, *30th IEEE Symposium on the Foundations of Computer Science, pp. 54-59, 1989.*
13. R.CANETTI, D.MICCIANCIO, O.REINGOLD: Perfectly One-Way Probabilistic Hash Functions, *30th ACM Symposium on Theory of Computing, 1998.*
14. J.FEIGENBAUM, L.FORTNOW: On the Random-Self-Reducibility of Complete Sets, *6th Annual IEEE Structure in Complexity Theory Conference, 1991.*

15. J.FEIGENBAUM, L.FORTNOW, C.LUND, D.SPIELMAN: The Power of Adaptiveness and Additional Queries in Random-Self-Reductions, *Computational Complexity, vol. 4, pp. 158-174, 1994.*

16. S.GOLDWASSER, O.GOLDREICH, S.MICALI: How to Construct Random Functions, *Journal of ACM, vol. 33, pp. 792-807, 1986.*

17. J.HÅSTAD, R.IMPAGLIAZZO, L.LEVIN, M.LUBY: Construction of Pseudorandom Generator from any One-Way Function, *to appear in SIAM Journal on Computing, preliminary versions in STOC'89 and STOC'90, 1989/1990.*

18. E.HEMASPAANDRA, A.NAIK, M.OGIHARA, A.SELMAN: P-Selective Sets, and Reducing Search to Decision vs. Self-Reducibility, *Journal of Computer and System Sciences, vol. 53, pp. 194-209, 1996.*

19. R.IMPAGLIAZZO, M.LUBY: One-Way Functions are Essential for Complexity Based Cryptography, *30th IEEE Symposium on Foundations of Computer Science, pp. 230-235, 1989.*

20. M.KEARNS, L.VALIANT: Cryptographic Limitations on Learning Boolean Formulae and Finite Automata, *Journal of ACM, vol. 41, pp. 67-95, 1994.*

21. M.KHARITONOV: Cryptographic Hardness of Distribution-Specific Learning, *25th ACM Symposium on the Theory of Computing, pp. 372-381, 1993.*

22. R.OSTROVSKY, A.WIGDERSON: One-Way Functions are Essential for Non-Trivial Zero-Knowledge, *Second IEEE Israel Symposium on Theory and Computing Systems, 1993.*

23. L.PITT, L.VALIANT: Computational Limitations on Learning from Examples, *Journal of ACM, vol. 35, pp. 965-984, 1988.*

24. L.PITT, M.WARMUTH: Prediction-Preserving Reducibility, *Journal of Computer and System Science, vol. 41, pp. 430-467, 1990.*

25. R.RIVEST, Y.L.LIN: Being Taught can be Faster than Asking Questions, *8th ACM Conference on Computational Learning Theory, 1995.*

26. C.P.SCHNORR: Optimal Algorithms for Self-Reducible Problems, *3rd International Colloqium on Automata, Languages, and Programming, pp. 322-347, Edingburgh University Press, 1976.*

27. L.VALIANT: A Theory of the Learnable, *Communications of ACM, vol. 27, pp. 1134-1142, 1984.*

28. J.VITTER, J.LIN: Learning in Parallel, *Information and Computation, vol. 92, pp. 179-202, 1992.*

29. A.YAO: Coherent Functions and Program Checkers, *22nd ACM Symposium on Theory of Computing, pp. 84-94, 1990.*

A   Proof of Lemma 2

Assume that there exists a pwm-algorithm L that weakly predicts C with respect to $\mathcal{D}$. Let $p(n)$ denote the polynomial such that L predicts correctly with probability at least $1/2 + 1/p(n)$ for infinitely many $n \in \mathbb{N}$.[1] Since L predicts C_n for all target concepts c_k, it also predicts C_n if we choose $k \in_R \{0,1\}^n$ and thus c_k at random. From L we construct a successful distinguisher D for the collection of pseudorandom functions $F = (F_n)_{n \in \mathbb{N}}$. D is given oracle access to a function

---

[1] Note that we only demand that L predicts correctly infinitely often. Weak predictability actually requires L to predict correctly for all sufficiently large n. This even strengthens our result.

$F_k(\cdot)$ in F_n, where $k \in_R \{0,1\}^n$ is chosen at random. Basically, D simulates L and for each membership query (x,j) of L algorithm D queries "on-line" the function oracle for x and, given the answer $z = F_k(x)$, returns $\pi_j(z)$ to L.

We start by showing that $y_k^{(1)}, \ldots, y_k^{(d(n))}$ are distinct with high probability. We use this fact to prove that the probability that the learning algorithm L queries $(y_k^{(d(n))}, j)$ for some j is negligible. If L does not query $(y_k^{(d(n))}, j)$ for any j then D is able to answer all queries of L using its oracle $F_k(\cdot)$. This is possible as $c_k(x,j) = \pi_j(F_k(x))$ except for $x = y_k^{(d(n))}$. If L queries $(y_k^{(d(n))}, j)$ for some j then D is supposed to return the j-th bit of the key k to L, because $c_k(y_k^{(d(n))}, j) = \pi_j(F_k^*(y_k^{(d(n))})) = \pi_j(k)$. But D does not know the secret key k and cannot guess it, because this would contradict the pseudorandomness of the underlying collection. Hence, if L queries $y_k^{(d(n))}$ then the simulation fails. Fortunately, the probability of this is negligible and, given that the simulation succeeds, it is easy to show that L cannot weakly predict the concept class.

CLAIM 1: The probability that $y_k^{(i)} = y_k^{(j)}$ for $i < j$ with $i,j \in \{0, \ldots, d(n)\}$ is negligible.

PROOF. We prove that otherwise there exist a polynomial-time algorithm D' that successfully predicts the value $F_k(y)$ for an appropriate y with probability at least $1/q'(n)$ for a polynomial $q'(n)$ and infinitely many $n \in \mathbb{N}$. Assume that the probability that there exist i,j as in the claim is not negligible. More precisely, let this probability be greater than $1/q(n)$ for a polynomial q and infinitely many n. For a fixed key k we call a pair (i,j) bad if $i < j$ and $y_k^{(i)} = y_k^{(j)}$. If a bad pair exist then there is also a minimal bad pair (i_0, j_0), i.e., such that there does not exist another bad pair (i,j) with $j < j_0$. We construct D' as follows. D' tries to guess (i_0, j_0) by choosing $J \in_R \{1, \ldots, d(n)\}$ and $I \in_R \{0, \ldots, J-1\}$ at random. Then D' computes $y_k^{(0)}, \ldots, y_k^{(J-1)}$ by querying the oracle $F_k(\cdot)$. If $y_k^{(J-1)} \neq y_k^{(0)}, \ldots, y_k^{(J-2)}$ then D' outputs $(y_k^{(J-1)}, y_k^{(I)})$. Else D' gives an arbitrary output. If there exist a (minimal) bad pair (i_0, j_0) then $(I, J) = (i_0, j_0)$ with probability at least $1/d^2(n)$. In this case, $y_k^{(J-1)} \neq y_k^{(0)}, \ldots, y_k^{(J-2)}$ because (i_0, j_0) is minimal. Additionally, $F_k(y_k^{(J-1)}) = y_k^{(J)} = y_k^{(I)}$. Hence, the prediction of D' is right with probability at least $1/d^2(n)q(n)$. This contradicts the unpredictability of F. □

We show that the probability (over the random choice of the target concept and the internal coin tosses of L) that L queries $y_k^{(d(n))}$ is less than any polynomial fraction.

CLAIM 2: The probability that L queries $(y_k^{(d(n))}, j)$ for some $j \in \{1, \ldots, n\}$ is negligible.

PROOF. Suppose, towards contradiction, that L asks a membership query for $(y^{(d(n))}, j)$ for some j with probability at least $1/q(n)$ for a polynomial q and infinitely many $n \in \mathbb{N}$. Then we derive a predictor D' for F with prediction probability $1/q'(n)$ for a polynomial q' and infinitely many n. First observe that the probability that $y_k^{(0)}, \ldots, y_k^{(d(n))}$ are pairwise different *and* that L queries $y_k^{(d(n))}$ is at least $1/2q(n)$ for infinitely many n; though these events are not necessarily independent we can assume by claim 1 that $y_k^{(0)}, \ldots, y_k^{(d(n))}$ are distinct with probability at least $1 - 1/2q(n)$ for sufficiently large n. The bound $1/2q(n)$ therefore follows from the fact that $\mathrm{Prob}[A \wedge B] \geq \mathrm{Prob}[A] - \mathrm{Prob}[\neg B]$ for any events A, B.

Recall that the query depth of L is $d(n)$. Thus, given that L queries $y_k^{(d(n))}$ and that $y_k^{(0)}, \ldots, y_k^{(d(n))}$ are pairwise different, there exist $i, r \in \{1, \ldots, d(n)\}$ such that L queries $y_k^{(i)}$ in round r without having queried $y_k^{(i-1)}$ in the proceding $r - 1$ rounds. Since D' does not necessarily know i and r it tries to guess these values by picking $I, R \in_R \{1, \ldots, d(n)\}$ uniformly at random. D' computes $y_k^{(1)}, \ldots, y_k^{(I-1)}$ via the function oracle and then simulates L until L has output the membership queries for round R. Let $p_L(n)$ denote the polynomial that bounds the running time of L and thus the number of queries in each round. D' uniformly picks a query (y, j) of the at most $p_L(n)$ queries. The value y will be the guess for $y_k^{(I)} = F_k(y_k^{(I-1)})$. If $y_k^{(I-1)}$ has not been among L's queries in the previous rounds, D' outputs the pair $(y_k^{(I-1)}, y)$. With probability at least $1/d^2(n)p_L(n)$, more specifically, if $I = i$ and $R = r$ and $y = y_k^{(I)}$, the value $y_k^{(I)}$ has not been queried previously. If $y_k^{(I-1)}$ has already been queried, D' outputs an arbitrary pair. Assume that $y_k^{(I-1)}$ has not appeared among the queries. Then D' predicts $F_k(y_k^{(I-1)})$ correctly with probability at least $1/2d^2(n)p_L(n)q(n)$ for infinitely many n, which is not negligble. The claim follows. □

We conclude that with probability at least $1 - 1/2p(n)$ (for large n) algorithm L does not query $(y_k^{(d(n))}, j)$ for any j. In this case, D is able to answer all queries correctly. After L has stopped and asked for a challenge, D generates a random $x \in_R \{0, 1\}^n$ and $j \in_R \{1, \ldots, n\}$. With probability $1 - (p_L(n) + 1) \cdot 2^{-n}$ we have $x \neq y_k^{(d(n))}$ and x has not been queried by L previously. We call such x fresh. Let x be D's challenge, i.e., D is given $F_k(x)$ and $r \in_R \{0, 1\}^n$ in random order (Q_0, Q_1). Let ℓ denote L's prediction for $c_k(x, j)$. D outputs a guess $g \in \{0, 1\}$ as follows:

- if $\pi_j(Q_0) = \pi_j(Q_1)$ then g is chosen at random
- if $\pi_j(Q_0) \neq \pi_j(Q_1)$ then define g such that $\pi_j(Q_g) = \ell$

We remark that each case occurs with probability $1/2$ since $\pi_j(r)$ is a random bit. In the former case, D is successful with probability $1/2$. In the latter case, D's guess is correct if and only if ℓ is. Note that we require that ℓ is correct *and* that L does not query $y_k^{(d(n))}$. Again, using the fact $\mathrm{Prob}[A \wedge B] \geq \mathrm{Prob}[A] - \mathrm{Prob}[\neg B]$, this happens with probability at least $1/2 + 1/2p(n)$ for infinitely many n.

It remains to analyze D's success probability. Let $\mathrm{not}(y_k^{(d(n))})$ denote the event that L does not query $y_k^{(d(n))}$, $\mathrm{fresh}(x)$ that x is fresh, and $\mathrm{correct}(\ell)$ that L's prediction is right. Furthermore, let case1 and case2 denote the events that the first case ($\pi_j(Q_0) = \pi_j(Q_1)$) resp. the other case ($\pi_j(Q_0) \neq \pi_j(Q_1)$) occurs. Then

$$
\begin{aligned}
\mathrm{Prob}[b = g] &\geq \mathrm{Prob}\left[b = g \wedge \mathsf{not}(y_k^{(d(n))}) \wedge \mathsf{fresh}(x)\right] \\
&= \mathrm{Prob}\left[b = g \wedge \mathsf{not}(y_k^{(d(n))}) \wedge \mathsf{fresh}(x) \wedge \mathsf{case1}\right] \\
&\quad + \mathrm{Prob}\left[b = g \wedge \mathsf{not}(y_k^{(d(n))}) \wedge \mathsf{fresh}(x) \wedge \mathsf{case2}\right] \\
&\geq \mathrm{Prob}\left[b = g \,\middle|\, \mathsf{not}(y_k^{(d(n))}) \wedge \mathsf{fresh}(x) \wedge \mathsf{case1}\right] \\
&\qquad \cdot \mathrm{Prob}\left[\mathsf{not}(y_k^{(d(n))}) \wedge \mathsf{fresh}(x) \wedge \mathsf{case1}\right] \\
&\quad + \mathrm{Prob}\left[b = g \,\middle|\, \mathsf{not}(y_k^{(d(n))}) \wedge \mathsf{correct}(\ell) \wedge \mathsf{fresh}(x) \wedge \mathsf{case2}\right] \\
&\qquad \cdot \mathrm{Prob}\left[\mathsf{not}(y_k^{(d(n))}) \wedge \mathsf{correct}(\ell) \wedge \mathsf{fresh}(x) \wedge \mathsf{case2}\right] \\
&\geq \frac{1}{2} \cdot \left(1 - \frac{1}{2p(n)}\right) \cdot \left(1 - \frac{p_L(n)+1}{2^n}\right) \cdot \frac{1}{2} \\
&\quad + \left(\frac{1}{2} + \frac{1}{2p(n)}\right) \cdot \left(1 - \frac{p_L(n)+1}{2^n}\right) \cdot \frac{1}{2} \\
&\geq \frac{1}{4} - \frac{1}{8p(n)} - \frac{p_L(n)+1}{4 \cdot 2^n} + \frac{1}{4} + \frac{1}{4p(n)} - \frac{p_L(n)+1}{4 \cdot 2^n} - \frac{p_L(n)+1}{4p(n) \cdot 2^n} \\
&\geq \frac{1}{2} + \frac{1}{16p(n)}
\end{aligned}
$$

for infinitely many $n \in \mathbb{N}$. That is, we obtain a distinguisher with distinguishing advantage that is not negligible. This contradicts the pseudorandomness of F.

Learning Unary Output Two-Tape Automata from Multiplicity and Equivalence Queries

Giovanna Melideo[1] and Stefano Varricchio[1]

[1] Dipartimento di Matematica Pura ed Applicata, Universita' di L'Aquila,
Via Vetoio, I-67100 L'Aquila, Italy
{melideo, varricch}@univaq.it

Abstract. We investigate the learning problem of unary output two-tape non deterministic finite automata (unary output 2-tape NFAs) from multiplicity and equivalence queries. Given an alphabet A and a unary alphabet $\{x\}$, a unary output 2-tape NFA accepts a subset of $A^* \times \{x\}^*$. In [6] Bergadano and Varricchio proved that the behavior of an unknown automaton with multiplicity in a field K (K-automaton) is exactly identifiable when multiplicity and equivalence queries are allowed. In this paper multiplicity automata are used to prove the learnability of unary output 2-tape NFA's. We shall identify the behavior of a unary output 2-tape NFA using an automaton with multiplicity in $K^{rat}\langle\langle x \rangle\rangle$. We provide an algorithm which is polynomial in the size of this automaton.

1 Introduction

The *exact learning* model was introduced by Angluin [3]. In this model we consider a learner that does not just passively receive data, but is able to ask queries. Some queries, called *membership queries*, may consist in asking an oracle whether a particular string belongs to the target language. Another possibility is found in *equivalence queries*, asking an oracle whether a guess is correct, and obtaining a counterexample if it is not. In particular, the following classes were shown to be learnable in this model: deterministic automata [3], various types of DNF formulas. Learnability in this model also implies learnability in the "PAC" model with membership queries [3,17]. The notion of a *multiplicity query* was introduced by Bergadano and Varricchio [6] who proved that the behavior of an unknown automaton with multiplicity in a field K (K-automaton) is exactly identifiable when multiplicity and equivalence queries are allowed. As a consequence, K-automata are PAC learnable from multiplicity queries under any distribution.

In this paper we consider a nontrivial extension of classical automata, that is two-tape non deterministic automata. In particular, we shall consider unary output two-tape non deterministic automata (*unary-output 2-tape NFAs*), and investigate the learning problem for this class. A two-tape non deterministic automaton (2-tape NFA) is a "finite-state machine" that scans two tapes containing words over two disjoint alphabets A and A_2. A 2-tape NFA accepts a subset of $A^* \times A_2^*$. A two-tape automaton can also be regarded as a transducer (cf. [9]): the first tape is the *input tape* and the second is the *output tape*. A unary-output

2-tape NFA is a 2-tape NFA which allows a unary alphabet $A_2 = \{x\}$ on the second tape, so accepts a subset of $A^* \times \{x\}^*$.

More in general, the notion of multi-tape finite automaton was introduced by Rabin and Scott in 1959 [15]. They showed that, unlike for ordinary finite automata, non deterministic multi-tape automata are more powerful than the deterministic ones. This holds already in the case of two tapes. As a central model of automata, multi-tape automata have gained plenty of attention. However, many important problems have remained open for long time. For non deterministic automata (even for two-tape) the equivalence problem is an undecidable problem (see [9]); Ibarra has proved that the equivalence problem for unary-output 2-tape NFAs is also undecidable [13]. Conversely, the equivalence problem of multi-tape deterministic automata has been expected to be decidable. Harju and Karhumaki [12] showed that for non deterministic multi-tape automata the *multiplicity equivalence problem* is decidable, that is we can decide if two automata accept the same n-tuples of words exactly the same number of times. In contrast to Ibarra's result the multiplicity equivalence problem for unary-output 2-tape NFAs is then decidable.

Based on a previous work by Bergadano and Varricchio [6], in this paper we identify the behavior of a unary output 2-tape NFA with the behavior of an automaton with multiplicity in the set of rational series over a one-letter alphabet $\{x\}$ $(K^{rat}\langle\langle x \rangle\rangle)$ and we provide an algorithm that is polynomial in the size of the automaton.

We remark that in [18] Yokomori has given a polynomial time algorithm that identifies any deterministic two-tape automaton from membership and equivalence queries. However, we consider non deterministic automata and use *multiplicity queries* instead of membership queries. We recall that a multiplicity query asks the number of accepting paths for a given pair of strings.

2 Rational series and Multiplicity automata

Let K be a field and A^* be the free monoid over the finite alphabet A. We consider the set $K\langle\langle A \rangle\rangle$ of all the applications $S : A^* \to K$. An element S of $K\langle\langle A \rangle\rangle$ is called a *formal series* with (non-commuting) variables in A or a K-*set* of A^*. For any $S \in K\langle\langle A \rangle\rangle$ and $u \in A^*$ we will denote $S(u)$ by (S, u).

Definition 1. *Let* $E \subseteq A^*$. *For any* $S, T \in K\langle\langle A \rangle\rangle$, *we say* $S \equiv_E T$ *if and only if* $(S, w) = (T, w)$ *for any* $w \in E$. $S \equiv T$ *stands for* $S \equiv_{A^*} T$.

A structure of a *semiring* is defined on $K\langle\langle A \rangle\rangle$. In fact, If S and T are two K-sets of A^*, then we can define the following operations, called *rational operations*: for each $w \in A^*$ and $a \in K$

- the *sum* $S + T$ is given by $(S + T, w) = (S, w) + (T, w)$;
- the *(Cauchy) product* ST is given by $(ST, w) = \sum_{uv=w}(S, u)(T, v)$;
- the external operation of K on $K\langle\langle A \rangle\rangle$ is defined as $(aS, w) = a(S, w)$;
- the *star* operation of S, denoted by S^*, is the sum $S^* = \sum_{n \geq 0} S^n$, if S is proper, that is $(S, \epsilon) = 0$.

Definition 2. *Let $K^{n \times n}$ be the monoid of the $n \times n$ square matrices equipped with the row by column product. A map $\mu : A^* \to K^{n \times n}$ is called a* morphism *if $\mu(\epsilon) = Id$, where Id is the identity matrix, and $\mu(w) = \mu(a_1) \ldots \mu(a_n)$, for any $w = a_1 \ldots a_n \in A^*$.*

Definition 3. *A K-set is called* recognizable *or* rational *if there exists a positive integer n, a row-vector $\lambda \in K^{1 \times n}$, a column-vector $\gamma \in K^{n \times 1}$, and a morphism $\mu : A^* \to K^{n \times n}$ such that, for any $w \in A^*$, $(S, w) = \lambda \mu(w) \gamma$. The triplet (λ, μ, γ) is called a* linear representation *of S of dimension n. We denote the family of these series with $K^{rat}\langle\langle A \rangle\rangle$.*

Definition 4. *For any string $u \in A^*$, and a K-set S of A^*, the formal series S_u and $_uS$ are defined by:*

$$(S_u, w) = (S, uw), \quad (_uS, w) = (S, wu), \quad \forall w \in A^*. \tag{1}$$

Definition 5. *Let S be a formal series of $K\langle\langle A \rangle\rangle$. The* Hankel matrix $H(S)$ *of S is the infinite matrix whose rows and columns are indexed by the words of A^*, where the element of indexes u e v is equal to (S, uv).*

It is known that a K-set S is recognizable if and only if the rank of S is finite [16]. Furthermore, if $rank(S) = r$ is finite, then there exists a linear representation of S of dimension r; conversely, if there exists a linear representation of S of dimension h, then $rank(S) \leq h$.

We remark that $K^{A^*} = K\langle\langle A \rangle\rangle$ is a vector space over K. Let S be a K-set; the dimension of the subspace of K^{A^*} generated by the columns of $H(S)$ is called the *rank of S* and denoted with $rank(S)$. We recall that $rank(S)$ is also equal to the dimension of the subspace of K^{A^*} generated by the rows of $H(S)$. Let $u \in A^*$, then the u th row and the u th column of $H(S)$ are the formal series S_u and $_uS$, respectively.

We recall now some definitions and notations on multiplicity automata. More details are in [10, 16, 11]. Let K be a field. An *automaton with multiplicity in K*, also called *multiplicity automaton*, is a 5-tuple $M = (Q, A, E, I, F)$, where A is a finite alphabet, Q is a finite set of states, $I, F : Q \to K$ are two mappings and $E : Q \times A \times Q \to K$ is a map that associates a multiplicity with each edge of M. The maps I and F represent for any state $q \in Q$ the multiplicity of q as *initial state* and *final state*, respectively. We will sometimes call M a K-automaton for brevity. Let $w = a_1 \ldots a_n \in A^*$. A *path* for w is a sequence

$$\pi = (p_1, a_1, p_2), (p_2, a_2, p_3), \ldots, (p_n, a_n, p_{n+1}),$$

where $p_i \in Q$ (for $i = 1, \ldots, n+1$). We denote the set of these paths for w as $\Pi(w)$. The *multiplicity* $Mult(\pi)$ of the path π is the product of the multiplicities of the edges of the path, i.e. $Mult(\pi) = \prod_{i=1}^{n} E(p_i, a_i, p_{i+1})$.

Definition 6. *The* behavior *of M is a mapping $S_M : A^* \to K$ defined as follows:*

$$S_M(w) = \sum_{\pi \in \Pi(w)} I(p_1) Mult(\pi) F(p_{n+1}) \quad \forall w = a_1 \ldots a_n \in A^*.$$

One can associate a linear representation (λ, μ, γ) of dimension n with a K-automaton $M = (\{q_1, q_2, \ldots, q_n\}, A, E, I, F)$ in the following way: for each $i, j = 1, \ldots, n$ and a in A, $\lambda_i = I(q_i)$, $\mu(a)_{i,j} = E(q_i, a, q_j)$ and $\gamma_i = F(q_i)$. One can easily prove that, for any $w \in A^*$, $\mu(w)_{i,j}$ is the sum of the multiplicities of the paths labelled by w from q_i to q_j and the *behavior* S_M of M is the recognizable K-set defined as $(S_M, w) = \lambda\mu(w)\gamma \ \forall w \in A^*$.

Any *non deterministic finite automaton* M can be represented as a $\mathbb{Q}$-automaton, since the initial states, the final states and the edges of the automaton can be represented by their characteristic functions. In this case, for any $w \in A^*$, $\mu(w)_{i,j}$ is the number of paths labelled with w from q_i to q_j and (S_M, w) is the number of different paths which are accepting for w.

In general a linear representation (λ, μ, γ) of dimension n of a recognizable K-set can be regarded as an "automaton" whose set of states is $Q = \{q_1, q_2, \ldots, q_n\}$, the initial and the final states are defined as K-sets of Q, while the edges are a K-sets of $Q \times A \times Q$. Indeed λ_i (resp. γ_i) represents the multiplicity of q_i as an initial state (resp. final state) and $\mu(a)_{i,j}$ the multiplicity of the edge (q_i, a, q_j).

3 Rational series in one variable

The set of rational series over a one-letter alphabet $\{x\}$ is denoted by $K^{rat}\langle\langle x \rangle\rangle$. We may indentify a series S in $K^{rat}\langle\langle x \rangle\rangle$ with a sequence $(a_n)_{n \geq 0}$ of elements of K where $a_n = (S, x^n)$ and we denote S by $\sum_{n \geq 0} a_n x^n$. We remark that the Hankel matrix $H(S)$ of S satisfies the following properties:

- $H(S)$ is the matrix $(a_{i+j})_{i,j \geq 0}$.
- The x^i th row coincides with the x^i th column, i.e. $S_{x^i} = {}_{x^i}S$, for all $i \geq 0$; thus the subspace of K^{A^*} generated by the columns of $H(S)$ coincides with the subspace of K^{A^*} generated by the rows of $H(S)$.
- The rank of $H(S)$ is the minimal dimension of a linear representation of S.

Theorem 1. *Let* $S = \sum_{n \geq 0} a_n x^n$ *be a series in* $K^{rat}\langle\langle x \rangle\rangle$. *If there are coefficients* $c_0, \ldots, c_{d-1} \in K$ *such that*

$$S_{x^d} \equiv \sum_{i=0}^{d-1} c_i S_{x^i}, \tag{2}$$

then for any $t \geq 0$ *and* $i = 0, 1, \ldots, d-1$

$$S_{x^{i+t}} \equiv \sum_{j=0}^{d-1} \hat{\mu}(x^t)_{i,j} S_{x^j} \tag{3}$$

where $\hat{\mu} : \{x\}^* \to K^{d \times d}$ *is the morphism defined as follows:*

$$\hat{\mu}(x)_{i,j} = 1 \text{ if } j = i+1, \text{ for } i = 0, \ldots, d-2$$
$$\hat{\mu}(x)_{i,j} = 0 \text{ if } j \neq i+i, \text{ for } i = 0, \ldots, d-2$$
$$\hat{\mu}(x)_{i,j} = c_j \text{ if } i = d-1$$

Proof. By induction on t. Since $\hat{\mu}(\epsilon)$ is the identity matrix, if $t = 0$, then for $i = 0, \ldots, d-1$, $S_{x^i} \equiv \sum_{j=0}^{d-1} \hat{\mu}(\epsilon)_{i,j} S_{x^j}$. If $t = 1$, then from the definition of $\hat{\mu}$ and Eq. (2) one easily derives that $S_{x^{i+1}} \equiv \sum_{j=0}^{d-1} \hat{\mu}(x)_{i,j} S_{x^j}$ for $i = 0, 1, \ldots, d-1$. We assume, by induction, that for any $k < t$, $S_{x^{i+k}} \equiv \sum_{j=0}^{d-1} \hat{\mu}(x^k)_{i,j} S_{x^j}$ for $i = 0, 1, \ldots, d-1$. Thus

$$S_{x^{i+t}} \equiv (S_{x^{i+t-1}})_x \equiv \sum_{j=0}^{d-1} \hat{\mu}(x^{t-1})_{i,j} (S_{x^j})_x \equiv \sum_{j=0}^{d-1} \hat{\mu}(x^{t-1})_{i,j} S_{x^{j+1}} \equiv$$

$$\sum_{j=0}^{d-1} \hat{\mu}(x^{t-1})_{i,j} \sum_{k=0}^{d-1} \hat{\mu}(x)_{j,k} S_{x^k} \equiv \sum_{k=0}^{d-1} \sum_{j=0}^{d-1} \hat{\mu}(x^{t-1})_{i,j} \hat{\mu}(x)_{j,k} S_{x^k} \equiv \sum_{k=0}^{d-1} \hat{\mu}(x^t)_{i,k} S_{x^k}.$$

□

Definition 7. *Let S be a series in $K^{rat}\langle\langle x \rangle\rangle$ and $H(S)$ be its Hankel matrix. For each $h \geq 1$ let $E_h = \{\epsilon, x, \ldots, x^{h-1}\}$. We denote by $H(S)|_h$ the infinite submatrix of $H(S)$ whose rows are indexed by the words of E_h, and $H(S)|_{h \times k}$ the finite submatrix of $H(S)$ whose rows are indexed by the words of E_h and whose columns are indexed by the words of E_k.*

Theorem 2. *If $S = \sum_{n \geq 0} a_n x^n \in K^{rat}\langle\langle x \rangle\rangle$ is a series with rank r, then there are coefficients $q_0, \ldots, q_{r-1}$ in K such that*

$$S_{x^r} \equiv \sum_{i=0}^{r-1} q_i S_{x^i}. \tag{4}$$

Proof. Since $S \in K^{rat}\langle\langle x \rangle\rangle$ has rank r, the $r+1$ rows of $H(S)$ with indexes in $\epsilon, x, \ldots, x^r$, that is the series $S, S_x, \ldots, S_{x^{r-1}}, S_{x^r}$, are linearly dependent. Hence, there are elements c_i's in K, not all zero, such that $\sum_{i=0}^{r} c_i S_{x^i} \equiv 0$. One has $c_r \neq 0$. If, by contradiction, we assume $c_r = 0$, then let k be the greatest index such that $c_k \neq 0$ and $c_j = 0$ for each $k < j \leq r$. Then $S_{x^k} = \sum_{i=0}^{k-1} c_i' S_{x^i}$ where $c_i' = -(c_k)^{-1} c_i$. By Theorem 1, since the x^k th row depends linearly on the rows with index in E_k, then all the rows depend linearly on the rows with index in E_k. Thus we may conclude that the rank of $H(S)$ must be at most $k < r$. This is a contradiction, since we know that the rank of $H(S)$ is r. Thus, $c_r \neq 0$ and we may write $S_{x^r} = \sum_{i=0}^{r-1} q_i S_{x^i}$ where $q_i = -(c_r)^{-1} c_i$ for $i = 0, \ldots, r-1$. □

Corollary 1. *Let $S = \sum_{n \geq 0} a_n x^n$ be a recognizable series of rank r and $\hat{\mu}$ be the morphism as in Theorem 1, taking in account the coefficients q_j's of Eq. (4). One has:*

$$S_{x^{i+t}} \equiv \sum_{j=0}^{r-1} \hat{\mu}(x^t)_{i,j} S_{x^j}, \ \forall t \geq 0 \text{ and } i = 0, 1, \ldots, r-1. \tag{5}$$

Proof. By Theorem 2 there are coefficients $q_0, \ldots, q_{r-1} \in K$ such that $S_{x^r} \equiv \sum_{i=0}^{r-1} q_i S_{x^i}$. By Theorem 1 the morphism $\hat{\mu}$ must satisfy Eq. (5). □

Corollary 2. *If $S = \sum_{n \geq 0} a_n x^n \in K^{rat}\langle\langle x \rangle\rangle$ is a series with rank r, then for each $h, k \geq r$ all finite matrices $H(S)|_{h \times k}$ of $H(S)$ have rank equal to $rank(S)$.*

Proof. By Corollary 1 all the rows of $H(S)$ depend linearly on the rows with indexes in E_r. Hence for any $h \geq r$ the infinite matrix $H(S)|_h$ has rank equal to $rank(S)$. Since for any $n \geq 0$ $S_{x^n} \equiv {}_{x^n}S$, Corollary 1 implies that all the columns of $H(S)|_h$ also depend linearly on the columns with indexes in E_r; thus for any $k \geq r$ the finite matrix $H(S)|_{h \times k}$ has rank equal to $rank(S)$. $\square$

We remark that if a series in one variable S has rank r then also the finite matrix $H(S)|_{r \times r}$ has rank r.

Corollary 3. *If $S = \sum_{n \geq 0} a_n x^n \in K^{rat}\langle\langle x \rangle\rangle$ is a series with rank r. then the system of r linear equations in the r unknowns q_i's*

$$S_{x^r} \equiv_{E_r} \sum_{i=0}^{r-1} q_i S_{x^i} \tag{6}$$

is compatible and has a single solution.

Proof. We can write the system of linear equations for $n = 0, \ldots, r-1$ as $\sum_{i=0}^{r-1} q_i(S_{x^i}, x^n) = (S_{x^r}, x^n)$, that is $\sum_{i=0}^{r-1} a_{i+n} q_i = a_{r+n}$, for $n = 0, \ldots, r-1$. The $r \times r$ matrix of the coefficents of the unknowns q_i coincide with the finite matrix $H(S)|_{r \times r}$ whereas the complete matrix of the coefficients of the system of linear equations coincides with the finite matrix $H(S)|_{r \times r+1}$. By Corollary 2 both matrices have rank r. This implies that the system of linear equations of r equations in the r unknowns q_i's has a single solution. $\square$

Theorem 3. *If $S = \sum_{n \geq 0} a_n x^n \in K^{rat}\langle\langle x \rangle\rangle$ is a series with rank r then*

$$S_{x^r} \equiv \sum_{i=0.}^{r-1} q_i S_{x^i} \Leftrightarrow S_{x^r} \equiv_{E_r} \sum_{i=0}^{r-1} q_i S_{x^i}, \tag{7}$$

Proof. The right implication is trivial. Conversely suppose that

$$S_{x^r} \equiv_{E_r} \sum_{i=0}^{r-1} q_i S_{x^i}. \tag{8}$$

Since S has rank r, by Theorem 2 there are coefficients $q_0', \ldots, q_{r-1}'$ in K such that $S_{x^r} \equiv \sum_{i=0}^{r-1} q_i' S_{x^i}$ and hence

$$S_{x^r} \equiv_{E_r} \sum_{i=0}^{r-1} q_i' S_{x^i}. \tag{9}$$

By Corollary 3 the systems of linear equations (8) and (9) have a single solution; thus $q_i = q_i'$ and $S_{x^r} \equiv \sum_{i=0}^{r-1} q_i S_{x^i}$. $\square$

Let $S \in K^{rat}\langle\langle x \rangle\rangle$. The following statements are equivalent (cf. [10, 16]):

1. S is recognizable (rational).
2. The sequence $(a_n)_{n \geq 0}$ satisfies a linear recurrence relation, i.e. there exist a positive integer m and coefficients $c_0, \ldots, c_{m-1}$ such that for all $n \geq 0$, $a_{m+n} = \sum_{j=0}^{m-1} c_j a_{n+j}$.
3. S has a generating function $p(x)/(1 - q(x))$, i.e. $S(1 - q(x)) = p(x)$, where p, q are polynomials, and $q(\epsilon) = 0$.

Let $S = \sum_{n \geq 0} a_n x^n$ be a series of rank r. Let $q_0, \ldots, q_{r-1}$ be r coefficients satisfying Eq. (6). By Theorem 3 they also satisfy Equation (4). Then we define a linear representation $(\hat{\lambda}, \hat{\mu}, \hat{\gamma})$ of dimension r. The morphism $\hat{\mu} : \{x\}^* \to K^{r \times r}$ is defined as in Theorem 1, taking in account the coefficients q_j's of Eq. (4). Moreover we set $\hat{\lambda} = (1, 0, \ldots, 0) \in K^{1 \times r}$ and $\hat{\gamma} = (a_0, \ldots, a_{r-1}) \in K^{r \times 1}$. One has:

Theorem 4. *The triplet $(\hat{\lambda}, \hat{\mu}, \hat{\gamma})$ is a linear representation of S.*

Proof. By Corollary 1, one has $S_{x^{i+t}} \equiv \sum_{j=0}^{r-1} \hat{\mu}(x^t)_{i,j} S_{x^j}$ for any $t \geq 0$ and for $i = 0, \ldots, r - 1$. Therefore

$$(S, x^t) = (S_{x^{0+t}}, \epsilon) = \sum_{j=0}^{r-1} \hat{\mu}(x^t)_{0,j} (S_{x^j}, \epsilon) = \hat{\lambda}\hat{\mu}(x^t)\hat{\gamma}, \ \forall t \geq 0.$$

$\square$

We remark that $(\hat{\lambda}, \hat{\mu}, \hat{\gamma})$ is a linear representation of S of minimal dimension.

Theorem 5. *Let $S = \sum_{n \geq 0} a_n x^n \in K^{rat}\langle\langle x \rangle\rangle$ be a series of rank r and let $q_0, \ldots, q_{r-1}$ be the coefficients satisying Eq. (6). Then the sequence $(a_n)_{n \geq 0}$ satisfies the following linear recurrence relation:*

$$\forall n \geq 0, \ a_{r+n} = \sum_{j=0}^{r-1} q_j a_{n+j}. \tag{10}$$

Proof. Eq. (6) implies that for any $n \geq 0$,

$$S_{x^{r+n}} \equiv \sum_{j=0}^{h-1} q_j S_{x^{j+n}}, \Rightarrow (S_{x^{r+n}}, \epsilon) = \sum_{j=0}^{r-1} q_j (S_{x^{j+n}}, \epsilon) \Rightarrow a_{r+n} = \sum_{j=0}^{r-1} q_j a_{n+j}.$$

$\square$

Theorem 6. *Let $S = \sum_{n \geq 0} a_n x^n \in K^{rat}\langle\langle x \rangle\rangle$ be a series of rank r and let $q_0, \ldots, q_{r-1}$ be the coefficients satisfying Eq. (6). Then $p/(1 - q)$ is a generating function of S, setting (we assume $a_k = 0$, for $k < 0$)*

$$q = q_{r-1}x + q_{r-2}x^2 + \ldots + q_0 x^r \quad and \quad p = \sum_{n=0}^{r-1}(a_n - \sum_{j=0}^{r-1} q_j a_{n-r+j})x^n.$$

Proof. By Theorem 5, for any $m \geq 0$, $a_{r+m} = \sum_{j=0}^{r-1} q_j a_{m+j}$, that implies, for any $n \geq r$, $a_n = \sum_{j=0}^{r-1} q_j a_{n-r+j}$. Hence, the polynomial p can be rewritten as a formal series

$$p = \sum_{n \geq 0} (a_n - \sum_{j=0}^{r-1} q_j a_{n-r+j}) x^n.$$

Therefore, one has

$$(1 - q)S = \sum_{n \geq 0} a_n x^n - (\sum_{j=0}^{r-1} q_j x^{r-j})(\sum_{n \geq 0} a_n x^n) =$$

$$\sum_{n \geq 0} a_n x^n - \sum_{n \geq 0} (\sum_{j=0}^{r-1} q_j a_{n-r+j}) x^n = \sum_{n \geq 0} (a_n - \sum_{j=0}^{r-1} q_j a_{n-r+j}) x^n = p.$$

□

4 Learning rational series in one variable

In this section we prove that rational series over a one-letter alphabet, having rank $\leq d$, are learnable in polynomial time when multiplicity queries are allowed. We provide an algorithm which is polynomial in d. The learning model we use is the exact learning model with multiplicity queries. In this model we consider a learner that is able to ask an oracle the value of the *target series S* for a given string in $\{x\}^*$. Moreover, we suppose that the positive integer d, which is an upper bound to the rank of the target series, is known to the learner.

By Theorems 4, 5 and 6, if we know the exact rank r of S, then we can compute the coefficients $q_0, \ldots, q_{r-1}$ of Eq. (6) to learn a linear representation of S, a linear recurrence relation satisfied by the sequence $(a_n)_{n \geq 0}$ and a generating function of S. To compute the coefficients $q_0, \ldots, q_{r-1}$, we can solve the system of r linear equations in the r unknowns q_i's (6). By Corollary 3 this linear system is compatible and has a single solution, then it can be solved with the Gauss' substitution method whose complexity is polynomial in r.

If instead of $rank(S)$ we know a parameter d such that $rank(S) \leq d$, by Corollary 2 the finite matrix $H(S)|_{d \times d}$ has rank equal to $rank(S)$, thus we can calculate the exact rank r of $H(S)$ computing the rank of $H(S)|_{d \times d}$.

We describe now the procedure for exactly identifying S with rank at most d from multiplicy queries. Let r be the rank of $H(S)|_{d \times d}$ and $E_r = \{\epsilon, x, x^2, \ldots, x^{r-1}\}$.

Algorithm $Learn_{1var}(d)$

- Compute the coefficients $q_0, q_2, \ldots, q_{r-1}$ satisfying Eq. (6).
- Compute the linear representation $(\hat{\lambda}, \hat{\mu}, \hat{\gamma})$ of S as in Theorem 4.
- Compute a linear recurrence relation for S as in Theorem 5:

$$\forall n \geq 0, \ a_{r+n} = \sum_{j=0}^{r-1} q_j a_{n+j}. \tag{11}$$

- Compute a generating function $p/1 - q$ of S as in Theorem 6: $q = q_{r-1}x + q_{r-2}x^2 + \ldots + q_0x^r$ and $p = \sum_{n=0}^{r-1}(a_n - \sum_{j=0}^{r-1} q_j a_{n-r+j})x^n$.

5   Unary output 2-tape NFA

A *non deterministic two-tape automaton* M (2-tape NFA) is a 7-tuple

$$M = (Q, A, A_2, E_1, E_2, I, F), \text{ where}$$

- Q is a finite set of states;
- A and A_2 are two disjoint finite alphabets called *first-tape* and *second-tape* alphabets, respectively;
- E_1 is the set of the transitions relative to the first tape, that is

$$E_1 \subseteq \{(p, a, \epsilon, q) \mid p, q \in Q, a \in A\};$$

- E_2 is the set of the transitions relative to the second tape, that is

$$E_2 \subseteq \{(p, \epsilon, b, q) \mid p, q \in Q, b \in A_2\};$$

- I and F are the sets of the initial and final states, respectively.

A *path* (p, x, y, q), labelled by $(x, y) \in A^* \times A_2^*$, with $xy \neq \epsilon$, is a sequence of transitions $(p_1, x_1, y_1, p_2)(p_2, x_2, y_2, p_3) \ldots (p_n, x_n, y_n, p_{n+1})$, where $x = x_1 x_2 \ldots x_n \in A^*$, $y = y_1 y_2 \ldots y_n \in A_2^*$, $p_1 = p$, $p_{n+1} = q$, and $(p_j, x_j, y_j, p_{j+1}) \in E_1 \cup E_2$, for $j = 1, 2, \ldots, n$. We say that (p, x, y, q) is an *accepting* path if $p \in I$ and $q \in F$.

A *unary output two-tape non deterministic finite automaton* (*unary output 2-tape NFA*) is a particular 2-tape NFA with a unary second-tape alphabet, that is $A_2 = \{x\}$.

Definition 8. *The behavior of a unary output 2-tape NFA M is the map*

$$S_M : (A^* \times \{x\}^*) - \{(\epsilon, \epsilon)\} \to \mathbb{Q}$$

such that, for any $(w, x^n) \in (A^* \times \{x\}^*) - \{(\epsilon, \epsilon)\}$, $(S_M, (w, x^n))$ is the number of the accepting paths labelled by (w, x^n).

Now, following [16], we show that S_M can be described by a map $S \in \mathbb{Q}^{rat}\langle\langle x\rangle\rangle^{rat}\langle\langle A\rangle\rangle$, i. e. S is a recognizable series over the alphabet A, with coefficients in $\mathbb{Q}^{rat}\langle\langle x\rangle\rangle$. In fact we set

$$((S, w), x^n) = (S_M, (w, x^n)) \ \forall w \in A^*, \ \forall n \geq 0. \tag{12}$$

Assume now that $S : A^* \to \mathbb{Q}^{rat}\langle\langle x\rangle\rangle^{rat}$ is a map associated with a unary 2-tape NFA M according to Eq. (12). We will show that S is a map from A^* to $\mathbb{Q}^{rat}\langle\langle x\rangle\rangle$ (i. e. a $(\mathbb{Q}^{rat}\langle\langle x\rangle\rangle)$-subset of A^*) and prove the existence of a linear representation (λ, μ, γ) of S. Let $M = (\{q_1, q_2, \ldots, q_n\}, A, \{x\}, E_1, E_2, I, F)$ and let $B = A \cup \{x\}$. We define the morphism $\mu' : B^* \to \mathbb{Q}^{n \times n}$ as follows: for $i, j = 1, 2, \ldots, n$, $a \in A$

$$\mu'(a)_{i,j} = 1 \text{ if } (q_i, a, \epsilon, q_j) \in E_1, \ \mu'(a)_{i,j} = 0 \text{ otherwise;} \tag{13}$$

$$\mu'(x)_{i,j} = 1 \text{ if } (q_i, \epsilon, x, q_j) \in E_2, \ \mu'(x)_{i,j} = 0 \text{ otherwise.} \tag{14}$$

For $i, j = 1, 2, \ldots, n$ we denote by $S_{i,j}$ the (recognizable) series over the alphabet $\{x\}$ defined as follows:

$$S_{i,j} = \sum_{n \geq 0} \mu'(x^n)_{i,j} x^n. \tag{15}$$

For any $n \geq 0$, $(S_{i,j}, x^n) = \mu'(x^n)_{i,j}$ is the number of the paths labelled by x^n on the second tape from the state q_i to the state q_j, that is the number of the paths like $(q_i, \epsilon, x^n, q_j)$ (Eq. (14)).

We define a linear representation (λ, μ, γ) of S as follows: for $i, j = 1, 2, \ldots, n$ and $a \in A$

- $\lambda_i = 1$ if $q_i \in I$, $\lambda_i = 0$ otherwise;
- $\gamma_i = 1$ if $q_i \in F$, $\gamma_i = 0$ otherwise;
- $\mu(a)_{i,j} = \sum_{h,k=1}^n S_{i,h} \mu'(a)_{h,k} S_{k,j} \in \mathbb{Q}^{rat} \langle\langle x \rangle\rangle$. By Eq. (13), we can note that for any $w \in A^*$, $\mu'(w)_{i,j}$ is the number of the paths labelled by w on the first tape from the state q_i to the state q_j, that is the number of the paths like (q_i, w, ϵ, q_j). By Eq. (15) one easily derives that $(\mu(a)_{i,j}, x^n)$ is the number of the paths of the kind (q_i, a, x^n, q_j). In fact a path labelled by (a, x^n) from the state q_i to the state q_j is of the kind $(q_i, \epsilon, x^m, q_h)(q_h, a, \epsilon, q_k)(q_k, \epsilon, x^{n-m}, q_j)$, with $q_h, q_k \in Q$ and $m \leq n$.

For any two states q_h, q_k of Q, and for $m = 0, 1, \ldots, n$ we obtain all the paths labelled by (a, x^n) from the state q_i to the state q_j and passing from q_h to q_k reading the letter a on the first tape. The sum of these paths is

$$\sum_{m=0}^n (S_{i,h}, x^m) \mu'(a)_{h,k} (S_{k,j}, x^{n-m}).$$

Ranking q_h and q_k in Q, we obtain all the paths labelled by (a, x^n) from the state q_i to the state q_j; thus the number of the paths like (q_i, a, x^n, q_j) is

$$\sum_{h,k=1}^n \sum_{m=0}^n (S_{i,h}, x^m) \mu'(a)_{h,k} (S_{k,j}, x^{n-m}) = (\mu(a)_{i,j}, x^n).$$

We conclude that

$$\mu(a)_{i,j} = \sum_{n \geq 0} \left(\sum_{h,k=1}^n \sum_{m=0}^n (S_{i,h}, x^m) \mu'(a)_{h,k} (S_{k,j}, x^{n-m}) \right) x^n =$$

$$\sum_{h,k=1}^n S_{i,h} \mu'(a)_{h,k} S_{k,j}.$$

Similarly one can prove that for any $w \in A^*$, $(\mu(w)_{i,j}, x^n)$ is the number of the paths of the kind (q_i, w, x^n, q_j). Therefore (λ, μ, γ) is a linear representation of S. We conclude by the following important:

Remark 1. A rational series $S \in Q^{rat}\langle\langle x \rangle\rangle$ has a generating function $p(x)/(1 - q(x))$, where p and q are polynomials and $q(\epsilon) = 0$. Thus, $Q^{rat}\langle\langle x \rangle\rangle \subseteq Q(x)$, i. e. we can embed the ring $Q^{rat}\langle\langle x \rangle\rangle$ into the field of rational functions $Q(x)$. From this point of view we can consider the series with coefficients in $Q^{rat}\langle\langle x \rangle\rangle$ as having the coefficients in the field $Q(x)$.

6 Learning unary output 2-tape NFA

We prove that unary output 2-tape NFA's are exactly identifiable, in poly-noimial time, when multiplicity and equivalence queries are allowed. We consider a learner that is able to ask an oracle whether a guess is correct, and obtaining a counterexample if it is not (equivalence queries), or to ask the number of ac-cepting paths of a pair of strings in $A^* \times \{x\}^*$. If S is the behavior of the target automaton, then we can obtain the answer to a query like

$$(S, (w, x^n)) =?, \text{ for } (w, x^n) \in w \in A^* \times \{x\}^*,$$

that is equivalent, by Eq. (12), to a query like:

$$((S, w), x^n) =?, \text{ for } (w, x^n) \in w \in A^* \times \{x\}^*.$$

Based on a previous work by Bergadano and Varricchio on automata with multiplicity on a field K [6], we show that the behaviors of unary output 2-tape NFA's may be identified in polynomial time when multiplicity and equivalence queries are allowed.

6.1 Base Algorithm

Let $S \in (Q^{rat}\langle\langle x \rangle\rangle)^{rat}\langle\langle A \rangle\rangle$ be the behavior of the target unary output 2-tape NFA M.

Definition 9. *By $SubDim_S(\lambda, \mu, \gamma)$ we mean the greatest rank of the entries of the linear representation (λ, μ, γ) of S, i.e. the greatest rank of the elements λ_i, γ_j, $\mu(a)_{i,j}$, for $i, j = 1, \ldots, n$ and $a \in A$.*

In this section we assume known the rank n of S, and the $SubDim_S(\lambda, \mu, \gamma) = m$ of the exact linear representation of S. One can prove the following:

Proposition 1. *Let $S \in Q^{rat}\langle\langle x \rangle\rangle^{rat}\langle\langle A \rangle\rangle$ be a series with rank n and let (λ, μ, γ) be a linear representation of S of dimension n where $\mu(a) \in Q^{rat}\langle\langle x \rangle\rangle^{n \times n}$ for any $a \in A$, $\lambda \in Q^{rat}\langle\langle x \rangle\rangle^{1 \times n}$ and $\gamma \in Q^{rat}\langle\langle x \rangle\rangle^{n \times 1}$. For any $w \in A^*$, if $SubDim_S(\lambda, \mu, \gamma) = m$ and $|w| = h$, then*

$$rank((S, w)) \leq ((h - 2)mn^2 + (2m + h - 1)n + 2m + 2)n^2 + 1.$$

that is $rank((S, w)) = O(hmn^4)$.

In the sequel we will denote this estimate of the maximal rank of the entries of (S, w) by $dim_w(n, m)$.

Theorem 7. *Let $S \in (\mathbb{Q}^{rat}\langle\langle x\rangle\rangle)^{rat}\langle\langle A\rangle\rangle$ be a target series. If the parameters n and m are known, then for any $w \in A^*$, the series $S^{(w)} = (S, w) \in \mathbb{Q}^{rat}\langle\langle x\rangle\rangle$ is exactly identifiable, when multiplicity queries are allowed, with an algorithm which is polynomial in n, m and $h = |w|$.*

Proof. Given the parameters n and m, we know that the rational series $S^{(w)} = (S, w) \in \mathbb{Q}^{rat}\langle\langle x\rangle\rangle$, have rank at most

$$dim_w(n, m) = ((h - 2)mn^2 + (2m + h - 1)n + 2m + 3)n^2 + 1.$$

The algorithm $Learn_{1var}(d)$ of Sec. 4, identifies, using multiplicity queries, a rational series $S' \in \mathbb{Q}^{rat}\langle\langle x\rangle\rangle$ with rank at most d in polynomial time with respect to d. Since, for any $w \in A^*$, the series $S^{(w)} = (S, w) \in \mathbb{Q}^{rat}\langle\langle x\rangle\rangle$ has rank at most $dim_w(n, m)$, we may identify $S^{(w)}$ with the learning algorithm $Learn_{1var}(dim_w(n, m))$. This algorithm is polynomial in $dim_w(n, m)$, that is in n, m and $h = |w|$. □

Let $S \in (\mathbb{Q}^{rat}\langle\langle x\rangle\rangle)^{rat}\langle\langle A\rangle\rangle$. Let $n = rank(S)$ and $m = SubDim_S(\lambda, \mu, \gamma)$, for any $w \in A^*$, we may describe the algorithm polynomial in n, m and $h = |w|$ for exactly identifying the series $S^{(w)} = (S, w) \in \mathbb{Q}^{rat}\langle\langle x\rangle\rangle$ when multiplicity queries are allowed:

Algorithm $Learn'_{1var}(w, n, m)$

– From Eq. (6.1) compute $d = dim_w(n, m)$;
– call $Learn_{1var}(d)$

We can consider the algorithm $Learn'_{1var}(w, n, m)$ as a multiplicity oracle for a target $\mathbb{Q}^{rat}\langle\langle x\rangle\rangle$-set S, if the parameters n and m are known. Moreover, by Remark 1, the ring $\mathbb{Q}^{rat}\langle\langle x\rangle\rangle$ is embedded in the field of rational functions in one variable. Thus, if the parameters n and m of the target $\mathbb{Q}^{rat}\langle\langle x\rangle\rangle$-set of A^* are known, then we can apply the learning algorithm of Bergadano and Varricchio [6].

Let $S \in (\mathbb{Q}^{rat}\langle\langle x\rangle\rangle)^{rat}\langle\langle A\rangle\rangle$.

Definition 10. *An observation table for S is a triplet $\tau = (P, E, T)$, where $P \subseteq A^*$ is a prefix-closed set of strings, $E \subseteq A^*$ is a suffix-closed set of strings and $T : (P \cup PA)E \to \mathbb{Q}^{rat}\langle\langle x\rangle\rangle$ is a map that gives the observed values of S, that is $T(w) = Learn'_{1var}(w, n, m)$ for any $w \in (P \cup PA)E$.*

The set P determines a set of rational series $\{S_u \mid u \in P\}$ that will be useful to define the target series S via linear dependencies.

Definition 11. *An observation table (P, E, T) is closed iff, for any $u \in P$ and $a \in A$, there is a series $\alpha_v \in \mathbb{Q}^{rat}\langle\langle x\rangle\rangle$, for each $v \in P$, such that*

$$S_{ua} \equiv_E \sum_{v \in P} \alpha_v S_v. \tag{16}$$

Definition 12. *An observation table (P, E, T) is consistent iff, for any choise of the rational series $\beta_v \in Q^{rat}\langle\langle x \rangle\rangle$, for $v \in P$,*

$$\sum_{v \in P} \beta_v S_v \equiv_E 0 \Rightarrow \sum_{v \in P} \beta_v S_{va} \equiv_E 0, \forall a \in A. \quad (17)$$

Definition 13. *P is a complete set of strings for S iff for any $u \in P$, and $a \in A$, there is a series $\lambda_v \in Q^{rat}\langle\langle x \rangle\rangle$, for each $v \in P$, such that*

$$S_{ua} \equiv \sum_{v \in P} \lambda_v S_v. \quad (18)$$

Here we only want to show how from such a table (P, E, T) we can guess a $Q^{rat}\langle\langle x \rangle\rangle$-set $M(P, E, T)$ by basing its representation upon the existing linear dependencies:

- Let $P = \{u_1, ..., u_k\}$, with $u_1 = \epsilon$.
- For all $a \in A$, compute $\hat{\mu}(a)$ satisfying

$$S_{u_i a} \equiv_E \sum_j \hat{\mu}(a)_{u_i, u_j} S_{u_j}. \quad (19)$$

Such a matrix exists because the table is closed.
- Let $\hat{\lambda} = (1, 0, \dots, 0)$ and $\hat{\gamma} = ((S_{u_1}, \epsilon), (S_{u_2}, \epsilon), \dots, (S_{u_k}, \epsilon))$. The value of (S_{u_j}, ϵ) is found in the table since $u_j \in P$ and $\epsilon \in E$. Obviously $\hat{\mu}(a)_{u_i, u_j}$ is the value at row i and column j of the matrix $\hat{\mu}(a)$. Let $\hat{\mu}(a_1 a_2 ... a_r) = \hat{\mu}(a_1)\hat{\mu}(a_2)...\hat{\mu}(a_r)$, $a_i \in A$. Define the $Q^{rat}\langle\langle x \rangle\rangle$-set M by $(M, w) = \hat{\lambda}\hat{\mu}(w)\hat{\gamma}$.

We may now describe an adaptation of the algorithm given in [6] for exactly identifiyng S from multiplicity and equivalence queries, if we known the rank n of the target series S and the subdimension m of a linear representation of S.

Base algorithm:

$\tau \leftarrow (\{\epsilon\}, \{\epsilon\}, T)$, where $(T, \epsilon) = Learn'_{1var}(\epsilon, n, m)$.

Repeat

- Make the table closed and consistent (P and E are extended and the entries of T are filled in by algorithm $Learn'_{1var}$). We remark that $Learn'_{1var}$ returns the correct entries iff the parameter n and m are correct.
- Make the hypothesized $Q^{rat}\langle\langle x \rangle\rangle$-set $M(P, E, T)$.
- Ask for a counterexample t to $M(P, E, T)$ by means of an equivalence query.
- Add t and its prefixes to P.

until correct

Bergadano and Varricchio showed [6] that this algorithm is correct and if $rank(S) = n$ then after at most n equivalence queries, we will have a correct guess, i.e. $M(P, E, T) \equiv S$. Hence after at most n iterations, the algorithm stops.

6.2 Closing a table

Given a table (P, E, T) and $u \in P$, we suppose S_{ua} is linearly independent from $\{S_v \mid v \in P\}$ with respect to E, in the sense that there are not $\lambda_{u,v} \in \mathbb{Q}^{rat}\langle\langle x \rangle\rangle$ such that $S_{ua} \equiv_E \sum_{v \in P} \lambda_{u,v} S_v$. In this case ua is added to P, and the table is again checked for closure.

This procedure must terminate. More precisely, if the correct $\mathbb{Q}^{rat}\langle\langle x \rangle\rangle$-set S is representable with $(S, x) = \lambda \mu(x) \gamma$, where $\lambda, \gamma \in \mathbb{Q}^{rat}\langle\langle x \rangle\rangle^n$ and $\mu : A^* \to \mathbb{Q}^{rat}\langle\langle x \rangle\rangle^{n \times n}$ is a morphism, then at most n strings can be added to P when closing the table. In fact, it should be noted that, when ua is added to P as indicated above, the dimension of $\{\lambda \mu(v) \mid v \in P\}$, as a subset of the vector space $\mathbb{Q}^{rat}\langle\langle x \rangle\rangle^n$, is increased by one. Otherwise, $\lambda \mu(ua)$ would be equal to $\sum_{v \in P} \beta_v \lambda \mu(v)$ for some $\beta_v \in \mathbb{Q}^{rat}\langle\langle x \rangle\rangle$ and

$$(S_{ua}, x) = (S, uax) = \lambda \mu(ua) \mu(x) \gamma = \sum \beta_v \lambda \mu(v) \mu(x) \gamma = \sum \beta_v (S_v, x)$$

i.e., S_{ua} would depend linearly on $\{S_v \mid v \in P\}$. Since the dimension of $\{\lambda \mu(v) \mid v \in P\}$ is at most n, we cannot close the table more than n times. The above discussion does not depend on E.

6.3 Making tables consistent

Given a table (P, E, T) and a symbol $a \in A$, consider the two systems of linear equations:

$$(1) \sum_{v \in P} \beta_v S_v \equiv_E 0 \quad (2) \sum_{v \in P} \beta_v S_{va} \equiv_E 0,$$

with β_v as unknowns. Check if every solution of system (1) is also a solution of system (2). In this case the table is consistent. Otherwise, let β_v', $v \in P$, be some solutions of (1) that are not solutions of (2) and $x \in E$ such that $\sum_{v \in P} \beta_v (S_{va}, x) \neq 0$. Add ax to E.

We suppose that S has a linear representation (λ, μ, γ) of dimension n; there cannot be more than n such additions to E, because every time a new string ax is added, the dimension of $\{\mu(w)\gamma \mid w \in E\}$ is increased by one. In fact, if $\mu(ax)\gamma = \sum_{w \in E} \delta_w \mu(w)\gamma$, then

$$\sum_{v \in P} \beta_v (S_{va}, x) = \sum_{v \in P} \beta_v \lambda \mu(v) \mu(ax) \gamma = \sum_{v \in P} \beta_v \lambda \mu(v) \sum_{w \in E} \delta_w \mu(w)\gamma =$$

$$\sum_{w \in E} \delta_w \sum_{v \in P} \beta_v \lambda \mu(vw)\gamma = \sum_{w \in E} \delta_w \sum_{v \in P} \beta_v (S_v, w) = 0$$

i.e., ax would not have been added to E.

6.4 Extended algorithm

The *algorithm* is correct iff we know the exact rank of target series S and the exact subdimension m of the correct linear representation for S. Otherwise the algorithm $Learn'_{1,ar}(w,n,m)$ may fail. In this case the stage in which the learning process builds a close and consistent table may not terminate; moreover also the base algorithm may not terminate. Bud we know that if the rank of the target series is n, then

 - we cannot close the table more than n times (cf. Sec. 6.2);
 - we cannot add more than n strings to E (cf. Sec. 6.3);
 - after at most n iterations the algorithm stops (cf. [6]).

Thus if we suppose that $rank(S) = n$ and $SubDim_S(\lambda, \mu, \gamma) = m$, we may conclude that they are wrong if the algorithm closes the table more than n times or adds more than n strings to E or does not stop after n iterations. In this case we may increase n and m and again execute the base algorithm supposing that they are correct.

Extended algorithm:

$n := 0$; $m := 0$; $Error := true$;

Repeat

 - If $Error$ then
    - $n := n + 1$; $m := m + 1$;
    - $\tau \leftarrow (\{\epsilon\}, \{\epsilon\}, T)$, where $(T, \epsilon) = Learn'_{1var}(\epsilon, n, m)$;
    - $Error := false$; $Control := 0$; $OldP := 0$;
 - while not(τ close and consistent) and $Control \leq n$ and $|E| \leq n$ do
    - Make the table closed;
    - If $|P| \geq OldP$ then $Control := Control + 1$; $OldP := |P|$;
    - Make the table consistent.
 - If $Control \leq n$ and $|E| \leq n$
    - then
       * Make the hypothsized $Q^{rat}\langle\langle x\rangle\rangle$-set $M(P, E, T)$.
       * Ask for a counterexample t to $M(P, E, T)$ by means of an equivalence query.
       * Add t and its prefixes to P"; $Controllo := Controllo + 1$;
    - else $Error := true$;

until correct

The correctness and the termination of the base algorithm showed by Bergadano and Varricchio [6] implies the correctness and the termination of the extended algorithm.

References

1. D. Angluin and Carl H. Smith, *Inductive Inference: Theory and Metods*, Computing Surveys, **15** (1983) pp. 237-269.
2. D. Angluin, *Learning regular sets from queries and counterexamples*, Information and Computation, **75** (1987), pp.87-106.
3. D. Angluin, *Queries and concept learning*, Machine Learning, **2** (1988), pp.319-342.
4. D. Angluin, *Computational Learning Theory: Survey and Selected Bibliography*, proceedings of the 24th ACM Symposium on the Theory of Computing (STOC 92), pp.351-369.
5. A. Beimel, F. Bergadano, N. H. Bshouty, E. Kushilevitz and S.Varricchio, *On the Applications of Multiplicity Automata in Learning*, 37th Annual Symposium on Foundations of Computer Science, (1996), pp.349-358.
6. F. Bergadano and S. Varricchio, *Learning Behaviors of automata from Multiplicity and Equivalence Queries* SIAM J. On Computing, **25** (1996), pp.1268-1280.
7. F. Bergadano, N. H. Bshouty, C. Tamon and S. Varricchio, *On Learning Branching Programs and Small Depth Circuits* Lectures Notes in Artififial Intelligence, 1208 (1997), pp.150-161.
8. F. Bergadano, D. Catalano and S. Varricchio, *Learning Sat-k-DNF Formulas from Membership Queries*, proceedings of the 28th ACM Symposium on the Theory of Computing (STOC 96), pp.126-131.
9. J. Berstel, *Trasductions and Languages context-free*, Stuttgard: Teubner, 1979.
10. J. Berstel and C. Reutenauer, *Rational series and their languages*, Springer-Verlag, Berlin, 1988.
11. S. Eilenberg, *Semirings, Automata, Languages and Machines*, Vol.A, Academic Press, New York, 1974.
12. T. Harju and J. Karhumaki, *The equivalence problem of multi-tape finite automata*, Theoretical Computer Science, **78** (1991), pp.347-355.
13. O. Ibarra, *Reversal-Bounded Multicounter Machines and their Decisions Problems*, J. Assoc. Comp. Machinery, **25** (1978), pp.116-133.
14. W. Kuich and A. Salomaa, *Semirings, Automata, Languages*, Springer-Verlag, Berlin.
15. M.Rabin and D. Scott, *Finite automata and their decision problems*, IBM J. Res. Develop., **3** (1959), pp.114-125.
16. A. Salomaa and M. Soittola *Automata theoretic aspects of formal power series*, Springer-Verlag, New York, 1978.
17. L.G. Valiant, *A theory of the learnable*, Communications of the ACM. **27(11)** (1984), pp.1134-1142.
18. T. Yokomori, *Learning Two-Tape Automata from Queries and Counterexamples*, Mathematical Systems Theory, **29(3)** (1996), pp.259-270.

Computational Aspects of Parallel Attribute-Efficient Learning

Peter Damaschke

FernUniversität, Theoretische Informatik II
58084 Hagen, Germany
Peter.Damaschke@fernuni-hagen.de

Abstract. We address the problem of nonadaptive learning of Boolean functions with few relevant variables by membership queries. In another recent paper [7] we have characterized those assignment families (query sets) which are sufficient for nonadaptive learning of this function class, and we studied the query number. However, the reconstruction of the given Boolean function from the obtained responses is an important matter as well in applying such nonadaptive strategies. The computational amount for this is apparently too high if we use our query families in a straightforward way. Therefore we introduce algorithms where also the computational complexity is reasonable, rather than the query number only. The idea is to apply our assignment families to certain coarsenings of the given Boolean function, followed by simple search and verification routines.

1 Introduction and Problem Statement

Attribute-efficient learning means the learning of Boolean functions f where only an unknown small subset $R \subset V$ of the variable set V is relevant. A variable $v \in V$ is called relevant if there exists an assignment of the remaining variables in $V \setminus \{v\}$ such that the function value of f changes if we switch the value of v only. In more simple words, v is relevant if it has an actual influence on f. Let $Rel(n, r)$ denote the class of Boolean functions of n variables, r or less of which are relevant.

We consider the model of exact learning by membership queries, that is, we may choose arbitrary assignments and ask an oracle about the value of f there. Our goal is to identify f. In parallel learning, the learning process consists of a sequence of stages. In every stage we may fix a set of queries which are asked simultaneously. The query set chosen in any stage may depend on the responses obtained in earlier stages. In the setting of adaptive learning we allow only one query per stage. The other extreme is nonadaptive learning where only one stage is allowed and all queries must be fixed beforehand. (The terminology in the literature may differ, cf. [4]. However, in the present paper let us use the terms as introduced above.)

Another view of nonadaptive learning is the concept of teaching [11] [12] [13] [14]. Assignment families which distinghuish pairwise between all functions from a given class are called universal identification sequences or universal teaching sets there, and several classes with polynomial-size universal teaching sets are known.

In the following, an assignment family means any subset of the 2^n possible assignments. In [7] we give a graph-theoretic characterization of assignment families A that are sufficient for nonadaptive learning of functions $f \in Rel(n, r)$, called r-wise bipartite connected families (see definitions below). Notice that, for trivial reasons, deciding whether $f \in Rel(n, r)$ would require asking all 2^n possible queries in the worst case. (Consider e.g. a constant function vs. a function whose value deviates on exactly one assignment – then we have $r = 0$ and $r = n$, respectively.) So we must be sure in advance that $f \in Rel(n, r)$, but this is a reasonable assumption in view of the interesting applications of attribute-efficient learning, such as fault detection, diagnosis systems, and combinatorial search [1] [2] [9] [10] [18]. Furthermore, parallelity of queries is essential in applications where the tests (queries) can be really performed simultaneuosly, but each test is time-consuming. This is the case e.g. in pooling in experimental molecular biology. We refer to the mentioned papers for background information. Other problems in the field of attribute-efficient learning are studied e.g. in [15] [3] [5].

Assume always that r is nothing more than a fixed small integer, but n may be huge. The problems are studied for general r only because the principal structures remain the same.

In [7] we study assignment families A being eligible for nonadaptive learning of function from $Rel(n, r)$. (That means, every function from this class can be identified from the $f(a)$, $a \in A$.) We prove the existence of such families of size $O(r^2 2^r + r 2^r \log n)$. Actually, a random family of that size is sufficient with high probability. We also proposed a pseudopolynomial explicit construction with slightly worse size of the results. On the other hand, $\Omega(2^r \log n)$ queries are necessary even for adaptive learning. Hence the pure query complexity of learning $Rel(n, r)$ is quite well understood. Constructing good families A needs some efforts, but this may be done once and for all, for given bounds of n and r, and the resulting A may be permanently stored. So this point is not an obstacle.

However, there remains another serious problem that cannot be ignored: In order to apply a nonadaptive learning algorithm A to several instances f, it is not enough to know that different functions f from $Rel(n, r)$ yield different response vectors $[f(a)]_{a \in A}$. We must also be able to perform the inverse transformation, i.e. to extract f from the response vector.

It is implicit in the proof of our characterization in [7] that the set R of relevant variables is the unique minimum (A, f)-feasible set (see definitions below). Once we know the set R, the function f is also learned, since our families A have the particular property that they induce all possible assignments on subsets of size r. (They are r-universal; see definitions below.) So we can focus attention on identifying R.

Clearly, (A, f)-feasibility of any subset can be recognized in $O(n|A|)$ time by lexicographic sorting. So we can find R naively by checking all (roughly) $n^r/r!$

candidate sets for (A, f)-feasibility. This gives a total computational amount of $O((r2^r/r!)n^{r+1}\log n) = O(\sqrt{r}(2e/r)^r n^{r+1}\log n)$ which is barely practicable because of the n^{r+1} term. Unfortunately, we did not find a better algorithm than exhaustive search, and even worse, we have the impression that such a fast transformation might not exist in general. Loosely speaking, it seems that the structure of our families A alone does not give enough hints how to find R. Trivially, all sets including R are (A, f)-feasible, but the difficulty is that many other sets are (A, f)-feasible, too, by inner dependencies in A.

Thus we should aim at such nonadaptive or parallel learning strategies where also the amount of auxiliary computations is reasonable. The above discussion does not imply that our r-wise bipartite connected families are of purely academic interest. On the contrary, in our favourite parallel algorithm we shall essentially make use of them again.

We remark that in the important special case of nonadaptive group testing [1] [2] [6], the analogous problem of reconstrucing the given function from the test results is almost trivial. (Group testing is learning of the disjunction of an unknown subset of variables, called the "defectives".)

The present note is understood as a supplement to [7]. We propose several solutions to our problem, based on the same idea. The choice of an algorithm for a concrete instance will depend on several circumstances such as the problem size, and the ratio of query costs and computation costs. (It may be assumed that queries are physical procedures, of whatever nature, outside a computer and therefore expensive, but computations are nowadays cheap and fast.) We do not provide novel techniques here, other than new compositions of the formerly known structures, but the issue is essential for making parallel attribute-efficient learning really accessible. For convenience we formulate our results thoroughly in O-notation, but the hidden factors are always moderate.

2 Special Assignment Families

First we list some definitions of useful combinatorial structures, as well as the basic lemmas. As explained in the introduction, we need not worry about explicit constructions of these combinatorial objects here, and we suppose that they are already available for given n and r. Throughout the paper, f means the given function from $Rel(n, r)$ that we wish to learn, V is the set of variables, and $R \subset V$ is the set of relevant variables of f.

Definition 1. *An assignment family A is called r-universal (or r-exhaustive) if each of the 2^r possible assignments on each subset of r variables is induced by some member of A. By convention, any nonempty assignment family is 0-universal.*

Lemma 1. *There exist r-universal families of size $O(r2^r \log n)$.* $\square$

This is proved in a straightforward way by the probabilistic method. Explicit constructions of slightly larger families are also known. See [17] for these matters. In the following we take the liberty to apply the $O(r2^r \log n)$ bound.

The following definition from [7] is not directly used in the sequel and may be skipped by the reader, but we include it here, in order to make this note more self-contained.

Definition 2. *An r-universal assignment family A on V is called r-wise bipartite connected if each bipartite graph $B(X, Y, z)$ is connected, where X, Y, Z are mutually disjoint subsets of V with $|X \cup Z| = |Y \cup Z| = r$, z is an assignment on Z, and $B(X, Y, z)$ is defined in the following way: The vertices are all possible assignments x on X and y on Y, respectively, and xy is an edge iff some assignment from A induces $x, y,$ and z on $X, Y,$ and Z, respectively.*

Definition 3. *Let f be a Boolean function and A an asignment family. The set $U \subset V$ is called (A, f)-feasible if, for all $a \in A$, $f(a)$ depends merely on the assignment induced by a on U.*

The central result of [7] is:

Theorem 1. *An assignment family A can learn functions from $Rel(n, r)$ nonadaptively if and only if A is r-wise bipartite connected. Moreover, there exist such families of size $O(r^2 2^r + r2^r \log n)$.[1] The set R of relevant variables of any $f \in Rel(n, r)$ is exactly the unique minimum (A, f)-feasible set.* $\Box$

From Theorem 3 and the remark in the introduction we get:

Theorem 2. *Functions from $Rel(n, r)$ can be learned nonadaptively by $O(r^2 2^r + r2^r \log n)$ queries followed by $O(\sqrt{r}(2e/r)^r n^{r+1} \log n)$ computations.* $\Box$

The next lemma shows how to test, by nonadaptive queries to f, whether a given set $S \subseteq R$ even satisfies $S = R$.

Lemma 2. *Let be $S \subseteq R$, $s = |S|$, and let A consist of all pairs of arbitrary assignments on S and assignments from an $(r - s)$-universal family on $V \setminus S$, respectively. Then there exist relevant variables outside S (i.e. $R \setminus S \neq \emptyset$) if and only if S is not (A, f)-feasible. The size of A can be bounded by $O(r2^r \log n)$.* $\Box$

Proof. The "if" direction is trivial, so we prove "only if".

Assume that $V \setminus S$ contains relevant variables. Since $|R| \leq r$ and $S \subseteq R$, these are at most $r - s$ variables. For any $v \in R \setminus S$, there exists an assignment on R such that f changes if v changes and the values on $R \setminus \{v\}$ remain fixed. Hence, due to $(r - s)$-universality, there exist two assignments $a, a' \in A$ agreeing on S but giving $f(a) \neq f(a')$. That means, S is not (A, f)-feasible.

If we take an $(r - s)$-universal family as in Lemma 1 then the number of assignments in A is $O(2^s (r - s) 2^{r-s} \log n)$ which implies the asserted bound. $\Box$

Definition 4. *We say that a partition of V into subsets, called bins, separates a subset $R \subset V$ if the elements of R get into pairwise distinct bins. An (r, b)-separating family is a family of partitions of V with $b \geq r$ bins each, such that every r-element subset of V is separated by at least one of these partitions.*

---

[1] In the preliminary version of [7] we claimed an $O(r2^r \log n)$ bound, but at the moment we can only prove the slightly weaker bound as stated here. However this is marginal.

Our separating families lie somewhere between shattering families (as in VC theory), splitters and perfect hash functions (see e.g. [17]); here we prefer the term "separating families" to avoid confusions with these similar concepts. Note that the bins are not required to be of equal size here.

Lemma 3. *There exist (r, r^2)-separating families of size $O(r \log n)$.*

Proof. This is a routine application of the probabilistic method. Each element of V is thrown independently and equiprobably into one of the b bins. Consider a fixed $R \subset V$ of size r. The probability of R to be separated is at least $(1 - r/b)^r \approx e^{-r^2/b}$. Hence the probability that some of the r-element subsets remains unseparated by t random partitions is less than $n^r(1-e^{-r^2/b})^t$. Choosing $t = O(e^{r^2/b}r \log n)$ keeps this probability below 1. Finally let $b = r^2$. $\square$

Definition 5. *For a Boolean function f and a partition π of V, the coarsening f_π is the function whose variables are the bins $y_1, \ldots, y_b$ of π, such that $f_\pi(y_1, \ldots, y_b)$ is defined to be the value of f when we assign the value of y_i to all variables in the i-th bin, for $i = 1, \ldots, b$. Bins that are relevant variables with respect to f_π are refered to as the relevant bins.*
A projection of f is any function obtained from f by fixing the assignment on a subset of the variables.

We need a further, rather trivial lemma as a basic step.

Lemma 4. *Functions $f \in Rel(n, 1)$ can be learned nonadaptively by $O(\log n)$ queries and $O(n \log n)$ computations. $\square$*

This is immediately clear, but it should also be noticed that the obvious strategy is not good for finding one out of several relevant variables, i.e. it may fail if $r > 1$.

3   Nonadaptive Attribute-Efficient Learning with Fair Total Complexity

In the following results we implicitly presume that the necessary ingredients (i.e. special assignment families) are already available, and so the time to construct them is not being counted. As already mentioned, the construction must be done only once for given n and r and can be applied then to several $f \in Rel(n, r)$. Thus, henceforth our input is the function $f \in Rel(n, r)$ to be learned, given as an oracle.

Theorem 3. *Functions from $Rel(n, r)$ can be learned nonadaptively using $O(r^4 2^r \log r \log^2 n)$ queries followed by $O((r^4 2^r \log r)n \log^2 n)$ computations.*

Proof. The construction consists of three nested structures.
   (1) Take an (r, b)-separating family with $b = r^2$ of size $O(r \log n)$, as given by Lemma 3.

(2) For every partition π, take an r-universal family on the set of bins of π as the ground set. By Lemma 1, the size is $O(r2^r \log b) = O(r2^r \log r)$. Now we have $O(r^2 2^r \log r \log n)$ "bin assignments" which may be also considered as assignments on V.

(3) Finally we replace every such assignment a with $O(r^2 \log n)$ assignments as follows: For every bin y, fix the assignment induced by a on $V \setminus y$, and replace the constant assignment (all 0 or all 1) on y by the members of a nonadaptive learning family for one relevant variable, as given by Lemma 5. This gives a total of $O(r^4 2^r \log r \log^2 n)$ assignments.

The learning algorithm works as follows: Query simultaneously all assignments produced above. For each π and each bin y of π, consider all $O(\log n)$ assignments introduced in (3). Whenever the straightforward search from Lemma 4 succeeds finding a relevant variable of the corresponding projection of f on y, this is, clearly, also a relevant variable of f.

The search will fail in many bins, since there are either no or more than one relevant variables. However make sure that all relevant variables are detected in this way: Among our partitions there is one, say π, that shatters R. For every relevant bin y of π, there exists a bin assignment a_0 on the relevant bins such that f_π changes if the assignment of y only changes. Due to r-universality, our family contains a bin assignment a inducing a_0 on the set of relevant bins. Finally, since we fix all values of a outside y, we find the unique relevant variable contained in y, just by applying Lemma 4. This holds for every relevant bin, thus we find all relevant variables. From the preceding discussion it follows also that our family is r-universal. Since R is learned, f is learned, too.

The very simple auxiliary "computations" are only required for setting up the query bits and for searching the bins, so the amount of computation is $O(n)$ times the query number. Details are straightforward. □

So the computational complexity does no longer contain the hardly acceptable n^{r+1} term. On the other hand, the query number is now rather large: The extra $r^3 \log r \log n$ factor is quite significant. Therefore it is nice that we get rid of some annoying factors by allowing two stages. This is presented in the next section.

4 Two-Stage Attribute-Efficient Learning

In our next result, notice especially the way in which the nonadaptive learning families are used.

Theorem 4. *Functions from $Rel(n, r)$ can be learned in two stages using $O(r^3 2^r \log n)$ queries and $O((2er)^r r^{7/2} \log r \log n + n \log n)$ computations.*

Proof. Take a separating family from Lemma 3, and consider any of the partitions π. Applying Theorem 2 to $b = r^2$ instead of n, we can learn f_π nonadaptively by $O(r^2 2^r)$ queries to f, followed by $O((2er)^r r^{5/2} \log r)$ computations. This is simultaneously done in all $O(r \log n)$ partitions π.

Once again, at least one π separates R. It is clear that we find one of them by taking any π such that $g := f_\pi$ has the maximum number of relevant bins.

Let us resume: After the first stage we know a partition that separates R, and for each of the (at most r) relevant bins y we also know a bin assignment such that g changes if we switch the value of y only. So we can apply Lemma 4 simultaneously in all relevant bins of g, in order to find the relevant variables of f. This needs $O(r \log n)$ queries and $O(n \log n)$ computations. The query number is dominated by the previous terms. Notice that we need only one further stage, thus we have a two-stage algorithm. $\square$

Note that the query number is reduced by a factor $r \log r \log n$ which might be crucial in applications with large n and expensive queries. We can further improve it with the help of randomness, as shown in the next section. Concerning the $(2er)^r$ term in the computational complexity, remember that only small fixed r are realistic anyway.

5 Randomization

Theorem 5. *Functions from $Rel(n,r)$ can be learned by a two-stage Monte Carlo algorithm using $O(r^2 2^r + r \log n)$ queries and $O((2er)^r r^{5/2} \log r \log n + n \log n)$ computations.*

Proof. We may presume $r > 1$.

Proceed as in Theorem 4, but replace the separating family by a random partition into r^2 bins. By the proof of Lemma 3 it separates R with constant positive probability. Again we learn the coarsening g applying Theorem 2. Then we search for the relevant variables in the relevant bins by $r \log n$ nonadaptive queries and $O(n \log n)$ computations.

This procedure can fail only if our random partition did not separate R. In this case the following happens: Either the search routine fails in some relevant bins containing more than one relevant variable (cf. the remark after Lemma 4), or we only detect a proper subset $S \subset R$. In the former case we recognize immediately that our random partition was bad, in the latter case the failure may be undetected. Therefore this strategy is of Monte Carlo type.

The bounds follow similarly as in the deterministic counterpart, but some factors are dropped. $\square$

For safety reasons it may be desirable to have a Las Vegas algorithm where we are sure that all relevant variables are found when the algorithm has stopped. Finally we propose such an algorithm. Of course, the stage number is no longer guaranteed to be 2, and the query number grows again, but it is still better than in our deterministic algorithms.

Theorem 6. *Functions $f \in Rel(n,r)$ can be learned by a Las Vegas algorithm having the following expected complexity parameters: $O(1)$ stages, $O(r^2 2^r + r 2^r \log n)$ queries, and $O((2er)^r r^{7/2} \log r \log n + r 2^r n \log n)$ computations.*

Proof. The only difference to Theorem 5 is the verification of the output of the two-stage strategy. Let $S \subseteq R$ be the set of relevant variables we found. With help of Lemma 2, check by $O(r2^r \log n)$ simultaneous queries whether $S = R$. This test is safe. Repeat the procedure until an affirmative result is obtained.

Since the two-stage learning algorithm in Theorem 5 succeeds with constant probability, we have $O(1)$ expected stages and $O(r2^r \log n)$ expected queries; it remains to add the query bound of Theorem 5. We need $O(r2^r n \log n)$ computations to analyze the $S = R$ tests. $\square$

6 Conclusions

We pointed out that computing a given Boolean function with few relevant variables from the outcome of a nonadaptive learning algorithm is a nontrivial problem, and we proposed various parallel learning algorithms for this function class, with reasonable amount of afterwards computations. Apparently, the most advisable solution at the moment is a two-stage method where an $O(r^2 2^r)$ nonadaptive learning strategy is applied to r^2 size coarsenings of the given function, one of which separates the relevant variables. This guarantees a query number not far from the optimum. We do not claim that the present complexity bounds are already the best. Further research may discover more clever combinations of the basic structures, or even an efficient solution to the original problem of computing the smallest (A, f)-feasible set from $[f(a)]_{a \in A}$.

In the introduction we mentioned the equivalence of nonadaptive learning and universal teaching sets. In contrast, a teaching set for a fixed function f with respect to a function class is an assignment family that distinguishes f from all other functions of that class. In $Rel(n, r)$, the problem of teaching can be easily settled: If f has $s < r$ relevant variables then the teacher presents a pairing of all 2^s possible assignments on S and an $(r - s)$-universal family on the remaining $n - s$ variables, similarly to Lemma 2. The latter is necessary, in order to convince the learner that no other relevant variables exist. So we have a teaching set of size $O((r - s)2^r \log n)$. Amazingly, if f has the full number of r relevant variables then a teaching set of size 2^r is sufficient, independent of n.

References

1. D.J. Balding, D.C.Torney: A comparative survey of non-adaptive pooling designs, in: Genetic Mapping and DNA Sequencing, *IMA Volumes in Mathematics and Its Applications*, Springer 1995, 133-155
2. D.J.Balding, D.C.Torney: Optimal pooling designs with error detection, *J. of Combinatorial Theory A* 74 (1996), 131-140
3. A.Blum, L.Hellerstein, N.Littlestone: Learning in the presence of finitely or infinitely many irrelevant attributes, *J. of Computer and System Sciences* 50 (1995), 32-40
4. N.H.Bshouty, R.Cleve: On the exact learning of formulas in parallel, 33rd IEEE Symposium on Foundations of Computer Science FOCS (1992), 513-522

5. N.H.Bshouty, L.Hellerstein: Attribute-efficient learning in query and mistake-bound models, *9th Computational Learning Theory COLT* (1996), 235-243

6. C.J.Colbourn, J.H.Dinitz: *The CRC Handbook of Combinatorial Designs*, CRC Press 1996, Section V6.1: Nonadaptive group testing

7. P.Damaschke: Adaptive vs. nonadaptive attribute-efficient learning, preliminary version in: *30th ACM Symposium on Theory of Computing STOC* (1998), 590-596

8. A.Dhagat, L.Hellerstein: PAC learning with irrelevant attributes, *35th IEEE Symposium on Foundations of Computer Science FOCS* (1994), 64-74

9. D.Z.Du, F.K.Hwang: *Combinatorial Group Testing and Its Applications*, World Scientific 1993

10. M.Farach, S.Kannan, E.Knill, S.Muthukrishnan: Group testing problems in experimental molecular biology, *Proc. of Sequences'97*

11. S.Goldman, M.Kearns: On the complexity of teaching, *J. of Computer and System Sciences* 50 (1995), 20-31

12. S.Goldman, M.Kearns, R.Schapire: Exact identification of read-once formulas using fixed points of amplification functions, *SIAM J. of Computing 22* (1993), 705-726

13. T.Hegedüs: Combinatorial results on the complexity of teaching and learning, *19th Symposium on Mathematical Foundations of Computer Science MFCS* (1994), *LNCS* 841 (Springer), 393-402

14. T.Hegedüs, P.Indyk: On learning disjunctions of zero-one threshold functions with queries, *8th Workshop on Algorithmic Learning Theory ALT* (1997), *LNAI 1316* (Springer), 446-460

15. N.Littlestone: Learning quickly when irrelevant attributes abound: A linear threshold algorithm, *Machine Learning 2* (1988), 285-318

16. R.Motwani, P.Raghavan: *Randomized Algorithms*, Cambridge Univ. Press 1995

17. M.Naor, L.J.Schulman, A.Srinivasan: Splitters and near-optimal derandomization, *36th IEEE Symposium on Foundations of Computer Science FOCS* (1995), 182-191

18. G.Seroussi, N.H.Bshouty: Vector sets for exhaustive testing of logic circuits, *IEEE Transactions on Information Theory* 34 (1988), 513-522

PAC Learning from Positive Statistical Queries[*]

François Denis

Bt. M3, LIFL, Universit de Lille I
59655 Villeneuve d'Ascq Cedex, France,
denis@lifl.fr

Abstract. Learning from positive examples occurs very frequently in natural learning. The PAC learning model of Valiant takes many features of natural learning into account, but in most cases it fails to describe such kind of learning. We show that in order to make the learning from positive data possible, extra-information about the underlying distribution must be provided to the learner. We define a PAC learning model from positive and unlabeled examples. We also define a PAC learning model from positive and unlabeled statistical queries. Relations with PAC model ([Val84]), statistical query model ([Kea93]) and constant-partition classification noise model ([Dec97]) are studied. We show that k-DNF and k-decision lists are learnable in both models, i.e. with far less information than it is assumed in previously used algorithms.

1 Introduction

The PAC learning model of Valiant ([Val84]) has become the reference model in computational learning theory. However, in spite of the importance of learning from positive examples in natural learning, extending the PAC model in order to modelize this kind of learning seems difficult. The reason for it is that it does not exist any good way to define the learning error. Suppose for example that f is the target concept, that h is a hypothesis and let μ be the underlying distribution. If the error is measured relatively to the positive examples of f, i.e. if $error(h) = \mu_f(f \Delta h)$, then over-generalization seems unavoidable: the "full" concept (Σ^* for languages, function 1 for boolean functions) is always a good answer. But if the error is measured over all the examples, i.e. if $error(h) = \mu(f \Delta h)$, the learner cannot differentiate between different distributions whose restrictions on the positive examples of f are equal. Consequently, the output concept must always be included into the target concept and the learning boils down to learning with one-sided error ([Nat87], [Nat91]). But since the underlying distribution can be equal to 0 on some positive examples of the target, a learning algorithm will not be able to use *missing* examples to infer *negative* ones. As a result, it is often impossible to be sure that a hypothesis is included into the target concept. To sum up, in most cases, positive examples provide not enough information

---

[*] This research was partially supported by "Motricité et Cognition : Contrat par objectifs région Nord/Pas-de-Calais"

to learn in the PAC framework ([Shv90]). The above discussion is detailed in section 3.

However, there exist classes of concepts satisfying the following property: there exists a (polynomial) collection of sets $(E_i)_{i \in I}$ such that for every concept f and g and for every distribution μ, if for every index i, $\mu_f(E_i) \simeq \mu_g(E_i)$ then $\mu(f \Delta g) \simeq 0$. This property does not mean that relative frequencies measured on the positive examples suffice to determine the target, but that the target is determined **relatively to the underlying distribution**. In other words, extra-information about the underlying distribution suffice to make the learning possible. These considerations lead us to define a PAC model of learning from positive examples where information about the distribution are given by unlabeled examples. Note that there are many situations in which it is natural to suppose that the learner is given positive and unlabeled data: for example, in marketing analysis context, if we want to know which customers are liable to ask for some specific service, we have at our disposal a population of customers who have already asked for these services (positive data) and the global population (unlabeled data). In medical context, a physician knows the patients who have developed a given disease (positive data) among his whole practice (unlabeled data).

A similar approach was taken in [BDL97] where a model of concept learning from unlabeled examples only is defined: the information about the target concept come through a dependence of the generating distribution upon this target.

We also define a model of learning from positive statistical queries where information about the distribution are given by unlabeled queries. Relations with PAC model ([Val84]), statistical query model ([Kea93]) and constant-partition classification noise model ([Dec97]) are studied in section 4. We show in section 5 that the classes of k-DNF and k-decision lists are learnable from positive statistical queries, i.e. with far less information than what is supposed in previously known algorithms ([Val84], [Kea93], [Riv87]).

A lot of work have been done on learning from positive examples only in Gold's model of learning in the limit ([Gol67], [Ang80], [Ber86], [Shi90], [ZL95]). The problems encountered in Gold framework, as over-generalizations, are clearly related to the questions studied here. But a systematic comparison between the two frameworks is out of the scope of this paper.

2 Preliminaries

Let $\mathcal{B}_n$ be the set of boolean functions from $X_n = \{0,1\}^n$ into $\{0,1\}$. Let $X = \cup_{n \geq 1} X_n$ and $\mathcal{B} = \cup_{n \geq 1} \mathcal{B}_n$. A *concept class* $\mathcal{C}$ over X is a subset of $\mathcal{B}$. We note $\mathcal{C}_n = \mathcal{C} \cap \mathcal{B}_n$.

A *representation scheme* for a concept class $\mathcal{C}$ is a function $R : \mathcal{C} \to 2^{\Sigma^*}$ where Σ is a finite alphabet and such that for each f and f' in $\mathcal{F}$, $R(f)$ is not empty and if $f \neq f'$, $R(f) \cap R(f') = \emptyset$. The *size* of a concept f is $size(f) = min\{|c| \| c \in R(f)\}$. We suppose that R is computable in polynomial-time, that is, there exists a polynomial-time deterministic algorithm which takes as input a pair of strings x and c and outputs 1 if $f(x) = 1$ with $c \in R(f)$, and 0 otherwise.

An *example* of a concept f is a pair $(x, f(x))$, where x is in the domain of f. An example $(x, f(x))$ is *positive* if $f(x) = 1$ and *negative* otherwise. We denote by $pos(f)$ (resp. $neg(f)$) the set of all x such that $f(x) = 1$ (resp. $f(x) = 0$). If μ is a probability distribution on X_n and if f is a boolean function defined on X_n, $\mu(f)$ denotes $\mu(pos(f))$. If $\mu(f) \neq 0$, let μ_f be the restriction of μ to $pos(f)$ defined as follows: $\mu_f(x) = \mu(x)/\mu(f)$ if $x \in pos(f)$ and 0 otherwise.

A *statistical query* over X_n is a mapping $\chi : X_n \times \{0,1\} \to \{0,1\}$. If $f \in B_n$, the query χ_f denotes the mapping defined by $\chi_f(x, y) = 1$ iff $y = f(x)$.

Definition 1. *Let C be a concept class over X. Let $f \in C_n$ and μ be a distribution over X_n.*

- *The oracle $EX(f, \mu)$ is a procedure that returns at each call an example $(x, f(x))$ drawn randomly according to μ.*
- *The oracle $UNL(\mu)$ is a procedure that returns at each call an unlabeled example x drawn randomly according to μ.*
- *The oracle $STAT(f, \mu)$ is a procedure that, for every statistical query χ and every $\tau \in (0, 1]$, with input (χ, τ) returns an approximation of $\mu(\{x | \chi(x, f(x)) = 1\})$ with an accuracy at least τ.*
- *The noisy oracle $EX^{\eta_+, \eta_-}(f, \mu)$ is a procedure which at each call draws an element x of X_n according to μ and returns (i) $(x, 1)$ with probability $1 - \eta_+$ and $(x, 0)$ with probability η_+ if $x \in pos(f)$, (ii) $(x, 0)$ with probability $1 - \eta_-$ and $(x, 1)$ with probability η_- if $x \in neg(f)$*

All these oracles run in unit time.

A *k-monomial* on the variables $x_1, \ldots, x_n$ is a conjunction of exactly k literals. When there is no ambiguity on the set of variables, we note k-MON the set of all k-monomials and for every boolean function f, we note $M_k(f)$ the set of all k-monomials m such that $m(x) = 1 \Rightarrow f(x) = 1$. The number of k-monomials over n variables is at most $(2n)^k$. A k-DNF is a disjunction of k-monomials. A k-decision list (k-DL) is an ordered sequence $f = (m_1, b_1), \ldots, (m_l, b_l)$ in which each m_i is a k-monomial, each $b_i \in \{0,1\}$ and $m_l = 1$. If $u \in X_n$, the value $f(u)$ is defined to be b_j, where j is the smallest index satisfying $m_j(u) = 1$. We choose representation schemes such that the size of a k-DNF or a k-DL over n variables is bounded by a polynomial in n. We note 1 the boolean function such that $1(u) = 1$ for every u.

We take the two basic following definitions in [KV94].

Definition 2. *Let C be a concept class over X. We say that C is **PAC learnable** if there exist a learning algorithm L and a polynomial $p(., ., ., .)$ with the following property: for any $f \in C$, for any distribution μ on X, and for any $0 < \epsilon < 1$ and $0 < \delta < 1$, if L is given access to $EX(f, \mu)$ and to inputs ϵ and δ, then with probability at least $1 - \delta$, L outputs a hypothesis concept $h \in C$ satisfying $\mu(f \triangle h) \leq \epsilon$ in time bounded by $p(1/\epsilon, 1/\delta, size(f), n)$.*

Definition 3. *Let C be a concept class over X. We say that C is* **learnable from statistical queries** *if there exist a learning algorithm L and polynomials $p(.,.,.), q(.,.,.)$ and $r(.,.,.)$ with the following property: for any $f \in C$, for any distribution μ over X, and for any $0 < \epsilon < 1$, if L is given access to $STAT(f, \mu)$ and to input ϵ, then*

- *For every query (χ, τ) made by L, the predicate χ can be evaluated in time $q(1/\epsilon, n, size(f))$, and $1/\tau$ is bounded by $r(1/\epsilon, n, size(f))$.*
- *L halts in time bounded by $p(1/\epsilon, n, size(f))$.*
- *L outputs a hypothesis $h \in C$ that satisfies $\mu(f \Delta h) \leq \epsilon$.*

The standard classification noise model is defined in [AL88]. It is generalized by the constant-partition classification noise (CPCN) model defined in [Dec97]. We give below a restricted variant of the CPCN model.

Definition 4. *Let C be a concept class over X. We say that C is* **CPCN learnable** *if there exist a learning algorithm L and a polynomial $p(.,.,.,.,.)$ with the following property: for any $f \in C$, for any distribution μ on X, and for any $0 \leq \eta_+, \eta_- < 1/2$ and $0 < \epsilon, \delta < 1$, if L is given access to $EX^{\eta_+,\eta_-}(f, \mu)$ and to inputs ϵ and δ, then with probability at least $1 - \delta$, L outputs a hypothesis concept $h \in C$ satisfying $\mu(f \Delta h) \leq \epsilon$ in time bounded by $p(1/\epsilon, 1/\delta, 1/\gamma, size(f), n)$ where $\gamma = min\{1/2 - \eta_+, 1/2 - \eta_-\}$.*

3   Is it possible to learn with positive examples only?

Let f be a target over X_n, let μ be the underlying distribution (such that $\mu(f) \neq 0$) and suppose that the only oracle available to the learner is $EX(f, \mu_f)$. Before saying whether he is able to learn, we have to define how the error will be evaluated.

The first idea could be to measure the error of a hypothesis h on the positive examples only. But if we do so, over-generalization will be unavoidable: 1 is a correct answer whatever the target is.

Then, it seems necessary to take negative examples into account. But if the error is measured in the standard way, taking $error(h) = \mu(f \Delta h)$, another problem appears: two distributions μ and μ' can have the same restriction on the positive examples of the target while they are very different on the negative examples. More precisely, let $x_0 \in X_n \setminus f$ and let $\alpha \in [0, 1)$ such that $|\alpha - \mu(x_0)| \geq 1/2$. Define

$$\mu'(x) = \begin{cases} \alpha & \text{if } x = x_0 \\ \frac{\mu(x)}{\mu(f)}(1 - \alpha) & \text{if } x \in f \\ 0 & \text{otherwise} \end{cases} \tag{1}$$

We have $\mu_f = \mu'_f$ and $|\mu(x) - \mu'(x_0)| \geq 1/2$. Therefore, as it is impossible to differentiate μ and μ' with the help of the oracle $EX(f, \mu_f)$, x_0 must not belong to the output hypothesis. That is, learning from positive examples requires the output hypothesis to be included into the target concept. But only for very constrained classes, as k-CNF or lattices, it will be possible to ensure that the output concept is included into the target concept. See ([Nat87], [Shv90]) for characterizations of such classes.

A related problem come from the following fact: as it is impossible to differentiate a negative example from a positive one on which the distribution is equal to 0, the learner cannot use missing examples to infer negative information.

Example 1. Consider the class of 1-DNF on two variables x_1 and x_2. Let $f = x_1$, $g = x_2$, μ and μ' such that $\mu(11) = \mu(01) = 1/2$ and $\mu'(11) = \mu'(10) = 1/2$. Whatever the pair *(target, distribution)* is among (f, μ) and (g, μ'), the sample will be $S = \{11\}$. Is 01 a negative example or a positive example on which the distribution is null? What must be learned?

Now, in order to make the learning possible, we could demand that each used distribution points out only one target concept. That is, we could demand the target to be the minimal concept consistent with a sufficiently large sample.

For example, if the target is $x_1 + x_2$, we should have $\mu(01), \mu(10)$ and $\mu(11)$ not too small. But, in addition to the fact that this restriction seems artificial, the simplest classes of concepts remain not learnable. We have shown (see [Den98]) that the problem of finding a minimal 1-DNF consistent with a *positive* sample is not polynomial (under the assumption $P \neq LOGSNP$).

So, isn't anything possible ? To our knowledge, the analysis of PAC learning from positive examples only usually stopped here. And yet, it is possible to go further. The following result shows that, with regard to k-DNF, the possible outputs are somehow determined by positive data.

Proposition 1. *For every $\epsilon \in [0, 1]$, for every integer n, for every k-DNF f and g over X_n and for every distribution μ over X_n such that $\mu(f) \neq 0$ and $\mu(g) \neq 0$, if for every k-monomial m,*

$$|\mu_f(m) - \mu_g(m)| < \alpha = \frac{\epsilon}{N(N+1)}$$

where $N = (2n)^k$, then

$$\mu(f \Delta g) < \epsilon$$

Proof. Let $m \in M_k(f)$ such that $\mu(m) \geq \mu(f)/N$. Such a monomial exists since the number of k-monomials is bounded by N.

We have

$$\mu_f(m) = \mu(m)/\mu(f) \leq \mu_g(m) + \alpha = \mu(m \cap g)/\mu(g) + \alpha \leq \mu(m)/\mu(g) + \alpha$$

that is,

$$\mu(g) \leq \mu(f) + \alpha\mu(f)\mu(g)/\mu(m) \leq \mu(f) + \alpha N$$

Symmetrically, we can get

$$\mu(f) \leq \mu(g) + \alpha N$$

and therefore

$$|\mu(g) - \mu(f)| \leq \alpha N$$

Now we have

$$\mu(f \setminus g) \leq \sum_{m \in M_k(f) \setminus M_k(g)} \mu(m \setminus g) = \sum_{m \in M_k(f) \setminus M_k(g)} [\mu(m \cap f) - \mu(m \cap g)]$$

$$= \sum_{m \in M_k(f) \setminus M_k(g)} [\mu(f)\mu_f(m) - \mu(g)\mu_g(m)]$$

$$\leq \sum_{m \in M_k(f) \setminus M_k(g)} [\mu(f)|\mu_f(m) - \mu_g(m)| + \mu_g(m)|\mu(f) - \mu(g)|]$$

$$\leq \sum_{m \in M_k(f) \setminus M_k(g)} [|\mu_f(m) - \mu_g(m)| + |\mu(g) - \mu(f)|]$$

Getting a similar bound for $\mu(g \setminus f)$ we get

$$\mu(f \Delta g) \leq \sum_{m \in M_k(f) \Delta M_k(g)} [|\mu_f(m) - \mu_g(m)| + |\mu(g) - \mu(f)|] \leq N\alpha(N+1) = \epsilon$$

$\square$

This result may seem quite paradoxical. Example 1 shows that it is impossible to differentiate $f = x_1$ from $g = x_2$ if the only available data is 11 and the previous proposition says that the target is determined by the frequencies on positive data. In fact, what is determined is not the target but **the target when the underlying distribution is known**. On the previous example, proposition 1 says that if the distribution is μ then the correct hypothesis must be f while if the distribution is μ', it must be g.

We think that this is the best we can expect from positive examples in the PAC framework: a learning algorithm has to return an approximation of the target concept as soon as extra-information about the underlying distribution are given.

4   Learning from positive examples

In the following definitions, the "positive" information about the target will be given by the oracles $EX(f, \mu_f)$ or $STAT(f, \mu_f)$ while the extra-information about the distribution will be given by $UNL(\mu)$ or $STAT(1, \mu)$.

Definition 5. *Let C be a concept class over X. We say that C is **PAC learnable from positive examples** if there exist a learning algorithm L and a polynomial $p(., ., ., .)$ with the following property: for any integer n, for any $f \in C_n$, for any distribution μ on X_n, and for any $0 < \epsilon < 1$ and $0 < \delta < 1$, if L is given access to $EX(f, \mu_f), UNL(\mu)$ and to inputs ϵ and δ, then with probability at least $1 - \delta$, L outputs a hypothesis concept $h \in C_n$ satisfying $\mu(f \Delta h) \leq \epsilon$ in time bounded by $p(1/\epsilon, 1/\delta, size(f), n)$.*

Remark that if a concept class C is PAC learnable and if there exists a learning algorithm for C which does not use negative examples of the target, then C is PAC learnable from positive examples. Therefore, k-CNF ([Val84]) and integer lattices ([HSW92]) are learnable from positive examples.

A similar approach has been taken in [BDL97]. A model of unsupervised learning is defined in which the task of the learner is to identify a probability distribution or more precisely, its high probability-density areas, from unlabeled examples. Then, a learning Without A Teacher model is proposed, in which it is assumed that "for points outside the target the distribution density is lower that a certain threshold α, while inside the target the density exceeds some value $\beta > \alpha$". A characterization of learnability is given, from an information-theoretic point of view; but the computational complexity of learning inside specific hypothesis spaces is not studied.

Definition 6. *Let C be a concept class over X. We say that C is **learnable from positive statistical queries** if there exist a learning algorithm L and polynomials $p(.,.,.), q(.,.,.)$ and $r(.,.,.)$ with the following property: for any integer n, for any $f \in C_n$, for any distribution μ over X_n, and for any $0 < \epsilon < 1$, if L is given access to $STAT(f, \mu_f)$ and $STAT(1, \mu)$ and to input ϵ, then*

- *For every query (χ, τ) made by L, the predicate χ can be evaluated in time $q(1/\epsilon, n, size(f))$, and $1/\tau$ is bounded by $r(1/\epsilon, n, size(f))$.*
- *L will halt in time bounded by $p(1/\epsilon, n, size(f))$.*
- *L will output a hypothesis $h \in C_n$ that satisfies $\mu(f \Delta h) \le \epsilon$.*

Proposition 2. *Let us note POSQ (resp. Q, CPCN, POSEX, PAC) the set of classes learnable with positive statistical queries (resp. statistical queries, constant partition classification noise, positive examples, positive and negative examples). Following relations hold:*

$$POSQ \subseteq Q \subseteq CPCN \subseteq POSEX \subseteq PAC$$

Proof. (sketch)

$POSQ \subseteq Q$: the oracles $STAT(1, \mu)$ and $STAT(f, \mu_f)$ can easily be simulated using the oracle $STAT(f, \mu)$ (see complete proof in [Den98]).

$Q \subseteq CPCN$: This result is proved in [Dec97].

$CPCN \subseteq POSEX$: (with the help of an anonymous referee). Let C be a concept class in CPCN, f be a concept of C_n, μ be a distribution over X_n such that $\mu(f) \neq 0$, $0 < \epsilon < 1$ and $0 < \delta < 1$. Let ν be the distribution defined by:

$$\nu(x) = \begin{cases} 2\mu_f(x)/3 + \mu(x)/3 & \text{if } x \in pos(f) \\ \mu(x)/3 & otherwise. \end{cases}$$

We can easily verify that the noisy oracle $EX^{\eta_+, \eta_-}(f, \nu)$ with $\eta_- = 0$ and $\eta_+ = \frac{\mu(f)}{2 + \mu(f)}$ can be simulated this way: with probability 2/3, get an example from $EX(f,\mu_f)$ and label it +, and with probability 1/3, get an example from $UNL(\mu)$ and label it -. A negative example of f is always labelled -: a positive example of f is labelled - with probability $\mu(f)/3$.

Note that $1/2 - \eta_+ \geq 1/6$ and that for every subset A of X_n, $\nu(A) \geq \mu(A)/3$. Therefore, in order to learn C from positive examples with accuracy parameter ϵ, run the CPCN algorithm with accuracy parameter $\epsilon/3$ and at each call of $EX^{\eta_+,\eta_-}(f,\mu)$, call $EX(f,\mu_f)$ with probability 2/3 and $UNL(\mu)$ with probability 1/3 and return the result according to the labelling defined above.

$POSEX \subseteq PAC$: the oracles $UNL(\mu)$ and $EX(f,\mu_f)$ can easily be simulated using the oracle $EX(f,\mu)$.

Remark that the class of parity functions can be learned in PAC model using positive examples uniquely ([HSW92], [Kea93]). It is proved in [Kea93] that it is not learnable with statistical queries. Therefore, the class of parity functions is in $POSEX$ but not in Q.

We can't prove that $POSEX$ (resp. $POSQ$) is strictly included into PAC (resp. Q). We conjecture that the class composed of complementary sets of lattices is not learnable from positive examples (while it is PAC learnable). □

As a corollary, the previous proposition proves that k-DNF and k-DL are learnable from positive examples since they are learnable from statistical queries [Kea93].

Moreover, if the learner knows the underlying distribution and can simulate it within polynomial time, he can learn any class in Q from positive examples only. For example,

Corollary 1. *The classes of k-DNF and k-DL are learnable from $EX(f, u_f)$ only under the uniform distribution u.*

Proof. The oracle $EX(1, u)$ can be simulated by tossing a coin. □

A concept class learnable from statistical queries can be not learnable from positive statistical queries with the same space of queries. For example, let $C = \{f, g\} \subset 2^{\{a,b\}}$ where $f = \{a, b\}$ and $g = \{a\}$ and let $\chi(x, y) = 1$ if $y = 1$ and $\chi(x, y) = 0$ otherwise. We have $STAT(f, \mu)(\chi, \tau) \simeq 1$ and $STAT(g, \mu)(\chi, \tau) \simeq \mu(a)$ while $STAT(f, \mu_f)(\chi, \tau) \simeq 1$ and $STAT(g, \mu_g)(\chi, \tau) \simeq 1$. Therefore, C is learnable using statistical query χ but it is not learnable using positive (restriction of) statistical query χ.

We prove in the next section that k-DNF and k-DL remains learnable from positive statistical queries.

5 Learning from positive statistical queries

Definition 7. *Let C be a concept class over X. We say that the weight of concepts of C can be estimated from positive statistical queries if there exist an*

algorithm W and a polynomial $p(.,.,.)$ with the following property: for any integer n, for any $f \in C_n$, for any distribution μ over X_n, and for any $0 < \epsilon < 1$, if W is given access to statistical queries oracles $STAT(f, \mu_f)$ and $STAT(1, \mu)$ and to input ϵ, then W outputs a number $\hat{\mu}(f)$ such that $|\hat{\mu}(f) - \mu(f)| \leq \epsilon$ and W halts in time bounded by $p(1/\epsilon, n, size(f))$.

Theorem 1. *Let C be a concept class over X learnable from statistical queries. If the weight of concepts of C can be estimated from positive statistical queries then C is learnable from positive statistical queries.*

Proof. Let L be the learning algorithm from statistical queries and let W be the algorithm which evaluates the weight of concepts of C. The following algorithm learns C from positive statistical queries.

Learning algorithm L'
Input: ϵ, n
Begin

    Run algorithm L
    Each time algorithm L asks the oracle $STAT(f, \mu)$
    in order to evaluate the query (χ, τ)

        Run $W(\tau/4)$ and let $\hat{\mu}(f)$ be the result
        Let χ^0 be the query defined by $\chi^0(x, y) = \chi(x, 0)$
        Let χ^1 be the query defined by $\chi^1(x, y) = \chi(x, 1)$
        Let $\hat{\mu}_{\chi^0} = STAT(1, \mu, \chi^0, \tau/4)$
        Let $\hat{\mu}^+_{\chi^0} = STAT(f, \mu_f, \chi^0, \tau/4)$
        Let $\hat{\mu}^+_{\chi^1} = STAT(f, \mu_f, \chi^1, \tau/4)$
        Return $\hat{\mu}_{\chi^0} + (\hat{\mu}^+_{\chi^1} - \hat{\mu}^+_{\chi^0})\hat{\mu}(f)$ to algorithm L

End
Output: the output of algorithm L

It is easy to verify that

$$\mu(\{x | \chi(x, f(x)) = 1\})$$
$$= \mu(\{x | \chi(x, 1) = 1 \wedge f(x) = 1\}) + \mu(\{x | \chi(x, 0) = 1 \wedge f(x) = 0\})$$
$$= \mu_f(\{x | \chi(x, 1) = 1\})\mu(f) + (\mu(\{x | \chi(x, 0) = 1\}) - \mu(\{x | \chi(x, 0) = 1 \wedge f(x) = 1\}))$$
$$= \mu(\{x | \chi(x, 0) = 1\}) + (\mu_f(\{x | \chi(x, 1) = 1\}) - \mu_f(\{x | \chi(x, 0) = 1\}))\mu(f)$$

The proposition follows. $\qquad\qquad\qquad\qquad\qquad\qquad\qquad\qquad\square$

We now apply this result to k-DNF and k-DL.

Proposition 3. *The class of k-DNF formulas is learnable from positive statistical queries.*

Proof. Let f be a k-DNF over n variables and m be a k-monomial over X_n. Let μ be a distribution over X_n such that $\mu(f) \neq 0$. We have

$$\mu_f(m) = \mu(f \cap m)/\mu(f) \leq \mu(m)/\mu(f)$$

i.e. for every $m \in k$-MON such that $\mu_f(m) \neq 0$,

$$\mu(f) = \mu(f \cap m)/\mu_f(m) \leq \mu(m)/\mu_f(m)$$

and if m is in $M_k(f)$, i.e. if $m \Rightarrow f$,

$$\mu(f) = \mu(m)/\mu_f(m)$$

Therefore, we get

$$\mu(f) = min\{\frac{\mu(m)}{\mu_f(m)}|m \in k\text{-MON}, \mu_f(m) \neq 0\}$$

and since there exists a monomial m in $M_k(f)$ such that $\mu_f(m) \geq 1/N$ (where $N = (2n)^k$), we have

$$\mu(f) = min\{\frac{\mu(m)}{\mu_f(m)}|m \in k\text{-MON}, \mu_f(m) \geq 1/N\}$$

The following algorithm computes an estimation of $\mu(f)$.

Learning the weight of a k-DNF
Input: ϵ, n
Begin
    Let $\tau = \frac{\epsilon}{(8N^2)}$
    For all k-monomial m
        compute $\hat{\mu}_f(m) = STAT(f, \mu_f, \chi_m, \tau)$
        $\{\chi_m(x,y) = 1$ iff $y = m(x)\}$
        compute $\hat{\mu}(m) = STAT(1, \mu, \chi_m, \tau)$
    EndFor
    Let $\hat{\mu}(f) = min\{\hat{\mu}(m)/\hat{\mu}_f(m)|m \in k\text{-MON}, \hat{\mu}_f(m) \geq 1/N - \tau\}$
End
Output: $\hat{\mu}(f)$

We have $\mu(f) = min\{\mu(m)/\mu_f(m)|m \in k\text{-MON}, \hat{\mu}_f(m) \geq 1/N - \tau\}$.
Verify that if $\hat{\mu}_f(m) \geq 1/N - \tau$,

$$|\hat{\mu}(m)/\hat{\mu}_f(m) - \mu(m)/\mu_f(m)| \leq 2\tau/(\hat{\mu}_f(m)\mu_f(m)) \leq 2\tau/[(1/N - \tau)(1/N - 2\tau)]$$

and since $1/N - \tau \geq 1/N - 2\tau \geq 1/(2N)$ we have

$$|\hat{\mu}(f) - \mu(f)| \leq 2\tau 4N^2 = \epsilon$$

We can now apply theorem 1. $\qquad\qquad\qquad\qquad\qquad\qquad\qquad\qquad\qquad\qquad\qquad\square$

We now prove an analogous result for k-decision lists. The proof is trickier in this case.

Theorem 2. *The class of k-decision lists is learnable from positive statistical queries.*

As in previous proposition, we just have to prove that the weight of k-decision lists can be estimated from positive statistical queries.

Let f be a k-DL over n variables and let μ be a distribution over X_n such that $\mu(f) \neq 0$.

Let

$$M_f^\mu = \{x \in X_n | \forall m \in k\text{-MON}, m(x) \Rightarrow \mu_f(m) \neq 0\}$$

Let $\overline{M_f^\mu}$ be the complementary set of M_f^μ. We have

$$\overline{M_f^\mu} = \bigcup \{m \in k\text{-MON} | \mu_f(m) = 0\}$$

We show below some properties of M_f^μ.

Lemma 1. *1. $\mu(f \setminus M_f^\mu) = 0$*

2. for every subset A of X_n, $\mu_f(A) \leq \mu(A \cap M_f^\mu)/\mu(f)$.

3. if $(m,1)$ is the first (positive) term of f such that $\mu_f(m) \neq 0$, then $\mu_f(m) = \mu(m \cap M_f^\mu)/\mu(f)$

4. $\mu(f) = min\{\mu(m \cap M_f^\mu)/\mu_f(m) | m \in k\text{-MON}, \mu_f(m) \neq 0\}$

Proof. 1. let $x \in f \setminus M_f^\mu$, and let $m \in k$-MON such that $m(x) = 1$ and $\mu_f(m) = 0$. As $x \in f$, we have $\mu(x) = 0$.

2. $\mu_f(A) = \mu(A \cap f)/\mu(f) \leq [\mu(A \cap (f \setminus M_f^\mu)) + \mu(A \cap M_f^\mu)]/\mu(f) \leq \mu(A \cap M_f^\mu)/\mu(f)$.

3. let $x \in m \cap M_f^\mu$ such that $\mu(x) \neq 0$. For every term (m',b) preceding $(m,1)$ in f, $\mu_f(m') = 0$ and since $x \in M_f^\mu$, we have $m'(x) = 0$. Therefore $x \in f$ and $\mu(m \cap M_f^\mu) = \mu(m \cap f)$.

4. apply the two previous points.

$\square$

The last relation is much less robust than the analogous one for k-DNF. This is because $\mu_f(m) = \mu(m \cap M_f^\mu)/\mu(f)$ can be true for only one monomial m, and moreover, the weight of m under μ can be very small. In the following learning algorithm, we build a distribution ν, close to μ and such that the first positive term $(m,1)$ of f such that $\nu_f(m) \neq 0$ has not too small a weight under ν.

Learning the weight of a k-decision list (WDL)
Input: ϵ, n
Begin

Let $N = (2n)^k$, $\alpha = \frac{\epsilon}{25N}$, $\tau_1 = \alpha/4$, $\tau_2 = (\epsilon\alpha^2)/64$
{We now build a set M such that for every k-monomial m,

$\mu_f(m \cap M)$ is null or not too small}
{$\overline{M}$ is the complementary set of M}
$\overline{M} = \emptyset$
$MON_\alpha = k\text{-MON}$
Loop
    For all k-monomials $m \in MON_c$
        ask $\hat{\mu}_f(m \cap M) = STAT(f, \mu_f, \chi_{m \cap M}, \tau_1)$
    EndFor
    If $\forall m \in MON_\alpha, \hat{\mu}_f(m \cap M) \geq \alpha$ **then**
        ExitLoop
    EndIf
    $AUX \leftarrow \{m \in MON_\alpha | \hat{\mu}_f(m \cap M) < \alpha\}$
    $\overline{M} \leftarrow \overline{M} \cup \bigcup \{m \in AUX\}$
    $MON_\alpha \leftarrow MON_\alpha \setminus AUX$
    {Note that $\overline{M}$ is a k-DNF and that
    the queries $\chi_{m \cap M}$ can be evaluated in polynomial time}
EndLoop
For all k-monomials m in MON_α **do**
    ask $\hat{\mu}(m \cap M) = STAT(1, \mu, \chi_{m \cap M}, \tau_2)$
    ask $\hat{\mu}_f(m \cap M) = STAT(f, \mu_f, \chi_{m \cap M}, \tau_2)$
EndFor
compute $\hat{\mu}(f) = min\{\frac{\hat{\mu}(m \cap M)}{\hat{\mu}_f(m \cap M)} | m \in MON_\alpha\}$
End
Output: $\hat{\mu}(f)$

Lemma 2. *The previous algorithm runs in polynomial time and outputs $\hat{\mu}(f)$ such that $|\hat{\mu}(f) - \mu(f)| \leq \epsilon$.*

The proof, a bit technical, relies on several lemmas.
Suppose in all the following that we have run the algorithm WDL.

Lemma 3. $\mu(\overline{M} \cap f) \leq N(\alpha + \tau_1)\mu(f) < 1$.

Proof. Each time a monomial m is added to $\overline{M}$ in the previous algorithm, this is because $\hat{\mu}_f(M \cap m) < \alpha$ which implies $\mu_f(M \cap m) < \alpha + \tau_1$. The quantity added to $\overline{M} \cap f$ is $\mu(M \cap m \cap f) < (\alpha + \tau_1)\mu(f)$. And because the number of k-monomials is less than N, we get the result. $\square$

Let ν be the distribution over X_n defined by :

$$\nu(x) = 0 \text{ if } x \in \overline{M} \cap f \text{ and } \nu(x) = \mu(x)/\mu(M \cup \overline{f}) \text{ otherwise.}$$

We prove some facts about ν which show that $\nu(f)$ is close to $\mu(f)$:

Lemma 4. *1. We have $M = M_f^\nu$.*
2. for every subset A of X_n, we have $|\nu(A) - \mu(A)| \leq 2N(\alpha + \tau_1)\mu(f)$.

3. we have $1 - 2N(\alpha + \tau_1) \leq \nu(f)/\mu(f) \leq 1 + 2N(\alpha + \tau_1)$.

Proof. 1. – Let $x \in \overline{M}$. There exists $m \in k$-MON such that $m(x) = 1$ and $m \subseteq \overline{M}$. Then, $\nu(m \cap f) = \nu_f(m) = 0$ and $x \in \overline{M_f^\nu}$.

– Let $x \in \overline{M_f^\nu}$. There exists $m \in k$-MON such that $m(x) = 1$ and $\nu_f(m) = \nu(m \cap f) = 0$. Then $\mu_f(m \cap M) = \mu(m \cap M \cap f)/\mu(f) = \mu(M \cup \overline{f})\nu(m \cap M \cap f)/\mu(f) = 0$. Therefore, m cannot be in MON_α since $\tau_1 < \alpha$. We have $x \in m \subseteq \overline{M}$.

2. we have

$$|\nu(A) - \mu(A)| \leq \sum_{x \in X_n} |\nu(x) - \mu(x)| \leq \sum_{x \in \overline{M} \cap f} |\nu(x) - \mu(x)| + \sum_{x \in M \cup \overline{f}} |\nu(x) - \mu(x)|$$

$$\leq \mu(\overline{M} \cap f) + \sum_{x \in M \cup \overline{f}} \mu(x)(1/\mu(M \cup \overline{f}) - 1)$$

$$\leq \mu(\overline{M} \cap f) + 1 - \mu(M \cup \overline{f}) \leq 2\mu(\overline{M} \cap f) \leq 2N(\alpha + \tau_1)\mu(f)$$

3. applying the last point, we get :

$$-2N(\alpha + \tau_1)\mu(f) \leq -\mu(f) + \nu(f) \leq 2N(\alpha + \tau_1)\mu(f)$$

that is

$$1 - 2N(\alpha + \tau_1) \leq \nu(f)/\mu(f) \leq 1 + 2N(\alpha + \tau_1)$$

$\square$

We can now prove the lemma 2.

Proof. First note that the algorithm runs in polynomial time.
The only thing to prove is that $|\mu(f) - \hat{\mu}(f)| \leq \epsilon$.

– From lemma 4, we have $|\frac{\nu(f)}{\mu(f)} - 1| \leq 2N(\alpha + \tau_1)$
– Let $m \in MON_\alpha$. We have

$$|\frac{\mu(m \cap M)}{\mu_f(m \cap M)} - \frac{\hat{\mu}(m \cap M)}{\hat{\mu}_f(m \cap M)}| \leq \frac{|\mu(m \cap M)\hat{\mu}_f(m \cap M) - \mu_f(m \cap M)\hat{\mu}(m \cap M)|}{\mu_f(m \cap M)\hat{\mu}_f(m \cap M)}$$

$$\leq \frac{2\tau_2}{\mu_f(m \cap M)\hat{\mu}_f(m \cap M)}$$

$$\leq \frac{2\tau_2}{(\alpha - \tau_1)(\alpha - \tau_1 - \tau_2)} \leq \frac{8\tau_2}{\alpha^2}$$

since $\tau_1 < \alpha/4$ and $\tau_2 < \alpha/4$
– We also have

$$\frac{\nu(m \cap M)}{\nu_f(m)} = \frac{\mu(m \cap M)}{\mu(M \cup \overline{f})} \frac{\nu(f)}{\nu(m \cap f)}$$

$$= \frac{\mu(m \cap M)}{\mu(M \cup \overline{f})} \frac{\mu(M \cup \overline{f})}{\mu(m \cap f \cap M)} \nu(f) = \frac{\mu(m \cap M)}{\mu(m \cap f \cap M)} \nu(f)$$

$$= \frac{\mu(m \cap M)}{\mu_f(m \cap M)} \frac{\nu(f)}{\mu(f)}$$

- Using this relation, we get

$$|\frac{\nu(m \cap M)}{\nu_f(m)} - \frac{\hat{\mu}(m \cap M)}{\hat{\mu}_f(m \cap M)}|$$

$$\leq \frac{\nu(f)}{\mu(f)}|\frac{\mu(m \cap M)}{\mu_f(m \cap M)} - \frac{\hat{\mu}(m \cap M)}{\hat{\mu}_f(m \cap M)}| + \frac{\hat{\mu}(m \cap M)}{\hat{\mu}_f(m \cap M)}|\frac{\nu(f)}{\mu(f)} - 1|$$

$$\leq 2|\frac{\mu(m \cap M)}{\mu_f(m \cap M)} - \frac{\hat{\mu}(m \cap M)}{\hat{\mu}_f(m \cap M)}| + 2|\frac{\nu(f)}{\mu(f)} - 1|$$

$$\leq \frac{16\tau_2}{\alpha^2} + 4N(\alpha + \tau_1)$$

for every $m \in MON_\alpha$

- Now, let $m_0 \in MON_\alpha$ such that $\nu(f) = \frac{\nu(m_0 \cap M)}{\nu_f(m_0)}$ and $m_1 \in MON_\alpha$ such that $\hat{\mu}(f) = \frac{\hat{\mu}(m_1 \cap M)}{\hat{\mu}_f(m_1 \cap M)}$.

$$|\nu(f) - \hat{\mu}(f)| = |\frac{\nu(m_0 \cap M)}{\nu_f(m_0)} - \frac{\hat{\mu}(m_1 \cap M)}{\hat{\mu}_f(m_1 \cap M)}|$$

$$\leq 2Max\{|\frac{\nu(m \cap M)}{\nu_f(m)} - \frac{\hat{\mu}(m \cap M)}{\hat{\mu}_f(m \cap M)}||m \in MON_\alpha\}$$

$$\leq \frac{32\tau_2}{\alpha^2} + 8N(\alpha + \tau_1)$$

- To end the proof,

$$|\mu(f) - \hat{\mu}(f)| \leq |\mu(f) - \nu(f)| + |\nu(f) - \hat{\mu}(f)|$$

and since $|\mu(f) - \nu(f)| \leq 2N(\alpha + \tau_1)$ from lemma 4,

$$|\mu(f) - \hat{\mu}(f)| \leq \frac{32\tau_2}{\alpha^2} + 10N(\alpha + \tau_1) \leq \epsilon$$

$\square$

As in corollary 1, if the learner knows the underlying distribution and can compute it within polynomial time, he can learn k-DNF and k-DL from positive queries only.

6 Conclusion

The models defined in this paper show that it is possible to describe learning from positive data in the PAC learning framework, as soon as information are given on the underlying distribution. Moreover, learning from positive and unlabeled data seems natural in many contexts. Lastly, these results show that many classes learnable in the PAC model are eventually learnable with much more severe constraints: positive and unlabeled queries provide far less information than positive and negative examples. In other words, classes which are learnable in the PAC framework are so not only because they meet the PAC model requirements but also others more restricting.

References

[AL88]   D. Angluin and P. Laird. Learning from noisy examples. *Machine Learning*, 2(4):343–370, 1988.

[Ang80]   D. Angluin. Inductive inference of formal languages from positive data. *Inform. Control*, 45(2):117–135, May 1980.

[BDL97]   Shai Ben-David and Michael Lindenbaum. Learning distributions by their density levels: A paradigm for learning without a teacher. *Journal of Computer and System Sciences*, 55(1):171–182, August 1997.

[Ber86]   R. Berwick. Learning from positive-only examples. In *Machine Learning, Vol. II*, pages 625–645. Morgan Kaufmann, 1986.

[Dec97]   S. E. Decatur. Pac learning with constant-partition classification noise and applications to decision tree induction. In *Proceedings of the Fourteenth International Conference on Machine Learning*, 1997.

[Den98]   F. Denis. Pac learning from positive statistical queries. Technical report, L.I.F.L., 1998. full version: http:\\www.lifl.fr\~denis.

[Gol67]   E.M. Gold. Language identification in the limit. *Inform. Control*, 10:447–474, 1967.

[HSW92]   D. Helmbold, R. Sloan, and M. K. Warmuth. Learning integer lattices. *SIAM J. COMPUT.*, 21(2):240–266, 1992.

[Kea93]   M. Kearns. Efficient noise-tolerant learning from statistical queries. In *Proceedings of the 25th ACM Symposium on the Theory of Computing*, pages 392–401. ACM Press, New York, NY, 1993.

[KV94]   M. J. Kearns and U. V. Vazirani. *An Introduction to Computational Learning Theory*. MIT Press, 1994.

[Nat87]   B. K. Natarajan. On learning boolean functions. In *Proceedings of the 19th Annual ACM Symposium on Theory of Computing*, pages 296–304. ACM Press, 1987.

[Nat91]   B. K. Natarajan. Probably approximate learning of sets and functions. *SIAM J. COMPUT.*, 20(2):328–351, 1991.

[Riv87]   R.L. Rivest. Learning decision lists. *Machine Learning*, 2(3):229–246, 1987.

[Shi90]   Takeshi Shinohara. Inductive inference from positive data is powerful. In *Proceedings of the Third Annual Workshop on Computational Learning Theory*, pages 97–110, Rochester, New York, 6–8 August 1990. ACM Press.

[Shv90]   Haim Shvayster. A necessary condition for learning from positive examples. *Machine Learning*, 5:101–113, 1990.

[Val84]   L.G. Valiant. A theory of the learnable. *Commun. ACM*, 27(11):1134–1142, November 1984.

[ZL95]   T. Zeugmann and S. Lange. A guided tour across the boudaries of learning recursive languages. In Lectures Notes in Artificial Intelligence, editor, *Algorithmic learning for knowledge-based systems*, volume 961, pages 190–258. 1995.

Structured Weight-Based Prediction Algorithms

Akira Maruoka and Eiji Takimoto

Graduate School of Information Sciences, Tohoku University
Sendai, 980-8579, Japan
{maruoka, t2}@ecei.tohoku.ac.jp

Abstract. Reviewing structured weight-based prediction algorithms (SWP for short) due to Takimoto, Maruoka and Vovk, we present underlying design methods for constructing a variety of on-line prediction algorithms based on the SWP. In particular, we shown how the typical expert model where the experts are considered to be arranged on one layer can be generalized to the case where they are laid on a tree structure so that the expert model can be applied to search for the best pruning in a straightforward fashion through dynamic programming scheme.

1 Introduction

Based on the mistake bound model, multiplicative weight-update prediction algorithms have been studied which predict the classification of an instance from environment at each time step (See [1],[2],[5],[7] and [8]). As opposed to the typical PAC learning model, the mistake bound model makes no assumptions about the way the sequence of instances, and hence the sequence of outcomes specifying the classification, is generated. Instead, in the mistake bound model we usually assume a pool of experts $\mathcal{E}$ which are supposed to make binary values so that, using these binary values the experts give, the prediction algorithms make its own prediction.

Although it seems that these models have been mainly investigated separately so far some topics having to do with both of these two models begin to be explored recently. In fact Freund and Schapire used the on-line prediction model to derive a new boosting algorithm [2]; Kearns and Mansour [4] constructed the efficient pruning algorithm that, in the PAC setting, enjoys a strong performance guarantee of the style of the prediction model. In this paper we give various multiplicative weight-update algorithms in [7] and present computational scheme behind these algorithms in as simple a form as possible. It is our hope that exploring the computational mechanism in the prediction model helps us establish results that share aspects from both the PAC and prediction models.

We start with explaining the aggregating algorithm due to Vovk ([8]). After reviewing Vovk's work, we give on on-line algorithm that finds the best pruning through dynamic programming scheme, and then present an on-line algorithm that is competitive not only with the best pruning but also with the best prediction values. Finally we notice that the later algorithm is so simple that it can be generalized to the case where, instead of using decision trees, data are classified in some arbitrarily fixed manner.

2 On-line prediction model

In the most primitive version of the prediction algorithm, which is called the weighted majority algorithm, the master algorithm produces its output based on the majority of weighted voting of the experts. In this algorithm, each of the N experts has initial weight 1, and in each trial the weights are multiplied by $0 \leq \beta < 1$ in the case of a mistake and are lefted unchanged otherwise. The weighted majority prediction model can be generalized to the case where it is allowed to hedge in predictions: The master algorithm and the experts are allowed to output values in $[0, 1]$ rather than binary values 0 or 1. In this paper we adopt the generalized prediction model described as follows. Let the *prediction space*, denoted $\hat{Y}$, be $[0, 1]$, and let the *outcome space*, denoted Y, be $\{0, 1\}$. And let the *instance space* be denoted by X. A prediction algorithm has the pool of experts denoted by $\mathcal{E} = \{\mathcal{E}_1, \ldots, \mathcal{E}_N\}$. At each trial $t = 1, 2, \cdots$ a prediction algorithm A receives an instance $x_t \in X$ and generates a prediction $\hat{y}_t \in [0, 1]$. Likewise, at each trial t, every expert $\mathcal{E}_i$ makes a prediction $\xi_i^t \in \hat{Y}$ for the instance x_t, and sends its prediction to the master algorithm. The algorithm somehow combines these predictions in order to make its own prediction $\hat{y}_t \in \hat{Y}$. After an outcome $y_t \in \{0, 1\}$ is observed (which can be thought of as the correct classification of x_t), the master algorithm and the experts suffer loss given in terms of a loss function denoted λ: the master algorithm suffers loss $\lambda(y_t, \hat{y}_t)$, whereas the ith expert suffers loss $\lambda(y_t, \xi_i^t)$. A typical example of such a loss function is given as $\lambda(y_t, \hat{y}_t) = |y_t - \hat{y}_t|$, which is called the *absolute loss function*. In the following arguments we'll see that the sequence of instances x_t's eventually does not play any essential role. Usually we start our argument assuming a sequence of outcomes arbitrarily given.

The prediction $\hat{y}_t \in [0, 1]$ can be typically interpreted as follows: The algorithm predicts $y_t = 1$ with probability $\hat{y}_t$ and $y_t = 0$ with probability $1 - \hat{y}_t$. The *cumulative loss* of a prediction algorithm A and that of the ith expert over T trials are given by $L_A(y) = \Sigma_{t=1}^T \lambda(y_t, \hat{y}_t)$ and $L_i(y) = \Sigma_{t=1}^T \lambda(y_t, \xi_i^t)$ for outcome sequence $y = (y_1, \ldots, y_T)$, respectively. The goal of the prediction algorithm A is to minimize the cumulative loss $L_A(y) = \Sigma_{t=1}^T \lambda(y_t, \hat{y}_t)$ for arbitrary outcome sequence $y = (y_1, \ldots, y_T)$, $T \geq 1$. The cumulative loss is simply called the loss of A.

We begin with reviewing Vovk's on-line prediction algorithms called the aggregating algorithm and the aggregating pseudo-algorithm. In the on-line prediction model, the prediction algorithm maintains a weight $w_i^t \in [0, 1]$ for each expert $\mathcal{E}_i$ that reflects the actual performance of the expert $\mathcal{E}_i$ up to time t. For simplicity, we assume that the weight is set to $w_i^1 = 1$ for $1 \leq i \leq N$ at time $t = 1$. It is crucial how to update the weights after time $t = 1$. In order to specify the update rule we introduce the parameter $\beta \in (0, 1)$ of the algorithm called the *exponential learning rate*. At each trial t, after receiving the predictions $\xi_1^t, \ldots, \xi_N^t$ from the experts, the master algorithm computes, for each $y \in Y$, the function $r(y)$ which is specified by

$$\beta^{r(y)} = \sum_{i=1}^{N} \beta^{\lambda(y,\xi_i^t)} \overline{w}_i^t,$$

or equivalently

$$r(y) = \log_\beta \sum_{i=1}^{N} \beta^{\lambda(y,\xi_i^t)} \overline{w}_i^t,$$

where $\overline{w}_i^t$ are the normalized weights:

$$\overline{w}_i^t = \frac{w_i^t}{\sum_{i=1}^{N} w_i^t}.$$

By definition, for each $y \in Y$, $r(y)$ gives the weighted average of losses of the experts. In other words, the function r does not provide information as to which outcome in Y is more likely to happen, but gives the weighted average of loss for both cases of $y_t = 0$ and $y_t = 1$. After receiving the correct classification $y_t \in Y$, the algorithm updates the weights of the experts according to the rule

$$w_i^{t+1} = w_i^t \beta^{\lambda(y_t,\xi_i^t)},$$

for $1 \leq i \leq N$ and $1 \leq t \leq T$. So the larger the expert $\mathcal{E}_i$'s loss is, the more its weight decreases. It will be seen later that, for any outcome sequence $y = (y_1, \ldots, y_T)$, $\sum_{t=1}^{T} r_t(y_t)$ is bounded from above in terms of the each expert loss $L_i(y) = \sum_{t=1}^{T} \lambda(y_t, \xi_i^t)$, where r_t is the weighted average of losses of the experts at time t. So in order to bound from above the loss of the prediction algorithm $L_A(y) = \sum_{t=1}^{T} \lambda(y_t, \hat{y}_t)$ in terms of loss of the best expert, we want to have an inequality of the form $\lambda(y_t, \hat{y}_t) \leq cr_t(y_t)$ that holds for *any* $y_t \in Y$ when *some* $\hat{y}_t \in \hat{Y}$ is chosen appropriately, where c is some constant. With the arguments above in mind, we define a β-*mixture* as the function $r : Y \to [0, \infty)$ defined as

$$r(y) = \log_\beta \sum_{\xi \in \hat{Y}} \beta^{\lambda(y,\xi)} P(\xi)$$

for a probability distribution P over $\hat{Y}$. Let $c(\beta)$ be the infimum of the real values c such that for any β-mixture r there exists $\hat{y} \in \hat{Y}$ such that $\lambda(y, \hat{y}) \leq cr(y)$ for any $y \in Y$. The constant $c(\beta)$ will be called the *mixability curve*. Throughout the paper we assume that the infimum in defining $c(\beta)$ is attained. Sufficient conditions for $c(\beta)$ to exist are given in [8]. By definition there exists a function, denoted Σ_β, from β-mixtures to $[0, \infty)$ such that

$$\lambda(y, \Sigma_\beta(r)) \leq c(\beta)r(y)$$

for any β-mixture r and any y. The function Σ_β will be called a *substitution function*. Note that $\Sigma_\beta(r)$ depends not only function r_t and constant β, but also the underlying loss function λ. The function r which gives the average loss of the experts for each outcome will be called a *pseudoprediction*, whereas a prediction (denoted ξ_i^t so far) given by an element in $\hat{Y}$ will be called a *genuine prediction* when we need to make it explicit that the prediction is not a pseudoprediction. The first type of the prediction algorithm yields a pseudoprediction and is called a Aggregating Pseudo-Algorithm (APA for short), whereas the second type of the algorithm produces a genuine prediction and is called a Aggregating Algorithm (AA for short).

The constant $c(\beta)$ and the substitution function $\Sigma_\beta(r)$ have been obtained for popular loss functions such as the absolute loss, the square loss and the log loss functions [8]. In particular, when we consider the absolute loss function $\lambda(y, \hat{y}) = |y - \hat{y}|$ for $y \in Y = \{0, 1\}$, $\hat{y} \in \hat{Y} = [0, 1]$, it was shown [8] that

$$c(\beta) = \frac{\ln(1/\beta)}{2\ln(2/(1+\beta))},$$

and

$$\sum_\beta (r) = \mathbf{I}_0^1 \left(\frac{1}{2} + c(\beta)\frac{r(0) - r(1)}{2} \right),$$

where

$$\mathbf{I}_0^1(t) = \begin{cases} 1, & \text{if } t > 1, \\ 0, & \text{if } t < 0, \\ t, & \text{otherwise.} \end{cases}$$

Note that the absolute loss $|y - \hat{y}|$ is exactly the probability of the probabilistically predicted bit differing from the true outcome y.

We consider that our prediction algorithms consist of two parts : one keeps track of $r_t(y)$, i.e., the average loss of the experts for each case of $y_t = 0$ and $y_t = 1$ which is computed provided that actual outcomes up to $t - 1$, and hence the actual weights up to $t - 1$, are known for the N experts; the other makes a prediction on outcome at time t by applying the substitution function Σ_β that selects good prediction based on the average $r_t(y)$ of losses over the experts when the outcome is y. We can say that the prediction at time t is made by fully exploiting the information the algorithm can get before the outcome at time t is revealed.

For ease of exposition we first give the prediction algorithm that consists of only the first part, and then present the algorithm that consists of both parts. As shown in the next section the first type of the algorithm will be useful when we don't need to produce a prediction in every trial. When we deal with the aggregating pseudo-algorithm, it is convenient to assume that not only the master algorithm but also the subordinate experts output pseudopredictions: for $y \in Y$ a pseudoprediction ξ takes the real value $\xi(y)$ which is interpreted as the loss of ξ for outcome y. We use the same symbol ξ which is used to represent a genuine prediction $\xi \in \hat{Y}$ as well. A genuine prediction $\xi \in \hat{Y}$ can also be viewed as the pseudoprediction $\xi' : Y \to [0, \infty)$ defined as $\xi'(y) = \lambda(y, \xi)$ for $y \in Y$. So the master algorithm computes the pseudoprediction based on the equation obtained by replacing $\lambda(y, \xi_i^t)$ in the equation $r(y) = \log_\beta \sum_{i=1}^N \beta^{\lambda(y, \xi_i^t)} \overline{w}_i^t$ by

$\xi_i^t(y)$:

$$r(y) = \log_\beta \sum_{i=1}^{N} \beta^{\xi_i^t(y)} \overline{w}_i^t.$$

The complete description of the algorithm APA due to Vovk ([8]) is given as follows.

Algorithm 1 (APA(β))
for $i \in \{1, \ldots, N\}$ **do**
  $w_i^1 := 1$
for $t := 1, 2, \ldots$ **do**
  receive $(\xi_1^t, \ldots, \xi_N^t)$
  for $y \in Y$ **do**
    $r_t(y) := \log_\beta \sum_i \beta^{\xi_i^t(y)} \overline{w}_i^t$
  output r_t
  receive y_t
  for $i \in \{1, \ldots, N\}$ **do**
    $w_i^{t+1} := w_i^t \beta^{\xi_i^t(y)}$

The loss of APA(β) and that of the expert $\mathcal{E}_i$ for $y = (y_1, \ldots, y_T)$ are given by

$$L_{\text{APA}(\beta)}(y) = \sum_{t=1}^{T} r_t(y_t)$$

and

$$L_i(y) = \sum_{t=1}^{T} \xi_i^t(y_t),$$

respectively. A described above, the loss for $y = (y_1, \ldots, y_T)$ is defined to be just the sum of the weighted average of losses for the outcomes y_i taken in trials. For an arbitrarily fixed outcome sequence $y = (y_1, \ldots, y_T) \in Y^*$, we have

$$
\begin{aligned}
L_{\text{APA}(\beta)}(y) &= \sum_{t=1}^{T} r_t(y_t) \\
&= \sum_{t=1}^{T} \log_\beta \left(\sum_{i=1}^{N} \beta^{\xi_i^t(y_t)} \overline{w}_i^t \right) \\
&= \sum_{t=1}^{T} \log_\beta \left(\frac{\sum_{i=1}^{N} w_i^{t+1}}{\sum_{i=1}^{N} w_i^t} \right) \\
&= \log_\beta \left(\sum_{i=1}^{N} w_i^{T+1} \right) - \log_\beta \left(\sum_{i=1}^{N} w_i^1 \right) \\
&= \log_\beta \left(\sum_{i=1}^{N} w_i^1 \beta^{L_i(y)} \right).
\end{aligned}
$$

Since $\beta < 1$, we have

$$L_{\text{APA}(\beta)}(y) \leq \log_\beta \left(\beta^{L_i(y)} w_i^1\right)$$
$$= \log_\beta \left(\beta^{L_i(y)} / N\right)$$

for any $1 \leq i \leq N$, which implies the following theorem.

Theorem 1. (Vovk, [8]) *Let $0 < \beta < 1$. Then, for any $N \geq 1$, any N experts $\mathcal{E}$ and for any $y \in Y^*$,*

$$L_{\text{APA}(\beta)}(y) = \sum_{t=1}^{T} r_t(y_t)$$
$$\leq \min_{1 \leq i \leq N} \left(L_i(y) + \frac{\ln N}{\ln(1/\beta)}\right).$$

When it is required for the algorithm to make prediction on an outcome for every trial, the algorithm computes $\Sigma_\beta(r_t)$ by using the pseudoprediction r_t and yields a genuine prediction. In this case the ith expert is also supposed to produce a genuine prediction, denoted ξ_i^t, for $1 \leq i \leq N$. In this way we have the aggregating algorithm ([8]) by replacing $\xi_i^t(y)$ in APA with $\lambda(y, \xi_i^t)$, and replacing output r_t in APA with output $\hat{y}_t := \Sigma_\beta(r)$.

Algorithm 2 (AA(β))
for $i \in \{1, \ldots, N\}$ **do**
$\quad w_i^1 := 1/N$
for $t := 1, 2, \ldots$ **do**
$\quad$ **receive** $(\xi_1^t, \ldots, \xi_N^t)$
$\quad$ **for** $y \in Y$ **do**
$\quad\quad r_t(y) := \log_\beta \sum_i \beta^{\lambda(y, \xi_i^t)} \overline{w}_i^t$
$\quad$ **output** $\hat{y}_t := \Sigma_\beta(r)$
$\quad$ **receive** y_t
$\quad$ **for** $i \in \{1, \ldots, N\}$ **do**
$\quad\quad w_i^{t+1} := w_i^t \beta^{\lambda(y_t, \xi_i^t)}$

The loss of the aggregating algorithm, denoted $L_{\text{AA}(\beta)}(y)$, is defined as

$$L_{\text{AA}(\beta)}(y) = \sum_{t=1}^{T} \lambda\left(y_t, \Sigma_\beta(r_t)\right).$$

By the definitions of the mixability curve $c(\beta)$ and the substitution function Σ_β, we immediately have an upper bound on the loss of the aggregating algorithm as follows.

$$L_{\text{AA}(\beta)}(y) = \sum_{t=1}^{T} \lambda(y_t, \Sigma_\beta(r_t))$$

$$\leq c(\beta) \sum_{t=1}^{T} r_t(y_t)$$

$$= c(\beta) L_{\text{APA}(\beta)}(y),$$

which, together with Theorem 1, establishes the following theorem. The above inequality follows from the fact that $\lambda(y_t, \Sigma_\beta(r_t)) \leq c(\beta) r_t(y_t)$. By definition it is clear that $\lambda(y_t, \Sigma_\beta(r_t)) \leq c(\beta) r_t(y_t)$, which holds because the pseudoprediction r_t easily shown to be a β-mixture.

Theorem 2. (Vovk, [8]) *Let $0 < \beta < 1$, and let $c(\beta)$ give the value of the mixability curve at β. Then, for any $N \geq 1$, any N experts $\mathcal{E}$ and for any $y \in Y^*$,*

$$L_{\text{AA}(\beta)}(y) = \sum_{t=1}^{T} \lambda(y_t, \Sigma_\beta(r_t))$$

$$\leq \min_{1 \leq i \leq N} \left(c(\beta) L_i(y) + \frac{c(\beta) \ln N}{\ln(1/\beta)} \right).$$

3 Applying the aggregating algorithm to prune decision trees

Among a variety of applications of the multiplicative weight-update prediction algorithm, is the problem of seeking for a "good" pruning of a given decision tree $\mathcal{T}$. By a good pruning we mean a pruning that is "not much worse" than the best pruning of a given decision tree. When given a label function, denoted V, which associates each node of $\mathcal{T}$ with an output in $\hat{Y}$, a pruned decision tree $\mathcal{P}$ can be naturally thought of as the expert who makes predictions. So we can enumerate all the pruned trees of a given decision tree and apply the AA with the pruned trees being taken as experts.

By applying simply the AA for the collection of the experts it follows from Theorem 2 that the loss of this naive prediction algorithm, denoted A_N, is at most

$$L_{A_N}(y) \leq \min_{\mathcal{P} \in \text{PRUN}(\mathcal{T})} c(\beta) L_{\mathcal{P},V}(y) + \frac{2 c(\beta) |\text{leaves}(\mathcal{T})| \ln 2}{\ln(1/\beta)}$$

for any $y \in Y^*$, where $L_{\mathcal{P},V}(y)$ denotes the loss of the pruning $\mathcal{P}$ when given V. Unfortunately this naive approach has a fatal drawback that we have to deal with the exponential number of the prunings of $\mathcal{T}$.

Elaborating a data structure, Helmbold and Schapire constructed an efficient prediction algorithm for the absolute loss that works in a manner equivalent to the naive algorithm without enumerating prunings. The performance of their algorithm is given as follows:

Theorem 3. (Helmbold and Schapire, [3]) *In the case of the absolute loss, there exists a prediction algorithm A such that for any $\mathcal{T}$, V and $y \in \{0,1\}^*$, when given $\mathcal{T}$ and V as input, A makes predictions for y so that the loss is at most*

$$L_A(y) \leq \min_{\mathcal{P} \in \mathrm{PRUN}(\mathcal{T})} \frac{L_{\mathcal{P},V}(y) \ln(1/\beta) + |\mathcal{P}| \ln 2}{2 \ln(2/(1+\beta))},$$

where $|\mathcal{P}|$ denotes the number of nodes of $\mathcal{P}$ minus $|\mathrm{leaves}(\mathcal{T}) \cap \mathrm{leaves}(\mathcal{P})|$. A generates a prediction at each trial t in time $O(|x_t|)$. Moreover, the label function V may depend on t.

The naive algorithm mentioned above considers each pruning of a decision tree as an expert. There is also a variety of choice as to what we think of as the experts. In the next section we consider as the experts agencies corresponding to blocks of a partition of the domain X, each making some fixed prediction for a block. In this section, we can consider the more complicated case that two kinds of mini-experts $\mathcal{E}_u = \{\mathcal{E}_{u\perp}, \mathcal{E}_{u\downarrow}\}$ are put on each internal node u in a tree, where one $\mathcal{E}_{u\perp}$ makes the decision to throw away the subtree below the node u and the other $\mathcal{E}_{u\downarrow}$ makes the decision to hold the edges downward from u. Then choosing one of the two mini-experts at each internal node clearly amounts to specifying a subtree of the tree given first. So putting the APA at each inner node u and applying the APA recursively we may compute a weighted subtree that has nearly the best performance.

To be more precise, let us introduce some notation about decision trees. Let Σ be a finite alphabet, $|\Sigma| > 1$. A template tree $\mathcal{T}$ over Σ is a rooted, $|\Sigma|$-ary tree. Thus we can identify each node of $\mathcal{T}$ with the sequence of symbols in Σ that forms a path from the root to that node. In particular, if a node u of $\mathcal{T}$ is represented by $x \in \Sigma^*$ (or a prefix of x), then we will say that x *reaches* the node u. The leaf l that x reaches is denoted by $l = \mathrm{leaf}_{\mathcal{P}}(x)$. Given a tree $\mathcal{T}$, the set of its nodes and that of its leaves are denoted by $\mathrm{nodes}(\mathcal{T})$ and $\mathrm{leaves}(\mathcal{T})$, respectively. A string in Σ^* that reaches any of the leaves of $\mathcal{T}$ is called an *instance*.

As in the usual setting, an instance includes a path from the root to a leaf according to the outcomes of classification tests done at the internal nodes on the path. So, without loss of generality, we can identify an instance with the path it induces and thus we do not need to explicitly specify classification rules at the internal nodes of $\mathcal{T}$. A label function V for template tree $\mathcal{T}$ is a function that maps the set of nodes of $\mathcal{T}$ to the prediction space $\hat{Y}$. A pruning $\mathcal{P}$ of the template tree $\mathcal{T}$ is a tree obtained by replacing zero or more of the internal nodes (and associated subtrees) of $\mathcal{T}$ by leaves. Note that $\mathcal{T}$ itself is a pruning of $\mathcal{T}$ as well. The pair $(\mathcal{P}, V)$ induces a pruned decision tree that makes its prediction $V(\mathrm{leaf}_{\mathcal{P}}(x))$ for instance x. The set of all pruning of $\mathcal{T}$ is denoted by $\mathrm{PRUN}(\mathcal{T})$.

Figure 1 shows an example of template tree $\mathcal{T}$ over alphabet $\Sigma = \{0, 1\}$ and a pruning $\mathcal{P}$ of $\mathcal{T}$ with $\hat{Y} = [0, 1]$. The numbers associated with the nodes are the values of the label function V for the nodes. For example, the predictions of $(\mathcal{T}, V)$ and $(\mathcal{P}, V)$ for instance (101) are 0.6 and 0.2, respectively.

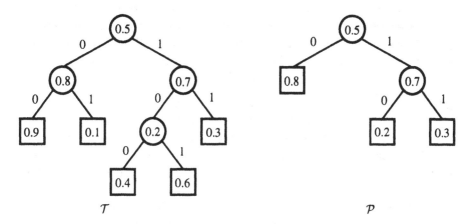

Fig. 1. Examples of a template tree $\mathcal{T}$ and a pruning $\mathcal{P}$ of $\mathcal{T}$ with a label function.

We shall explore how to use the APA in the previous section to construct an algorithm that seeks for a weighted combination of the mini-experts located at the inner nodes of a decision tree given so that the weighted combination of the mini-experts performs nearly as well as the best pruning of the decision tree.

Our algorithm is in some sense a quite straightforward implementation of the dynamic programming. To explain how it works, we still need some more notations. Recall that each node of $\mathcal{T}$ is identified with the string in Σ^* that forms the path from the root to that node. In particular, the root is specified by the empty string ϵ. For node $u \in \Sigma^*$, let $\mathcal{T}_u$ denote the subtree of $\mathcal{T}$ rooted at u. For an outcome sequence $y \in Y^*$, the loss suffered at u, denoted $L_u(y)$, is defined as follows:

$$L_u(y) = \sum_{t:x_t \text{ reaches } u} \lambda(y_t, V(u)).$$

Then, for any pruning $\mathcal{P}_u$ of $\mathcal{T}_u$, the loss suffered by $\mathcal{P}_u$, denoted $L_{\mathcal{P}_u}(y)$, can be represented by the sum of $L_l(y)$ for all leaves l of $\mathcal{P}_u$. In other words, we can write $L_{\mathcal{P}_u}(y) = L_u(y)$ if $\mathcal{P}_u$ consists of a single leaf u and $L_{\mathcal{P}_u(y)} = \Sigma_{a \in \Sigma} L_{\mathcal{P}_{ua}}(y)$ otherwise. Here $\mathcal{P}_{ua}$ is the subtree of $\mathcal{P}_u$ rooted at ua. Since the losses $L_{\mathcal{P}_{ua}}(y)$ for $a \in \Sigma$ are independent of each other, we can minimize the loss $L_{\mathcal{P}_u}(y)$ by minimizing each loss $L_{\mathcal{P}_{ua}}(y)$ independently. We therefore have for any internal node u of $\mathcal{T}$

$$\min_{\mathcal{P}_u \in \text{PRUN}(\mathcal{T}_u)} L_{\mathcal{P}_u}(y) = \min \left\{ L_u(y), \sum_{a \in \Sigma} \min_{\mathcal{P}_{ua} \in \text{PRUN}(\mathcal{T}_{ua})} L_{\mathcal{P}_{ua}}(y) \right\}.$$

Since dynamic programming can be applied to solve the minimization problem of this type, we can efficiently compute $\mathcal{P}_\epsilon \in \mathrm{PRUN}(\mathcal{T}_\epsilon)$ that minimize $L_{\mathcal{P}_\epsilon}(y)$, which is the best pruning of $\mathcal{T}$. But if we try to solve the minimization problem based on the formula above in a straightforward way, we have to have the sequence of outcomes $y = (y_1, \ldots, y_T)$ ahead of time.

In the rest of this section we try to construct an algorithm that solves the minimization problem in an on-line fashion by applying aggregating pseudo-algorithm recursively on the decision trees. As mentioned before, we associate two mini-experts $\mathcal{E}_u = \{\mathcal{E}_{u\perp}, \mathcal{E}_{u\downarrow}\}$ with each internal node u, one $\mathcal{E}_{u\perp}$ corresponding to making the node u a leaf and the other $\mathcal{E}_{u\downarrow}$ corresponding to making the node u an internal node. To combine these experts we apply the APA recursively, which is placed on each inner node of $\mathcal{T}$: The APA at an inner node u, denoted $\mathrm{APA}_u(\beta)$, combines the pseudopredictions of the experts $\mathcal{E}_{u\perp}$ and $\mathcal{E}_{u\downarrow}$ to obtain its own pseudoprediction r_u^t, and pass it to the APA at the parent node of u. More precisely, when given an instance x_t that goes through u and ua, the first expert $\mathcal{E}_{u\perp}$ generates $V(u)$ and the second expert $\mathcal{E}_{u\downarrow}$ generates r_{ua}^t, i.e., the pseudoprediction made by $\mathrm{APA}_{ua}(\beta)$, the APA at node ua. Then, taking the weighted average of these pseudopredictions $V(u)$ and r_{ua}^t according to the multiplicative weight-update rule (recall that the genuine prediction $V(u)$ is regarded as a pseudoprediction), $\mathrm{APA}_u(\beta)$ obtains the pseudoprediction r_u^t at u. To obtain the genuine prediction $\hat{y}_t$, our algorithm applies the β–substitution function to the pseudoprediction only at the root during every trial, that is, $\hat{y}_t = \Sigma_\beta(r_\epsilon^t)$: in the internal nodes we combine not genuine predictions but pseudopredictions using the APA.

We present below the prediction algorithm constructed this way, which we call *Structured Weight-based Prediction algorithm* (SWP(β) for short). Here, $\mathrm{path}(x_t)$ denotes the set of the nodes of $\mathcal{T}$ that x_t reaches. In other words, $\mathrm{path}(x_t)$ is the set of the prefixes of x_t. For node u, $|u|$ denotes the depth of u, i.e, the length of the path from the root to u.

Algorithm 3 ($\mathrm{APA}_u(\beta)$)
procedure PSEUDOPRED(u, x_t)
    if $u \in \mathrm{leaf}(\mathcal{T})$ **then**
        for $y \in Y$ **do**
            $r_u^t(y) := \lambda(y, V(u))$
    else
        choose $a \in \Sigma$ such that $ua \in \mathrm{path}(x_t)$
        $r_{ua}^t := \mathrm{PSEUDOPRED}(ua, x_t)$
        for $y \in Y$ **do**
$$r_u^t(y) := \log_\beta\left(\overline{w}_{u\perp}^t \beta^{\lambda(y, V(u))} + \overline{w}_{u\downarrow}^t \beta^{r_{ua}^t(y)}\right)$$
    return r_u^t

procedure UPDATE(u, y_t)
    if $u \in \mathrm{leaf}(\mathcal{T})$ **then**
        return
    else

choose $a \in \Sigma$ such that $ua \in \text{path}(x_t)$
$w_{u\perp}^{t+1} := w_{u\perp}^t \beta^{\lambda(y_t, V(u))}$
$w_{u\downarrow}^{t+1} := w_{u\downarrow}^t \beta^{r_{ua}^t(y_t)}$
return

Algorithm 4 (algorithm SWP(β))

for $u \in \text{nodes}(\mathcal{T})\backslash\text{leaves}(\mathcal{T})$ **do**
  $w_{u\perp}^1 := 1/2$
  $w_{u\downarrow}^1 := 1/2$
for $t = 1, 2, \ldots$ **do**
  receive x_t
  $r_\epsilon^t := \text{PSEUDOPRED}(\epsilon, x_t)$
  $\hat{y}_t := \Sigma_\beta(r_\epsilon^t)$
  output $\hat{y}_t$
  receive y_t
  for $u \in \text{path}(x_t)$ **do**
    UPDATE(u, y_t)

Let the loss suffered by $\text{APA}_u(\beta)$ be denoted by $\hat{L}_u(y)$. That is,

$$\hat{L}_u(y) = \sum_{t:u\in\text{path}(x_t)} r_u^t(y_t).$$

Since the first expert $\mathcal{E}_{u\perp}$ suffers the loss $L_u(y)$ and the second expert $\mathcal{E}_{u\downarrow}$ suffers the loss $\Sigma_{a\in\Sigma}\hat{L}_{ua}(y)$, Theorem 2 says that for any internal node u of $\mathcal{T}$,

$$\hat{L}_u(y) \leq \min\left\{L_u(y), \sum_{a\in\Sigma}\hat{L}_{ua}(y)\right\} + (\ln 2)/(\ln(1/\beta)).$$

By the similarity between the inequality above and the equation

$$\min_{\mathcal{P}_u \in \text{PRUN}(\mathcal{T}_u)} L_{\mathcal{P}_u}(y) = \min\left\{L_u(y), \sum_{a\in\Sigma}\min_{\mathcal{P}_{ua}\in\text{PRUN}(\mathcal{T}_{ua})} L_{\mathcal{P}_{ua}}(y)\right\}$$

for the minimization problem, we can roughly say that $\hat{L}_u(y)$ is not much larger than the loss of the best pruning of $\mathcal{T}_u$. More precisely, applying the inequality recursively, we obtain the following upper bound on the loss $\hat{L}_\epsilon(y)$ at the root:

$$\hat{L}_\epsilon(y) \leq L_\mathcal{P}(y) + |\mathcal{P}|(\ln 2)/(\ln(1/\beta))$$

for any pruning $\mathcal{P} \in \text{PRUN}(\mathcal{T})$. This is because every node of $\mathcal{P}$ that is not $\mathcal{T}$'s leaf gives an extra loss of $(\ln 2)/(\ln(1/\beta))$. Recall that $|\mathcal{P}|$ denotes the number of such nodes. Since r_u^t in $\text{APA}_u(\beta)$ is shown to be a β-mixture for any $u \in \text{nodes}(\mathcal{T})$ and hence $\lambda(y_t, \Sigma_\beta(r_u^t)) \leq c(\beta)r_u^t(y_t)$ for any $1 \leq t \leq T$ and $u \in \text{nodes}(\mathcal{T})$, the cumulative loss of the SWP, denoted $L_{\text{SWP}(\beta)}(y)$, is given as follows:

$$L_{\text{SWP}(\beta)}(y) = \sum_{t=1}^{T} \lambda(y_t, \Sigma_\beta(y_\epsilon^t))$$

$$\leq c(\beta) \sum_{t=1}^{T} r_\epsilon^t(y_t)$$

$$= c(\beta)\hat{L}_\epsilon(y)$$

$$\leq c(\beta)(L_{\mathcal{P}}(y) + |\mathcal{P}|(\ln 2)/(\ln(1/\beta)))$$

for any $\mathcal{P} \in \text{PRUN}(\mathcal{T})$ and $y \in Y^T$. Thus we have the following theorem.

Theorem 4. ([7], cf.[6]) *There exists a prediction algorithm A such that for any $\mathcal{T}$, V and $y \in Y^*$, when $\mathcal{T}$ and V are given as input, A makes predictions for y so that loss is at most*

$$L_A(y) \leq \min_{\mathcal{P} \in \text{PRUN}(\mathcal{T})} \left(c(\beta) L_{\mathcal{P}, V}(y) + \frac{c(\beta)\ln 2}{\ln(1/\beta)} |\mathcal{P}| \right).$$

We now go further forward exploiting the idea of putting mini-experts at each node in a decision tree in order to make prediction. If we consider putting at each node the mini-experts deciding not only to throw away the subtree below a node, but also to make prediction on values in prediction space $\hat{Y}$, then we may construct an algorithm to yield a pruning that is competitive with best pruning having the best prediction at its leaves.

In fact, if $\hat{Y}$ is finite, it can be done by associating $|\hat{Y}| + 1$ experts with each internal node u, one predicting the value that the subtree below u predicts, and the others predicting different values in prediction space $\hat{Y}$; we also need to associate $|\hat{Y}|$ experts with each leaf, each predicting different values in $\hat{Y}$. We shall deal with infinite prediction space $\hat{Y}$ and give an algorithm that is competitive not only with the best pruning $\mathcal{P}$ but also with the best node labeling V. To do so, we assume that the node label function V is time invariant (V does not depend on t), and that the loss function λ is taken to be the absolute loss function. Since the loss function is assumed to be the absolute loss function, the loss suffered at the node l (which is not necessarily a leaf) of $\mathcal{T}$ under a label function V, which is denoted by $L_{l,V}(y)$, is given by

$$L_{l,V}(y) = \sum_{t:x_t \text{reaches } l} |y_t - V(l)|,$$

for an outcome sequence $y = (y_1, \ldots, y_T) \in \{0,1\}^T$. Then the loss of a pruning $\mathcal{P}$ of $\mathcal{T}$ and a label function V can be represented by

$$L_{\mathcal{P}, V}(y) = \sum_{l \in \text{leaves}(\mathcal{P})} L_{l,V}(y).$$

Let l be a node of $\mathcal{T}$. And for a label function V, let V_0 and V_1 denote the label functions obtained by replacing the value $V(l)$ by 0 and 1, respectively (with the values of the other nodes unchanged). Then it is easy to see that, for any $y \in \{0,1\}^*$,

$$\min\{L_{l,V_0}(y), L_{l,V_1}(y)\} \leq L_{l,V}(y)$$

holds.

By applying the above inequality repeatedly, we have the next lemma which says that without loss of generality we can assume that the label function V takes only binary values in $\{0,1\}$.

Lemma 1. *Let $\mathcal{T}$ be a template tree and let V be a label function from* nodes($\mathcal{T}$) *to* $[0,1]$. *Then, for any $y \in \{0,1\}^*$ there exists a label function V_B from* nodes(V) *to* $\{0,1\}$ *such that*

$$L_{\mathcal{T},V}(y) \geq L_{\mathcal{T},V_B}(y).$$

So we assume that $\hat{Y} = \{0,1\}$. Then since $\hat{Y}$ is finite we can apply our strategy for the decision tree with the weighted mini-experts placed at its nodes: two mini-experts $\{\mathcal{E}_0, \mathcal{E}_1\}$ placed at each leaf in leaves($\mathcal{T}$) and three mini-experts $\{\mathcal{E}_0, \mathcal{E}_1, \mathcal{E}_{u\downarrow}\}$ placed at each inner node u in nodes($\mathcal{T}$), where $\mathcal{E}_0$ and $\mathcal{E}_1$ identically predict 0 and 1, respectively, and $\mathcal{E}_{u\downarrow}$ predicts the value that the subtree below u predicts. So it is clear that the modified algorithm achieves the same loss bounds as in Theorem 4 except that $(\ln 2)|\mathcal{P}|$ in the loss bound is replaced by

$$(\ln 3)|\mathcal{P}| + (\ln 2)|\text{leaves}(\mathcal{P}) \cap \text{leaves}(\mathcal{T})|.$$

Thus, since the mixability curve for the absolute loss is given by $c(\beta) = \ln(1/\beta)/(2\ln(2/(1+\beta)))$, we have established the following theorem in a similar way to the proof of Theorem 4.

Theorem 5. ([7], cf.[6]) *In the case of the absolute loss, there exists a prediction algorithm A such that for any $\mathcal{T}$ and $y \in \{0,1\}^*$, when given $\mathcal{T}$ as input, A makes predictions for y so that the loss is at most*

$$L_A(y) \leq \min_{\mathcal{P} \in \text{PRUN}(\mathcal{T})} \min_{V:\text{nodes}(\mathcal{T}) \to [0,1]}$$

$$\frac{L_{\mathcal{P},V}(y)\ln(1/\beta) + |\mathcal{P}|\ln 3 + |\text{leaves}(\mathcal{T}) \cap \text{leaves}(\mathcal{P})|\ln 2}{2\ln(2/(1+\beta))}.$$

Finally we mention that, instead of searching for a good pruning with a good label function, we can seek for a good label function for the template tree to obtain the same mistake bound. In this case we can greatly simplify the algorithm putting the mini-experts only on the leaves of the template tree.

Let pruning $\mathcal{P}_m$ of $\mathcal{T}$ and label function V_m be those that minimize $L_{\mathcal{P},V}(y)$ for $y \in \{0,1\}^{\mathcal{T}}$. That is,

$$L_{\mathcal{P}_m,V_m}(y) = \min_{\mathcal{P} \in \text{PRUN}(\mathcal{T})} \min_{V:\text{nodes}(\mathcal{T}) \to [0,1]} L_{\mathcal{P},V}(y).$$

By Lemma 5 we can assume that V_m is a function from nodes($\mathcal{P}_m$) to $\{0,1\}$. On the other hand, it is easy to see that, if we define the label function V^* by $V^*(l') = V_m(l)$ for any leaf l' of $\mathcal{T}$ that is a descendant of l, then we have

$$L_{\mathcal{T},V^*}(y) = L_{\mathcal{P}_m,V_m}(y).$$

Since the loss of a decision tree $\mathcal{T}$ for a label function V is represented as

$$L_{\mathcal{T},V}(y) = \sum_{l \in \text{leaves}(\mathcal{T})} L_{l,V}(y)$$

and that the loss $L_{l,V}(y)$ at leaf l is independent of the labels $V(l')$ for leaves $l' \neq l$, we have

$$\min_{V:\text{leaves}(\mathcal{T})\to\{0,1\}} L_{\mathcal{T},V}(y) = \sum_{l \in \text{leaves}(\mathcal{T})} \min_{V:\{l\}\to\{0,1\}} L_{l,V}(y)$$
$$= L_{\mathcal{T},V^*}(y)$$

which says that, in order to find the best V^*, it suffices to find the best values (0 or 1) at each leaf l of $\mathcal{T}$ independently.

In this way the problem of minimizing $L_{\mathcal{P},V}(y)$ over label function V and pruning $\mathcal{P}$ of $\mathcal{T}$ can be reduced to the problem of minimizing $L_{\mathcal{T},V}(y)$ over label function V. We will give an algorithm that solves the latter minimization problem. To solve the problem, we associate two mini-experts $\mathcal{E} = \{\mathcal{E}_0, \mathcal{E}_1\}$ with each leaf l of $\mathcal{T}$, the one $\mathcal{E}_0$ who identically predicts 0 and the other $\mathcal{E}_1$ who identically predicts 1, and then place the aggregating algorithm $\text{AA}_l(\beta)$ at each leaf l which works for the instances that reach the leaf l.

Let a leaf l of $\mathcal{T}$ be fixed. Put the both initial weights of $\mathcal{E}_0$ and $\mathcal{E}_1$ to $1/2$. Since the losses that these experts suffer at each trial are 0 or 1, the weights of the experts depend on the number of times when the mini-experts make mistakes. More precisely, denoting the weights of $\mathcal{E}_0$ and $\mathcal{E}_1$ at the beginning of trial t by w_0^t and w_1^t, respectively, these weights are given by

$$w_0^t = w_0^1 \beta^{|N_{l,1}^t|}$$

and

$$w_1^t = w_1^1 \beta^{|N_{l,0}^t|},$$

where

$$N_{l,1}^t = \{t'|x_{t'} \text{ reaches } l \text{ and } y_{t'} = 1, 1 \leq t' < t\}$$

and

$$N_{l,0}^t = \{t'|x_{t'} \text{ reaches } l \text{ and } y_{t'} = 0, 1 \leq t' < t\}.$$

Then the weighted average r of the predictions of the experts is given by

$$r(0) = \log_\beta(\beta^{|N_{l,1}^t|} + \beta^{|N_{l,0}^t|+1}),$$
$$r(1) = \log_\beta(\beta^{|N_{l,1}^t|+1} + \beta^{|N_{l,0}^t|}),$$

where the re-normalization is skipped. Since the prediction output by the AA_l only depends on the difference

$$r(0) - r(1) = \log_\beta \frac{\beta^{|N_{l,1}^t|} + \beta^{|N_{l,0}^t|+1}}{\beta^{|N_{l,1}^t|+1} + \beta^{|N_{l,0}^t|}} = \log_\beta \frac{\beta^{|N_{l,1}^t|-|N_{l,0}^t|} + \beta}{\beta^{|N_{l,1}^t|-|N_{l,0}^t|+1} + 1},$$

the algorithm AA_l works well by only maintaining an integer $a = |N_{l,1}^t| - |N_{l,0}^t|$ rather than the weights. Theorem 2 says that the loss of AA_l for y is given by

$$L_{A_l}(y) \leq \min_{V:\{l\}\to\{0,1\}} \frac{L_{l,V}(y)\ln(1/\beta) + \ln 2}{2\ln(2/(1+\beta))}.$$

The complete algorithm, denoted A^*, that is competitive with the best pruning associated with the best label function is given as follows.

Algorithm 5 (prediction algorithm A^*)
$c := (\ln(1/\beta))/(2\ln(2/(1+\beta)))$
for $l \in \text{leaves}(\mathcal{T})$ **do**
  $a_l := 0$
for $t := 1, 2, \ldots$ **do**
  receive x_t
  $l := \text{leaf}_\mathcal{T}(x_t)$
  $\hat{y}_t = \mathbf{I}_0^1\left(\frac{1}{2} + \frac{c}{2}\log_\beta \frac{\beta^{a_l}+\beta}{\beta^{a_l+1}+1}\right)$
  output $\hat{y}_t$
  receive y_t
  if $y_t = 1$ **then**
    $a_l := a_l + 1$
  else
    $a_l := a_l - 1$

It is clear that

$$L_{A^*}(y) = \sum_{l\in\text{leaves}(\mathcal{T})} L_{A_l}(y)$$

$$\leq \sum_{l\in\text{leaves}(\mathcal{T})} \min_{V:\{l\}\to\{0,1\}} \frac{L_{l,V}(y)\ln(1/\beta) + \ln 2}{2\ln(2/(1+\beta))}$$

$$= \min_{V:\text{leaves}(\mathcal{T})\to\{0,1\}} \frac{L_{\mathcal{T},V}(y)\ln(1/\beta) + |\text{leaves}(\mathcal{T})|\ln 2}{2\ln(2/(1+\beta))}.$$

Thus we have the following theorem.

Theorem 6. *Let the absolute loss function be assumed. For any $\mathcal{T}$ and for any $y \in \{0,1\}^*$,*

$$L_{A^*}(y) \leq \min_{\mathcal{P}\in\text{PRUN}(\mathcal{T})} \min_{V:\text{nodes}(\mathcal{T})\to[0,1]} \frac{L_{\mathcal{P},V}(y)\ln(1/\beta) + |\text{leaves}(\mathcal{T})|\ln 2}{2\ln(2/(1+\beta))}.$$

Having constructed the prediction algorithm which is competitive with the best pruning as well as the best node labeling, you can see that the tree $\mathcal{T}$ could be thought of as specifying how to partition the instance space Σ^* into subclasses and how to assign a prediction value to each subclass. Because our algorithm does not use the internal structure of $\mathcal{T}$ but only uses the subclasses defined by $\mathcal{T}$, it can easily be generalized for any given rule that partitions the instance space into subclasses.

Acknowledgment

The authors would like to thank Volodya Vovk for sharing his insights that led to this work. We are also thankful Prof. Thomas Zeugmann for his patience.

References

1. N. Cesa-Bianchi, Y. Freund, D. Helmbold, D. Haussler, R. Schapire and M. Warmuth, How to use expert advice, JACM **44**(3) (1997) 427–485.
2. Y. Freund and R. E. Schapire, A decision-theoretic generalization of on-line learning and an application to boosting, in: P. Vitányi, ed., Computational Learning Theory, Lecture Notes in Computer Science, Vol. 904 (Springer, Berlin, 1995) 23–37. To appear in J. Computer System Sciences.
3. D. Helmbold and R. Schapire, Predicting nearly as well as the best pruning of a decision tree, Machine Learning, **27** (1997) 51–68.
4. M. Kearns and Y. Mansour, A fast, bottom-up decision tree pruning algorithm with near-optimal generalization, To appear in the Machine Learning Conference,
5. N. Littlestone and M. K. Warmuth, The weighted majority algorithm, Inform. Computation **108** (1994) 212–261.
6. E. Takimoto, K. Hirai and A. Maruoka, A simple algorithm for predicting nearly as well as the best pruning labeled with the best prediction values of a decision tree, in: M. Li and A. Maruoka, eds., Algorithmic Learning Theory, Lecture Notes in Artificial Intelligence, Vol. 1316 (1997) 385–400.
7. E. Takimoto, A. Maruoka and V. Vovk, Predicting nearly as well as the best pruning of a decision tree through dynamic programming scheme, submitted.
8. V. Vovk, Aggregating strategies, in: Proc. 3rd COLT (Morgan Kaufmann, San Mateo, CA, 1990) 371–383.
9. V. Vovk, A game of prediction with expert advice, accepted for publication in J. Comput. Inform. Syst. Short version in: Proc. 8th COLT (Assoc. Comput. Mach., New York, 1995) 51–60.
10. L. G. Valiant, A theory of the learnable, Comm. ACM27 (1084) 1134-1142.

Learning from Entailment of Logic Programs with Local Variables

M. R. K. Krishna Rao   and   A. Sattar

School of Computing and Information Technology
Faculty of Information and Communication Technology
Griffith University, Brisbane 4111, Australia.
e-mail: {krishna,sattar}@cit.gu.edu.au

Abstract. In this paper, we study exact learning of logic programs from entailment and present a polynomial time algorithm to learn a rich class of logic programs that allow local variables and include many standard programs like append, merge, split, delete, member, prefix, suffix, length, reverse, append/4 on lists, tree traversal programs on binary trees and addition, multiplication, exponentiation on natural numbers. Grafting a few aspects of incremental learning [9] onto the framework of learning from entailment [3], we generalize the existing results to allow local variables, which play an important role of sideways information passing in the paradigm of logic programming.

1   Introduction

Starting with the seminal work of Shapiro [16, 17], the problem of learning logic programs from examples and queries has attracted a lot of attention in the last fifteen years. Many techniques and systems for learning logic programs are developed and used in many applications. See [11] for a survey. In this paper, we consider the framework of *learning from entailment* [1-7,13,14] and present a polynomial time algorithm to learn a rich class of logic programs that allow local variables and include many standard programs from Sterling and Shapiro's book [18].

Our work has been inspired by the recent work of Arimura [3] presenting a polynomial time algorithm to learn a class of logic programs called acyclic constrained Horn programs. This class includes an impressive set of standard programs with recursion like append, merge, split, delete, member, prefix, suffix, length and add besides many nonrecursive programs. The main property of these programs is that all the terms in the body of a clause are subterms of the terms in the head. This means that local variables are not allowed. However, local variables play an important role of *sideways information passing* in the paradigm of logic programming and there is an urgent need to extend the results for classes of programs which allow local variables.

In this paper, we extend the results of Arimura [3] for one such class of programs, using moding annotations and background knowledge. Our background knowledge is nothing but a logic program already learnt, perhaps using the framework of learning from entailment itself. In other words, we graft a few aspects of incremental learning [9] to the framework of learning from entailment [3]. To summerize the results of this paper, (1) a class of logic programs as background knowledge is identified together with (2) a class of logic programs (called *finely-moded programs*) learnable in polynomial time from entailment is introduced, (3) some results about the complexity of subsumption and entailment problem for these classes are obtained and (4) a learning algorithm is presented. We also prove that the class of finely-moded programs properly contains the class of acyclic constrained Horn programs.

The rest of the paper is organized as follows. The next section gives preliminary definitions and section 3 defines the class of finely-moded programs and proves some characteristic properties of them. Section 4 presents a few results about subsumption and entailment and section 5 presents the learning algorithm for finely-moded programs. Section 6 provides correctness proof of the learning algorithm and section 7 concludes with a discussion.

2 Preliminaries

Assuming that the reader is familiar with the basic terminology of first order logic and logic programming [10], we use the first order logic language with a finite set Π of predicate symbols and a finite set Σ of function symbols. The arity of a predicate/function symbol f is denoted by $arity(f)$. Function symbols of arity zero are also called constants. The size of a term/atom/clause/program is defined as the number of (occurrences of) variables, predicate and function symbols in it.

Definition 1 A *mode* m of an n-ary predicate p is a function from $\{1, \cdots, n\}$ to the set $\{in, out\}$. The sets $in(p) = \{j \mid m(j) = in\}$ and $out(p) = \{j \mid m(j) = out\}$ are the sets of input and output positions of p respectively.

A moded program is a logic program with each predicate having a unique mode associated with it. In the following, $p(\mathbf{s}; \mathbf{t})$ denotes an atom with input terms $\mathbf{s}$ and output terms $\mathbf{t}$. The set of varaibles occuring in $\mathbf{t}$ is denoted by $Var(\mathbf{t})$.

Definition 2 A definite clause

$$p_0(\mathbf{s_0}; \mathbf{t_0}) \leftarrow p_1(\mathbf{s_1}; \mathbf{t_1}), \cdots, p_k(\mathbf{s_k}; \mathbf{t_k})$$

$k \geq 0$ is *well-moded* if (a) $Var(\mathbf{t_0}) \subseteq Var(\mathbf{s_0}, \mathbf{t_1}, \cdots, \mathbf{t_k})$ and (b) $Var(\mathbf{s_i}) \subseteq Var(\mathbf{s_0}, \mathbf{t_1}, \cdots, \mathbf{t_{i-1}})$ for each $i \in [1, k]$. A logic program is *well-moded* if each clause in it is well-moded.

The class of well-moded programs is extensively studied in the literature and the following lemma is one of the well-known facts about well-moded programs.

Lemma 1 Let P be a well-moded program and Q be the query $\leftarrow p(\mathbf{s}; \mathbf{t})$ with ground input terms $\mathbf{s}$. *If there is an SLD-refutation of $P \cup \{Q\}$ with θ as computed answer substitution then $\mathbf{t}\theta$ is ground as well.*

Definition 3 A predicate p defined in a well-moded program P is *deterministic* if $\mathbf{t}_1 \equiv \mathbf{t}_2$ whenever $P \models p(\mathbf{s}; \mathbf{t}_1)$ and $P \models p(\mathbf{s}; \mathbf{t}_2)$ for any sequence of ground input terms $\mathbf{s}$.

In this paper, we only consider deterministic well-moded programs. Without loss of generality, we assume that each predicate has at most one output position.[1]

3 Finely-Modeled Programs

As mentioned in the introduction, our learning algorithm takes a logic program as background knowledge. In this section, we present our assumptions about the background knowledge and the class of finely-moded programs.

Definition 4 Let program B be a background knowledge and t be a ground term. The *dependent set* $D_B(t)$ of t w.r.t. B is defined as

1. $t \in D_B(t)$,

2. if $u \in D_B(t)$ and $B \models p(\mathbf{s}; u)$ for some predicate p in B and ground input terms $\mathbf{s}$ then every term in $\mathbf{s}$ is in $D_B(t)$ and

3. if $u \in D_B(t)$ then every subterm of u is in $D_B(t)$.

The following lemma is useful in the sequel.

Lemma 2 Let t be a ground term. Then $D_B(s) \subseteq D_B(t)$ *if s is a subterm of t or $s \in D_B(t)$.*

Proof : Easy.   □

---

[1] A predicate symbol with $k > 1$ output positions can be replaced by a predicate symbol with 1 output position (and same number of input positions) using a k-tupling operator. An atom $p(s_1, \ldots, s_n; t_1, \ldots, t_k)$ with k output positions will be replaced by the corresponding atom $p'(s_1, \ldots, s_n; f(t_1, \ldots, t_k))$ with 1 output position, where f is a fresh function symbol of arity k.

Definition 5 A background knowledge B is *regular* if (a) for every ground term t, $|D_B(t)|$ is bounded by a polynomial in the size of t, and (b) the size of the SLD-tree for any query $\leftarrow A$ is bounded by a polynomial in the size of A.

Example 1 Consider the following append program.

```
moding: app(in,in, out).

app([ ],Ys,Ys) ←
app([X|Xs], Ys, [X|Zs]) ← app(Xs, Ys, Zs)
```

This program is *well-moded* and deterministic. For a list L, $D(L)$ is the set of sublists of L. The number of sublists[2] of a list L of length n is $(n+1)_{C_2}+1$, which is of the order $O(n^2)$. It is clear that the size of the SLD-tree for any query $\leftarrow A$ is bounded by a polynomial (in fact, linear) in the size of A. Therefore, B is *regular*. □

Example 2 It is easy to verify that standard programs for multiplication and addition can be served as regular background knowledge. □

In this paper, we only deal with regular background knowledge and use **B** to denote the background knowledge under consideration.

Now, we go about presenting the class of finely-moded programs. We partition Π into Π_0 and Π_1 such that Π_0 contains the predicate symbols (say, k_0) defined in **B** and Π_1 contains the rest of the predicate symbols (say, k_1). We assume that maximum arity of a predicate symbol in Π is k_2.

Definition 6 A well-moded clause

$$p_0(s_0; t_0) \leftarrow p_1(s_1; t_1), \cdots, p_n(s_n; t_n)$$

$n \geq 0$ is *finely-moded* if there is an integer $m \in [1, n]$ such that

1. predicate symbols $p_1, \cdots, p_m$ are in Π_1 and $p_{m+1}, \cdots, p_n$ are in Π_0,

2. for each $i \in [1, m]$, every term in s_i is a subterm of a term in s_0 and t_i is either a subterm of t_0 or a (local) variable occurring in $s_{m+1}, \cdots, s_n$ and

3. for each $i \in [m+1, n]$, t_i is a subterm of t_0 and every term in s_i is either a subterm of a term in s_0 or a (local) variable in $t_1, \cdots, t_m$.

Definition 7 A well-moded program P is *finely-moded* if each clause in it is finely-moded.

---

[2] Basically, a non-empty sublist of L can be identified by its two end-points. The number of possible ways of choosing two distinct points on a line with $n+1$ points is $(n+1)_{C_2}$. Therefore, the number of sublists of a list L of length n is $(n+1)_{C_2}+1$.

Example 3 The following program for multiplication is finely-moded w.r.t. the regular background knowledge about addition.

moding: a(in,in, out) and m(in,in, out).

a$(0,$ Y, Y$)$ ←
a$($s$($X$),$ Y, s$($Z$))$ ← a$($X, Y, Z$)$

m$(0,$ Y, $0)$ ←
m$($s$($X$),$ Y, Z$)$ ← m$($X, Y, Z1$),$ a$($Y, Z1, Z$)$

Example 4 The following program for reverse is finely-moded w.r.t. the regular background knowledge about append-last.

moding: app-last(in,in, out) and rev(in, out).

app-last$($[ ], Y, [Y]$)$ ←
app-last$($[X|Xs], Y, [X|Zs]$)$ ← app-last$($Xs,Y, Zs$)$

rev$($[ ],[ ]$)$ ←
rev$($[X|Xs], Zs$)$ ← rev$($Xs, Ys$),$ app-last$($Ys,X, Zs$)$

We present two characteristic theorems about finely-moded programs below. In view of the background knowledge, we adapt SLD-computations as follows.

Definition 8 Let **B** be a regular background knowledge, P be a finely-moded program and Q be a query ← $p(s; t)$ with ground input terms s. An adapted SLD-derivation of $P \cup \{Q\}$ is a sequence of queries $Q_0 = Q, Q_1, Q_2, \ldots$ such that each Q_i, $i > 0$ satisfies one of the following:

1. Q_{i-1} is ← $A_1, \ldots, A_n$, the predicate symbol of the selected atom A_1 is in Π_1, the head H of a clause $H \leftarrow B_1, \ldots, B_m$ in P unifies with A_1 through a most general unifier σ and Q_i is

$$\leftarrow B_1\sigma, \ldots, B_m\sigma, A_2\sigma, \ldots, A_n\sigma.$$

2. Q_{i-1} is ← $A_1, \ldots, A_n$, the predicate symbol of the selected atom A_1 is in Π_0, **B** $\models A_1\sigma$ and Q_i is

$$\leftarrow A_2\sigma, \ldots, A_n\sigma.$$

An adapted SLD-derivation $Q_0, \ldots, Q_n$ is called an adapted SLD-refutation if Q_n is an empty query. The notion of an adapted SLD-tree is defined similarly.

The following two theorems are characteristic facts about finely-moded programs.

Theorem 1 Let **B** be a regular background knowledge, P be a finely-moded program and Q be a ground query $\leftarrow p(\mathbf{s};t)$ with predicate $p \in \Pi_1$. Then *every input term of any atom* $q(\mathbf{u};v)$ *in an adapted SLD-derivation of* $P \cup \{Q\}$ *is a subterm of a term in* $\mathbf{s}$ *if* $q \in \Pi_1$.

Proof : Induction on the length l of the adapted SLD-derivation. Use the fact that input terms of an atom with predicate in Π_1 in the body of a finely-moded clause are subterms of the input terms of its head. $\qquad\square$

Theorem 2 Let **B** be a regular background knowledge, P be a finely-moded program and Q be a ground query $\leftarrow p(\mathbf{s};t)$ with predicate $p \in \Pi_1$. *If* $q(\mathbf{u};v)$ *is an atom in any adapted SLD-refutation of* $P \cup \{Q\}$ *with answer substitution* θ *and* $q \in \Pi_0$ *then* $v\theta \in D_B(t)$.

Proof : Induction on the length l of the adapted SLD-refutation.

Basis : $l = 1$. There is nothing to prove in this case.

Induction Hypothesis : Assume that the theorem holds for all SLD-refutations of length $l < k$.

Induction Step : Now, we establish that it holds for $l = k$. Let $p_0(\mathbf{s_0};t_0) \leftarrow p_1(\mathbf{s_1};t_1), \cdots, p_n(\mathbf{s_n};t_n)$ be the input clause used in the first resolution step. There are two cases: (1) all predicate symbols $p_1, \cdots, p_n$ are in Π_1 or (2) there is an $m < n$ such that $p_1, \ldots, p_m$ are in Π_1 and $p_{m+1}, \ldots, p_n$ are in Π_0.

Case (1): By the definition of finely-moded clauses, each term in $\mathbf{s_1}, \cdots, \mathbf{s_n}$ is a subterm of a term in $\mathbf{s_0}$ and each t_i is a subterm of t_0. Since Q is a ground query, $\mathbf{s_0}\theta \equiv \mathbf{s}$ and $t_0\theta \equiv t$ and hence each atom $p_i(\mathbf{s_i};t_i)\theta$ is ground. It is easy to see that each atom in the adapted SLD-refutation of $P \cup \{Q\}$ is also an atom in an adapted SLD-refutation of $P \cup \{\leftarrow p_i(\mathbf{s_i};t_i)\theta\}$ for some $i \in [1,n]$. The length of the adapted SLD-refutation of $P \cup \{\leftarrow p_i(\mathbf{s_i};t_i)\theta\}$ is clearly less than k and by the induction hypothesis, $v\theta \in D_B(t_i\theta) \subseteq D_B(t)$ for each atom $q(\mathbf{u};v)$ in any adapted SLD-refutation of $P \cup \{\leftarrow p_i(\mathbf{s_i};t_i)\theta\}$ if $q \in \Pi_0$.

Case (2): We have 2 subcases: $m = 0$ and $m > 0$. In the former subcase, there are no local variables and $t_1, \cdots, t_n$ are subterms of t_0. Further, $p_1(\mathbf{s_1};t_1)\theta, \cdots, p_n(\mathbf{s_n};t_n)\theta$ are the only atoms in the adapted SLD-refutation of $P \cup \{Q\}$. Since Q is a ground query, $\mathbf{s_0}\theta \equiv \mathbf{s}$ and $t_0\theta \equiv t$. Hence, output terms of these atoms are subterms of t and therefore members of $D_B(t)$.

Now, consider the subcase $m > 0$. By the definition of finely-moded clauses, $t_{m+1}, \ldots, t_n$ are subterms of t_0 and hence $t_{m+1}\theta, \ldots, t_n\theta$ are subterms of $t_0\theta = t$ and therefore members of $D_B(t)$. For each atom $q(\mathbf{u};v)$ (not a member of $p_{m+1}(\mathbf{s_{m+1}};t_{m+1})\theta, \cdots, p_n(\mathbf{s_n};t_n)\theta$) in the adapted SLD-refutation of $P \cup \{Q\}$ with $q \in \Pi_0$, it is clear that $q(\mathbf{u};v)\theta$ is an atom in an adapted SLD-refutation of $P \cup \{\leftarrow p_i(\mathbf{s_i};t_i)\theta\}$, for some $i \in [1,m]$. The length of the adapted SLD-refutation of $P \cup \{\leftarrow p_i(\mathbf{s_i};t_i)\theta\}$ is clearly less than k and by the induction hypothesis, $v\theta \in D_B(t_i\theta)$. Now, we prove that $D_B(t_i\theta) \subseteq D_B(t)$ for each $i \in [1,m]$. By the definition of finely-moded clauses, $t_1, \ldots, t_m$ are subterms of terms in $t_0, \mathbf{s_{m+1}}, \ldots, \mathbf{s_n}$. If t_i is a subterm of t_0 then $D_B(t_i\theta) \subseteq D_B(t_0\theta) = D_B(t)$. Consider the case that t_i is a subterm of a term in $\mathbf{s_{m+j}}$ for some $j \in [1, n-m]$. Since $\mathbf{B} \models p_{m+j}(\mathbf{s_{m+j}}; t_{m+j})\theta$, it follows that each term in $\mathbf{s_{m+j}}\theta$ is a member of $D_B(t_{m+j}\theta) \subseteq D_B(t_0\theta) = D_B(t)$. Therefore, $D_B(t_i\theta) \subseteq D_B(t)$ as t_i is a subterm of a term in $\mathbf{s_{m+j}}$. $\qquad\square$

It may be noted that unlike Theorem 1, this Theorem does not hold for any arbitrary adapted SLD-derivation, but holds only for SLD-refutations. In particular, it does not hold if $P \not\models p(\mathbf{s}; t)\theta$.

4 Subsumption and Entailment

Definition 9 Let C_1 and C_2 be clauses $H_1 \leftarrow Body_1$ and $H_2 \leftarrow Body_2$ respectively. We say C_1 *subsumes* C_2 and write $C_1 \succeq C_2$ if there exists a substitution θ such that $H_1\theta \equiv H_2$ and $Body_1\theta \subseteq Body_2$.

Definition 10 A program P_1 is a *refinement* of program P_2, denoted by $P_1 \sqsubseteq P_2$ if $(\forall C_1 \in P_1)(\exists C_2 \in P_2)C_2 \succeq C_1$. Further, P_1 is a *conservative refinement* of P_2 if P_1 is a refinement of P_2 and each C in P_2 has at most one $C' \in P_1$ such that $C \succeq C'$.

Definition 11 A program P *entails* a clause C, denoted by $P \models C$, if C is a logical consequence of P.

The relation between subsumption and entailment is discussed below.

Definition 12 A *derivation* of a clause C from a program P is a finite sequence of clauses $C_1, \ldots, C_k = C$ such that each C_i is either an instance of a clause in P or a resolvent of two clauses in $C_1, \ldots, C_{i-1}$. If such a derivation exists, we write $P \vdash_d C$.

The following theorem is proved in Nienhuys-Cheng and de Wolf [12].

Theorem 3 (Subsumption Theorem)
Let P be a program and C be a clause. Then $P \models C$ *if and only if one of the following holds:*
(1) C is a tautology or
(2) there exists a clause D such that $P \vdash_d D$ and D subsumes C.

When C is ground, the above theorem can be reformulated as follows.

Theorem 4 Let P be a program and C be a ground clause $A \leftarrow B_1, \cdots, B_n$. Then $P \models C$ *if and only if one of the following holds.*
(1) C is a tautology.
(2) C is subsumed by a clause in P.
(3) There is a minimal SLD-refutation of $P' \cup \{\leftarrow A\}$, where
$$P' = P \cup \{B_i \leftarrow \; \mid \; i \in [1, n]\}.$$

Definition 13 An SLD-refutation is *minimal* if selected atoms are resolved with unit clauses whenever possible.

Even though (2) is covered by (3) in the above theorem, we explicitly mention (2) in view of its importance in our learning algorithm.

Lemma 3 If C_1 and C_2 are two finely-moded clauses, $C_1 \succeq C_2$ is decidable in polynomial time over the sizes of C_1 and C_2.

5   Learning Algorithm

In this section, we present an algorithm **Learn-FM** for exact learning of **terminating** finely-moded programs from entailment using equivalence, subsumption and request-for-hint queries. The oracle (teacher) answers 'yes' to an *entailment equivalence query* $EQUIV(H)$ if H is equivalent to the target program H^*, i.e., $H \models H^*$ and $H^* \models H$. Otherwise, it produces a ground atom A such that $H^* \models A$ but $H \not\models A$ or $H^* \not\models A$ but $H \models A$. A *subsumption query* $SUBSUME(C)$ produces an answer 'yes' if the clause C is subsumed by a clause in H^*, otherwise answer 'no'. When C is a ground clause $A \leftarrow B_1, \cdots, B_n$ such that $H^* \models C$, the request-for-hint query $REQ(C)$ returns (1) an answer 'subsumed' if C is subsumed by a clause in H^*, otherwise returns (2) an atom (hint) $B\theta$ in a minimal adapted SLD-refutation of $H' \cup \{\leftarrow A\}$ with answer substitution θ such that $B\theta \notin \{B_1, \cdots, B_n\}$, where $H' = H^* \cup \{B_i \leftarrow \ | \ i \in [1,n]\}$.

Algorithm **Learn-FM** uses the notions of saturation [8, 15] and least general generalization.

Definition 14 A clause C is a saturation of an example E w.r.t. a theory (program) H if and only if C is a reformulation of E w.r.t. H and $C' \Rightarrow C$ for every reformulation C' of E w.r.t. H. A clause D is a reformulation of E w.r.t. H if and only if $H \wedge E \Leftrightarrow H \wedge D$.

We are concerned with finely-moded programs and clauses and define saturation of an example $E \equiv p_0(\mathbf{s_0}; t_0)$ w.r.t. H as $E \leftarrow Closure_H(E)$, where $Closure_H(E) = S_1 \cup S_2$ such that S_1 is the set of ground atoms $\{p(\mathbf{s};t) \mid p \in \Pi_1,$ each term in $\mathbf{s}$ is a subterm of a term in $\mathbf{s_0}$ and $H \models p(\mathbf{s};t)\}$ and S_2 is the set of ground atoms $\{q(\mathbf{u};v) \mid q \in \Pi_0, v$ is a subterm of $t_0, H \models q(\mathbf{u};v)$ and each term in $\mathbf{u}$ is either a subterm of a term in $\mathbf{s_0}$ or an output term of an atom in $S_1\}$.

Definition 15 Let C_1 and C_2 be two finely-moded clauses $A_1 \leftarrow Body_1$ and $A_2 \leftarrow Body_2$ respectively. The least general generalization $C_1 \sqcup C_2$ of C_1 and C_2 is defined as a finely-moded clause $A \leftarrow Body$ such that (1) $A \equiv p_0(\mathbf{s_0}; t_0)$ is the least general generalization of A_1 and A_2 and $A_i \equiv A\sigma_i, i \in [1,2]$, (2) $Body = S_1 \cup S_2$ is the largest set of atoms such that (a) $S_1 = \{p(\mathbf{s};t) \mid p \in \Pi_1,$ $p(\mathbf{s};t)\sigma_i \in Body_i, i \in [1,2]$, each term in $\mathbf{s}$ is a subterm of a term in $\mathbf{s_0}$ and t is either a subterm of t_0 or a local variable} and (b) $S_2 = \{p(\mathbf{s};t) \mid p \in \Pi_0,$ $p(\mathbf{s};t)\sigma_i \in Body_i, i \in [1,2], t$ is a subterm of t_0 and each term in $\mathbf{s}$ is either a subterm of a term in $\mathbf{s_0}$ or an output variable (local) of an atom in $S_1\}$.

Now, we are in a position to present our algorithm **Learn-FM**.

Procedure **Learn-FM**;
begin $H := \mathbf{B}$;
while $EQUIV(H) \neq$ 'yes' **do**
  begin $A := EQUIV(H)$;
    $C := A \leftarrow Closure_H(A)$;
    while $REQ(C)$ returns a hint B **do** $C := B \leftarrow Closure_H(B)$;
    % This **while** loop exits when C is subsumed by a clause in H^*. %
    $C := \mathbf{Reduce}(C)$;
    if $SUBSUME(C \sqcup D)$ returns 'yes' for some clause $D \in H$ **then**
        generalize H by replacing D with $\mathbf{Reduce}(C \sqcup D)$
      else generalize H by adding C to H
  end;
$Return(H)$
end Learn-FM;

Function **Reduce**($A \leftarrow Body$);
% Removes irrelevant literals in the body of a clause. %
begin
    for each atom $B \in Body$ **do**
        if $SUBSUME(A \leftarrow (Body - \{B\}))$ **then** $Body := (Body - \{B\})$;
    $Return(A \leftarrow Body)$
end Reduce;

Remark: It may be noted the application of the above function **Reduce** (from Reddy and Tadepalli [14]) is not mandatory for the correctness of the algorithm **Learn-FM**, but it improves the efficiency. In particular, checking subsumption of reduced clauses is easier than that of non-reduced clauses.

Lemma 4 If a clause C is subsumed by a clause in the target program H^* then **Reduce**(C) $= C'\theta$ for some clause C' in H^* and a substitution θ.

Example 5 We illustrate the working of **Learn-FM** by considering the standard multiplication program given in Example 3. The program for addition is given as the background knowledge **B**. For presentation purposes, we consider counterexamples of small size. **Learn-FM** starts with $H = \mathbf{B}$ as the initial hypothesis and query $EQUIV(H)$ returns a counterexample, say $A = \mathbf{m(s(s(0)), s(s(0)), s(s(s(s(0)))))}$.

The inner **while** loop asks $REQ(A \leftarrow Body)$, where $Body = \mathbf{a(0,0,0)}$, $\mathbf{a(0,s(0),s(0))}$, $\mathbf{a(s(0),0,s(0))}$, $\mathbf{a(0,s(s(0)),s(s(0)))}$, $\mathbf{a(s(s(0)),0,}$ $\mathbf{s(s(0)))}$, $\mathbf{a(s(0),s(0),s(s(0)))}$, $\mathbf{a(s(0),s(s(0)),s(s(s(0))))}$, $\mathbf{a(s(s(0)),s(0),s(s(s(0))))}$, $\mathbf{a(s(s(0)),s(s(0)),s(s(s(s(0)))))}$.

This results in a hint $m(0, s(s(0)), 0)$. Now, the inner **while** loop asks $REQ(m(0, s(s(0)), 0) \leftarrow a(0, 0, 0))$, which returns answer 'subsumed'. The function **Reduce** is applied to the clause $m(0, s(s(0)), 0) \leftarrow a(0, 0, 0)$ and **the resulting clause $C_0 : m(0, s(s(0)), 0) \leftarrow$ is added to H.**

The outer **while** loop asks $EQUIV(H)$ and gets a counterexample, say $A_1 = m(s(0), s(s(0)), s(s(0)))$. The inner **while** loop asks $REQ(A_1 \leftarrow Body_1)$, where $Body_1 = m(0, s(s(0)), 0)$, $a(0, 0, 0)$, $a(0, s(0), s(0))$, $a(s(0), 0, s(0))$, $a(0, s(s(0)), s(s(0)))$, $a(s(s(0)), 0, s(s(0)))$, $a(s(0), s(0), s(s(0)))$. The query $REQ(A_1 \leftarrow Body_1)$ returns answer 'subsumed' and **Reduce**$(A_1 \leftarrow Body_1)$ is the clause $C_1 : m(s(0), s(s(0)), s(s(0))) \leftarrow m(0, s(s(0)), 0), a(s(s(0)), 0, s(s(0)))$. **The clause C_1 is added to H as $SUBSUME(C_0 \sqcup C_1)$ returns 'no.'**

The outer **while** loop asks $EQUIV(H)$ and gets a counterexample, say $A_2 = m(s(s(0)), s(s(0)), s(s(s(0))))$. The inner **while** loop asks $REQ(A_2 \leftarrow Body_2)$, where $Body_2 = m(0, s(s(0)), 0)$, $m(s(0), s(s(0)), s(s(0)))$, $a(0, 0, 0)$, $a(0, s(0), s(0))$, $a(0, s(s(0)), s(s(0)))$, $a(s(s(0)), 0, s(s(0)))$ $a(s(0), 0, s(0))$, $a(s(0), s(0), s(s(0)))$, $a(s(0), s(s(0)), s(s(s(0))))$, $a(s(s(0)), s(0), s(s(s(0))))$, $a(s(s(0)), s(s(0)), s(s(s(s(0)))))$. The query $REQ(A_2 \leftarrow Body_2)$ returns answer 'subsumed' and **Reduce**$(A_2 \leftarrow Body_2)$ is the clause $m(s(s(0)), s(s(0)), s(s(s(0)))) \leftarrow m(s(0), s(s(0)), s(s(0)))$, $a(s(s(0)), s(s(0)), s(s(s(0)))))$. The lgg of this clause and C_1 is $C_3 : m(s(X), s(s(0)), s(s(Z))) \leftarrow m(X, s(s(0)), Z1), a(s(s(0)), Z1, s(s(Z)))$. The query $SUBSUME(C_3)$ returns answer 'yes' and **clause C_1 in H is replaced by C_3.**

The outer **while** loop asks $EQUIV(H)$ and gets a counterexample, say $m(s(0), s(0), s(0))$. The inner **while** loop asks $REQ(m(s(0), s(0), s(0)) \leftarrow a(0, 0, 0)$, $a(0, s(0), s(0)), a(s(0), 0, s(0)))$, which returns a hint $m(0, s(0), 0)$. Then inner **while** loop asks $REQ(m(0, s(0), 0) \leftarrow a(0, 0, 0))$, which returns answer 'subsumed' and **Reduce**$(m(0, s(0), 0) \leftarrow a(0, 0, 0))$ is $m(0, s(0), 0) \leftarrow$. The lgg of this clause and C_0 is $C_4 : m(0, Y, 0) \leftarrow$. As $SUBSUME(C_4)$ returns answer 'yes,' **clause C_0 in H is replaced by C_4.**

The outer **while** loop asks $EQUIV(H)$ and (say) gets the above counterexample $m(s(0), s(0), s(0))$. The inner **while** loop asks $REQ(m(s(0), s(0), s(0)) \leftarrow m(0, s(0), 0), a(0, 0, 0), a(0, s(0), s(0)), a(s(0), 0, s(0)))$, which returns answer 'subsumed.' An application of **Reduce** returns the clause $m(s(0), s(0), s(0)) \leftarrow m(0, s(0), 0), a(s(0), 0, s(0))$. The lgg of this clause and C_3 is $C_5 : m(s(U), s(V), s(W)) \leftarrow m(U, s(V), Z1), a(s(V), Z1, s(W))$. The query $SUBSUME(C_5)$ returns answer 'yes' and **clause C_3 in H is replaced by C_5.**

The outer **while** loop asks $EQUIV(H)$ and gets a counterexample, say $m(s(s(s(0))), 0, 0)$. The inner **while** loop asks $REQ(m(s(s(s(0))), 0, 0) \leftarrow m(0, 0, 0), a(0, 0, 0))$, which returns a hint $m(s(0), 0, 0)$. Then inner **while** loop asks $REQ(m(s(0), 0, 0) \leftarrow m(0, 0, 0), a(0, 0, 0))$, which returns answer 'subsumed' and **Reduce** does not delete any literal but returns the same clause. The lgg of this clause and C_5 is $C_6 : m(s(X), Y, Z) \leftarrow m(X, Y, Z1), a(Y, Z1, Z)$. The query

$SUBSUME(C_6)$ returns answer 'yes' and **clause C_5 in H is replaced by** C_6. The algorithm terminates as the query $EQUIV(H)$ returns answer 'yes' and the final program learnt is the following.

$$m(0, Y, 0) \leftarrow$$
$$m(s(X), Y, Z) \leftarrow m(X, Y, Z1), a(Y, Z1, Z) \qquad \square$$

6   Correctness of the Learning Algorithm

First we prove that oracle answers all the three types of queries in polynomial time.

Lemma 5 The query $SUBSUME(C)$ can be answered in polynomial time over the size of the target program and the size of C.

Proof : Follows from Lemma 3. $\qquad \square$

Lemma 6 The query $EQUIV(H)$ can be answered in polynomial time over the size of the target program and the size of H.

Proof : This can be done by checking that each clause in H is subsumed by a clause in the target program H^* and each clause in H^* is subsumed by a clause in H. Each such subsumption check can be done in polynomial time and hence $EQUIV(H)$ can be answered in polynomial time. $\qquad \square$

Before proving that the query $REQ(A \leftarrow Closure_H(A))$ can be answered in polynomial time over the size of the target program and the size of A, we prove that the clause $A \leftarrow Closure_H(A)$ can be constructed in polynomial time over the size of A.

Lemma 7 If A is a ground atom then $|Closure_H(A)|$ is bounded by a polynomial over $|A|$.

Proof : Let n be the size of A. By definition, each input term of an atom $p(\cdots) \in Closure_H(A)$ with $p \in \Pi_1$ is a subterm of an input term of A. The number of subterms of a term is bounded by its size. Since H is a deterministic program, the sequence of input terms of an atom uniquely determines the output term. Therefore, the number of atoms $p(\cdots) \in Closure_H(A)$ with $p \in \Pi_1$ is bounded by $k_1 n^{k_2}$, a polynomial in n. By definition, output term of an atom $p(\cdots) \in Closure_H(A)$ with $p \in \Pi_0$ is a subterm of the output term of A. Since the back ground knowledge $\mathbf{B}$ is regular, the number of atoms $p(\mathbf{u}; v)$ such that $\mathbf{B} \models p(\mathbf{u}; v)$ is bounded by a polynomial over the size of v. Therefore, $|Closure_H(A)|$ is bounded by a polynomial over the size of A. $\qquad \square$

Lemma 8 Let A be either a positive example returned by an equivalence query or a hint returned by a request-for-hint query. The query $REQ(A \leftarrow Closure_H(A))$ can be answered in polynomial time over the size of the target program and the size of A.

Proof : It is easy to see that $H^* \models A$ if A is a positive example or A is a hint returned by a request-for-hint query. Therefore, there is an adapted SLD-refutation of $H^* \cup \{\leftarrow A\}$ with answer substitution θ such that each atom $p(\mathbf{u}; v)$ in it satisfies (a) $p \in \Pi_1$ and each term in $\mathbf{u}$ is a subterm of an input term of A or (b) $p \in \Pi_0$ and $v\theta \in D_B(t)$. Let S be the set of all atoms of the form $p(\mathbf{u}; v)$ such that $H^* \models p(\mathbf{u}; v)$ and either (1) $p \in \Pi_1$ and each term in $\mathbf{u}$ is a subterm of an input term of A or (2) $p \in \Pi_0$ and $v \in D_B(t)$. Note that each atom in S need not be there in any adapted SLD-refutation of $H^* \cup \{\leftarrow A\}$, though the converse holds. Since $|D_B(t)|$ is bounded by a polynomial over $|t|$, it follows that $|S|$ is bounded by a polynomial over the size of A and we can compute S in polynomial time over the size of A in a bottom-up fashion. Now, we can construct an adapted SLD-refutation of $H^* \cup \{\leftarrow A\}$ in polynomial time by resolving each selected atom with a ground instance of a clause whose body-atoms are all members of S. □.

Remark: It may be noted that the main idea of the above proof, namely, bottom-up construction of potential atoms in an SLD-refutation, can be used for proving Lemma 5 of Arimura [3]. That lemma is very important for the results of [3], but the proof given there is wrong in the following respect. In their lemma, an attempt is made to prove that entailment problem $H \models C$ is polynomial solvable for acyclic constrained Horn programs. They Skolemize $C = A \leftarrow Body$ by applying a Skolem substitution σ, construct the set $ground_\sigma(H)$ of all the ground clauses obtained from H by substituting for the variables in H arbitrary subterms of the head $A\sigma$ and check whether $ground_\sigma(H) \models C\sigma$ or not. They *incorrectly* claim that $size(ground_\sigma(H))$ is bounded by a polynomial in $size(H)$ and $size(C)$. The upper bound on the number of variables in H is a linear function over $size(H)$ (it is easy to that a term of size n can have $n - 1$ variables). The number of subterms of the head $A\sigma$ is bounded by $size(A\sigma)$, which is again a linear function over $size(C)$. Each variable can be substituted by any of these subterms. Therefore, $size(ground_\sigma(H))$ is bounded by $size(C)^{size(H)}$, which is not a polynomial in $size(H)$ but an exponential in $size(H)$.

We now proceed onto the correctness proof of **Learn-FM**. Let H^* be the target program, $H_0, H_1, \cdots$ be the sequence of hypotheses proposed in the equivalence queries and $A_1, A_2, \cdots$ be the sequence of counterexamples returned by those queries.

Theorem 5 For each $i \geq 0$, hypothesis H_i is a conservative refinement of H^* and counterexample A_{i+1} is positive.

Proof : Proof by induction on i. For $i = 0$, H_i is **B** and the theorem obviously holds. We prove the theorem holds for $i = m$ if it holds for $i = m - 1$. Consider m^{th} iteration of the main **while** loop. Since A is a positive counterexample, $H^* \models A$ and hence $H^* \models A \leftarrow Closure_{H_{m-1}}(A)$. Each hint B is an atom in an adapted SLD-refutation of $H' \cup \{\leftarrow A\}$ where $H' = H^* \cup \{B' \leftarrow \ \ | \ B' \in Closure_{H_{m-1}}(A)\}$. By induction hypothesis, H_{m-1} is a conservative refinement of H^* and hence $H^* \models B'$ for each $B' \in Closure_{H_{m-1}}(A)$. Therefore each hint

B is an atom in an adapted SLD-refutation of $H^* \cup \{\leftarrow A\}$ and $H^* \models B \leftarrow Closure_H(B)$. By definition, $H \not\models B$ for any hint B. That is, $H^* \models C$ and $H_{m-1} \not\models C$ for each clause C considered in this iteration, in particular for the clause C at the exit of the inner **while** loop. We have two cases: (a) there is a clause $D \in H_{m-1}$ such that $C \sqcup D$ is subsumed by a clause $C^* \in H^*$ and $H_m = H_{m-1} \cup \{\mathbf{Reduce}(C \sqcup D)\} - D$ or (b) there is no such clause D and $H_m = H_{m-1} \cup \{C\}$.

By hypothesis, H_{m-1} is a conservative refinement of H^* and it is easy to see that H_m is a conservative refinement of H^* in case (b). Consider case (a) now. Since H_{m-1} is a conservative refinement of H^*, D is the unique clause in H_{m-1} subsumed by C^*. As H_m is obtained from H_{m-1} by replacing D with $\mathbf{Reduce}(C \sqcup D)$, it is clear that H_m is a conservative refinement of H^*. Since each hypothesis is a refinement, each counterexample is positive. □

Now, we establish polynomial time complexity of the learning algorithm **Learn-FM**.

Lemma 9 If C is a clause of size n, then the sequence $C = C_0 \prec C_1 \prec C_2 \prec \cdots$ is of length no more than $2n$.

Proof: When $C_i \prec C_{i+1}$, one of the following holds: (1) $size(C_{i+1}) = size(C_i)$ and $|Var(C_{i+1})| > |Var(C_i)|$, i.e., a constant or an occurrence of a variable (which occurs in C_i more than once) is replaced by a new variable or (2) $size(C_{i+1}) < size(C_i)$. The change (1) can occur at most n times as the number of variables in a clause is less than its size. The change (2) can occur at most n times as the size of any clause is positive. □

Theorem 6 For any counterexample A of size n, the inner **while** loop of **Learn-FM** iterates for no more than $k_1 n^{k_2}$ (a polynomial in n) times.

Proof: Since each hint B is an atom in an adapted SLD-refutation of $H^* \cup \{\leftarrow A\}$, the input terms of B are subterms of the input terms of A by Theorem 1. There are at most $k_1 n^{k_2}$ such atoms. As the target program H^* is a terminating program, no atom B is returned as hint more than once. Therefore the inner **while** loop iterates for no more than $k_1 n^{k_2}$ times. □

Theorem 7 The algorithm **Learn-FM** exactly identifies any finely-moded program with m clauses in a polynomial time over m and n, where n is the size of the largest counterexample provided.

Proof: Termination condition of the main **while** loop is $H \leftrightarrow H^*$. Therefore **Learn-FM** exactly identifies the target program H^* if **Learn-FM** terminates. Now, we prove that the number of iterations of the main **while** loop is bounded by a polynomial over m and n.

By Theorem 5, H is always a conservative refinement of H^* and hence H has at most m clauses. The size of each clause in H is bounded by a polynomial in n by Lemma 7. Each iteration of the main **while** loop either adds a clause to

H or generalizes a clause in H. By Lemma 9, the number of times a clause can be generalized is bounded by twice the size of the clause. Therefore, the number of iterations of the main **while** loop is bounded by $m.poly(n)$, where $poly(n)$ is a polynomial in n. Each iteration takes polynomial time as (1) saturation and lgg are polynomial time computable, (2) each query is answered in polynomial time and (3) by Theorem 6, the number of iterations of the inner **while** loop is bounded by a polynomial in n. Therefore, **Learn-FM** exactly identifies any finely-moded program with m clauses in a polynomial time over m and n.　□

7　Discussion

In this paper, we studied exact learning of logic programs from entailment and presented a polynomial time algorithm to learn a rich class of logic programs that allow local variables and include many standard programs from Sterling and Shapiro's book [18].

The following theorem establishes that the class of acyclic constrained Horn programs is properly contained in the class of finely-moded programs and our main result is a generalization of the main result of [3].

Theorem 8 Every acyclic constrained Horn program is a terminating finely-moded program with respect to the moding in which every predicate has no output position.

Proof : By acyclicity, every acyclic constrained Horn program is a terminating program. Now we prove that any acyclic constrained Horn clause $p_0(s_0) \leftarrow p_1(s_1), \cdots, p_n(s_n)$ is finely-moded. Only condition (2) of the definition of finely-moded clauses is relevent as no predicate has any output position. Condition (2) requires that each term in $s_1, \cdots, s_m$ is a subterm of a term in s_0 and this is true of any acyclic constrained Horn clause.　□

As in [3], we can replace request-for-hint queries with membership queries to learn a class of finely-moded programs whose termination can be proved using a particular well-founded ordering.

Reddy and Tadepalli [14] independently studied exact learning of logic programs with local variables from entailment and introduced the class of acyclic Horn (AH) programs. The main restriction AH-programs is that each term occurring in the head of a clause is a subterm of a term in the body. This is a strong restriction from the programming point of view and excludes even simple programs like append and member. However, Reddy and Tadepalli [14] argue that the class of acyclic Horn (AH) programs is quite useful for representing planning knowledge. Further, they do not need moding annotations.

Acknowledgements: The authors wish to acknowledge the financial support from the Australian Research Council (ARC) under the ARC Large Grant Scheme (No. A49601783).

References

1. D. Angluin (1988), *Learning with hints*, Proc. COLT'88, pp. 223-237.
2. D. Angluin (1988), *Queries and concept learning*, Machine Learning **2**, pp. 319-342.
3. H. Arimura (1997), *Learning acyclic first-order Horn sentences from entailment*, Proc. ALT'97, Lecture Notes in Artificial intelligence **1316**, pp. 432-445.
4. W. Cohen and H. Hirsh (1992), *Learnability of description logics*, Proc. COLT'92, pp. 116-127.
5. S. Dzeroski, S. Muggleton and S. Russel (1992), *PAC-learnability of determinate logic programs*, Proc. of COLT'92, pp. 128-135.
6. M. Frazier and L. Pitt (1993), *Learning from entailment: an application to propositional Horn sentences*, Proc. ICML'93, pp. 120-127.
7. M. Frazier and L. Pitt (1994), *CLASSIC learning*, Proc. COLT'94, pp. 23-34.
8. P. Idestam-Almquist (1996), *Efficient induction of recursive definitions by structural analysis of saturations*, pp. 192-205 in L. De Raedt (ed.), *Advances in inductive logic programming*, IOS Press.
9. M.R.K. Krishna Rao (1995), *Incremental Learning of Logic Programs*, Proc. of Algorithmic Learning Theory, ALT'95, LNCS **997**, pp. 95-109. Revised version in *Theoretical Computer Science* special issue on ALT'95, Vol **185**, 193-213.
10. J. W. Lloyd (1987), *Foundations of Logic Programming*, Springer-Verlag.
11. S. Muggleton and L. De Raedt (1994), *Inductive logic programming: theory and methods*, J. Logic Prog. **19/20**, pp. 629-679.
12. S.H. Nienhuys-Cheng and R. de Wolf (1995), *The subsumption theorem for several forms of resolution*, Tech. Rep. EUR-FEW-CS-96-14, Erasmus University, Rotterdam.
13. C.D. Page and A.M. Frish (1992), *Generalization and learnability: a study of constrained atoms*, in Muggleton (ed.) Inductive Logic programming, pp. 29-61.
14. C. Reddy and P. Tadepalli (1998), *Learning first order acyclic Horn programs from entailment*, to appear in Proc. of International Conference on Machine Learning, ICML'98.
15. C. Rouveirol (1992), *Extensions of inversion of resolution applied to theory completion*, in Muggleton (ed.) Inductive Logic programming, pp. 63-92.
16. E. Shapiro (1981), *Inductive inference of theories from facts*, Tech. Rep., Yale Univ.
17. E. Shapiro (1983), *Algorithmic Program Debugging*, MIT Press.
18. L. Sterling and E. Shapiro (1994), *The Art of Prolog*, MIT Press.

Logical Aspects of Several Bottom-Up Fittings

Akihiro YAMAMOTO

Division of Electronics and Information Engineering
and
Meme Media Laboratory
Hokkaido University
N 13 W 8, Kita-ku
Sapporo 060-8628 JAPAN
yamamoto@meme.hokudai.ac.jp

Abstract. This research is aimed at giving a bridge between the two research areas, Inductive Logic Programming and Computational Learning. We focus our attention on four fittings (learning methods) invented in the two areas: Saturant Generalization, V^*-operation with Generalization, Bottom Generalization, and Inverse Entailment. Firstly we show that each of them can be represented as an instance of a common schema. Secondly we compare the four fittings. By modifying Jung's result, we show that all definite hypotheses derived by V^*-operation with Generalization can be derived by Bottom Generalization and vice versa, but that some hypotheses cannot be derived by Saturant Generalization. We also give a hypotheses of a general clause which can be derived Bottom Generalization but not by V^*-operation with Generalization. We show Inverse Entailment is more powerful than other three fittings both in definite and in general clausal logic. In our papers presented at the IJCAI'97 workshops and the 7th ILP workshop, Bottom Generalization was called "Inverse Entailment," but after the workshops we found it differs from Muggleton's original Inverse Entailment. We renamed it "Bottom Generalization" in order to reduce confusion and allow fair comparison of the fitting to others.

1 Introduction

This research is aimed at giving a bridge between the two research areas, Inductive Logic Programming and Computational Learning.

We are giving logical foundations of systems which learn clausal theories from entailment. Such a system M works as follows: At first M is given an initial *background theory*, and takes many positive examples as its input one by one. The background theory is a clausal theory (a conjunction of clauses) and each positive example is a clause. The system revises its current background theory B whenever $B \not\models E$. One of the revision operations is to add a clause called a *hypothesis* to B. A hypothesis H is said to be *correct* if $B \wedge H \models E$. A method to find correct hypotheses with is called a *fitting*.

In this paper we clarify the relationship among four fittings developed in the area of ILP (Inductive Logic Programming): Saturant Generalization, V^*-operation with Generalization, Bottom Generalization, and Inverse Entailment. Firstly we show that each of these can be represented as an instance of a common schema for various fitting procedures. According to this result, we can compare the fittings by comparing the sets which consists of correct hypotheses generated by each fitting.

Saturant Generalization was developed by Rouveirol [15, 16], in the ILP community, in order to find hypotheses which cannot be found with Muggleton's V-operator [9, 12]. She assumed that every background theory should be a definite logic program, and that every example should be a definite clause. Saturant Generalization can generate only definite clauses as hypotheses. The V^*-*operation* was proposed by Muggleton in his invited talk at the first ALT workshop [9]. He presented a fitting by combining it with the inverse of subsumption, and Jung [6] showed that the fitting is an extension of Saturant Generalization. Muggleton defined the fitting without the assumption for Saturant Generalization, and allowed non-definite clauses to be derived as hypotheses. Later he proposed another fitting *Inverse Entailment*, which is again an extension of Saturant Generalization. While we were analyzing Inverse Entailment, we happened to find a new fitting *Bottom Generalization* [19]. It can be regard another extension of Saturant Generalization. Bottom Generalization as well as Inverse Entailment allows non-definite clauses to appear in background theories, examples, and hypotheses.

In the COLT communities, Angluin et al.[1] invented Saturant Generalization in their algorithm which learns propositional definite programs from entailment efficiently. Since they did not use the word "saturant," we should conjecture that they invented Saturant Generalization without referring Rouveirol's work. Arimura [2] developed an algorithm learning first-order definite clauses, based on his analysis of Angluin's algorithm. He presented the algorithm at the last ALT workshop. Cohen [4, 5] analyzed the complexity of Saturant Generalization in the first-order definite clause logic, by using the PAC-learning framework.

Now we must notice that a quite interesting problem has left unsolved: Can we develop any algorithm which learns non-definite clausal theories from entailment, by using the three extensions of Saturant Generalization? In this paper we give the first step for the solutions to this problem. The result that the four fittings can be regarded as instances of a common shama means that we may use the three fittings as well as Saturant Generalization for learning from entailment. The comparison of the four shows, from a logical viewpoint, how the three extensions are more complicated than Saturant Generalization. This information should be helpful when we design the intended learning algorithms.

This paper is organized as follows: After preparing some terminology in logic in Section 2, we show in Section 3 that each of the four fitting can be represented as an instance of a procedure BU-FIT-MAIN. In Section 4 we compared each of them with others, with referring some previous results given by Jung [6] and by ourselves [17, 19, 21]. In Section 5, we give some additional comments to our discussion.

In our papers presented at the IJCAI'97 workshops and the 7th ILP workshop, our fitting was called "Inverse Entailment," but after the workshops we found it differs from Muggleton's original Inverse Entailment. We renamed it "Bottom Generalization" in order to reduce confusion and allow fair comparison of our fitting to others.

2 Preliminaries

We assume that readers are familiar with first-order logic and logic programming. When more precise definitions are needed, they should consult some textbooks on the areas(e.g. [8, 13]).

Let $\mathcal{L}$ be a first-order language. For each variable x we prepare a new constant symbol c_x called the *Skolem constant* of x. We let $\mathcal{L}^s$ denote the language whose alphabet is obtained by adding all the Skolem constants to that of $\mathcal{L}$.

A *clausal theory* is a finite conjunction of clauses. In this paper a *clause* is a formula of the form

$$C = \forall x_1 \ldots x_k (A_1 \vee A_2 \vee \ldots \vee A_n \vee \neg B_1 \vee \neg B_2 \vee \ldots \vee \neg B_m)$$

where $n \geq 0$, $m \geq 0$, A_i's and B_j's are all atoms, and $x_1, \ldots, x_k$ are all variables occurring in the atoms. We represent the clause C in the form of implication:

$$A_1, A_2, \ldots, A_n \leftarrow B_1, B_2, \ldots, B_m \ .$$

The *complement* of F is a clausal theory

$$\neg(C\sigma_C) = (\neg A_1 \wedge \neg A_2 \wedge \ldots \wedge \neg A_m \wedge B_1 \wedge B_2 \wedge \ldots \wedge B_m)\sigma_C$$

where σ_C is a substitution which replaces each variable in C with its Skolem constant. We will write the substitution with σ if it makes no ambiguity.

A *definite clause* is a clause of the form $A_0 \leftarrow A_1, \ldots, A_n$. A clausal theory consisting of definite clauses is called a *definite program*.

Definition 1. A clause D *subsumes* a clause C if there is a substitution θ such that every literal in $D\theta$ occurs in C.

We apply this definition to the case when C is a (possibly infinite) set of literals. Note that D subsumes C iff there are a clause F and a substitution θ such that every literal in F belongs to C and $D\theta = F$. Therefore to make a clause D subsuming C is to apply the inverse of instantiation to a clause made of some literals in C.

For a first-order language $\mathcal{L}$, we introduce some notations: $\mathrm{GL}(\mathcal{L})$ for the set of all ground literals in $\mathcal{L}$, $\mathrm{CT}(\mathcal{L})$ for the set of all clausal theories in $\mathcal{L}$, $\mathrm{C}(\mathcal{L})$ for the set of all clauses in $\mathcal{L}$, $\mathrm{DP}(\mathcal{L})$ for the set of all definite programs in $\mathcal{L}$, and $\mathrm{D}(\mathcal{L})$ for the set of all definite clauses in $\mathcal{L}$. For a set S of literals, S^+ (S^-) denotes the set of all positive (negative, resp.) literals in S. The set $\mathrm{GL}(\mathcal{L})^+$, which is the *Herbrand base* of $\mathcal{L}$, is denoted by $\mathrm{HB}(\mathcal{L})$.

3 Bottom-Up Fittings

In the theory of ILP three languages should be distinguished: the language $\mathcal{L}_B$ for background knowledge, the observational language $\mathcal{L}_E$, and the hypothesis language $\mathcal{L}_H$. Each element of $\mathcal{L}_B$ is called a *background theory*, each of $\mathcal{L}_E$ is called an *example*, and each of $\mathcal{L}_H$ is called a *hypothesis*. The tuple $S = (\mathcal{L}_B, \mathcal{L}_E, \mathcal{L}_H)$ is called a *language structure* for an ILP theory. The language structure $S_G = (\mathrm{CT}(\mathcal{L}), \mathrm{C}(\mathcal{L}), \mathrm{C}(\mathcal{L}))$ is called the *general structure* of $\mathcal{L}$, and the structure $S_D = (\mathrm{DP}(\mathcal{L}), \mathrm{D}(\mathcal{L}), \mathrm{D}(\mathcal{L}))$ is the *definite structure* of $\mathcal{L}$.

Definition 2. Let S be a language structure. A *fitting procedure* (or a *fitting*, for short) $\mathcal{F}$ is a procedure which generates hypotheses H from a given example E with the support of a background theory B. The set of all such hypotheses is denoted by $\mathcal{F}(E, B)$.

The fittings we are now discussing can be represent one main routine and two sub-procedures. The first sub-procedure derives a highly specific clause and the second generalizes it. We give formal definitions.

Definition 3. A *base enumerator* Λ is a procedure which takes an example E and a background theory B as its input and enumerates a subset of $\mathrm{GL}(\mathcal{L}^s)$. This subset is denoted by $\Lambda(E, B)$ and called a *base set*.

Definition 4. A *generalizer* Γ takes a ground clause F in $\mathrm{C}(\mathcal{L}^s)$ and generates clauses in $\mathcal{L}_H$. The set of all clauses generated by Γ is denoted by $\Gamma(F)$.

Procedure BU-FIT-MAIN$_{\Lambda, \Gamma}(E, B)$

1. Choose non-deterministically literals $L_1, \ldots, L_n$ from $\Lambda(E, B)$.
2. Return non-deterministically clauses in $\Gamma(L_1 \vee \ldots \vee L_n)$.

If at least one of the sets $\Lambda(E, B)$ and $\Gamma(F)$ is infinite, we must adopt some dovetailing method in order to enumerate all elements in the sets. In our discussion we need not mind how the dovetailing method is implemented.

The followings are fittings we analyze logical aspects in this paper.

3.1 Saturant Generalization

We define Saturant Generalization as an instance of BU-FIT-MAIN, which is denoted by SATG.

At first, for a definite clause $C = A \leftarrow B_1, B_2, \ldots, B_m$, we define clauses C^+ and C^- as follows:

$$C^+ = A \leftarrow ,$$
$$C^- = \leftarrow B_1, B_2, \ldots, B_m .$$

Definition 5. The *saturant* of a definite clause E w.r.t. a definite program B is defined as

$$\text{Satu}(E, B) = \{E^+\sigma\} \cup \{\neg A \mid A \in \text{HB}(\mathcal{L}) \text{ and } B \wedge \neg(E^-\sigma) \models A\} \ .$$

The generalizer for SATG is the inverse of instantiation. We formally define the generalizer in the form of a set

$$\text{IIns}(K) = \{C \mid C\theta = K \text{ for some substitution } \theta\} \ .$$

The clause C in $\text{IIns}(K)$ is usually called *generalization* of K.

We put

$$\text{SATG} = \text{BU-FIT-MAIN}_{\text{Satu,IIns}} \ .$$

The set of the hypotheses generated by SATG is represented as

$$\text{SATG}(E, B) = \{H \mid H\theta \text{ subsumes Satu}(E, B)\} \ .$$

3.2 $V*$-operation with Generalization

As proposed by Muggleton [9] and Jung [6], the repeated use of Muggleton's *most specific V-operation* (*MSV-operation* for short) can be regarded as generating a base set.

The original definition of MSV-operator in [9] is in a operational form and is not convenient for discussing the derivability of hypotheses. With focusing on the results of the operator, we give a new definition suitable to our discussion.

Definition 6. Let D and E be clauses. A clause C is *V-derivable* from E with the support of D if there is a substitution θ and a literal L such that

1. L is in a factor D' of D,
2. $C = E \vee \neg L\theta$, and
3. every literal in $(D' - \{L\})\theta$ occurs in E.

If D is a ground instance of a set of clauses B, we say C is *V-derivable* from E with the support of B.

Next we inductively define a set $V^n(E, B)$ for every non-negative integer n:

$$V^0(E, B) = \{E\sigma_E\} \ ,$$
$$V^{n+1}(E, B) = \left\{H \in C(\mathcal{L}^s) \ \middle| \ \begin{array}{l} H \text{ is V-derivable from a clause } F \in V^n(E, B) \\ \text{with the support of } B \end{array}\right\}$$
$$(n \geq 0) \ .$$

By using the sets $V^n(E, B)$ $(n = 0, 1, 2, \ldots)$, we define a base set

$$\text{Vbot}(E, B) = \{L \in \text{GL}(\mathcal{L}^s) \mid L \text{ occurs in some } H \in V^n(E, B) \text{ for some } n\} \ .$$

and a fitting

$$\text{VNG} = \text{BU-FIT-MAIN}_{\text{Vbot,IIns}} \ .$$

From the definition it holds that

$$\text{VNG}(E, B) = \{H \mid H\theta \text{ subsumes Vbot}(E, B)\} \ .$$

3.3 Bottom Generalization

The base set of Bottom Generalization is the bottom set $\mathrm{Bot}(E, B)$, which was originally introduced by Muggleton [10] in an informal manner. We give its formal definition.

Definition 7. Let B be a background theory and E be an example. The *bottom set*(or *bottom*, for short) for E w.r.t. B is a set of literals

$$\mathrm{Bot}(E, B) = \{L \in \mathrm{GL}(\mathcal{L}^s) \mid B \wedge \neg(E\sigma) \models \neg L\} \ .$$

We adopt the inverse of the subsumption as the generalizer for BOTG, that is, we define

$$\mathrm{BOTG} = \mathrm{BU\text{-}FIT\text{-}MAIN}_{\mathrm{Bot,IIns}},$$

and therefore,

$$\mathrm{BOTG}(E, B) = \{H \in \mathcal{L}_{\mathrm{H}} \mid H \text{ subsumes } \mathrm{Bot}(E, B)\} \ .$$

From the note on the subsumption relation in Section 2, the generalizer can be a procedure for inverting instantiation.

3.4 Inverse Entailment

A fitting INVE for Inverse Entailment [10] is defined as

$$\mathrm{INVE} = \mathrm{BU\text{-}FIT\text{-}MAIN}_{\mathrm{Bot,IImp}} \ ,$$

where IImp is a procedure for inverting logical implication of clauses.
    The set of the hypotheses derived by INVE is represented as

$$\mathrm{INVE}(E, B) = \left\{ H \in \mathcal{L}_{\mathrm{H}} \ \middle| \ \begin{array}{l} \text{There is a clause } K \text{ such that } H \models K \\ \text{and } K \text{ consists of literals in } \mathrm{Bot}(E, B) \end{array} \right\} \ .$$

The set

$$\mathrm{IImp}(F) = \{H \in C(\mathcal{L}) \mid H \models F\}$$

could be recursively enumerable with some generate-and-test method. We do not mind how efficiently generate the elements of the set.

4 Logical Aspects of the Fittings

4.1 Correctness and Completeness of Fittings

We give the formal definition of the correctness of hypotheses generated by a fitting according to our previous works [19].

Definition 8. Let B be a background theory and E an example. A hypothesis H is *correct* for E w.r.t. B if $B \wedge H$ is consistent and $B \wedge H \models E$.

Definition 9. A fitting procedure $\mathcal{F}$ is *correct* in a language structure $S = (\mathcal{L}_B, \mathcal{L}_E, \mathcal{L}_H)$ if $H \in \mathcal{F}(E, B)$ implies $B \wedge H \models E$ for any pair of $B \in \mathcal{L}_B$ and $E \in \mathcal{L}_E$.

Generally speaking, the inference power of a fitting $\mathcal{F}$ is analyzed in two ways: The first one is to find a structure S in which every H such that $B \wedge H \models E$ must be in $\mathcal{F}(E, B)$. The second approach is to find a relation among B, E, and H which is equivalent to $H \in \mathcal{F}(E, B)$ in the structure S. This means that we show the completeness of $\mathcal{F}$ relative to the relation.

According to the second approach, we define the completeness of fittings relative to a generalization relation.

Definition 10. Let $\mathcal{B}$ and $\mathcal{H}$ be sets of formulas. A ternary relation $\succeq \in \mathcal{B} \times \mathcal{H} \times \mathcal{H}$ is a *generalization relation* on $\mathcal{H}$ parameterized with $\mathcal{B}$ if $\succeq (B, H, E)$ implies $B \wedge H \models E$. In the followings we write $H \succeq E\,(B)$ instead of $\succeq (B, H, E)$.

Definition 11. A fitting $\mathcal{F}$ is *complete* in a language structure S w.r.t. a generalization relation $\succeq$ if $\mathcal{F}$ is correct and every hypothesis H such that $H \succeq E\,(B)$ can be derived from E w.r.t. B with $\mathcal{F}$ whenever $B \not\models E$.

From the definition, a relation $\succeq_I$ defined as

$$H \succeq_I E\,(B) \iff B \wedge H \models E$$

is a generalization relation. We call it the *relative implication relation*.

Both Plotkin's relative subsumption and Buntine's generalized subsumption are also generalization relations [13].

Definition 12 (Plotkin [14]). Let H and E be two clauses. H *subsumes* E *relative to* B if there is a clause F such that

$$B \models \forall y_1 \ldots y_n (E' \leftrightarrow F')$$

and H subsumes F, where E' and F' are obtained by removing universal quantifiers from E and F respectively, and $y_1, \ldots, y_n$ are all variables occurring in E' and F'.

Definition 13. Let A be a ground atom and I be an Herbrand interpretation. A definite clause $A_0 \leftarrow A_1, \ldots, A_m$ *covers* A in I if there is a substitution θ such that $A_0 \theta = A$ and $A_i \theta$ is true in I for every $i = 1, \ldots, n$.

Definition 14 (Buntine [3]). Let H and E be two definite clauses. H *subsumes* E *w.r.t.* B if, for any Herbrand model M of B and for any ground atom A, H covers A in M whenever E covers A.

When H subsumes E relative (w.r.t.) B, we write $H \succeq_P E\,(B)$ ($H \succeq_B E\,(B)$, resp.). To demonstrate the main result visually, we introduce the following two sets of hypotheses:

$$\succeq_P (E, P) = \{H \mid H \succeq_P E\,(B)\}\,,$$
$$\succeq_B (E, B) = \{H \mid H \succeq_B E\,(B)\}\,.$$

4.2 Results

Now we demonstrate the current analysis of correctness and completeness of the fittings explained in Section 3.

Theorem 1 (Correctness). *The fitting* SATG *is correct in* S_D, *and all of* VNG, INVE, *and* BOTG *are as well in* S_G.

Theorem 2 (Completeness). *Let us assume the structure* S_D. *Then, for every background theory* B *and ever example* E *such that* $B \not\models E$, *the followings hold in general:*

$$\mathrm{SATG}(E,B) = \succeq_B (E,B) \subsetneqq \mathrm{VNG}(E,B) = \mathrm{BOTG}(E,B) = \succeq_P (E,B)$$
$$\subsetneqq \mathrm{INVE}(E,B) \ .$$

If S_G *is assumed, the followings hold in general for every* B *and every* E *such that* $B \not\models E$:

$$\mathrm{VNG}(E,B) \subsetneqq \mathrm{BOTG}(E,B) = \succeq_P (E,B) \subsetneqq \mathrm{INVE}(E,B) \ .$$

[1] Proof of the Correctness Theorem
Since we will prove the completeness theorem, all that we must show is the next lemma.

Lemma 1. *The procedure* INVE *is correct in the general structure* S_G.

Proof. Let H be a hypothesis in $\mathrm{INVE}(E,B)$ and

$$F = A_1, A_2, \ldots, A_n \leftarrow B_1, B_2, \ldots, B_m$$

be a clause such that every literal in F belongs to $\mathrm{Bot}(E,B)$ and $H \models F$.
  Since the clause F is ground, no quantifiers are occurring in $\neg F$, that is,

$$\neg F = (\neg A_1 \wedge \neg A_2 \wedge \ldots \wedge \neg A_m \wedge B_1 \wedge B_2 \wedge \ldots \wedge B_m)\theta \ .$$

From the definition of the bottom set, it holds that $B \wedge \neg(E\sigma) \models \neg F$. Since all the literals in $\neg(E\sigma)$ and $\neg F$ are ground, it is equivalent to an assertion that $B \wedge F\theta \models E\sigma$. Because $H \models F$ and σ is the Skolemizing substitution for E, we obtain that $B \wedge H \models E$. □

[2] Proof of the Completeness Theorem
We divide the Completeness Theorem into several Lemmas and give their proofs.
  The completeness of Saturant Generalization was proved by Jung, and that of Bottom Generalization was proved in our previous work,

Lemma 2 (Jung [6]). SATG *is complete w.r.t. Buntine's generalized subsumption in* S_D.

Lemma 3 (Yamamoto[19]). BOTG *is complete w.r.t. Plotkin's relative subsumption in* S_G.

Because $H \succeq_P E(B)$ implies $H \succeq_B E(B)$ but the converse does not hold in general [3], we have the next lemma.

Lemma 4. *In the definite structure* S_D, $\text{BOTG}(E, B) \supseteq \text{SATG}(E, B)$ *if* $B \not\models E$. *However,* $\text{SATG}(E, B) \not\supseteq \text{BOTG}(E, G)$ *in general.*

We gave in [17, 18, 21] more precise discussion on the comparison of BOTG and SATG.

If a clause H subsumes another F, it also logically implies F. We have already shown in [20] that $H \succeq_I E(B)$ is not equivalent to $H \in \text{INVE}(E, B)$ in S_G. By combining the two results, we obtain the following:

Lemma 5. *In the structure* S_G, $\text{BOTG}(E, B) \subseteq \text{INVE}(E, B)$ *if* $B \not\models E$. *The inclusion holds in the* S_D *as well.*

The problem whether or not $\text{INVE}(E, B) = \text{BOTG}(E, B)$ has not been solved yet. The following example shows that the answer is negative.

Example 1. Let $E_1 = p(s(s(0)) \leftarrow p(0)$ and $B_1 = \emptyset$. The hypotheses

$$H_1 = p(s(x)) \leftarrow p(x)$$

logically implies E_1, but does not subsume it. Therefore we conclude

$$\text{INVE}(E_1, B_1) - \text{BOTG}(E_1, B_1) \neq \emptyset .$$

Now we compare VNG with BOTG. As Jung [6] showed, applying V-operator iteratively is inverting linear input resolution. With the completeness of linear input resolution for definite programs, the following two propositions hold.

Lemma 6 (Jung [6]). *It holds that, in* S_D, $\text{VNG}(E, B) = \succeq_P (E, B)$ *if* $B \not\models E$.

It is also obtained that $\text{VNG}(E, B) \supseteq \succeq_P (E, B)$ in S_G, but the problem whether or not $\text{VNG}(E, B) = \succeq_P (E, B)$ has been open. The following example shows that $\text{BOTG}(E, B) \neq \text{VNG}(E, G)$ in S_G, and consequently that BOTG is superior to VNG in the point its completeness holds in a wider language structure.

Example 2. Consider the following E_2 and B_2:

$$E_2 = p \leftarrow ,$$
$$B_2 = (p, q \leftarrow r) \wedge (p \leftarrow q, r) \wedge (q \leftarrow p, r) \wedge (\leftarrow p, q, r) .$$

If any clause is V-derivable from E_2 with the support of a clause in B_2, it must have a factor of the form

$$p, r \leftarrow$$

because every clause in B_2 has $\neg r$ but E_2 has no r in it. However, we cannot derive E_2 from any pair of such a clause and a clause in B_4. Therefore $\text{Vbot}(E_2, B_2) = \{p\}$. On the other hand, we can easily show that $\text{Bot}(E_2, B_2) = \{p, r\}$. This concludes that $\text{Bot}(E_2, B_2) \neq \text{Vbot}(E_2, B_2)$.

5 Concluding Remarks

Jung defined of the set $V^{n+1}(E, B)$ as follows:

$$V^{n+1}(E, B) = \left\{ H \in C(\mathcal{L}^s) \,\middle|\, \begin{array}{l} H \text{ is V-derivable from a clause } F \in V^n(E, B) \\ \text{with the support of an instance } D \text{ of} \\ \text{a clause in } B \end{array} \right\}$$

$$(n \geq 0) .$$

In his definition hypotheses in $V^{n+1}(E, B)$ are not always ground even if $V^n(E, B)$ contains ground clauses only. To keep all the clauses in $V^n(E, B)$ ground, he assumed that the background theory B should be a strongly generative logic program. We need not assume that strong generativeness because we restricted the supporting clause D as a ground clause.

In our personal communication with Muggleton [11], he gave a conjecture that $H \in \text{INVE}(E, B)$ is equivalent to $H \succeq_P E$. The conjecture is equivalent to $\text{INVE}(E, B) = \text{BOTG}(E, B)$, and has been refuted by our result.

Now we are at the point where our result to analyzing computational aspects of learning. For example, it is in our future plans to investigate how to use Bottom Generalization in extending the algorithms based on Saturant Generalization presented at COLT and ALT workshops.

Acknowledgments

The author thanks to Dr. Steve Muggleton for his kind introduction of Inverse Entailment and Progol, and Prof.Dr. Nada Lavrač, Prof.Dr. Shan-Hwei Nienhuys-Cheng, and Dr. J.-K. Kietz for their kind providing of documents. This work was partly supported by Grant-in-Aid for Scientific Research No.10780213 from the Ministry of Education, Science and Culture, Japan.

References

1. D. Angluin, M. Frazier, and L. Pitt. Learning Conjunctions of Horn Clauses. *Machine Learning*, 9:147–164, 1992.
2. H. Arimura. Learning Acyclic First-order Horn Sentences From Implication. In *Proceedings of the 8th International Workshop on Algorithmic Learning Theory (LNAI 1316)*, pages 432–445, 1997.
3. W. Buntine. Generalized Subsumption and its Applications to Induction and Redundancy. *Artificial Intelligence*, 36:149–176, 1988.
4. W. W. Cohen. PAC-learning Recursive Logic Programs: Efficient Algorithms. *J. of Artificial Intelligence Research*, 2:501–539, 1995.
5. W. W. Cohen. PAC-learning Recursive Logic Programs: Negative Results. *J. of Artificial Intelligence Research*, 2:541–573, 1995.
6. B. Jung. On Inverting Generality Relations. In *Proceedings of the 3rd International Workshop on Inductive Logic Programming*, pages 87–101, 1993.

7. J.-U. Kietz. *Inductive Analyse relationaler Daten*. PhD thesis, Technische Universität Berlin, 1996. (in German).

8. J. W. Lloyd. *Foundations of Logic Programming : Second, Extended Edition*. Springer - Verlag, 1987.

9. S. Muggleton. Inductive Logic Programming. In S. Arikawa and S. Goto and S. Ohsuga and T. Yokomori, editor, *Proceedings of the First International Workshop on Algorithmic Learning Theory*, pages 42–62. JSAI, 1990.

10. S. Muggleton. Inverse Entailment and Progol. *New Generation Computing*, 13:245–286, 1995.

11. S. Muggleton. Personal Communication, 1996.

12. S. H. Muggleton and W. Buntine. Machine Invention of First-Order Predicates by Inverting Resolution. In *Proceeding of the Fifth International Conference on Machine Learning*, pages 339–352. Morgan Kaufmann, 1988.

13. S.-H. Nienhuys-Cheng and R. de Wolf. *Foundations of Inductive Logic Programming (LNAI 1228)*. Springer, 1997.

14. G. D. Plotkin. *Automatic Methods of Inductive Inference*. PhD thesis, Edinburgh University, 1971.

15. C. Rouveirol. Completeness for Inductive Procedures. In *Proceedings of the 8th International Workshop on Machine Learning*, pages 452–456. Morgan Kaufmann, 1991.

16. C. Rouveirol. Extentions of Inversion of Resolution Applied to Theory Completion. In S. Muggleton, editor, *Inductive Logic Programming*, pages 63–92. Academic Press, 1992.

17. A. Yamamoto. Representing Inductive Inference with SOLD-Resolution. In *Proceedings of the IJCAI'97 Workshop on Abduction and Induction in AI*, pages 59 – 63, 1997.

18. A. Yamamoto. Theoretical Foundations of Inductive Logic Programming. *The Journal of Japanese Society for Artificial Intelligence*, 12(5):665–674, 1997. (In Japanese).

19. A. Yamamoto. Which Hypotheses Can Be Found with Inverse Entailment? In *Proceedings of the Seventh International Workshop on Inductive Logic Programming (LNAI 1297)*, pages 296 – 308, 1997. The extended abstract is in *Proceedings of the IJCAI'97 Workshop on Frontiers of Inductive Logic Programming, pp.19-23 (1997)*.

20. A. Yamamoto. Revising the Logical Foundations of Inductive Logic Programming Systems with Ground Reduced Programs. To appear in *New Generation Computing*, 1998.

21. A. Yamamoto. Using Abduction for Induction based on Bottom Generalization. To appear in A. Kakas and P. Flach (eds.) *Abductive and Inductive Reasoning : Essays on their Relation and Integration*, 1998.

Learnability of Translations
from Positive Examples

Noriko Sugimoto

Department of Artificial Intelligence,
Kyushu Institute of Technology,
Kawazu 680-4, Iizuka 820-8502, JAPAN
E-mail: `sugimoto@ai.kyutech.ac.jp`

Abstract. One of the most important issues in machine translations is deducing unknown rules from pairs of input-output sentences. Since the translations are expressed by elementary formal systems (EFS's, for short), we formalize learning translations as the process of guessing an unknown EFS from pairs of input-output sentences. In this paper, we propose a class of EFS's called linearly-moded EFS's by introducing local variables and linear predicate inequalities based on mode information, which can express translations of context-sensitive languages. We show that, for a given input sentence, the set of all output sentences is finite and computable in a translation defined by a linearly-moded EFS. Finally, we show that the class of translations defined by linearly-moded EFS's is learnable under the condition that the number of clauses in an EFS and the length of the clause are bounded by some constant.

1   Introduction

In machine translation, many formal systems have been developed to translate a language into another. One well-known system, *syntax-directed translation scheme* (SDTS, for short) [1, 2, 8, 9], has sufficient power to express the relations of two context-free languages. The SDTS has been investigated from the viewpoint of designing compilers for programming languages. On the other hand, the expressive power of SDTSs is insufficient to deal with more complicated languages, such as context-sensitive or natural languages.

One of the most important issues in machine translations is deducing unknown rules from pairs of input-output sentences. This issue can be formalized in the framework of learning binary relations from strings. In this paper, we adopt an *elementary formal system*(EFS, for short) [5, 14] instead of an SDTS, and discuss the learnability of translations over context-sensitive languages. The EFS is flexible enough to define various classes of formal languages corresponding to Chomsky hierarchy, and is an adequate tool for learning formal languages [5, 12]. An EFS is a kind of logic program on strings, and consists of the clauses of the form $A \leftarrow B_1, \ldots, B_n$ as Prolog programs. Here, the sequence $B_1, \ldots, B_n$ is called a *body* of the clause. In EFS's, we deal with strings as the argument's terms of a predicate symbol. Specifically, the binary relation of a translation can be expressed by the binary predicate symbol in an EFS. Therefore, we can formalize the learning translations as the process of guessing an unknown EFS, which defines a translation, from pairs of input-output sentences.

In general, a variable is said to be *local* if it occurs only in the body of a clause. An EFS is generally defined as a finite set of clauses without having local variables. While this definition is sufficient for us to regard EFS's as acceptors of formal languages, it is not useful in terms of translations. For example, suppose that two translations are defined by EFS's with binary predicate symbols q_1 and q_2, and consider composing them. If we deal with standard EFS's, we need to generate a new EFS representing the composition. On the other hand, if we deal with EFS's with local variables, we can define the composition as a simple clause $q(x, z) \leftarrow q_1(x, y), q_2(y, z)$. Clearly, unconditionally introducing local variables does not preserve the computability of computations for EFS's. Hence, in this paper, we extend the form of EFS's by introducing local variables while preserving the computability of computations from input sentences to output sentences.

It is not surprising that there are no so-called negative examples in learning translations from examples, because it is difficult to obtain negative and meaningful examples in any translation. Therefore, we discuss learning translations from only positive examples. The learning in this setting is applied to various targets [3, 4, 7, 11, 12]. In particular, Arimura and Shinohara [6] have shown that the class of *linearly covering programs*, which is a useful subclass of logic programs with local variables, is learnable from positive examples. The linearly covering program is defined by the information of an input-output mode. Furthermore, Rao [10] has extended the class by using *linear predicate inequalities*, which is so large to express standard Prolog programs as quick-sort or merge-sort.

In this paper, we present a class of EFS's, called *linearly-moded EFS's*. The linearly-moded EFS's are EFS's with local variables and linear predicate inequalities. By the linearly-moded EFS's, we can define translations over context-sensitive languages. Then, we show that, given an input sentence, the set of all output sentences is finite and computable on the translation defined by a linearly-moded EFS. Furthermore, we show that the class of translations defined by linearly-moded EFS's is learnable from positive examples under the condition that the number of clauses in an EFS and the length of a clause are bounded by some constant.

2 Preliminaries

In this section, we give some basic definitions. Let Σ, X and Π be mutually disjoint sets. We assume that Σ is finite. We refer to each element of Σ as a *constant symbol*, to each element of X as a *variable*, and to each element of Π as a *predicate symbol*. Each predicate symbol is associated with a non-negative integer called its *arity*. For a set A, we denote the set of all finite strings of symbols from A by A^* and the set $A^* - \{\varepsilon\}$ by A^+, where ε is an empty string. A *term* is an element of $(\Sigma \cup X)^+$. A term is said to be *ground* if it is an element of Σ^+. An *atomic formula* (*atom*, for short) is of the form $p(s_1, s_2, \ldots, s_n)$, where p is a predicate symbol with arity n and each s_i is a term $(1 \le i \le n)$. An atom $p(s_1, s_2, \ldots, s_n)$ is said to be *ground* if all $s_1, s_2, \ldots, s_n$ are ground. In this paper, constant symbols are denoted by $a, b, \ldots$, variables by $x, y, \ldots$, terms or sequences of terms by $s, t, \ldots$, and atoms by $A, B, \ldots$.

A *definite clause* (*clause*, for short) is of the form $A \leftarrow B_1, \ldots, B_n$ $(n \ge 0)$, where $A, B_1, \ldots, B_n$ are atoms. The atom A and the sequence $B_1, \ldots, B_n$ of atoms are called the *head* and the *body* of the clause, respectively. We refer to either a term, a finite sequence of terms, an atom or a clause as an *expression*. For an expression E, the set of all variables occurring in E is denoted by $v(E)$. For an expression E and a variable x, the number of occurrence of x in E is denoted by $oc(x, E)$. An *elementary formal system* (*EFS*, for short) [13] is a finite set of clauses and denoted by Γ.

For an EFS Γ, the set of all predicate symbols occurring in Γ is denoted by Π_Γ. A *substitution* is a finite set of the form $\{x_1/s_1, \ldots, x_n/s_n\}$, where $x_1, \ldots, x_n$ are distinct variables and each s_i is a term distinct from x_i $(1 \le i \le n)$. Let E be an expression. For a substitution $\theta = \{x_1/s_1, \ldots, x_n/s_n\}$, $E\theta$, called an *instance* of E, is the expression obtained from E by simultaneously replacing each occurrence of the variable x_i in E with the term s_i $(1 \le i \le n)$.

We give two semantics of EFS's, *provability* and *fixpoint* semantics.

First, we introduce the provability semantics. Let Γ and C be an EFS and a clause. Then, the provability relation $\Gamma \vdash C$ is defined inductively as follows:

1. If $C \in \Gamma$ then $\Gamma \vdash C$.
2. If $\Gamma \vdash C$ then $\Gamma \vdash C\theta$ for any substitution θ.
3. If $\Gamma \vdash A \leftarrow B_1, \ldots, B_m$ and $\Gamma \vdash B_m \leftarrow$ then $\Gamma \vdash A \leftarrow B_1, \ldots, B_{m-1}$.

A clause C is *provable from* Γ if $\Gamma \vdash C$. The *provability semantics* of an EFS Γ is the set:
$$PS(\Gamma) = \{A \mid A \text{ is ground and } \Gamma \vdash A \leftarrow\}.$$

The second semantics is based on the least fixpoint of the functions T_Γ. Let Γ and S be an EFS and the set of ground atoms. Then, the function T_Γ is defined as follows:

$$T_\Gamma(S) = \{A \mid \text{there exists a ground instance } A \leftarrow B_1, \ldots, B_n \text{ of a clause in } \Gamma$$
$$\text{such that } B_i \in S \text{ for any } i(1 \le i \le n)\}.$$

Clearly, the function T_Γ is monotonic for any EFS Γ. The *fixpoint semantics* $T_\Gamma{\uparrow}\omega$ of an EFS Γ is defined as follows:

1. $T_\Gamma{\uparrow}0 = \emptyset$,
2. $T_\Gamma{\uparrow}n = T_\Gamma(T_\Gamma{\uparrow}(n-1))$ for $n \ge 1$,
3. $T_\Gamma{\uparrow}\omega = \bigcup_{n \ge 0} T_\Gamma{\uparrow}n$.

We can show that the two semantics are equivalent for every EFS [15].

3   Linealy-moded EFS's

Rao [10] has proposed the class of Prolog programs based on moding information and linear predicate inequalities. Here, the inequality has been defined as an inclusion over the multisets corresponding to terms. In this section, we redefine an inequality as a relation over the length of each term. Then, we introduce the class of EFS's with linear predicate inequalities. The EFS in this class includes some local variables, which occurs in only the body of each clause under some conditions.

First, we define a partial order over finite sequences of terms. Note that we deal with not only terms but also finite sequences of terms in the following definition.

Let s and t be finite sequences of terms. Then, we denote $s \geq t$ if $|s\theta| \geq |t\theta|$ for any substitution θ. We can easily show that $s \geq t$ if and only if $|s| \geq |t|$ and $oc(x, s) \geq oc(x, t)$ for any $x \in v(t)$. Hence, the following lemma obviously holds.

Lemma 1. *For any pair (s, t) of finite sequences of terms, the problem of deciding whether $s \geq t$ or not is solvable.*

For an n-ary predicate symbol p, a *mode* F_p of p is a function from $\{1, \ldots, n\}$ to $\{\text{in}, \text{out}\}$. The ith argument of p is called an *input* (resp., *output*) *argument* if $F_p(i) = \text{in}$ (resp., out). In order to simplify notations, we assume that, for any i and j, if $F_p(i) = \text{in}$ and $F_p(j) = \text{out}$, then it holds that $i < j$. Then, we separate input arguments in an atom from output ones by the special symbol ";", that is, we denote an atom by $p(t_1, \ldots, t_m; t_{m+1}, \ldots, t_n)$, where $F_p(i) = \text{in}$ for any i $(1 \leq i \leq m)$ and $F_p(j) = \text{out}$ for any j $(m + 1 \leq j \leq n)$. For a predicate symbol p, the set of all i such that $F_p(i) = \text{in}$ is denoted by $in(p)$. An EFS is said to be a *moded* EFS if a mode is defined for every predicate symbol in the EFS.

Let Γ be a moded EFS and q_0 be a binary predicate symbol in Π_Γ such that $F_{q_0}(1) = \text{in}$ and $F_{q_0}(2) = \text{out}$. Then, a *translation defined by* Γ, denoted by $Trans(\Gamma)$, is defined as follows:

$$Trans(\Gamma) = \{(s, t) \in \Sigma^+ \times \Sigma^+ \mid q_0(s; t) \in PS(\Gamma)\}.$$

Let Γ be a moded EFS. Then, an *input selection* I of Γ is a function from Π_Γ to the set of natural numbers such that $I(p) \subseteq in(p)$ for any predicate symbol p in Π_Γ.

Definition 1. Let Γ be a moded EFS and I be an input selection of Γ. Then, for an atom $A = p(s_1, \ldots, s_m; t)$, $LI(A, I)$ is defined as the set of all substitutions θ such that $(s_{i_1}, \ldots, s_{i_n})\theta \geq t\theta$, where $I(p) = \{i_1, \ldots, i_n\}$.

Note that, in the above definition, the set $LI(A, I)$ can be regarded as the set of all answers to the inequality $s_{i_1}, \ldots, s_{i_n} \geq t$ for two sequences $s_{i_1}, \ldots, s_{i_n}$ and t of terms. Then, the class of EFS's with linear inequalities is defined as follows.

Definition 2. Let Γ be an EFS and I be an input selection of Γ. Then, the EFS Γ is *linearly-moded w.r.t. I* if each clause

$$p_0(s_0; t_0) \leftarrow p_1(s_1; t_1), \ldots, p_m(s_m; t_m)$$

in Γ satisfies the following conditions:

1. if $\theta \in LI(p_i(s_i; t_i), I)$ for any i $(1 \le i \le j - 1)$, then $s_0\theta \ge s_j\theta$ for each $j (1 \le j \le m)$, and
2. if $\theta \in LI(p_i(s_i; t_i), I)$ for any i $(1 \le i \le m)$, then $\theta \in LI(p_0(s_0; t_0), I)$.

The EFS Γ is *linearly-moded* if there exists a function I such that Γ is linearly-moded w.r.t. I.

For a linearly-moded EFS's, each clause in the EFS may have local variables under some conditions, which is a useful to express binary relations by EFS's.

Example 1. Let $I(q_0) = I(q_1) = I(q_2) = 1$ and Γ be an EFS defined as follows:

$$\Gamma = \left\{ \begin{array}{l} q_0(xx; yz) \leftarrow q_1(x; y), q_2(y; z), \\ q_1(axb; ayb) \leftarrow q_1(x; y), \\ q_1(ab; ab) \leftarrow, \\ q_2(ax; ya) \leftarrow q_2(x; y), \\ q_2(bx; yb) \leftarrow q_2(x; y), \\ q_2(a; a) \leftarrow, \\ q_2(b; b) \leftarrow \end{array} \right\}.$$

In the first clause of Γ, $(1)xx \ge x$, $(2)x \ge y$ implies $xx \ge y$, and $(3)x \ge y$ and $y \ge z$ implies $xx \ge yz$, where (1) and (2) are corresponding to 1, while (3) is to 2 in Definition 2. Since all clauses in Γ satisfy the conditions of linearly-moded EFS's, Γ is a linealy-moded EFS. The translation defined by Γ is

$$\{(a^n b^n a^n b^n, a^n b^{2n} a^n) \mid n \ge 1\}.$$

By Definition 2, the following lemma holds:

Lemma 2. *If Γ is a linearly-moded EFS, then each clause*

$$p_0(s_0; t_0) \leftarrow p_1(s_1; t_1), \ldots, p_m(s_m; t_m)$$

in Γ satisfies the following conditions:

1. *if $m = 0$ then $v(t_0) \subseteq v(s_0)$, and*
2. *$v(s_i) \subseteq v(s_0) \cup v(t_1) \cup \cdots \cup v(t_{i-1})$ for any i $(1 \le i \le m)$.*

Since the relation $s \ge t$ is based on the length of each instance of s and t, it can be regarded as the inequality over the set of integers. Therefore, the following proposition holds.

Proposition 1. *For any moded EFS Γ, the problem of deciding whether Γ is a linearly-moded or not is solvable.*

Proof. For a term s, define the following expression $[s]$:

$$[s] = \sum_{x \in v(s)} oc(x, s)x + k,$$

where k is the number of constant symbols occurring in s. Then, the problem of deciding whether $|s| \geq |t|$ or not is reduced the satisfiability problem of the linear inequality $[s] \geq [t]$ over the set of integers. Hence, for a given input selection I, the problem of deciding whether Γ is linearly-moded w.r.t. I or not is solvable. Since the number of possible input selections I is finite for a given moded EFS Γ, the problem is solvable. □

4 Properties of linearly-moded EFS's

We can characterize linearly-moded EFS's by the relationship between input and output sentences generated by them. In this section, we show some properties for the translation defined by a linearly-moded EFS.

Lemma 3. *For every linearly-moded EFS Γ, if a ground atom $A = p(s; t)$ is an element of $PS(\Gamma)$, then it holds that $|s| \geq |t|$.*

Proof. We show that if $p(s; t) \in T_\Gamma{\uparrow}i$ then $|s| \geq |t|$ by the induction on i.

If $i = 1$ then there exists a clause $A' = p(s'; t') \leftarrow \in \Gamma$ such that $A = A'\theta$ for a substitution θ. By Definition 2, $|s'\sigma| \geq |t'\sigma|$ for any substitution σ. Hence, $|s| = |s'\theta| \geq |t'\theta| = |t|$.

Assume that $A \in T_\Gamma{\uparrow}k$. Then, there exists a clause $A' \leftarrow B_1, \ldots, B_m \in \Gamma$ such that $A = A'\theta$ and $B_i\theta \in T_\Gamma{\uparrow}(k-1)$. By the induction hypothesis, $|s_i\theta| \geq |t_i\theta|$ for any $p_i(s_i; t_i) = B_i$ ($1 \leq i \leq m$). Hence, it holds that $\theta \in LI(B_i, I)$ for any i ($1 \leq i \leq m$). Since $\theta \in LI(A', I)$ by Definition 2, it holds that $|s| = |s'\theta| \geq |t'\theta| = |t|$. □

By Lemma 3, the class of translations defined by linearly-moded EFS's is incomparable with the class of translations defined by all SDTS's, because the SDTS can express a translation in which the length of an output sentence is greater than the length of its input sentence.

By the following theorem, it is shown that the translation defined by a linearly-moded EFS is recursive.

Theorem 1. *Let A be a ground atom and Γ be a linearly-moded EFS. Then, the problem of deciding whether $\Gamma \vdash A \leftarrow$ or not is solvable.*

Proof. Suppose that $|A| = n$ and let k be $|\Pi_\Gamma| \cdot \sum_{i=1}^{n} |\Sigma|^n$. If $A \in T_\Gamma{\uparrow}(k+1) - T_\Gamma{\uparrow} k$, then, for any i ($1 \leq i \leq k$), there exists an atom $B_i \in T_\Gamma{\uparrow}i - T_\Gamma{\uparrow}(i-1)$ such that $|B_i| \leq n$ by the definition of T_Γ and Definition 2. Since the number of all ground atoms whose length is at most n is at most k, there exist two atoms C and D in the sequence $A, B_k, \ldots, B_1$ such that $C = D$. This fact contradicts to the monotonicity of T_Γ. Hence, if $A \in T_\Gamma{\uparrow}\omega$ then $A \in T_\Gamma{\uparrow}k$ for some k.

For a set S, we denote the set $\{A \in S \mid |A| \leq j\}$ by S/j. Then, we can easily show that $T_\Gamma{\uparrow}(i+1)/j = T_\Gamma(T_\Gamma{\uparrow}i/j)/j$ for any $i \geq 0$ and $j \geq 0$. Since the set $T_\Gamma{\uparrow}i/j$ is finite and computable for any $i \geq 0$ and $j \geq 0$, and $\Gamma \vdash A \leftarrow$ if and only if $A \in T_\Gamma{\uparrow}k/n$, the problem is solvable. $\quad\Box$

It is shown that all of the output sentences can be computed from input sentences by the following two propositions.

Proposition 2. *Let Γ be a linearly-moded EFS, and $p(s;t)$ be an atom such that $\Gamma \vdash p(s;t) \leftarrow$. If s is ground, then so is t.*

Proof. We say that a clause C is k-*provable* from Γ if C is provable from Γ using at most k applications of the rules in the definition of the relation $\Gamma \vdash C$. We prove the statement by induction on k.

Suppose that $p(s;t) \leftarrow$ is 1-provable from Γ. Then, $p(s;t) \leftarrow \in \Gamma$. By Definition 2, it holds that $v(t) \subseteq v(s)$. Since s is ground, t is ground.

Suppose that $p(s;t) \leftarrow$ is k-provable ($k \geq 2$) from Γ. Then, there exists a clause $p(s_0;t_0) \leftarrow q_1(s_1,t_1), \ldots, q_m(s_m;t_m) \in \Gamma$ and a substitution θ such that $p(s_0;t_0)\theta = p(s;t)$ and all of the atoms $q_1(s_1,t_1)\theta, \ldots, q_m(s_m;t_m)\theta$ are $(k-1)$-provable from Γ. For any i ($m \geq i \geq 1$), if all of the atoms $q_1(s_1,t_1)\theta, \ldots, q_{i-1}(s_{i-1};t_{i-1})\theta$ are ground, so is $q_i(s_i;t_i)\theta$ by Lemma 2 and the induction hypothesis. Then, all of the atoms $q_1(s_1,t_1)\theta, \ldots, q_m(s_m;t_m)\theta$ are ground. Since $v(t_0) \subseteq v(s_0) \cup v(t_1) \cup \cdots \cup v(t_m)$, $t_0\theta$ is ground. $\quad\Box$

Proposition 3. *Let Γ be a linearly-moded EFS. Then, for any ground term s, the set $\{t \in \Sigma^+ \mid (s;t) \in Trans(\Gamma)\}$ is finite and computable.*

Proof. We can easily show that $(s;t) \in Trans(\Gamma)$ if and only if $q_0(s;t) \in T_\Gamma{\uparrow}\omega$. Furthermore, if $q_0(s;t) \in T_\Gamma{\uparrow}\omega$ then $q_0(s;t) \in T_\Gamma{\uparrow}k/2n$, where $k = |\Pi_\Gamma| \sum_{i=1}^{2n} |\Sigma|^i$. Since the set $T_\Gamma{\uparrow}k/2n$ is finite and computable, the set $\{t \in \Sigma^+ \mid (s;t) \in Trans(\Gamma)\}$ is also finite and computable. $\quad\Box$

The expressive power of the linearly-moded EFS's is characterized by Lemma 3 and the following proposition.

Proposition 4. *A linearly-moded EFS can define the binary relation over context-sensitive languages.*

Proof. Consider the class of linearly-moded EFS's in which each clause is of the form $p_0(s_0;) \leftarrow p_1(s_1;), \ldots, p_m(s_m;)$. The class contains all of the length-bounded EFS's [5], which can define context-sensitive languages. $\quad\Box$

5 Learnability of linearly-moded EFS's from positive examples

In this section, we discuss the learnability of two classes of EFS's from positive examples. One is the linearly-moded EFS's, and the other is the slightly larger class of linearly-moded EFS's.

Let $\Gamma_1, \Gamma_2, \ldots$ be any recursive enumeration of linearly-moded EFS's. Then, the class $C = \mathit{Trans}(\Gamma_1), \mathit{Trans}(\Gamma_2), \ldots$ is an indexed family of recursive sets. A translation is a subset of $\Sigma^+ \times \Sigma^+$. A *semantic mapping* is a mapping from EFS's to translations. A semantic mapping M is *monotonic* if $\Gamma' \subseteq \Gamma$ implies $M(\Gamma') \subseteq M(\Gamma)$. An EFS Γ is *reduced w.r.t.* a set S of atoms if for any $\Gamma' \subset \Gamma$, $S \subseteq M(\Gamma)$ but $S \not\subseteq M(\Gamma')$. A *concept defining framework* is a triple (U, E, M) of a universe U of objects, a universe E of expressions, and a semantic mapping M.

Definition 3. A concept defining framework (U, E, M) has *bounded finite thickness* if M is monotonic, and for any finite set $S \subseteq U$ and any n $(n \geq 0)$, the set

$$\{ M(\Gamma) \mid \Gamma \text{ is reduced w.r.t. } S \text{ and } |\Gamma| \leq n \}$$

is finite.

Shinohara [11] has shown that if a concept defining framework $C = (U, E, M)$ has bounded finite thickness, then the class

$$C_k = \{ M(\Gamma) \mid \Gamma \subseteq E \text{ and } |\Gamma| \leq k \}$$

is learnable from positive examples.

We denote the set of all linearly-moded EFS's in which each clause has at most m atoms in its body by E^m. Consider the concept defining framework $(\Sigma^+ \times \Sigma^+, E^m, \mathit{Trans})$. Then the following theorem holds.

Theorem 2. *For any $k \geq 0$, the class*

$$E_k^m = \{ \mathit{Trans}(\Gamma) \mid \Gamma \subseteq E^m \text{ and } |\Gamma| \leq k \}$$

is learnable from positive examples.

Proof. We show that the concept defining framework $(\Sigma^+ \times \Sigma^+, E^m, \mathit{Trans})$ has bounded finite thickness for any $m \geq 1$.

Since the function PS is monotonic, so is the function Trans. Let n be a positive integer, S be a finite subset of $\Sigma^+ \times \Sigma^+$, and l be the maximum length of s such that $(s, t) \in S$. If a linearly-moded EFS Γ is reduced w.r.t. S and $|\Gamma| \leq n$, then each clause $p_0(s_0; t_0) \leftarrow p_1(s_1; t_1), \ldots, p_i(s_i; t_i) \in \Gamma$ satisfies the condition that $|s_j| \leq l$ and $|t_j| \leq l$ for any j $(0 \leq j \leq i)$. Since $i \leq m$ and the number of all predicate symbols in Γ is at most n, the set

$$\{ \mathit{Trans}(\Gamma) \mid \Gamma \text{ is reduced w.r.t. } S \text{ and } |\Gamma| \leq n \}$$

is finite. By Shinohara's theorem [11], the class E_k^m is learnable from positive examples. $\square$

Consider the learnability of the larger class of linearly-moded EFS's. Let s and t be finite sequences of terms, and l be a positive integer. Then, we denote $s \geq^l t$ if $|s\theta| + l \geq |t\theta|$ for any substitution θ. For example, $x \geq^1 ax$ and $ab \geq^1 aab$.

An l-*linearly-moded EFS* is defined by replacing $\geq$ with $\geq^l$ in Definition 1 and Definition 2. For the translation defined by an l-linearly-moded EFS, the length of each output sentence is at most l greater than the length of its input sentence.

Let $F(l)^m$ be the class of all l-linearly-moded EFS's in which each clause has at most m atoms in its body. Then, the following theorem holds.

Theorem 3. *Suppose that $m \geq 2$ and $k \geq 3$. Then, the class*

$$F(l)^m_k = \{ Trans(\Gamma) \mid \Gamma \subseteq F(l)^m \text{ and } |\Gamma| \leq k \}$$

is not learnable from positive examples for any $l \geq 1$.

Proof. The class $F(1)^2_3$ contains the following EFS's Γ_n $(n \geq 1)$ and Γ_∞:

$$\Gamma_n = \left\{ \begin{array}{l} q_0(a^n; a^n) \leftarrow, \\ q_0(x; x) \leftarrow suc(x; y), q_0(y; z), \\ suc(x; ax) \leftarrow \end{array} \right\},$$

$$\Gamma_\infty = \left\{ \begin{array}{l} q_0(a; a) \leftarrow, \\ q_0(ax; ay) \leftarrow q_0(x; y) \end{array} \right\}.$$

Note that only the third clause of Γ_n does not satisfy the conditions in Definition 2, because $|x\theta| + 1 = |ax\theta|$ for any substitution θ. Then, $Trans(\Gamma_n) = \{(a^i, a^i) \mid 1 \leq i \leq n\}$ and $Trans(\Gamma_\infty) = \{(a^i, a^i) \mid i \geq 1\}$. Since $Trans(\Gamma_i) \subseteq Trans(\Gamma_{i+1})$ and $Trans(\Gamma_i) \subseteq Trans(\Gamma_\infty)$ for any $i \geq 1$, the class $F(l)^2_3$ is superfinite. Hence, it is not learnable from positive examples [7]. $\qquad\square$

6 Conclusion

In this paper, we have introduced a linearly-moded EFS with local variables and linear predicate inequalities based on mode information. The class of linearly-moded EFS's is so large as to express translations over context-sensitive languages. For the translation defined by a linearly-moded EFS, the set of all output sentences is finite and computable for each input sentence. Furthermore, we have shown that the class of translations defined by linearly-moded EFS's is learnable from positive examples under the condition that the number of clauses in the EFS's and the length of each clause are bounded by some constant.

As a further extension of EFS's, we have formalized an l-linearly-moded EFS. For the translations defined by an l-linearly-moded EFS, the length of each output sentence is at most l greater than the length of its input sentence. It is a natural extension, because the 0-linearly-moded EFS is equivalent to that of a linearly-moded EFS. However, the class of translations defined by l-linearly-moded EFS's is not learnable from positive examples for any $l \geq 1$ even if both the number of clauses in each EFS and the length of bodies of each clause are bounded some constant. Therefore, we need another investigation to extend the learnability of translations without the restriction on the relationship between the lengths of input-output sentences.

Acknowledgements

I wish to thank Dr. Hiroki Ishizaka for motivating this research. I am grateful to Dr. Kouichi Hirata for his comments on this paper. I would also like to thank the anonymous referees for their valuable comments to improve this paper.

References

1. A. V. Aho and J. D. Ullman. Properties of syntax directed translations. *Journal of Computer and System Sciences* 3:319–334, 1969.
2. A. V. Aho and J. D. Ullman. Syntax directed translation and the pushdown assembler. *Journal of Computer and System Sciences* 3:37–56, 1969.
3. D. Angluin. Inductive inference of formal languages from positive data. *Information and Control* 45:117–135, 1980.
4. D. Angluin. Inference of reversible languages. *Journal of the ACM* 29:741–765, July 1982.
5. S. Arikawa, T. Shinohara, and A. Yamamoto. Learning elementary formal systems. *Theoretical Computer Science* 95:97–113, 1992.
6. H. Arimura and T. Shinohara. Inductive inference of prolog programs with linear data dependency from positive data. *Proc. Information Modelling and Knowledge Bases V*, 1994.
7. E. Gold. Language identification in the limit. *Information and Control* 10:447–474, 1967.
8. E. Irons. A syntax directed compiler for ALGOL-60. *Communications of the ACM* 4:51–55, 1961.
9. P. M. Lewis and R. E. Stearns. Syntax-directed transduction. *Journal of the ACM* 15:465–488, 1968.
10. M. K. Rao. A class of prolog programs inferable from positive data. *Lecture Notes in Artificial Intelligence 1160*, 272–284, 1996.
11. T. Shinohara. Inductive inference of monotonic formal systems from positive data. *New Generation Computing*, 8:371–384, 1991.
12. T. Shinohara. Rich classes inferable from positive data: length-bounded elementary formal system. *Information and Computation* 108:175–186, 1994.
13. R. Smullyan. Theory of formal systems. *Princeton Univ. Press*, 1961.
14. N. Sugimoto, K. Hirata and H. Ishizaka. Constructive learning of translations based on dictionaries. *Lecture Notes in Artificial Intelligence 1160*, 177–184, 1996.
15. A. Yamamoto. Procedural semantics and negative information of elementary formal system. *Journal of Logic Programming* 13:89–97, 1992.

Analysis of Case-Based Representability of Boolean Functions by Monotone Theory

Ken Satoh

Division of Electronics and Information, Hokkaido University
N13W8 Kita-ku, Sapporo, 060-8628, Japan
Email:ksatoh@db-ei.eng.hokudai.ac.jp

Abstract. Classification is one of major tasks in case-based reasoning(CBR) and many studies have been done for analyzing properties of case-based classification [1, 14, 10, 15, 12, 9, 13, 7]. However, these studies only consider numerical similarity measures whereas there are other kinds of similarity measure for different tasks. Among these measures, HYPO system [2, 3] in a legal domain uses a similarity measure based on set inclusion of differences of attributes in cases.

In this paper, we give an analysis of representability of boolean functions in case-based classification using the above set inclusion based similarity. We show that such case-based classification has a strong connection between monotone theory studied in [4, 11]. Monotone theory is originated from computational learning theory and is used to show learnability of boolean function with polynomial DNF size and polynomial CNF size [4] and is used for deductive reasoning as well [11]. In this paper, we analyze a case-based representability of boolean functions by using the above relationship between the case-based classification by set inclusion based similarity and the monotone theory. We show that any boolean function is representable by a casebase whose size is bounded in polynomial of its DNF size and its CNF size and thus, k-term DNF, k-clause CNF can be efficiently representable in a casebase using set inclusion similarity.

1 Introduction

In this paper, we show a correspondence between case-based classification using set inclusion similarity and monotone theory [4, 11] in learning of boolean functions and analyze case-based representability of boolean functions by using the correspondence.

Classification is one of the main tasks of case-based reasoning(CBR). For example, CBR has been used for classfication of pronunciation of unknown English words[17], a telex classification[8], and the census classification task[6].

For case-based classification, we introduce a distance measure between cases and retrieve the most similar case to the current case and regard the classification label of the retrieved case as the label of the current case. This kind of usage of CBR is sometimes called memory-based reasoning [17], instance-based learning [1], or the its origin, nearest-neighbor classification [5].

This way of learning contrasts with the usual inductive learning mechanism where we extract abstract regularity which reflects tendency of examples. Although it is more desirable to induce abstract information from examples, if we focus on a classification task only, we do not need such information. Actually, [1] shows that the performance of instance-based learning for several classification tasks is compatible with other inductive learning mechanism such as Quinlan's C4. Moreover, instance-based learning has advantages of its simple and lazy manner of learning.

To understand the behavior of case-based classifiers, many theoretical analyses have been done [1, 14, 10, 15, 12, 9, 13, 7]. Among these studies, [10, 15, 7] give analyses of representativity of concepts in a case-based manner. [10] analyzes case-based representability of pattern languages, [15] gives upper and lower bounds on sample complexity to present various concept classes in the nearest neighbor algorithm and [7] investigates efficient case-based representations for some classes of boolean functions. A motivation of these analyses of case-based classifier is explained in [15]; we would like to know how many cases are needed for the system to "learn" the concept exactly. Another motivation is that we should analyze representability before analyzing learnability since if the concept cannot be represented efficiently, the concept cannot be learned efficiently [10]. Although the results of the above studies are important in their own rights, considered case-based classifiers in these studies are based on numerical similarity measures.

On the other hand, there are other similarity measures used in different tasks of CBR. Among existing CBR systems, a legal CBR system, HYPO [2, 3] uses a similarity measure based on set inclusion of differences of attributes in cases. The original usage of HYPO is to retrieve similar or contrasting precedents for an input case to create an arguments for the input case. However, we can use this similarity measure for classification as follows. The current case is classified as positive if there is a positive case which shares a set of factors with the current case and there is no negative case such that the set of shared factors between the negative case and the current case includes the set of shared factors between the positive case and the current case. This idea is actually implemented in abductive logic programming [16] to decide whether an input case is preferable to plaintiff side or defendant side.

In this paper, we show that case-based reasoning with the set inclusion based similarity is closely related to monotone theory studied in [4, 11]. Monotone theory is originated from computational learning theory and is used to show learnability of boolean function with polynomial DNF size and polynomial CNF size. Moreover, [11] shows that the idea is also applicable to deductive reasoning task. We use the monotone theory for a different purpose, that is, an analysis of representability of case-based classifier using set inclusion similarity. Specifically, we show that a boolean function defined by a casebase with our similarity measure is a complement of a monotone extension [4] such that a set of positive cases in the casebase is called *basis* in [4] and negative cases are assignments in the monotone extension. By using this relationship, we show that any boolean function f is representable by a casebase whose size is bounded in polynomial of its DNF size and its CNF size. The above implies that interesting classes such as k-term DNF, k-clause CNF can be efficiently representable in case-based classifier using set inclusion similarity measure.

The structure of the paper is as follows. In Section 2, we give preliminary definitions. In Section 3, we propose a new similarity measure based on set inclusion for case-based classification and give some properties of the similarity. In Section 4, we show a correspondence between set inclusion based case-based classification and monotone theory. In Section 5, we discuss representability of boolean function by using the above correspondence. Finally, we conclude our paper by summarizing our contribution and future research.

2 Preliminaries

We consider a boolean function $\{0,1\}^n \mapsto \{0,1\}$. To represent a boolean function syntactically, we use a boolean formula in the usual way which consists of a tuple of boolean variables $\langle X_1, ..., X_n \rangle$ and logical connectives such as $\wedge$, $\vee$ and $\neg$ which denotes boolean AND, OR and NOT operator respectively. We denote a negation of a formula F as $\overline{F}$ called the complement of F. A literal is either a variable X_i (called a positive literal) or its negation $\neg X_i$ (called a negative literal). A clause is a disjunction of literals. We say that a variable appears positively in a clause if a positive literal of the variable appears in the clause and a variable appears negatively in a clause if a negative literal of the variable appears in the clause. A CNF formula is a conjunction of clauses and a DNF formula is a disjunction of conjunctions of literals. Note that there are many CNF representations of the same boolean function and many DNF representations of the same boolean function. We denote the DNF size of a boolean function f as $|DNF(f)|$ meaning the minimum possible number of conjunctions in any DNF representation of f and the CNF size of a boolean function f as $|CNF(f)|$ meaning the minimum possible number of clauses in any CNF representation of f.

We use a bit vector $x \in \{0,1\}^n$ to give a value of a boolean function represented by a formula. We assign the value of the i-th component of x, $x[i]$, to the variable X_i and interpret a formula in the usual way. We say that an assignment x satisfies boolean function f if $f(x) = 1$. We sometimes regard a boolean function f as a set of assignments satisfying f, that is, for an assignment x, we write $x \in f$ in stead of $f(x) = 1$. We also regard a set of assignments S as a boolean function, that is, for an assignment x, we write $S(x) = 1$ if and only if $x \in S$. We use an interpretation function ϕ from a formula to a boolean function represented by the formula. If F is a representation of a boolean function f, then $\phi(F) = f$. For a boolean function f, $\overline{f}$ expresses the complement of f which defines as $\overline{f}(x) = 1$ if and only $f(x) = 0$ for every assignment x. Note that for a set representation of boolean function, $\overline{f} = \{0,1\}^n - f$.

3 Case-Based Classification

We regard an assignment vector in $\{0,1\}^n$ as a case. This means that a case is represented as an n boolean-valued attributes.

Definition 1. For cases c_1, c_2, we define $d(c_1, c_2)$ as $c_1 \oplus c_2$ where $\oplus$ is a bitwise EXCLUSIVE-OR operation $((c_1 \oplus c_2)[i] = 1$ if and only if $c_1[i] \neq c_2[i])$.

We write $d(c_1, c) \preceq d(c_2, c)$ where $\preceq$ denotes a partial order over a vector $x, y \in \{0,1\}^n$ such that $x \preceq y$ if and only if $\forall i (1 \leq i \leq n), x[i] \leq y[i]$.

We write $d(c_1, c) \prec d(c_2, c)$ if $d(c_1, c) \preceq d(c_2, c)$ and $d(c_1, c) \neq d(c_2, c)$.

In the above definition, d expresses a difference set of a pair of cases and $\preceq$ is based on set-inclusion relation expressing that difference set of a pair is included in the difference set of the other pair.

Definition 2. Let CB be a pair of two disjoint sets of cases $\langle CB^+, CB^- \rangle$.

We call CB a *casebase*, CB^+ a set of *positive cases* and CB^- a set of *negative cases* respectively.

Let CB a casebase $\langle CB^+, CB^- \rangle$. We say that *a boolean function* f_{CB} *is represented by a casebase* CB if

$$f_{CB} = \{c | \exists c_{ok} \in CB^+ \text{ s.t. } \forall c_{ng} \in CB^- \ d(c_{ng}, c) \npreceq d(c_{ok}, c)\}$$

Note that in the above definition f_{CB} is represented as a set of assignments. For a function representation, $f_{CB}(c) = 1$ if and only if $c \in f_{CB}$. We can recognize the analogue to instance-based learning by numerical-valued similarity. However, note that $d(c_{ng}, c) \npreceq d(c_{ok}, c)$ does not always imply $d(c_{ok}, c) \prec d(c_{ng}, c)$.

Example 1. Let $\{X_1, X_2, X_3, X_4\}$ be a set of variables. We consider a boolean function $f : \{0,1\}^4 \mapsto \{0,1\}$ such that a representation of f in a CNF formula is

$$(\neg X_1 \lor \neg X_2 \lor \neg X_3) \land (X_2 \lor \neg X_3 \lor \neg X_4).$$

Then, assignments satisfying f are:

$$\{0000, 0001, 0010, 0100, 0101, 0110, 0111, 1000, 1001, 1010, 1100, 1101\},$$

where an assignment are represented as a sequence $b_1 b_2 b_3 b_4$ meaning that b_i is the assigned value to X_i.

Let CB be a casebase $\langle CB^+, CB^- \rangle$ where $CB^+ = \{0010, 0101\}$ and $CB^- = \{0011, 1110, 1111\}$. We can show that f is represented by CB, that is, $f_{CB} = f$ by checking for every $c \in f$ there exists some $c_{ok} \in CB^+$ such that every $c_{ng} \in CB^-$, $d(c, c_{ng}) \npreceq d(c, c_{ok})$.

For example, let us consider an assignment $1000 \in f$ and $0010 \in CB^+$. Note that $d(0010, 1000) = 1010$. Then,

- for $0011 \in CB^-$, $d(0011, 1000) = 1011$ means $d(0011, 1000) \npreceq d(0010, 1000)$.
- for $1110 \in CB^-$, $d(1110, 1000) = 0110$ means $d(1110, 1000) \npreceq d(0010, 1000)$.
- for $1111 \in CB^-$, $d(1111, 1000) = 0111$ means $d(1111, 1000) \npreceq d(0010, 1000)$.

Therefore, $1000 \in f_{CB}$.

On the other hand, let us consider an assignment $1011 \notin f$. For $0010 \in CB^+$, there exists $0011 \in CB^-$, $d(0011, 1011) \preceq d(0010, 1011)$ and for $0101 \in CB^+$, there exists $1111 \in CB^-$, $d(1111, 1011) \preceq d(0101, 1011)$. Therefore, $1011 \notin f_{CB}$.

A combination of the above d and $\preceq$ leads to the following important property which will be used for correspondence between case-based classification and monotone theory.

Lemma 3. *Let* c, c_1, c_2 *be cases.* $d(c_1, c) \preceq d(c_2, c)$ *if and only if* $d(c_1, c_2) \preceq d(c, c_2)$

Proof: Clearly, $x \preceq y$ if and only if $x = x \& y$ where $=$ is a bitwise equality and $\&$ is a bitwise AND operation. Therefore, $d(c_1, c) \preceq d(c_2, c)$ if and only if $(c_1 \oplus c) = (c_1 \oplus c) \& (c_2 \oplus c)$.

Then, this is equivalent to $c_1 = (c_1 \& c_2) \oplus (c \& c_2) \oplus (c_1 \& c)$ by using that $c \& c = c$, and $c_1 \oplus c = X \oplus c$ if and only $c_1 = X$.

Similarly, $d(c_1, c_2) \preceq d(c, c_2)$ if and only if $c_1 = (c_1 \& c_2) \oplus (c \& c_2) \oplus (c_1 \& c)$ $\square$.

Note that if a difference function is defined as numerical-valued function, we do not have the above symmetrical property.

Lemma 4. *Let* CB *be a casebase* $\langle CB^+, CB^- \rangle$. *Let* f_{CB} *be a boolean function represented by* CB.
$$f_{CB} = \{c | \exists c_{ok} \in CB^+ \text{ s.t. } \forall c_{ng} \in CB^- \ d(c_{ng}, c_{ok}) \npreceq d(c, c_{ok})\}$$

Proof: By Lemma 3. $\square$

Note that the above lemma is important if we use a casebase for classification task. When we decide to fix a casebase, given a new case c to be classified, we need to compute both of $d(c, c_{ng})$ and $d(c, c_{ok})$ in the original definition of representation of boolean function. However, by the above Lemma, we can "precompile" a fixed casebase for efficient classification, that is, we can compute $d(c_{ng}, c_{ok})$ in advance. Then, we only need to compute $d(c, c_{ok})$ for a classification task.

We can detect redundant negative cases by using the following lemma.

Lemma 5. *Let* CB *be a casebase* $\langle CB^+, CB^- \rangle$. *Let* f_{CB} *be a boolean function represented by* CB. *Let* $C_{ng} \in CB^-$ *and* $CB' = \langle CB^+, CB'^- \rangle$ *where* $CB'^- = CB^- - \{C_{ng}\}$. *If for all* $c_{ok} \in CB^+$, *there exists* $c_{ng} \in CB'^-$ *s.t.* $d(c_{ng}, c_{ok}) \preceq d(C_{ng}, c_{ok})$. *Then* $f_{CB} = f_{CB'}$.

Proof: Clearly, $f_{CB} \subseteq f_{CB'}$. Suppose that $f_{CB} \neq f_{CB'}$. Then, there exists some C such that $C \notin f_{CB}$ and $C \in f_{CB'}$. This means:

- $\forall c'_{ok} \in CB^+ \exists c_{ng} \in CB^-$ s.t. $d(c_{ng}, C) \preceq d(c'_{ok}, C)$.
- $\exists c_{ok} \in CB^+ \forall c_{ng} \in CB'^-$ s.t. $d(c_{ng}, C) \npreceq d(c_{ok}, C)$. Let C_{ok} be such c_{ok}.

Then, $d(C_{ng}, C) \preceq d(C_{ok}, C)$. By Lemma 3, this means $d(C_{ng}, C_{ok}) \preceq d(C, C_{ok})$. However, since there exists $c_{ng} \in CB'^-$, $d(c_{ng}, C_{ok}) \preceq d(C_{ng}, C_{ok})$ by the condition of C_{ng}, there exists $c_{ng} \in CB'^-$, $d(c_{ng}, C_{ok}) \preceq d(C, C_{ok})$. This implies $d(c_{ng}, C) \preceq d(C_{ok}, C)$ again by Lemma 3 and leads to contradiction. □

Example 2. Consider the same boolean function f, CB^+ and CB^- in Example 1. Note that $\overline{f} = CB^- \cup \{1011\}$. For $0010 \in CB^+$, there exists $0011 \in CB^-$ such that $d(0011, 0010) \preceq d(1011, 0010)$ and for $0101 \in CB^+$, there exists $1111 \in CB^-$ such that $d(1111, 0101) \preceq d(1011, 0101)$. Then, $f_{CB} = f_{CB'}$ where $f_{CB} = \langle CB^+, \overline{f} \rangle$ and $f_{CB'} = \langle CB^+, CB^- \rangle$ as Lemma 5 states.

Definition 6. Let S be a set of cases and c be a case. We define the nearest cases of S from c, $NN(c, S)$, as follows.
$$NN(c, S) = \{c' \in S | \neg \exists c'' \in S \text{ s.t. } d(c, c'') \preceq d(c, c')\}$$

Corollary 7. *Let CB be a casebase $\langle CB^+, CB^- \rangle$.*
Let $CB' = \langle CB^+, \bigcup_{c_{ok} \in CB^+} NN(c_{ok}, CB^-) \rangle$. Then, $f_{CB} = f_{CB'}$.

Proof: Suppose $c_{ng} \notin \bigcup_{c_{ok} \in CB^+} NN(c_{ok}, CB^-)$. Then, for every $c_{ok} \in CB^+$, $c_{ng} \notin NN(c_{ok}, CB^-)$. This means that there exists $c'' \in CB^-$ s.t. $d(c_{ok}, c'') \preceq d(c_{ok}, c_{ng})$. Therefore, by Lemma 5, $f_{CB} = f_{CB''}$ where $CB'' = \langle CB^+, (CB^- - \{c_{ng}\}) \rangle$. Even after removing c_{ng} from CB^-, $\bigcup_{c_{ok} \in CB^+} NN(c_{ok}, (CB^- - \{c_{ng}\})) = \bigcup_{c_{ok} \in CB^+} NN(c_{ok}, CB^-)$, since otherwise, c_{ng} was in $\bigcup_{c_{ok} \in CB^+} NN(c_{ok}, CB^-)$. Therefore, we can remove all c_{ng} such that $c_{ng} \notin \bigcup_{c_{ok} \in CB^+} NN(c_{ok}, CB^-)$ from CB^- without changing f_{CB} and thus, $f_{CB} = f_{CB'}$. □

This corollary also helps speedup of classification together with Lemma 4, since we do not need to compute $d(c_{ng}, c_{ok})$ for redundant negative cases. However, note that when a positive case is added, we must check redundancy for unused negative cases again.

4 Relation Between Case-Based Classification and Monotone Theory

We follow the definition by [4, 11].

Let z, x and b be assignments. We define $z \preceq_b x$ as $d(z, b) \preceq d(x, b)$. Let f be a boolean function. The *b-monotone boolean function of f* is $\mathcal{M}_b(f) = \{x | \exists z \in f, z \preceq_b x\}$.

Let f be a boolean function and S be sets of assignments. We write $\mathcal{M}_S(f) = \bigcap_{b \in S} \mathcal{M}_b(f)$. We call $\mathcal{M}_S(f)$ *monotone extension of boolean function f* w.r.t. S.

The following is the main theorem of this paper expressing a relationship between case-based resoning and monotone theory.

Theorem 8. *Let CB be a casebase $\langle CB^+, CB^- \rangle$. We regard CB^- as a boolean function such that for an assignment x, $CB^-(x) = 1$ if and only if $x \in CB^-$. Then, $f_{CB} = \mathcal{M}_{CB^+}(CB^-)$.*

Proof:

$$f_{CB} = \{c | \exists c_{ok} \in CB^+ \text{ s.t. } \forall c_{ng} \in CB^- \ d(c_{ng}, c_{ok}) \not\preceq d(c, c_{ok})\} \text{ (by Lemma 4)}$$
$$= \overline{\{c | \neg \forall c_{ok} \in CB^+ \exists c_{ng} \in CB^- \ c_{ng} \preceq_{c_{ok}} c\}}$$
$$= \overline{\{c | \forall c_{ok} \in CB^+ \exists c_{ng} \in CB^- \ c_{ng} \preceq_{c_{ok}} c\}}$$
$$= \overline{\bigcap_{c_{ok} \in CB^+} \{c | \exists c_{ng} \in CB^- \ c_{ng} \preceq_{c_{ok}} c\}}$$
$$= \overline{\bigcap_{c_{ok} \in CB^+} \mathcal{M}_{c_{ok}}(CB^-)}$$
$$= \overline{\mathcal{M}_{CB^+}(CB^-)} \ \square$$

Therefore, a boolean function represented by case-based classification using set inclusion similarity is the complement of monotone extension of negative cases w.r.t. positive cases.

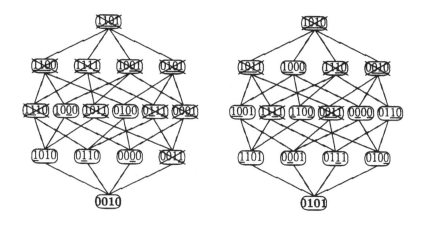

Fig. 1. $\mathcal{M}_{0010}(\{1111, 1110, 0011\})$ and $\mathcal{M}_{0101}(\{1111, 1110, 0011\})$

Example 3. Let $CB^+ = \{0010, 0101\}$ and $CB^- = \{0011, 1110, 1111\}$ as in Example 1. In each lattices of Figure 1 is induced by difference between an assignment in a node and the assignment in the bottom node. Underlined bits of an assignment express a difference from an assignment of the bottom node and crossed nodes of the lattice on the left express $\mathcal{M}_{0010}(CB^-)$ and one on the right express $\mathcal{M}_{0101}(CB^-)$. Note that $\mathcal{M}_{CB^+}(CB^-) = \mathcal{M}_{0010}(CB^-) \cap \mathcal{M}_{0101}(CB^-) = \{0011, 1011, 1110, 1111\}$ which coincides with $\overline{f}$ in Example 1.

By using the above correspondence, we can apply findings from monotone theory to analysis of case-based classification. In the sequel, we paraphrase results and proofs in the study of monotone theory in terms of case-based learning.

The following is a dual of Claim 4.7 [11] which is related to the size of CB^+.

Lemma 9. *Let CB^+ be a set of cases and $D_1 \vee \ldots \vee D_k$ be a DNF represenation of a boolean function f. Suppose that for every D_i, there exists $c_{ok} \in CB^+$ such that $c_{ok} \in \phi(D_i)$. Then, $f = f_{CB}$ where $CB = \langle CB^+, \overline{f} \rangle$.*

Proof:

Since $f_{CB} = \overline{\mathcal{M}_{CB^+}(\overline{f})}$ by Theorem 8, we show $f = \overline{\mathcal{M}_{CB^+}(\overline{f})}$. Since it is always the case that $\overline{f} \subseteq \mathcal{M}_{CB^+}(\overline{f})$, $\overline{\mathcal{M}_{CB^+}(\overline{f})} \subseteq f$ and so, it is sufficient to show that for every c satisfying f, there is some positive case $c_{ok} \in CB^+$ such that $c \notin \mathcal{M}_{c_{ok}}(\overline{f})$.

Suppose c satisfies f. Then, there exists a conjunct D of the above DNF formula which does not contain a positive literal and a negative literal of the same variable simultaneously such that $c \in \phi(D)$. This means that $i(1 \leq i \leq n)$,

- $c[i] = 1$ if X_i appears in D.
- $c[i] = 0$ if $\neg X_i$ appears in D.

Let $c_{ok} \in CB^+$ be a case satisfying $c_{ok} \in \phi(D)$. This also means that for every $i(1 \leq i \leq n)$,

- $c_{ok}[i] = 1$ if X_i appears in D.
- $c_{ok}[i] = 0$ if $\neg X_i$ appears in D.

Now, we show that $c \notin \mathcal{M}_{c_{ok}}(\overline{f})$. Suppose that $c \in \mathcal{M}_{c_{ok}}(\overline{f})$. Then, there exists a case z satisfying $\overline{f}$ such that $d(z, c_{ok}) \preceq d(c, c_{ok})$. This means that if $c[i] = c_{ok}[i]$ then $z[i] = c_{ok}[i]$ Therefore, $i(1 \leq i \leq n)$,

- $z[i] = 1$ if X_i appears in D.
- $z[i] = 0$ if $\neg X_i$ appears in D.

This means $z \in f$ and this leads to contradition. Thus, $f \subseteq \overline{\mathcal{M}_{CB^+}(\overline{f})}$. $\square$

Example 4. Consider the same boolean function f in Example 1. A DNF representation of f is

$$(\neg X_1 \wedge X_2) \vee (\neg X_1 \wedge \neg X_4) \vee (\neg X_2 \wedge \neg X_4) \vee \neg X_3.$$

Then, for every conjunct D in the above representation there exists $c_{ok} \in CB^+$ in Example 1 such that $c_{ok} \in \phi(D)$. Let CB be a casebase $\langle CB^+, \overline{f} \rangle$. We can easily check that $f = f_{CB}$ as Lemma 9 states.

For the next lemma, we use a set of cases $PNN(b, \overline{f})$ defined as follows:

$\{c | c \notin f$ s.t. there is no $c' \notin f$ s.t. $d(c', b) \preceq d(c, b)$ and
    there exists l s.t. $c[l] \neq c'[l]$ and $c[j] = c'[j]$ for $j \neq l(1 \leq j \leq n)\}$

$PNN(b, \overline{f})$ is a set of pseudo nearest neighbor assignments from b with respect to $\overline{f}$. Note that $NN(b, \overline{f}) \subseteq PNN(b, \overline{f})$.

The following is a dual of Claim 4.8 [11] which is related to the size of CB^-.

Lemma 10. *Suppose that $D_1 \wedge ... \wedge D_k$ be a CNF represenation for a boolean function f and b be a case. Then, $|PNN(b, \overline{f})| \leq k$.*

Proof:

Let D be any clause in the above CNF representation. If D contains the positive literal and the negative literal of the same variable, then it becomes 1 and can be ignored. Otherwise, we define a case $c_{min}(D)$ w.r.t. a clause D in the above CNF representation of f as follows. For every $j(1 \leq j \leq n)$,

- $c_{min}(D)[j] = 1$ if X_j appears negatively in D.
- $c_{min}(D)[j] = 0$ if X_j appears positively in D.
- $c_{min}(D)[j] = b[j]$ if X_j does not appear in D.

Consider such c that for some l, $c_{min}(D)[l] \neq c[l]$, and $c_{min}(D)[j] = c[j]$ for $j \neq l (1 \leq j \leq n)$.

- If X_l appears negatively in D, then $c[l] = 0$ and so, $c \in f$.
- If X_l appears positively in D, then $c[l] = 1$ and so, $c \in f$
- If X_l does not appear in D, then $c[l] \neq b[l]$ and so, $d(c_{min}(D), b) \prec d(c, b)$

Therefore, $c_{min}(D) \in PNN(b, \overline{f})$.

Suppose $c' \in \overline{f}$. Then, there exists some clause D' in the above CNF representation of f such that for every $j (1 \leq j \leq n)$,

- $c'[j] = 1$ if X_j appears negatively in D'.
- $c'[j] = 0$ if X_j appears positively in D'.

Suppose $c' \neq c_{min}(D')$. Then, c' is different from $c_{min}(D')$ only in such j-th values that X_j does not appear in D'. This means $d(c_{min}(D'), b) \prec d(c', b)$. Therefore, $PNN(b, \overline{f}) = \{c_{min}(D) | D$ is a clause in the above CNF representation of $f\}$ and thus $|PNN(b, \overline{f})| \leq k$. (Note that $c_{min}(D)$ might be equal to other $c_{min}(D')$ for other D'). $\square$

Corollary 11. *Let f be a boolean function which has a CNF representation $D_1 \wedge \ldots \wedge D_k$ and b be a case. For every case b, $|NN(b, \overline{f})| \leq k$. Especially, $|NN(b, \overline{f})| \leq |CNF(f)|$.*

Proof: $NN(b, \overline{f}) \subseteq PNN(b, \overline{f})$ and by Lemma 10.

5 Representability

We modify the definition of [7] of polynomial representability so that we confine similarity measure to the one based on set inclusion.

Let S be a set of cases or assignments. Then, we denote the number of cases or assignments in S as $|S|$. Let CB be a casebase $\langle CB^+, CB^- \rangle$. We denote the sum of $|CB^+| + |CB^-|$ as $|CB|$ which we call *the size of the casebase CB.*

Definition 12. *Let $\mathcal{F}_n$ be a class of boolean function from $\{0, 1\}^n$ to $\{0, 1\}$. Let $\mathcal{F} = \bigcup_{i=1}^n \mathcal{F}_n$. $\mathcal{F}$ is called polynomially representable iff there exists a polynomial $p(\cdot)$ such that, for every n and every $f \in \mathcal{F}_n$, there exists a casebase CB_n that satisfies $f_{CB_n} = f$ and $|CB_n| \leq p(n)$.*

The following theorem gives the upper bound of representability of boolean functions.

Theorem 13. *Let f be a boolean function. Then, there exists a casebase $CB = \langle CB^+, CB^- \rangle$ such that $|CB^+| \leq |DNF(f)|$, $|CB^-| \leq |DNF(f)| \cdot |CNF(f)|$ and $|CB| \leq |DNF(f)|(1 + |CNF(f)|)$.*

Proof: There is a DNF representation $D_1 \vee ... \vee D_k$ of f such that $k = |DNF(f)|$. If we take a set of cases each of which satisfies each D_i as CB^+, then by Lemma 9, there exists $f = f_{CB'}$ where $CB' = \langle CB^+, \overline{f} \rangle$ and $|CB^+| \leq |DNF(f)|$. Then, by Corollary 7, $f = f_{CB}$ where $CB = \langle CB^-, CB^- \rangle$ where $CB^- = \bigcup_{c_{ok} \in CB^+} NN(c_{ok}, \overline{f})$. Then, since by Corollary 11, for each $c_{ok} \in CB^+$, $|NN(c_{ok}, \overline{f})| \leq |CNF(f)|$,

$$|CB^-| \leq \sum_{c_{ok} \in CB^+} |CNF(f)| \leq |DNF(f)| \cdot |CNF(f)|.$$

$\square$

Corollary 14. *Let $\mathcal{F}_n$ be a class of boolean function from $\{0,1\}^n$ to $\{0,1\}$. Let $\mathcal{F} = \bigcup_{i=1}^{n} \mathcal{F}_n$. If for every $f \in \mathcal{F}_n$, $|DNF(f)|$ and $|CNF(f)|$ is polynomial of n, then $\mathcal{F}$ is polynomially representable.*

There are interesting classes of boolean function which have the above property.

Theorem 15. *The class of k-term DNF is a class of boolean functions whose DNF contains at most k conjunctions. k-term DNF is polynomially representable.*

Proof: For every n-ary boolean function f in k-term DNF class, $|DNF(f)| \leq k$ and $|CNF(f)| \leq n^k$. Therefore, by Theorem 13, there exists a casebase CB such that $f = f_{CB}$ and $|CB| \leq n^k(k+1)$. $\square$

In a similar way, the class of k-clause CNF (a class of boolean functions whose CNF contains at most k clauses) is polynomially representable.

So far, we are concerned about a boolean function to be represented as a casebase. Suppose that a casebase represents a boolean function correctly. If we can decode the boolean function in a rule form, it might be useful for a user to get a hint of a structure of the boolean function. For example, if we apply our case-based learning to domain of legal reasoning, then to extract a rule from the casebase corresponds to make a case law which tells a lawyer when the previous case can be applied to the current case. This kind of decoding can be done as follows.

Definition 16. Let CB be a casebase $\langle CB^+, CB^- \rangle$. For every $c_{ok} \in CB^+$, we construct CNF formula as follows and combine them with $\vee$ to result in a formula denoted as F_{CB}.

For every $c_{ng} \in CB^-$, we construct a clause in the CNF as follows.
- If $c_{ng}[i] = 0$ and $c_{ok}[i] = 1$, then X_i is in the clause.
- If $c_{ng}[i] = 1$ and $c_{ok}[i] = 0$, then $\neg X_i$ is in the clause.

Theorem 17. *Let CB be a casebase and F_{CB} is constructed in a way of Definition 16. Then, $\phi(F_{CB}) = f_{CB}$.*

Proof: Let $CB = \langle CB^+, CB^- \rangle$.

(1) $\phi(F_{CB}) \subseteq f_{CB}$

Suppose $c \in \phi(F_{CB})$. Then, there is a CNF formula $D \in F_{CB}$ defined in Definition 16 such that $c \in \phi(D)$.

Let c_{ok} be a corresponding case with D. This means that for every clause E in D, $c \in \phi(E)$. and so, there is $i(1 \leq i \leq n)$ s.t. either $c[i] = 1$ and $X_i \in E$ or $c[i] = 0$ and $\neg X_i \in E$. Therefore, for every $c_{ng} \in CB^-$, there is i s.t. either $c[i] = 1$ and $c_{ng}[i] = 0$ and $c_{ok}[i] = 1$ or $c[i] = 0$ and $c_{ng}[i] = 1$ and $c_{ok}[i] = 0$. This means that for every $c_{ng} \in CB^-$, $d(c, c_{ng}) \not\preceq d(c, c_{ok})$. Therefore, $c \in f_{CB}$.

(2) $f_{CB} \subseteq \phi(F_{CB})$

Suppose $c \in f_{CB}$. Then, there is $c_{ok} \in CB^+$ such that for every $c_{ng} \in CB^-$, $d(c, c_{ng}) \not\preceq d(c, c_{ok})$.

This means that for every $c_{ng} \in CB^-$, there is i s.t. $c[i] = c_{ok}[i]$ and $c[i] \neq c_{ng}[i]$. This means that for such i, $c[i] = 1$ and $c_{ok}[i] = 1$ and $c_{ng}[i] = 0$ or $c[i] = 0$ and $c_{ok}[i] = 0$ and $c_{ng}[i] = 1$.

Let D be a corresponding a CNF formula $D \in F_{CB}$ with c_{ok} defined in Definition 16. Let E be a clause in D which corresponds with $c_{ng} \in CB^-$. By the construction of E, we can show that $c \in \phi(E)$. Therefore, $c \in \phi(F_{CB})$. $\square$

Example 5. Consider Example 1 again. Note that $CB^+ = \{0010, 0101\}$ and $CB^- = \{0011, 1110, 1111\}$. For $0010 \in CB^+$, we produce the following CNF formula:

$\neg X_4 \wedge (\neg X_1 \vee \neg X_2) \wedge (\neg X_1 \vee \neg X_2 \vee \neg X_4)$.

And for $0101 \in CB^+$, we produce the following CNF formula:

$(X_2 \vee \neg X_3) \wedge (\neg X_1 \vee \neg X_3 \vee X_4) \wedge (\neg X_1 \vee \neg X_3)$.

By combining these two CNF formulas by $\vee$, we have a formula which is logically equivalent to the formula in Example 4.

6 Conclusion

We believe that the following are contributions of this paper.

- We propose a new similarity measure for case-based classification based on set inclusion and show properties which can be used for reduction of redundant cases.
- We show a correspondence between a boolean function represented by a casebase with the proposed similarity measure and a boolean function defined by monotone theory.
- By using the correspondence, we show that for every function f, we can represent f in a casebase whose size is bounded by $|DNF(f)|(1+|CNF(f)|)$.
- We show how to construct a formula which is equivalent to a boolean function represented by a casebase.

As future research, we would like to do the following.

- In [4], boolean functions are learned by membership query and equivalence query. Equivalence query can be replaced by sampling oracle for PAC learning framework. We study this method for active construction of casebase.

- We would like to extend our method to represent other kinds of concept such as concept with numerical attributes.
- We would like to apply our method to real applications for evaluation.

References

1. Aha, D. W., Kibler, D., and Albert, M. K.: Instance-Based Learning Algorithms. *Machine Learning* **2** (1991) 37–66
2. Ashley, K. D.: *Modeling Legal Argument: Reasoning with Cases and Hypotheticals* MIT press (1990)
3. Ashley, K. D., and Aleven, V.: A Logical Representation for Relevance Criteria. S. Wess, K-D. Althoff and M. Richter (eds.) *Topics in Case-Based Reasoning, LNAI 837* (1994) 338–352
4. Bshouty, N. H.: Exact Learning Boolean Functions via the Monotone Theory. *Information and Computation* **123** (1995) 146–153
5. Cover, T., and Hart, P.: NN pattern classification. *IEEE Trans. on Information Theory* **13** (1967) 21–27
6. Creecy, R. H., Masand, B. M., Smith, S. J. and Waltz, D. L.: Trading MIPS and Memory for Knowledge Engineering. *Communications of the ACM* **35** No. 8 (1992) 48–64
7. Globig, C., and Lange, S.: Case-Based Representability of Classes of Boolean Functions. *Proceedings of ECAI'96* (1996) 117–121
8. Goodman, M.: Prism: A Case-Based Telex Classifier. A. Rappaport and R. Smith (eds.) *Innovative Applications of Artificial Intelligence 2* (1990) 86–90
9. Griffiths, A .D., and Bridge, D. G.: On Concept Space and Hypothesis Space in Case-Based Learning. *Proceedings of ECML-95, LNAI 912* (1995) 161–173
10. Jantke, K. P. and S. Lange.: Case-based Representation and Learning of Pattern Languages. *Theoretical Computer Science* **137** (1995) 25–51
11. Khardon, R., and Roth, D.: Reasoning with Models. *Artificial Intelligence* **87** (1996) 187–213
12. Okamoto, S., and Satoh, K.: An Average Predictive Accuracy of the Nearest Neighbor Classifier. J-P. Haton, M. Keane, and M. Manago (eds.) *Advances in Case-Based Reasoning, LNAI 984* (1995) 101–112
13. Okamoto, S., and Satoh, K.: An Average Analysis of k-Nearest Neighbor Classifier. M. Veloso and A. Aamodt (eds.) *Case-Based Reasoning Research and Development, LNAI 1010* (1995) 253–264
14. Rachlin, J., Kasif, S., Salzberg, S., and Aha, D. W.: Towards a Better Understanding of Memory-based Reasoning Systems. *Machine Learning: Proceedings of the Eleventh International Conference* (1994) 242–250.
15. Salzberg, S., Delcher, A. L., Heath, D., and Kasif, S.: Best-Case Results for Nearest-Neighbor Learning. *IEEE Trans. on Pattern Analysis and Machine Intelligence* **17** (1995) 599–608
16. Satoh, K.: Translating Case-Based Reasoning into Abductive Logic Programming. *Proceedings of ECAI'96* (1996) 142–146
17. Stanfill, C., and Waltz, D.: Toward Memory-based Reasoning. *Communications of the ACM* **29** No. 12 (1986) 1213–1228

Locality, Reversibility, and Beyond: Learning Languages from Positive Data

Tom Head[1]   Satoshi Kobayashi[2]   Takashi Yokomori[3]

[1]Department of Mathematics, Binghamton University
Binghamton, New York 13902-6000, USA,
e-mail:tom@math.binghamton.edu
[2]Department of Information Science, Tokyo Denki University
Ishizaka, Hatoyama-cho, Hiki-gun, Saitama 350-0394, JAPAN
e-mail:satoshi@j.dendai.ac.jp
[3]Department of Mathematics, School of Education, Waseda University
1-6-1, Nishiwaseda, Shinjuku, Tokyo 169-8050, JAPAN
e-mail:yokomori@mn.waseda.ac.jp

Abstract. In algorithmic learning theory fundamental roles are played by the family of languages that are locally testable in the strict sense and by the family of reversible languages. These two families are shown to be the first two members of an infinite sequence of families of regular languages the members of which are learnable in the limit from positive data only. A uniform procedure is given for deciding, for each regular language R and each of our specified families, whether R belongs to the family. The approximation of arbitrary regular languages by languages belonging to these families is discussed. Further, we will give a uniform scheme for learning these families from positive data. Several research problems are also suggested.

Keywords: reversible languages, local languages, regular languages, identification in the limit from positive data, approximate learning

1   Introduction

In several natural ways one can provide, with a single definition, the global specification of exactly one binary irreflexive relation in the set of states of every automaton. We will use each such globally specified class of binary relations to define a family of regular languages. Two trivial examples will provide clarification of what we mean by such a global specification: the *empty* relation, and the relation of *inequality*. We will see that these two extremes provide the upper and lower range, respectively, of the families of languages definable by the means we propose. The empty relation provides the family of all regular languages and the relation of inequality provides the family of languages that are locally testable in the strict sense. The family of reversible languages is an intermediate example of a family definable in the suggested manner.

We use this general technique to provide a sequence of language families $\{DB_n \mid n$ is a non-negative integer$\}$ for which DB_0 coincides with the family of languages that are locally testable in the strict sense and DB_1 is the family of reversible languages. A foundational fact given by D. Angluin ([2]) is that each reversible language contains a constructable finite subset that determines the language from among the members of its family at its level. Each such subset she called a characteristic sample of the language. We observe that characteristic samples exist not only for the reversible languages, but for all members of our sequence DB_n. The significance of Angluin's characteristic samples is that they provide the basis for an algorithm for learning the languages that contain them in the limit from positive data only. Thus her results tell us that her learning procedure could be generalized to work also for all of the members of our sequence DB_n $(n \geq 0)$.

We provide an elementary algorithm that decides in an entirely uniform manner whether a given regular language is a member of a given family of any of the types defined here. For each regular language R and for each of the language families DB_n, we construct a minimal member (at the k-th level) of the family that contains R. This construction is also done in an elementary and uniform manner for all families. For an understanding of the significance of this construction for the theory of approximate learning, see [9].

Results reported here are related to research on biomolecular phenomena through the applications of learning theory to the semantics of DNA ([13] and [15]) and through the methodological similarity with work on splicing systems ([5], [6] and [7]) which model DNA recombinant behaviors.

2 Preliminaries

Let A be a finite alphabet. By A^*, we denote the set of all strings over A. By 1, we denote the null string. A subset of A^* is called a *language* over A. A set of languages is called a *family of languages*. For a language L and a string w, by $w \backslash L$, we denote the set $\{x \in A^* \mid wx \in L\}$. We write $w_1 \pi_L w_2$ if $w_1 \backslash L = w_2 \backslash L$.

For an equivalence relation π over A^* and a string w, by $[w]_\pi$, we denote an equivalence class of π containing w. For equivalence relations π_1 and π_2 over A^*, π_1 is said to be *finer* than π_2 if for any $s, t \in A^*$, $s\pi_1 t$ implies $s\pi_2 t$. An equivalence relation π over A^* is called a *right congruence* if for any $s, t \in A^*$ and $a \in A$, $s\pi t$ implies $sa\pi ta$. Note that for any language L, π_L is a right congruence.

By an automaton over A, we mean a formal system $M = (A, S, I, F, E)$, where A is a finite set that serves as the input alphabet, S is a finite set of states, I is the set of initial states, F is the set of final states, and E is the set of directed edges labeled by elements of A. Thus I and F are subsets of S and we may regard E as a subset of $S \times A \times S$. In case that the cardinality of I is 1 and for every $p \in S$ and $a \in A$, $(p, a, q_1), (p, a, q_2) \in E$ implies $q_1 = q_2$, M is said to be *deterministic*. We allow the set of initial states to contain more than one element of S, but minimal automata will be assumed to have only a single initial state. For a state p and a string w, pw will denote the set of all states which are accessible from the state p with the transition w. In case that pw is a singleton $\{q\}$, we simply write $pw = q$. $L(M)$ will denote the language *recognized* by M, i.e., $L(M) = \{w \in A^* \mid \exists p_0 \in I \text{ such that } p_0w \text{ contains some element in } F\}$. An automaton is said to be *trimmed* if every state is accessible from an initial state and, for every state q, there is a final state which is accessible from q. A language is *regular* if it is recognized by a finite automaton.

For a language L over A, by $Pre(L)$, we denote the set of all prefixes of elements of L. Let π be a right congruence which is finer than π_L. Then, it is straightforward to see that for a given language L, we can construct a trimmed automaton $M_{\pi,L} = (A, S, I, F, E)$ such that $L(M_{\pi,L}) = L$ using π as follows:

$$S = \{[w]_\pi \mid w \in Pre(L)\},$$
$$I = \{[1]_\pi\},$$
$$F = \{[w]_\pi \mid w \in L\},$$
$$E = \{([w_1]_\pi, a, [w_1a]_\pi) \mid w_1 \in Pre(L)\}.$$

It is well known that $M_{\pi_L,L}$ is a trimmed minimal automaton of L. This construction of an automaton for a given language L will be used in Section 6.

Let $M_1 = (A, S_1, I_1, F_1, E_1)$ and $M_2 = (A, S_2, I_2, F_2, E_2)$ be trimmed automata. We write $M_1 \preceq M_2$ if and only if there exists a function θ from S_1 to S_2 such that (1) $\theta(I_1) \subseteq I_2$, (2) $\theta(F_1) \subseteq F_2$, (3) for any $p \in S_1$ and $a \in A$, $\theta(pa) \subseteq \theta(p)a$ holds.

Proposition 1. $M_1 \preceq M_2$ implies $L(M_1) \subseteq L(M_2)$. $\qquad\qquad\square$

The following argument gives a method for constructing a new finer right congruence from a given right congruence. Let π be any right congruence over A^*. A string $w_1 = a_1 \cdots a_n$ ($a_i \in A$) is said to be π-*reduced* to a string w_2 at positions (i, j) if $a_1 \cdots a_i \; \pi \; a_1 \cdots a_j$, $1 \leq i < j \leq n$ and $w_2 = a_1 \cdots a_i a_{j+1} \cdots a_n$. Let w_2 be a π-reduction of w_1 at positions (i, j). Then, w_2 is called a *left-most π-reduction* of w_1 if there exists no π-reduction of w_1 at positions (i', j') such that $j' < j$. Such a left-most π-reduction is determined uniquely. We write $w_1 \xrightarrow{\pi} w_2$ if w_2 is a left-most π-reduction of w_1. Let $\xrightarrow{\pi} *$ be a reflexive and transitive closure of $\xrightarrow{\pi}$. Then, we write $x \; \overline{\pi} \; y$ if there exists some string w such that $x \xrightarrow{\pi} * w$ and $y \xrightarrow{\pi} * w$. Note that $\overline{\pi}$ is a right congruence which is finer than π. A string x is said to be *minimal with respect to π* if there exists no string y such that $x \neq y$ and $x \xrightarrow{\pi} y$.

An interesting right congruence, which plays an significant role in this article, will be defined bellow. For a string w, by $suf_k(w)$, we denote the k-length suffix of w. In case that the length of w is less than k, $suf_k(w)$ is defined as w itself. For a non-negative integer k and a language L, we write $w_1 \pi_{L,k} w_2$ if $w_1 \setminus L = w_2 \setminus L$ and $suf_k(w_1) = suf_k(w_2)$. In case of $k = 0$, $\pi_{L,0}$ coincides with π_L. Note that $\pi_{L,k}$ is a right congruence for each k and L and $\pi_{L,k}$ is finer than π_L. For a given language L and a non-negative integer k, the right congruence $\overline{\pi_{L,k}}$ will be used in Section 7 to show the existence of a characteritic sample of L with respect to the family of $\mathcal{DB}_n$ languages at its kth level.

3 The Definition Chosen for the *LTS* Language and the Reversible Languages

The concept of a language that is locally testable in the strict sense (*LTS*) was first defined by R. McNaughton and S. Papert ([11]). Most authors are now using modifications of their definition. Unfortunately, a language such as $ab * a$, which is in *LTS* by the original definition, is not *LTS* according to some current definitions. This situation is confusing. For simplicity we will use as our definition a property that is easily confirmed to hold for all of the definitions of the family *LTS* that are currently in use. For this purpose Schutzenberger's concept of a constant ([12]) will be used: A string w in A^* is a *constant relative to* a language L if, whenever uwv and swt are in L, both uwt and swv are also in L. It is easy to see that if w is a constant relative to L, then for any strings $x, y \in A^*$, xwy is also a constant relative to L. The following proposition is easily verified:

Proposition 2. A string w is a constant relative to a language L, if and only if for any $uw, sw \in Pre(L)$, $uw \setminus L = sw \setminus L$ holds. □

Recall that a string x is a factor of a language L if there are w and y in A^* for which wxy is in L. We let $Fac(L) = \{x \in A^* \mid x$ is a factor of $L\}$. For additional evidence of the appropriateness of the following definition see [10].

Definition 1. A language L is *k-locally testable in the strict sense* (*k-LTS*), for a non-negative integer k, if every string of length k in A^* (equivalently, in $Fac(L)$) is a constant relative to L. We say that L is *locally testable in the strict sense* (*LTS*) if it is *k-LTS* for some k.

Note: With this choice the family of *LTS* languages coincides with the family of null context splicing languages ([5], [6] and [7]).

We take the characterization of the concept of a *k*-reversible language given by Angluin (Theorem 14 in [2]) as the basis of our definition, but we prefer to give her definition in a slightly different form to allow us to emphasize what we believe is a fundamental concept lying at the core of her definition (characterization). This new concept is a generalization of Schutzenberger's concept of a constant: A string w in A^* is a *semiconstant relative to a language L* if, whenever uwv, swt, and uwt are in L, swv is also in L. This allows the following equivalent of Angluin's definition:

Definition 2. A regular language L is *k-reversible*, for a non-negative integer k, if every string of length k in A^* (equivalently, in $Fac(L)$) is a semiconstant relative to L. We say that L is *reversible* if it is *k*-reversible for some k.

The versions of the definitions given here underscore the fact that the concept of reversibility is a generalization of the *LTS* concept — in the same sense that the concept of a semiconstant is a generalization of the concept of a constant.

Thus by our definition of the family k-LTS, each k-LTS language is also k-reversible. For the definition of McNaughton and Papert ([11]) it is known that each LTS language is reversible ([8]) and that each k-LTS language is $(k+1)$-reversible (lemma 13 in [15]).

4 A Broader Context for the *LTS* and the Reversible Families

The following concept provides the basis for the embedding of the algorithmics of the LTS languages and the reversible languages into a common context. By an *irreflexive class* B we will mean a globally defined class of irreflexive binary relations, one for each automaton, defined on the set of states of the automaton. Recall that one such irreflexive class is provided by the empty relation and another is provided by inequality.

Definition 3. With each irreflexive class B we associate the family $\mathcal{D}B$ of regular languages: A regular language R belongs to the family $\mathcal{D}B$ if, for the *trimmed minimal* automaton of R with a state set S, the set $Bad(B, R) = \{w \in A^* \mid \exists\, p, q \in S,\ pw$ is defined, qw is defined, and $pwBqw\}$ is finite.

Note: Since in the definition above we have required that the minimal automaton is trimmed, replacing $w \in A^*$ by $w \in Fac(R)$ does not change the meaning of the definition.

Several notations are required for adequate discussion of examples.

With each automaton $M = (A, S, I, F, E)$ we associate several additional automata and make fundamental use of the languages they recognize. The set of all factors of the regular language R that is recognized by the automaton M is the regular language $Fac(R) = L((A, S, S, S, E))$. With each state q in S we associate the regular languages $I(q) = L((A, S, \{q\}, F, E))$ and $F(q) = L((A, S, S, \{q\}, E))$. Thus $I(q)$ consists of the strings that initiate at q and terminate at a state in F, and $F(q)$ consists of the strings that initiate anywhere in S and terminate at q.

Note: Suppose that pBp holds for some state p of a trimmed minimal automaton M. Then, $L(M)$ does belong to $\mathcal{D}B$ only if $I(p)$ is finite. This observation moves our attention to the *irreflexive* class B in Definition 3.

Example 1. For each non-negative integer n, let B_n be the irreflexive class globally specified in the state set of each trimmed automaton by:
$B_n = \{(p, q) \mid p$ and q are distinct and $I(p) \cap I(q)$ contains at least n strings$\}$.

Note that B_0 is simply the set of all pairs of distinct states in the trimmed automaton considered. The examples above are central to the significance of this article. The following observations have motivated this presentation.

Proposition 3. The family $\mathcal{DB}_0$ coincides with the family of LTS languages.

Proof. For a language $L \in \mathcal{DB}_0$, $M_{\pi_L,L}$ satisfies the condition of Def. 3. Thus, $Bad(B_0, L)$ is finite, and let k be the maximum length of strings in $Bad(B_0, L)$. (In case of $Bad(B_0, L)$ being empty, we set $k = -1$.) Let w be any string of length $k + 1$ and assume that uwv and swt are in L. Then, the states $[uw]_{\pi_L}$ and $[sw]_{\pi_L}$ of $M_{\pi_L,L}$ must be equivalent, since otherwise, $[uw]_{\pi_L} B_0 [sw]_{\pi_L}$ implies $w \in Bad(B_0, L)$, a contradiction. Therefore, uwt and swv are in L, which implies that every string of length $k + 1$ is a constant relative to L. Thus, $L \in LTS$.

For a language $L \in LTS$, there exists a non-negative integer k such that L is k-locally testable in the strict sense. Thus, every string of length k is a constant relative to L. Consider the trimmed minimal automaton $M_{\pi_L,L}$ of L. Let w be any string of length greater than k. Note that w is a constant relative to L. Then, $w \notin Bad(B_0, L)$ holds, since by Prop. 2, for any states $[u]_{\pi_L}$ and $[s]_{\pi_L}$ of $M_{\pi_L,L}$, $[uw]_{\pi_L}$ and $[sw]_{\pi_L}$ must be equivalent, i.e., $\neg([uw]_{\pi_L} B_0 [sw]_{\pi_L})$. Therefore, $Bad(B_0, L)$ is finite, which implies $L \in \mathcal{DB}_0$. $\square$

Proposition 4. The family $\mathcal{DB}_1$ coincides with the family of reversible languages.

Proof. Omitted. Similar argument of the proof of Proposition 3 can be applied. $\square$

Our principle result for machine learning appears in Section 7 and confirms that each $\mathcal{DB}_n$ shares the excellent learnability properties of $\mathcal{DB}_0$ and $\mathcal{DB}_1$.

Example 2. The following examples are given only to indicate the ease with which additional natural examples of irreflexive classes can be generated. We have not explored the significance of these examples.
(1) $BNC = \{(p,q) \mid$ Neither of $I(p)$ and $I(q)$ is contained in the other$\}$.
(2) $BII = \{(p,q) \mid I(p)$ and $I(q)$ are distinct, but have infinite intersection$\}$.
(3) $BFN = \{(p,q) \mid$ Precisely one of the states p and q is a final state$\}$.
(4) $BNG = \{(p,q) \mid$ Precisely one of the languages $I(p)$ and $I(q)$ is non-counting$\}$.

In the remainder of this section we provide an algorithm for deciding whether a given regular language R is a $\mathcal{DB}$ language or not in a uniform manner. By definition, the question "$R \in \mathcal{DB}$?" is equivalent to ask whether $Bad(B, R)$ is finite or not. It is easily verified that the computation of $Bad(B, R)$ is carried out in the following way:

Algorighm 1. For each regular language R and each irreflexive class B, decide whether R lies in $\mathcal{DB}$ as follows:
Construct the two regular languages using a trimmed minimal automaton of R:
$Good(B, R) = \bigcap\{\overline{(F(p) \cap F(q))} \mid pBq\}$,
$Bad(B, R) = Fac(R) \backslash Good(B, R)$.
Decide if the regular language $Bad(B, R)$ is finite.
R lies in $\mathcal{DB}$ if and only if $Bad(B, R)$ is finite.

Note:

(1) Any word that is not a factor of L is vacuously 'good'. Consequently we also have $Bad(B, R) = A^* \backslash Good(B, R)$, i.e., Good and Bad partition of A^*.

(2) For every B and every R, $A^* Good(B, R) = Good(B, R)$, i.e., Good is always a left ideal of A^*. However, for the irreflexive classes B_n given in Example 1 above, it is easily confirmed that $A^* Good(B_n, R) A^* = Good(B_n, R)$, i.e., Good is a two sided ideal.

(3) For local testability in the strict sense, constants are 'good', others are 'bad'. For reversibility, semiconstants are 'good', others are 'bad'. Constants have proven to be of great value in the study of splicing systems well beyond their use in generating LTS languages ([7]). This suggests that semiconstants will prove to be of value beyond the theory of reversible languages.

Algorithm 1 allows a non-negative integer, $\#B(R)$, to be associated with each $\mathcal{DB}$ language R: If $Bad(B, R)$ is empty, $\#B(R) = 0$, otherwise $\#B(R)$ is $1 +$ the length of the longest string in $Bad(B, R)$. This definition allows us to say: For a $\mathcal{DB}$ language all factors of length at least $\#B(R)$ are 'good'.

Definition 4. Let k be a non-negative integer. A $\mathcal{DB}$ language is called a k-$\mathcal{DB}$ *language* if $\#B(R) \leq k$.

Theorem 1. If a regular language R is in $\mathcal{DB}$ it must be in k-$\mathcal{DB}$ for $k = n^2$, where n is the number of states in the trimmed minimal automaton of R.

Proof. Suppose that R is in $\mathcal{DB}$ but not in k-$\mathcal{DB}$ for $k = n^2$. Then there is a pair of states p, q and a word w of length at least k for which $pwBqw$. Since length w is at least n^2 and there are only n^2 ordered pairs of states, there must be a factorization $w = xyz$, with y not null, such that the ordered pair (px, qx) is identical with (pxy, qxy). It follows that, for every non-negative integer i, $pxy^i z B qxy^i z$. This means that $Bad(B, R)$ is not finite and consequently that we have arrived at the contradiction: R is not $\mathcal{DB}$. $\square$

Corollary 1. If a regular language R is LTS it must be n^2-LTS where n is the number of states in the trimmed minimal automaton of R. $\square$

Corollary 2. If a regular language R is reversible it must be n^2-reversible where n is the number of states in the trimmed minimal automaton of R. $\square$

Proposition 5. In case of $\#A \geq 2$, for any nonnegative integers k, l, n, k-$\mathcal{DB}_{n+1} - l$-$\mathcal{DB}_n \neq \emptyset$ holds.

Proof. Let a, b be distinct elements in A. Let F_1 and F_2 be finite sets of strings of length $n + 1$ such that $\#(F_1 \cap F_2) = n$ and $F_1 - F_2 \neq \emptyset$. Let v be any string of length l and let $L = avF_1 + bvF_2$.

Then, it is straightforward to see that for any nonnegative integer k, $L \in (k$-$\mathcal{DB}_{n+1} - l$-$\mathcal{DB}_n)$ holds. $\square$

Thus, for any nonnegative integer k and n, k-$\mathcal{DB}_n$ is a proper subset of k-$\mathcal{DB}_{n+1}$.

5 Characterizations of k-$\mathcal{DB}_n$ Languages

In this section, we give some characterizations of the k-$\mathcal{DB}_n$ families, where we will introduce a generalized notion of a constant or a semiconstant.

Let $\mathcal{F}_n$ be the set of all finite subsets of A^* whose cardinality is equal to n. The first characterization is given as follows:

Theorem 2. A regular language L is a k-$\mathcal{DB}_n$language if and only if for any strings $u_1, u_2 \in A^*$, any string w of length k such that $u_1 w, u_2 w \in Pre(L)$, and any element $F \in \mathcal{F}_n$, $u_1 w F \subseteq L$ and $u_2 w F \subseteq L$ imply $u_1 w \setminus L = u_2 w \setminus L$.

Proof. Assume that L is a k-$\mathcal{DB}_n$language. Then, the maximum length of strings in $Bad(B_n, L)$ is bounded by $k-1$. Let u_1, u_2, w be any strings such that $\mid w \mid = k$, and F be any element in $\mathcal{F}_n$. Suppose that $u_1 w F \subseteq L$ and $u_2 w F \subseteq L$. Then, the states $[u_1 w]_{\pi_L}$ and $[u_2 w]_{\pi_L}$ of the trimmed minimal automaton $M_{\pi_L, L}$ should be equivalent, since otherwise $[u_1]_{\pi_L} w = [u_1 w]_{\pi_L} B_n [u_2 w]_{\pi_L} = [u_2]_{\pi_L} w$ holds and therefore $w \in Bad(B_n, L)$, a contradiction. Therefore, we have $u_1 w \setminus L = u_2 w \setminus L$.

Assume that the 'if' condition of the claim holds. Let w be any string of length greater than or equal to k. Consider any distinct states $[u_1]_{\pi_L}$ and $[u_2]_{\pi_L}$ of the minimal trimmed automaton $M_{\pi_L, L}$. In case that $I([u_1 w]_{\pi_L}) \cap I([u_2 w]_{\pi_L})$ contains at most $n-1$ strings, $\neg([u_1 w]_{\pi_L} B_n [u_2 w]_{\pi_L})$ holds. In case that $I([u_1 w]_{\pi_L}) \cap I([u_2 w]_{\pi_L})$ contains some $F \in \mathcal{F}_n$, by the assumption, we have $u_1 w \setminus L = u_2 w \setminus L$. Therefore, $[u_1 w]_{\pi_L} = [u_2 w]_{\pi_L}$ holds, which implies $\neg([u_1 w]_{\pi_L} B_n [u_2 w]_{\pi_L})$. Thus, in any case we have $\neg([u_1 w]_{\pi_L} B_n [u_2 w]_{\pi_L})$. Therefore, $w \notin Bad(B_n, L)$, i.e., L is a k-$\mathcal{DB}_n$language. $\square$

For a non-negative integer k and a language L, a string w is an *n-weak constant relative to* L if, whenever (1) $uwv, swt \in L$ and (2) $\exists F \in \mathcal{F}_n$ such that $uwF \subseteq L$ and $swF \subseteq L$, it holds that uwt and swv are also in L. The notion of 0-weak constant coincides with that of a constant. Further, the notion of 1-weak constant coincides with that of a semiconstant. In this sense, the notion of an n-weak constant is a natural hierachical generalization of a constant.

The following proposition is straightforward:

Proposition 6. A string w is an n-weak constant relative to a language L if and only if for any strings $u_1 w, u_2 w \in Pre(L)$ and any element $F \in \mathcal{F}_n$, $u_1 w F \subseteq L$ and $u_2 w F \subseteq L$ imply $u_1 w \setminus L = u_2 w \setminus L$. $\square$

Theorem 3. A regular language L is a k-$\mathcal{DB}_n$language for a non-negative integer k, if and only if every string of length k in A^* (equivalently, in $Fac(L)$) is an n-weak constant relative to L.

Proof. By Th. 2 and Prop. 6. $\square$

We introduce a class of automata, which could be used to characterize k-$\mathcal{DB}_n$languages. An automaton M is called a k-$\mathcal{DB}_n$ *automaton* if it is trimmed, deterministic and for any states p, q of M and any string w of length k, $\neg(pwB_nqw)$ holds. The class of k-$\mathcal{DB}_1$ automata coincides with the class of k-reversible automata ([2]). The following proposition is immediate from Def. 3 and Def. 4.

Proposition 7. A language L is a k-$\mathcal{DB}_n$language if and only if the trimmed minimal automaton of L is a k-$\mathcal{DB}_n$automaton. □

It is known that L is k-reversible if and only if L is accepted by *some* k-reversible automaton. The next characterization gives the generalization of these properties.

Theorem 4. A language L is a k-$\mathcal{DB}_n$language if and only if L is recognized by *some* k-$\mathcal{DB}_n$automaton.

Proof. Prop. 7 gives the proof of 'only if' direction.

Assume that there exists a k-$\mathcal{DB}_n$automaton $M = (A, S, \{p_0\}, F, E)$ recognizing L. Let π_M be a right congruence defined by $s\pi_M t$ if and only if $p_0 s = p_0 t$. Then, it is easily verified that $M_{\pi_M, L}$ is equivalent to M itself by allowing the renaming of the states. Recall that π_M is finer than π_L since M recognizes L.

Let u_1, u_2, w be any strings and F be any element of $\mathcal{F}_n$ such that $\mid w \mid = k$, $u_1 w F \subseteq L$ and $u_2 w F \subseteq L$ hold. Then, since $M \ (=M_{\pi_M, L})$ is a k-$\mathcal{DB}_n$automaton, for the states $[u_1]_{\pi_M}$ and $[u_2]_{\pi_M}$ of $M_{\pi_M, L}$, we have $\neg([u_1]_{\pi_M} w B_n [u_2]_{\pi_M} w)$. Therefore, we have $\neg([u_1 w]_{\pi_M} B_n [u_2 w]_{\pi_M})$, which implies, by $u_1 w F \subseteq L$ and $u_2 w F \subseteq L$, $[u_1 w]_{\pi_M} = [u_2 w]_{\pi_M}$. Thus, we have $u_1 w \pi_M u_2 w$. Since π_M is finer than π_L, we also have $u_1 w \pi_L u_2 w$. This implies, by Th. 2, that L is a k-$\mathcal{DB}_n$language. □

With this theorem, we can conclude that the class of k-$\mathcal{DB}_1$ languages coincides with the class of k-reversible languages, since the class of k-$\mathcal{DB}_1$ automata is equivalent to the class of k-reversible automata.

6 k-$\mathcal{DB}_n$ Approximation of Regular Language

For a language L and a string $w \in Pre(L)$, we will select a string w' such that $ww' \in L$, and denote it by $tail(w)$.

Let k and n be any non-negative integers.

Define the sets:

$$T(R, k) = \{(s_1, t, s_2) \mid s_1 t s_2 \xrightarrow{\pi_{R,k}} s_1 s_2 \in Pre(R) \ \wedge$$
$$s_1 s_2 \text{ is minimal with respect to } \pi_{R,k}\},$$
$$A(R, n, k) = \{s_1 t^i s_2 tail(s_1 s_2) \mid (s_1, t, s_2) \in T(R, k), 0 \leq i \leq n\}.$$

Note: For an element $s_1 t^i s_2 tail(s_1 s_2) \in A(R, n, k)$, there is a $\pi_{R,k}$ reduction: $s_1 t^i s_2 tail(s_1 s_2) \xrightarrow{\pi_{R,k}} s_1 t^{i-1} s_2 tail(s_1 s_2) \xrightarrow{\pi_{R,k}} \cdots \xrightarrow{\pi_{R,k}} s_1 s_2 tail(s_1 s_2) \in R$. Since $\overline{\pi_{R,k}}$ is finer than π_R, every element of $A(R, n, k)$ is also in R. Therefore, we have $A(R, n, k) \subseteq R$.

Lemma 1. Let R be any language. Let L be any k-$\mathcal{DB}_n$language containing $A(R, n, k)$. For any strings $u_1, u_2 \in Pre(R)$, $u_1 \overline{\pi_{R,k}} u_2$ implies $u_1 \pi_L u_2$.

Proof. Let u be any string in $Pre(R)$ and w be a minimal string for u with respect to $\pi_{R,k}$. Assume that i ($i \geq 0$) is the number of steps of the left-most reductions from u to w. We will prove $u \setminus L = w \setminus L$ by induction on i.

In case of $i = 0$, $u = w$, which immediately implies the claim.

Assume that the claim holds for $i \leq l$, and consider the case of $i = l + 1$. Let $s_1 t a s_2 \overset{\pi_{R,k}}{\to} s_1 s_2 = w$ be the last left-most $\pi_{R,k}$-reduction when u is left-most $\pi_{R,k}$-reduced to w, where $s_1, s_2, t \in A^*$ and $a \in A$. Then, by the definition of the left-most reduction, there exists some $u' \in A^*$ such that $u = u' a s_2$ and $u' \overset{\pi_{R,k}}{\to} * s_1 t$, where $s_1 t$ is minimal with respect to $\pi_{R,k}$. By the induction hypothesis, $u' \setminus L = s_1 t \setminus L$ holds. Since $\overline{\pi_{R,k}}$ is finer than $\pi_{R,k}$, by $s_1 t a s_2 \overset{\pi_{R,k}}{\to} s_1 s_2$, we have $s_1 t a \pi_{R,k} s_1$. Then, by the definition of $A(R, n, k)$, both of $s_1 t a \setminus L$ and $s_1 \setminus L$ contain the set $\{(ta)^j s_2 tail(s_1 s_2) \mid 0 \leq j \leq n - 1\}$. Furhter, by $s_1 t a \pi_{R,k} s_1$, we have $suf_k(s_1 t a) = suf_k(s_1)$. Therefore, by the k-DB_nproperty of L (Th. 2), we have $s_1 t a \setminus L = s_1 \setminus L$. Thus, we have $u \setminus L = u' a s_2 \setminus L = s_1 t a s_2 \setminus L = s_1 s_2 \setminus L = w \setminus L$ holds, completing the induction step.

For the string $u_1, u_2 \in Pre(R)$, by $u_1 \overline{\pi_{R,k}} u_2$, we have $u_1 \setminus L = u_2 \setminus L$. This completes the proof. $\square$

Corollary 3. Let R be any regular language. Let L be any k-DB_nlanguage containing R. For any strings $u_1, u_2 \in Pre(R)$, $u_1 \overline{\pi_{R,k}} u_2$ implies $u_1 \pi_L u_2$.

Proof. By Lem. 1 and $A(R, n, k) \subseteq R$. $\square$

Algorithm 2. Given a regular language R and a non-negative integer k, construct the minimal k-DB_nlanguage containing R as follows:

Construct $M_{\overline{\pi_{R,k}}, R}$.

Assign i the value 0. Assign $M(i)$ the value $M_{\overline{\pi_{R,k}}, R}$.

[Label]

IF there exists no pair of distinct states p and q in the state set of $M(i)$ satisfying either of the following condition (a) or (b), then halt.

ELSE, construct $M(i + 1)$ from $M(i)$ by merging states p_1 and p_2 in $M(i)$ into a new state q:

    (a) $p_1 B_n p_2$ holds and $F(p_1) \cap F(p_2)$ contains a k-length string,

    (b) there exists $a \in A$ and a state r in $M(i)$ such that $p_1 \in ra$ and $p_2 \in ra$.

Assign i the value $i + 1$.

Go to [Label].

Theorem 5. Algorithm 2 outputs an automaton recognizing the minimal k-DB_nlanguage containing the given regular language R.

Proof. Note that any language recognized by an automaton which has only one state could be a k-DB_nlanguage. Therefore, the algorithm terminates because the number of states of $M(0)$ is an upper bound for the number of times the loop can be traversed. Further, the output of the algorithm is a k-DB_nautomaton, since it has no pair of states satisfying conditions (a) or (b).

Let L be any k-DB_nlanguage containing R and $M_{\pi_L, L} = (A, S, \{p_0\}, F, E)$ be the minimal trimmed automaton of L. By Prop. 1, it suffices to show that for every $i \geq 0$, $M(i) \preceq M_{\pi_L, L}$ holds. We will prove this claim by induction on i.

In case of $i = 0$, define θ_0 as $\theta_0([w]_{\overline{\pi_{R,k}}}) = [w]_{\pi_L}$. By Cor. 3, this mapping is well-defined and it is straightforward to see $M(0) \preceq M$.

Assume that $M(l) \preceq M_{\pi_L,L}$ and let θ_l be a mapping from S_l to S ensuring the relation $M(l) \preceq M_{\pi_L,L}$, where S_l is the state set of $M(l)$. $M(l+1)$ will be constructed by merging states p_1 and p_2 satisfying the condition (a) or (b). Let $p_1' = \theta_l(p_1)$ and $p_2' = \theta_l(p_2)$. In case of (a), by the induction hypothesis and by the fact that $M_{\pi_L,L}$ is a k-$\mathcal{DB}_n$ automaton, $p_1' = p_2'$ holds, since otherwise $F(p_1') \cap F(p_2')$ contains a k-lenth string and $p_1' B_n p_2'$ holds, which contradicts the definition of k-$\mathcal{DB}_n$ automaton. In case of (b), by the induction hypothesis and by the determinisity of $M_{\pi_L,L}$, $p_1' = p_2'$ holds. Thus, in both cases, we have $p_1' = p_2'$.

Then, we will construct a new mapping θ_{l+1} from S_{l+1} to S, where S_{l+1} is the state set of $M(l+1)$ written as $(S_l - \{p_1, p_2\}) \cup \{q\}$, defined by: $\theta_{l+1}(p) = \theta_l(p_1)$ if $p = q$, otherwise, $\theta_{l+1}(p) = \theta_l(p)$. By $p_1' = p_2'$, θ_{l+1} ensures the relation $M(l+1) \preceq M_{\pi_L,L}$, which completes the induction step. $\quad\square$

Although a minimal k-DB language containing an arbitrary regular language R exists for each non-negative integer k, there may be no minimal $\mathcal{DB}$ language containing R. This fundamental fact is illustrated in the following:

Example 3. For the language $L = ca^*(b + e) + da^*(b + f)$, one can confirm that, for each non-negative integer k, the minimal k-$\mathcal{DB}_1$ language containing L is the language $L_k = \{ca^i(b + e) \mid 0 \le i \le k - 1\} \cup \{da^i(b + f) \mid 0 \le i \le k - 1\} \cup \{(c + d)a^i(b + e + f) \mid i \ge k\}$. Consequently, the sequence $\{L_k \mid k = 0, 1, 2, ...\}$ is a strictly descending infinite nest of languages. Thus L is not contained in a minimal $\mathcal{DB}_1$ language. It is interesting to note that the intersection of this nest is precisely L, a non-$\mathcal{DB}_1$ language.

7 Learnability Results for the Families k-$\mathcal{DB}_n$

For a language L over A, a *positive presentation* of L is an infinite sequence $\sigma = w_1, w_2, ...$ such that $\{w_i \in A^* \mid i \ge 1\} = L$.

Let $\mathcal{C}$ be a family of languages over A. Consider a *class of representations* $\mathcal{R}$ for $\mathcal{C}$ with the following properties:

1. $\mathcal{R}$ is a recursively enumerable language (over some fixed alphabet).
2. For every $L \in \mathcal{C}$, there exists an $r \in \mathcal{R}$ such that r represents L (denoted by $L(r) = L$).
3. There exists a recursive function f such that for all $r \in \mathcal{R}$ and $w \in \Sigma^*$,

$$f(r, w) = \begin{cases} 1 \ if \ w \in L(r) \\ 0 \ otherwise \end{cases}$$

Thus, $L(r)$ is the language represented by r. Note that $\{L(r) \mid r \in \mathcal{R}\}$ could be regarded as an *indexed family of recursive languages*(cf. [1]), if we encode each $r \in \mathcal{R}$ into positive integer.

Let C_1 and C_2 be families of languages, and R be a class of representations for C_2. Let L be any language in C_1. We say that an algorithm M *upper approximately identifies L in the limit from positive data using C_2 and R* if for any positive presentation of L, the infinite sequence, $g_1, g_2, g_3, \ldots$ ($g_i \in R$), produced by M converges to an element $r \in R$ such that $L(r)$ is a minimal language in C_2 containing L. A family C_1 is *upper approximately identifiable in the limit from positive data using C_2 and R* if there exists an algorithm M such that M identifies upper approximately identify every concept in C_1 in the limit from positive data using C_2 and R.

Note: In case of $C_1 = C_2$, we simply say that C_1 is *identifiable in the limit from positive data using R*. This coincides with the original definition by [2] and [4].

Example 4. For the families DB_n or $k\text{-}DB_n$, we can use the representation class of finite automata. In the sequel, we will use this finite automata representation for these families of languages, and R is omitted if the context allows.

The following notion of characteristic sample, introduced by [2], plays an essential role in the theory of learning from positive data.

Let C be a family of languages. For any language L of A^*, a finite subset F of L is called a *characteristic sample* of L with respect to C if for any $X \in C$, $F \subseteq X$ implies $L \subseteq X$.

Theorem 6. Let R be a regular language, and let n and k be non-negative integers. Then, there exists a characteristic sample of R with respect to the family of $k\text{-}DB_n$ languages.

Proof. Since R is regular, the number m of equivalence classes of $\pi_{R,k}$ is finite. Therefore, the number of elements of $T(R, k)$ is finite, since for each $(s_1, t, s_2) \in T(R, k)$, the lengths of s_1, t and s_2 are bounded by m. Thus, $A(R, n, k)$ is also finite. We will prove that this finite set $A(R, n, k)$ is a characteristic sample of R with respect to the family of $k\text{-}DB_n$ languages.

Let L be any $k\text{-}DB_n$ language containing $A(R, n, k)$ and let $M_{\pi_L,L} = (A, S_1, \{p_0\}, F_1, E_1)$. Consider an automaton $M_{\overline{\pi_{R,k}},R} = (A, S_2, I_2, F_2, E_2)$ which recognizes R. Define a mapping θ from S_2 to S_1 such that for each state $[w]_{\overline{\pi_{R,k}}} \in S_2$, $\theta([w]_{\overline{\pi_{R,k}}}) = [w]_{\pi_L}$ holds. (Note that we can take w from the set $Pre(A(R, n, k))$.) Then, by Lem. 1 and by the fact that every final state of $M_{\overline{\pi_{R,k}},R}$ is accessible from the initial state by the transition using some string in $A(R, n, k)$, it is straightforward to see that the mapping θ ensures the relation $M_{\overline{\pi_{R,k}},R} \preceq M_{\pi_L,L}$. Therefore, by Prop. 1, we have $R \subseteq L$. This completes the proof. $\qquad\square$

Theorem 7. The family of regular languages is upper approximately identifiable in the limit from positive data using each of the families $k\text{-}DB_n$.

Proof. The learning device M for this approximate learning is given as follows: For a new input w_i, M outputs the previous conjecture g_{i-1} if $L(g_{i-1})$ contains w_i, otherwise we will construct a trimmed minimal automaton M' accepting precisely the union of $\{w_i\}$ and the previous inputs $\{w_1, \ldots, w_{i-1}\}$ and applies the

Algorithm 2. The output of Algorithm 2 is the new conjecture at the stage i of M.

It holds that at each stage i $(i \geq 1)$, the output M_i of M represents a minimal language containing $\{w_1, ..., w_i\}$. By Theorem 6, there exists some stage j $(j \geq 1)$ such that $\{w_1, ..., w_j\}$ contains a characteristic sample F of the target regular language L with respect to the family of k-$\mathcal{DB}_n$ languages. At the stage j, M outputs a conjecture representing a minimal k-$\mathcal{DB}_n$ language containing L, since $L(M_j)$ is a minimal k-$\mathcal{DB}_n$ language containing $\{w_1, ..., w_j\}$ $(\supseteq F)$ and thus for any k-$\mathcal{DB}_n$ language L' containing L, $F \subseteq \{w_1, ..., w_j\} \subseteq L \subseteq L(M_j) \subseteq L'$ holds. Therefore, after the stage j, M does not change its conjecture. This completes the proof. $\qquad\square$

Note: It should be noted that the learning algorithm of Th. 7 has several good properties such as consistency, conservativeness, responsiveness. (See [2].)

8 Problems

1. Consider some (all?) significant families of regular languages for possible representation by means of irreflexive classes.
2. Generate new families of regular languages by specifying potentially interesting irreflexive classes B and investigate the language families $\mathcal{DB}$ they determine for potential significance.
3. For each family $\mathcal{DB}$: [i] Are there additional algorithms for treating the languages in $\mathcal{DB}$? [ii] Are there new properties of these languages that can be discovered based on the new definition? [iii] Are there previously known properties that can be demonstrated in a simpler way, or with greater generality so that the property is seen to hold for additional $\mathcal{DB}$ families?
4. Characterize by abstract properties the families of regular languages that admit definitions by irreflexive classes as discussed here. This may be possible using a reformulation of our method in which one forms, for each regular language R, the product automaton $M \times M$, where M is the minimal automaton recognizing R. The irreflexive relation then becomes a set of states of $M \times M$ that is disjoint from the diagonal. Special attention may be given to those irreflexive classes B for which $Good(B, R)$ is a two-sided ideal for each regular language R.
5. Whether a language is regular or not, it has a unique minimal automaton, although the number of states will be infinite if the language is not regular. Are there tractable families of non-regular languages that can be defined in the present manner using (trimmed?) minimal automata having an infinite number of states?
6. What role might the semiconstant strings relative to a language play beyond the context of the present investigation?

204

Acknowledgement

We are grateful to anonymous referees for their valuable comments. The first author is grateful to M. Hagiya and the Molecular Computing Project members for inviting him to Japan. This research was supported in part by "Research for the Future" Program No. JSPS-RFTF 96I00101 from the Japan Society for the Promotion of Science and by the National Science Foundation of the United States through grant CCR-9509831.

References

[1] D. Angluin, Inductive inference of formal languages from positive data, *Information and Control* **45** (1980) 117-135.

[2] D. Angluin, Inference of reversible languages, *Journal of the ACM* **29** (1982) 741-765.

[3] E. W. Dijkstra, A note on two problems in connection with graphs, *Numerishe Mathematik*, **1** (1959) 269-271.

[4] E. Mark Gold, Language identification in the limit, *Information and Control*, **10** (1967), 447-474.

[5] Head, T, Formal language theory and DNA: an analysis of the generative capacity of specific recombinant behaviors, *Bulletin of Mathematical Biology*, **49** (1987) 737-759.

[6] T. Head, Splicing representations of strictly locally testable languages, submitted for publication. (1997)

[7] T. Head, Splicing languages generated with one-sided context, submitted for publication. (1997)

[8] S. Kobayashi and T. Yokomori, Families of non-counting languages and their learnability from positive data, *Intern. Journal of Foundations of Computer Science*, **7** 309-327 (1996).

[9] S. Kobayashi and T. Yokomori, Learning approximately regular languages with reversible languages, *Theoretical Computer Science*, **174** (1997) 251-257.

[10] De Luca, A. and A. Restivo, A characterization of strictly locally testable languages and its application to subsemigroups of a free semigroup, *Information and Control*, **44** (1980) 300-319.

[11] R. McNaughton and S. Papert, *Counter-Free Automata*, MIT Press, Cambridge, Massachusetts (1971).

[12] M. P. Schutzenberger, Sur certaines operations de fermeture dans les languages rationnels, *Symposium Mathematicum*, **15** (1975) 245-253.

[13] T. Yokomori, N. Ishida, and S. Kobayashi, Learning local languages and its application to protein alpha-chain identification, In *Proc. of 27th Hawaii Intern. Conf. on System Sciences*, IEEE Press, 113-122 (1994).

[14] T. Yokomori, On polynomial-time learnability in the limit of strictly deterministic automata, *Machine Learning*, **19** (1995) 153-179.

[15] T. Yokomori and S. Kobayashi, Learning local languages and its application to DNA sequence analysis, *IEEE Transactions on Pattern Analysis and Machine Intelligence, to appear*.

Synthesizing Learners Tolerating Computable Noisy Data

John Case[1] and Sanjay Jain[2]

[1] Department of CIS
University of Delaware
Newark, DE 19716, USA
Email: case@cis.udel.edu
[2] Sanjay Jain
Department of ISCS
National University of Singapore
Singapore 119260
Email: sanjay@iscs.nus.edu.sg

Abstract. An *index for an r.e. class of languages* (by definition) generates a sequence of grammars defining the class. An *index for an indexed
family of languages* (by definition) generates a sequence of decision procedures defining the family.

F. Stephan's model of noisy data is employed, in which, roughly, correct
data crops up infinitely often, and incorrect data only finitely often.

In a completely computable universe, all data sequences, even noisy ones,
are computable. New to the present paper is the restriction that noisy
data sequences be, nonetheless, computable!

Studied, then, is the synthesis *from indices for r.e. classes and for indexed
families of languages* of various kinds of *noise-tolerant* language-learners
for the corresponding classes or families indexed, *where the noisy input
data sequences are restricted to being computable.*

Many positive results, as well as some negative results, are presented
regarding the existence of such synthesizers.

The main positive result is surprisingly more positive than its analog
in the case the noisy data is not restricted to being computable: grammars for *each* indexed family *can* be learned behaviorally correctly from
computable, noisy, positive data! The proof of another positive synthesis result yields, as a pleasant corollary, a strict subset-principle or tell-
tale style characterization, for the *computable* noise-tolerant behaviorally
correct learnability of grammars from positive and negative data, of the
corresponding families indexed.

1 Introduction

Ex*-learners*, when successful on an object input, (by definition) find a final correct program for that object after at most finitely many trial and error attempts
[Gol67,BB75,CS83,CL82].[1]

---
[1] **Ex** is short for *explanatory*.

For function learning, there is a learner-synthesizer algorithm **lsyn** so that, if **lsyn** is fed any procedure that lists programs for some (possibly infinite) class S of (total) functions, then **lsyn** outputs an **Ex**-learner successful on S [Gol67]. The learners so synthesized are called *enumeration techniques* [BB75,Ful90]. These enumeration techniques yield many positive learnability results, for example, that the class of all functions computable in time polynomial in the length of input is **Ex**-learnable.[2]

For language learning *from positive data and with learners outputting grammars*, [OSW88] provided an amazingly negative result: there is *no* learner-synthesizer algorithm **lsyn** so that, if **lsyn** is fed a *pair* of grammars g_1, g_2 for a language class $\mathcal{L} = \{L_1, L_2\}$, then **lsyn** outputs an **Ex**-learner successful, from positive data, on $\mathcal{L}$.[3] [BCJ96] showed how to circumvent *some* of the sting of this [OSW88] result by resorting to more general learners than **Ex**. Example more general learners are: **Bc**-*learners*, which, when successful on an object input, (by definition) find a final (possibly infinite) *sequence* of correct programs for that object after at most finitely many trial and error attempts [B̄74,CS83].[4] Of course, if suitable learner-synthesizer algorithm **lsyn** is fed procedures for listing *decision procedures* (instead of mere grammars), one also has more success at synthesizing learners. In fact the computational learning theory community has shown considerable interest (spanning at least from [Gol67] to [ZL95]) in language classes defined by r.e. listings of decision procedures. These classes are called *uniformly decidable* or *indexed families*. As is essentially pointed out in [Ang80], all of the formal language style example classes *are* indexed families. A sample result from [BCJ96] is: there *is* a learner-synthesizer algorithm **lsyn** so that, if **lsyn** is fed any procedure that lists decision procedures defining some indexed family $\mathcal{L}$ of languages *which can be* **Bc**-*learned from positive data with the learner outputting grammars*, then **lsyn** outputs a **Bc**-learner successful, from positive data, on $\mathcal{L}$. The proof of this positive result yielded the surprising characterization [BCJ96]: for indexed families $\mathcal{L}$, $\mathcal{L}$ can be **Bc**-learned from positive data with the learner outputting grammars iff

$$(\forall L \in \mathcal{L})(\exists S \subseteq L \mid S \text{ is finite})(\forall L' \in \mathcal{L} \mid S \subseteq L')[L' \not\subset L]. \tag{1}$$

(1) is Angluin's important Condition 2 from [Ang80], and it is referred to as the *subset principle*, in general a necessary condition for preventing overgeneralization in learning from positive data [Ang80,Ber85,ZLK95,KB92,Cas96].

[CJS98a] considered language learning from both *noisy* texts (only positive data) and from *noisy* informants (both positive and negative data), and adopted,

---

[2] The reader is referred to Jantke [Jan79a,Jan79b] for a discussion of synthesizing learners for classes of computable functions that are not necessarily recursively enumerable.

[3] Again for language learning from positive data and with learners outputting grammars, a somewhat related negative result is provided by Kapur [Kap91]. He shows that one cannot algorithmically find an **Ex**-learning machine for **Ex**-*learnable* indexed families of recursive languages from an index of the class. This is a bit weaker than a closely related negative result from [BCJ96].

[4] **Bc** is short for *behaviorally correct*.

as does the present paper, Stephan's [Ste95,CJS98b] noise model. Roughly, in this model correct information about an object occurs infinitely often while incorrect information occurs only finitely often. Hence, this model has the advantage that noisy data about an object nonetheless uniquely specifies that object.[5]

In the context of [CJS98a], *where the noisy data sequences can be uncomputable*, the presence of noise plays havoc with the learnability of many concrete classes that can be learned without noise. For example, the well-known class of *pattern languages* [Ang80][6] can be **Ex**-learned from texts but cannot be **Bc**-learned from unrestricted noisy texts even if we allow the final grammars each to make finitely many mistakes. While, it is possible to **Ex**-learn the pattern languages *from informants* in the presence of noise, a mind-change complexity price must be paid: any **Ex**-learner succeeding on the pattern languages from unrestricted noisy informant must change its mind an unbounded finite number of times about the final grammar. However, some learner can succeed on the pattern languages from noise-*free* informants *and on its first guess as to a correct grammar* (see [LZK96]). The class of languages formed by taking the union of two pattern languages can be **Ex**-learned from texts [Shi83]; however, this class cannot be **Bc**-learned from unrestricted noisy informants even if we allow the final grammars each to make finitely many mistakes.

In [CJS98a], the proofs of most of the positive results providing *existence* of learner-synthesizers which synthesize *noise-tolerant* learners also yielded pleasant characterizations which look like strict versions of the subset principle (1).[7] Here is an example. If $\mathcal{L}$ is an indexed family, then: $\mathcal{L}$ can be noise-tolerantly **Ex**-learned from positive data with the learner outputting grammars (iff $\mathcal{L}$ can

---

[5] Less roughly: in the case of noisy informant each false item may occur a finite number of times; in the case of text, it is mathematically more interesting to require, as we do, that the *total* amount of false information has to be finite. The alternative of allowing *each* false item in a text to occur finitely often is too restrictive; it would, then, be impossible to learn even the class of all singleton sets [Ste95] (see also Theorem 8).

[6] [Nix83] as well as [SA95] outline interesting applications of pattern inference algorithms. For example, pattern language learning algorithms have been successfully applied for solving problems in molecular biology (see [SSS+94,SA95]). Pattern languages and finite unions of pattern languages [Shi83,Wri89] turn out to be subclasses of Smullyan's [Smu61] Elementary Formal Systems (EFSs). [ASY92] show that the EFSs can also be treated as a logic programming language over strings. The techniques for learning finite unions of pattern languages have been extended to show the learnability of various subclasses of EFSs [Shi91]. Investigations of the learnability of subclasses of EFSs are important because they yield corresponding results about the learnability of subclasses of logic programs. [AS94] use the insight gained from the learnability of EFSs subclasses to show that a class of linearly covering logic programs with local variables is **TxtEx**-learnable. These results have consequences for Inductive Logic Programming [MR94,LD94].

[7] For $\mathcal{L}$ either an indexed family or defined by some r.e. listing of grammars, the prior literature has many interesting characterizations of $\mathcal{L}$ being **Ex**-learnable from noise-free positive data, with and without extra restrictions. See, for example, [Ang80,Muk92,LZK96,dJK96].

be noise-tolerantly **Bc**-learned from positive data with the learner outputting grammars) iff

$$(\forall L, L' \in \mathcal{L})[L \subseteq L' \Rightarrow L = L'].\tag{2}$$

(2) is easily checkable (as is (1) above, but, (2) is more restrictive, as we saw in the just previous paragraph).

In a completely computable universe, all data sequences, even noisy ones, are computable. In the present paper, we are concerned with learner-synthesizer algorithms which operate on procedures which list either grammars or decision procedures but, significantly, *we restrict the noisy data sequences to being computable.*

Herein, our main and surprising result (Theorem 7 in Section 4.1 below) is: there *is* a learner-synthesizer algorithm **lsyn** so that, if **lsyn** is fed any procedure that lists decision procedures defining *any* indexed family $\mathcal{L}$ of languages, then **lsyn** outputs a learner which, from *computable,* noisy, positive data on any $L \in \mathcal{L}$, outputs a sequence of grammars eventually all correct for L! This result has the following corollary (Corollary 1 in Section 4.1 below): for *every* indexed family $\mathcal{L}$, there *is* a machine for **Bc**-learning $\mathcal{L}$, where the machine outputs grammars and the input is *computable* noisy positive data! Essentially Theorem 7 is a constructive version of this corollary: not only can each indexed family be **Bc**-learned (outputting grammars on computable noisy positive data), but one can *algorithmically find* a corresponding **Bc**-learner (of this kind) from an *index* for any indexed family! As a corollary to Theorem 7 we have that the class of finite unions of pattern languages *is* **Bc**-learnable from *computable* noisy texts, where the machine outputs grammars (this contrasts sharply with the negative result mentioned above from [CJS98a] that even the class of pattern languages is not learnable from *unrestricted* noisy texts)!

Another main positive result of the present paper is Corollary 3 in Section 4.1 below. It says that an indexed family $\mathcal{L}$ can be **Bc**-learned from *computable* noisy *informant* data by outputting grammars iff

$$(\forall L \in \mathcal{L})(\exists z)(\forall L' \in \mathcal{L} \mid \{x \leq z \mid x \in L\} = \{x \leq z \mid x \in L'\})[L' \subseteq L].\tag{3}$$

Corollary 2 in the same section is the constructive version of Corollary 3 and says one can algorithmically find such a learner from an index for any indexed family so learnable. (3) is easy to check too and intriguingly differs slightly from the characterization in [CJS98a] of the same learning criterion applied to indexed families *but with the noisy data sequences unrestricted:*

$$(\forall L \in \mathcal{L})(\exists z)(\forall L' \in \mathcal{L} \mid \{x \leq z \mid x \in L\} = \{x \leq z \mid x \in L'\})[L' = L].\tag{4}$$

Let N denote the set of natural numbers. Then $\{L \mid \operatorname{card}(N - L)$ is finite $\}$ satisfies (3), but not (4)! However, $\mathcal{L} =$ the class of all unions of two pattern languages satisfies *neither* (3) nor (4).

As might be expected, for several learning criteria considered here and in previous papers on synthesis, the restriction to *computable* noisy data sequences may, in some cases, reduce a criterion to one previously studied, but, in other cases (e.g., the one mentioned at the end of the just previous paragraph), not. Section 3 below, then, contains many of the comparisons of the criteria of this paper to those of previous papers.

As we indicated above, Section 4.1 below contains the main results of the present paper, and, in general, the results of this section are about synthesis from indices for indexed families and, when appropriate, corresponding characterizations. Section 4.2 below contains our positive and negative results on synthesis from r.e. indices for r.e. classes.

Finally Section 5 gives some directions for further research.

2 Preliminaries

2.1 Notation and Identification Criteria

The recursion theoretic notions are from the books of Odifreddi [Odi89] and Soare [Soa87]. $N = \{0, 1, 2, \ldots\}$ is the set of all natural numbers, and this paper considers r.e. subsets L of N. $N^+ = \{1, 2, 3, \ldots\}$, the set of all positive integers. All conventions regarding range of variables apply, with or without decorations[8], unless otherwise specified. We let c, e, i, j, k, l, m, n, q, s, t, u, v, w, x, y, z, range over N. $\emptyset, \in, \subseteq, \supseteq, \subset, \supset$ denote empty set, member of, subset, superset, proper subset, and proper superset respectively. $\max(), \min(), \text{card}()$ denote the maximum, minimum, and cardinality of a set respectively, where by convention $\max(\emptyset) = 0$ and $\min(\emptyset) = \infty$. $\text{card}(S) \leq *$ means cardinality of set S is finite. a, b range over $N \cup \{*\}$. $\langle \cdot, \cdot \rangle$ stands for an arbitrary but fixed, one to one, computable encoding of all pairs of natural numbers onto N. $\langle \cdot, \cdot, \cdot \rangle$, similarly denotes a computable, 1-1 encoding of all triples of natural numbers onto N. $\overline{L}$ denotes the complement of set L. χ_L denotes the characteristic function of set L. $L_1 \Delta L_2$ denotes the symmetric difference of L_1 and L_2, i.e., $L_1 \Delta L_2 = (L_1 - L_2) \cup (L_2 - L_1)$. $L_1 =^a L_2$ means that $\text{card}(L_1 \Delta L_2) \leq a$. Quantifiers $\forall^\infty, \exists^\infty$, and $\exists!$ denote for all but finitely many, there exist infinitely many, and there exists a unique respectively.

$\mathcal{R}$ denotes the set of total computable functions from N to N. f, g, range over total computable functions. $\mathcal{E}$ denotes the set of all recursively enumerable sets. L ranges over $\mathcal{E}$. $\mathcal{L}$ ranges over subsets of $\mathcal{E}$. φ denotes a standard acceptable programming system (acceptable numbering). φ_i denotes the function computed by the i-th program in the programming system φ. We also call i a program or index for φ_i. For a (partial) function η, domain(η) and range(η) respectively denote the domain and range of partial function η. We often write $\eta(x)\downarrow$ ($\eta(x)\uparrow$) to denote that $\eta(x)$ is defined (undefined). W_i denotes the domain of φ_i. W_i is considered as the language enumerated by the i-th program in φ system, and we say that i is a grammar or index for W_i. Φ denotes a standard Blum complexity measure [Blu67] for the programming system φ. $W_{i,s} = \{x < s \mid \Phi_i(x) < s\}$.

A *text* is a mapping from N to $N \cup \{\#\}$. We let T range over texts. content(T) is defined to be the set of natural numbers in the range of T (i.e. content(T) =

---

[8] Decorations are subscripts, superscripts, primes and the like.

range$(T) - \{\#\})$. T is a *text for* L iff content$(T) = L$. That means a text for L is an infinite sequence whose range, except for a possible $\#$, is just L.

An *information sequence or informant* is a mapping from N to $(N \times \{0,1\}) \cup \{\#\}$. We let I range over informants. content(I) is defined to be the set of pairs in the range of I (i.e. content$(I) = $ range$(I) - \{\#\}$). An *informant for* L is an informant I such that content$(I) = \{(x,b) \mid \chi_L(x) = b\}$. It is useful to consider the canonical information sequence for L. I is a canonical information sequence for L iff $I(x) = (x, \chi_L(x))$. We sometimes abuse notation and refer to the canonical information sequence for L by χ_L.

σ and τ range over finite initial segments of texts or information sequences, where the context determines which is meant. We denote the set of finite initial segments of texts by SEG and set of finite initial segments of information sequences by SEQ. We use $\sigma \preceq T$ (respectively, $\sigma \preceq I, \sigma \preceq \tau$) to denote that σ is an initial segment of T (respectively, I, τ). $|\sigma|$ denotes the length of σ. $T[n]$ denotes the initial segment of T of length n. Similarly, $I[n]$ denotes the initial segment of I of length n. Let $T[m:n]$ denote the segment $T(m), T(m+1), \ldots, T(n-1)$ (i.e. $T[n]$ with the first m elements, $T[m]$, removed). $I[m:n]$ is defined similarly. $\sigma \diamond \tau$ (respectively, $\sigma \diamond T$, $\sigma \diamond I$) denotes the concatenation of σ and τ (respectively, concatenation of σ and T, concatenation of σ and I). We sometimes abuse notation and say $\sigma \diamond w$ to denote the concatenation of σ with the sequence of one element w.

A *learning machine* $\mathbf{M}$ is a mapping from initial segments of texts (information sequences) to N. We say that $\mathbf{M}$ converges on T to i, (written: $\mathbf{M}(T)\!\downarrow = i$) iff, for all but finitely many n, $\mathbf{M}(T[n]) = i$. If there is no i such that $\mathbf{M}(T)\!\downarrow = i$, then we say that M diverges on T (written: $\mathbf{M}(T)\!\uparrow$). Convergence on information sequences is defined similarly.

Let ProgSet$(\mathbf{M}, \sigma) = \{\mathbf{M}(\tau) \mid \tau \subseteq \sigma\}$.

Definition 1 Suppose $a, b \in N \cup \{*\}$.
(a) Below, for each of several learning criteria $\mathbf{J}$, we define what it means for a machine $\mathbf{M}$ to $\mathbf{J}$-*identify* a language L from a text T or informant I.
- [Gol67,CL82] $\mathbf{M}$ $\mathbf{TxtEx}^a$-*identifies* L *from text* T iff $(\exists i \mid W_i =^a L)[\mathbf{M}(T)\!\downarrow = i]$.
- [Gol67,CL82] $\mathbf{M}$ $\mathbf{InfEx}^a$-*identifies* L *from informant* I iff $(\exists i \mid W_i =^a L)[\mathbf{M}(I)\!\downarrow = i]$.
- [B̄74,CL82]. $\mathbf{M}$ $\mathbf{TxtBc}^a$-*identifies* L *from text* T iff $(\forall^\infty n)[W_{\mathbf{M}(T[n])} =^a L]$.
- [B̄74,CL82]. $\mathbf{M}$ $\mathbf{InfBc}^a$-*identifies* L *from informant* I iff $(\forall^\infty n)[W_{\mathbf{M}(I[n])} =^a L]$.

(b) Suppose $\mathbf{J} \in \{\mathbf{TxtEx}^a, \mathbf{TxtBc}^a\}$. $\mathbf{M}$ $\mathbf{J}$-*identifies* L iff, for all texts T for L, $\mathbf{M}$ $\mathbf{J}$-identifies L from T. In this case we also write $L \in \mathbf{J}(\mathbf{M})$.

We say that $\mathbf{M}$ $\mathbf{J}$-identifies $\mathcal{L}$ iff $\mathbf{M}$ $\mathbf{J}$-identifies each $L \in \mathcal{L}$.

$\mathbf{J} = \{\mathcal{L} \mid (\exists \mathbf{M})[\mathcal{L} \subseteq \mathbf{J}(\mathbf{M})]\}$.

(c) Suppose $\mathbf{J} \in \{\mathbf{InfEx}^a, \mathbf{InfBc}^a\}$. $\mathbf{M}$ $\mathbf{J}$-*identifies* L iff, for all information sequences I for L, $\mathbf{M}$ $\mathbf{J}$-identifies L from I. In this case we also write $L \in \mathbf{J}(\mathbf{M})$.

We say that $\mathbf{M}$ $\mathbf{J}$-identifies $\mathcal{L}$ iff $\mathbf{M}$ $\mathbf{J}$-identifies each $L \in \mathcal{L}$.

$\mathbf{J} = \{\mathcal{L} \mid (\exists \mathbf{M})[\mathcal{L} \subseteq \mathbf{J}(\mathbf{M})]\}$.

We often write $\mathbf{TxtEx}^0$ as $\mathbf{TxtEx}$. A similar convention applies to the other learning criteria of this paper.

Next we prepare to introduce our noisy inference criteria, and, in that interest, we define some ways to calculate the number of occurrences of words in (initial segments of) a text or informant. For $\sigma \in \mathrm{SEG}$, and text T, let

$$\mathrm{occur}(\sigma, w) \overset{\mathrm{def}}{=} \mathrm{card}(\{j \mid j < |\sigma| \wedge \sigma(j) = w\}) \text{ and}$$
$$\mathrm{occur}(T, w) \overset{\mathrm{def}}{=} \mathrm{card}(\{j \mid j \in N \wedge T(j) = w\}).$$

For $\sigma \in \mathrm{SEQ}$ and information sequence I, $\mathrm{occur}(\cdot, \cdot)$ is defined similarly except that w is replaced by (v, b).

For any language L, $\mathrm{occur}(T, L) \overset{\mathrm{def}}{=} \Sigma_{x \in L} \mathrm{occur}(T, x)$. It is useful to introduce the set of positive and negative occurrences in (initial segment of) an informant. Suppose $\sigma \in \mathrm{SEQ}$

$$\mathrm{PosInfo}(\sigma) \overset{\mathrm{def}}{=} \{v \mid \mathrm{occur}(\sigma, (v, 1)) \geq \mathrm{occur}(\sigma, (v, 0)) \wedge \mathrm{occur}(\sigma, (v, 1)) \geq 1\}$$

$$\mathrm{NegInfo}(\sigma) \overset{\mathrm{def}}{=} \{v \mid \mathrm{occur}(\sigma, (v, 1)) < \mathrm{occur}(\sigma, (v, 0)) \wedge \mathrm{occur}(\sigma, (v, 0)) \geq 1\}$$

That means, that $\mathrm{PosInfo}(\sigma) \cup \mathrm{NegInfo}(\sigma)$ is just the set of all v such that either $(v, 0)$ or $(v, 1)$ occurs in σ. Then $v \in \mathrm{PosInfo}(\sigma)$ if $(v, 1)$ occurs at least as often as $(v, 0)$ and $v \in \mathrm{NegInfo}(\sigma)$ otherwise. Similarly,

$$\mathrm{PosInfo}(I) = \{v \mid \mathrm{occur}(I, (v, 1)) \geq \mathrm{occur}(I, (v, 0)) \wedge \mathrm{occur}(I, (v, 1)) \geq 1\}$$

$$\mathrm{NegInfo}(I) = \{v \mid \mathrm{occur}(I, (v, 1)) < \mathrm{occur}(I, (v, 0)) \wedge \mathrm{occur}(I, (v, 0)) \geq 1\}$$

where, if $\mathrm{occur}(I, (v, 0)) = \mathrm{occur}(I, (v, 1)) = \infty$, then we place v in $\mathrm{PosInfo}(I)$ (this is just to make the definition precise; we will not need this for criteria of inference discussed in this paper).

Definition 2 [Ste95] An information sequence I is a *noisy information sequence* (or *noisy informant*) for L iff $(\forall x) [\mathrm{occur}(I, (x, \chi_L(x))) = \infty \wedge \mathrm{occur}(I, (x, \chi_{\overline{L}}(x))) < \infty]$. A text T is a *noisy text* for L iff $(\forall x \in L)[\mathrm{occur}(T, x) = \infty]$ and $\mathrm{occur}(T, \overline{L}) < \infty$.

On the one hand, both concepts are similar since $L = \{x \mid \mathrm{occur}(I, (x, 1)) = \infty\} = \{x \mid \mathrm{occur}(T, x) = \infty\}$. On the other hand, the concepts differ in the way they treat errors. In the case of informant every false item $(x, \chi_{\overline{L}}(x))$ may occur a finite number of times. In the case of text, it is mathematically more interesting to require, as we do, that the total amount of false information has to be finite.[9]

Definition 3 [Ste95,CJS98b] *Suppose* $a \in N \cup \{*\}$. *Suppose* $\mathbf{J} \in \{\mathbf{TxtEx}^a, \mathbf{TxtBc}^a\}$. *Then* $\mathbf{M}$ $\mathbf{NoisyJ}$-*identifies* L *iff, for all noisy texts* T *for* L, $\mathbf{M}$ $\mathbf{J}$-*identifies* L *from* T. *In this case we write* $L \in \mathbf{NoisyJ}(\mathbf{M})$.

$\mathbf{M}$ $\mathbf{NoisyJ}$-*identifies a class* $\mathcal{L}$ *iff* $\mathbf{M}$ $\mathbf{NoisyJ}$-*identifies each* $L \in \mathcal{L}$.

$\mathbf{NoisyJ} = \{\mathcal{L} \mid (\exists \mathbf{M})[\mathcal{L} \subseteq \mathbf{NoisyJ}(\mathbf{M})]\}$.

---

[9] As we noted in Section 1 above, the alternative of allowing each false item in a text to occur finitely often is too restrictive; it would, then, be impossible to learn even the class of all singleton sets [Ste95].

Inference criteria for learning from noisy informants are defined similarly.

Note that in all the learning criteria formally defined thus far in this section, the (possibly noisy) texts or informants may be of arbitrary complexity. In a completely computable universe all texts and informants (even noisy ones) must be recursive (synonym: computable). As noted in Section 1 above, this motivates our concentrating in this paper on recursive texts and informants.

When a learning criterion is restricted to requiring learning from *recursive texts/informants only*, then we name the resultant criteria by adding, in an appropriate spot, 'Rec' to the name of the unrestricted criterion. For example, **RecTxtEx**-identification is this restricted variant of **TxtEx**-identification. Formally, **RecTxtEx**-identification may be defined as follows.

Definition 4 M RecTxtEx^a-identifies L *iff, for all* recursive *texts T for L,* **M TxtEx^a** *-identifies L from T.*

One can similarly define **RecInfEx^a**, **RecTxtBc^a**, **RecInfBc^a**, **NoisyRecTxtEx^a**, **NoisyRecTxtBc^a**, **NoisyRecInfEx^a**, **NoisyRecInfBc^a**.

RecTxtBc^a $\neq$ **TxtBc^a** [CL82,Fre85]; however, **TxtEx^a** = **RecTxtEx^a** [BB75,Wie77,Cas96]. [CJS98b] showed that, for $a \in N \cup \{*\}$, **NoisyInfBc^a** $\cup$ **NoisyTxtBc^a** $\subseteq$ **TxtBc^a** and **NoisyInfEx^a** $\cup$ **NoisyTxtEx^a** $\subseteq$ **TxtEx^a**. The proof of the above also shows: **NoisyRecInfBc^a** $\cup$ **NoisyRecTxtBc^a** $\subseteq$ **RecTxtBc^a** and **NoisyRecInfEx^a** $\cup$ **NoisyRecTxtEx^a** $\subseteq$ **RecTxtEx^a**. In Section 3 below, we indicate the remaining comparisons.

2.2 Recursively Enumerable Classes and Indexed Families

This paper is about the synthesis of algorithmic learners for r.e. classes of r.e. languages and of indexed families of recursive languages. To this end we define, for all i, $C_i \stackrel{\text{def}}{=} \{W_j \mid j \in W_i\}$. Hence, C_i is *the r.e. class with index i*. For a decision procedure j, we let $U_j \stackrel{\text{def}}{=} \{x \mid \varphi_j(x) = 1\}$. For a decision procedure j, we let $U_j[n]$ denote $\{x \in U_j \mid x < n\}$. For all i,

$$\mathcal{U}_i \stackrel{\text{def}}{=} \begin{cases} \{U_j \mid j \in W_i\}, & \text{if } (\forall j \in W_i)[j \text{ is a decision procedure}]; \\ \emptyset, & \text{otherwise.} \end{cases}$$

Hence, $\mathcal{U}_i$ is *the indexed family with index i*.

3 Comparisons

In this section we consider the comparisons between the inference criteria introduced in this paper among themselves and with the related inference criteria from the literature. We omit the proofs of these theorems due to lack of space.

The next theorem says that for **Bc***-learning, with computable noise, from either texts or informants, some machine learns grammars for all the r.e. languages. It improves a similar result from [CL82] for the noise-free case.

Theorem 1. *(a)* $\mathcal{E} \in$ **NoisyRecTxtBc***.
   (b) $\mathcal{E} \in$ **NoisyRecInfBc***.

The next result says that for **Ex**-style learning with noisy texts or informants, restricting the data sequences to be computable does not help us.

Theorem 2. *Suppose* $a \in N \cup \{*\}$.
   (a) **NoisyTxtEx**^{a} = **NoisyRecTxtEx**^{a}.
   (b) **NoisyInfEx**^{a} = **NoisyRecInfEx**^{a}.

Theorem 3. *Suppose* $n \in N$.
   (a) **NoisyTxtEx** − **NoisyRecInfBc**$^n \neq \emptyset$.
   (b) **NoisyInfEx** − **NoisyRecTxtBc**$^n \neq \emptyset$.

Theorem 4. *Suppose* $n \in N$. *(a)* **NoisyTxtBc**$^{n+1}$ − **RecInfBc**$^n \neq \emptyset$.
   (b) **NoisyInfBc**$^{n+1}$ − **RecInfBc**$^n \neq \emptyset$.

Theorem 5. *(a)* **NoisyRecTxtBc** − **TxtBc***$ \neq \emptyset$.
   (b) **NoisyRecInfBc** − **TxtBc***$ \neq \emptyset$.

It is open at present whether, for $m \leq n$, (i) **NoisyRecTxtBc**^{m} − **InfBc**$^n \neq \emptyset$? and whether (ii) **NoisyRecInfBc**^{m} − **InfBc**$^n \neq \emptyset$? In this context note that

Theorem 6. **RecTxtBc**$^a \cap 2^{\mathcal{R}} \subseteq$ **InfBc**^{a}.

4 Principal Results on Synthesizers

Since $\mathcal{E} \in$ **NoisyRecTxtBc*** and $\mathcal{E} \in$ **NoisyRecInfBc***, the only cases of interest are regarding when **NoisyRecTxtBc**^{n} and **NoisyRecInfBc**^{n} synthesizers can be obtained algorithmically.

4.1 Principal Results on Synthesizing from Uniform Decision Indices

The next result is the main theorem of the present paper.

Theorem 7. $(\exists f \in \mathcal{R})(\forall i)[\mathcal{U}_i \subseteq$ **NoisyRecTxtBc**$(\mathbf{M}_{f(i)})]$.

Proof. Let $\mathbf{M}_{f(i)}$ be such that, $\mathbf{M}_{f(i)}(T[n]) = prog(T[n])$, where, $W_{prog(T[n])}$ is defined below. Construction of *prog* will easily be seen to be algorithmic in i.

If $\mathcal{U}_i$ is empty, then trivially $\mathbf{M}_{f(i)}$ **NoisyRecTxtBc**-identifies $\mathcal{U}_i$. So suppose $\mathcal{U}_i$ is nonempty (in particular, for all $j \in W_i$, φ_j is a decision procedure). In the construction below, we will thus assume without loss of generality that, for each $j \in W_i$, φ_j is a decision procedure.

Let g be a computable function such that, range$(g) = \{\langle j, k \rangle \mid j \in W_i \wedge k \in N\}$. Intuitively, for an input noisy recursive text T for a language L, think of m such that $g(m) = \langle j, k \rangle$ as representing the hypothesis: (i) $L = U_j$, (ii) $\varphi_k = T$, and (iii) $T[m : \infty]$ does not contain any element from $\overline{L}$. In the procedure below, we just try to collect "non-harmful" and "good" hypothesis in P_n and Q_n^s (more details on this in the analysis of $prog(T[n])$ below). Let P1 and P2 be recursive functions such that $g(m) = \langle \mathrm{P1}(m), \mathrm{P2}(m) \rangle$.

$W_{prog(T[n])}$

1. Let $P_n = \{m \mid m \le n\} - [\{m \mid \text{content}(T[m : n]) \nsubseteq U_{P1(m)}\} \cup \{m \mid (\exists k < n)[\Phi_{P2(m)}(k) \le n \ \wedge \ \varphi_{P2(m)}(k) \ne T(k)]\}]$.

(* Intuitively, P_n is obtained by deleting $m \le n$ which represent a clearly wrong hypothesis. *)

(* Q_n^s below is obtained by refining P_n so that some further properties are satisfied. *)

2 Let $Q_n^0 = P_n$.

Go to stage 0.

3. Stage s

3.1 Enumerate $\bigcap_{m \in Q_n^s} U_{P1(m)}$.

3.2 Let $Q_n^{s+1} = Q_n^s - \{m' \mid (\exists m'' \in Q_n^s)(\exists k \le s)[m'' < m' \le k \ \wedge \ [\Phi_{P2(m'')}(k) \le s \ \wedge \ \varphi_{P2(m'')}(k) \notin U_{P1(m')}]]\}$.

3.3 Go to stage $s + 1$.

End stage s.

End

Let T be a noisy text for $L \in \mathcal{U}_i$. Let m be such that $U_{P1(m)} = L$, $T[m : \infty]$ is a text for L, and $\varphi_{P2(m)} = T$. Note that there exists such an m (since φ is acceptable numbering, and T is a noisy recursive text for L). Consider the definition of $W_{prog(T[n])}$ for $n \in N$ as above.

Claim. For all $m' \le m$, for all but finitely many n, if $m' \in P_n$ then

(a) $L \subseteq U_{P1(m')}$, and

(b) $(\forall k)[\varphi_{P2(m')}(k)\uparrow \ \vee \ \varphi_{P2(m')}(k) = T(k)]$.

Proof. Suppose $m' \le m$.

(a) If $W_{P1(m')} \nsupseteq L$, then there exists a $k > m'$ such that $T(k) \notin W_{P1(m')}$. Thus, for $n > k$, $m' \notin P_n$.

(b) If there exists a k such that $[\varphi_{P2(m')}(k)\downarrow \ne T(k)]$, then for all $n > \max(\{k, \Phi_{P2(m')}(k)\})$, $m' \notin P_n$.

The claim follows. □

Claim. For all but finitely many n: $m \in P_n$.

Proof. For $n \ge m$, clearly $m \in P_n$. □

Let n_0 be such that, for all $n \ge n_0$, (a) $m \in P_n$, and (b) for all $m' \le m$, if $m' \in P_n$, then $L \subseteq W_{P1(m')}$ and $(\forall k)[\varphi_{P2(m')}(k)\uparrow \ \vee \ \varphi_{P2(m')}(k) = T(k)]$. (There exists such a n_0 by Claims 4.1 and 4.1.)

Claim. Consider any $n \ge n_0$. Then, for all s, we have $m \in Q_n^s$. It follows that $W_{prog(T[n])} \subseteq L$.

Proof. Fix $n \ge n_0$. The only way m can be missing from Q_n^s, is the existence of $m'' < m$, and $t > m$ such that $m'' \in P_n$, and $\varphi_{P2(m'')}(t)\downarrow \notin L$. But then $m'' \notin P_n$ by the condition on n_0. Thus $m \in Q_n^s$, for all s. □

Claim. Consider any $n \geq n_0$. Suppose $m \leq m' \leq n$. If $(\exists^\infty s)[m' \in Q_n^s]$, then $L \subseteq U_{\mathrm{P1}(m')}$. Note that, using the condition on n_0, this claim implies $L \subseteq W_{prog(T[n])}$.

Proof. Fix any $n \geq n_0$. Suppose $(\exists^\infty s)[m' \in Q_n^s]$. Thus, $(\forall s)[m' \in Q_n^s]$. Suppose $L \not\subseteq U_{\mathrm{P1}(m')}$. Let $y \in L - U_{\mathrm{P1}(m')}$. Let $k \geq m'$ be such that $T(k) = y$. Note that there exists such a k, since y appears infinitely often in T. But then $\varphi_{\mathrm{P2}(m)}(k)\downarrow \notin U_{\mathrm{P1}(m')}$. This would imply that $m' \notin Q_n^s$, for some s, by step 3.2 in the construction. Thus, $L \subseteq U_{\mathrm{P1}(m')}$, and claim follows. $\square$

From Claims 4.1 and 4.1 it follows that, for $n \geq n_0$, $W_{prog(T[n])} = L$. Thus, $\mathbf{M}_{f(i)}$ **NoisyRecTxtBc**-identifies $\mathcal{U}_i$. ∎

Corollary 1 *Every indexed family belongs to* **NoisyRecTxtBc***.*

As noted in Section 1 above, then, the class of finite unions of pattern languages is **NoisyRecTxtBc**-learnable!

Remark 1. In the above theorem, learnability is *not* obtained by learning the rule for generating the noise. In fact, in general, it is *impossible* to learn (in the **Bc**-sense) the rule for noisy text generation (even though the noisy text is computable)!

While the **NoisyRecTxtBc**^{a}-hierarchy collapses *for indexed families*, we see below that the **NoisyRecInfBc**^{a}-hierarchy does not so collapse.

Definition 5 $\mathrm{Inf}[S, L] \stackrel{\text{def}}{=} \{\tau \mid (\forall x \in S)\,[occur(\tau, (x, \chi_{\overline{L}}(x))) = 0]\}$.

Lemma 1. *Let $n \in N$.*

*(a) Suppose L is a recursive language, and $\mathbf{M}$ **NoisyRecInfBc**^{n}-identifies L. Then there exists a σ and z such that $(\forall \tau \in \mathrm{Inf}[\{x \mid x \leq z\}, L])[card(W_{\mathbf{M}(\sigma \diamond \tau)} - L) \leq n]$.*

*(b) Suppose $\mathcal{L}$ is an indexed family in **NoisyRecInfBc**^{n}. Then, for all $L \in \mathcal{L}$, there exists a z such that, for all $L' \in \mathcal{L}$, $[(\{x \leq z \mid x \in L\} = \{x \leq z \mid x \in L'\}) \Rightarrow (card(L' - L) \leq 2n)]$.*

We omit the proof due to lack of space. An easy application of above lemma yields the following theorem.

Theorem 8. *Suppose $n \in N$. $\{L \mid card(L) \leq 2(n+1)\} \in$ **NoisyInfBc**$^{n+1}$ − **NoisyRecInfBc**^{n}.*

We will see in Corollary 2 below that it is possible to algorithmically synthesize learners for **NoisyRecInfBc**-learnable indexed families.

Theorem 9. *There exists $f \in \mathcal{R}$ such that the following is satisfied. Suppose $(\forall L \in \mathcal{U}_i)(\exists z)(\forall L' \in \mathcal{U}_i)[(\{x \leq z \mid x \in L\} = \{x \leq z \mid x \in L'\}) \Rightarrow L' \subseteq L]$. Then, $[\mathcal{U}_i \in$ **NoisyRecInfBc**$(\mathbf{M}_{f(i)})]$.*

As a corollary to Lemma 1(b) and Theorem 9 we have the second main, positive result of the present paper:

Corollary 2

$(\exists f \in \mathcal{R})(\forall i \mid \mathcal{U}_i \in \mathbf{NoisyRecInfBc})[\mathcal{U}_i \subseteq \mathbf{NoisyRecInfBc}(\mathbf{M}_{f(i)})]$.

The following corollary to Lemma 1(b) and Theorem 9 provides the very nice characterization of indexed families in **NoisyRecInfBc**.[10]

Corollary 3 $\mathcal{U}_i \in \mathbf{NoisyRecInfBc} \Leftrightarrow$ *for all* $L \in \mathcal{U}_i$, *there exists a* z *such that,* *for all* $L' \in \mathcal{U}_i$, $[(\{x \leq z \mid x \in L\} = \{x \leq z \mid x \in L'\}) \Rightarrow L' \subseteq L]$.

For $n > 0$, we do not know about synthesizing learners for $\mathcal{U}_i \in$ **NoisyRecInfBc**^{n}.

4.2 Principal Results on Synthesizing From R.E. Indices

Theorem 10. $\neg(\exists f \in \mathcal{R})(\forall i \mid \mathcal{C}_i \in \mathbf{NoisyTxtEx} \cap \mathbf{NoisyInfEx})[\mathcal{C}_i \subseteq \mathbf{RecTxtBc}^n(\mathbf{M}_{f(x)})]$.

Proof. Theorem 17 in [CJS98a] showed $\neg(\exists f \in \mathcal{R})$ $(\forall i \mid \mathcal{C}_i \in \mathbf{NoisyTxtEx} \cap$ **NoisyInfEx**) $[\mathcal{C}_i \subseteq \mathbf{TxtBc}^n(\mathbf{M}_{f(x)})]$. The proof of this given in [CJS98a] also shows that $\neg(\exists f \in \mathcal{R})(\forall i \mid \mathcal{C}_i \in \mathbf{NoisyTxtEx} \cap \mathbf{NoisyInfEx})[\mathcal{C}_i \subseteq \mathbf{RecTxtBc}^n(\mathbf{M}_{f(x)})]$. ∎

Corollary 4 $\neg(\exists f \in \mathcal{R})(\forall i \mid \mathcal{C}_i \in \mathbf{NoisyTxtEx} \cap \mathbf{NoisyInfEx})[\mathcal{C}_i \subseteq$ **NoisyRecTxtBc**$^n(\mathbf{M}_{f(x)})]$.

Corollary 5 $\neg(\exists f \in \mathcal{R})(\forall i \mid \mathcal{C}_i \in \mathbf{NoisyTxtEx} \cap \mathbf{NoisyInfEx})[\mathcal{C}_i \subseteq$ **NoisyRecInfBc**$^n(\mathbf{M}_{f(x)})]$.

5 Conclusions and Future Directions

In a completely computable universe, all data sequences, even noisy ones, are computable. Based on this, we studied in this paper the effects of having computable noisy data as input. In addition to comparing the criteria so formed within themselves and with related criteria from the literature, we studied the problem of synthesizing learners for r.e. classes and indexed families of languages. The main result of the paper (Theorem 7) showed that *all* indexed families of languages can be learned (in **Bc**-sense) from computable noisy texts. Moreover, one can algorithmically find a learner doing so, from an index for any indexed family! Another main positive result of the paper, Corollary 3, gives a characterization of indexed families which can be learned (in **Bc**-sense) from computable noisy informant. In addition to the results presented in the paper, we have related results for synthesis in the case of computable data (texts and informants) when there is no noise in the input. Due to lack of space we omit these results.

---

[10] Hence, as was noted in Section 1 above, we have: $\{L \mid \mathrm{card}(N - L)$ is finite $\} \in$ (**NoisyRecInfBc** − **NoisyInfBc**).

It is interesting to extend the study to the case where the texts have some other restriction than the computability restriction we considered in this paper. In this regard we have considered limiting recursive texts.[11] One of the results we have here is that **TxtBc** = **LimRecTxtBc** and **NoisyTxtBc** = **LimRecNoisyTxtBc** (where the **LimRec** in **LimRecTxtBc** and **LimRecNoisyTxtBc** denotes that identification is supposed to be from limiting recursive texts, noise-free and noisy, respectively). One can also similarly consider texts from natural *subrecursive* classes [RC94], linear-time computable and above. From [Gol67,Cas86], in that setting, some machine learns $\mathcal{E}$. *However*, it remains to determine the possible tradeoffs between the complexity of the texts and useful complexity features of the resultant learners. [Cas86] mentions that, in some cases, subrecursiveness of texts forces infinite repetition of data. Can this be connected to complexity tradeoffs? [Cas86] further notes that, if the texts we present to children, contain many repetitions, that would be consistent with a restriction in the world to subrecursive texts.

References

[Ang80] D. Angluin. Inductive inference of formal languages from positive data. *Information and Control*, 45:117–135, 1980.

[AS94] H. Arimura and T. Shinohara. Inductive inference of Prolog programs with linear data dependency from positive data. In *Proc. Information Modelling and Knowledge Bases V*, pages 365–375. IOS Press, 1994.

[ASY92] S. Arikawa, T. Shinohara, and A. Yamamoto. Learning elementary formal systems. *Theoretical Computer Science*, 95:97–113, 1992.

[B̃74] J. Bārzdiņš. Two theorems on the limiting synthesis of functions. In *Theory of Algorithms and Programs, vol. 1*, pages 82–88. Latvian State University, 1974. In Russian.

[BB75] L. Blum and M. Blum. Toward a mathematical theory of inductive inference. *Information and Control*, 28:125–155, 1975.

[BCJ96] G. Baliga, J. Case, and S. Jain. Synthesizing enumeration techniques for language learning. In *Proceedings of the Ninth Annual Conference on Computational Learning Theory*, pages 169–180. ACM Press, 1996.

[Ber85] R. Berwick. *The Acquisition of Syntactic Knowledge*. MIT Press, 1985.

[Blu67] M. Blum. A machine-independent theory of the complexity of recursive functions. *Journal of the ACM*, 14:322–336, 1967.

[Cas86] J. Case. Learning machines. In W. Demopoulos and A. Marras, editors, *Language Learning and Concept Acquisition*. Ablex Publishing Company, 1986.

[Cas96] J. Case. The power of vacillation in language learning. Technical Report LP-96-08, Logic, Philosophy and Linguistics Series of the Institute for Logic, Language and Computation, University of Amsterdam, 1996. To appear revised in *SIAM Journal on Computing*.

---

[11] The *limiting recursive* texts are in between the computable and the arbitrarily uncomputable. Informally, they are the ones computed by *limiting-programs*, programs that "change their minds" finitely many times about each output before getting it right [Sha71,Soa87].

[CJS98a] J. Case, S. Jain, and A. Sharma. Synthesizing noise-tolerant language learners. *Theoretical Computer Science A*, 1998. Accepted.

[CJS98b] J. Case, S. Jain, and F. Stephan. Vacillatory and BC learning on noisy data. *Theoretical Computer Science A*, 1998. Accepted.

[CL82] J. Case and C. Lynes. Machine inductive inference and language identification. In M. Nielsen and E. M. Schmidt, editors, *Proceedings of the 9th International Colloquium on Automata, Languages and Programming*, volume 140 of *Lecture Notes in Computer Science*, pages 107–115. Springer-Verlag, 1982.

[CS83] J. Case and C. Smith. Comparison of identification criteria for machine inductive inference. *Theoretical Computer Science*, 25:193–220, 1983.

[dJK96] D. de Jongh and M. Kanazawa. Angluin's thoerem for indexed families of r.e. sets and applications. In *Proceedings of the Ninth Annual Conference on Computational Learning Theory*, pages 193–204. ACM Press, July 1996.

[Fre85] R. Freivalds. Recursiveness of the enumerating functions increases the inferrability of recursively enumerable sets. *Bulletin of the European Association for Theoretical Computer Science*, 27:35–40, 1985.

[Ful90] M. Fulk. Robust separations in inductive inference. *31st Annual IEEE Symposium on Foundations of Computer Science*, pages 405–410, 1990.

[Gol67] E. M. Gold. Language identification in the limit. *Information and Control*, 10:447–474, 1967.

[Jan79a] K. Jantke. Automatic synthesis of programs and inductive inference of functions. In *Int. Conf. Fundamentals of Computations Theory*, pages 219–225, 1979.

[Jan79b] K. Jantke. Natural properties of strategies identifying recursive functions. *Electronische Informationverarbeitung und Kybernetik*, 15:487–496, 1979.

[Kap91] S. Kapur. *Computational Learning of Languages*. PhD thesis, Cornell University, 1991.

[KB92] S. Kapur and G. Bilardi. Language learning without overgeneralization. In *Proceedings of the Ninth Annual Symposium on Theoretical Aspects of Computer Science*, volume 577 of *Lecture Notes in Computer Science*. Springer-Verlag, 1992.

[LD94] N. Lavarač and S. Džeroski. *Inductive Logic Programming*. Ellis Horwood, New York, 1994.

[LZK96] S. Lange, T. Zeugmann, and S. Kapur. Monotonic and dual monotonic language learning. *Theoretical Computer Science A*, 155:365–410, 1996.

[MR94] S. Muggleton and L. De Raedt. Inductive logic programming: Theory and methods. *Journal of Logic Programming*, 19/20:669–679, 1994.

[Muk92] Y. Mukouchi. Characterization of finite identification. In K. Jantke, editor, *Analogical and Inductive Inference, Proceedings of the Third International Workshop*, pages 260–267, 1992.

[Nix83] R. Nix. Editing by examples. Technical Report 280, Department of Computer Science, Yale University, New Haven, CT, USA, 1983.

[Odi89] P. Odifreddi. *Classical Recursion Theory*. North-Holland, Amsterdam, 1989.

[OSW88] D. Osherson, M. Stob, and S. Weinstein. Synthesising inductive expertise. *Information and Computation*, 77:138–161, 1988.

[RC94] J. Royer and J. Case. *Subrecursive programming systems: Complexity & succinctness*. Birkhäuser, 1994.

[SA95] T. Shinohara and A. Arikawa. Pattern inference. In Klaus P. Jantke and Steffen Lange, editors, *Algorithmic Learning for Knowledge-Based Systems*, volume 961 of *Lecture Notes in Artificial Intelligence*, pages 259–291. Springer-Verlag, 1995.

[Sha71]   N. Shapiro. Review of "Limiting recursion" by E.M. Gold and "Trial and error predicates and the solution to a problem of Mostowski" by H. Putnam. *Journal of Symbolic Logic*, 36:342, 1971.

[Shi83]   T. Shinohara. Inferring unions of two pattern languages. *Bulletin of Informatics and Cybernetics*, 20:83–88., 1983.

[Shi91]   T. Shinohara. Inductive inference of monotonic formal systems from positive data. *New Generation Computing*, 8:371–384, 1991.

[Smu61]   R. Smullyan. *Theory of Formal Systems, Annals of Mathematical Studies, No. 47*. Princeton, NJ, 1961.

[Soa87]   R. Soare. *Recursively Enumerable Sets and Degrees*. Springer-Verlag, 1987.

[SSS+94] S. Shimozono, A. Shinohara, T. Shinohara, S. Miyano, S. Kuhara, and S. Arikawa. Knowledge acquisition from amino acid sequences by machine learning system BONSAI. *Trans. Information Processing Society of Japan*, 35:2009–2018, 1994.

[Ste95]   F. Stephan. Noisy inference and oracles. In *Algorithmic Learning Theory: Sixth International Workshop (ALT '95)*, volume 997 of *Lecture Notes in Artificial Intelligence*, pages 185–200. Springer-Verlag, 1995.

[Wie77]   R. Wiehagen. Identification of formal languages. In *Mathematical Foundations of Computer Science*, volume 53 of *Lecture Notes in Computer Science*, pages 571–579. Springer-Verlag, 1977.

[Wri89]   K. Wright. Identification of unions of languages drawn from an identifiable class. In R. Rivest, D. Haussler, and M.K. Warmuth, editors, *Proceedings of the Second Annual Workshop on Computational Learning Theory, Santa Cruz, California*, pages 328–333. Morgan Kaufmann Publishers, Inc., 1989.

[ZL95]   T. Zeugmann and S. Lange. A guided tour across the boundaries of learning recursive languages. In K. Jantke and S. Lange, editors, *Algorithmic Learning for Knowledge-Based Systems*, volume 961 of *Lecture Notes in Artificial Intelligence*, pages 190–258. Springer-Verlag, 1995.

[ZLK95]   T. Zeugmann, S. Lange, and S. Kapur. Characterizations of monotonic and dual monotonic language learning. *Information and Computation*, 120:155–173, 1995.

Characteristic Sets for Unions of Regular Pattern Languages and Compactness

Masako Sato, Yasuhito Mukouchi and Dao Zheng

Department of Mathematics and Information Sciences
College of Integrated Arts and Sciences
Osaka Prefecture University, Sakai, Osaka 599-8531, Japan
e-mail: {sato, mukouchi}@mi.cias.osakafu-u.ac.jp

Abstract. The paper deals with the class $\mathcal{RP}^k$ of sets of at most k regular patterns. A semantics of a set P of regular patterns is a union $L(P)$ of languages defined by patterns in P. A set Q of regular patterns is said to be a more general than P, denoted by $P \sqsubseteq Q$, if for any $p \in P$, there is a more general pattern q in Q than p. It is known that the syntactic containment $P \sqsubseteq Q$ for sets of regular patterns is efficiently computable. We prove that for any sets P and Q in $\mathcal{RP}^k$, (i) $S_2(P) \subseteq L(Q)$, (ii) the syntactic containment $P \sqsubseteq Q$ and (iii) the semantic containment $L(P) \subseteq L(Q)$ are equivalent mutually, provided $\sharp\Sigma \geq 2k - 1$, where $S_n(P)$ is the set of strings obtained from P by substituting strings with length at most n for each variable. The result means that $S_2(P)$ is a characteristic set of $L(P)$ within the language class for $\mathcal{RP}^k$ under the condition above. Arimura et al. showed that the class $\mathcal{RP}^k$ has compactness with respect to containment, if $\sharp\Sigma \geq 2k + 1$. By the equivalency above, we prove that $\mathcal{RP}^k$ has compactness if and only if $\sharp\Sigma \geq 2k - 1$.

The results obtained enable us to design efficient learning algorithms of unions of regular pattern languages such as already presented by Arimura et al. under the assumption of compactness.

1 Introduction

A pattern is a string consisting of constant symbols in a fixed alphabet Σ and variables. For example, $p = axbx$ is a pattern, where a and b are constant symbols, and x is a variable. The language $L(p)$ defined by a pattern p is the set of constant strings obtained from the pattern by substituting nonempty constant strings for variables in p. For example, the language defined by the above pattern is $L(p) = \{awbw \mid w \in \Sigma^+\}$.

The class $\mathcal{PL}$ of pattern languages was introduced by Angluin[1] as a class inductively inferable from positive data based on identification in the limit due to Gold[7]. The class $\mathcal{PL}$ is one of the most basic class in the framework of elementary formal systems which was introduced by Smullyan[13] to develop a new theory of recursive functions, and was proposed as a unifying framework for language learning by Arikawa et al.[3]. That is, an elementary formal system consisting of only one definite clause defines a pattern language. In some practical applications such as genome informatics, pattern languages are paid much attentions (cf. Arikawa et al.[4]).

Angluin[2] showed that the class $\mathcal{PL}$ has a property of so-called finite thickness. Wright[14] introduced a notion of finite elasticity for a language class, which is a natural extension of that of finite thickness, and showed that a class with finite elasticity is inferable from positive data and moreover, the property is closed under union operation. As a result, it was shown that for any fixed k, the class $\mathcal{PL}^k$ of unions of at most k pattern languages is also inferable from positive data. On the other hand, Sato[11] introduced a notion of finite cross property characterizing a class with finite elasticity. The property of finite cross property is closely related with a characteristic set. A nonempty finite set S of strings is said to be a characteristic set of a language L within a class $\mathcal{L}$, when L is the least language within $\mathcal{L}$ containing the set S. We show that a language L has a finite cross property within $\mathcal{L}$ if and only if there is a characteristic set of L within the class $\mathcal{L}$. Thus if a class $\mathcal{L}$ has a finite elasticity, then for any language $L \in \mathcal{L}$, there is a characteristic set of L within $\mathcal{L}$.

Let $\mathcal{D}$ be a set of descriptions which can be partially ordered by an effectively computable relation $\sqsubseteq$, and let $\mathcal{L} = \{L(P) \mid P \in \mathcal{D}\}$ be the language class defined by descriptions of $\mathcal{D}$. We assume that the syntactic containment $P \sqsubseteq Q$ implies the semantic containment $L(P) \subseteq L(Q)$ for any $P, Q \in \mathcal{D}$. Assume that the class $\mathcal{L}$ has finite elasticity. Thus for any description $P \in \mathcal{D}$, there is a characteristic set of $L(P)$ within $\mathcal{L}$. If the problem of finding one of the characteristic sets and the membership problem for languages in $\mathcal{L}$ are efficiently computable, then the containment for languages of $\mathcal{L}$ is also efficiently computable. Furthermore, if the semantic containment $L(P) \subseteq L(Q)$ implies the syntactic containment $P \sqsubseteq Q$, the containment for languages of $\mathcal{L}$ is efficiently computable.

A pattern is said to be regular, if each variable in the pattern appears at most once. In this paper, we deal with the class $\mathcal{RP}^k$ of sets of at most k regular patterns as a class of descriptions, and develop the above discussion for $\mathcal{RP}^k$. A pattern q is a generalization of a pattern p, denoted by $p \preceq q$, when q is obtained from p by substituting patterns for variables in p. For example, a pattern $q = axy$ is a generalization of a pattern $p = axbx$, i.e., $axbx \preceq axy$. The set $\mathcal{P}$ of patterns is a partially ordered set under the relation $\preceq$, provided we identify patterns obtained by renaming variables. Clearly the syntactic containment $p \preceq q$ implies the semantic containment $L(p) \subseteq L(q)$, but not always the converse. Mukouchi showed that the converse is valid for the class $\mathcal{RP}$ of regular patterns.

A set $P = \{p_1, \cdots, p_n\}$ of regular patterns defines a language $L(P) = L(p_1) \cup \cdots \cup L(p_n)$. Let $\mathcal{RPL}^k$ be the class defined by the description class $\mathcal{RP}^k$. For sets $P, Q \in \mathcal{RP}^k$, we define a relation $\sqsubseteq$ as follows: $P \sqsubseteq Q$ if and only if for any $p \in P$, there is a regular pattern $q \in Q$ such that $p \preceq q$. Clearly $P \sqsubseteq Q$ implies $L(P) \subseteq L(Q)$. The relation $\sqsubseteq$ is an efficiently computable and partially ordered relation by restricting to sets in $\mathcal{RP}^k$ of canonical form (cf. Arimura et al.[5]).

The class $\mathcal{RPL}^k$ as well as the class $\mathcal{PL}$ have finite elasticity. Thus for each $P \in \mathcal{RP}^k$, there is a characteristic set of $L(P)$ within $\mathcal{RPL}^k$. Let $S_n(P) =$

$\bigcup_{p \in P} S_n(p)$, where $S_n(p)$ is the set of strings obtained from p substituting non-empty constant strings with length at most n for each variable. Then there is a positive number n such that $S_n(P)$ is a characteristic set of $L(P)$ within $\mathcal{RPL}^k$. We are interested in the positive number n for given $P \in \mathcal{RP}^k$. We first prove that (i) $S_1(P) \subseteq L(Q)$, (ii) $P \sqsubseteq Q$ and (iii) $L(P) \subseteq L(Q)$ are equivalent mutually, provided $\sharp\Sigma \geq 2k + 1$. The result is not always valid, if $\sharp\Sigma \leq 2k$. We show, however, that the above equivalency for (i') $S_2(P) \subseteq L(Q)$ instead of (i) is valid, provided $\sharp\Sigma \geq 2k - 1$. Thus $S_2(P)$ is a characteristic set of $L(P)$ within $\mathcal{RPL}^k$. It is known that the membership problem for regular pattern languages is polynomial time computable (cf. Shinohara[12]), although it is NP-complete for general pattern languages (cf. Angluin[1]). Thus the containment for languages of $\mathcal{RPL}^k$ is efficiently computable.

On the other hand, Arimura et al.[5] gave an efficient algorithm of languages in $\mathcal{RPL}^k$ under the condition that the class has compactness with respect to containment. The class $\mathcal{RP}^k$ has compactness with respect to containment, if $L(P) \subseteq L(Q)$ implies $P \sqsubseteq Q$ for $P, Q \in \mathcal{RP}^k$. Arimura and Shinohara[6] showed the compactness of $\mathcal{RP}^k$, if $\sharp\Sigma \geq 2k + 1$. In terms of the above equivalency, it can be shown that $\mathcal{RP}^k$ has compactness w.r.t. containment, if $\sharp\Sigma \geq 2k - 1$. Moreover, a counter-example is given so that $\mathcal{RP}^k$ does not have compactness w.r.t. containment, if $\sharp\Sigma < 2k - 1$. Consequently, the containment for languages of $\mathcal{RPL}^k$ reduces to that for $\mathcal{RP}^k$, and thus it is efficiently computable.

2 Regular Pattern Languages

Let Σ be a finite set of *constant* symbols containing at least two symbols, and $X = \{x, y, x_1, x_2, \cdots\}$ be a countable set of *variable* symbols. We assume $\Sigma \cap X = \phi$.

A *pattern* is a string in $(\Sigma \cup X)^*$. Note that we consider the empty string ε as a pattern, for convenience. By $\mathcal{P}$ we denote the set of all patterns. The *length* of a pattern p, denoted by $|p|$, is just the number of symbols composing it. A *substitution* θ is a homomorphism from patterns to patterns that maps every constant to itself. For a pattern p and a substitution θ, we denote by $p\theta$ the image of p by θ. A pattern q is a *generalization* of a pattern p, or p is an *instance* of q, denoted by $p \preceq q$, if there is a substitution θ such that $p = q\theta$. For two patterns p and q, if $p \preceq q$ and $q \preceq p$, then p equals q, denoted by $p \equiv q$, except for labeling variables in them. The set $(\mathcal{P}, \preceq)$ constitutes a partial ordering set with respect to $\equiv$.

The language defined by a pattern p is the set $L(p) = \{w \in \Sigma^* \mid w \preceq p\}$. Clearly if $p \equiv q$, then $L(p) = L(q)$. A language L over Σ is a *pattern language*, if $L = L(p)$ for some pattern p. We denote by $\mathcal{PL}$ the class of all pattern languages.

In this paper, we are especially concerned with a subclass of $\mathcal{P}$. A pattern p is *regular*, if each variable appears at most once in p. A *regular pattern language* is a pattern language defined by a regular pattern. We denote by $\mathcal{RP}$ the set of all regular patterns, and by $\mathcal{RPL}$ the set of all regular pattern languages.

Concerning regular patterns, the next fundamental result has been shown:

Lemma 1 (Mukouchi[10]). *Let p and q be regular patterns. Then $p \preceq q$ if and only if $L(p) \subseteq L(q)$.*

Note that "if" part of the lemma above is not always valid for general patterns, although "only if" part is always valid.

By the result above, the containment problem for regular pattern languages is reduced to the decision problem of partial ordering for regular patterns, which is polynomial time computable (cf. Shinohara[12]).

Now we consider unions of languages defined by patterns. By $\mathcal{P}^+$ we denote the class of all nonempty finite subsets of $\mathcal{P}$. For $k \geq 1$, let $\mathcal{P}^k$ be the class of sets consisting of at most k patterns. By $\mathcal{PL}^k$ we denote the class of unions of at most k pattern languages, that is,

$$\mathcal{PL}^k = \{L(P) \mid P \in \mathcal{P}^k\},$$

where $L(P) = \bigcup_{p \in P} L(p)$. In a similar way, we also define $\mathcal{RP}^+$, $\mathcal{RP}^k$ and $\mathcal{RPL}^k$, respectively.

For $P, Q \in \mathcal{P}^+$, we define the binary relation $P \sqsubseteq Q$ as follows: $P \sqsubseteq Q$ if and only if for any $p \in P$, there is $q \in Q$ such that $p \preceq q$. It is easy to see that $P \sqsubseteq Q$ implies $L(P) \subseteq L(Q)$. However the converse is not valid in general.

Definition 2. A class $\mathcal{C} \subseteq \mathcal{P}^+$ has *compactness with respect to containment*, if for any pattern $p \in \mathcal{P}$ and any set $Q \in \mathcal{C}$, $L(p) \subseteq L(Q)$ implies $L(p) \subseteq L(q)$ for some $q \in Q$.

In a similar way, we also define compactness for a class $\mathcal{C} \subseteq \mathcal{RP}^+$.

For a class $\mathcal{C} \subseteq \mathcal{RP}^+$ with compactness, it is easy to see by Lemma 1 that for any $P, Q \in \mathcal{C}$, $P \sqsubseteq Q$ if and only if $L(P) \subseteq L(Q)$.

In this paper, we show the compactness of the class $\mathcal{RP}^k$ as a corollary of stronger property than the compactness as follows: For some particular finite subset S of $L(p)$, $S \subseteq L(Q)$ implies $L(p) \subseteq L(q)$ for some $q \in Q$. Note that $S \subseteq L(Q)$ implies also $L(p) \subseteq L(Q)$. Such a set S is called a characteristic set for $L(p)$, which is defined as follows:

Definition 3. Let $\mathcal{L}$ be a class of languages and L be a language. A set $S \subseteq \Sigma^+$ is a *characteristic set* for L within $\mathcal{L}$, if S is a finite subset of L and for any $L' \in \mathcal{L}$, $S \subseteq L'$ implies $L \subseteq L'$.

If S is a characteristic set for $L \in \mathcal{L}$, L is the least language among $\mathcal{L}$ containing S in the set-containment ordering, and any finite superset of S contained in L is also a characteristic set for L. Furthermore a finite language $L \in \mathcal{L}$ is a characteristic set for itself.

The notion of a characteristic set has very closed relation with that of finite elasticity due to Wright[14] as well as that of finite cross property due to Sato[11] defined as follows:

Definition 4 (Wright[14] and Motoki et al.[9]). A class $\mathcal{L}$ of languages has *finite elasticity*, if there does not exist an infinite sequence $(w_i)_{i \geq 0}$ of strings and an infinite sequence $(L_i)_{i \geq 1}$ of languages in $\mathcal{L}$ such that for any $i \geq 1$,

$$\{w_0, \cdots, w_{i-1}\} \subseteq L_i, \quad \text{but} \quad w_i \notin L_i.$$

A condition for a class to have finite elasticity is characterized by the notion of finite cross property of a language as follows:

Definition 5 (Sato[11]). Let $\mathcal{L}$ be a class of languages. A language L has *finite cross property within* $\mathcal{L}$, if there does not exist an infinite sequence $(T_n)_{n \geq 1}$ of finite sets of strings and an infinite sequence $(L_i)_{i \geq 1}$ of languages in $\mathcal{L}$ such that
(i) $T_1 \subsetneq T_2 \subsetneq \cdots$,   (ii) $\bigcup_{i=1}^{\infty} T_i = L$,   (iii) $T_i \subseteq L_i$, but $T_{i+1} \not\subseteq L_i$ $(i \geq 1)$.

Lemma 6 (Sato[11]). *A class $\mathcal{L}$ of languages has finite elasticity if and only if every language L has finite cross property within $\mathcal{L}$.*

Furthermore, by their definitions, it is easy to see that the following lemma is valid:

Lemma 7. *Let $\mathcal{L}$ be a class of languages and L be a language. Then L has finite cross property within $\mathcal{L}$ if and only if there is a characteristic set for L within $\mathcal{L}$.*

By Lemmas 6 and 7, we see that a class $\mathcal{L}$ has finite elasticity if and only if for any language L, there is a characteristic set for L within $\mathcal{L}$. Note that this result has already shown in Kobayashi and Yokomori[8].

Wright[14] showed that the class $\mathcal{PL}^k$ has finite elasticity, and so is the subclass $\mathcal{RPL}^k$. Thus, by the lemmas above, we see that for any language $L \in \mathcal{RPL}^k$, there is a characteristic set for L within $\mathcal{RPL}^k$.

Now we define a particular finite subset of a regular pattern language which plays an important role in our paper. For a regular pattern p with just m variables $x_1, \cdots, x_m$ and for $n \geq 1$, we define a finite subset $S_n(p)$ of $L(p)$ as follows: Let $S_n(p)$ be the set of all strings obtained from p by substituting strings in Σ^+ with length at most n for each variable in p.

For a nonempty finite set P of regular patterns, we define

$$S_n(P) = \bigcup_{p \in P} S_n(p).$$

Clearly $S_n(P) \subseteq S_{n+1}(P) \subseteq L(P)$ for any $n \geq 1$.

Since a characteristic set for $L(P)$ is a finite set, we have the following theorem:

Theorem 8. *For any $P \in \mathcal{RP}^k$, there is $n \geq 1$ such that $S_n(P)$ is a characteristic set for $L(P)$ within $\mathcal{RPL}^k$.*

In Section 4, we will show that 2 is sufficient for the number n in the theorem above, under the assumption that the number of constants is not less than $2k-1$.

3 $S_1(P)$ as a Characteristic Set

In this section, we will give some simple characteristic set for each language in $\mathcal{RPL}^k$. The key is the set $S_1(p)$ of strings with the shortest length for a regular pattern p.

Let $p_1 r p_2 \preceq q$ for regular patterns p_1, r, p_2 and q, and let $x_1, \cdots, x_n$ be variables appearing in q. The subpattern r in $p_1 r p_2$ is *generated from q by variable substitution*, if there exists a variable x_i in q and a substitution $\theta = \{x_1 := r_1, \cdots, x_i := r'rr'', \cdots, x_n := r_n\}$ such that $p_1 = (q_1\theta)r'$, $p_2 = r''(q_2\theta)$ for $q = q_1 x_i q_2$. Note that if the pattern r in $p_1 r p_2$ is generated from q by variable substitution, clearly $p_1 x p_2 \preceq q$ holds. In particular, if $p_1 a p_2 \preceq q$ but $p_1 x p_2 \not\preceq q$ for some $a \in \Sigma$, then the constant a in $p_1 a p_2$ is not generated from q by variable substitution, and moreover $q = q_1 a q_2$ holds for some q_1 and q_2 such that $p_j \preceq q_j$ ($j = 1, 2$). Furthermore, if $p_1 x p_2 \preceq q$, then the variable x in $p_1 x p_2$ is always generated from q by variable substitution.

For a pattern p, by $\text{head}(p)$ and $\text{tail}(p)$ we denote the first symbol and the last symbol of p, respectively.

We first give two fundamental lemmas useful in this paper.

Lemma 9. *Let $p = p_1 x p_2$ and $q = q_1 q_2 q_3$, where p, q, p_1, p_2, q_1, q_2 and q_3 are regular patterns and x is a variable. Then if $p_1 \preceq q_1 q_2$, $p_2 \preceq q_2 q_3$ and q_2 contains some variables, then $p \preceq q$ holds.*

Proof. Let y be any fixed variable appearing in q_2 and $q_2 = q_2' y q_2''$ for some q_2' and q_2''. By $p_1 \preceq q_1(q_2' y q_2'')$, we can put $p_1 = p_1' p_1''$ for some p_1' and p_1'' such that $p_1' \preceq q_1 q_2'$ and $p_1'' \preceq y q_2''$. Similarly, by $p_2 \preceq (q_2' y q_2'')q_3$, we can put $p_2 = p_2' p_2''$ for some p_2' and p_2'' such that $p_2' \preceq q_2' y$ and $p_2'' \preceq q_2'' q_3$. Now we consider a substitution $\theta = \{y := p_1'' x p_2'\}$. Then we have $p = p_1 x p_2 = p_1'(p_1'' x p_2')p_2'' \preceq q_1 q_2'(p_1'' x p_2')q_2'' q_3 = q\theta \preceq q$. $\qquad\square$

By the result above, if $p_1 \preceq q_1 q_2$ and $p_2 \preceq q_2 q_3$ but $p \not\preceq q$, then q_2 contains no variable, i.e., $q_2 \in \Sigma^*$.

Lemma 10. *Suppose $\sharp\Sigma \geq 3$. Let p and q be regular patterns. Then if $p\{x := a\} \preceq q$, $p\{x := b\} \preceq q$ and $p\{x := c\} \preceq q$ for distinct constants a, b and c, then $p \preceq q$ holds.*

Proof. If p does not contain the variable x, then it is clearly true. Thus we consider $p = p_1 x p_2$ for some regular patterns p_1 and p_2.

Suppose $p \not\preceq q$. As mentioned above, if the constant a in $p_1 a p_2$ is generated by variable substitution from q, then by $p_1 a p_2 \preceq q$, $p \preceq q$ holds, which is a contradiction. Thus we can put $q = q_a^{(1)} a q_a^{(2)}$ for some $q_a^{(1)}$ and $q_a^{(2)}$ such that $p_j \preceq q_a^{(j)}$ ($j = 1, 2$). Similarly, from $p_1 b p_2 \preceq q$ and $p_1 c p_2 \preceq q$, we can put $q = q_b^{(1)} b q_b^{(2)} = q_c^{(1)} c q_c^{(2)}$ for some $q_b^{(1)}, q_b^{(2)}, q_c^{(1)}$ and $q_c^{(2)}$ such that $p_j \preceq q_b^{(j)}$ and $p_j \preceq q_c^{(j)}$ ($j = 1, 2$).

Without loss of generality, we can put $q = q_1 a q_2 b q_3 c q_4$, where

$$(1)\ p_1 \preceq q_a^{(1)} = q_1, \qquad\qquad (1')\ p_2 \preceq q_a^{(2)} = q_2 b q_3 c q_4,$$
$$(2)\ p_1 \preceq q_b^{(1)} = q_1 a q_2, \qquad\quad (2')\ p_2 \preceq q_b^{(2)} = q_3 c q_4,$$
$$(3)\ p_1 \preceq q_c^{(1)} = q_1 a q_2 b q_3, \qquad (3')\ p_2 \preceq q_c^{(2)} = q_4.$$

As easily seen, both q_2 and q_3 contain no variable. In fact, by (2) and (1'), $p_1 \preceq (q_1 a) q_2$ and $p_2 \preceq q_2 (b q_3 c q_4)$. Thus if q_2 contains some variables, it implies by Lemma 9 that $p \preceq q$, which contradicts the assumption. Therefore q_2 contains no variable. Similarly we can show that q_3 contains no variable.

Put $w = q_2$ and $w' = q_3$. By (2) and (3), both aw and $awbw'$ are suffixes of p_1. Therefore if $|w| = |w'|$, then $aw = bw'$ holds, which contradicts the assumption that $a \neq b$.

Assume $|w| < |w'|$. Then aw is a suffix of w', so $w' = w_1 aw$ for some $w_1 \in \Sigma^*$. Similarly, by (1') and (2'), both $wbw'c$ and $w'c$ are prefixes of p_2. Thus wb is a prefix of w', so $w' = wbw_2$ for some $w_2 \in \Sigma^*$, and thus $|w_1| = |w_2|$. This implies $a = c$, because both $wbw'c = wbw_1 awc$ and $w'c = wbw_2 c$ are prefixes of p_2, which contradicts the assumption that $a \neq c$.

We can also show a contradiction similarly for the case of $|w'| < |w|$. This completes our proof. $\qquad\qquad\square$

Theorem 11. *Suppose $\sharp\Sigma \geq 2k + 1$. Let $P \in \mathcal{RP}^+$ and $Q \in \mathcal{RP}^k$. Then the following three propositions are equivalent:*

(i) $S_1(P) \subseteq L(Q)$,   (ii) $P \sqsubseteq Q$,   (iii) $L(P) \subseteq L(Q)$.

Proof. Clearly (ii) implies (iii) and (iii) implies (i). Now we prove (i) implies (ii). It suffices to show that for any regular pattern p, $S_1(p) \subseteq L(Q)$ implies $p \preceq q$ for some $q \in Q$.

The proof is done by a mathematical induction on the number n of variables in p. In case $n = 0$, $p \in L(Q)$, and so $p \in L(q)$ for some $q \in Q$. Let $n \geq 0$ and assume that it is valid for any regular pattern with n variables. Let p be a regular pattern with $(n + 1)$ variables such that $S_1(p) \subseteq L(Q)$, and let x be any fixed variable in p. Put $p_a = p\{x := a\}$ for each $a \in \Sigma$. Note that p_a has just n variables and $S_1(p_a) \subseteq L(Q)$ holds. Thus by the induction hypothesis, $p_a \preceq q_a$ for some $q_a \in Q$. Since $\sharp\Sigma \geq 2k + 1$ and $\sharp Q \leq k$, there exists at least one regular pattern $q \in Q$ such that $p_{a_j} \preceq q$ for some distinct constants $a_j \in \Sigma$ ($j = 1, 2, 3$). By Lemma 10, it implies $p \preceq q$. $\qquad\qquad\square$

As a direct corollary of this theorem, we have:

Corollary 12. *Suppose $\sharp\Sigma \geq 3$. Let p and q be regular patterns. Then the following three propositions are equivalent:*

(i) $S_1(p) \subseteq L(q)$,   (ii) $p \preceq q$,   (iii) $L(p) \subseteq L(q)$.

Note that Theorem 11 is not valid in general if $\sharp\Sigma \leq 2k$. Before illustrating a counter-example, we give the following lemma:

Lemma 13. *Suppose* $\sharp \Sigma \geq 3$. *Let* p *and* q *be regular patterns. Then if* $p\{x := a\} \preceq q$ *and* $p\{x := b\} \preceq q$ *for distinct constants* a *and* b *but* $p \not\preceq q$, *then there exist regular patterns* p_1, p_2, q_1 *and* q_2 *and a string* $w \in \Sigma^*$ *such that*

$$p = p_1 A w x w B p_2, \quad q = q_1 A w B q_2, \quad p_j \preceq q_j \ (j = 1, 2),$$
$$p_1 A w \preceq q_1, \quad w B p_2 \preceq q_2,$$

where $A = a$, $B = b$ *or* $A = b$, $B = a$.

Proof. Clearly p contains the variable x. Let $p = p_1' x p_2'$ for some regular patterns p_1' and p_2'. Similarly to the proof of Lemma 10, we can show that there exist regular patterns q_1 and q_2 and a string $w \in \Sigma^*$ such that $q = q_1 A w B q_2$, $p_j' \preceq q_j$ $(j = 1, 2)$, $p_1' \preceq q_1 A w$ and $p_2' \preceq w B q_2$. Hence we can put $p_1' = p_1 A w$ and $p_2' = w B p_2$ for some p_1 and p_2 such that $p_j \preceq q_j$ $(j = 1, 2)$. It implies $p = p_1 A w x w B p_2$. □

By the result above, we can construct the following counter-example for Theorem 11:

Example 1. Let $\Sigma = \{a_1, \cdots, a_k, b_1, \cdots, b_k\}$ be an alphabet with just $2k$ constants. We consider a regular pattern p and a set $Q = \{q_1, \cdots, q_k\} \in \mathcal{RP}^k$ given by

$$p = x_1 a_1 w_1 x w_1 b_1 x_2, \quad q_i = x_1 a_i w_i b_i x_2 \ (i = 1, 2, \cdots, k),$$

where $w_1, \cdots, w_k$ are defined recursively as follows:

$$w_i = w_{i+1} b_{i+1} a_{i+1} w_{i+1} \ (i = 1, 2, \cdots, k - 1), \quad w_k = \varepsilon.$$

For instance, in case $k = 3$, $w_3 = \varepsilon, w_2 = b_3 a_3$ and $w_1 = (b_3 a_3) b_2 a_2 (b_3 a_3)$,

$$p = x_1 a_1 ((b_3 a_3) b_2 a_2 (b_3 a_3)) x ((b_3 a_3) b_2 a_2 (b_3 a_3)) b_1 x_2,$$
$$q_1 = x_1 a_1 ((b_3 a_3) b_2 a_2 (b_3 a_3)) b_1 x_2, \quad q_2 = x_1 a_2 (b_3 a_3) b_2 x_2, \quad q_3 = x_1 a_3 b_3 x_2.$$

We will show that $p\{x := a_i\} \preceq q_i$ and $p\{x := b_i\} \preceq q_i$ $(i = 1, 2, \cdots, k)$. For $i = 1$, we have $p\{x := a_1\} = (x_1 a_1 w_1) a_1 (w_1 b_1 x_2) = q_1 \{x_1 := x_1 a_1 w_1\} \preceq q_1$ and, similarly, $p\{x := b_1\} = q_1 \{x_2 := w_1 b_1 x_2\} \preceq q_1$.

Next for $i \geq 2$, as easily seen, by the definition of w_i, we can put $w_1 = (w_i b_i) w^{(i)} = w'^{(i)} (a_i w_i)$ for some strings $w^{(i)}$ and $w'^{(i)}$. Thus for each $i \geq 2$,

$$\begin{aligned} p\{x := a_i\} &= (x_1 a_1 w_1) a_i (w_1 b_1 x_2) = (x_1 a_1 w_1) a_i (w_i b_i w^{(i)}) b_1 x_2 \\ &= (x_1 a_1 w_1)(a_i w_i b_i)(w^{(i)} b_1 x_2) \\ &= q_i \{x_1 := x_1 a_1 w_1, \ x_2 := w^{(i)} b_1 x_2\} \\ &\preceq q_i, \quad \text{similarly,} \\ p\{x := b_i\} &= q_i \{x_1 := x_1 a_1 w'^{(i)}, \ x_2 := w_1 b_1 x_2\} \\ &\preceq q_i. \end{aligned}$$

Hence $S_1(p) \subseteq L(Q)$. On the other hand, clearly $p \not\preceq q_i$, and so $L(p) \not\subseteq L(q_i)$ $(i = 1, \cdots, k)$. □

4 $S_2(P)$ and Compactness

In this section, we show that $S_2(P)$ is a characteristic set for $L(P)$ within $\mathcal{RPL}^k$, under the condition $\#\Sigma \geq 2k - 1$. As a result, the class $\mathcal{RP}^k$ has compactness with respect to containment.

Lemma 14. *Suppose $\#\Sigma \geq 3$. Let p and q be regular patterns. Then if $p\{x := r\} \preceq q$ for any $r \in D$, then $p\{x := xy\} \preceq q$ holds, where D is either one of the followings:*

(i) $D = \{ay, by\}$, or $D = \{ya, yb\}$, where $a \neq b$,

(ii) $D = \{a_1 b_1, a_2 b_2, a_3 b_3\}$, where $a_i \neq a_j$ and $b_i \neq b_j$ for $i \neq j$.

Proof. If p does not contain the variable x, then it is clearly true. Thus we consider $p = p_1 x p_2$ for some regular patterns p_1 and p_2. We prove only for the case (i) that if $p_1 a y p_2 \preceq q$ and $p_1 b y p_2 \preceq q$, then $p_1 x y p_2 \preceq q$ holds. We can prove for other cases similarly.

Assume $p_1 x y p_2 \not\preceq q$. Let us put $p_2' = y p_2$ and $p' = p_1 x y p_2 = p_1 x p_2'$. Since $p'\{x := a\} \preceq q$, $p'\{x := b\} \preceq q$ but $p' \not\preceq q$, by Lemma 13, there exist regular patterns p_1'', p_2'', q_1 and q_2 and a string $w \in \Sigma^*$ such that $p_1 = p_1'' A w$, $p_2' = w B p_2''$ and $q = q_1 A w B q_2$, where $\{A, B\} = \{a, b\}$. By $p_2' = w B p_2''$, head(p_2') must be a constant, which contradicts that $p_2' = y p_2$. □

Lemma 15. *Suppose $\#\Sigma \geq 3$. Let p and q be regular patterns. Then if $p\{x := a\} \preceq q$ for some $a \in \Sigma$ and $p\{x := xy\} \preceq q$, then $p \preceq q$ holds, where y is a variable not appearing in p.*

Proof. If p does not contain the variable x, then it is clearly true. Thus we consider $p = p_1 x p_2$ for some regular patterns p_1 and p_2.

Assume the converse that $p_1 a p_2 \preceq q$ and $p_1 x y p_2 \preceq q$ but $p_1 x p_2 \not\preceq q$. Similarly to the proof of Lemma 10, we can show that there exist regular patterns q_1 and q_2 and a string $w \in \Sigma^*$ such that

$$q = q_1 A w B q_2, \quad p_j \preceq q_j \ (j = 1, 2), \quad p_1 \preceq q_1 A w, \quad p_2 \preceq w B q_2,$$

where $\{A, B\} = \{a, xy\}$.

Let $A = a$ and $B = xy$. By $p_1 \preceq q_1 a w$ and $p_2 \preceq w x (y q_2)$, we can put $p_1 = p_1' a w$ and $p_2 = w p_2' p_2''$ for some p_1', p_2' and p_2'' such that $p_1' \preceq q_1$, $p_2' \preceq x$ and $p_2'' \preceq y q_2$. Consider a substitution $\theta = \{x := x w p_2'\}$. Then $p_1 x p_2 = p_1' a w x w p_2' p_2'' \preceq (q_1) a w x w p_2' (y q_2) = ((q_1 a w) x (y q_2))\theta = q\theta \preceq q$, which contradicts the assumption.

Similarly, we can show a contradiction for the case of $A = xy$ and $B = a$. □

For a nonempty finite set D of regular patterns, we denote

$$\text{head}(D) = \{\text{head}(p) \mid p \in D\}, \quad \text{tail}(D) = \{\text{tail}(p) \mid p \in D\}.$$

Lemma 16. *Suppose $\#\Sigma \geq 3$. Let p and q be regular patterns. Then if $p\{x := r\} \preceq q$ for any $r \in D$, then $p \preceq q$ holds, where D is either one of the followings:*

(i) $D = \{a, b, cy\}$, or $D = \{a, b, yc\}$, where $a \neq b$,

(ii) $D = \{a, by, cy\}$, or $D = \{a, yb, yc\}$, where $b \neq c$.

Proof. If p does not contain the variable x, then it is clearly true. Thus we consider $p = p_1 x p_2$ for some regular patterns p_1 and p_2.

For the case (ii), by Lemma 14 (i), we have $p_1 x y p_2 \preceq q$. Since $p_1 a p_2 \preceq q$, we have $p \preceq q$ by Lemma 15.

We prove for $D = \{a, b, cy\}$ of the case (i). Assume the converse that $p_1 a p_2 \preceq q$, $p_1 b p_2 \preceq q$ and $p_1 cy p_2 \preceq q$ but $p_1 x p_2 \not\preceq q$. Then clearly the constant a in $p_1 a p_2$ is not generated by variable substitution from q, and so are b in $p_1 b p_2$ and cy in $p_1 cy p_2$. If $p_1 x y p_2 \preceq q$, since $p_1 a p_2 \preceq q$, it follows by Lemma 15 that $p \preceq q$, and a contradiction. Thus we have $p_1 x y p_2 \not\preceq q$. Similarly to the proof of Lemma 10, we can show that there exist regular patterns q_1 and q_2 and strings w and w' such that

(1) $q = q_1 A w B w' C q_2$, $p_i \preceq q_i$ $(i = 1, 2)$,
(2) $p_1 \preceq q_1 A w$, $p_1 \preceq q_1 A w B w'$,
(3) $p_2 \preceq w B w' C q_2$, $p_2 \preceq w' C q_2$,

where $D = \{A, B, C\} = \{a, b, cy\}$. Note that head$(D) = \{a, b, c\}$ and tail$(D) = \{a, b, y\}$ (possibly $c = a$ or $c = b$, but $a \neq b$). Since Aw is a suffix of $AwBw'$ by (2) and $w'C$ is a prefix of $wBw'C$ by (3), it follows that $|w| \neq |w'|$ and $w, w' \neq \varepsilon$. Assume $|w| < |w'|$. Then there exist strings $w_1, w_2 \in \Sigma^+$ such that $w' = w_1 w = w w_2$, and so A is a suffix of $AwBw_1$ and $w_2 C$ is a prefix of $Bw_1 wC$.

If $A = cy$, then tail$(w_1) = $ tail$(A) = y$, which contradicts that w_1 is a constant string.

If $B = cy$, then $w_2 C$ contains the variable y, because B is a prefix of $w_2 C$. In this case, $C = a$ or b, and thus $w_2 C$ is a constant string. It is a contradiction.

Finally, if $C = cy$, then $w_2 cy$ is a prefix of the constant string $Bw_1 w$, and a contradiction.

We can prove for the case of $|w| > |w'|$ similarly. $\qquad\qquad\square$

Now we present the main theorem in this paper.

Theorem 17. *Suppose $k \geq 3$ and $\sharp\Sigma \geq 2k - 1$. Let $P \in \mathcal{RP}^+$ and $Q \in \mathcal{RP}^k$. Then the following three propositions are equivalent:*
(i) $S_2(P) \subseteq L(Q)$,   (ii) $P \sqsubseteq Q$,   (iii) $L(P) \subseteq L(Q)$.

Proof. It suffices to show the case of $\sharp Q = k$ and $\sharp\Sigma = 2k - 1$ and that of $\sharp Q = k$ and $\sharp\Sigma = 2k$. Other cases can be reduced to Theorem 11.

We show that for any regular pattern p, $S_2(p) \subseteq L(Q)$ implies $p \preceq q$ for some $q \in Q$, when $\sharp Q = k$ and $\sharp\Sigma = 2k - 1$. The case of $\sharp Q = k$ and $\sharp\Sigma = 2k$ can be shown similarly. Put $Q = \{q_1, \cdots, q_k\}$.

The proof is done by a mathematical induction on the number n of variables in p. In case $n = 0$, $S_2(p) = \{p\}$, and so $p \in L(Q)$. Hence $p \preceq q$ for some $q \in Q$. Let $n \geq 0$ and assume that it is valid for any regular pattern with n variables. Let p be a regular pattern with $(n + 1)$ variables such that $S_2(p) \subseteq L(Q)$.

Assume $p \not\preceq q_i$ $(i = 1, \cdots, k)$. Let x be any fixed variable in p and $p = p_1 x p_2$ for some p_1 and p_2. For $a, b \in \Sigma$, put $p_a = p\{x := a\}$ and $p_{ab} = p\{x := ab\}$. Note that both p_a and p_{ab} contain just n variables and that $S_2(p_a) \subseteq L(Q)$ and

$S_2(p_{ab}) \subseteq L(Q)$ hold. By the induction hypothesis, for any $a, b \in \Sigma$, there exist $i, i' \leq k$ such that $p_a \preceq q_i$ and $p_{ab} \preceq q_{i'}$.

For each $i \leq k$, put $D_i = \{a \in \Sigma \mid p_a \preceq q_i\}$ and define a bigraph $G_i = (V, E_i)$, where the set V of vertices consists of two sets Σ and $\overline{\Sigma} = \{\overline{a} \mid a \in \Sigma\}$ and the set E_i of edges is defined by $E_i = \{(a, \overline{b}) \mid p_{ab} \preceq q_i\}$. Note that any cycle in a bigraph has even length. For each $a, b \in \Sigma$, $\deg_i(a)$ (resp., $\deg_i(\overline{b})$) means the number of b's (resp., a's) such that $p_{ab} \preceq q_i$. We note that, as easily seen, $\bigcup_{i=1}^{k} D_i = \Sigma$ and $\bigcup_{i=1}^{k} E_i = \Sigma \times \overline{\Sigma}$ hold.

If $\sharp D_i \geq 3$ for some i, then $p \preceq q_i$ by Lemma 10, and a contradiction. Thus $\sharp D_i \leq 2$ for any $i \leq k$. Moreover, since $\sharp \Sigma = 2k - 1$ and $\bigcup_{i=1}^{k} D_i = \Sigma$, it follows that $\sharp D_i \geq 1$ for any $i \leq k$.

Here we note that for the case of $\sharp D_i = 2$, by Lemma 16 (i), $p_1 a y p_2 \npreceq q_i$ and $p_1 y b p_2 \npreceq q_i$ hold for any $a, b \in \Sigma$. Therefore, by Lemma 10, there exist neither distinct constants a_j ($j = 1, 2, 3$) nor b_j ($j = 1, 2, 3$) such that $p_{a b_j} \preceq q_i$ and $p_{a_j b} \preceq q_i$, and thus $\deg_i(a) \leq 2$ and $\deg_i(\overline{b}) \leq 2$ for any $a, b \in \Sigma$. These mean that any connected component of the bigraph G_i is a cycle with even length or a chain.

For the case of $\sharp D_i = 1$, by Lemma 16 (ii), the following four cases are possible:

(1) $p_1 a y p_2 \npreceq q_i$ and $p_1 y b p_2 \npreceq q_i$ for any $a, b \in \Sigma$,
(2) $p_1 a y p_2 \npreceq q_i$ and $p_1 y b p_2 \npreceq q_i$ for any $a \in \Sigma - \{a_0\}$, $b \in \Sigma - \{b_0\}$,
(3) $p_1 a y p_2 \npreceq q_i$ and $p_1 y b p_2 \npreceq q_i$ for any $a \in \Sigma - \{a_0\}$, $b \in \Sigma$,
(4) $p_1 a y p_2 \npreceq q_i$ and $p_1 y b p_2 \npreceq q_i$ for any $a \in \Sigma$, $b \in \Sigma - \{b_0\}$,

where $a_0, b_0 \in \Sigma$ are some constant symbols.

For the case (1), any connected component of G_i is similarly shown to be a cycle with even length or a chain. For the case (2), we consider a bigraph G_i' obtained from the bigraph G_i by deleting the vertices a_0 and $\overline{b}_0$. Clearly $\deg_i(a) \leq 2$ and $\deg_i(\overline{b}) \leq 2$ in the bigraph G_i' for any $a \in \Sigma - \{a_0\}$ and any $b \in \Sigma - \{b_0\}$. Thus any connected component of the bigraph is a cycle with even length or a chain. For the cases (3) and (4), we can similarly get subbigraphs of G_i whose connected components are all cycles with even lengths or chains.

Hereafter, we prove the following claim:

Claim: For some $i_0 \leq k$, the bigraph G_{i_0} contains at least three edges $(a_j, \overline{b}_j)$, $j = 1, 2, 3$ such that $a_j \neq a_{j'}$, $\overline{b}_j \neq \overline{b}_{j'}$ for $j \neq j'$.

Proof of the claim. Since $\sharp \Sigma = 2k - 1$ and $\bigcup_{i=1}^{k} D_i = \Sigma$, it follows that $\sharp D_i = 2$ for at least $(k - 1)$ i's, say, $1, 2, \cdots, k - 1$, and $\sharp D_k = 1$ or 2.

(i) In case $\sharp D_i = 2$ for any $i \leq k$. As noted above, for any $i \leq k$, all connected components of the bigraph G_i are cycles with even lengths and chains. As mentioned above, for any $a, b \in \Sigma$, there exists $i \leq k$ such that $p_{ab} \preceq q_i$, and thus for any edge $(a, \overline{b})$, there exists $i \leq k$ such that $(a, \overline{b}) \in E_i$. Since there are $(2k - 1)^2$ possible edges, there exists $i_0 \leq k$ such that the bigraph G_{i_0} contains at least $(4k - 3)$ ($\geq (2k - 1)^2 / k$) edges. Since $\deg_{i_0}(a) \leq 2$ for any $a \in \Sigma$, it means that $\deg_{i_0}(a) = 2$ for at least $(2k - 2)$ a's, and $\deg_{i_0}(a) \leq 1$ for at most one a. Hence the bigraph G_{i_0} consists of some cycles with even lengths and at most one chain. Note that a cycle with length $2l$ contains distinct l edges which are not adjacent mutually. As easily seen, G_{i_0} contains a set of edges $(a_j, \bar{b}_j)$, $j = 1, \cdots, 2k-1$ which are not adjacent mutually. Since $k \geq 3$, we have $2k - 1 \geq 5$, and thus our claim is valid.

(ii) In case $\sharp D_i = 2$ for any $i < k$ and $\sharp D_k = 1$. For the case (1) mentioned above, we can show similarly to (i). Let us consider the case (2) above. For any $i \leq k$, let G_i' be a subbigraph obtained from G_i by deleting the vertices a_0 and $\bar{b}_0$. Then for any $i \leq k$, any connected component of the bigraph G_i' is a cycle with even length or a chain. Similarly to (i), since there are $(2k - 2)^2$ possible edges $(a, \bar{b})$ each of which is contained in at least one bigraph considered, there exists $i_0 \leq k$ such that the bigraph G_{i_0}' contains at least $4k - 7$ ($\geq (2k-2)^2/k$) edges. It implies that $\deg_{i_0}(a) = 2$ for at least $(2k-5)$ a's and $\deg_{i_0}(a) \leq 1$ for at most three a's. In particular, if $\deg_{i_0}(a) = 2$ for just $(2k-5)$ a's, $\deg_{i_0}(a) = 1$ for the other three a's. Moreover, if $\deg_{i_0}(a) = 2$ for just $(2k-4)$ a's, $\deg_{i_0}(a) = 1$ for at least one a. In any case, G_{i_0} contains a set of edges $(a_j, \bar{b}_j)$, $j = 1, \cdots, 2k-3$, which are not adjacent mutually. Since $k \geq 3$, we have $2k - 3 \geq 3$, and thus our claim is valid.

We can prove our claim for the cases (3) and (4) similarly. ∎

Appealing to Lemma 14, we have $p_1 x y p_2 \preceq q_{i_0}$, and thus $p \preceq q_i$ by Lemma 15. This contradicts our assumption. □

As a direct corollary of this theorem, we have:

Corollary 18. *Suppose $k \geq 3$ and $\sharp \Sigma \geq 2k - 1$. Let $P \in \mathcal{RP}^+$. Then $S_2(P)$ is a characteristic set for the language $L(P)$ within $\mathcal{RPL}^k$.*

Lemma 19. *If $\sharp \Sigma \leq 2k - 2$, then the class $\mathcal{RP}^k$ does not have compactness with respect to containment.*

Proof. Let $\Sigma = \{a_1, \cdots, a_{k-1}, b_1, \cdots, b_{k-1}\}$ be an alphabet with just $(2k - 2)$ constants. Let p, q_i and w_i ($i = 1, \cdots, k - 1$) be regular patterns and strings defined in Example 1, where $w_{k-1} = \varepsilon$. Then let $q_k = x_1 a_1 w_1 x y w_1 b_1 x_2$.

As shown in Example 1, $p\{x := a_i\} \preceq q_i$ and $p\{x := b_i\} \preceq q_i$ for $i = 1, 2, \cdots, k-1$, and thus $S_1(p) \subseteq \bigcup_{i=1}^{k-1} L(q_i)$. On the other hand, clearly, for any string w with $|w| \geq 2$, $p\{x := w\} \preceq q_k$. These mean $L(p) \subseteq L(Q)$. However, clearly, $p \not\preceq q_i$, and so $L(p) \not\subseteq L(q_i)$ ($i = 1, 2, \cdots, k$). Therefore $\mathcal{RP}^k$ does not have compactness w.r.t. containment. □

By Theorem 17 and Lemma 19, we have the following theorem:

Theorem 20. *Suppose $k \geq 3$. Then the class $\mathcal{RP}^k$ has compactness with respect to containment if and only if $\sharp \Sigma \geq 2k - 1$.*

Note that, independent of ours, Arimura and Shinohara[6] showed that if $\sharp \Sigma \geq 2k + 1$, then the class $\mathcal{RP}^k$ has compactness w.r.t. containment, and so is not if $\sharp \Sigma = k + 1$. Theorem 20 completely fills the gap on the number of constant symbols.

The following example is a counter-example for Theorem 17 in case $k = 2$.

Example 2. Let $\Sigma = \{a, b, c\}$ be an alphabet with just 3 constants. We consider regular patterns p, q_1 and q_2 given by

$$p = x_1 a x b x_2, \quad q_1 = x_1 a b x_2, \quad q_2 = x_1 c x_2.$$

For any $w \in \Sigma^+$, if c appears in w, then $p\{x := w\} \preceq q_2$ holds. Otherwise, as easily seen, $p\{x := w\} \preceq q_1$ holds. It implies that $L(p) \subseteq L(q_1) \cup L(q_2)$, but clearly $p \npreceq q_i$ $(i = 1, 2)$. $\qquad\square$

Thus Theorem 17 is not always valid for $k = 2$. However, we obtain the following result for the case of $k = 2$.

Theorem 21. *Suppose* $\sharp\Sigma \geq 4$. *Let* $P \in \mathcal{RP}^+$ *and* $Q \in \mathcal{RP}^2$. *Then the following three propositions are equivalent:*

(i) $S_2(P) \subseteq L(Q)$, *(ii)* $P \sqsubseteq Q$, *(iii)* $L(P) \subseteq L(Q)$.

Proof. We can prove similarly to the proof of Theorem 17. $\qquad\square$

As direct corollaries of this theorem, we have:

Corollary 22. *Suppose* $\sharp\Sigma \geq 4$. *Let* $P \in \mathcal{RP}^+$. *Then* $S_2(P)$ *is a characteristic set for the language* $L(P)$ *within* $\mathcal{RPL}^2$.

Corollary 23. *Suppose* $\sharp\Sigma \geq 4$. *Then the class* $\mathcal{RP}^2$ *has compactness with respect to containment.*

The following corollary would be very useful in the theory of inductive inference of recursive languages from positive data from the view point of efficiency:

Corollary 24. *Suppose* $k \geq 3$ *and* $\sharp\Sigma \geq 2k - 1$. *Let* $P \in \mathcal{RP}^+$ *and* $Q \in \mathcal{RP}^k$. *Then for any subset* S *of* $L(Q)$, *if* $S_2(P) \subseteq S$, *then* $P \sqsubseteq Q$ *holds.*

Furthermore, because for any regular patterns p and q, whether or not $p \preceq q$ is computable in time polynomial of the sum of lengths of p and q (cf. Shinohara[12]), it follows that containment problem for unions are efficiently computable, that is, we have the following corollary:

Corollary 25. *Suppose* $k \geq 3$ *and* $\sharp\Sigma \geq 2k - 1$. *For any* $P \in \mathcal{RP}^+$ *and* $Q \in \mathcal{RP}^k$, *whether or not* $L(P) \subseteq L(Q)$ *is computable in time polynomial of the total length of patterns appearing in* P *and* Q.

References

1. Angluin, D.: *Finding patterns common to a set of strings*, in Proceedings of the 11th Annual Symposium on Theory of Computing (1979) 130–141.
2. Angluin, D.: *Inductive inference of formal languages from positive data*, Information and Control **45** (1980) 117–135.

3. Arikawa, S., Shinohara, T. and Yamamoto, A.: *Elementary formal systems as a unifying framework for language learning*, in Proceedings of the 2nd Annual ACM Workshop on Computational Learning Theory (1989) 312–327.
4. Arikawa, S., Kuhara, S., Miyano S., Mukouchi, Y., Shinohara, A. and Shinohara, T.: *A machine discovery from amino acid sequences by decision trees over regular patterns*, in Proceedings of the International Conference on Fifth Generation Computer Systems (1992) 618–625 (also in New Generation Computing **11**(3, 4) (1993) 361–375).
5. Arimura, H., Shinohara, T. and Otsuki, S.: *Finding minimal generalizations for unions of pattern languages and its application to inductive inference from positive data*, in Proceedings of the 11th Symposium on Theoretical Aspects of Computer Science, Lecture Notes in Computer Science **775** (1994) 646–660.
6. Arimura, H. and Shinohara, T.: *Compactness for unions of regular pattern languages*, in Proceedings of the Symposium on Language and Automaton, Research on Computational Models and Complexity, RIMS Koukyuroku **950** (1996) 246–249 (in Japanese).
7. Gold, E.M.: *Language identification in the limit*, Information and Control **10** (1967) 447–474.
8. Kobayashi, S. and Yokomori, T.: *Identifiability of subspaces and homomorphic images of zero-reversible languages*, in Proceedings of the 8th International Workshop on Algorithmic Learning Theory, Lecture Notes in Artificial Intelligence **1316** (1997) 48–61.
9. Motoki, T., Shinohara, T. and Wright, K.: *The correct definition of finite elasticity: corrigendum to identification of unions*, in Proceedings of the 4th Annual ACM Workshop on Computational Learning Theory (1991) 375–375.
10. Mukouchi, Y.: *Characterization of pattern languages*, in Proceedings of the 2nd Workshop on Algorithmic Learning Theory (1991) 93–104.
11. Sato, M.: *Inductive inference of formal languages*, Bulletin of Informatics and Cybernetics **27**(1) (1995) 85–106.
12. Shinohara, T.: *Polynomial time inference of pattern languages and its applications*, in Proceedings of the 7th IBM Symposium on Mathematical Foundations of Computer Science (1982) 191–209.
13. Smullyan, R.M.: "Theory of formal systems," Princeton University Press, 1961.
14. Wright, K.: *Identification of unions of languages drawn from an identifiable class*, in Proceedings of the 2nd Annual Workshop on Computational Learning Theory (1989) 328–333.

Finding a One-Variable Pattern from Incomplete Data

Hiroshi SAKAMOTO

hiroshi@i.kyushu-u.ac.jp
Department of Informatics, Kyushu University Fukuoka 812-8581, Japan

Abstract. The present paper deals with the problem of finding a consistent one-variable pattern from incomplete positive and negative examples. The studied problems are called an *extension* E, a *consistent extension* CE and a *robust extension* RE, respectively. Problem E corresponds to the ordinary problem to decide whether there exists a one-variable pattern that is consistent with the given positive and negative examples. As for the other problems, an example string is allowed to contain some unsettled symbols that can potentially match with every constant symbol. For the problem CE, one has to decide whether there exists a suitable assignment for these unsettled symbols as well as a one-variable pattern consistent with the examples with respect to the assignment chosen. Problem RE is the universal version of problem CE, i.e., now one has to decide whether there exists a one-variable pattern that is consistent with the examples under *every* assignment for the unsettled symbols. The decision problems defined are closely connected to the learnability of one-variable pattern languages from positive and negative examples. The computational complexity of the decision problems defined above is studied. In particular, it shown that RE is NP-complete.

1 Introduction

A pattern is a non-null string over $\Sigma \cup X$, where Σ is a finite alphabet of *constants* and $X = \{x_0, x_1, \ldots\}$ a countably infinite alphabet of *variables*. For example, $ax_0x_1x_0bx_0$ and $bbx_0aax_0x_1x_1$ are patterns over $\{a, b\} \cup X$. A pattern π is said to be a k-variable pattern if at most k different $x_i \in X$ appear in π. The language $L(\pi)$ generated by a pattern π is the set of all constant strings obtained by substituting nonempty strings for the variables of π (cf. [1]). In order to motivate our research, we shortly recall results concerning the learnability of pattern languages and their relation to decision and constructibility problems. For any background concerning the definitions and properties of relevant learning models we refer the interested reader to [9, 13, 15].

A string w is called a positive example of a pattern π if $w \in L(\pi)$. Furthermore, every infinite sequence of positive examples eventually exhausting $L(\pi)$ is said to be a *positive presentation* for $L(\pi)$. The set of all pattern languages is an important and prominent language family that can be learned in the limit from positive presentations. The first result in this regard goes back to Angluin [1] who showed that any algorithm computing a descriptive pattern on input a finite sample of positive examples can be transformed into a learner for the whole class of pattern languages from positive presentations. Here, a pattern π is called *descriptive* for a finite set S of strings, if $S \subseteq L(\pi)$ and for any other pattern π' such that $S \subseteq L(\pi')$, $L(\pi') \not\subseteq L(\pi)$ (cf. [1]). However, no polynomial-time algorithm computing descriptive patterns is known, and finding a descriptive pattern of maximum possible length is known to be NP-complete (cf. [1]).

As for the special case of one-variable patterns, descriptive patterns can be computed in time $O(n^2 \log n)$, where n is the size of the input sample (cf. [4]). Nevertheless, the resulting learner is not optimal with respect to the expected overall time taken until convergence (cf. [11]). Giving up the idea to find descriptive one-variable patterns at all enabled Reischuk and Zeugmann [11] to design a learner achieving *linear* total learning time, that is $O(|\pi|)$, with probability 1 for a huge class of probability distributions.

Moreover, Angluin [1] also proposed to study the complexity of the inclusion problem for pattern languages, i.e., given any patterns π and τ, to decide whether $L(\pi) \subseteq L(\tau)$. Recently, Jiang *et al.* [8] have shown the inclusion problem to be undecidable, and this has also negative consequences concerning the learnability of all pattern languages from positive presentations under certain monotonicity constraints (cf. [16]).

Next, we turn our attention to problems more closely related to the research presented in this paper. A string w is called a negative example of a pattern π provided $w \notin L(\pi)$. Given two finite sets $\mathcal{P}$ and $\mathcal{N}$, the *consistency* problem is to *decide* whether there is a pattern π such that $\mathcal{P} \subseteq L(\pi)$ and $\mathcal{N} \cap L(\pi) = \emptyset$. This problem is sometimes also referred to as separability. Let *SEP* denote the separability problem and *CSEP* the problem to *construct* a separating pattern. Wiehagen and Zeugmann [14] showed *CSEP* to be NP-hard. Additionally, the latter result implies that the class of all pattern languages is not inferable from positive and negative data by a learner achieving both polynomial update time and outputting exclusively consistent hypotheses, unless P = NP (cf. [14]). Furthermore, their result also sharpens the previously known fact that Gold's [6] *identification by enumeration* principle cannot be used for computing a separating pattern in polynomial time, since Angluin [1] has proved the *membership* problem for the pattern languages to be NP-complete. Here, the membership problem is defined as follows. Given as input a string w and a pattern π, decide whether $w \in L(\pi)$.

Note that *CSEP* and *SEP* are also closely related to the PAC-learnability of all pattern languages. If *CSEP* would be in P, then the class of pattern languages would be PAC learnable with respect to the hypothesis space consisting of all pattern languages. On the other hand, since the membership problem for patterns is NP-complete, the set of all patterns does not constitute a polynomial time evaluable hypothesis space as usually required in PAC learning. But the pattern languages are also known to be not PAC learnable for any such polynomial time evaluable hypothesis space, unless $P/_{poly} = NP/_{poly}$ (cf. [12]).

On the other hand, the pattern languages have already found highly non-trivial applications for real world data sets (cf. [2]). Thus, understanding what makes the decision and constructibility problems outlined above hard, is of major importance. We continue along this line of research by looking at the class of one-variable patterns. While it has been known that membership and inclusion are decidable in polynomial time, the complexity of the consistency problem remains open. We attack this problem by adapting the notion of monotone extensions introduced in [3] in the setting of learning Boolean concepts.

Besides the motivation given in Boros *et al.* [3] it may also be helpful to look at the problems *extension, consistent extension,* and *robust extension* from the point of view how noisy data may influence the complexity of learning. These problems are defined as follows. Given a set of positive data $\mathcal{P}$ and a set of negative data $\mathcal{N}$, a one-variable pattern π such that $\mathcal{P} \subseteq L(\pi)$ and $\mathcal{N} \cap L(\pi) = \emptyset$ is called an extension. The problem of deciding whether there exists an extension for the data given is denoted by E, i.e., E is just the consistency problem for one-variable patterns. Since real world data may be noisy, e.g., by containing indefinite values it is only natural to look at the following versions of E. Allowing strings to contain indefinite values can be modeled by introducing a wild card $\star$ as a placeholder. Thus, now we are given strings over the alphabet of constants plus $\star$. There are two kinds of interpretations. One is that we consider an establishment of the indefinite values to be critical for our hypothesis. In this case, we must settle all the indefinite values such that there exists an extension with respect to the settlement. The other is that the value does not influence our hypothesis. In this case, our requirement is an extension that is consistent with the data with respect to every settlement. The resulting decision problems are called consistent extension CE and robust extension RE, respectively. Moreover, allowing indefinite values directly yields two natural versions of the membership problem. We study the complexity of all these problems. In particular, we show that RE is NP-complete.

2   Preliminaries

For each finite set S, the cardinality of S is denoted by $\|S\|$. An alphabet is a finite set of symbols, denoted by Σ. The free monoid over Σ is denoted by Σ^*, and the set of all nonempty strings is denoted by Σ^+, where $\Sigma^* = \Sigma^+ \cup \{\varepsilon\}$, and ε is the empty string (cf., e.g., [7]). In particular, for each $n \geq 1$, we denote the set of all strings of length n over Σ by Σ^n.

Let w be a string of the form $\alpha\beta\gamma$. Then α, β, and γ are called substrings of w. A substring of w is said to be a proper substring if it is not equal to w. Furthermore, we refer to α and γ as to a a prefix and a suffix of w, respectively. The string α is called a proper prefix if $\alpha \neq w$, and a proper suffix is defined similarly. Let α and β be strings. By $\sharp(\alpha, \beta)$, we denote the number of occurrences of β in α. The length of a string α is denoted by $|\alpha|$. The i-th symbol of α from the left is denoted by $\alpha[i]$.

Let x be a symbol not belonging to Σ. Every $\pi \in (\Sigma \cup \{x\})^+$ is called a *one-variable pattern* and x is referred to as the pattern variable of π. If $\sharp(\pi, x) \geq 1$, then the pattern π is called proper. The set of all one-variable patterns is denoted by *Pat*. For any $\pi \in Pat$ and $u \in \Sigma^+$, the expression $\pi[x/u]$ denotes the string $w \in \Sigma^+$ which is obtained by replacing all occurrences of x in π by string u. The string u is called a substitution[1] for x. For every $\pi \in Pat$, we define the language of π by

$$L(\pi) =_{df} \{w \in \Sigma^+ \mid w = \pi[x/u], u \in \Sigma^+\}.$$

Let $\star$ be a special symbol not belonging to $\Sigma \cup \{x\}$. A string $w \in (\Sigma \cup \{\star\})^+$ is called *incomplete* if $\sharp(w, \star) \geq 1$. Let $\mathcal{P}$ and $\mathcal{N}$ be finite subsets of $(\Sigma \cup \{\star\})^+$ such that $\mathcal{P} \cap \mathcal{N} = \emptyset$. A member of $\mathcal{P}$ is called a positive example and a member of $\mathcal{N}$ is said to be a negative example. For an alphabet Σ, Φ_Σ denotes the set of all partial functions $\varphi : (\Sigma \cup \{\star\})^+ \mapsto \Sigma^+$ such that $\varphi \in \Phi_\Sigma$ iff for each $w \in (\Sigma \cup \{\star\})^+$, if $\sharp(w, \star) = 0$, then $\varphi(w) = w$, and if $\sharp(w, \star) \geq 1$, then $\varphi(w)$ is a string $w' \in \Sigma^{|w|}$ such that for any $1 \leq i \leq |w|$ and $w[i] \neq \star$, $w'[i] = w[i]$.

Next, we define the decision problems mainly studied in this paper. Let $\mathcal{P}$, $\mathcal{N}$ be finite sets of positive examples and of negative examples, respectively, such that $\mathcal{P}$, $\mathcal{N} \subseteq \Sigma^+$. A pattern $\pi \in Pat$ is said to be *consistent* with $\mathcal{P} \cup \mathcal{N}$ if $\mathcal{P} \cup \mathcal{N} \subset \Sigma^+$, $\mathcal{P} \subseteq L(\pi)$ and $\mathcal{N} \cap L(\pi) = \emptyset$. Thus, if there is a consistent pattern for $\mathcal{P} \cup \mathcal{N}$, then such a pattern can be thought of as *explaining* the data given. Moreover, since every pattern language generated by a proper pattern is infinite, a consistent pattern for $\mathcal{P} \cup \mathcal{N}$ can be also regarded as a generalization or extension of the data sets $\mathcal{P}$ and $\mathcal{N}$. Following Boros *et al.* [3], we call therefore call a consistent pattern an *extension*.

Now, let $\mathcal{P}$, $\mathcal{N} \subseteq (\Sigma \cup \{\star\})^+$ be any finite sets. We say that there is a *consistent extension* for $\mathcal{P} \cup \mathcal{N}$ iff there are a $\varphi \in \Phi_\Sigma$ and a pattern $\pi \in Pat$ such that π is consistent with $\varphi(\mathcal{P}) \cup \varphi(\mathcal{N})$. Finally, there is a *robust extension* for $\mathcal{P} \cup \mathcal{N}$ provided there exists a pattern $\pi \in Pat$ such that π is consistent with $\varphi(\mathcal{P}) \cup \varphi(\mathcal{N})$ for all $\varphi \in \Phi_\Sigma$.

Definition 1. The *decision* problem *extension*, denoted by E is the problem to decide, on input any sets $\mathcal{P}$, $\mathcal{N} \subseteq \Sigma^+$ whether there exists an extension for $\mathcal{P} \cup \mathcal{N}$.

Consistent extension (abbr. CE) is the problem to decided, on input any sets $\mathcal{P}$, $\mathcal{N} \subseteq (\Sigma \cup \{\star\})^+$, whether there exists a consistent extension for $\mathcal{P} \cup \mathcal{N}$.

Finally, *robust extension* (abbr. RE) is the problem to decided, on input any sets $\mathcal{P}$, $\mathcal{N} \subseteq (\Sigma \cup \{\star\})^+$, whether there exists a robust extension for $\mathcal{P} \cup \mathcal{N}$.

Clearly, the complexity of these problems is measured in the length of the input. Next, we exemplify these problems.

Example 1. Let $\Sigma = \{a, b, c\}$, $\mathcal{P} = \{abacababacacabaca, abacabaca\}$ and $\mathcal{N} = \{aabaacabaca\}$. Then, there are three patterns $\pi_1 = x$, $\pi_2 = xbxcabaca$ and

---

[1] In this study, no erasing is assumed, i.e., any possible substitution is not ε.

$\pi_3 = abacabxcx$ that are consistent with $\mathcal{P}$, but π_1 and π_2 are not consistent with $\mathcal{N}$ because $\pi_1[x/aabaacabaca] = \pi_2[x/aa] = aabaacabaca$. On the other hand, π_3 is consistent with $\mathcal{P} \cup \mathcal{N}$, and thus, there exists an extension of $\mathcal{P} \cup \mathcal{N}$.

Next, let $\mathcal{P} = \{abacababacacabaca, abacabaca\}$ and let $\mathcal{N} = \{\star abb \star cabaca\}$. Then, the answer to CE is "yes," since $\pi = xbxcabaca$ is consistent with $\mathcal{P} \cup \varphi(\mathcal{N})$ for $\varphi(\star abb \star cabaca) = aabbacabaca$ such that π_2 is consistent with $\mathcal{P}$ and $\varphi(\mathcal{N})$.

Finally, let $\mathcal{P} = \{a \star b, ab \star aba \star cb\}$ and $\mathcal{N} = \{bb \star cba\}$. Then, the $\pi = axb$ is consistent with $\varphi(\mathcal{P})$ and $\varphi(\mathcal{N})$ for every $\varphi \in \Phi_\Sigma$. Thus, in this case, there exists a robust extension.

In this study, we generally assume that $\|\Sigma\| \geq 2$ because of the following reasons. Let Σ consist of one symbol, say $\Sigma = \{a\}$. Then, there exist trivial reductions from CE to E and from RE to E by replacing all $\star$ in given strings by the same symbol a. For each $w \in \Sigma^+$, let $L_w(i,j) = \{\pi \in Pat \mid \sharp(\pi, a) = i, \sharp(\pi, x) = j, \pi[x/u] = w, |u| = (|w| - i)/j\}$. Since $\|\Sigma\| = 1$, for any $w, w' \in \Sigma^+$ and $1 \leq i, j \leq \min\{|w|, |w'|\}$, it holds that $L_w(i,j) = L_{w'}(i,j)$ iff $L_w(i,j) \cap L_{w'}(i,j) \neq \emptyset$. Thus, if $\|\Sigma\| = 1$, then the problem E, CE and RE are decidable in polynomial time in the size of the sum of the length of given strings.

3 Comparing the difficulty of E and CE

In this section, we study the complexity of problems E and CE. First of all, we would like to establish an upper bound for the complexity of these problems, i.e., we aim to show that both are in NP. This is straightforward for E, since membership for one-variable patterns is in P (cf. [1]). Thus, we may just guess a pattern π and check whether or not all strings from $\mathcal{P}$ are contained in $L(\pi)$, and none of the strings from $\mathcal{N}$ does behave thus. Therefore, it is only natural to try the same approach for CE. However, this immediately leads us to the following version of the membership problem.

Definition 2. For any given $w \in (\Sigma \cup \{\star\})^+$ and $\pi \in Pat$, the *existential membership problem*, denoted by $\exists Mem(\pi, w)$, is the problem of deciding whether there exists a $\varphi \in \Phi_\Sigma$ such that $\varphi(w) \in L(\pi)$.

Lemma 1. $\exists Mem(\pi, w) \in P$.

Proof. Let $\pi = v_1 x v_2 x \cdots v_n x v_{n+1}$ be the input pattern, where $v_i \in \Sigma^*$ for all $1 \leq i \leq n+1$. First, we check whether or not $|w| \geq |\pi|$ in $O(|\pi| + |w|)$ time. If $|w| < |\pi|$, then $\varphi(w) \notin L(\pi)$ for all $\varphi \in \Phi_\Sigma$. If $|w| \geq |\pi|$, then we compute $m = |w| - \sum_{1 \leq i \leq n+1} |v_i|$ and test whether or not m/n is a positive integer. This can be done in $O(|w|)$ time. If m/n is not a positive integer, then there exists no substitution u such that $\pi[x/u] = w$. Now, let $k = m/n$ be a positive integer. Then, w is of the form $w = w_1 s_1 w_2 s_2 \cdots w_n s_n w_{n+1}$ such that for each $1 \leq i \leq n+1$, $|w_i| = |v_i|$ and $|s_1| = \cdots = |s_n| = k$.

We can check whether or not there exists an $1 \leq i \leq n+1$ and a $1 \leq j \leq |v_i|$ such that $v_i[j] \neq w_i[j]$ and $w_i[j] \neq \star$ in $O(|w|)$. If there exists such i and j, then

$\varphi(w) \notin L(\pi)$ for any $\varphi \in \Phi_\Sigma$. If not, for each $1 \leq j \leq n$, we next compute the string $\alpha_j = s_1[j]s_2[j] \cdots s_n[j]$. If an α_j contains two different constants, then there exists no $\varphi \in \Phi_\Sigma$ that maps all $s_1[j], \ldots, s_n[j]$ to the same constant. Thus, $\varphi(w) \notin L(\pi)$ for any $\varphi \in \Phi_\Sigma$. Conversely, if for each j, the α_j contains at most one constant, then there exists a $\varphi \in \Phi_\Sigma$ such that $\varphi(w) \in L(\pi)$. The time to check all the α_j is $O(kn) = O(m) \leq O(|w|)$. Hence, the time to decide whether there exists $\varphi \in \Phi_\Sigma$ such that $\varphi(w) \in L(\pi)$ is $O(\max\{|\pi| + |w|\})$.   Q.E.D.

Consequently, Lemma 1 implies that, with respect to polynomial-time, incomplete strings do not make the membership problem for one-variable patterns difficult. Moreover, Lemma 1 directly allows the following corollary.

Corollary 1. CE $\in$ NP.

Clearly, the next question arising naturally is whether or not CE is even in P or NP-complete. However, while we must leave this problem open, our next result will shed some additional light on the question which problem is more difficult, E or CE. For that purpose, we assume the restriction to CE that the given sets of positive examples $\mathcal{P}$ contain only constant strings, i.e., $\mathcal{P} \subseteq \Sigma^+$. The restricted problem is denoted by RCE. The next theorem clarifies the relation between RCE and E.

Theorem 1. E and RCE are equivalent with respect to polynomial-time reductions.

Proof. Clearly, E is polynomial-time reducible to RCE. For the opposite direction, suppose a finite set $\mathcal{P} \subseteq \Sigma^+$ and a finite set $\mathcal{N} \subseteq (\Sigma \cup \{\star\})^+$, where $\|\Sigma\| \geq 2$. We want to construct sets $\mathcal{P}'$ and $\mathcal{N}'$ such that the answer to E, on input $\mathcal{P}'$ and $\mathcal{N}'$, is "yes" iff RCE is answered thus on input $\mathcal{P}$ and $\mathcal{N}$. We set $\mathcal{P}' = \mathcal{P}$ and $\Sigma' = \Sigma \cup \{0, 1\}$, where $\Sigma \cap \{0, 1\} = \emptyset$. For each $w \in \mathcal{N}$, define w' over Σ' such that for each $1 \leq i \leq |w|$, $w'[i] = w[i]$ if $w[i] \in \Sigma$, $w'[i] = 0$ if $w[j] \in \Sigma$ for all $j < i$ and $w'[i] = 1$ otherwise. That is if $w \in \Sigma^+$, then $w' = w$ and if $\sharp(w, \star) \geq 1$, then w' is obtained by replacing the first $\star$ in w by 0 and by replacing all other $\star$ in w by 1. Finally, we define $\mathcal{N}'$ to be the set of all w' obtained.

Since $\mathcal{P} = \mathcal{P}' \subseteq \Sigma^+$, any pattern containing 0 or 1 is not consistent with $\mathcal{P}'$. Thus, it is sufficient to show that there exist a $\pi \in (\Sigma \cup \{x\})^+$ and a $\varphi \in \Phi_\Sigma$ such that $\varphi(\mathcal{N}) \cap L(\pi) = \emptyset$ iff there exists a $\pi' \in (\Sigma \cup \{x\})^+$ such that $\mathcal{N}' \cap L(\pi') = \emptyset$. Moreover, since for any $w \in \mathcal{N}$, $w \in \Sigma^+$ iff $w \in \mathcal{N}'$, we can assume that each string in $\mathcal{N}$ contains at least one $\star$. Thus, for each $w' \in \mathcal{N}'$, $\sharp(w', 0) = 1$.

First, assume that there are a $\varphi \in \Phi_\Sigma$ and a pattern $\pi \in (\Sigma \cup \{x\})^+$ such that $\varphi(\mathcal{N}) \cap L(\pi) = \emptyset$.

Let $\sharp(\pi, x) \geq 2$. Since $\sharp(\pi, 0) = \sharp(\pi, 1) = 0$ and for each $w' \in \mathcal{N}'$, $\sharp(w', 0) = 1$, then, there exists no substitution $u \in \Sigma'^+$ such that $\pi[x/u] \in \mathcal{N}'$. Thus, in this case, $\mathcal{N}' \cap L(\pi) = \emptyset$.

Let $\sharp(\pi, x) = 1$. Then π is of the form $\pi = \alpha x \beta$, where $\alpha\beta \in \Sigma^+$. Since $\varphi(\mathcal{N}) \cap L(\pi) = \emptyset$, for any $w \in \mathcal{N}$, there exist the following three cases.

Case 1: $|w| < |\pi|$, *Case* 2: There exists a prefix α' of w such that $|\alpha'| = |\alpha|$ and $\alpha' \neq \alpha$ and *Case* 3: There exists a suffix β' of w such that $|\beta'| = |\beta|$ and $\beta' \neq \beta$. Let the string $w \in \mathcal{N}$ be reduced to a $w' \in \mathcal{N}'$. In *Case* 1, since $|w'| = |w|$, it is clear that $w' \notin L(\pi)$. In *Case* 2, either $\alpha' \in \Sigma^+$ or $\sharp(\alpha', \star) \geq 1$. If $\alpha' \in \Sigma^+$, then it is also a prefix of w'. Thus, $\pi[x/u] \neq w'$ for any $u \in \Sigma'^+$. If $\sharp(\alpha', \star) \geq 1$, then there exists an $1 \leq i \leq |\alpha'|$ such that $w'[i] \in \{0, 1\}$. Thus, $\pi[x/u] \neq w'$ for any $u \in \Sigma'^+$. *Case* 3 is analogous. Hence, there exists a $\pi \in (\Sigma \cup \{x\})^+$ such that $\mathcal{N}' \cap L(\pi) = \emptyset$.

Conversely assume that there is a $\pi \in (\Sigma \cup \{x\})^+$ such that for any $w' \in \mathcal{N}'$, $w' \notin L(\pi)$. Let the string $w' \in \mathcal{N}'$ be reduced from a $w \in \mathcal{N}$. Let $\pi = v_1 x v_2 x \cdots v_n x v_{n+1}$, where $v_i \in \Sigma^*$ for each $1 \leq i \leq n + 1$. Since $|w'| = |w|$, if $m = (|w'| - (|\pi| - n))/n$ is not a positive integer, then $\varphi(w) \notin L(\pi)$ for any $\varphi \in \Phi_\Sigma$. If m is a positive integer, then $w = w_1 s_1 w_2 s_2 \cdots w_n s_n w_{n+1}$ and $w' = w_1' s_1' w_2' s_2' \cdots w_n' s_n' w_{n+1}'$ such that for each $1 \leq i \leq n + 1$, $|w_i| = |w_i'| = |v_i|$ and $|s_1| = \cdots = |s_n| = |s_1'| = \cdots = |s_n'| = m$.

If there exist an $1 \leq i \leq n + 1$ and a $1 \leq j \leq |w_i'|$ such that $w_i'[j] \in \Sigma$ and $w_i'[j] \neq v_i[j]$, then, since $w_i[j] = w_i'[j]$, for any $\varphi \in \Phi_\Sigma$, $\varphi(w) \notin L(\pi)$.

If there exist an $1 \leq i \leq n + 1$ and a $1 \leq j \leq |w_i'|$ such that $w_i'[j] \in \{0, 1\}$, then $w_i[j] = \star$. Thus, there exists a $\varphi \in \Phi_\Sigma$ such that it maps the $w_i[j]$ to a symbol not equal to the $v_i[j] \in \Sigma$. It follows that $\varphi(w) \notin L(\pi)$.

Thus, we can assume that $v_i = w_i' = w_i$ for all $1 \leq i \leq n + 1$. The remaining parts are *Case* (a): $\sharp(\pi, x) = 1$ and *Case* (b): $\sharp(\pi, x) \geq 2$.

In *Case* (a), $w' = w_1' s_1' w_2'$. It follows that $w' \in L(\pi)$; a contradiction. In *Case* (b), there exist $s_i', s_j' \in \{s_1', s_2', \ldots, s_n'\}$ such that $i \neq j$ and $s_i'[k] = 0$, where $1 \leq k \leq |s_i'|$. Since $s_i[k] = \star$, if $s_j[k] \in \Sigma$, then there exists a $\varphi \in \Phi_\Sigma$ such that it maps the $s_i[k]$ to a symbol not equal to the $s_j[k]$, and if $s_j[k] = \star$, then there exists a $\varphi \in \Phi_\Sigma$ such that it maps the $s_i[k]$ and $s_j[k]$ to different symbols. Hence, there exist a $\pi \in (\Sigma \cup \{x\})^+$ and a $\varphi \in \Phi_\Sigma$ such that $\varphi(\mathcal{N}) \cap L(\pi) = \emptyset$. Therefore, there exist a $\pi \in (\Sigma \cup \{x\})^+$ and a $\varphi \in \Phi_\Sigma$ such that $\varphi(\mathcal{N}) \cap L(\pi) = \emptyset$ iff there exists a $\pi' \in (\Sigma \cup \{x\})^+$ such that $\mathcal{N}' \cap L(\pi') = \emptyset$. $\qquad$ Q.E.D.

From this Theorem, it seems that incomplete strings as negative examples cause the difficulty of the consistency problem. However, it is open whether there is a gap between RCE and CE. Moreover, there is a chance that E and RCE are members inside NP, e.g., E and RCE in randomized P or P.

4 Analyzing the complexity of RE

The aim of this section is to show the NP-completeness of problem RE. Again, we begin with a version of membership adapted to RE as follows.

Definition 3. For any given $w \in (\Sigma \cup \{\star\})^+$ and $\pi \in Pat$, the *universal membership problem*, denoted by $\forall Mem(\pi, w)$, is the problem of deciding whether for each $\varphi \in \Phi_\Sigma$, $\varphi(w) \in L(\pi)$.

Lemma 2. $\forall Mem(\pi, w) \in$ P.

Proof. Let $\pi = v_1 x v_2 x \cdots v_n x v_{n+1}$ be the input pattern, where $v_i \in \Sigma^*$ for all $1 \leq i \leq n+1$. The test whether or not $|w| \geq |\pi|$ can be done in $O(|\pi|+|w|)$ time. If $|w| \geq |\pi|$, then similarly to Lemma 1, we compute $m = |w| - \sum_{1 \leq i \leq n+1} |v_i|$ and check whether or not m/n is a positive integer in $O(|w|)$ time. Let $m/n = k$ be a positive integer. Then, w is of the form $w = w_1 s_1 w_2 s_2 \cdots w_n s_n w_{n+1}$ such that for each $1 \leq i \leq n+1$, $|w_i| = |v_i|$ and $|s_1| = \cdots = |s_n| = k$.

We can check whether or not there exists an $1 \leq i \leq n+1$ such that $v_i \neq w_i$ in $O(|w|)$ time. If there exist such v_i and w_i, then $\varphi(w) \notin L(\pi)$ for a $\varphi \in \Phi_\Sigma$. If not, for each $1 \leq j \leq n$, we next compute the string $\alpha_j = s_1[j]s_2[j] \cdots s_n[j]$. Since we have $v_i = w_i$, for each $\varphi \in \Phi_\Sigma$, $\varphi(w) \in L(\pi)$ iff for each $1 \leq j \leq n$, $s_1[j] = \cdots = s_n[j]$. The time to check all the α_j is $O(kn) = O(m) \leq O(|w|)$. Hence, the time to decide whether $\varphi(w) \in L(\pi)$ for all $\varphi \in \Phi_\Sigma$ is $O(\max\{|\pi| + |w|\})$. Q.E.D.

We recall the problem of the robust extension RE for one-variable patterns in Definition 1. This problem requires the universal consistency of a one-variable pattern for every $\varphi \in \Phi_\Sigma$. Now, we give a log-space reduction from the 3-SAT to RE below.

Lemma 3. 3-SAT is log-space reducible to RE.

Proof. Let $C = C_1 \wedge C_2 \wedge \cdots \wedge C_m$ be a 3-CNF of n variables $x_1, x_2, \ldots, x_n$ such that $C_i = (\ell_{i_1} \vee \ell_{i_2} \vee \ell_{i_3})$, where each ℓ_{i_j} denotes a positive or negative literal of x_{i_j}, that is, $\ell_{i_j} \in \{x_{i_j}, \neg x_{i_j}\}$, $1 \leq i \leq n$ and $1 \leq j \leq 3$. Let us fix an alphabet consisting of $n+3$ symbols such that $\Sigma = \{a_1, a_2, \ldots, a_{n+1}\} \cup \{A, B\}$. First, we compute the strings $\alpha_1, \alpha_2, \alpha_3$ and α_4 as follows.

$$\alpha_1 = a_1 A^2 a_2 B a_n A^2 a_{n+1},$$
$$\alpha_2 = a_1 A a_2 A a_3 \cdots a_n A a_{n+1},$$
$$\alpha_3 = a_1 A^2 a_2 A^2 a_3 \cdots a_n A^2 a_{n+1} \text{ and}$$
$$\alpha_4 = a_1 A^3 a_2 A^3 a_3 \cdots a_n A^3 a_{n+1}.$$

Next, for each clause $C_i = (\ell_{i_1} \vee \ell_{i_2} \vee \ell_{i_3})$, we compute the string $\beta_i = a_1 \gamma_1 a_2 \gamma_2 a_3 \cdots a_n \gamma_n a_{n+1}$ such that for each $1 \leq j \leq n$, $\gamma_j = BA$ if $x_j \in \{\ell_{i_1}, \ell_{i_2}, \ell_{i_3}\}$, $\gamma_j = AB$ if $\neg x_j \in \{\ell_{i_1}, \ell_{i_2}, \ell_{i_3}\}$ and $\gamma_j = \star\star$ otherwise. Finally, we output $\mathcal{P} = \{\alpha_3, \alpha_4\}$ as the set of positive examples and $\mathcal{N} = \{\alpha_1, \alpha_2\} \cup \{\beta_k \mid 1 \leq k \leq m\}$ as the set of negative examples. The idea for the string $\beta_k \in \mathcal{N}$ is illustrated in Fig.1. We first prove the following *Claim*.

Claim: If a pattern $\pi \in Pat$ is consistent with the strings $\alpha_1, \alpha_2, \alpha_3$, and α_4, then the π is of the form $\pi = a_1 X_1 a_2 X_2 a_3 \cdots a_n X_n a_{n+1}$, where $X_i \in \{Ax, xA\}$ and $1 \leq i \leq n$.

Suppose that there exists a pattern $\pi \in Pat$ consistent with the $\alpha_1, \alpha_2, \alpha_3$, and α_4. There are the following cases for a substitution $u \in \Sigma^+$ such that $\pi[x/u] \in \{\alpha_1, \alpha_2, \alpha_3, \alpha_4\}$.

Case 1: A substitution u contains an $a_i \in \{a_1, a_2, \ldots, a_{n+1}\}$ such that $\pi[x/u] \in \mathcal{P}$. Since any a_i appears in the strings at most once, the π must be of the

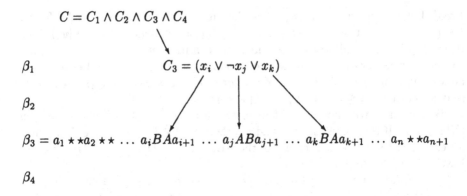

Negative examples

Fig. 1. Negative examples computed from a 3-CNF C of n-variable.

form wxw' such that $w \in \{a_1, a_1 A, a_1 AA\}$ and $w' \in \{a_{n+1}, Aa_{n+1}, AAa_{n+1}\}$. For any possible w and w', the π is not consistent with the negative example α_1. Thus, *Case 1* is removed.

Case 2: $\pi[x/AA] = \alpha_3$. Then, $\pi = a_1 X_1 a_2 X_2 a_3 \cdots a_n X_n a_{n+1}$, where $X_i \in \{AA, x\}$ and $1 \leq i \leq n$. If $X_j = AA$ for a $1 \leq j \leq n$, then the π contains $a_j AA a_{j+1}$. Since $\sharp(\alpha_4, a_j AA a_{j+1}) = 0$, it is a contradiction. Thus, in this case, the π is of the form $a_1 x a_2 x a_3 \cdots a_n x a_{n+1}$. This pattern is inconsistent with the negative example α_2.

Case 3: $\pi[x/AA] = \alpha_4$. Then the π contains one of the strings $a_i A^3 a_{i+1}$, $a_i Ax a_{i+1}$ and $a_i x A a_{i+1}$. In case of $a_i A^3 a_{i+1}$, the π is not consistent with the α_3. It is a contradiction. Thus, for each $1 \leq i \leq n$, the substring of π between a_i and a_{i+1} must be Ax or xA. This π satisfies the *Claim* and it is consistent with all $\alpha_1, \alpha_2, \alpha_3$, and α_4.

Case 4: $\pi[x/A] = \alpha_3$. If the π contains a substring $a_i AA a_{i+1}$, then it is not consistent with α_4. Thus, the π satisfies the *Claim*.

Case 5: $\pi[x/A] = \alpha_4$. In this case, the π contains one of $a_i A^3 a_{i+1}$, $a_i x A^2 a_{i+1}$ and $a_i A^2 x a_{i+1}$. Since it is not consistent with α_3, this case is removed. Thus, the *Claim* is true.

We set $PI = \{\pi \in Pat \mid \alpha_3, \alpha_4 \in L(\pi), \alpha_1, \alpha_2 \notin L(\pi)\}$. By the above *Claim*, the proof of the theorem is now reduced to the consistency that the 3-CNF C is satisfiable iff there exists a $\pi \in PI$ such that $\varphi(\mathcal{N}) \cap L(\pi) = \emptyset$ for all $\varphi \in \Phi_\Sigma$.

Assume that the CNF C is satisfiable. There exists a truth assignment $f : \{x_1, x_2, \ldots, x_n\} \mapsto \{0, 1\}$ such that for each clause $C_i = (\ell_{i_1} \vee \ell_{i_2} \vee \ell_{i_3})$ $(1 \leq i \leq m)$, at least one $\ell' \in \{\ell_{i_1}, \ell_{i_2}, \ell_{i_3}\}$ fulfills exactly one of the following conditions.

Case (a): $\ell' = x_j \in \{x_1, \ldots, x_n\}$ and $f(x_j) = 1$, or
Case (b): $\ell' = \neg x_j$ and $f(x_j) = 0$.

There exists a one-to-one mapping from truth assignments f for $x_1, \ldots, x_n$ to the set PI such that for each $1 \leq i \leq n$, $f(x_i) = 0$ iff π contains $a_i x A a_{i+1}$ and $f(x_i) = 1$ iff π contains $a_i A x a_{i+1}$.

If an f satisfies each clause C_i, then there exists a negative example $\beta_i \in \mathcal{N}$ constructed from the C_i such that $x_j \in \{\ell_{i_1}, \ell_{i_2}, \ell_{i_3}\}$ iff β_i contains $a_j B A a_{j+1}$ and $\neg x_j \in \{\ell_{i_1}, \ell_{i_2}, \ell_{i_3}\}$ iff β_i contains $a_j A B a_{j+1}$.

In *Case* (a), a $\pi \in PI$ corresponding to the f contains $a_j A x a_{j+1}$ and the β_i constructed from C_i contains $a_j B A a_{j+1}$. We note that for any $\pi \in PI$ and $\beta_i \in \mathcal{N}$, $|\pi| = |\beta_i|$. Thus, as compared with the strings $a_j A x a_{j+1}$ and $a_j B A a_{j+1}$, no substitution $u \in \Sigma^+$ and no $\varphi \in \Phi_\Sigma$ satisfy $\pi[x/u] = \varphi(\beta_i)$.

In *Case* (b), analogously a π corresponding to the f contains $a_j x A a_{j+1}$ and the β_i constructed from C_i contain $a_j A B a_{j+1}$. Thus, there is no substitution u and φ for $\pi[x/u] = \varphi(\beta_i)$.

Hence, if C is satisfiable, then there exists a $\pi \in PI$ such that $\varphi(\mathcal{N}) \cap L(\pi) = \emptyset$ for all $\varphi \in \Phi_\Sigma$.

Conversely, let the CNF C be unsatisfiable. Then, for any truth assignment f, there exists a clause C_i of C such that for any literal ℓ' of C_i, either $\ell' = x_j \in \{x_1, \ldots, x_n\}$ and $f(x_j) = 0$ or $\ell' = \neg x_j$ and $f(x_j) = 1$.

Then, for each $\ell' \in \{\ell_{i_1}, \ell_{i_2}, \ell_{i_3}\}$, the π contains $a_j x A a_{j+1}$ and the $\beta_i \in \mathcal{N}$ contains $a_j B A a_{j+1}$ if $\ell' = x_j \in \{x_1, \ldots, x_n\}$ and the π contains $a_j A x a_{j+1}$ and the β_i contains $a_j A B a_{j+1}$ if $\ell' = \neg x_j$.

Finally, we define $\varphi(\beta_i) = w$ such that for each $1 \leq k \leq |\beta_i|$,

$$w[k] = \begin{cases} B, & \text{if } \pi[k] = x. \\ \pi[k], & \text{otherwise.} \end{cases}$$

It follows $\varphi(\beta_i) \in L(\pi)$ for the substitution B. Hence, if C is unsatisfiable, then for any $\pi \in PI$, there exists a $\varphi \in \Phi_\Sigma$ such that $\varphi(\mathcal{N}) \cap L(\pi) \neq \emptyset$. Thus, we conclude that the 3-CNF C is satisfiable iff there exists a robust extension for $\mathcal{P}$ and $\mathcal{N}$. $\qquad$ Q.E.D.

Theorem 2. RE is NP-complete, even if $\|\Sigma\| = 2$.

Proof. Analogously, we reduce a 3-CNF C to RE. Let C consist of m clauses $C_1, C_2, \ldots, C_m$ and defined by n variables $x_1, x_2, \ldots, x_n$. Initially, we set $\Sigma = \{A, B\}$ and $\mathcal{P} = \{\alpha_1 = A^{2n}, \alpha_2 = A^{3n}\}$. The set $\mathcal{N}$ of negative examples over Σ is the sum of the sets N_1, N_2 and N_3 defined as follows.

$N_1 = \{A^n\} \cup \{\beta_i = A^{2n+i} \mid i \in \{1, \ldots, 2n\} \setminus \{n, 2n\}\}$,
$N_2 = \{\beta_j = \star^{2j-2} B B \star^{2(n-i)} \mid 1 \leq i \leq n\}$ and
$N_3 = \{\beta_k = \gamma_{k_1} \cdots \gamma_{k_n} \mid 1 \leq k \leq m\}$ such that

$$1 \leq \forall k \leq m \text{ and } 1 \leq \forall j \leq n, \; \gamma_{k_j} = \begin{cases} BA, & \text{if } x_j \text{ is a literal of } C_k, \\ AB, & \text{if } \neg x_j \text{ is a literal of } C_k \text{ and} \\ \star\star, & \text{otherwise.} \end{cases}$$

We define the set $PI \subseteq Pat$ such that $\pi \in PI$ iff $\pi = X_1 X_2 \cdots X_n$, where $X_i \in \{Ax, xA\}$ and $1 \leq i \leq n$. Then, we prove the following *Claim*.

Claim: $\pi \in PI$ iff $\pi \in Pat$ is consistent with $\mathcal{P}$ and $N_1 \cup \varphi(N_2)$ for all $\varphi \in \Phi_\Sigma$.

First, assume $\pi \in PI$. Then, clearly, $\mathcal{P} \subseteq L(\pi)$. For each $A^{2n+i} \in N_1$, $\pi[x/u] \neq A^{2n+i}$ because $i \in \{1, \ldots, 2n\} \setminus \{n, 2n\}$ and $\sharp(\pi, A) = \sharp(\pi, x) = n$. Thus, $N_1 \cap L(\pi) = \emptyset$. For each odd number i such that $1 \leq i \leq 2n-1$, $\pi[i]\pi[i+1] = Ax$ or $\pi[i]\pi[i+1] = xA$. On the other hand, for any $\beta_j \in N_2$, there exists exactly one odd number i such that $\beta_j[i]\beta_j[i+1] = BB$. Since $|\pi| = |\beta_j|$, there exists no $\varphi \in \Phi_\Sigma$ such that $\varphi(\beta_j) \in L(\pi)$. Thus, if $\pi \in PI$, then π is consistent with $\varphi(\mathcal{P})$ and $\varphi(N_1 \cup N_2)$ for all $\varphi \in \Phi_\Sigma$.

Suppose to the contrary that there exists a $\pi \in Pat$ and $\pi \notin PI$ such that π is consistent with $\mathcal{P}$ and $N_1 \cup \varphi(N_2)$ for all $\varphi \in \Phi_\Sigma$. If π contains a B, then clearly, $\mathcal{P} \cap L(\pi) = \emptyset$. Thus, we can assume $\pi \in \{A, x\}^+$.

We first show that π must satisfy $\pi[x/A] = \alpha_1 = A^{2n}$. Assume that $\pi[x/u] = A^{2n}$ and $u = A^r$, where $2 \leq r \leq 2n$. Then, $\sharp(\pi, x) = n' \leq n$ and $\sharp(\pi, A) = 2n - rn'$. If $n' = n$, then $\pi = x^n$. Since $x^n[x/A] = A^n \in N_1$, it is a contradiction. Thus, $n' \leq n - 1$. For each $1 \leq n' \leq n - 1$, there exists a $\beta_{n'} \in N_1$ such that $\beta_{n'} = A^{2n+n'} = A^{(r+1)n'}A^{2n-rn'}$. It follows the contradiction $\pi[x/A^{r+1}] = \beta_{n'}$. Thus, $\pi[x/A] = A^{2n}$.

Second, we show that π must satisfy $\sharp(\pi, x) = n$. Assume that $\sharp(\pi, x) = n' \neq n$. In case of $n' \leq n - 1$, there exists $\beta_{n'} \in N_1$ such that $\beta_{n'} = A^{2n+n'} = A^{2n}A^{2n-n'}$. Thus, $\beta_{n'} \in L(\pi)$ for the substitution A^2. In case of $\sharp(\pi, x) = n' \geq n + 1$, since $\alpha_1, \alpha_2 \in L(\pi)$, it holds that $n' \leq 2n - 1$. Thus, there exists $\beta_{n'} \in N_1$ such that $\beta_{n'} = A^{2n+n'} = A^{2n'}A^{2n-n'}$. It follows the contradiction $\pi[x/A^2] = \beta_{n'}$. Thus, $\sharp(\pi, x) = n$. By the condition that $\pi[x/A] = A^{2n}$ and $\sharp(\pi, x) = n$, the π must satisfy that $\sharp(\pi, A) = \sharp(\pi, A) = n$.

Since $\pi \in \{A, x\}^+$, $\pi \notin PI$ and $\sharp(\pi, A) = \sharp(\pi, A) = n$, there exists an odd number i and $1 \leq i \leq 2n - 1$ such that $\pi[i]\pi[i+1] = xx$. On the other hand, since $(i+1)/2$ is a positive integer, there is a the string $\beta_{(i+1)/2} \in N_2$ such that it is of the form $\star^{i-1} BB \star^{2n-i-1}$. Thus, there exists a $\varphi \in \Phi_\Sigma$ such that for each $1 \leq k \leq 2n$, $\varphi(\beta_{(i+1)/2})[k] = B$ if $\pi[k] = x$ and $\varphi(\beta_{(i+1)/2})[k] = A$ otherwise. It follows the contradiction $\pi[x/B] = \beta_{(i+1)/2}$. Hence, if a $\pi \in Pat$ consistent with $\mathcal{P}$ and $N_1 \cup \varphi(N_2)$ for all $\varphi \in \Phi_\Sigma$, then $\pi = X_1 X_2 \cdots X_n$ such that $X_\ell \in \{Ax, xA\}$ and $1 \leq \ell \leq n$ and the *Claim* is true.

Similarly to the proof of Lemma 3, we can see that the 3-CNF is satisfiable iff there exists a $\pi \in PI$ consistent with $\varphi(N_3)$ for all $\varphi \in \Phi_\Sigma$. Thus, we conclude that the RE is NP-complete, even if $\|\Sigma\| = 2$. Q.E.D.

Example 2. Let C be a 3-CNF of 5 variables. Then, $\mathcal{P} = \{A^{10}, A^{15}\}$. The N_1 and N_2 in Theorem 2 are defined as follows.

$N_1 = \{A^5, A^{11}, A^{12}, \ldots, A^{14}, A^{16}, \ldots, A^{19}\}$ and
$N_2 = \{BB\star^8, \star^2 BB\star^6, \star^4 BB\star^4, \star^6 BB\star^2, \star^8 BB\}$.

Let us take a $\pi \in Pat$ such that $\pi[x/u] = A^{10}$ for a substitution $u \in \{A\}^+$. If $u \neq A$, then $u = A^n$ for some $2 \leq n \leq 10$. Let $\natural(\pi, x) = m$, where $1 \leq m \leq 5$. If $m = 5$, then $\pi = x^5$ and $A^5 \in L(\pi)$. Thus, this π is inconsistent with N_1. For each $2 \leq n \leq 10$ and $1 \leq m \leq 4$ such that $\pi[x/A^n] = A^{10}$ and $\natural(\pi, x) = m$, there exists a $w \in N_1$ such that $\pi[x/A^{n+1}] = w$. Thus, if a π is consistent with N_1, then $\pi[x/A] = A^{10}$.

If $\natural(\pi, x) < 5$, then there exists $1 \leq n' \leq 4$ such that $A^{10+n'} \in N_1 \cap L(\pi)$ and if $\natural(\pi, x) > 5$, then there exists $6 \leq n' \leq 9$ such that $A^{10+n'} \in N_1 \cap L(\pi)$. Thus, these π are inconsistent with N_1. It follows that if a π is consistent with N_1, then $\natural(\pi, x) = 5$. Hence, $\natural(\pi, x) = \natural(\pi, A) = 5$.

For example, let $\pi = xAxxAAxAAx \notin PI$. Then, there exists a $\varphi \in \Phi_\Sigma$ and $w = \star^2 BB\star^6 \in N_2$ such that $\varphi(w) = BABBAABAAB \in L(\pi)$. Let $\pi = xAxAAxAxxA \in PI$. Then, there exists no $w \in N_2$ and $\varphi \in \Phi_\Sigma$ such that $\varphi(w) \in L(\pi)$.

5 Conclusions

We have studied the decision problems E, CE and RE as well as the membership problems $\exists\mathrm{Mem}(\pi, w)$ and $\forall\mathrm{Mem}(\pi, w)$ for one-variable patterns with respect to incomplete strings. Although the problem RE is shown to be NP-complete even if the size of an alphabet is 2, it is still an open question whether the problem CE is in a subclass of NP. Also, the tractability of problem E remains open.

In the first part of this paper, we showed the equivalence of E and RCE for polynomial-time reductions. This means that incomplete negative examples make problem RCE no more difficult than problem E. Then, our next interest is whether there is a computational gap between CE and E. Since $\exists\mathrm{Mem}(\pi, w) \in P$, we can check whether a one-variable pattern is consistent with given positive and negative examples in polynomial time for both problems. The critical part to be overcome is an effective representation of all consistent one-variable patterns for given incomplete strings.

For constant strings, Angluin [1] introduced the one-variable pattern automata. They can be thought of as a clever data structure to represent exponentially many consistent patterns in polynomial space. Let $L(A)$ denote the set of one-variable patterns accepted by A. Then, for any given one-variable pattern automata A and B, we can compute a one-variable pattern automaton A' such that $L(A') = L(A) \cap L(B)$ in time polynomial in the size of A and B (cf. [1]). Thus, we can find a descriptive pattern for a given set of strings by enumerating at most polynomially many patterns. Hence, for attacking CE and E further, it may be promising to generalize Angluin's [1] one-variable pattern automata to our incomplete strings.

Acknowledgement

The author wishes to heartily thank the ALT'98 program committee and the subreferees involved for their useful comments and hints helping to enhance the quality of the present paper.

References

1. D. Angluin. Finding patterns common to a set of strings. *Journal of Computer and System Sciences* 21:46–62, 1980.

2. S. Arikawa, S. Miyano, A. Shinohara, S. Kuhara, Y. Mukouchi and T. Shinohara. A machine discovery from amino acid sequences by decision trees over regular patterns. *New Generation Computing* 11:361–375, 1993.

3. E. Boros, T. Ibaraki and K. Makino. Monotone extensions of Boolean data sets. In *Proc. 8th International Workshop on Algorithmic Learning Theory*, Lecture Notes in Artificial Intelligence 1316, pp. 161–175, Berlin, 1997. Springer-Verlag.

4. T. Erlebach, P. Rossmanith, H. Stadtherr, A. Steger and T. Zeugmann. Learning one-variable pattern languages very efficiently on average, in parallel, and by asking queries. In *Proc. 8th International Workshop on Algorithmic Learning Theory*, Lecture Notes in Artificial Intelligence 1316, pp. 260–276, Berlin, 1997. Springer-Verlag.

5. M.R. Garey and D.S. Johnson. *Computers and Intractability*. W.H. Freeman and company, 1983.

6. M.E. Gold. Language identification in the limit. *Information and Control* 10:447–474.

7. J.E. Hopcroft and J.D. Ullman. *Introduction to Automata Theory, Languages, and Computation*. Addison-Wesley Publ., 1979.

8. T. Jiang, A. Salomaa, K. Salomaa and S. Yu. Inclusion is undecidable for pattern languages. In *Proc. 20th ICALP*, Lecture Notes in Computer Science 700, pp. 301–312, Berlin, 1993. Springer-Verlag.

9. M.J. Kearns and U.J. Vazirani. *An Introduction to Computational Learning Theory*. The MIT Press, Cambridge, MA 1994.

10. C.H. Papadimitriou. *Computational complexity*. Addison-Wesley Publ., 1994.

11. R. Reischuk and T.·Zeugmann. Learning One-variable pattern languages in linear average time. In *Proc. 11st Ann. Conference on Computational Learning Theory*, 1998, to appear.

12. R.E. Schapire. Pattern languages are not learnable. In M.A. Fulk and J. Case, editors, *Proc. 3rd Annual ACM Workshop on Computational Learning Theory*, pp. 122 – 129, 1990. Morgan Kaufmann Publishers Inc., San Mateo.

13. T. Shinohara and S. Arikawa. Pattern inference. In *Algorithmic Learning for Knowledge-Based Systems*, Lecture Notes in Artificial Intelligence 961, pp. 259–291, Berlin, 1995. Springer-Verlag.

14. R. Wiehagen and T. Zeugmann. Ignoring data may be the only way to learn efficiently. *Journal of Experimental and Theoretical Artificial Intelligence* 6:131–144, 1994.

15. T. Zeugmann and S. Lange. A guided tour across the boundaries of learning recursive languages. In *Algorithmic Learning for Knowledge-Based Systems*, (K.P. Jantke and S. Lange, Eds.), Lecture Notes in Artificial Intelligence 961, pp. 193–262, Berlin, 1995. Springer-Verlag.

16. T. Zeugmann, S. Lange and S. Kapur. Characterizations of monotonic and dual monotonic language learning. *Information and Computation* 120(2):155–173.

A Fast Algorithm for Discovering Optimal String Patterns in Large Text Databases

Hiroki Arimura, Atsushi Wataki*, Ryoichi Fujino, and Setsuo Arikawa

Department of Informatics, Kyushu University
Hakozaki 6-10-1, Fukuoka, 812-8581 Japan
{arim,wataki,fujino,arikawa}@i.kyushu-u.ac.jp
http://www.i.kyushu-u.ac.jp/~arim/

Abstract. We consider a data mining problem in a large collection of unstructured texts based on association rules over subwords of texts. A two-words association pattern is an expression such as

$$(\texttt{TATA, 30, AGGAGGT}) \Rightarrow C$$

that expresses a rule that if a text contains a subword $\texttt{TATA}$ followed by another subword $\texttt{AGGAGGT}$ with distance no more than 30 letters then a property C will hold with high probability. The optimized confidence pattern problem is to compute frequent patterns (α, k, β) that optimize the confidence with respect to a given collection of texts. Although this problem is solved in polynomial time by a straightforward algorithm that enumerates all the possible patterns in time $O(n^5)$, we focus on the development of more efficient algorithms that can be applied to large text databases. We present an algorithm that solves the optimized confidence pattern problem in time $O(\max\{k, m\}n^2)$ and space $O(kn)$, where m and n are the number and the total length of classification examples, respectively, and k is a small constant around $30 \sim 50$. This algorithm combines the suffix tree data structure in combinatorial string matching and the orthogonal range query technique in computational geometry for fast computation. Furthermore for most random texts like DNA sequences, we show that a modification of the algorithm runs very efficiently in time $O(kn \log^3 n)$ and space $O(kn)$. We also discuss some heuristics such as sampling and pruning as practical improvement. Then, we evaluate the efficiency and the performance of the algorithm with experiments on genetic sequences. A relationship with efficient Agnostic PAC-learning is also discussed.

1 Introduction

The recent progress of communication and network technologies, e.g., electronic mail, World Wide Web, and inter/intra networks makes it easy for computer users to accumulate a large collection of unstructured or semi-structured texts on their computers at a low cost [1]. Such *text databases* may be collections of

---

* Presently working for Fujitsu LTD.

web pages or SGML documents (OPENTEXT Index [26]), protein databases in molecular biology (GenBank [11]), online dictionary (OED [13]), or plain texts on a file system. There has been a potential demand for efficient discovery of useful information from text databases beyond the power of the present access methods in information retrieval [1, 19, 28].

Data mining is a research area that aims at development of semi-automatic tools for discovering useful information from large databases. Data mining has emerged in early 1990's and has been extensively studied in both practice and theory [2, 10, 15]. However, the present data mining technologies mainly deal with well-structured data such as relational databases with Boolean or numeric attributes [2, 10, 15], and thus are not directly applicable to those unstructured text data. Because, a text database is simply a collection of unstructured strings and the amount of the data is huge, which typically ranges from mega (10^6) bytes to tera (10^{12}) bytes. We concentrate on efficient and robust discovery methods that work for a large collection of unstructured texts [9, 19, 23, 28].

In this paper, we consider the discovery of very simple patterns called k-proximity two-words association patterns. Given a collection S of texts and an objective condition C over S, a k-proximity two-words association pattern is an expression of the form

$$(\texttt{TATA, 30, AGGAGGT}) \Rightarrow C$$

that represent a rule that if a text contains a subword TATA followed by another subword AGGAGGT with distance no more than $k = 30$ letters then the objective condition C will hold with a probability. Although this class of rules seems very restricted, they are more flexible to describe a local similarity in text data with context information than unordered collections of keywords or single subwords. Hence, this kind of rules are frequently used for applications in bioinformatics [12], bibliographic search [13], and Web search [26]. Further, the simplicity of the class allows robust and efficient learning in noisy environment as we will show in this paper.

As the framework of data mining, we adopt the *optimal pattern discovery* recently proposed by Fukuda *et al.* [10]. In their framework, a discovery algorithm receives a sample set S with an objective condition $C : S \to \{0, 1\}$ and finds all/some patterns P that maximize a certain criterion. Based on this framework, we consider the efficient solvability of the *optimized confidence pattern problem* in data mining (Fukuda *et al.* [10]) and the *empirical error minimization problem* in computational learning theory (Kearns,Shapire, Sellie [17]; Maass [20]).

The optimized confidence patterns can be computed in time $O(n^5)$ by a straightforward algorithm that enumerates $O(n^4)$ possible two-words association patterns since there are at most possible $O(n^2)$ subwords of A. However, this polynomial is too large to apply this algorithm to real applications. To the problem, in Section 3 and in Section 4, we present variations of algorithms that compute all the two-words association patterns (α, k, β) using data structures from string matching and computational geometry, the *suffix tree* and the *orthogonal range query*. The idea is to reduce the discovery of such patterns to that of axes-parallel rectangles over the 2-dimensional plane of suffix ranks.

In Section 3, we present an algorithm that runs in time $O(mn^2 \log^2 n)$ and in space $O(kmn \log n)$. where m and n are the number and the total size of texts, respectively, and k is a proximity. Next in Section 4, implementing the orthogonal range queries directly over the suffix tree, we give a modified version of the algorithm that runs in time $O(\max\{k, m\}n^2)$ and space $O(kn)$ in the worst case. For most of nearly random texts like DNA sequences, it is known that the depth of the suffix tree is bounded by $O(\log n)$. Then, we show that our algorithm can be modified to run very quickly in time $O(kn \log^3 n)$ for such random texts.

In Section 5, we describe an application to computational learning theory. We show that the algorithm in Section 4 can be modified to efficiently solve the empirical error minimization problem. As a corollary, we obtain an efficient Agnostic PAC-learner for the class of k-proximity two-words association patterns. Nakanishi *et al.* [25] study the consistency problem, which is a special case of the empirical error minimization problem, for the class of single substrings. Since a single substring is a special k-proximity two-words association pattern, our result also generalizes their result.

In Section 6, we introduce some heuristics and examine their performances. In Section 7, we evaluate the efficiency and the performance of our algorithm from the empirical view point with experiments on genetic sequences from GenBank databases. Finally, Section 8 concludes the results.

2 Preliminaries

2.1 Texts and patterns

Let Σ be a finite alphabet. We always assume a fixed total order on the letters in Σ. For a string s and a set S of strings, we denote by $|s|$ and by $size(S)$ the length of s and the total length of the strings in S. If there exist some $u, v, w \in \Sigma^*$ such that $t = uvw$ then we say that u, v and w are a *prefix*, a *subword* and a *suffix* of t, respectively. A *text* is any string t over Σ. For $1 \leq i \leq |t|$, we denote the i-th letter of t by $t[i]$. An *occurrence* of $s \in \Sigma^*$ in t is a positive integer i such that $t[i] \cdots t[i + |t| - 1] = s$.

Let k be a nonnegative integer. A *k-proximity two-words association pattern* (or pattern, for short) is a triple $P = (\alpha, k, \beta)$, where $\alpha, \beta \in \Sigma^*$ are strings over Σ and $k \geq 0$ is called a *proximity*. A proximity two-words association pattern P *matches* a string $t \in \Sigma^*$ if there exist a pair of integers p and q such that p and q are the occurrences of α and β in t, respectively, and satisfy $0 \leq q - p \leq k$. The pair (p, q) is called an *occurrence* of P in t. For a set S, $card(S)$ denotes the number of elements in S. For nonnegative integers i, j, $[i..j]$ denotes the interval $\{i, i + 1, \ldots, j\}$ if $i \leq j$ and $\emptyset$ otherwise.

2.2 Data mining problem

A *sample* is a finite set $S = \{s_1, \ldots, s_m\}$ of strings over Σ and an *objective condition over* S is a binary labeling function $C : S \to \{0, 1\}$. Each string $s_i \in S$ is a *document* and $C(s_i)$ is its *label*. A document s_i is *positive* if $C(s_i) = 1$ and *negative* otherwise. Let $\alpha \in \{0, 1\}$ be any label. We denote the set $\{ s \in S | C(s) = \alpha \}$ by S_α. For a subset T of S, we define $count(P, T)$ to be the number of documents $s \in T$ that P matches.

The first problem to consider is the confidence maximization [10]. For a pattern P, we define the *support* of P by $supp_S(P) = count(P, S_1)/card(S)$ and the *confidence* of P by $conf_S(P) = count(P, S_1)/count(P, S)$. A *minimum support* is any real number $0 \le \sigma \le 1$. A pattern P is said to be σ-*frequent* if $supp_S(P) \ge \sigma$.

Definition 1. OPTIMIZED CONFIDENCE PATTERN PROBLEM
An instance is a five-tuple $(\Sigma, S, C, k, \sigma)$ *of an alphabet* Σ, *a sample set* S, *an objective condition* C *over* S, *constants* $k \ge 0$ *and* $0 \le \sigma \le 1$. *The problem is to find a* σ-*frequent* k-*proximity two-words association pattern* P *that maximizes* $conf_S(P)$.

Intuitively, the optimized confidence pattern problem is to find an implication $P \Rightarrow C$ with highest conditional probability among those rules that can apply to at least σ percent of the documents in S. In Section 3 and Section 4, we give algorithms for efficiently solving the optimized confidence pattern problem.

The second problem to consider is the empirical error minimization [17, 20]. Let S be a sample, C an *objective condition over* S and P a k-proximity two-words association pattern over Σ. We define $P(s) \in \{0, 1\}$ is 1 iff P occurs in s. The *empirical error* of a pattern P with respect to S and C is the number of the documents in S misclassified by P, that is, $error_{S,C}(P) = \sum_{s \in S} |P(s) - C(s)|$.

Definition 2. EMPIRICAL ERROR MINIMIZATION PROBLEM
An instance is a four-tuple (Σ, S, C, k) *of an alphabet* Σ, *a sample set* S, *an objective condition* C *over* S, *a constant* $k \ge 0$. *The problem is to find a* k-*proximity two-words association pattern* P *that minimizes* $error_{S,C}(P)$.

As we will see in Section 5, the empirical error minimization problem is closely related to a learning problem in noisy environments.

2.3 Suffix trees

A suffix tree is a data structure for storing all subwords of a given text in very economical way (McCreight [24]). Let $A = a_1 a_2 \cdots a_{n-1}\$$ be a text of length n. We assume that the text always terminates with a special symbol $\$ \notin \Sigma$ distinct from any letter including itself. For each $1 \le p \le n$, we define the suffix starting at position p by $A_p = a_p \cdots a_{n-1}\$$.

Then, the *suffix tree* for text A is exactly the *compact trie* for all the suffices of A, that is, obtained from a trie for A by iteratively removing the internal nodes with only one child and merging the labels of the removed edges.

More precisely, the suffix tree for A is a rooted tree $Tree_A$ that satisfies the following conditions. (i) Each edge is labeled by a subword α of A, which is encoded by a pair (p, q) of positions that points an occurrence of α in A, that is, $A[p]A[p+1]\cdots[q] = \alpha$. (ii) The labels of any two edges leaving from the same node start with mutually *distinct* letters. (iii) Each node v represents the string $Word(v)$ obtained by concatenating the labels on the path from the root to v in this order. (iv) For $1 \le i \le n$, the i-th leaf l_i represents the suffix of rank i in the lexicographic order over all the suffices of A.

Let α be a subword of A. The *locus* of α in $Tree_A$, denoted by $Locus(\alpha)$, is the unique node v of $Tree_A$ such that α is a prefix of $Word(v)$ and $Word(w)$ is a proper prefix of α, where w is the parent of v.

From (iv) and (iii) above $Tree_A$ has exactly n leaves and at most $n-1$ internal nodes, and thus from (i) it requires $O(n)$ space representing $O(n^2)$ subwords of A. Furthermore, McCreight (1976) gives an elegant algorithm that computes $Tree_A$ in linear time and space. It is known that the average height of a suffix tree for a random string of length n is $O(\log n)$ [7]. This is also the case for genetic sequences.

2.4 Orthogonal range query

Let n be a positive integer. Assume that we are given a finite collection X of points over a discrete two-dimensional plane $[1..n] \times [1..n]$. An *orthogonal range query* is to find all the points in X that are included in a given rectangle $[x_1..x_2] \times [y_1..y_2]$.

Several solutions have been proposed for the problem, and among them we adopt a method described in Preparata and Shamos [27] for its simplicity although it is not optimum in computation time. Their solution uses a data structure called the *orthogonal range tree* that requires $O(m \log m)$ space, $O(m \log m)$ preprocessing time, and $O(\log^2 m)$ time per query, where m is the number of points in X. For the algorithm in Section 4, we extend this data structure to search over the suffix tree.

3 The Mining Algorithm

In this section, we first show that there exists an efficient algorithm that computes optimized confidence patterns in time $O(mn^2 \log^2 n)$ and space $O(kmn \log n)$ using the suffix tree and the orthogonal range tree as its data structures. Then, in the next section, we show that we can make orthogonal range queries directly over the suffix tree instead of the range tree. This yields a faster algorithm for the optimized confidence pattern problem.

Figure 1 shows our data mining algorithm *Find_Optimal*, which finds the optimized confidence patterns. The keys of the algorithm are steps to enumerate patterns in canonical form and to compute $supp(P)$ and $conf(P)$ quickly. Let $(\Sigma, S, C, k, \sigma)$ be an instance of the optimized confidence pattern problem.

Procedure: *Find_Optimal;*
Given: a sample $S = \{s_1, \ldots, s_m\}$, an objective condition C,
a proximity $k \geq 0$ and a minimum support $0 \leq \sigma \leq 1$.
Output: the optimized confidence patterns (α, k, β) in canonical form.
Variable: a priority queue Q.

  begin
1    $Q := \emptyset$;
2    $A := s_1\$ \cdots \$s_m\$$ and compute *doc*;
3   Build the suffix tree $Tree_A$ and suffix arrays *suf, pos*.
4   Compute $Diag_k$ and $Rank_k$ from A.
5   Foreach node v do compute $I(v)$;
6   Foreach node u in $Tree_A$ do   /* Traversing $Tree_A$ from the root to the leaves */
7   Foreach node v in $Tree_A$ do   /* Traversing $Tree_A$ from the root to the leaves */
8      $P := (Word(u), k, Word(v))$;
9   Compute $count(P, S_1)$ and $count(P, S_0)$ by making
10   an orthogonal range query $I(u) \times I(v)$ for $Rank_k$;
11   Compute $supp(P)$ and $conf(P)$;
12   if $supp(P) \geq \sigma$ then insert P into the priority queue Q with the key $conf(P)$;
13   **end**;
14 **end**;
15 Output all the optimized confidence patterns in Q;
  end

Fig. 1. An algorithm for discovering the optimized confidence patterns

3.1 Enumerating the patterns in canonical form using a suffix tree

Let $\$ \notin \Sigma$ be a symbol such that $\$ \neq \$$. Given $S = \{s_1, \ldots, s_m\}$ and $C : S \to \{0, 1\}$ as input, our algorithm computes a single text $A = s_1\$ \cdots \$s_m\$$ called an *input text* by concatenating all documents in S delimited with $\$$. Let $n = |A|$. For each $1 \leq p \leq n$, we define $doc(p) = i$ if if i-th text $s_i \in S$ includes p. Without loss of generality, we assume that there exists some $1 \leq p \leq m$ such that $C(s_i) = 1$ for all $1 \leq i \leq p$ and $C(s_i) = 0$ for all $p < i \leq m$.

Next, we build the suffix tree $Tree_A$ for input text A by using a linear time algorithm in [24]. This tree $Tree_A$ is isomorphic to the *generalized suffix tree* (GST), that is, the compacted trie for all the suffices of documents in S, except the labels of the edges directed to the leaves (Amir *et al.* [3]). Then, for each leaf v, we redefine $Word(v)$ as the longest prefix of the suffix represented by v that contains no $\$$'s. This is actually a standard method to build GST in linear time [3].

Now, we introduce an equivalence relation $\equiv_A$ as follows. For strings α, β, $\alpha \equiv_A \beta$ iff $Occ_A(\alpha) = Occ_A(\beta)$. For k-proximity two-words association patterns $P = (\alpha_1, k, \alpha_2), Q = (\beta_1, k, \beta_2)$, $P \equiv_A Q$ iff $\alpha_1 \equiv_A \beta_1$ and $\alpha_2 \equiv_A \beta_2$. If $P \equiv_A Q$ then we say that P and Q are *equivalent*.

Lemma 1. *Equivalent patterns give the same value for $supp_S(P)$ and $conf_S(P)$.*

Proof. By definition, equivalent patterns P, Q have the same set of the occurrences for any text A. Thus, $count(P, T) = count(Q, T)$ for any subset $T \subseteq S$. Since $supp_S(P)$ and $conf_S(P)$ are defined through $count$, the result follows. $\square$

A pattern is said to be in *canonical form* if it has the form $(Word(u), k, Word(v))$ for some nodes u, v of $Tree_A$. By definition, the number of k-proximity two-words association patterns is $O(n^2)$. Let $\perp_S \in \Sigma^*$ be an arbitrary string whose length is $\max\{|s| \mid s \in S\} + 1$. Clearly, $\Delta_{S,\xi}(\perp_S) = 0$.

Lemma 2. *For any k-proximity two-words association pattern P, if P matches a document in S then there exists a equivalent pattern in canonical form.*

Proof. Let $P = (\alpha, k, \beta)$. We show that for any subword α of A, there exists a node w of $Tree_A$ such that $\alpha \equiv_A Word(w)$ as follows. Suppose that we have the uncompacted suffix trie $\widehat{Tree}_A$ for A. Then, there exists a node v of $\widehat{Tree}_A$ that represents α. Let w be the highest descendant of v that has at least two children. Now, we map the nodes in $Tree_A$ into those in $\widehat{Tree}_A$ in a standard way. Then, we can easily see that v and w are mapped on a same edge in the compacted version $Tree_A$. We know that $subtree(v)$ and $subtree(w)$ have the same set of leaves, and thus they have the same set of occurrences in A. Since $w = Locus(\alpha)$ in $Tree_A$, we have $Word(w) \equiv_A \alpha$. Hence, the lemma follows. $\square$

Lemma 3. *For any optimized confidence pattern among k-proximity two-words association patterns, there is an equivalent pattern P that is either in canonical form or $\perp_S$.*

3.2 Computing the support values using range queries

In this section, we show how to quickly compute the support and the confidence by using orthogonal range queries. The technique used here is basically due to Manber and Baeza-Yates [21]. The idea is to reduce the discovery of optimized confidence patterns to the discovery of 2-dimensional axes-parallel rectangles over the space consisting of the ranks of the lexicographically ordered suffices.

Let $A_{p_1}, A_{p_2}, \ldots, A_{p_n}$ be the sequence obtained by arranging all the suffices of A in the lexicographic order over Σ^*. Here, A_p is the suffix of A starting at position p. Then, we store the indexes $p_1, p_2, \ldots, p_n$ in an array $suf : [1..n] \to [1..n]$ of length n in this order, and define the array $pos : [1..n] \to [1..n]$ as the inverse mapping of suf. These arrays are called the *suffix array* (Gonnet and Baeza-Yates [14]; Manber and Myers [22]). By definition, $suf(i)$ is the position of the suffix of rank i and $pos(p)$ is the rank of the suffix A_p.

First, we observe that for any node v of $Tree_A$, the set of the occurrences of $Word(v)$ occupy a contiguous subinterval $I(v) = [x_1..x_2]$ in array suf.

Lemma 4. *The subintervals $I(v)$ for all nodes v are computed in $O(n)$ time.*

Proof. $I(v)$ is computed by traversing $Tree_A$ from the leaves to the root in, e.g., depth-first search. Scanning the leaves from left to right, let $I(v_i) = [i..i]$ for the i-th leaf $(i = 1, \ldots, n)$. Then, traversing $Tree_A$ from the leaves to the root, we visit each internal node v with its children $v_1, \ldots, v_h$ and let $I(v) = [L..R]$, where L and R are the left boundary of $I(v_1)$ and the right boundary of $I(v_h)$. □

Secondly, the algorithm builds from S and C the *diagonal set of width k*, that is, the set of 2-dimensional labeled points

$$Diag_k = \{ (p, q; doc(p)) \mid 1 \leq p, q \leq n, 0 \leq (q - p) \leq k, doc(p) = doc(q) \}.$$

Then, the algorithm transforms $Diag_k$ into the following set of 2-dimensional labeled points:

$$Rank_k = \{ (pos(p), pos(q); i) \mid (p, q; i) \in Diag_k \}.$$

For a k-proximity two-words association pattern $P = (\alpha, k, \beta)$, we associate a 2-dimensional axis-parallel rectangle $Rect(P) = I(\alpha) \times I(\beta)$, and define $count(Rect(P), Q)$ to be the number of distinct i such that $(x, y; i) \in Q \cap Rect(P) \times [1..m]$, where Q is any subset of $Rank_k$.

Lemma 5. *For any k-proximity two-words association pattern P, $count(P, S) = count(Rect(P), Rank_k)$.*

From Lemma 5, the problems of computing $supp_S(P)$ and $conf_S(P)$ reduces to the problem of computing $count(Rect(P), Rank_k)$. From [27], a standard argument show the following lemma.

Lemma 6. *Let l be any integer, $Q \subseteq [1..l]^2 \times [1..m]$ be a set of 2-dimensional labeled points and $R \subseteq [1..n]^2$ be any rectangle. Then, $count(R, Q)$ is computable in time $O(m \log^2 n)$ and space $O(mn \log n)$ with preprocessing time $O(n \log n)$, where n is the number of points in Q.*

Theorem 1. *Let $(\Sigma, S, C, k, \sigma)$ be an instance of the optimized confidence pattern problem. Then, the algorithm Find_Optimal in Figure 1 computes all the optimized confidence patterns in canonical form with proximity k and support threshold σ in time $O(mn^2 \log^2 n)$ and space $O(kmn \log n)$, where $m = card(S)$ and $n = size(S)$.*

Proof. First we build the suffix tree $Tree_A$ in linear time and space. Then, compute intervals $I(v)$ for all node v in time $O(n)$ with dynamic programming (Preparata and Shamos 1985). From Lemma 1 and Lemma 3, it suffices to search at most $O(n^2)$ canonical patterns $P = (Word(u), k, Word(v))$ by enumerating a pair u, v of nodes of $Tree_A$. Then, we can see from Lemma 5 and Lemma 6 that for each P, we can compute $supp(P)$ and $conf(P)$ in $O(kmn \log n)$ preprocessing time, $O(kmn \log n)$ space, and $O(m \log^2 n)$ time per query. Note that the number of $Rank_k$ is at most kn. Since the number of possible patterns in canonical form is $O(n^2)$, this proves the result. □

4 Modified algorithm

In this section, we present a modified version of our algorithm, that runs in time $O(\max\{k, m\}n^2)$ and space $O(kn)$, In the algorithm, we implement an orthogonal range query mechanism over the suffix tree itself instead of a range tree and compute the value of $count(Rect(P), Rank_k)$ by a dynamic programming in a similar way as Maass [20]. Figure 2 shows a modified version of our algorithm.

Procedure: *Modified_Find_Optimal;*
Given: a sample $S = \{s_1, \ldots, s_m\}$, an objective condition C, constants $k \geq 0$, and $0 \leq \sigma \leq 1$.
Output: the optimized confidence patterns (α, k, β) in canonical form.
Variable: a priority queue Q;
  begin
1   Compute $A = s_1 \$ \cdots \$ s_m \$$, and *doc*; $Q := \emptyset$;
2   Build the suffix tree $Tree_A$ and suffix arrays suf, pos;
3   Compute $Diag_k$ and $Rank_k$ from S.
4   **Foreach** node u in $Tree_A$ traversing from the leaves to the root **do**
5   **if** u is the x-th leaf l_x **then**
6         $B(l_x) := \{\langle y, z \rangle \mid \langle x, y, z \rangle \in Rank_k, \exists y, \exists z\}$;
7   **if** u is an internal node with children $u_1, \ldots, u_h$ **then**
8         $B(u) := B(u_1) \cup \cdots \cup B(u_h)$, and then discard $B(u_1), \ldots, B(u_h)$;
9   **Foreach** node v in $Tree_A$ traversing from the leaves to the root **do**
10   **if** v is the y-th leaf l_y **then**
11      $C(l_y) := \{\langle z \rangle \mid \langle y, z \rangle \in B(u), \exists z\}$;
12   **if** v is an internal node with children $v_1, \ldots, v_h$ **then**
13      $C(v) := C(v_1) \cup \cdots \cup C(v_h)$ and then discard $C(v_1), \ldots, C(v_h)$;
14      $P := (Word(u), k, Word(v))$;
15   Compute $count(P, S_1)$ and $count(P, S_0)$ from $C(v)$;
16   **if** $supp(P) \geq \sigma$ **then**
17   Insert P into Q with the key $conf(P)$;
18   **end**;
19 **end**;
20 Output all the optimized confidence patterns in Q;
  end

Fig. 2. A modified algorithm for discovering the optimized confidence patterns

Each node v of $Tree_A$ has linear list $B(v)$ and $C(v)$. Elements of $B(v)$ are pairs $\langle y, z \rangle \in [1..n] \times [1..m]$ and are sorted in the y-coordinate y. Similarly, Elements of $C(v)$ are labels $\langle z \rangle \in [1..m]$ and are sorted in the z-coordinate z. For any $x \in [1..n]$, we denote by l_x the x-th leaf.

Lemma 7. *Suppose the algorithm Modified_Find_Optimal visits node u in the loop at Line 4, visits node v in the loop at Line 9, and reaches Line 15. Then, $C(v)$ is the ordered list of the z's such that $(x, y; z) \in Rank_k \cap Rect(P) \times [1..m]$.*

Proof. Proved by induction on the height of the node u and v in a similar way as in Lemma 4. □

Theorem 2. *Let $(\Sigma, S, C, k, \sigma)$ be an instance of the optimized confidence pattern problem. Then, the algorithm Modified_Find_Optimal in Figure 2 computes all the optimized confidence patterns in canonical form with proximity k and support threshold σ in time $O(\max\{k, m\}n^2)$ and space $O(kn)$, where $m = card(S)$, $n = size(S)$.*

Proof. The correctness follows from Lemma 1, Lemma 3, Lemma 5, and Lemma 7. Then, we estimate the running time. Line 1 to Line 3 take time $O(n + kn)$. Since $Tree_A$ contains $O(n)$ nodes, the outer loop at Line 4 is executed $O(n)$ times, and thus the inner loop at Line 9 is executed $O(n^2)$ times. At each visit to a node u in the outer loop, each merge operation at Line 8 takes time at most $O(kn)$ because the length of the resulting list $B(u)$ is obviously bounded by $kn = card(Rank_k)$. Line 6 takes total time $O(kn)$ in scanning all leaves. Similarly, at each visit to a node v in the inner loop, each merge operation at Line 13 takes time $O(hm)$ because each $C(v_i)$ are sorted and its length is bounded by m, where h is the number of children. Since the sum of the number of the children at all nodes is $O(n)$, amortized total time of Line 13 is $O(mn)$ and that of Line 11 is $O(kn)$ in scanning all leaves for a fixed u. Combining these observations, the total running time of the algorithm is $T(n) = O(kn) + O(kn) + n \cdot (O(kn) + O(mn)) = O(\max\{k, m\}n^2)$. □

It is known that the height of the suffix tree is $O(\log n)$ for random texts generated by a uniform distribution [7]. By Theorem 3 below, we expect an algorithm to run very efficiently in time $O(kn \log^3 n)$ with a high probability for such random texts.

Theorem 3. *Let $(\Sigma, S, C, k, \sigma)$ be an instance of the optimized confidence pattern problem. Then, there exists an algorithm that computes all the optimized confidence patterns in canonical form with proximity k and support threshold σ in time $O(kd^2 n \log n)$ and space $O(kn)$, where $n = size(S)$ and d is the height of the suffix tree.*

Proof. We observe that each layer, the set of nodes at the same level, of a suffix tree contains totally $N = kn$ elements in $B(u)$ ($C(v)$). In the modified algorithm, we attach with each node the pointer to its parent and a sorted list $C(v)$ and $B(u)$ of points $\langle y, z \rangle$ and $\langle x, y, z \rangle$. We use a balanced tree to represent each list $C(v)$ so that we can perform both the insertion of an element and the counting of positive-labeled or negative-labeled elements in time $\log l$ for $l = card(C(v))$. By using these, we traverse the tree levelwise from the leaves to the root. Thus, at each node u with list $B(u)$, we can compute all $C(v)$ in time $O(dn_0 \log n_0)$ from Line 10 to Line 17 in Figure 2, where $n_0 = card(B(u))$. Repeatedly using this idea, we can derive the time $O(kd^2 n \log n)$ in k, d, n. We omit the details. □

5 Agnostic PAC-learning and the empirical error minimization

Agnostic PAC-learning is a generalization of a well known PAC-learning model in computational learning theory, which is intended to capture learning situations in real world [16, 17, 20]. In agnostic PAC-learning, a learning algorithm must work robustly with noisy environments, and even have the capability to *approximate* arbitrary unknown probability distributions.

Haussler [16] and Kearns *et al.* [17] showed a close link between Agnostic PAC-learning and the empirical error minimization problem defined above. The *Vapnik-Chervonenkis dimension* (VC-dimension) is a measure of the complexity of a concept class (See, e.g. [16, 17] for the definition). The class of k-proximity two-words association patterns obviously has polynomial VC-dimension for any fixed $k \geq 0$.

Lemma 8 (Kearns *et al.* [17]). *For any hypothesis class with polynomial VC-dimension, the polynomial time solvability of the empirical error minimization problem and the efficient agnostic PAC-learnability are equivalent.*

Now, we show that we can modify the algorithm *Modified_Find_Optimal* to solve the empirical error minimization problem in the same time and space complexity as the original version.

Theorem 4. *Let S be a sample, C be an objective condition over S, $k \geq 0$ be a fixed constant. Then, there exists an algorithm that solves the empirical error minimization problem for k-proximity two-words association patterns in time $O(kd^2 n \log n)$ and space $O(kn)$, where $n = size(S)$ and d is the height of the suffix tree.*

Proof. We can easily show that the empirical error minimization is obviously equivalent to the maximization of the difference $\Delta_{S,C}(P) = count(P, S_1) - count(P, S_0)$. It is not hard to see that $\Delta_{S,C}$ is maximized by either a pattern in canonical form or $\perp_S$ as in Lemma 3. Now, we modify the algorithm *Modified_Find_Optimal* in Figure 2 to compute a pattern P that maximizes $\Delta_{S,C}(P)$. At Line 15 of the algorithm, we compute the quantities $count(P, S_1)$ and $count(P, S_0)$, and then compute $\Delta_{S,C}(P)$. We skip the test at Line 16, and then at Line 17 we insert P into a priority queue Q with $\Delta_{S,C}(P)$ as the key. This modification correctly works, and hence the theorem follows from Theorem 3. □

Although the empirical error minimization problem is intractable for most concept classes, recently some geometrical patterns, e.g. *axis-parallel rectangles* and *convex k-gons* on Euclidean plain, are shown to be efficiently agnostic PAC-learnable [8, 20]. From Lemma 8 and Theorem 4, we know that there exists an agnostic learning algorithm that runs in time $O(kn \log^3 n)$ if an input sample is ensured to be random. Hence, our result is one of a few results on the efficient agnostic learnability for nontrivial concept classes other than geometric patterns.

6 Pruning and sampling

Pruning: Based on the monotonicity of the support of patterns in canonical form $(W(u), k, W(v))$,

- If u is a parent of v then $supp_S(u) \geq supp_S(v)$,
- If $\min\{supp_S(W(u)), supp_S(W(v))\} < \sigma$ then $supp_S(\langle W(u), k, W(v) \rangle) \leq \sigma$,

we incorporate two pruning heuristics in the first algorithm: (1) Local pruning. Prune the descendants of u if $supp_S(W(u)) \leq \sigma$ at some u. (2) Global pruning. Prune the descendants of v if $supp_S(\langle W(u), k, W(v) \rangle) \leq \sigma$, where $supp(\alpha)$ is the support of a subword α. The local pruning is also possible in the second algorithm. By a similar argument to the proof of Theorem 2, we know that there are at most kd^2n canonical patterns of nonzero support for the height d of the suffix tree. Thus, we can expect that the efficiency of the first algorithm is improved with pruning for nearly random texts.

Sampling: The modified algorithm in Section 4 achieves $O(mn^2)$ time but it is not fast enough to be applied for huge text databases of several giga bytes. The following procedure approximates the solutions by using a random sampling technique.

Given: a sample S consisting of n examples.
  begin
    Draws m documents from S according to the uniform
    distributions. Let S_m be the obtained sample.
    By using algorithm *Find_Optimal*, compute the optimized
    confidence patterns P with respect to S_m, and output P.
  end

We set the sample size m to be, say, $O(n^{1/3})$ so that the algorithm works in almost linear time in n. The patterns computed by random sampling may give lower confidence than the patterns obtained from the original sample S. Therefore, we present empirical evaluations of the sampling heuristics by experiments.

7 Experimental results

We run experiments on genetic data to evaluate the efficiency and the performance of our algorithms. The program was written in C based on the second algorithm in Section 4 and run on Sun Ultra 1 workstation under the Sun Solaris 2.5 operating system. The data were amino acid sequences of totally $24KB$ from GenBank database [11]. We obtained 450 positive sequences related to the signal peptide and 450 negative sequences 450 from other sequences, and preprocessed the data by transforming twenty amino acids into three symbols $0, 1, 2$ by indices due to Kyte and Doolittle (1982). For each $m = 10 \sim 100$ and each trial, we randomly drawn m positive and m negative sequences from the original sample S, and compute the optimum patterns for the obtained sample.

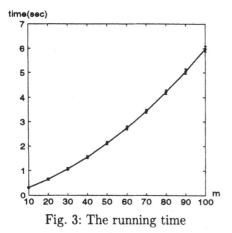

Fig. 3: The running time

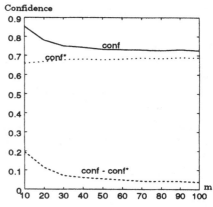

Fig. 4: The performance of sampling

Running time. Figure 3 shows the dependency of the running time to the number m of documents, which is proportional to the sample size n. We see that the growth of the running time is slower than that we expected from Theorem 2. For a larger sample of 24KB ($m = 450$), the algorithm takes one minute and over twenty mega bytes of main memory to find 37 optimal patterns with testing 676 locally frequent patterns within 577296729 possible patterns. Examples of the optimal patterns are "12222"*"2" and "0"*"2222" that achieve high confidence 69% and 66% with support around 65%.

Random sampling. Figure 4 show the performance of sampling heuristics for varying sample size. For each trial, first compute the best ten patterns for the sample S_m and then evaluate the empirical confidence $conf$ on S_m and the real confidence $cond^*$ on S. We plotted the average of the confidence through 100 trials for each m. The parameters were $k = 5$ and $\sigma = 0.6$. In Figure 4, we can see that the error is 5% for the confidence by 10% sampling. For the support, we had a similar result (12% error for the support).

Table 1. The performance of pruning heuristics

σ %	Sample size(bytes)	Candidates	Locally frequent	Globally frequent
90%	2,701	7,295,401	121	40
50%	2,754	7,584,516	1,444	64
30%	2,764	7,639,696	6,241	88

Pruning. Table 1 shows the efficiency of the pruning heuristics. The sample consists of 50 positive and 50 negative sequences of totally 2.7KB. The first and the second columns show the minimum support and the sample size, and the third, the fourth, and the fifth columns show the number of candidate patterns remain at the initial, after local pruning, and after global pruning. We can see that only a small fraction of patterns can be solutions for nearly random sequences.

8 Conclusion

In this paper, we considered the problem of finding association rules over subwords, and gave efficient algorithms that compute optimized confidence rules from a large collection of unstructured text data for the class of two-words association patterns. We discussed the performance of search heuristics and run experiments on genetic data.

The algorithms presented in this paper extensively use the *suffix array* data structure, which is a variant of the suffix tree that is more space efficient and suitable for implementing advanced search functions in large text databases (Gonnet and Baeza-Yates [14]; Manber and Myers [22]). Thus, it is a future problem to develop scalable implementation techniques over suffix arrays that enables us to incorporate our algorithms into existing text databases [13, 26]. The study of secondary storage directed algorithms and the speed-up by parallel execution are other future problems.

We developed efficient learning algorithm for classes of structured patterns [4–6]. It will be interesting to extend the framework of this paper for the structured patterns.

Acknowledgments

The authors would like to thank anonymous referees for their suggestions that greatly improve the correctness and the presentation of this paper. We also thank Shinichi Shimozono, Masayuki Takeda, Ayumi Shinohara, Takeshi Shinohara and Thomas Zeugmann for their valuable discussions and comments concerning this work. The first author would like to thank Esko Ukkonen and Heikki Mannila for directing his interests in this area. This research is partly supported from the Ministry of Education, Science and Culture, Japan by Grant-in-Aid for Scientific Research on Priority Area "Advanced Databases" and by Grant-in-Aid for Scientific Research on Priority Area "Discovery Science."

References

1. S. Abiteboul, Querying semi-structured data. In Proc. ICDT'97 (1997).
2. R. Agrawal, T. Imielinski, A. Swami, Mining association rules between sets of items in large databases. In Proc. the 1993 ACM SIGMOD Conference on Management of Data, 207–216 (1993).
3. A. Amir, M. Farach, Z. Galil, R. Giancarlo, K. Park, Dynamic Dictionary Matching. *JCSS*, 49 (1994), 208–222.
4. H. Arimura, R. Fujino, T. Shinohara, and S. Arikawa. Protein motif discovery from positive examples by minimal multiple generalization over regular patterns *Proc. Genome Informatics Workshop 1994*, 39–48, 1994.
5. H. Arimura, H. Ishizaka, T. Shinohara, Learning unions of tree patterns using queries, *Theoretical Computer Science*, 185 (1997) 47–62.
6. H. Arimura, T. Shinohara, S. Otsuki. Finding minimal generalizations for unions of pattern languages and its application to inductive inference from positive data. In Proc. the 11th STACS, LNCS 775, (1994) 649–660.

7. L. Devroye, W. Szpankowski, B. Rais, A note on the height of the suffix trees. *SIAM J. Comput.*, 21, 48–53 (1992).

8. D. P. Dobkin and D. Gunopulos, Concept learning with geometric hypothesis. In Proc. COLT95 (1995) 329–336.

9. R. Feldman and I. Dagan, Knowledge Discovery in Textual Databases (KDT). In Proc. KDD-95 (1995).

10. T. Fukuda, Y. Morimoto, S. Morishita, and T. Tokuyama, Data mining using two-dimensional optimized association rules. In Proc. the 1996 ACM SIGMOD Conference on Management of Data, (1996) 13–23.

11. GenBank, GenBank Release Notes, IntelliGenetics Inc. (1991).

12. G. Gras and J. Nicolas, FOREST, a browser for huge DNA sequences. In Proc. the 7th Workshop on Genome Informatics (1996).

13. G. Gonnet, PAT 3.1: An efficient text searching system, User's manual. UW Center for the New OED, University of Waterloo (1987).

14. G. Gonnet, R. Baeza-Yates, Handbook of Algorithms and Data Structures, Addison-Wesley (1991).

15. J. Han, Y. Cai, N. Cercone, Knowledge discovery in databases: An attribute-oriented approach. In Proc. the 18th VLDB Conference, 547–559 (1992).

16. D. Haussler, Decision theoretic generalization of the PAC model for neural net and other learning applications. Information and Computation 100 (1992) 78–150.

17. M. J. Kearns, R. E. Shapire, L. M. Sellie, Toward efficient agnostic learning. *Machine Learning*, 17(2–3), 115–141, 1994.

18. J. Kyte and R. F. Doolittle, In J. Mo. Biol., 157 (1982), 105–132.

19. D. D. Lewis, Challenges in machine learning for text classification. In Proc. 9th Computational Learning Theory (1996), pp. 1.

20. W. Maass, Efficient agnostic PAC-learning with simple hypothesis, In Proc. COLT94 (1994), 67–75.

21. U. Manber and R. Baeza-Yates, An algorithm for string matching with a sequence of don't cares. IPL 37, 133–136 (1991).

22. U. Manber and E. Myers, "Suffix arrays": a new method for on-line string searches. In Proc. the 1st ACM-SIAM Symposium on Discrete Algorithms (1990)319–327.

23. H. Mannila, H. Toivonen, Discovering generalized episodes using minimal occurrences. In Proc. KDD'96 (1996) 146–151.

24. E. M. McCreight, A space-echonomical suffix tree constructiooon algorithm. JACM 23 (1976), 262–272.

25. M. Nakanishi, M. Hashidume, M. Ito, A. Hashimoto, A linear-time algorithm for computing characteristic strings. In Proc. the 5th International Symposium on Algorithms and Computation (1994), 315-23.

26. OPENTEXT Index. http://index.opentext.net (1997).

27. F. P. Preparata, M. I. Shamos, Computational Geometry. Springer-Verlag (1985).

28. J. T.-L. Wang, G.-W. Chirn, T. G. Marr, B. Shapiro, D. Shasha, K. Zhang. Combinatorial Pattern Discovery for Scientific Data: Some preliminary results. In Proc. 1994 SIGMOD (1994) 115–125.

A Comparison of Identification Criteria for Inductive Inference of Recursive Real-Valued Functions

Eiju Hirowatari[1] and Setsuo Arikawa[2]

[1] Center for Information Processing Research and Education, Kitakyushu University,
Kitakyushu 802-8577, Japan
e-mail: eiju@cc.kitakyu-u.ac.jp
[2] Department of Informatics, Kyushu University, Fukuoka 812-8581, Japan
e-mail: arikawa@i.kyushu-u.ac.jp

Abstract. In this paper we investigate inductive inference of recursive real-valued functions from data. A recursive real-valued function is regarded as a computable interval mapping, which has been introduced by Hirowatari and Arikawa (1997), and modified by Apsītis et al (1998). The learning model we consider in this paper is an extension of the Gold's inductive inference. We first introduce some criteria for successful inductive inference of recursive real-valued functions. Then we show a recursively enumerable class of recursive real-valued functions which is not inferable in the limit. This should be an interesting contrast to the result by Wiehagen (1976) that every recursively enumerable subset of recursive functions from N to N is consistently inferable in the limit. We also show that every recursively enumerable class of recursive real-valued functions on a fixed rational interval is consistently inferable in the limit. Furthermore we show that our consistent inductive inference coincides with the ordinary inductive inference, when we deal with recursive real-valued functions on a fixed closed rational interval.

1 Introduction

This paper investigates inductive inference of real-valued functions from examples. Examples of real-valued functions obtained by experiments and observations are numerical data which inevitably involve some ranges of errors. Hence such numerical data are represented by pairs of rational numbers approximating an exact value and an error bound respectively. Each of the numerical data can also be represented as a pair of an upper and lower bounds to the exact value. Thus it is regarded as an interval number [1, 11], i.e. a closed interval containing the exact value. Hence it is reasonable to regard real-valued functions as computable interval mappings.

Recursive real-valued functions as interval mapping has been introduced by Hirowatari and Arikawa [9], and then modified by Apsītis et al [2], in order to study learning of real-valued functions. On the other hand, computable real functions was introduced by Grzegorczyk [6], and several other formulations, different from but equivalent to his, have been reported in [7, 10, 12, 13]. The formulations of computable real functions are convenient for discussing the computational complexity of such functions. However it is not always suitable to learning or inductive inference from examples. Our functions are implemented by recursive mappings of intervals, in contrast with the computable real functions. Furthermore our functions can enjoy the merits of not only computable interval functions but also computable real functions. Every partial computable real function is a recursive real-valued function [2]. These are why our functions are suitable for algorithmic learning.

In [3] two approaches were exhibited for the learning of real-valued functions from examples by using computable analytic functions and arbitrary computable functions of recursive real numbers respectively. It was proved there that the set of continuous functions defined over an interval is learnable if and only if the interval is closed on both ends, and that the same is true for monotonic functions. Furthermore, Haussler [8] considered the problem of learning functions from X into Y, as a generalization of the PAC learning model. In his model, the learner receives randomly drawn examples $(x, h_0(y)) \in X \times Y$ for some unknown target function h_0, and tries to find a decision rule $h : X \to A$, in order to minimize the expectation of a loss $l(y, a)$, where X, Y and A are arbitrary sets of reals, and l is a real-valued function. Our learning model, first presented in [9], differs from these models in [3, 8].

Our model is an extension of the Gold model [5] of inductive inference (called $REALEX$-inference) to handle inference of real-valued functions. This is a process of hypothesizing recursive real-valued functions intended to explain the received numerical data. An inference machine requests input data from time to time, and identifies an algorithm which computes the target function in the limit. As we deal with real-valued functions as target functions, we need to consider the precision of the guesses from the inference machine. For this purpose, we introduce the notion of consistent inductive inference of recursive real-valued functions (called $REALCONS$-inference) as a successful identification criterion. In [9] we have shown that every recursively enumerable class of recursive real-valued functions on a fixed rational interval is $REALCONS$-inferable in the limit.

In this paper we first propose some criteria for successful inference, and compare the classes resulting from the criterion of $REALCONS$ that is the set of all consistently inferable classes of recursive real-valued functions. Then we show that $REALCONS$ is properly included in $REALEX$, and show that $REALNUM$, the collection of all recursively enumerable sets of recursive real-valued functions, is not included in $REALCONS$. $REALNUM$ is not included in $REALEX$, although Wiehagen showed that every recursively enumerable subset of recursive functions from N to N is consistently inferable in the limit [14]. We then consider inferability of recursive real-valued functions on a fixed domain. We will focus our attention on functions on a rational interval. In the context of inference of recursive real-valued functions on a fixed open or half-open rational interval, we show that *REALNUM* is properly included in *REALCONS*, which makes an interesting contrast with the above result that *REALNUM* is not included in *REALEX*. Furthermore, we show that *REALCONS* is properly included in *REALEX*, in the context of inference of recursive real-valued functions on a fixed open or half-open rational interval. On the other hand, we show that *REALCONS* coincides with *REALEX*, in the context of inference of recursive real-valued functions on a fixed closed rational interval.

2 Recursive Real-Valued Functions

Let N, Q and R be the sets of all natural numbers, rational numbers and real numbers respectively. By N^+ and Q^+ we denote the sets of all positive natural numbers and rational numbers respectively.

A recursive real number is a pair of two sequences of rational numbers converging to the number and rational numbers converging to zero.

Definition 1. *Let f be a function from N to Q, and g be a function from N to Q^+. A pair $\langle f, g \rangle$ is an approximate expression of a real number x, if f and g satisfy the following conditions:*

1. $\lim_{n \to \infty} g(n) = 0$.
2. $|f(n) - x| \le g(n)$ for any n.

The number x is recursive real, if there is an approximate expression $\langle f, g \rangle$ of x such that f and g are recursive.

$f(n)$ and $g(n)$ show an approximate value of the real number and an error bound at each point respectively.

In this section we propose *recursive real-valued functions* which are closely related with computable real functions [6, 7, 10, 12, 13]. They are implemented via recursive mappings of intervals.

By a rational interval we mean an interval whose end points are rational. We sometimes call it just an interval when no confusion occurs. Let $h : S \to R$ be a real-valued function, where $S \subseteq R$ is the domain of h. Given S, we introduce a collection of rational intervals: $Dom_S \subseteq Q \times Q^+$ which contains all sufficiently short intervals contained in S. Given Dom_S, we also introduce a function $\mathcal{A}_h : Dom_S \to Q \times Q^+$ which maps rational intervals $\langle p, \alpha \rangle \in Dom_S$ to rational intervals showing where the value $h(x)$ is, provided that $x \in [p - \alpha, p + \alpha]$. The rationalized function $\mathcal{A}_h$ maps short intervals to short intervals, so that h can be computed with arbitrary precision.

Definition 2. *Let $S \subseteq R$ be a domain of some function. We say that $Dom_S \subseteq Q \times Q^+$ is a rationalized domain of S, if it satisfies the following conditions:*

1. *Every interval in Dom_S is contained in S: If $\langle p, \alpha \rangle \in Dom_S$, then $[p - \alpha, p + \alpha] \subseteq S$.*
2. *Dom_S covers the whole S: For any $x \in S$ there is $\langle p, \alpha \rangle \in Dom_S$ such that $x \in [p - \alpha, p + \alpha]$. Especially, if $x \in S$ is an interior point, then there is $\langle p, \alpha \rangle \in Dom_S$ such that $x \in (p - \alpha, p + \alpha)$.*
3. *Dom_S is closed under subintervals: If $\langle p, \alpha \rangle \in Dom_S$ and $[q - \beta, q + \beta] \subseteq [p - \alpha, p + \alpha]$, then $\langle q, \beta \rangle \in Dom_S$.*

There exist rationalized domains Dom_S, if and only if S can be expressed as unions of closed rational intervals. The same S can have different rationalized domains Dom_S.

Definition 3. *Let $h : S \to R$ be a real-valued function, and let S have a rationalized domain Dom_S. A rationalized function of h, denoted by $\mathcal{A}_h$, is a computable function from Dom_S to $Q \times Q^+$ which satisfies the following condition:*

For any $x \in S$ and any approximate expression $\langle f, g \rangle$ of a number x, there exists an approximate expression $\langle f_0, g_0 \rangle$ of the number $h(x)$ such that for all $n \in N$, $\langle f(n), g(n) \rangle \in Dom_S$ implies $\mathcal{A}_h(\langle f(n), g(n) \rangle) = \langle f_0(n), g_0(n) \rangle$.

If f and g are recursive, then there exist recursive functions f_0 and g_0 satisfying the above. Thus the function h above satisfies the condition that $h(x)$ is recursive real for any recursive real $x \in S$.

Definition 4. *Let $h : S \to R$ be a real-valued function. Then h is said to be a recursive real-valued function, if there exists a rationalized domain Dom_S of S, and a rationalized function $\mathcal{A}_h : Dom_S \to Q \times Q^+$ of h. We demand that $\mathcal{A}_h(\langle p, \alpha \rangle)$ does not halt for all $\langle p, \alpha \rangle \notin Dom_S$.*

From these definitions we can design $\mathcal{A}_h$ as the following algorithm: For h, $\mathcal{A}_h$ takes a pair $\langle p, \alpha \rangle \in Q \times Q$ as an input, and produces $\mathcal{A}_h(\langle p, \alpha \rangle)$ and stops if $\langle p, \alpha \rangle \in Dom_S$, else it never halts. Thus we sometimes say that $\mathcal{A}_h$ is an *algorithm which computes h*.

A real-valued function $h : S \to R$ is computable if $h(x)$ is recursive real for any recursive real $x \in S$ and there exists an efficient procedure to find $h(x)$ from the given x. Thus our recursive real-valued function is computable. Furthermore the recursive real-valued functions satisfy the conditions required in the interval analysis [11].

Let h be a recursive real-valued function, and $\mathcal{A}_h$ be the algorithm that computes h. By $\mathcal{A}_h(\langle p, \alpha \rangle)$, we denote the output of the algorithm for an input $\langle p, \alpha \rangle$.

By φ_j we denote a partial recursive function from N to N computed by a program j. Thus the set $\mathcal{P} = \{\varphi_0, \varphi_1, \varphi_2, \cdots\}$ is the set of all partial recursive functions from N to N. By $\Phi_j(i)$, we denote the step number to compute $\varphi_j(i)$ for a program j received an input i. For this set $\{\varphi_0, \varphi_1, \varphi_2, \cdots\}$, the following recursion theorem holds:

Theorem 1. *For any recursive function h from N to N, there exists a number $i \in N$ such that $\varphi_{h(i)} = \varphi_i$.*

We can extend $\varphi_j \in P$ to a stair function defined bellow, and then treat φ_j as a kind of recursive real-valued functions.

Definition 5. *Let $\varphi_j \in P$ and let S_0 be the domain of φ_j. A function $h : S \to R$ is a stair function of φ_j, if h satisfies the conditions:*

(1) $S = \bigcup_{i \in S_0}(i - \frac{1}{2}, i + \frac{1}{2})$,
(2) $h(x) = \varphi_j(i)$ for any $x \in (i - \frac{1}{2}, i + \frac{1}{2})$, $i \in S_0$.

Proposition 1. *Let $\varphi_j \in P$ and let h be a stair function of φ_j. Then h is a recursive real-valued function.*

Proof. Let S_0 and S be the domain of φ_j and h respectively. We define Dom_S as the set of all $\langle p, \alpha \rangle \in Q \times Q^+$ such that $[p - \alpha, p + \alpha] \subseteq (l - \frac{1}{2}, l + \frac{1}{2})$ and $\Phi_j(l) \leq \frac{1}{\alpha}$ for an $l \in S_0$, and a computable function $A_h : Dom_S \to Q \times Q^+$ by $A_h(\langle p, \alpha \rangle) = \langle \varphi_j(m), \alpha \rangle$, where $m \in N$, $|p - m| \leq \frac{1}{2} - \alpha$. Then Dom_S is a rationalized domain of S. Therefore we show that A_h is a rationalized function of h. Let $x \in S$, and $\langle f, g \rangle$ be approximate expression of x. Now we construct the following functions f_0 and g_0 from N to Q:

$$f_0(n) = \varphi_j(K)$$

$$g_0(n) = g(n)$$

where $K \in S_0$, $|x - K| \leq \frac{1}{2}$. Note that K can be computed uniquely, because there is a number t such that $[f(t) - g(t), f(t) + g(t)] \subseteq (K - \frac{1}{2}, K + \frac{1}{2})$. Therefore $\langle f_0, g_0 \rangle$ is an approximate expression of $h(x)$. Furthermore it holds that $\langle f(n), g(n) \rangle \in Dom_S$ implies $A_h(\langle f(n), g(n) \rangle) = \langle f_0(n), g_0(n) \rangle$. Hence A_h is a rationalized function of h. □

For any given algorithm A that computes a stair function of $\varphi_j \in P$, we can easily construct a program j which receives $n \in N$ as an input, and works as follows: If an input $n \in N$ is in the domain of φ_j, then j outputs $\varphi_j(n)$ else it never stops.

```
program: j
begin
    let n ∈ N be an input;  i := 0;  j := 0;  n := 0;  T := 0;
    while T = 0 do begin
        if A((n, 1/2^i)) has an output in at most j steps then ⟨q, β⟩ := A((n, 1/2^i));
        while l + 1/2 ≤ q + β do l := l + 1;
        if [q − β, q + β] ⊆ (l − 1/2, l + 1/2 then output l and T := 1
        else j := j − 1 and i := i + 1;
        if j < 0 then n := n + 1, j := n and i := 0
    end
end.
```

3 The Model of Learning

In our scientific activities we cannot observe the exact value of a real number x, but we can observe approximations of x. Such approximations can be captured by a pair $\langle p, \alpha \rangle$ of rational numbers such that p is an approximate value of the number x and α is its error bound, i.e., $x \in [p - \alpha, p + \alpha]$. We call such a pair $\langle p, \alpha \rangle$ a datum of x.

Definition 6. *Let $S \subseteq R$, and let $h : S \to R$ be a function. A datum of a function h is a pair $\langle \langle p, \alpha \rangle, \langle q, \beta \rangle \rangle$ such that there is an $x \in S$ such that $\langle p, \alpha \rangle$ and $\langle q, \beta \rangle$ are the data of the numbers $x \in S$ and $h(x)$ respectively.*

Definition 7. *A presentation of the function h is an infinite sequence $w_1, w_2, \cdots$ of data of h in which, for any number x in the domain of h and any $\zeta > 0$, there is a $w_k = \langle \langle p_k, \alpha_k \rangle, \langle q_k, \beta_k \rangle \rangle$ such that $x \in [p_k - \alpha_k, p_k + \alpha_k]$, $h(x) \in [q_k - \beta_k, q_k + \beta_k]$, and $\alpha_k, \beta_k \leq \zeta$. By σ we denote such a presentation, and by $\sigma[n]$ we denote the σ's initial segment of length n.*

Definition 8. *An inductive inference machine (IIM) is a procedure that requests inputs from time to time and produces algorithms that compute recursive real-valued functions from time to time. These algorithms produced by the machine while receiving data are called* conjectures.

The notion of a datum and a presentation for a real-valued function is more relaxed than that of rationalized function A_h. We do not require that a datum $\langle \langle p, \alpha \rangle, \langle q, \beta \rangle \rangle$ should satisfy $h([p - \alpha, p + \alpha]) \subseteq [q - \beta, q + \beta]$. Neither has the interval $[p - \alpha, p + \alpha]$ to be wholly contained in the domain S. We now require a graph of h just to intersect each data box at some point.

For an IIM $\mathcal{M}$ and a finite sequence $\sigma[n] = \langle w_1, w_2, \cdots, w_n \rangle$, by $\mathcal{M}(\sigma[n])$ we denote the last conjecture of the IIM $\mathcal{M}$ after requesting data $w_1, w_2, \cdots, w_n$ as inputs. In this paper we assume that $\mathcal{M}(\sigma[n])$ is defined for any n.

Definition 9. *Let σ be a presentation for some function h. An IIM $\mathcal{M}(\sigma[n])$ converges to an algorithm $A_{h'}$, if there exists a number $n_0 \in N$ such that $\mathcal{M}(\sigma[m])$ equals $A_{h'}$ for any $m \geq n_0$.*

A set $\mathcal{T}$ of recursive real-valued functions is said to be recursively enumerable if there is a recursive function Ψ such that the set $\mathcal{T}$ is equal to the set of all functions computed by algorithms $\Psi(1), \Psi(2), \cdots$.

Definition 10. *Let S_0 and S be subsets of R, h_0 be a function from S_0 to R, and h be a function from S to R. The h_0 is a restriction of h (denoted by $h_0 = h|_{S_0}$), if $S_0 \subseteq S$ and $h_0(x) = h(x)$ for any $x \in S_0$. We also say that h is an* extension *of h_0.*

Since we do not distinguish a function from its extensions, we claim the success in learning even when an IIM converges to an extension of the target. A similar technique was used previously in [4].

Let $\varphi_j \in \mathcal{P}$ be a recursive function from N to N, and let h be a stair function of φ_j. We define that $\sigma = \langle 0, \varphi_j(0) \rangle, \langle 1, \varphi_j(1) \rangle, \cdots$. For each $\langle i, \varphi_j(i) \rangle$, we can define a constant function h_i from $(i - \frac{1}{2}, i + \frac{1}{2})$ to $\{\varphi_j(i)\}$. Let $\rho^i = w_1^i, w_2^i, \cdots$ be a presentation of h_i with $w_n^i = \langle \langle i - \frac{1}{2} + \frac{m}{2^k}, \frac{1}{2^k} \rangle, \langle \varphi_j(i), \frac{1}{2^{k+1}} \rangle \rangle$ such that $k, m \in N$, $2^k - k \leq n < 2^{k+1} - (k+1)$ and $m = n + k + 1 - 2^k$. Furthermore let $\rho_h = w_1, w_2, \cdots$ be a presentation of h with $w_n = w_{(s-t)}^t$ such that $s, t \in N$, $\frac{1}{2}s(s-1) \leq n - 1 < \frac{1}{2}s(s+1)$ and $t = \frac{1}{2}s(s+1) - n$. We call ρ_h a *stair presentation* of h.

4 Learning Criteria

An IIM $\mathcal{M}$ succeeds in learning a function h, if the algorithm $\mathcal{A}_{h'}$, to which $\mathcal{M}$ converges, computes an extension h' of h. In this paper we introduce different *criteria of success* to formalize the statement that an IIM $\mathcal{M}$ learns a target function h. Such criteria are *REALEX*, *REALCONS REALSCONS*, *REALFIN* and *REALNUM*. Two of them, *REALEX* and *REALCONS*, are from [2].

Definition 11. *Let h be recursive real-valued function. An IIM $\mathcal{M}$ is said to learn h in the limit (denoted by $h \in REALEX(\mathcal{M})$), if for any presentation σ of h $\mathcal{M}$ converges to an algorithm $\mathcal{A}_{h'}$ that computes an extension of h.*

A class $\mathcal{T}$ of recursive real-valued functions is *REALEX*-inferable, if there is an IIM $\mathcal{M}$ which learns every $h \in \mathcal{T}$ in the limit. By *REALEX* we denote the collection of all *REALEX*-inferable classes $\mathcal{T}$ of recursive real-valued functions.

Consistent inductive inference was first studied by Wiehagen [14] to require that any program produced by an IIM be correct on all the data seen so far. This notion is extended to the case of real-valued functions in [2].

Definition 12. *Let $\mathcal{T}$ be a class of recursive real-valued functions. An IIM $\mathcal{M}$ is said to* consistently infer *$\mathcal{T}$ in the limit, if $h \in REALEX(\mathcal{M})$ and for any conjecture $h_n = \mathcal{M}(\sigma[n])$ and any $\langle \langle p, \alpha \rangle, \langle q, \beta \rangle \rangle \in \sigma[n]$ such that $[p - \alpha, p + \alpha] \subseteq S$, there is an $x \in [p - \alpha, p + \alpha]$ such that $h_n(x) \in [q - 2\beta, q + 2\beta]$.*

A class $\mathcal{T}$ is *REALCONS*-inferable, if there is an IIM $\mathcal{M}$ which consistently infers every function $h \in \mathcal{T}$ in the limit. By *REALCONS* we denote the collection of all *REALCONS*-inferable classes $\mathcal{T}$ of recursive real-valued functions.

We can also formalize the consistency requirement in the sense of Wiehagen [14].

Definition 13. *Let $\mathcal{T}$ be a class of recursive real-valued functions. An IIM $\mathcal{M}$ is said to* strongly consistently infer *$\mathcal{T}$ in the limit, if $h \in REALEX(\mathcal{M})$ and $\sigma[n]$ is a set of data of h_n for any conjecture $h_n = \mathcal{M}(\sigma[n])$.*

A class $\mathcal{T}$ is *REALSCONS*-inferable, if there is an IIM $\mathcal{M}$ which strongly consistently infers every function $h \in \mathcal{T}$ in the limit. By *REALCONS* we denote the collection of all *REALSCONS*-inferable classes $\mathcal{T}$ of recursive real-valued functions.

We recall that an IIM is a procedure that requests inputs from time to time and produces an algorithm that computes recursive real-valued function from time to time. Now we admit that an IIM requests input data from time to time and produces a unique algorithm that computes a recursive real-valued function.

Definition 14. *Let T be a class of recursive real-valued functions. An IIM M is said to* finitely infer T, *if for any $h \in T$ and any presentation σ of h, the IIM M presented σ's data outputs a unique algorithm that computes an extension of h after some finite time.*

A class T is *REALFIN*-inferable, if there is an IIM M which finitely infers every function $h \in T$. By *REALFIN* we denote the collection of all *REALFIN*-inferable classes T of recursive real-valued functions. By *REALNUM*, we denote the collection of all recursively enumerable sets of recursive real-valued functions.

5 A Comparison of Identification Criteria

In this section we compare identification criteria for inductive inference of recursive real-valued functions. It is obvious that $REALSCONS \subseteq REALCONS \subseteq REALEX$.

Theorem 2. $REALCONS \subsetneq REALEX$.

Proof. We show that $REALEX \setminus REALCONS \neq \emptyset$. Let U be the set of all recursive functions h from N to N such that there exists a number $l \in N$ such that $h(l-1) = 0$, $h(l) = j$, $h(n) > 0$ for any $n \geq l$, and $\varphi_j = h$ for a number $j \in N$, and let T be the set of all stair functions of functions in U. Then $T \in REALEX$. Now we show that $T \notin REALCONS$. Assume that there is an IIM M that $REALCONS$-infers T. Let $\sigma = w_1, w_2, \cdots$ be a presentation and w be a datum. By $M(\sigma[n], w)$ we denote the last conjecture of the IIM M requested data $w_1, w_2, \cdots, w_n, w$ as inputs. For each $i \in N$, we define a stair function η_i which satisfies the following conditions:

$$\eta_i(0) = 0,$$
$$\eta_i(1) = i,$$

$$\eta_i(k+1) = \begin{cases} 1 & \text{if } M(\rho_{\eta_i}[\frac{1}{2}k(k+1)]) \neq M(\rho_{\eta_i}[\frac{1}{2}k(k+1)], d_1), \\ 2 & \text{if } M(\rho_{\eta_i}[\frac{1}{2}k(k+1)]) = M(\rho_{\eta_i}[\frac{1}{2}k(k+1)], d_1) \\ & \text{and } M(\rho_{\eta_i}[\frac{1}{2}k(k+1)]) \neq M(\rho_{\eta_i}[\frac{1}{2}k(k+1)], d_2), \end{cases}$$

where $k \in N^+, d_1 = \langle\langle k+1, \frac{1}{2}\rangle, \langle 1, \frac{1}{8}\rangle\rangle$, $d_2 = \langle\langle k+1, \frac{1}{2}\rangle, \langle 2, \frac{1}{8}\rangle\rangle$, and ρ_{η_i} is a stair presentation of η_i. For each $i \in N$, η_i is a recursive real-valued function, because $M(\rho_{\eta_i}[\frac{1}{2}k(k+1)], \langle\langle k+1, \frac{1}{2}\rangle, \langle 1, \frac{1}{8}\rangle\rangle) \neq M(\rho_{\eta_i}[\frac{1}{2}k(k+1)], \langle\langle k+1, \frac{1}{2}\rangle, \langle 2, \frac{1}{8}\rangle\rangle)$ for any $k \in N$. By the recursion theorem, there is a number $t \in N$ such that $\varphi_t = \eta_t$. Thus it holds that $\eta_t \in T$ and the progression $\{M(\rho_{\eta_t}[n])\}_{n \in N}$ does not converge, which is contradiction. Hence $T \notin REALCONS$. $\square$

Theorem 3. $REALSCONS \subsetneq REALCONS$.

Proof. The $\mathcal{P} = \{\varphi_0, \varphi_1, \varphi_2, \cdots\}$ is the set of all partial recursive functions from N to N. Let $\mathcal{R}^{PRIM}$ be the set of all primitive recursive functions from N to $\{0,1\}$, and let z be a function defined by $z(n) = 0$ for any $n \in N$. There is a recursive function a from N to N such that $\mathcal{R}^{PRIM} = \{\varphi_{a(0)}, \varphi_{a(1)}, \varphi_{a(2)}, \cdots\}$. Note that the set $\{i \in N \mid \varphi_{a(i)} = z\}$ is not recursively enumerable.

It is trivial that $REALSCONS \subseteq REALCONS$. Therefore it suffices to show that $REAL\,CONS \setminus REALSCONS \neq \emptyset$. For any $i \in N$, we define a function h_i from $[0,1]$ to R by $h_i(x) = \sum_{n=0}^{\infty} \frac{\varphi_{a(i)}(n)}{n!}$. Since $\sum_{n=0}^{\infty} \frac{\varphi_{a(i)}(n)}{n!}$ is a recursive real number for any $i \in N$, h_i is a recursive real-valued function. Let $\mathcal{T} = \{h_0, h_1, h_2, \cdots\}$. Then $\mathcal{T} \in REALCONS$. Assume that there is an IIM $\mathcal{M}$ which $REALSCONS$-infers $\mathcal{T}$. For any $i \in N$, we define a presentation $\sigma_i = w_1^i, w_2^i, \cdots$ of h_i with $w_n^i = \langle\langle \frac{m}{2^l}, \frac{1}{2^l}\rangle, \langle \sum_{j=0}^{n} \frac{h_i(j)}{j!}, \frac{3}{n!}\rangle\rangle$ such that $k, l, m \in N$, $2^k - k \leq l < 2^{k+1} - k - 1$ and $m = n - 2^k - n + 1$. By $\mathcal{M}(\sigma[n], w)$ we denote the last conjecture of the IIM $\mathcal{M}$ requested data $w_1, w_2, \cdots, w_n, w$ as inputs. Since $\mathcal{M}$ $REALSCONS$-infers $\mathcal{T}$, $h_i(x) = 0$ for any $x \in [0,1]$ iff there is a number $l \in N$ such that $\sum_{j=0}^{n} \frac{h_i(j)}{j!} - \frac{3}{n!} \leq 0 \leq \sum_{j=0}^{n} \frac{h_i(j)}{j!} + \frac{3}{n!}$ for any $n \leq l$ and $\mathcal{M}(\sigma_i[l]) = \mathcal{M}(\sigma_i[l], d)$, where $d = \langle\langle \frac{1}{2}, \frac{1}{2}\rangle, \langle \frac{-1}{2}, \frac{1}{2}\rangle\rangle$. Thus $\{i \in N \mid h_i(x) = 0$ for any $[0,1]\}$ is recursively enumerable. It holds that $h_i(x) = 0$ for any $x \in [0,1]$ iff $\varphi_{a(i)} = z$ for any $i \in N$. Therefore $\{i \in N \mid \varphi_{a(i)} = z\}$ is recursively enumerable, which is contradiction. Hence $\mathcal{T} \notin REALSCONS$. $\qquad\square$

Theorem 4. $REALFIN \subsetneq REALSCONS$.

Proof. It is obvious that $REALFIN \subseteq REALSCONS$. Therefore we just show that $REAL\,FIN \setminus REALSCONS \neq \emptyset$. Let $\mathcal{T}$ be the set of all constant functions from $[0,1]$ to Q. Then $\mathcal{T} \in REASCONS$. Assume that there is an IIM $\mathcal{M}$ which $REALFIN$-infers $\mathcal{T}$. Let $C_r \in \mathcal{T}$ be a target function defined by $C_r(x) = r$, and $w_1, w_2, \cdots$ be a presentation of C_r such that $q_n - \beta_n < r < q_n + \beta_n$, where $w_n = \langle\langle p_n, \alpha_n\rangle, \langle q_n, \beta_n\rangle\rangle$ for any $n \in N$. Since $\mathcal{M}$ $REALFIN$-infers $\mathcal{T}$, $\mathcal{M}$ requested $w_1, w_2, \cdots, w_k$ outputs an algorithm which computes C_r for a $k \in N$. Put $l := \max\{q_1 - \beta_1, \cdots, q_k - \beta_k\}$ and $u := \min\{q_1 + \beta_1, \cdots, q_k + \beta_k\}$. Then $l < r < u$. Since there exists a $j \in Q$ such that $l < j < u$ and $j \neq r$, $w_1, \cdots, w_k$ are data of a constant function C_j. Let $w_1', w_2', \cdots$ be a presentation of C_j such that $w_1 = w_1', \cdots, w_k = w_k'$. Then $\mathcal{M}$ requested $w_1', \cdots, w_k'$ outputs an algorithm which computes C_r, which is contradiction. Hence $\mathcal{T} \notin REALFIN$. Consequently $REALFIN \subsetneq REALSCONS$. $\qquad\square$

Now we recall a result on identification criteria for inductive inference of recursive functions from N to N. Let $\mathcal{R}$ be the set of all recursive functions from N to N. Every recursively enumerable subset of $\mathcal{R}$ is consistently inferable in the limit [14], whereas the following theorem asserts that there exists a recursively enumerable class of recursive real-valued functions which is not $REALEX$-inferable.

Theorem 5. $REALNUM \setminus REALEX \neq \emptyset$.

Proof. The $\mathcal{P} = \{\varphi_0, \varphi_1, \varphi_2, \cdots\}$ is the set of all partial recursive functions from N to N. Let $\mathcal{S}$ be the set of all stair functions of functions in $\mathcal{P}$. It is obvious that $\mathcal{S} \in REALNUM$. Assuming that there is an IIM $\mathcal{M}$ which $REALEX$-infers $\mathcal{S}$.

Let φ_j be a target function in $\mathcal{P}$, and h be the stair function of φ_j. We define that $Image(\varphi_j) = \{\langle n, \varphi_j(n)\rangle \mid n$ is in the domain of $\varphi_j\}$, and we call a sequence $\sigma = \langle x_0, \varphi_j(x_0)\rangle, \langle x_1, \varphi_j(x_1)\rangle, \cdots$ data of φ_j if $\{\langle x_0, \varphi_j(x_0)\rangle, \langle x_1, \varphi_j(x_1)\rangle, \cdots\} = Image(\varphi_j)$. For each $\langle x_i, \varphi_j(x_i)\rangle$ in the domain of φ_j, we can define a constant function h_i from $(x_i - \frac{1}{2}, x_i + \frac{1}{2})$ to $\{\varphi_j(x_i)\}$. Let $\rho^i = w_1^i, w_2^i, \cdots$ be an infinite sequence of data of h_i such that $w_n^i = \langle\langle i - \frac{1}{2} + \frac{m}{2^k}, \frac{1}{2^k}\rangle, \langle\varphi_j(x_i), \frac{1}{2^{k+1}}\rangle\rangle$, where k and m are natural numbers such that $2^k - k \leq n < 2^{k+1} - (k+1)$ and $m = n + k + 1 - 2^k$. Furthermore let $\rho_h = w_1, w_2, \cdots$ be an infinite sequence of data of h such that $w_n = w_{(s-t)}^t$, where s and t are natural numbers such that $\frac{1}{2}s(s-1) \leq n - 1 < \frac{1}{2}s(s+1)$ and $t = \frac{1}{2}s(s+1) - n$. Since ρ^i is a presentation of h_i for any $i \in N$, ρ_h is a presentation of h. Note that we can construct ρ_h for any given σ.

Since IIM $\mathcal{M}$ which $REALEX$-infers $\mathcal{S}$, $\mathcal{M}(\rho_h)$ converges to an algorithm A_h which computes an extension of h. Since h is a stair function of $\varphi_j \in \mathcal{P}$, we can construct a program j which receives $n \in N$ as an input, and works as follows: If an input $n \in N$ is in the domain of φ_j, then j outputs $\varphi_j(n)$ else it never stops. Thus there exists an IIM $\mathcal{M}_0$ that infers every $\varphi_j \in \mathcal{P}$ in the limit, for any input data σ of φ_j, which is contradiction. Hence $REALNUM \setminus REALEX \neq \emptyset$. □

Example 1. For each $i \in N$, we define recursive real-valued functions h_i and $\hat{h}_i$ by

$$h_i(x) = \begin{cases} 1 & \text{if } x \leq 0, \\ 0 & \text{if } x > \frac{1}{2^i}, \end{cases} \qquad \hat{h}_i(x) = \begin{cases} 1 & \text{if } x < 0, \\ 0 & \text{if } x > \frac{1}{2^i}. \end{cases}$$

We also define a recursive real-valued function $\hat{h}$ by

$$\hat{h}(x) = \begin{cases} 1 & \text{if } x < 0, \\ 0 & \text{if } x > 0. \end{cases}$$

Let $\mathcal{T} = \{\hat{h}, h_0, h_1, h_2, \cdots\}$. Then $\mathcal{T} \in REALNUM \setminus REALEX$.

Now let $\hat{\sigma}_i = \hat{w}_1^i, \hat{w}_2^i, \hat{w}_3^i, \cdots$ be a presentation of $\hat{h}_i$ with $\hat{w}_{2j-1}^i = \langle\langle 0, \frac{1}{2^j}\rangle, \langle 1, \frac{1}{2^j}\rangle\rangle$ such that $j \in N^+$. Then $\hat{\sigma}_i$ is also a presentation of h_i for each $i \in N$. Therefore we can construct a presentation $\sigma_i = w_1^i, w_2^i, w_3^i, \cdots$ of h_i for each $i \in N$ as follows:

$$w_j^i = \begin{cases} \hat{w}_j^0 & \text{if } i = 0, \\ w_j^{i-1} & \text{if } i > 0 \text{ and } 1 \leq j \leq n_{i-1}, \\ w_{n_i+k}^{i-1} & \text{if } i > 0 \text{ and } j = n_{i-1} + 2k, \\ \hat{w}_k^i & \text{if } i > 0 \text{ and } j = n_{i-1} + 2k - 1, \end{cases}$$

where $k \in N^+$, and n_i is the least natural number such that $\mathcal{M}(\sigma_i[n]) = \mathcal{M}(\sigma_i[n_i])$ for any $n \geq n_i$. Let $\sigma_* = \lim_{i\to\infty} \sigma_i$. Since σ_i is also a presentation of $\hat{h}_i$ for each $i \in N$, σ_* is a presentation of $\hat{h}$. By the definition of σ_*, the progression $\{\mathcal{M}(\sigma_*[n])\}_{n\in N}$ does not converge. Thus $\mathcal{T} \notin REALEX$. □

Theorem 6. *REALFIN* ∩ *REALNUM* $\neq \emptyset$.

Proof. Let T be the set of all constant function from $[0,1]$ to N. Since T is recursively enumerable, $T \in REALNUM$. For any constant functions $C_i, C_j \in T$, it holds that $|i - j| \geq 1$ iff $i \neq j$. Thus $T \in REALFIN$. Consequently *REALFIN* ∩ *REALNUM* $\neq \emptyset$. □

Theorem 7. *REALFIN* \ *REALNUM* $\neq \emptyset$.

Proof. Let U be the set of all recursive functions h from N to N such that $\varphi_{h(0)} = h$, and let T be the set of all stair functions of functions in U. Then $T \in REALFIN$. Since T is not recursively enumerable, we have that $T \notin REALNUM$. Consequently *REALFIN* \ *REALNUM* $\neq \emptyset$. □

6 Learning Functions on a Fixed Rational Interval

In the previous section we have considered several criteria for learning recursive real-valued functions. In each of the criteria we have not cared about domains of the functions to be learnt. In this section we discuss inferability of recursive real-valued functions on a fixed domain. Hence we can assume that the IIM knows the domain of functions to be learnt. We focus our attention to functions on a rational interval.

Let I be a rational interval, and T be a class of recursive real-valued functions on I. In order to emphasize the I, we say that a class T is $REALEX_I$-inferable, if $T \in REALEX$, and by $REALEX_I$ we denote the collection of all $REALEX_I$-inferable classes T of recursive real-valued functions. Similarly we define $REALCONS_I$, $REALSCONS_I$, $REALFIN_I$ and $REALNUM_I$ to emphasize the interval I. Then we have the same results as in the previous section:

Theorem 8. *Let I be a rational interval. Then*

(1) $REALCONS_I \subseteq REALEX_I$,

(2) $REALSCONS_I \subsetneq REALCONS_I$,

(3) $REALFIN_I \subsetneq REALSCONS_I$,

(4) $REALFIN_I$ \ $REALNUM_I \neq \emptyset$.

Proof. (1) is obvious. (2) We recall T in the proof of Theorem 3. Every $h_i \in T$ is a constant function on the same closed interval $[0,1]$. For any $h_i \in T$, we construct a function $\hat{h}_i$ from I to R by $\hat{h}_i(x) = h_i(0)$. Let $T_0 = \{\hat{h}_i \mid h_i \in T\}$. Then $T_0 \in REALCONS_I$ \ $REALSCONS_I$. Hence $REALSCONS_I \subsetneq REALCONS_I$. (3) Let T be the set of all constant function from I to Q. In the same way as in the proof of Theorem 4, it holds that $T \in REALSCONS_I$ \ $REALFIN_I$. Hence $REALFIN_I \subsetneq REALSCONS_I$. (4) Let $U \subseteq N$ be a not recursively enumerable set, and let T be the set of all constant function from I to U. Then $T \notin REALNUM_I$ and $T \in REALFIN_I$. □

Proposition 2. *Let $I = [0, 1)$. Then $REALCONS_I \subsetneq REALEX_I$.*

Proof. It is obvious that $REALCONS_I \subseteq REALEX_I$. We show that $REALEX_I \setminus REALCONS_I \neq \emptyset$. Let $\mathcal{T}$ be the set of all recursive real-valued functions η_j from $[0, 1)$ to R defined by $\eta_j(x) = 2^{i+1}(1 - \frac{1}{2^{i+1}} - x)h(i) + 2^{i+1}(x - 1 + \frac{1}{2^i})h(i + 1)$ if $x \in [1 - \frac{1}{2^i}, 1 - \frac{1}{2^{i+1}})$, where h is a recursive function from N to N such that there exists a number $l \in N$ such that $h(l - 1) = 0$, $h(l) = j$ and $h(n) > 0$ for any $n \geq l$, $\varphi_j = h$ for a number $j \in N$. Then $\mathcal{T} \in REALEX_I$. Assume that there is an IIM $\mathcal{M}$ that $RIALCONS_I$-infers $\mathcal{T}$. Let $\eta \in \mathcal{T}$ be a target function. Since $\eta|_{[1 - \frac{1}{2^i}, 1 - \frac{1}{2^{i+1}})}$ is a recursive real-valued function for each $i \in N$, there exists a presentation $\sigma_i = w_1^i, w_2^i, \cdots$ of $\eta|_{[1 - \frac{1}{2^i}, 1 - \frac{1}{2^{i+1}})}$ such that $w_1^i = \langle\langle 1 - \frac{1}{2^i}, \frac{1}{2^{i+1}}\rangle, \langle \eta(1 - \frac{1}{2^i}), \frac{1}{8}\rangle\rangle$. Let $\sigma_\eta = w_1, w_2, \cdots$ be a presentation of η such that $w_n = w_{(s-t)}^t$, where $s, t \in N$ that $\frac{1}{2}s(s - 1) \leq n - 1 < \frac{1}{2}s(s + 1)$ and $t = \frac{1}{2}s(s + 1) - n$. By $\mathcal{M}(\sigma[n], w)$ we denote the last guess of the IIM $\mathcal{M}$ requested data $w_1, w_2, \cdots, w_n, w$ as inputs. For each $i \in N$, we define a function $\hat{\eta}_i \in \mathcal{T}$ satisfies the following conditions:

$$\hat{\eta}_i(0) \quad = 0,$$

$$\hat{\eta}_i(1) \quad = i,$$

$$\hat{\eta}_i(k + 1) = \begin{cases} 1 & \text{if } M_0(\sigma_{\hat{\eta}_i}[\frac{1}{2}k(k + 1)]) \neq M_0(\sigma_{\hat{\eta}_i}[\frac{1}{2}k(k + 1)], d_1), \\ 2 & \text{if } M_0(\sigma_{\hat{\eta}_i}[\frac{1}{2}k(k + 1)]) = M_0(\sigma_{\hat{\eta}_i}[\frac{1}{2}k(k + 1)], d_1) \\ & \text{and } M_0(\sigma_{\hat{\eta}_i}[\frac{1}{2}k(k + 1)]) \neq M_0(\sigma_{\hat{\eta}_i}[\frac{1}{2}k(k + 1)], d_2), \end{cases}$$

where $k \in N^+$, $d_1 = \langle\langle k + 1, \frac{1}{2}\rangle, \langle 1, \frac{1}{4}\rangle\rangle$, and $d_2 = \langle\langle k + 1, \frac{1}{2}\rangle, \langle 2, \frac{1}{4}\rangle\rangle$. For each $i \in N$, $\hat{\eta}_i$ is a recursive real valued function, because of $\mathcal{M}_0(\sigma_{\hat{\eta}_i}[\frac{1}{2}k(k + 1)], \langle\langle k + 1, \frac{1}{2}\rangle, \langle 1, \frac{1}{4}\rangle\rangle) \neq M_0(\sigma_{\hat{\eta}_i}[\frac{1}{2}k(k + 1)], \langle\langle k + 1, \frac{1}{2}\rangle, \langle 2, \frac{1}{4}\rangle\rangle)$ for any $k \in N$. By the recursion theorem, there is a number $a \in N$ such that $\varphi_a = \hat{\eta}_a$. Thus it holds that $\hat{\eta}_a \in \mathcal{T}$ and the progression $\{M_0(\sigma_{\hat{\eta}_a}[n])\}_{n \in N}$ does not converge, which is contradiction. Hence $\mathcal{T} \notin RIALCONS$. $\qquad\square$

The following theorem asserts that every recursively enumerable class of recursive real-valued functions is $REALCONS_I$-inferable, which is an interesting contrast to the result in Theorem 5.

Theorem 9. *$REALNUM_I \subsetneq REALCONS_I$ for every rational interval I.*

Proof. Let $\mathcal{T}$ be a recursively enumerable set of recursive real-valued functions on a fixed closed or open rational interval I. According to [2, 9], $\mathcal{T} \in REALCONS$. Similarly we have $\mathcal{T} \in REALCONS$, even if I is a half-open rational interval. Thus $REALNUM_I \subseteq REALCONS_I$ for every rational interval I. By Theorem 8, $REALNUM_I \subsetneq REALCONS_I$ for every rational interval I. $\qquad\square$

Theorem 10. *$REALNUM_I \setminus REALSCONS_I \neq \emptyset$ for every rational interval I.*

Proof. We recall $\mathcal{T}$ in the proof of Theorem 3. Every $h \in \mathcal{T}$ is a constant function from $[0, 1]$ to R. For any $h \in \mathcal{T}$, we construct a function h_0 from

I to R by $h_0(x) = h(0)$. Let $\mathcal{T}_0 = \{h_0 \mid h \in \mathcal{T}\}$. Then $\mathcal{T}_0 \in REALNUM_I$ and $\mathcal{T}_0 \in REALSCONS_I$. Hence $REALNUM_I \setminus REALSCONS_I \neq \emptyset$ for every rational interval I. $\qquad\square$

If the IIM knows that the domain of the target function is a closed rational interval, $REALEX$-inferability coincides with $REALCONS$-inferability, which is again an interesting contrast to the result in Proposition 2.

Theorem 11. $REALCONS_I = REALEX_I$ *for every closed rational interval I.*

Proof. Let $I = [p - \alpha, p + \alpha]$ be a closed rational interval, where $\langle p, \alpha \rangle \in Q \times Q^+$. By Theorem 8 $REALCONS_I \subseteq REALEX_I$. We show that $REALEX_I \subseteq REALCONS_I$. Let $\mathcal{T} \in REALEX_I$. Then there is an IIM $\mathcal{M}$ which $REALEX_I$-infers $\mathcal{T}$. For any $h \in \mathcal{T}$ and any presentation $\sigma = w_1, w_2, \cdots$ of h, there is an $l \in N$ such that $\mathcal{M}(\sigma[n]) = \mathcal{M}(\sigma[l])$ for any $n \geq l$, and $\mathcal{M}(\sigma[l])$ is an algorithm which computes h. Let h_n be a function the algorithm $\mathcal{M}(\sigma[n])$ computes for each $n \in N$, and let $\mathcal{A}_{h_n} = \mathcal{M}(\sigma[n])$. Then there exists a $k \in N$ such that h_n is defined on I for any $n \geq k$, that is, $I \subseteq \bigcup_{\langle a, \gamma \rangle \in D_\delta^n} [a - \gamma, a + \gamma]$ for any $n \geq k$, where D_δ^n is the n-th division set of I w.r.t. $\mathcal{A}_{h_n}$ and $\delta > 0$ defined as follows:

$$A^n = \{a \ : \ a = p + \alpha \tfrac{k}{2^n} \ \text{ for some integer } k, \ -2^n \leq k \leq 2^n\},$$
$$B^n = \{\langle a, \gamma \rangle \in Q \times Q^+ \ : \ a \in A^n, \gamma = \tfrac{\alpha}{2^n}, \text{ and }$$
$$\mathcal{A}_{h_n}(\langle a, \gamma \rangle) \text{ halts in at most } n \text{ steps}\},$$
$$D_\delta^n = \{\langle a, \gamma \rangle \in \textstyle\bigcup_{i=0}^n B^i \ : \ \mathcal{A}_{h_n}(\langle a, \gamma \rangle) = \langle b, \beta \rangle \text{ and } \beta < \tfrac{\delta}{2}\}.$$

Therefore we can determine whether there is an x such that $h_n(x) \in [q - 2\beta, q + 2\beta]$, for each datum $\langle \langle p, \alpha \rangle, \langle q, \beta \rangle \rangle \in \sigma[n]$ with $[p - \alpha, p + \alpha] \subseteq I$. Thus we can construct an IIM $\mathcal{M}_0$ which $REALCONS$-infers $\mathcal{T}$ as follows:

```
IIM: M₀
begin
   n := 1;  D := ∅;  δ := 1;
   repeat
      read wₙ and D := D ∪ {wₙ};
      let D_δ^n be the n-th division set of I w.r.t. M(σ[n]) and δ;
      if I ⊆ ∪_{⟨a,γ⟩∈D_δ^n} [a − γ, a + γ] and
         there exists an x such that hₙ(x) ∈ [q − 2β, q + 2β],
               for each datum ⟨⟨p, α⟩, ⟨q, β⟩⟩ ∈ D with [p − α, p + α] ⊆ I
            then output M(σ[n]) else output linear(D);
      n := n + 1
   forever
end,
```

where $linear(D)$ is an algorithm which computes a function h such that D is a finite set of data of h. Hence $REALEX_I \subseteq REALCONS_I$. Consequently, for every closed rational interval I, $REALCONS_I = REALEX_I$. $\qquad\square$

7 Conclusions

In this paper we have considered learning recursive real-valued functions from data. We have shown that $REALCONS \subsetneq REALEX$ and $REALNUM \setminus REALEX \neq \emptyset$. We have also discussed the relationship between different criteria based on whether the inference machine knows the domains of functions to be learnt. More exactly we have shown that if the functions are defined on a fixed rational open or half-open interval, it holds that $REALCONS \subsetneq REALEX$ and $REALNUM \subsetneq REALCONS$, and if they are defined on a fixed rational closed interval, it holds that $REALCONS = REALEX$.

References

1. G. Alefeld and J. Herzberger. *Introduction to Interval Computations.* Academic Press, London, England, 1983.
2. K. Apsītis, S. Arikawa, R. Freivalds, E. Hirowatari, and C. H. Smith. Inductive inference of real functions. (to appear in TCS).
3. K. Apsītis, R. Freivalds, and C. H. Smith. On the inductive inference of real valued functions. In *Proceedings of the Eighth Annual Conference on Computational Learning Theory*, pp. 170–177, 1995.
4. L. Blum and M. Blum. Toward a mathematical theory of inductive inference. *Information and Control*, Vol. 28, pp. 125–155, 1975.
5. E.M. Gold. Language identification in the limit. *Information and Control*, Vol. 10, pp. 447–474, 1967.
6. A. Grzegorczyk. Computable functionals. *Fundamenta Mathematicae*, Vol. 42, pp. 168–202, 1955.
7. A. Grzegorczyk. On the definitions of computable real continuous functions. *Fundamenta Mathematicae*, Vol. 44, pp. 61–71, 1957.
8. D. Haussler. Decision theoretic generalizations of the PAC model for neural net and other learning applications. *Information and Computation*, Vol. 100, pp. 78–150, 1992.
9. E. Hirowatari and S. Arikawa. Inferability of recursive real-valued functions. In *Proceedings of International Workshop on Algorithmic Learning Theory*, (*Lecture Notes in Artificial Intelligence 1316 Springer-Verlag*), pp. 18–31. Springer-Verlag, 1997.
10. K. Ko. *Complexity Theory of Real Functions.* Birkhäuser, 1991.
11. R.E. Moore. *Interval Analysis.* Prentice-Hall, 1966.
12. A. Mostowski. On computable sequences. *Fundamenta Mathematicae*, Vol. 44, pp. 37–51, 1957.
13. M. B. Pour-El and J.I. Richards. *Computability in Analysis and Physics.* Springer-Verlag, 1988.
14. R. Wiehagen. Limes-erkennung rekursiver Funktionen durch spezielle Strategien. *Elektronische Informationsverarbeitung und Kybernetik*, Vol. 12, pp. 93–99, 1976.

Predictive Learning Models for Concept Drift

John Case[1], Sanjay Jain[2], Susanne Kaufmann[3],
Arun Sharma[4] and Frank Stephan[5]

[1] Department of Computer and Information Sciences, University of Delaware,
101A Smith Hall, Newark, DE 19716-2586, USA, case@cis.udel.edu
[2] Department of Information Systems and Computer Science, National University of
Singapore, Singapore 119260, Republic of Singapore, sanjay@iscs.nus.edu.sg
[3] Institut für Logik, Komplexität und Deduktionssysteme, Universität Karlsruhe,
76128 Karlsruhe, Germany, EU, kaufmann@ira.uka.de
[4] School of Computer Science and Engineering, University of New South Wales,
Sydney, NSW 2052, Australia, arun@cse.unsw.edu.au
[5] Mathematisches Institut, Universität Heidelberg, Im Neuenheimer Feld 294,
69120 Heidelberg, Germany, EU, fstephan@math.uni-heidelberg.de

Abstract. *Concept drift* means that the concept about which data is
obtained may shift from time to time, each time after some minimum permanence. Except for this minimum permanence, the concept shifts may
not have to satisfy any further requirements and may occur infinitely
often. Within this work is studied to what extent it is still possible to
predict or learn values for a data sequence produced by drifting concepts.
Various ways to measure the quality of such predictions, including martingale betting strategies and density and frequency of correctness, are
introduced and compared with one another. For each of these measures
of prediction quality, for some interesting concrete classes, usefully established are (nearly) optimal bounds on permanence for attaining learnability. The concrete classes, from which the drifting concepts are selected,
include regular languages accepted by finite automata of bounded size,
polynomials of bounded degree, and exponentially growing sequences defined by recurrence relations of bounded size. Some important, restricted
cases of drifts are also studied, e.g., the case where the intervals of permanence are computable. In the case where the concepts shift only among
finitely many possibilities from certain infinite, arguably practical classes,
the learning algorithms can be considerably improved.

1 Introduction

In many machine learning situations, the concepts to be learned or the concepts
auxiliarily useful to learn may drift with time [2, 3, 5, 6, 8, 16]. As in the just
previous references, to sufficiently track drifting concepts to permit learning
something of them at all, it is necessary to consider some restrictions on the
nature of the drift. For example, Helmbold and Long [8] bound the probability
of disagreement between subsequent concepts. Blum and Chalasani [3] place
some constraints on how many different concepts may be used, or the frequency
of concept switches. Bartlett, Ben-David and Kulkarni [2] consider 'class of legal

function sequences' based on some constraints (such as being formed from a walk on a directed graph).

Most of the above work was in a setting similar to PAC learning. Our work addresses drift in a more general computability setting. In the present paper we consider some pleasantly modest restrictions on the rate with which one concept changes into another, model concepts as functions and employ as our principal learning vehicle (computable) martingale betting strategies [9, 14].

$\mathcal{N}$ denotes the set of natural numbers $\{0, 1, 2, \ldots\}$. Functions (as concepts) considered in this paper have domain $\mathcal{N}$ or, in some special cases, the set of binary strings $\{0, 1\}^*$ which is identified with $\mathcal{N}$ in a standard way. The range of the functions is normally $\mathcal{N}$, but it is sometimes $\{0, 1\}$ (in the case of computable languages represented as characteristic functions)[6] or the set of integers $\mathcal{I}$ or rationals $\mathcal{Q}$ (in the cases of some concrete examples).

It is not possible to predict the next values of a rapidly shifting concept if, in each time step, the concept changes without restriction. For example, a drift which randomly vacillates between the constantly 0 function and the constantly 1 function can produce as a data sequence any $\{0, 1\}$-valued function, and, hence, the class of such data sequences cannot be usefully predicted.

Therefore, given a class $\mathcal{S}$ of functions, the learning tasks we consider involve data sequences for segments of members of $\mathcal{S}$ where these segments do not change from one member of $\mathcal{S}$ to another too often. We require that any concept/function from such an $\mathcal{S}$ in a drifting data sequence be present for some minimal number of successive data points. We call a function p computing this minimal number the *permanence*. The class of data sequences with segments from members of $\mathcal{S}$ with each segment required to be present with permanence p is called $\mathcal{S}[p]$. The formal definition follows immediately.

Definition 1. Let $\mathcal{S}$ be a class of computable functions. A function f is said to be *obtained from $\mathcal{S}$ by concept drift with permanence p* if and only if, for each x, there is an interval I_x containing x and a function $g_x \in \mathcal{S}$ such that $|I_x| \geq p(\min(I_x))$ and $f(y) = g_x(y)$, for all $y \in I_x$. $\mathcal{S}[p]$ denotes the class of all such functions f.

We only consider permanence p such that p is non-decreasing and $\{1, 2, 3, \ldots\}$-valued function. We always assume such restriction on p without explicitly saying so.

Learning deals normally not with a single concept but with a class of concepts. Therefore it is necessary to define when a class of objects is learnable under a given criterion. As we see in the immediately following definition, learnability of a class is defined in terms of learnability of the single objects in it.

Definition 2. A class $\mathcal{S}$ of functions can be *learned under a given criterion with permanence p* if and only if there is a computable and total machine M which succeeds on every function $f \in \mathcal{S}[p]$ under the given criterion.[7]

---

[6] We sometimes call $\{0, 1\}$-valued functions, *binary functions.*

[7] Here and below "total" means that the machine always has defined output.

So it suffices, then, to define various criteria under which a learner M is said to succeed on a *single* function f. Shortly below we define three such criteria of success.

Learning is normally modeled as a process to identify an underlying global concept which describes the observed behavior. Under concept drift, this underlying global description does not exist or is too complicated. Therefore, the learner can be expected to give local descriptions only. Within this paper, the local behavior is mostly described by just guessing the next value(s).[8] Because of the unpredictable drifts of the concept, it is unavoidable to err infinitely often. So the learning criteria considered, in effect, involve the ratios of successes and failure during the learning process. The learners studied in the sequel are always total and computable devices which give predictions for the values $f(x+1)$ from the data $f(0), f(1), \ldots, f(x)$. The criteria of correctness for such devices differ in how the quantity of correct and incorrect predictions are measured and compared. The next three definitions introduce learning criteria each of which quantify the amount of correct prediction which is required of a successful learner M operating on a function f (normally in $S[p]$).

Definition 3. A learner M *learns* a function f (or *predicts* f) *with frequency a out of b* if and only if, for each x, at least a of the equations

$$f(y+1) = M(f(0)f(1)\ldots f(y))$$

are correct, where y ranges over the b arguments $x, x+1, \ldots, x+b-1$. We refer to such learners as *frequency learners*.

We say that a class is *frequency learnable* if and only if some learner predicts all functions in the class with frequency a out of b, for some a, b, with $1 \le a \le b$.

The requirement that, for each interval of length b, at least a of the predictions are correct is quite restrictive. This could be alleviated somewhat by aiming for a particular ratio between a and b in a limiting sense instead of requiring it for each interval. In other words, the set X of all correct predictions need only be of some *minimum* "density." We employ a notion of density introduced by Tennenbaum [12, §9.5/9-38] in formalizing this approach to frequency learners. Tennenbaum called the limit inferior[9] of the sequence $\frac{1}{x+1} \cdot (A(0) + A(1) + \ldots + A(x))$ the *density* of the set A.[10] Royer [13] introduced the related notion of *uniform density* of a set A to be the limit inferior of the sequence $\min\{\frac{1}{x+1} \cdot (A(y) + A(y+1) + \ldots + A(y+x)) : y \in \mathcal{N}\}$. These notions are incorporated in the next definition.

---

[8] Since we deal almost always with "learning by prediction" we often just write "M learns f" as a short hand notation for "M learns f by predicting values of f" and so on.

[9] The definition of the limit inferior can be found in most advanced calculus text books, for example, [15]. The limit inferior of a sequence $a_0, a_1, \ldots$, is the supremum r of all rational numbers q which are below almost all a_n: $r = \text{supremum}\{q : (\forall^\infty n)\,[q < a_n]\}$

[10] For $A \subseteq \mathcal{N}$, $A(x) = 1$ if $x \in A$ and $A(x) = 0$ if $x \notin A$.

Definition 4. A learner M *learns* a function f (or *predicts* f) *with* (*uniform*) *density* q if and only if the (uniform) density of the set $\{x : M(f(0)f(1)\ldots f(x)) = f(x+1)\}$ is at least q. We refer to such learners as (*uniform*) *density learners*.

It may be argued that in the criteria introduced so far, the learner is unnecessarily penalized by being required to make a prediction at all times. The learner is not allowed to use any knowledge about the times when predictions are easy and when they are difficult. The learner may be bogged down by difficult predictions even if it has some restricted knowledge which is enough to correctly predict the majority of values. A well-known setting that models such a case is the world of gambling [9]. Here a gambler may decide whether and how much to bet on a certain prediction coming true or whether to pass if it is too difficult to make a prediction with a reasonable chance of success. Such a gambling learner is said to succeed if and only if it can extract enough information about the values of f so that successive betting (predicting) allows it to accumulate arbitrarily large amount of money. The following definition introduces this criterion via martingales.

Definition 5. A *martingale* is a computable function m from strings to positive rational numbers such that, for every σ, there is an a and a q which satisfy

$-\ 0 \le q < m(\sigma);$
$-\ m(\sigma a) = m(\sigma) + q$ and $m(\sigma b) = m(\sigma) - q$, for $b \ne a$.

The martingale m *learns* a function f (or *succeeds on* f or *wins on* f) if and only if the function $x \to m(f(0)f(1)\ldots f(x))$ is not bounded by any constant.

Intuitively, the martingale calculates the accumulated wealth of a player who, for every sequence or string σ, bets an amount of money q that (a number) a will follow σ and receives it in the case of success and loses it otherwise. This definition includes the ability to pass by betting 0 and also the ability to bet arbitrary small amounts of money. That is, there is no smallest unit like a "Cent" which cannot be split into smaller pieces. On the other hand the player cannot (in our definition) go broke by playing at some time his total accumulation at that time. This latter constraint is for expository convenience in the present paper — we avoid having to test for going broke — and our results hold with or without it.

   A martingale wins iff — according to the previous example — the gambler has arbitrary large amounts of money at some suitable time. This analogy becomes more striking by the fact, that the definition of martingale learning is invariant under the following change of definition.

   A martingale m *learns* f iff the limit inferior of $m(f(0)f(1)\ldots f(x))$ is ∞, that is, iff, for all c, for all but finitely many x, $m(f(0)f(1)\ldots f(x)) > c$.

This is interesting since, when successful, the money of the gambler exceeds any given bound c *almost always* and *not only infinitely often*.

Any of the above criteria requires that the learner correctly predicts infinitely often on functions to be learned. One might say that this is an essential precondition for any kind of learning process. Hence we call a learning criterion *reasonable*, if it explicitly as above or at least implicitly requires that the learner M predicts each function to be learned infinitely often correctly. The class of all binary functions is not learnable with respect to a reasonable criterion: if M is a learner then one constructs a binary function f inductively by $f(0) = 0$; $f(x+1) = 1$, if $M(f(0)f(1)\ldots f(x)) \downarrow = 0$, and $f(x+1) = 0$, otherwise. This function f disagrees with every prediction of M. So any criterion which allows to learn the class of all the binary functions is not reasonable. Frequency learning, martingale learning, and learning with a density $q > 0$ are reasonable criteria; learning with density 0 is not reasonable since the requirement for success is void.

In the sequel we proceed as follows.

In Section 2, we compare the relative predictive ability of martingale learners, frequency learners and density learners. We show that frequency learners are the most restrictive, while martingale learners and density learners with low density (below $\frac{1}{2}$) are incomparable generalizations of them.

In Section 3, we analyze the learnability of several interesting concrete concept classes under the various criteria introduced in the present section. Our upper bounds on permanence are also shown to be (nearly) optimal.

We show that, for all $h \in \mathcal{N} - \{0\}$, if constant permanence p satisfies $p > (3h+3)\log(h+3)$ then $\mathcal{S}[p]$ is frequency learnable, where $\mathcal{S}$ is the class of the regular languages over the alphabet $\{0, 1\}$ accepted by finite automata with up to h states.

While polynomials of bounded degree are shown to be learnable with reasonable constant permanence under all our criteria, we show that the natural concept class of pattern languages [1] *with erasing* separates martingale learners from density learners (also from frequency learners and uniform density learners). A martingale learner succeeds on the erasing pattern languages already at the small constant permanence 7.

Fibonacci and other sequences defined by similar recurrence relations grow exponentially, yet we show such classes defined by bounded size of recurrence relations are learnable with reasonable constant permanence under all our criteria.

While Sections 2 and 3 deal with drifts having no restrictions except for permanence bounds, Section 4 is devoted to some natural restrictions on drift like (a) the resulting function has to be computable, (b) the set $\mathcal{N}$ is *computably* partitioned into disjoint intervals $I_0, I_1, \ldots$ such that each I_n has at least $p(\min(I_n))$ elements and each $f \in \mathcal{S}[p]$ presented to the learner agrees on each interval I_n with some function $g_n \in \mathcal{S}$ and (c) the drift vacillates between a finite number of functions in $\mathcal{S}$. In each case, it is shown that there are classes $\mathcal{S}$ and permanences p such that the class $\mathcal{S}[p]'$ consisting of all functions $f \in \mathcal{S}[p]$ satisfying an additional restriction on the drift can be learned with some smaller permanence or sharper learning criterion than the class $\mathcal{S}[p]$. Hence, there are always situations where that restriction on the drift pays off, that is, where knowledge of some regularity within the drift allows construction of *better* learning algorithms.

In the subsequent sections, logarithms are all base 2. Any computability terminology used below and not explained herein may be found in [12]. Due to space limitations, we only give a few sample proofs.

2 Martingale, Frequency and Density Learners

The first result states that everything that can be learned by a frequency learner can also be learned by a martingale learner. The strategy employed by the martingale learner is the well known doubling-algorithm which sometimes ruins gamblers but which nicely works in this case. We omit the proof.

Proposition 6. *Suppose a class, S, of functions (possibly but not necessarily generated by some concept drift) is frequency learnable. Then S can be learned by a martingale.*

The next result investigates the inclusion relation on frequency learning for different parameters. We first introduce some definitions. In the following the natural numbers a, b, c, d always satisfy $1 \leq a \leq b$ and $1 \leq c \leq d$. Let $F_{a,b}(bx + y) = ax$, for $y = 0, 1, \ldots, b - a$, and $F_{a,b}(bx + y) = ax + y$, for $y = -a + 1, \ldots, 0$. Note that, for every natural number d, it is possible to find $x \in \mathcal{N}$, $y \in \mathcal{I}$ with $-a < y \leq b - a$, such that $d = bx + y$. For all a, b and d it holds that $\frac{ad}{b} - a < F_{a,b}(d) \leq \frac{ad}{b}$.

Theorem 7. *Every class learnable with frequency a out of b is also learnable with frequency c out of d if $c \leq F_{a,b}(d)$. If $c > F_{a,b}(d)$, then there exists a class of functions which is learnable with frequency a out of b, but not with frequency c out of d.*

Proof. For the first part, let $c \leq F_{a,b}(d)$ and suppose M predicts S with frequency a out of b. We claim that M also predicts S with frequency c out of d. Let f be an arbitrary function in S. Suppose $d = bx + y$, where $-a < y \leq b - a$. Proof now proceeds based on whether y is positive.

(a): $y \geq 0$. Then $F_{a,b}(d) = ax$. Since M predicts correctly a values of f on every interval of length b, M also predicts correctly ax values of f on every interval of length bx which can be viewed upon as a union of x disjoint intervals. Since $d \geq bx$ it follows that M predicts at least $ax = F_{a,b}(d)$ values correctly on an interval of length d.

(b): $y < 0$. Then $F_{a,b}(d) = ax + y$. For the ease of notation let $z = -y$ and $d = bx - z$, z is positive. Again one knows that M predicts correctly ax values of f on an interval of length bx. From these predictions at most z can be correct on the last z arguments. So M makes at least $F_{a,b}(d) = ax - z$ correct predictions on any interval of length $d = bx - z$.

So in both cases M predicts f correctly on each interval of length d at least $F_{a,b}(d)$ times, in particular at least c times. So M learns f with frequency c out of d.

For the second part of the theorem, consider the class of all primitive recursive functions which take the value 0 on the set $X = \{xb + y : y \in \{0, 1, \ldots, a-1\}\}$. $S[p]$ is then the set of all functions (also the noncomputable ones) which are 0 on the set X. For every learner M, there is a function $f \in S[p]$ which differs from the predicted value on every $z \notin X$. So starting with any input of the form $z = xb + a - 1$, M correctly predicts $f(z+u)$, for $u = 1, 2, \ldots, d$, only if $z + u$ is in X. Thus the number of correct predictions is at most $|X \cap \{xb + a, xb + a + 1, \ldots, xb + a + d - 1\}| = F_{a,b}(d)$. This completes the proof. ∎

Fact 8. *For the notion of predicting with density and uniform density the following results hold.*
(a) If $S[p]$ is learnable with uniform density q, then $S[p]$ is also learnable with density q. On the other hand, there is a class S such that, for every permanence p, $S[p]$ is learnable with density 1 but not with any uniform density $q > 0$.
(b) If $S[p]$ is learnable with frequency a out of b, then $S[p]$ is also learnable with uniform density $\frac{a}{b}$.
(c) Some $S[p]$ is learnable with density $\frac{1}{2}$ but not by any martingale.
(d) If $S[p]$ is learnable with density $q > \frac{1}{2}$, then it is also learnable by a martingale.

Proof. (a): This implication of learning with uniform density towards learning with normal density follows directly from the definition. The separation follows ideas of Royer [13]. Consider the class S of all primitive recursive functions which are 0 on the set $X = \{x : (\exists y)\,[2^y < x < 2^{y+1} - y]\}$. Then $S[p]$ contains all total functions which are 0 on X. So an algorithm which predicts 0 everywhere is correct on X. On the other hand, for any M, there is an $f \in S[p]$ which differs from the predictions on every input outside X. So $S[p]$ can be learned with density 1 (since X has density 1) but not with positive uniform density (since X has the uniform density 0).

(b): Let M be any learner which predicts all $f \in S[p]$ with frequency a out of b. Then, for any interval of length d, M predicts all $f \in S[p]$ with frequency $F_{a,b}(d)$ out of d. Since $F_{a,b}(d) > \frac{ad}{b} - a$, it follows that M learns $S[p]$ with uniform density $\lim_{d \to \infty} \frac{1}{d} \cdot F_{a,b}(d) = \frac{a}{b}$.

(c): Let $p(x) = 2x$. Let S be the class of all primitive recursive $\{0,1\}$-valued functions g which satisfy $\frac{x+1}{2} - 2\log(x) \le g(0) + g(1) + \ldots + g(x) \le \frac{x+1}{2} + 2\log(x)$, for all $x \ge 1$. There is a random function f which also satisfies this relation for all $x \ge 1$ [11]. This f is in $S[p]$, for any permanence p, since every prefix of f is extended by some $g \in S$. On the other hand this sequence is not learnable by a martingale because of its randomness. The proof can now be completed by showing that just predicting 1 gives correctness density $\frac{1}{2}$ or more, details are omitted due to space limitations.

(d): Schnorr [14, Section 10] shows that every binary function not learnable by a martingale satisfies the law of large numbers, that is, the density of 1's converges to $\frac{1}{2}$. Furthermore he showed that if the density of 1's is larger than $\frac{1}{2}$, then some martingale succeeds by always betting a suitable amount of money on 1. Similarly one can argue, for $S[p]$ learnable by M with density $q > 1/2$, that some martingale succeeds on $S[p]$, by betting always a suitable amount of money on the value predicted by M (since these predictions are correct on a set of density $q > \frac{1}{2}$). ∎

The results of Fact 8 have some straightforward extensions: Learnability by martingales can also be obtained if S contains only functions f which are learnable via some fixed machine under some uniform density $q_f > 0$ — or, equivalently, which are learnable under some frequency 1 out of b_f. That means, that it is more important that all functions in the given class are learnable by the same learner than that they are learnable with respect to the same parameters. The other way, to fix the parameter but not the machine, does not help since every computable function is predictable with frequency 1 out of 1 — by its own program — but the class of all computable functions is not learnable by a martingale [14].

3 Concrete Classes

In this section optimal and nearly optimal bounds are derived for the permanence necessary and sufficient to learn certain concrete classes under drift.

Suppose S is a class of up to k binary functions. We first investigate for which (constant depending on k) permanence p the class $S[p]$ is frequency learnable.

Looking at the class of all binary functions which repeat with period $\lfloor \log(k) \rfloor$ one sees directly that the condition $p > \log(k)$ is *necessary* — otherwise the class $S[p]$ contains every binary function and is not learnable under every reasonable criterion. On the other hand, there is an upper bound that is only a bit above this lower bound. The problem which gives an upper bound slightly larger than the expected value $\lfloor \log(k) + 1 \rfloor$, is that one does not explicitly know the intervals on which f coincides with some g from the concept class. So the learner intuitively has to assume that these intervals may be chosen by an adversary. The implicit bound on p in the next theorem could also be made a bit more explicit by taking stronger sufficient conditions such as $p \geq \log(k) + 2 \log \log(k+1) + 10$ or $p \geq \log(k) + \log \log(k+1) + 2 \log \log \log(k+3) + 10$.

Theorem 9. *Suppose S contains up to k computable $\{0, 1\}$-valued functions and nothing else. Then $S[p]$ is frequency learnable if $p - \log(p) > \log(k)$.*

Proof. Fix k and corresponding p. Since all functions in S are computable and permanence is constant, it is possible to compute on any interval $x + 1, x + 2, \ldots, x + b$, the finite set F_x of all possible value-vectors $(f(x + 1), f(x + 2), \ldots, f(x + b))$, where f ranges over $S[p]$. Whenever there is a constant b such that $|F_x| < 2^b$, for all x, then one can predict one of the values in the given interval by the well-known halving algorithm. By restarting this process after any successful prediction one can show that $S[p]$ is predictable with frequency 1 out of b. So it remains to find such a b.

Let $b = 2p - 1$. Any interval I' of length b contains a subinterval I of length p on which f equals some $g \in S$. Now f on I' can be described by the starting point of I, which is among the first p positions of the interval, the index of the function $g \in S$ which coincides with f on I, and $p - 1$ binary bits to represent the remaining values of f. Thus, there are $k \cdot p \cdot 2^{p-1}$ possibilities which f can take on the interval I'. Since $\log(k) < p - \log(p)$, we have $\log(k) + \log(p) < p$, $k \cdot p < 2^p$ and $k \cdot p \cdot 2^{p-1} < 2^b$ which is the desired combinatorial condition. ∎

As an application of this theorem, the class of all regular languages accepted by some deterministic finite automaton having at most h states, can be learned in the presence of concept drift with *constant* permanence (where, of course, the constant depends on h). We omit the details.

Example 10. *Suppose S is the class of the regular languages over the alphabet $\{0, 1\}$ accepted by deterministic finite automata with up to h states. Then, $S[p]$ is frequency learnable, if $p - \log(p) > 3h \log(h + 1)$.[11] For $p \leq h$, $S[p]$ is not learnable under any reasonable learning criterion, since $S[p]$ is the class of all the binary functions. We omit the proof.*

Finding the best permanence often requires considerable combinatorics. Some classes, such as polynomials, are easier to handle where a full solution of the possible learning frequencies in dependence of the allowed degree and permanence is possible. The proof of Theorem 11 (c) furthermore gives the more general result that a class, which contains a function extending every function with finite domain, is not learnable under concept drift. The same principle holds if only the binary functions with finite domain are extended. Thus, one can obtain another proof for the second statement in the previous example.

Theorem 11. *Let k be a natural number and S be the class of all polynomials of degree up to k.*
(a) $S[k + 1]$ contains every function and thus S cannot be learned with permanence $k + 1$ under any reasonable learning criterion.
(b) If $h > k + 1$, then $S[h]$ is learnable with frequency a out of b iff $a \leq F_{h-k-1,h}(b)$.
(c) Let S be the class of all polynomials. Then, for every permanence p, the class $S[p]$ contains all total functions and thus is not learnable under any reasonable criterion.

Proof. (a): Let $I_n = \{n(k + 1), n(k + 1) + 1, \ldots, n(k + 1) + k\}$; the intervals I_0, I_1, ... form a partition of $\mathcal{N}$ and each interval contains exactly $k + 1$ elements. Given any function f, one can find for each n a polynomial g_n of degree up to k which is equal to f on I_n. Thus,

$$(\forall f)\,(\forall n)\,(\exists g_n \in S)\,(\forall x \in I_n)\,[g_n(x) = f(x)]$$

and $S[k + 1]$ contains all the total functions.

(b): For the positive result, with $a \leq F_{h-k-1,h}(b)$, it is sufficient to show that S can be frequency learned with frequency $h - k - 1$ out of h. The learner M

---

[11] For example, $p - \log(p) > 3h \log(h + 1)$ holds if $p \geq (3h + 3) \log(h + 3)$.

predicts 0 for $f(0), f(1), \ldots, f(k)$ and M predicts $g_x(x+k+1)$ for $f(x+k+1)$, where g_x is the polynomial of least degree which coincides with f on $f(x)$, $f(x+1), \ldots, f(x+k)$. Let $I = \{y, y+1, \ldots, y+h-1\}$ be an interval of length h and assume that $y+u$ is the first place where the prediction algorithm makes an error. $y+u$ must belong to some interval J of length h on which f coincides with some polynomial g of degree up to k. Since M errs, u must be among the first $k+1$ elements of J. So M makes at least $h-k-1$ correct predictions on the input $y+u, y+u+1, \ldots, y+u+h-1$. Since M makes in total $u+h-k-1$ correct predictions on the interval $\{y, y+1, \ldots, y+u+h-1\}$, it follows that M makes at least $h-k-1$ correct predictions on the interval $\{y, y+1, \ldots, y+h-1\}$.

Now consider the converse direction. Given any learner M, one can use the intervals $I_n = \{hn, hn+1, \ldots, hn+h-1\}$ and find, for each n, a polynomial g_n of degree not above k, such that $g_n(hn+u) = M(f(0)f(1) \ldots f(hn+u-1))+1$, for $u = 0, 1, \ldots, k$. Let $f = g_n$ on I_n. This inductive procedure gives a function f such that M fails to predict $f(x)$ correctly, whenever x is in $\{0, 1, \ldots, k\}$ modulo h. It follows that, if M learns f with frequency a out of b, then $a \leq F_{h-k-1,h}(b)$ must hold.

(c): This is similar to case (a). The growing permanence is compensated by the absence of any degree bound. Choosing a partition $I_0, I_1, \ldots$ of $\mathcal{N}$, respecting the permanence, one can find, for each function f and each natural number n, a polynomial g_n, which agrees with f on I_n. Thus, $\mathcal{S}[p]$ contains every total function. ∎

The values of polynomials can be computed from the preceding ones. So a linear function satisfies the equation $f(x+2) = 2f(x+1)-f(x)$ and a quadratic function satisfies $f(x+3) = 3f(x+2) - 3f(x+1) + f(x)$. The functions satisfying such equations are a natural generalization of polynomials. The Fibonacci numbers, given by $f(x+2) = f(x)+f(x+1)$, and the powers of 2, given by $f(x+1) = 2f(x)$, cannot be represented by polynomials and demonstrate that the generalization is proper. In the case of polynomials, it was necessary to bound the degree in order to achieve learnability. For the generalization, this bound is given by the number of terms on the right-hand side of the recurrence relation (1). We omit the details.

Example 12. *Let $\mathcal{S}$ be the class of functions defined by a finite recurrence relation*

$$f(x+k+1) = a_0 f(x) + a_1 f(x+1) + \ldots + a_k f(x+k), \tag{1}$$

where the values $f(0), f(1), \ldots, f(k)$ can be chosen arbitrarily. This class $\mathcal{S}$ is frequency learnable with permanence $2k+3$ but not with permanence $k+2$.

It is quite natural to ask whether the lower bound can be lifted to $2k+2$. The following example illustrates that a lower bound $2k+2$ would need some nontrivial properties of the space of the values which perhaps are present in the field $\mathcal{Q}$ and in the ring $\mathcal{I}$ of the integers but which are certainly not present in the Boolean field $\{0, 1\}$. Again, we omit the details.

Example 13. *Let S be the class of functions defined by a finite recurrence relation*

$$g(x + k + 1) = a_0 g(x) + a_1 g(x + 1) + \ldots + a_k g(x + k),$$

over the Boolean field $\{0, 1\}$ where the multiplication is the "Boolean and", the addition is the "Boolean exclusive or" and the values $g(0), g(1), \ldots, g(k)$ can be chosen arbitrarily. This class S is frequency learnable with permanence $2k + 2$.

The pattern languages [1] are a prominent and natural language class. We consider a known natural extension with the aim of showing that some natural class S separates the ability to learn by a martingale from that to learn by a frequency learner.

Let each Boolean string σ be identified with the number x such that 1σ is the dual code for $x + 1$; so 00 is identified with 3 and 111 is identified with 14. A pattern is a schema consisting of variables and constants. It generates the language of all words which can be obtained by replacing each variable by a fixed binary string. A pattern language [1] is called *erasing* if the variables in the defining pattern may be replaced by the empty string. So the pattern $0x1xy$ generates words like 01, 010, 011, 0010, 00100, 00101 and so on, but it does not generate the words 0000 and 11111 since the constants 0 and 1 cannot be removed. The proof is quite detailed and is omitted due to lack of space.

Example 14. *If S is the class of all erasing pattern languages then $S[7]$ can be learned by a martingale but $S[p]$ is not frequency learnable even for very fast growing permanences. For constant permanence it is also impossible to learn $S[p]$ with some density $q > 0$.*

4 Restrictions on Drift

The previous section dealt with arbitrary drift and therefore the learning algorithms intuitively had to compensate for drifts produced by an arbitrarily unpleasant adversary. One might argue that nature does not always follow the worst case but is sometimes more pleasant and well behaved. In particular, drifting concepts might follow some rules and laws; the next three sub-sections are devoted to discussing the influence of such rules on the ability to learn under concept drift. So we derive conditions under which the subclass $S[p]' \subseteq S[p]$ of the functions resulting from restricted drift may be (and are) easier to learn. Due to space limitation, we omit proofs of most results in this section.

4.1 Drifts Preserving Computability

Let REC be the set of all computable functions. The present section investigates the case where the drift results in computable functions, that is, where $S[p]' = S[p] \cap \text{REC}$. The results of Sections 2 and 3 carry over to the case where $S[p]'$ is used instead of $S[p]$; provided that in the places where something is "not learnable under any reasonable learning criterion", this statement is weakened to "not learnable under any criterion which does not permit the learnability of all binary recursive functions." That the inclusions in the previous results go through is quite obvious but the noninclusions requires some additional work: instead of taking an arbitrary function for diagonalization one has to construct, for every computable learner, a specific computable function in $S[p]$ on which this learner fails.

Some criteria like learning with a fixed frequency a out of b either succeed on a function f or fail already on some finite prefix of f. So whenever such a learner fails on some f one can abstain from changing the concept after this failure. So, if a given learner fails on some $f \in S[p]$, then it also fails on some computable f from the same class. Thus the question whether $S[p]$ is learnable with frequency a out of b does not depend on the decision whether all or only the computable functions in $S[p]$ have to be learned.

For the other learning criteria it is decidable in the limit whether the learner is successful or not. So one can, for certain problems, compensate early errors by a lot of good predictions. For these criteria it can be an essential difference whether the learner has to cope with the whole class $S[p]$ or only the subclass $S[p]'$ of all computable functions in $S[p]$. In particular the next theorem shows that there are classes where this transition allows a large improvement in learnability.

Theorem 15. *There is a class S such that, for any p, the class $S[p]$ cannot be learned under any reasonable learning criterion, since, for each learner M, there is a function $f \in S[p]$ which is never correctly predicted by M. However, the subclass $S[p]' \subseteq S[p]$ consists only of functions with finite support and is therefore learnable with uniform density 1.*

4.2 Equality on Computable Intervals

The second model limits the drift by requiring *computable* intervals on which the function to be predicted equals some concept in S. (We use $S[p]'$ to denote the drift class formed in this fashion). This allows, for example, a reduction in the upper bound from Theorem 9.

Example 16. *If S contains up to k finite functions and $p > \log(k)$, then the functions in $S[p]$ respecting the computable intervals $I_0, I_1, \ldots$, are frequency learnable by just using the majority vote algorithm on each interval I_n. The frequency is 1 out of $2\lfloor \log(k) \rfloor + 1$.*

One might argue that such an improvement is due only to the ease of finding an algorithm and not to any real difference between the two concepts. The next example shows that there is a class S such that $S'[2]$ is frequency learnable for computable intervals while the general class $S[2]$ is not learnable under any reasonable criterion for arbitrary drift.

Example 17. *Let S be the class of all increasing binary functions, that is, $S = \{0^n 1^\infty : n \in \mathcal{N}\}$. Let $I_0, I_1, \ldots$ be a computable partition of $\mathcal{N}$ such that every* *interval I_n contains at least two elements. Let $S[2]'$ be the class of all functions $f \in S[2]$ which in addition coincide with some $g_n \in S$ on every interval I_n. Now $S[2]'$ is frequency learnable while $S[2]$ itself is not learnable under any reasonable learning criterion since $S[2] = 0 \cdot \{0,1\}^\infty$.*

In the above proof we used disjoint intervals of consistency. The next example shows that disjointness itself (and a little more) can yield advantages in terms of learnability with higher frequencies.

Example 18. *Let S contain all functions which are 0 at all but one argument. Then the subclass $S[2]'$ of all functions $f \in S[2]$ which coincide with functions in S on disjoint intervals of length at least 2 is learnable with frequency 2 out of 5. The whole class $S[2]$ is not learnable with frequency 2 out of 5, though it is learnable with frequency 2 out of 6. The corresponding densities of the best possible learning algorithms are $\frac{1}{2}$ and $\frac{1}{3}$.*

4.3 Vacillating Drift

There are cases where, in principle, a drifting concept might involve any members of some infinite class but, in reality, the drift is only between finitely many of them. In this case, this knowledge can be exploited to achieve real improvements in learnability.

As in the case of computable drift, vacillation cannot be exploited for frequency learners. However an improvement can be observed for other types of learning considered in this paper, that is for martingale learners, learners with some density and learners with uniform density.

It should be noted that such an improvement is possible on many practical classes and not only on some artificially constructed examples as in the case of computable drift. These examples are the class of all polynomials for the case of constant permanence and any uniformly enumerable class for the case of nonconstant permanence.

Example 19. *Let p be constant and $S[p]'$ denote the class of all functions which vacillate between a finite number of polynomials with permanence p. Then $S[p]'$ can be learned with uniform density $\frac{p-1}{p}$.*

Proof. Let $g_0, g_1, \ldots$ be a 1-1 enumeration of all the polynomials. Now the learner M searches on input $f(0)f(1)\ldots f(x)$ for the first k such that $g_k(x) = f(x)$. Then M outputs $g_k(x+1)$ as a prediction for the next value:

$$M(f(0)f(1)\ldots f(x)) = g_{\min\{k:g_k(x)=f(x)\}}(x+1).$$

For the verification of this algorithm, fix $f \in S[p]'$. There is an h such that f vacillates only between the functions $g_0, g_1, \ldots, g_h$. Any two distinct polynomials agree on only finitely many arguments. So there is a y such that all the polynomials $g_0, g_1, \ldots, g_h$ are different at each $x \geq y$.

Now let $x \geq y$ and assume that the prediction for $f(x+1)$ fails. There is a unique $k \leq h$ with $f(x+1) = g_k(x+1)$. By assumption $f(x) \neq g_k(x)$ since the prediction failed. Now f and g_k coincide at an interval of length p containing $x+1$ and not x. Thus the predictions for f at $x+2, x+3, \ldots, x+p$ are correct. Hence, each wrong prediction is followed by at least $p-1$ correct ones. It follows that M, on an interval of length x, makes at most $y + \frac{x}{p}$ mistakes. Thus M learns this f and also all other functions in $\mathcal{S}[p]'$ with uniform density $\frac{p-1}{p}$. ∎

The above algorithm works for the special case of polynomials and there is no directly general equivalent. For example, if $\mathcal{S}$ is the class of all periodic functions, then no learner achieves some minimum density on all functions in $\mathcal{S}[p]'$ for constant permanence p. Hereby a function is periodic if there is a y such that $f(x+y) = f(x)$ for all x. However, in the case of unbounded permanence, that is, in the case that p is not decreasing and not bounded by any constant, it is possible to learn the class $\mathcal{S}[p]'$ with uniform density 1.

Theorem 20. *Let $\mathcal{S} = g_0, g_1, \ldots$ be an effectively enumerable class of total functions and let p be a computable non-decreasing and unbounded permanence. Then the class $\mathcal{S}[p]'$ of all functions in $\mathcal{S}[p]$ which vacillate between finitely many functions in $\mathcal{S}$ can be learned with uniform density 1.*

5 Some Concluding Remarks

Finally, we would like to note that there is a connection between our model and the mistake-bound learning model of Littlestone [10].[12] Consider the setting in which a machine M predicts the values of a function f on a sequence of arguments $x_0, x_1, x_2, \ldots$ as follows: M is given x_0, M predicts the value of f at x_0, M is given $f(x_0)$, M is given x_1, M predicts the value of f at x_1, M is given $f(x_1)$, M is given x_2, and so on. We say that M learns a class $\mathcal{S}$ of functions with mistake-bound c if M predicts, for each sequence $x_0, x_1, x_2, \ldots$ and each function $f \in \mathcal{S}$, the function $i \to f(x_i)$ at all but at most c places correctly. Since this literal restriction of the mistake-bound model is restrictive, we make the model somewhat more interesting by additionally requiring the sequence $x_0, x_1, x_2 \ldots$ to be increasing. An example class of functions learnable with mistake-bound c is $\mathcal{S}_c = \{\text{decreasing } f : f(0) \leq c\}$.

Now the following can be shown to hold: If a class $\mathcal{S}$ is learnable with a mistake-bound of c and if $b \leq p$ for some constant permanence p, then $\mathcal{S}[p]$ is learnable with frequency a out of b where $a = b - 2c - 1$. Furthermore, the class $\mathcal{S}_c[p]$ cannot be learned with frequency $a+1$ out of b, so the bound is tight.

Acknowledgement

We are especially grateful to Matthias Ott for his suggestions and encouragement regarding the present paper. We thank referees for several helpful comments. Arun Sharma was supported in part by Australian Research Council

---

[12] We are grateful to an anonymous referee of COLT for pointing out this connection.

Grants A49600456 and A49803051. Frank Stephan was supported in part by the Deutsche Forschungsgemeinschaft (DFG) grants Am 90/6-2.

References

1. D. Angluin. Finding patterns common to a set of strings. *Journal of Computer and System Sciences*, 21:46–62, 1980.
2. P. Bartlett, S. Ben-David, and S. Kulkarni. Learning changing concepts by exploiting the structure of change. In *Proceedings of the Ninth Annual Conference on Computational Learning Theory, Desenzano del Garda, Italy*. ACM Press, July 1996.
3. A. Blum and P. Chalasani. Learning switching concepts. In *Proceedings of the fifth Annual Workshop on Computational Learning Theory, Pittsburgh, Pennsylvania*, pages 231–242. ACM Press Computer Society Press, 1992.
4. J. Case and C. Smith. Comparison of identification criteria for machine inductive inference. *Theoretical Computer Science*, 25:193–220, 1983.
5. M. Devaney and A. Ram. Dynamically adjusting concepts to accommodate changing contexts. In *Proceedings of the ICML-96 Pre-Conference Workshop on Learning in Context-Sensitive Domains, Bari, Italy*, 1994. Journal submission.
6. Y. Freund and Y. Mansour. Learning under persistent drift. In S. Ben-David, editor, *Proceedings of the Third European Conference on Computational Learning Theory (EuroCOLT'97)*, volume 1208 of *Lecture Notes in Artificial Intelligence*, pages 94–108. Springer-Verlag, Berlin, 1997.
7. M. Fulk and S. Jain. Approximate inference and scientific method. *Information and Computation*, 114(2):179–191, November 1994.
8. D. Helmbold and P. Long. Tracking drifting concepts by minimizing disagreements. *Machine Learning*, 14:27–46, 1994.
9. S. Kaufmann and F. Stephan. Robust learning with infinite additional information. In S. Ben-David, editor, *Proceedings of the Third European Conference on Computational Learning Theory (EuroCOLT'97)*, volume 1208 of *Lecture Notes in Artificial Intelligence*, pages 316–330. Springer-Verlag, Berlin, 1997.
10. N. Littlestone. *Mistake Bounds and Logarithmic Linear-threshold Learning Algorithms*. PhD thesis, University of California, Santa Cruz, 1989.
11. M. Li and P. Vitanyi. *An Introduction to Kolmogorov Complexity and Its Applications*. Springer Verlag, Heidelberg, second edition, 1997.
12. H. Rogers. *Theory of Recursive Functions and Effective Computability*. McGraw Hill, New York, 1967. Reprinted, MIT Press, 1987.
13. J. Royer. Inductive inference of approximations. *Information and Control*, 70:156–178, 1986.
14. C. Schnorr. *Zufälligkeit und Wahrscheinlichkeit*. Lecture Notes in Mathematics. Springer-Verlag, Berlin, 1971.
15. D. Widder. *Advanced Calculus*. Prentice-Hall, NJ, second edition, 1961.
16. S. Wrobel. *Concept Formation and Knowledge Revision*. Kluwer Academic Publishers, 1994.

Learning with Refutation

Sanjay Jain[1]

Department of ISCS
National University of Singapore
Singapore 119260
Email: sanjay@iscs.nus.edu.sg

Abstract. In their pioneering work, Mukouchi and Arikawa modeled a learning situation in which the learner is expected to refute texts which are not representative of $\mathcal{L}$, the class of languages being identified. Lange and Watson extended this model to consider justified refutation in which the learner is expected to refute texts only if it contains a finite sample unrepresentative of the class $\mathcal{L}$. Both the above studies were in the context of indexed families of recursive languages. We extend this study in two directions. Firstly, we consider general classes of recursively enumerable languages. Secondly, we allow the machine to either identify or refute the unrepresentative texts (respectively, texts containing finite unrepresentative samples). We observe some surprising differences between our results and the results obtained for learning indexed families by Lange and Watson.

1 Introduction

Consider the identification of formal languages from positive data. A text for a language is a sequential presentation (in arbitrary oder) of all and only the elements of the language. In a widely studied identification paradigm, called **TxtEx**-identification, a learning machine is fed texts for languages, and, as the machine is receiving the data, it outputs a (possibly infinite) sequence of hypotheses. A learning machine is said to **TxtEx**-identify a language L just in case, when presented with a text for L, the sequence of hypotheses output by the machine converges to a grammar for L (formal definitions of criteria of inference informally presented in this section are given in Sections 2 and 3). A learning machine **TxtEx**-identifies a class, $\mathcal{L}$, of languages if it **TxtEx**-identifies each language in $\mathcal{L}$. This model of identification was introduced by Gold [Gol67] and has since then been explored by several researchers.

For the following, let $\mathcal{L}$ denote a class of languages which we want to identify. The model of identification presented above puts no constraint on the behaviour of the machine on texts for languages not in $\mathcal{L}$. However, we may want a machine to be able to detect that it cannot identify an input text for at least two reasons. Firstly, once a machine detects that it cannot identify an input text, we can use the machine for other useful purposes. Secondly, we may employ another machine to identify the input text, so as to further enhance the class of languages that can be identified. These are very useful considerations in the design of a practical learning system. Further, it is philosophically interesting to study machines which know their limitations.

In their pioneering work, Mukouchi and Arikawa [MA93] modeled such a scenario. They required that in addition to identifying all languages in $\mathcal{L}$, the machine should *refute* texts for languages not in $\mathcal{L}$ (i.e. texts which are "unrepresentative" of $\mathcal{L}$). We refer to this identification criterion as **TxtRef**. Mukouchi and Arikawa showed that **TxtRef** constitutes a serious drawback on the learning capabilities of machines. For example, a machine working as above cannot identify any infinite language.[1] This led Lange and Watson [LW94] (see also [MA95]) to consider justified refutation in which they require a machine to refute a text iff some initial segment of the text is enough to determine that the input text is not for a language in $\mathcal{L}$, i.e., the input text contains a finite sample "unrepresentative" of $\mathcal{L}$. We call this criteria of learning **TxtJRef**. Lange and Watson also considered a modification of justified refutation model (called **TxtJIRef**, for immediate justified refutation) in which the machine is required to refute the input text as soon as the initial segment contains an unrepresentative sample (formal definitions are given in Section 3). For further motivation regarding learning with refutation and its relationship with Popper's Logic for scientific inference, we refer the reader to [MA93] and [LW94]. Jantke [Jan95] and Grieser [Gri96] have studied criteria similar to those studied in this paper for function learning. Ben-David studied refutation model for PAC learning in [BD92].

[MA93] and [LW94] were mainly concerned with learning indexed families of recursive languages, where the hypothesis space is also an indexed family. In this paper, we extend the study in two directions. Firstly, we consider general classes of r.e. languages, and use the class of all computer programs (modeling accepting grammars) as the hypothesis space. Secondly, we allow a learning machine to either identify or refute unrepresentative texts (texts containing finite unrepresentative samples). Note that in the models of learning with refutation considered by [MA93] and [LW94] described above, the machine has to refute all texts which contain samples unrepresentative of $\mathcal{L}$. Thus, a machine which may identify some of these texts is disqualified.[2] For learning general classes of r.e. languages we feel that it is more reasonable to allow a machine to either identify or refute such texts (in most applications identifying an unrepresentative text is not going to be a disadvantage). This motivation has led us to the models described in the present paper. We refer to these criteria by attaching an **E** (for extended) in front of the corresponding criteria considered by [MA93, LW94].

We now highlight some important differences in the structure of results obtained by us, and those in [LW94]. In the context of learning indexed families of

---

[1] A machine working as above, cannot refute a text for any subset of a language it identifies; this along with a result due to Gold [Gol67] (which says that no machine can **TxtEx**-identify an infinite language and all of its finite subsets) shows that no machine can **TxtRef**-identify a class containing an infinite language.

[2] This property and the restriction to indexed families is crucially used in proving some of the results in [LW94].

recursive languages, Lange and Watson (in their model, see also [MA95]) showed that **TxtJIRef = TxtJRef** (i.e. requiring machines to refute as soon as the initial segment becomes unrepresentative of $\mathcal{L}$, is not a restriction). Similar result was also shown by them for learning from informants[3]. We show that requiring immediate refutation is a restriction if we consider general classes of r.e. languages (in both our (extended) and Lange and Watson's models of justified refutation, and for learning from texts as well as informants). We also consider a variation of our model in which "unrepresentative" is with respect to what a machine identifies and not with respect to the class $\mathcal{L}$. In this variation, for learning from texts, (immediate) justified refutation model has the same power as **TxtEx** — a surprising result in the context of results in [LW94] and other results in this paper. However, in the context of learning from informants, even this variation fails to capture the power of **InfEx** (which is a criterion of learning from informants; see Section 2).

We now proceed formally.

2 Preliminaries

The recursion theoretic notions not explained below are from [Rog67]. $N = \{0, 1, 2, \ldots\}$ is the set of all natural numbers, and this paper considers r.e. subsets L of N. All conventions regarding range of variables apply, with or without decorations[4], unless otherwise specified. We let $c, e, i, j, k, l, m, n, p, s, t, u, v, w, x, y, z$, range over N. Symbols $\emptyset, \in, \subseteq, \supseteq, \subset, \supset$ denote empty set, member of, subset, superset, proper subset, and proper superset respectively. Notation $\max(), \min()$, and $\operatorname{card}()$ denote the maximum, minimum, and cardinality of a set respectively, where by convention $\max(\emptyset) = 0$ and $\min(\emptyset) = \infty$. $\langle \cdot, \cdot \rangle$ stands for an arbitrary, one to one, computable encoding of all pairs of natural numbers onto N. Quantifiers $\forall^\infty, \exists^\infty$, and $\exists!$ denote for all but finitely many, there exist infinitely many, and there exists a unique respectively.

$\mathcal{R}$ denotes the set of total recursive functions from N to N. f and g range over total recursive functions. $\mathcal{E}$ denotes the set of all recursively enumerable (r.e.) sets. L ranges over $\mathcal{E}$. $\overline{L}$ denotes the complement of set L (i.e. $\overline{L} = N - L$). χ_L denotes the characteristic function of set L. $L_1 \Delta L_2$ denotes the symmetric difference of L_1 and L_2, i.e., $L_1 \Delta L_2 = (L_1 - L_2) \cup (L_2 - L_1)$. $\mathcal{L}$ ranges over subsets of $\mathcal{E}$. φ denotes a standard acceptable programming system (acceptable numbering) [Rog67]. φ_i denotes the function computed by the i-th program in the programming system φ. We also call i a program or index for φ_i. For a (partial) function η, domain(η) and range(η) respectively denote the domain and range of partial function η. We often write $\eta(x)\downarrow$ ($\eta(x)\uparrow$) to denote that $\eta(x)$ is defined (undefined). W_i denotes the domain of φ_i. W_i is considered as the language enumerated by the i-th program in φ system, and we say that i

---

[3] An informant for a language L is a sequential presentation of the elements of the set $\{(x, 1) \mid x \in L\} \cup \{(x, 0) \mid x \notin L\}$; see formal definition in Section 2.

[4] Decorations are subscripts, superscripts, primes and the like.

is a grammar or index for W_i. Φ denotes a standard Blum complexity measure [Blu67] for the programming system φ. $W_{i,s} = \{x < s \mid \Phi_i(x) < s\}$.

FIN denotes the class of finite languages, $\{L \mid card(L) < \infty\}$. **INIT** denotes the class of initial segments of N, that is $\{\{x \mid x < l\} \mid l \in N\}$. L is called a *single valued total language* iff $(\forall x)(\exists! y)[\langle x, y \rangle \in L]$. **svt** $= \{L \mid L$ is a single valued total language $\}$. If $L \in$ **svt**, then we say that L represents the total function f such that $L = \{\langle x, f(x) \rangle \mid x \in N\}$. **K** denotes the set $\{x \mid \varphi_x(x)\downarrow\}$. Note that **K** is r.e. but $\overline{\textbf{K}}$ is not.

A *text* is a mapping from N to $N \cup \{\#\}$. We let T range over texts. content(T) is defined to be the set of natural numbers in the range of T (i.e. content$(T) =$ range$(T) - \{\#\}$). T is a *text for* L iff content$(T) = L$. That means a text for L is an infinite sequence whose range, except for a possible $\#$, is just L.

An infinite *information sequence or informant* is a mapping from N to $(N \times \{0,1\}) \cup \{\#\}$. We let I range over informants. content(I) is defined to be the set of pairs in the range of I (i.e. content$(I) =$ range$(I) - \{\#\}$). By PosInfo(I) we denote the set $\{x \mid (x,1) \in$ content$(I)\}$. By NegInfo(I) we denote the set $\{x \mid (x,0) \in$ content$(I)\}$. For this paper, we only consider informants I such that PosInfo(I) and NegInfo(I) partition the set of natural numbers.

An *informant for* L is an informant I such that PosInfo$(I) = L$. It is useful to consider canonical information sequence for L. I is a canonical information sequence for L iff $I(x) = (x, \chi_L(x))$. We sometimes abuse notation and refer to the canonical information sequence for L by χ_L.

σ, τ, and γ range over finite initial segments of texts or informants, where the context determines which is meant. We denote the set of finite initial segments of texts by SEG and set of finite initial segments of informants by SEQ. We define content$(\sigma) =$ range$(\sigma) - \{\#\}$ and, for $\sigma \in$ SEQ, PosInfo$(\sigma) = \{x \mid (x,1) \in$ content$(\sigma)\}$, and NegInfo$(\sigma) = \{x \mid (x,0) \in$ content$(\sigma)\}$

We use $\sigma \preceq T$ (respectively, $\sigma \preceq I$, $\sigma \preceq \tau$) to denote that σ is an initial segment of T (respectively, I, τ). $|\sigma|$ denotes the length of σ. $T[n]$ denotes the initial segment of T of length n. Similarly, $I[n]$ denotes the initial segment of I of length n. $\sigma \diamond \tau$ (respectively, $\sigma \diamond T$, $\sigma \diamond I$) denotes the concatenation of σ and τ (respectively, concatenation of σ and T, concatenation of σ and I). We sometimes abuse notation and say $\sigma \diamond w$ to denote the concatenation of σ with the sequence of one element w.

A *learning machine* (also called *inductive inference machine*) **M** is an algorithmic mapping from initial segments of texts (informants) to $(N \cup \{?\})$. We say that **M** converges on T to i, (written: $\mathbf{M}(T)\downarrow = i$) iff, for all but finitely many n, $\mathbf{M}(T[n]) = i$. Convergence on informants is defined similarly.

We now present the basic models of identification from texts and informants.

Definition 1. [Gol67, CL82]

   (a) **M TxtEx**-*identifies text* T iff $(\exists i \mid W_i =$ content$(T))[\mathbf{M}(T)\downarrow = i]$.

   (b) **M TxtEx**-identifies L (written: $L \in$ **TxtEx(M)**) iff **M TxtEx**-identifies each text T for L.

   (c) **M TxtEx**-identifies $\mathcal{L}$ iff **M TxtEx**-identifies each $L \in \mathcal{L}$.

   (d) **TxtEx** $= \{\mathcal{L} \mid (\exists \mathbf{M})[\mathbf{M}$ **TxtEx**-identifies $\mathcal{L}]\}$.

Definition 2. [Gol67]

(a) **M** **TxtFin**-*identifies text* T iff $(\exists i \mid W_i = \text{content}(T))(\exists n)[(\forall m < n)[\mathbf{M}(T[m]) =?] \wedge (\forall m \geq n)[\mathbf{M}(T[m]) = i]]$.

(b) **M** **TxtFin**-identifies L (written: $L \in \mathbf{TxtFin}(\mathbf{M})$) iff **M** **TxtFin**-identifies each text T for L.

(c) **M** **TxtFin**-identifies $\mathcal{L}$ iff **M** **TxtFin**-identifies each $L \in \mathcal{L}$.

(d) **TxtFin** $= \{\mathcal{L} \mid (\exists \mathbf{M})[\mathbf{M} \ \mathbf{TxtFin}\text{-identifies } \mathcal{L}]\}$.

Intuitively, for finite identification, **M** outputs just one grammar, which must be correct.

Definition 3. [Gol67, CL82]

(a) **M** **InfEx**-*identifies informant* I iff $(\exists i \mid W_i = \text{PosInfo}(I))[\mathbf{M}(I)\downarrow = i]$.

(b) **M** **InfEx**-identifies L (written: $L \in \mathbf{InfEx}(\mathbf{M})$) iff **M** **InfEx**-identifies each informant I for L.

(c) **M** **InfEx**-identifies $\mathcal{L}$ iff **M** **InfEx**-identifies each $L \in \mathcal{L}$.

(d) **InfEx** $= \{\mathcal{L} \mid (\exists \mathbf{M})[\mathbf{M} \ \mathbf{InfEx}\text{-identifies } \mathcal{L}]\}$.

Definition 4. [Gol67]

(a) **M** **InfFin**-*identifies informant* I iff $(\exists i \mid W_i = \text{PosInfo}(I))(\exists n)[(\forall m < n)[\mathbf{M}(I[m]) =?] \wedge (\forall m \geq n)[\mathbf{M}(I[m]) = i]]$.

(b) **M** **InfFin**-identifies L (written: $L \in \mathbf{InfFin}(\mathbf{M})$) iff **M** **InfFin**-identifies each informant I for L.

(c) **M** **InfFin**-identifies $\mathcal{L}$ iff **M** **InfFin**-identifies each $L \in \mathcal{L}$.

(d) **InfFin** $= \{\mathcal{L} \mid (\exists \mathbf{M})[\mathbf{M} \ \mathbf{InfFin}\text{-identifies } \mathcal{L}]\}$.

The next two definitions introduce reliable identification. A reliable machine diverges on texts (informants) it does not identify. Though a reliable machine does not refute a text (informant) it does not identify, it at least doesn't give false hope by converging to a wrong hypothesis. This was probably the first constraint imposed on machine's behaviour on languages outside the class being identified. We give two variations of reliable identification based on whether the machine is expected to diverge on every text which is for a language not in $\mathcal{L}$, or just on texts it does not identify.

For the rest of the paper, for criteria of inference, **J**, we will only define what it means for a machine to **J**-identify a class of languages $\mathcal{L}$. The identification class **J** is then implicitly defined as $\mathbf{J} = \{\mathcal{L} \mid (\exists \mathbf{M})[\mathbf{M} \ \mathbf{J}\text{-identifies } \mathcal{L}]\}$.

Definition 5. [Min76]

(a) **M** **TxtRel**-identifies $\mathcal{L}$ iff

(a.1) **M** **TxtEx**-identifies $\mathcal{L}$ and

(a.2) $(\forall T \mid \text{content}(T) \notin \mathcal{L})[\mathbf{M}(T)\uparrow]$.

(b) **M** **InfRel** identifies $\mathcal{L}$ iff

(b.1) **M** **InfEx**-identifies $\mathcal{L}$ and

(b.2) $(\forall I \mid \text{PosInfo}(I) \notin \mathcal{L})[\mathbf{M}(I)\uparrow]$.

(c) **M** **ETxtRel**-identifies $\mathcal{L}$ iff

(c.1) **M** **TxtEx**-identifies $\mathcal{L}$ and

(c.2) $(\forall T \mid$ M does not **TxtEx**-identify $T)[\mathbf{M}(T)\uparrow]$.
(d) **M EInfRel** identifies $\mathcal{L}$ iff
    (d.1) **M InfEx**-identifies $\mathcal{L}$ and
    (d.2) $(\forall I \mid$ M does not **InfEx**-identify $I)[\mathbf{M}(I)\uparrow]$.

The following propositions are some known facts about the identification criteria discussed above, which we will be using in this paper. First two propositions are based on results due to Gold [Gol67].

Proposition 6. *Suppose L is any infinite r.e. language, and* M *a learning machine. Let σ be such that* content$(\sigma) \subseteq L$. *Then there exists an r.e. L',* content(σ) $\subseteq L' \subseteq L$ *such that* M *does not TxtEx-identify L'.*

Proposition 7. *Suppose L is any infinite r.e. language, and* M *a learning machine. Let σ be such that PosInfo$(\sigma) \subseteq L$. Then there exists an r.e. L', PosInfo(σ) $\subseteq L' \subseteq L$ such that* M *does not InfEx-identify L'.*

Proposition 8. *[Gol67, Sha98]* **TxtFin** $\subset$ **InfFin** $\subset$ **TxtEx** $\subset$ **InfEx**.

3 Learning with Refutation

In this section we introduce the refutation models for learning. For learning with refutation we allow learning machines to output a special refutation symbol denoted $\perp$. We assume that if $\mathbf{M}(\sigma) = \perp$, then, for all τ, $\mathbf{M}(\sigma \diamond \tau) = \perp$. Intuitively output of $\perp$ denotes that **M** is declaring the input to be "unrepresentative". In the following definitions we consider the different criteria mentioned in the introduction. It is useful to define $\mathbf{Cons}_{\mathcal{L}} = \{\sigma \mid (\exists L \in \mathcal{L})[\text{content}(\sigma) \subseteq L]\}$.

The following definition introduces learning with refutation for general classes of r.e. languages.

Definition 9. [MA93] **M TxtRef** identifies $\mathcal{L}$ iff
    (a) **M TxtEx**-identifies $\mathcal{L}$ and
    (b) $(\forall T \mid \text{content}(T) \notin \mathcal{L})[\mathbf{M}(T)\downarrow = \perp]$.

If $\mathbf{M}(T)\downarrow = \perp$, then we often say that **M** refutes the text T. The following definitions introduce identification with justified refutation for general classes of r.e. languages. Below **JRef** stands for justified refutation, and **JIRef** stands for justified immediate refutation.

Definition 10. [LW94] **M TxtJRef** identifies $\mathcal{L}$ iff
    (a) **M TxtEx**-identifies $\mathcal{L}$ and
    (b) $(\forall T \mid \text{content}(T) \notin \mathcal{L}$ and $(\exists \sigma \preceq T)[\sigma \notin \mathbf{Cons}_{\mathcal{L}}])[\mathbf{M}(T)\downarrow = \perp]$.

Intuitively, in the above definition, **M** is required to refute a text T only if T contains a finite sample which is unrepresentative of $\mathcal{L}$. Following definition additionally requires that **M** refutes an initial segment of T as soon as it contains an unrepresentative sample.

Definition 11. [LW94] M **TxtJIRef** identifies $\mathcal{L}$ iff
  (a) M **TxtEx**-identifies $\mathcal{L}$ and
  (b) $(\forall T \mid \text{content}(T) \notin \mathcal{L})(\forall \sigma \preceq T \mid \sigma \notin \mathbf{Cons}_\mathcal{L})[\mathbf{M}(\sigma) = \perp]$.

We now present the above criteria for learning from informants. It is useful to define the following analogue of **Cons**. $\mathbf{ICons}_\mathcal{L} = \{\sigma \mid (\exists L \in \mathcal{L})[\text{PosInfo}(\sigma) \subseteq L \wedge \text{NegInfo}(\sigma) \subseteq \overline{L}]\}$.

Definition 12.
(a) [MA93] M **InfRef** identifies $\mathcal{L}$ iff
  (a.1) M **InfEx**-identifies $\mathcal{L}$ and
  (a.2) $(\forall I \mid \text{PosInfo}(I) \notin \mathcal{L})[\mathbf{M}(I){\downarrow} = \perp]$.
(b) [LW94] M **InfJRef** identifies $\mathcal{L}$ iff
  (b.1) M **InfEx**-identifies $\mathcal{L}$ and
  (b.2) $(\forall I \mid \text{PosInfo}(I) \notin \mathcal{L} \text{ and } (\exists \sigma \preceq I)[\sigma \notin \mathbf{ICons}_\mathcal{L}])[\mathbf{M}(I){\downarrow} = \perp]$.
(c) [LW94] M **InfJIRef** identifies $\mathcal{L}$ iff
  (c.1) M **InfEx**-identifies $\mathcal{L}$ and
  (c.2) $(\forall I \mid \text{PosInfo}(I) \notin \mathcal{L})(\forall \sigma \preceq I \mid \sigma \notin \mathbf{ICons}_\mathcal{L})[\mathbf{M}(\sigma) = \perp]$.

We now present our extended definition for learning with refutation. Intuitively, we extend the above definitions of [MA93, LW94] by allowing a machine to identify an unrepresentative text.

The following definition is a modification of the corresponding definition in [MA93]. E in the beginning of criteria of inference, such as **ETxtRef**, stands for extended.

Definition 13. M **ETxtRef** identifies $\mathcal{L}$ iff
  (a) M **TxtEx**-identifies $\mathcal{L}$ and
  (b) $(\forall T \mid \mathbf{M} \text{ does not } \mathbf{TxtEx}\text{-identify } T)[\mathbf{M}(T){\downarrow} = \perp]$.

Intuitively, in the above definition we require the machine to refute the input text, only if it does not **TxtEx**-identify it.

The following definitions on identification by justified refutation are modifications of corresponding definitions considered by [LW94].

Definition 14. M **ETxtJRef** identifies $\mathcal{L}$ iff
  (a) M **TxtEx**-identifies $\mathcal{L}$ and
  (b) $(\forall T \mid \mathbf{M} \text{ does not } \mathbf{TxtEx}\text{-identify } T \text{ and } (\exists \sigma \preceq T) [\sigma \notin \mathbf{Cons}_\mathcal{L}]) [\mathbf{M}(T) = \perp]$.

Intuitively, in the above definition, M is required to refute a text T only if M does not identify T, and T contains a finite sample which is unrepresentative of $\mathcal{L}$. In the following definition, we additionally require that M refute an initial segment of T as soon as it contains an unrepresentative sample.

Definition 15. M **ETxtJIRef** identifies $\mathcal{L}$ iff
  (a) M **TxtEx**-identifies $\mathcal{L}$ and
  (b) $(\forall T \mid \mathbf{M} \text{ does not } \mathbf{TxtEx}\text{-identify } T)(\forall \sigma \preceq T \mid \sigma \notin \mathbf{Cons}_\mathcal{L})[\mathbf{M}(\sigma) = \perp]$.

We now present the above criteria for learning from informants.

Definition 16.
(a) **M EInfRef** identifies $\mathcal{L}$ iff
   (a.1) **M InfEx**-identifies $\mathcal{L}$ and
   (a.2) $(\forall I \mid \mathbf{M} \text{ does not } \mathbf{InfEx}\text{-identify } I)[\mathbf{M}(I)\!\downarrow =\perp]$.
(b) **M EInfJRef** identifies $\mathcal{L}$ iff
   (b.1) **M InfEx**-identifies $\mathcal{L}$ and
   (b.2) $(\forall I \mid \mathbf{M} \text{ does not } \mathbf{InfEx}\text{-identify } I \text{ and } (\exists \sigma \preceq I) \, [\sigma \notin \mathbf{ICons}_{\mathcal{L}}])$
$[\mathbf{M}(I)\!\downarrow =\perp]$.
(c) **M EInfJIRef** identifies $\mathcal{L}$ iff
   (c.1) **M InfEx**-identifies $\mathcal{L}$ and
   (c.2) $(\forall I \mid \mathbf{M} \text{ does not } \mathbf{InfEx}\text{-identify } I)(\forall \sigma \preceq I \mid \sigma \notin \mathbf{ICons}_{\mathcal{L}})[\mathbf{M}(\sigma) =\perp]$.

4 Results

We next consider the relationship between different identification criteria defined in this paper. The results presented give a complete relationship between all the criteria of inference introduced in this paper.

4.1 Containment Results

The following containments follow immediately from the definitions.

Proposition 17. TxtRef $\subseteq$ TxtRel $\subseteq$ TxtEx.
   TxtRef $\subseteq$ TxtJRef $\subseteq$ TxtEx.
   TxtJIRef $\subseteq$ TxtJRef $\subseteq$ TxtEx.
   InfRef $\subseteq$ InfRel $\subseteq$ InfEx.
   InfRef $\subseteq$ InfJRef $\subseteq$ InfEx.
   InfJIRef $\subseteq$ InfJRef $\subseteq$ InfEx.
   TxtRef $\subseteq$ InfRef $\subseteq$ InfEx.
   TxtRel $\subseteq$ InfRel $\subseteq$ InfEx.

Proposition 18. ETxtRef $\subseteq$ ETxtRel $\subseteq$ TxtEx.
   ETxtRef $\subseteq$ ETxtJRef $\subseteq$ TxtEx.
   ETxtJIRef $\subseteq$ ETxtJRef $\subseteq$ TxtEx.
   EInfRef $\subseteq$ EInfRel $\subseteq$ InfEx.
   EInfRef $\subseteq$ EInfJRef $\subseteq$ InfEx.
   EInfJIRef $\subseteq$ EInfJRef $\subseteq$ InfEx.
   ETxtRef $\subseteq$ EInfRef $\subseteq$ InfEx.
   ETxtRel $\subseteq$ EInfRel $\subseteq$ InfEx.

Proposition 19. *(a)* **TxtJIRef** = **ETxtJIRef**.
   (b) **InfJIRef** = **EInfJIRef**.

Proof. (a) It suffices to show **ETxtJIRef $\subseteq$ TxtJIRef**. Suppose **M ETxtJIRef**-identifies $\mathcal{L}$.

Claim 20. For all σ such that $\sigma \notin \mathbf{Cons}_{\mathcal{L}}$, $\mathbf{M}(\sigma) = \perp$.

Proof. (of Claim) Suppose by way of contradiction that there is a σ such that $\sigma \notin \mathbf{Cons}_{\mathcal{L}}$ and $\mathbf{M}(\sigma) \neq \perp$. Let T be an extension of σ such that $\mathbf{M}$ does not **TxtEx**-identify T. Note that by Proposition 6 there exists such a T. But then by definition of **ETxtJIRef**, $\mathbf{M}(\sigma) = \perp$. A contradiction. Thus claim holds. $\square$

It immediately follows from the claim that $\mathbf{M}$ also **TxtJIRef**-identifies $\mathcal{L}$.

Part (b) can be proved in a manner similar to part (a). $\blacksquare$

Theorem 21. *Suppose X is a set not in Σ_2. Let $\mathcal{L} = \{\{i\} \mid i \in X\}$. Suppose $\mathbf{J} \in \{$ **TxtRef, TxtRel, TxtJRef, InfRef, InfRel, InfJRef** $\}$. Then $\mathcal{L} \in \mathbf{EJ}$ but $\mathcal{L} \notin \mathbf{J}$.*

Proof. It is easy to construct a machine which identifies all texts for empty or singleton languages and refutes/diverges on all texts for languages containing at least 2 elements. Thus, we have that $\mathcal{L} \in \mathbf{EJ}$.

Now, suppose by way of contradiction that $\mathbf{M}$ $\mathbf{J}$-identifies $\mathcal{L}$. Then, $i \in X$ iff $(\exists\sigma \mid \text{content}(\sigma) = \{i\})(\forall\tau \mid \sigma \preceq \tau \wedge \text{content}(\tau) = \{i\})[\mathbf{M}(\sigma) = \mathbf{M}(\tau) \wedge \mathbf{M}(\sigma) \in N]$. A contradiction to the fact that X is not in Σ_2. $\blacksquare$

Theorem 22. *Suppose $\mathbf{J} \in \{$ **TxtRef, TxtRel, TxtJRef, InfRef, InfRel, InfJRef** $\}$. Then, $\mathbf{J} \subset \mathbf{EJ}$.*

4.2 Separation Results

We now proceed to show the separation results. The next two theorems show the advantages of finite identification over reliable identification and identification with refutation. For the proof of first theorem, we need the following proposition, which follows immediately from definitions.

Proposition 23. *Suppose $\mathcal{L}$ is such that:*
(a) $\mathcal{L} \in \mathbf{EInfJRef}$, and
(b) For all $L_1, L_2 \in \mathcal{L}$, either $L_1 \cap L_2 = \emptyset$ or $L_1 = L_2$.
Then $\mathcal{L} \in \mathbf{EInfRef}$ (and thus in $\mathbf{EInfRel}$).

Let $\mathbf{M}_0, \mathbf{M}_1, \ldots$, denote a recursive enumeration of all machines.

Theorem 24. $\mathbf{TxtFin} - (\mathbf{EInfRel} \cup \mathbf{EInfJRef}) \neq \emptyset$.

Proof. For each i, we will define below a nonempty language L_i with the following properties:
(a) $L_i \subseteq \{\langle i, n \rangle \mid n \in N\}$;
(b) either $\mathbf{M}_i$ is not reliable, or $L_i \notin \mathbf{InfEx}(\mathbf{M}_i)$.
(c) a grammar for L_i can be obtained effectively in i.

We take $\mathcal{L} = \{L_i \mid i \in N\}$. Clearly, $\mathcal{L} \in \mathbf{TxtFin}$ (since a grammar for L_i can be found effectively from i). Further, (using clause (b) above) we have that $\mathcal{L} \notin \mathbf{EInfRel}$. It thus follows from Proposition 23 that $\mathcal{L} \notin \mathbf{EInfJRef}$.

We will define L_i in stages below. Let L_i^s denote L_i defined before stage s. Let $L_i^0 = \{\langle i, 0 \rangle\}$. Let $x^0 = \langle i, 1 \rangle$. Go to stage 0.

Stage s

1. Suppose, I_1^s is the canonical information sequence for L_i^s and I_2^s is the canonical information sequence for $L_i^s \cup \{x^s\}$.

2. Search for $n > x^s$ such that either $\mathbf{M}_i(I_1^s[n]) \neq \mathbf{M}_i(I_1^s[x^s])$ or $\mathbf{M}_i(I_2^s[n]) \neq \mathbf{M}_i(I_2^s[x^s])$.

   If and when such an n is found proceed to step 3.

3. Let n be as found in step 2. If $\mathbf{M}_i(I_2^s[n]) \neq \mathbf{M}_i(I_2^s[x^s])$, then let $L_i^{s+1} = L_i^s \cup \{x^s\}$; otherwise let $L_i^{s+1} = L_i^s$.

   Let $x^{s+1} \in \{\langle i, z \rangle \mid z \in N\}$ be such that $x^{s+1} > n$.

   Go to stage $s+1$.

End stage s

It is easy to verify that L_i can be enumerated effectively in i. Fix i. We consider two cases in the definition of L_i.

Case 1: There exist infinitely many stages.

In this case $\mathbf{M}_i$ on canonical informant for L_i makes infinitely many mind changes.

Case 2: Stage s starts but does not end.

In this case $\mathbf{M}_i$ converges to the same grammar for both L_i and $L_i \cup \{x^s\}$ (which are distinct languages). Thus $\mathbf{M}_i$ is not reliable.

The above cases show that $\mathcal{L}$ is not **EInfRel**-identified by $\mathbf{M}_i$. ∎

Theorem 25. TxtFin − ETxtJRef ≠ ∅.

The following theorem shows the advantages of identification with refutation over finite identification.

Theorem 26. (TxtRef ∩ TxtJIRef ∩ InfJIRef) − InfFin ≠ ∅.

Proof. Let $\mathcal{L} = \{L \mid \mathrm{card}(L) \leq 2\}$. It is easy to verify that $\mathcal{L}$ witnesses the separation. ∎

The following theorem shows the advantages of justified refutation and reliable identification over the case when the learning machine has to refute all unidentified texts (informants).

Theorem 27. (TxtRel ∩ TxtJIRef ∩ InfJIRef) − InfRef ≠ ∅.

Proof. It is easy to verify that **FIN** witnesses the separation. ∎

The following theorem shows the disadvantages of immediate refutation. Note that for learning indexed families of recursive languages, Lange and Watson have shown that **TxtJRef = TxtJIRef** and **InfJRef = InfJIRef**, and thus the following result does not hold for learning indexed families of recursive languages.

Theorem 28. *(a)* **TxtRef − EInfJIRef ≠ ∅.**
   (b) **TxtRef − ETxtJIRef ≠ ∅.**

Proof. Let $\mathcal{L} = \{\{i\} \mid i \notin \mathbf{K}\}$. It is easy to verify that $\mathcal{L} \in \mathbf{TxtRef}$. We show that $\mathcal{L} \notin \mathbf{ETxtJIRef}$. A similar proof also shows that $\mathcal{L} \notin \mathbf{EInfJIRef}$. Suppose by way of contradiction that $\mathbf{M}$ $\mathbf{ETxtJIRef}$-identifies $\mathcal{L}$. Then the following claim shows that $\overline{\mathbf{K}}$ is r.e., a contradiction. Thus $\mathcal{L} \notin \mathbf{ETxtJIRef}$.

Claim 29. $i \in \overline{\mathbf{K}} \Leftrightarrow (\exists \sigma \mid \mathrm{content}(\sigma) = \{i\})[\mathbf{M}(\sigma){\downarrow} \neq {\perp}]$.

Proof. Suppose $i \in \overline{\mathbf{K}}$. Then, since $\mathbf{M}$ $\mathbf{TxtEx}$-identifies $\{i\} \in \mathcal{L}$, there must exist a σ such that $\mathrm{content}(\sigma) = \{i\}$ and $\mathbf{M}(\sigma){\downarrow} \neq {\perp}$. On the other hand suppose by way of contradiction that $i \notin \overline{\mathbf{K}}$, and σ is such that $\mathrm{content}(\sigma) = \{i\}$ and $\mathbf{M}(\sigma){\downarrow} \neq {\perp}$. Let T be an extension of σ such that $\mathbf{M}$ does not $\mathbf{TxtEx}$-identify T (there exists such a T by Proposition 6). But then, since $\sigma \notin \mathbf{Cons}_{\mathcal{L}}$, by definition of $\mathbf{ETxtJIRef}$, $\mathbf{M}(\sigma)$ must be equal to ${\perp}$; a contradiction. This proves the claim, and completes the proof of the theorem. $\blacksquare$

In the context of learnability of indexed families, Lange and Watson (in their model of learning with refutation) had shown that immediate refutation is not a restriction, i.e. $\mathbf{TxtJRef} = \mathbf{TxtJIRef}$ and $\mathbf{InfJRef} = \mathbf{InfJIRef}$. The following corollary shows that immediate refutation is a restriction in the context of learning general classes of r.e. languages! Note that this restriction holds for both extended and unextended models of justified refutation (for general classes of r.e. languages).

Corollary 30. *(a)* $\mathbf{InfJIRef} \subset \mathbf{InfJRef}$.
 (b) $\mathbf{TxtJIRef} \subset \mathbf{TxtJRef}$.
 (c) $\mathbf{EInfJIRef} \subset \mathbf{EInfJRef}$.
 (d) $\mathbf{ETxtJIRef} \subset \mathbf{ETxtJRef}$.

The following theorem shows the advantages of justified refutation over reliable identification.

Theorem 31. $(\mathbf{TxtJIRef} \cap \mathbf{InfJIRef}) - \mathbf{EInfRel} \neq \emptyset$.

Proof. For $f \in \mathcal{R}$, let $L_f = \{\langle x, y \rangle \mid f(x) = y\}$. Let $\mathcal{L} = \{L_f \mid \varphi_{f(0)} = f\} \cup \{L \mid L \in \mathbf{FIN} \wedge (\exists x, y, z \mid y \neq z)[\langle x, y \rangle \in L \wedge \langle x, z \rangle \in L]\}$. It is easy to verify that $\mathcal{L} \in \mathbf{TxtEx}$ (and thus $\mathbf{InfEx}$). Since, $\mathbf{ICons}_{\mathcal{L}} = \mathbf{SEQ}$, it follows that $\mathcal{L} \in \mathbf{TxtJIRef} \cap \mathbf{InfJIRef}$. Essentially the proof in [CJNM94] to show that $\{f \mid \varphi_{f(0)} = f\}$ cannot be identified by a reliable machine (for function learning) translates to show that $\mathcal{L} \notin \mathbf{EInfRel}$. $\blacksquare$

The following theorem shows the advantages of reliable identification over justified refutation.

Theorem 32. *(a)* $\mathbf{TxtRel} - \mathbf{ETxtJRef} \neq \emptyset$.
 (b) $\mathbf{TxtRel} - \mathbf{EInfJRef} \neq \emptyset$.

The following theorem shows the advantages of having an informant over texts.

Theorem 33. $(\mathbf{InfRef} \cap \mathbf{InfJIRef}) - \mathbf{TxtEx} \neq \emptyset$.

Proof. $\mathbf{INIT} \cup \{N\}$ witnesses the separation. ∎

5 A Variation of Extended Justified Refutation Criteria

In the definitions for (extended) criteria of learning with justified refutation, we required the machines to either identify or (immediately) refute any text (informant) which did not contain a finite sample representative of the class, $\mathcal{L}$, being learned. For example, in **ETxtJRef**-identification we required that the machine either identify or refute every text which starts with an initial segment not in $\mathbf{Cons}_{\mathcal{L}}$. Alternatively, we could place such a restriction only for texts which are not representative of what the machine identifies (note that this gives more freedom to the machine). In other words, in the definitions for **ETxtJRef, ETxtJIRef, EInfJRef, EInfJIRef**, we could have taken $\{T[n] \mid n \in N \text{ and M } \mathbf{TxtEx}\text{-identifies } T\}$, instead of $\mathbf{Cons}_{\mathcal{L}}$ and $\{I[n] \mid n \in N \text{ and M } \mathbf{InfEx}\text{-identifies } I\}$, instead of $\mathbf{ICons}_{\mathcal{L}}$. Let these new classes formed be called **ETxtJRef′, EInfJRef′, ETxtJIRef′, EInfJIRef′**. Note that a similar change does not effect the classes **ETxtRef, ETxtRel, EInfRef, EInfRel**.

An easy to show interesting property of the classes **ETxtJRef′, EInfJRef′, ETxtJIRef′, EInfJIRef′** is that they are closed under subset operation (i.e., if $\mathcal{L} \in \mathbf{ETxtJRef′}$, then every $\mathcal{L}′ \subseteq \mathcal{L}$ is in **ETxtJRef′**). Note that **ETxtJIRef, ETxtJRef, EInfJIRef, EInfJRef** are not closed under subset operation — this follows immediately from Theorem 32 and the fact that **FIN** belongs to each of these inference criteria.

We now show a result that **ETxtJIRef′** and **ETxtJRef′** obtain the full power of **TxtEx**! This is a surprising result given the results in [LW94] and this paper (**ETxtJRef** and **EInfJRef** do not even contain **TxtFin**, as shown in Theorem 24 and Theorem 25).

Theorem 34. *(a)* $\mathbf{TxtEx} = \mathbf{ETxtJRef′} = \mathbf{ETxtJIRef′}$.
(b) $\mathbf{EInfJRef′} = \mathbf{EInfJIRef′}$.

Proof. For part (a), it is enough to show that $\mathbf{TxtEx} \subseteq \mathbf{ETxtJIRef′}$. Consider any class $\mathcal{L} \in \mathbf{TxtEx}$. If $N \in \mathcal{L}$, then it immediately follows that $\mathcal{L} \in \mathbf{ETxtJIRef′}$ (since $\mathbf{Cons}_{\mathcal{L}} = \mathbf{SEG}$). If $N \notin \mathcal{L}$, then let $\mathcal{L}′ = \mathcal{L} \cup \mathbf{INIT}$. It was shown by Fulk [Ful90] that, if $\mathcal{L} \in \mathbf{TxtEx}$ and $\mathcal{L}$ does not contain N, then $\mathcal{L}′$ as defined above is in **TxtEx**. Since $\mathcal{L}′$ contains a superset of every finite set, it follows that $\mathcal{L}′ \in \mathbf{ETxtJIRef′}$ (since $\mathbf{Cons}_{\mathcal{L}′} = \mathbf{SEG}$). Part (a) now follows using the fact that **ETxtJIRef′** is closed under subset operation.

(b) It is sufficient to show that $\mathbf{EInfJRef′} \subseteq \mathbf{EInfJIRef′}$. Suppose M **EInfJRef′**-identifies $\mathcal{L}$. We construct an M′ which **EInfJIRef′**-identifies $\mathcal{L}$. Let g denote a recursive function such that, for all finite sets S, $W_{g(S)} = S$. On any input $I[n]$, M′ behaves as follows. If $\mathbf{M}(I[n]) \neq \perp$, then $\mathbf{M}′(I[n]) = \mathbf{M}(I[n])$ (this ensures that M′ **InfEx**-identifies $\mathcal{L}$). If $\mathbf{M}(I[n]) = \perp$, then let m be the smallest number such that $M(I[m]) = \perp$. If $PosInfo(I[n]) = PosInfo(I[m])$, then $M'(I[n])$ outputs $g(PosInfo(I[n]))$. Otherwise $M'(I[n])$ outputs $\perp$. We claim that for every σ, either $M'(\sigma) = \perp$ or there exists an extension I of σ such that M' **InfEx**-identifies I. So suppose $M'(\sigma) \neq \perp$. We consider the following cases.

Case 1: $M(\sigma) \neq \perp$.

If **M InfEx**-identifies some extension of σ, then clearly M' does too. So suppose that **M** does not **InfEx**-identify any extension of σ. This implies that **M** refutes every informant which begins with σ. Let I be an informant, extending σ, for $PosInfo(\sigma)$. Let n be the least number such that $M(I[n]) = \perp$. Note that $I[n]$ must be an extension of σ. It now follows from the definition of M' that M' **InfEx**-identifies I.

Case 2: $M(\sigma) = \perp$.

Let τ be the smallest prefix of σ such that $M'(\tau) = \perp$. It follows from the definition of M' that $PosInfo(\tau) = PosInfo(\sigma)$. Let I, extending σ, be an informant for $PosInfo(\sigma)$. It follows from the definition of M' that $M'(I)$ is a grammar for $PosInfo(\tau) = PosInfo(I)$.

From the above cases, it follows that M' **EInfJIRef'**-identifies $\mathcal{L}$. ∎

However, unlike the case for texts, **EInfJRef'**, is not equal to **InfEx**.

Theorem 35. **TxtEx** − **EInfJRef'** $\neq \emptyset$.

Following corollary can be obtained from the (omitted) proof of the above theorem.

Corollary 36. **TxtJIRef** − **EInfJRef'** $\neq \emptyset$.

The following theorem, however, shows that **EInfJRef'** contains **InfRel**.

Theorem 37. **InfRel** $\subseteq$ **EInfJIRef'**

Proof. Note that **InfRel** is closed under finite union. Also **FIN** $\in$ **InfRel**. Now suppose $\mathcal{L} \in$ **InfRel**. Thus $(\mathcal{L} \cup \textbf{FIN}) \in$ **InfRel** $\subseteq$ **InfEx**. It follows that $(\mathcal{L} \cup \textbf{FIN}) \in$ **EInfJIRef'** (since $ICons_{\mathcal{L} \cup \textbf{FIN}} = SEQ$). Now, **EInfJIRef'** is closed under subset operation, and thus it follows that $\mathcal{L} \in$ **EInfJIRef'**. ∎

6 Conclusions

Mukouchi and Arikawa modeled a learning situation in which the learner is expected to refute texts which are not representative of $\mathcal{L}$, the class of languages being identified. Lange and Watson extended this model to consider justified refutation in which the learner is expected to refute texts only if it contains a finite sample unrepresentative of the class $\mathcal{L}$. Both the above studies were in the context of indexed families of recursive languages. In this paper we extended this study in two directions. Firstly, we considered general classes of recursively enumerable languages. Secondly, we allowed the machine to either identify or refute the unrepresentative texts (respectively, texts containing finite unrepresentative samples). We observed some surprising differences between our results and the results obtained for learning indexed families by Lange and Watson. For example, in the context of learning indexed families of recursive languages, Lange and Watson (in their model) showed that **TxtJIRef = TxtJRef** (i.e. requiring machines to refute as soon as the initial segment becomes unrepresentative of $\mathcal{L}$, is not a restriction). Similar result was also shown by them for learning from informants. We showed that requiring immediate refutation is a restriction if we consider general classes of r.e. languages (in both our (extended) and Lange and Watson's models of justified refutation, and for learning from texts as well as informants). We also considered a variation of our model in which "unrepresentative" is with respect to what a machine identifies and not with respect to the class $\mathcal{L}$. In this variation, for learning from texts, (immediate) justified refutation model has the same power as **TxtEx** — a surprising result in the context of results in [LW94] and other results in this paper. However, in the context of learning from informants, even this variation fails to capture the power of **InfEx**.

It would be useful to find interesting characterizations of the different inference classes studied in this paper. An anonymous referee suggested the following problems. When we do not require immediate refutation (as in **TxtJRef**) the delay in refuting the text may be arbitrarily large. It would be interesting to study any hierarchy that can be formed by "quantifying" the delay. Note that if one just considers the number of excess data points needed before refuting, then the hierarchy collapses — except for the * (unbounded but finite) case. As extensions of criteria considered in this paper, one could consider the situation when a machine approximately identifies [KY95, KY97, Muk94] a text T in the cases when it doesn't identify or refute a text.

7 Acknowledgments

We thank Arun Sharma for helpful discussions and comments. Anonymous referees provided several comments which improved the presentation of this paper.

References

[BD92]   S. Ben-David. Can finite samples detect singularities of real-valued functions. In *Symposium on the Theory of Computation*, pages 390–399, 1992.

[Blu67]   M. Blum. A machine-independent theory of the complexity of recursive functions. *Journal of the ACM*, 14:322–336, 1967.

[CJNM94] J. Case, S. Jain, and S. Ngo Manguelle. Refinements of inductive inference by Popperian and reliable machines. *Kybernetika*, 30:23–52, 1994.

[CL82]   J. Case and C. Lynes. Machine inductive inference and language identification. In M. Nielsen and E. M. Schmidt, editors, *Proceedings of the 9th International Colloquium on Automata, Languages and Programming*, volume 140 of *Lecture Notes in Computer Science*, pages 107–115. Springer-Verlag, 1982.

[Ful90]   M. Fulk. Prudence and other conditions on formal language learning. *Information and Computation*, 85:1–11, 1990.

[Gol67]   E. M. Gold. Language identification in the limit. *Information and Control*, 10:447–474, 1967.

[Gri96]   G. Grieser. Reflecting inductive inference machines and its improvement by therapy. In S. Arikawa and A. Sharma, editors, *Algorithmic Learning Theory: Seventh International Workshop (ALT '96)*, volume 1160 of *Lecture Notes in Artificial Intelligence*, pages 325–336. Springer-Verlag, 1996.

[Jan95]   K. P. Jantke. Reflecting ans self-confident inductive inference machines. In *Algorithmic Learning Theory: Sixth International Workshop (ALT '95)*, volume 997 of *Lecture Notes in Artificial Intelligence*, pages 282–297. Springer-Verlag, 1995.

[KY95]   S. Kobayashi and T. Yokomori. On approximately identifying concept classes in the limit. In *Algorithmic Learning Theory: Sixth International Workshop (ALT '95)*, volume 997 of *Lecture Notes in Artificial Intelligence*, pages 298–312. Springer-Verlag, 1995.

[KY97]   S. Kobayashi and T. Yokomori. Learning approximately regular languages with reversible languages. *Theoretical Computer Science A*, 174:251–257, 1997.

[LW94]   S. Lange and P. Watson. Machine discovery in the presence of incomplete or ambiguous data. In S. Arikawa and K. Jantke, editors, *Algorithmic learning theory: Fourth International Workshop on Analogical and Inductive Inference (AII '94) and Fifth International Workshop on Algorithmic Learning Theory (ALT '94)*, volume 872 of *Lecture Notes in Artificial Intelligence*, pages 438–452. Springer-Verlag, 1994.

[MA93]   Y. Mukouchi and S. Arikawa. Inductive inference machines that can refute hypothesis spaces. In K.P. Jantke, S. Kobayashi, E. Tomita, and T. Yokomori, editors, *Algorithmic Learning Theory: Fourth International Workshop (ALT '93)*, volume 744 of *Lecture Notes in Artificial Intelligence*, pages 123–136. Springer-Verlag, 1993.

[MA95]   Y. Mukouchi and S. Arikawa. Towards a mathematical theory of machine discovery from facts. *Theoretical Computer Science A*, 137:53–84, 1995.

[Min76]   E. Minicozzi. Some natural properties of strong identification in inductive inference. *Theoretical Computer Science*, pages 345–360, 1976.

[Muk94]   Y. Mukouchi. Inductive inference of an approximate concept from positive data. In S. Arikawa and K. Jantke, editors, *Algorithmic learning theory: Fourth International Workshop on Analogical and Inductive Inference (AII '94) and Fifth International Workshop on Algorithmic Learning Theory (ALT '94)*, volume 872 of *Lecture Notes in Artificial Intelligence*, pages 484–499. Springer-Verlag, 1994.

[Rog67]   H. Rogers. *Theory of Recursive Functions and Effective Computability*. McGraw-Hill, 1967. Reprinted by MIT Press in 1987.

[Sha98]   A. Sharma. A note on batch and incremental learnability. *Journal of Computer and System Sciences*, 1998. to appear.

Comparing the Power of Probabilistic Learning and Oracle Identification Under Monotonicity Constraints

Léa Meyer

Institut für Informatik und Gesellschaft,
Albert-Ludwigs-Universität Freiburg,
79098 Freiburg, Germany.
lea@modell.iig.uni-freiburg.de

Abstract. In the setting of learning indexed families, probabilistic learning under monotonicity constraints is more powerful than deterministic learning under monotonicity constraints even if the probability is close to 1 provided the learning machines are restricted to proper or class preserving hypothesis spaces (cf. [19]). In this paper, we investigate the relation between probabilistic learning and oracle identification under monotonicity constraints. In particular, we deal with the question how much "additional information" provided by oracles is necessary in order to compensate the additional power of probabilistic learning.

If the oracle machines have access to $\mathcal{K}$-oracle, then they can compensate the power of monotonic (conservative) probabilistic machines completely, provided the probability p is greater than 2/3 (1/2). Furthermore, we show that for every recursively enumerable oracle A, there exists a learning problem which is strong-monotonically learnable by an oracle machine having access to A, but not conservatively or monotonically learnable with any probability $p > 0$. A similar result holds for Peano-complete oracles. However, probabilistic learning under monotonicity constraints is "rich" enough to encode every recursively enumerable set in a characteristic learning problem, i.e., for every recursively enumerable set A, and every $p > 2/3$, there exists a learning problem $\mathcal{L}_A$ which is monotonically learnable with probability p, and monotonically learnable with oracle B if and only if A is Turing-reducible to B. The same result holds for conservative probabilistic learning with $p > 1/2$, and strong-monotonic learning with probability $p = 2/3$. In particular, it follows that probabilistic learning under monotonicity constraints cannot be characterized in terms of oracle identification. Moreover, we close an open problem that appeared in [19] by showing that the probabilistic hierarchies of class preserving monotonic and conservative probabilistic learning are dense.

Finally, we show that these probability bounds are *strict*, i.e., in the case of monotonic probabilistic learning with probability $p = 2/3$, conservative probabilistic learning with probability $p = 1/2$, and strong-monotonic probabilistic learning with probability $p = 1/2$, $\mathcal{K}$ is *not sufficient to compensate the power of probabilistic learning under monotonicity constraints.*

1 Introduction

Many human learning processes are *inductive*, i.e., the learner tries to generate a solution of a problem, a concept, or a grammar for a language on the basis of *incomplete or ambiguous information*. In order to understand the special quality of inductive learning, it turned out to be useful to investigate abstract learning models which try to reflect the human ability to learn natural languages.

A well studied approach in this field is the theory of formal language learning first introduced by Gold [9]. The general situation investigated in *language identification in the limit* can be described as follows. An inductive inference machine is an algorithmic device that is fed more and more information about a language to be inferred. This information can consist of positive and negative examples or only positive ones. In this paper we consider the case where the learner is fed all strings belonging to the language to be inferred but no other strings, i.e., *learning from text*. When fed a text for a language L, the inductive inference machine has to produce hypotheses about L. The hypotheses the learner produces have to be members of an admissible set of hypotheses; every such admissible set is called *hypothesis space*. The hypothesis space may be a set of grammars or a set of decision procedures for the languages to be learned. Finally, the sequence of hypotheses has to converge to a hypothesis correctly describing the language L to be learned. If the learner converges for every positive presentation for L to a correct description of L, then it is said to *identify the language in the limit from text*. A learner *identifies a collection of languages in the limit from text* if and only if it identifies each member of this collection in the limit from text.

With respect to potential applications, we do not consider arbitrary collections of recursive languages but restrict ourselves to enumerable families of recursive languages with uniformly decidable membership, i.e., *indexed families of uniformly recursive languages* (cf. [1], [17], [31], and the references therein).

As mentioned above, we require the learners to produce grammars for the languages to be learned. However, we do not allow every set of grammars as hypothesis space but only *enumerable families of grammars with uniformly decidable membership* (cf. for example [31]). Let $\mathcal{L} = L_0, L_1, \ldots$ be an enumerable family of target languages. Obviously, $\mathcal{L}$ itself may be used as hypothesis space. This leads to the notion of *proper learning*, i.e., a learner identifies $\mathcal{L}$ properly if it learns $\mathcal{L}$ with respect to $\mathcal{L}$ itself. Since the requirement to learn properly in general leads to a decrease of the learning power, we additionally consider *class preserving probabilistic learning*, i.e., $\mathcal{L}$ has to be inferred with respect to some hypothesis space having the same range as $\mathcal{L}$. Since it may be appropriate to allow the learner to "construct" new hypotheses or to "amalgamate" hypotheses already guessed to new hypotheses during the learning process until a correct description of the language to be learned is found, we also consider the case of *class comprising learning*. Thereby, $\mathcal{L}$ is identifiable with respect to a class comprising hypothesis space if and only if there are an inductive inference machine M and a hypothesis space $\mathcal{G}$ which has a range comprising $range(\mathcal{L})$ such that M learns $\mathcal{L}$ and only chooses hypotheses from $\mathcal{G}$. For more information about the impact of the hypothesis space on the learning power of inductive or probabilistic inference machines, we refer the reader, for example, to [17], [19] or [31].

When observing human inference processes, we notice that people often accept that their learning processes fail with a certain probability in order to gain learning power. Moreover, they enhance their learning capabilities by using external sources such as databases or teachers. Finally, people use various *learning strategies* to "improve" their hypotheses, i.e., they reject a hypothesis only if they are convinced that the new hypothesis is "better" than the previous conjecture. Obviously, the learning model described above does not reflect these human abilities. Thus, it seems only natural to define and investigate learning models which try to formalize the special characteristics of human inference processes. For an overview on the various modifications and refinements of the learning model of Gold investigated in the last decades, see [2], [4] or [23].

In this paper, we deal with *probabilistic learning models* and formal models of *learning with additional information*. In both cases, we claim the learning machines to fulfil *monotonicity constraints* as learning strategies.

Generalization strategies belong to the most important learning heuristics that are used to guarantee the improvement of the hypotheses during the learning process. Thereby, a learning algorithm *generalizes on a presentation for a language L* provided it starts by hypothesizing a grammar for a language "smaller" than the language L to be learned, and "refines" this hypothesis gradually until a correct hypothesis for L is found. Jantke [13] defined the strongest notion of generalization, namely *strong-monotonicity*. Thereby, the learner, when successively fed a text for the language to be inferred, has to produce a chain of hypotheses such that $L_i \subseteq L_j$ in case j is guessed later than i. Since strong-monotonicity is a very restrictive constraint on the behavior of an inductive inference machine (cf. [16]), There are several weaker formalizations of the generalization principle. One of them is due to Wiehagen [28], namely *monotonicity*. Informally, the learner, when successively fed a text for the language L to be inferred, learns *monotonically* if it produces a chain of hypotheses such that for any two hypotheses, the hypothesis produced later is as least as good as the earlier one with respect to L. More precisely, we require that $L_i \cap L \subseteq L_j \cap L$, if j is conjectured after i. Furthermore, we consider *weak-monotonic learning* (cf. [13]). Weak-monotonicity can be described as follows. If the learner conjectures j after i and the set of strings seen by the learner when j is guessed is a subset of L_i, then $L_i \subseteq L_j$. For more information about monotonic learning of recursive or recursively enumerable languages, we refer the reader to [12], [13], [14], [28], and [31]. Notice that in the setting of indexed families, weak-monotonicity is equivalent to conservative learning as defined in [1].

Probabilistic inference of recursive functions was introduced by Freivalds [5], and further investigated, for example, by Pitt [24], and Wiehagen *et al.* [29], [30]. In many cases (cf. e.g. [5], and [24]), the probabilistic learning models investigated induce probabilistic hierarchies with a "gap". In particular, each collection of recursive languages identifiable from text with probability $p > 2/3$ is deterministically identifiable (cf. [24]). Within the setting of probabilistic inference under monotonicity constraints, the picture completely changes provided the machines are restricted to proper or class preserving hypothesis spaces (cf. [19]). It turned out that the learning capabilities of probabilistic inference devices working under monotonicity constraints are strictly larger than the learning capabilities of their deterministic counterparts even if the probability has to be *close to* 1. Moreover, the learning power is strictly decreasing when the probability increases.

In order to describe how much learning power is gained, we investigate how much *additional information* is necessary for a deterministic learner to achieve at least the learning power of its probabilistic counterpart. There are several formalizations of *learning with additional information*, for example *learning by teaching* (cf. e.g. [7], [8])), or *oracle identification* (cf. [6], [15], [25], [27]). In the setting of *oracle identification*, the learning machines are allowed to ask questions of the form "$x \in A$" to an oracle $A \subseteq \mathbb{N}$. Thereby, the information given by the oracle is independent from the problem to be learnt. For example, the learner may ask questions to the "halting problem" $\mathcal{K}$. In this paper, we restrict ourselves to oracles which are either recursively enumerable or Peano-complete.

2   Preliminaries

We denote the natural numbers by $\mathbb{N} = \{0, 1, 2, \ldots\}$. Let M_0, $M_1, \ldots$ be a standard list of all Turing machines, and let φ_0, $\varphi_1, \ldots$ be the resulting acceptable programming system, i.e., φ_i denotes the partial recursive function computed by M_i. Let Φ_0, Φ_1, $\ldots$ be any associated complexity measure (cf. [3]). Without loss of generality we may assume that $\Phi_k(x) \geq 1$ for all $k, x \in \mathbb{N}$. Furthermore, let $k, x \in \mathbb{N}$. If $\varphi_k(x)$ is defined, we say that $\varphi_k(x)$ converges and write $\varphi_k(x) \downarrow$; otherwise $\varphi_k(x)$ diverges and we write $\varphi_k(x) \uparrow$.

Let $A, B \subseteq \mathbb{N}$. For the complement of A in $\mathbb{N}$, we write $\overline{A}$. A is *Turing-reducible* to B ($A \leq_T B$) if and only if the characteristic function χ_A of A can be computed by a machine which has access to an infinite database which supplies for each $x \in \mathbb{N}$ whether $x \in B$ or not. Such a database is called an *oracle*. In particular, the set $\mathcal{K} := \{k|\varphi_k(k) \downarrow\}$ is an oracle. By $\mathcal{TOT}$, we denote the set $\{k|\varphi_k \text{ is total}\}$. The class $\{A|A \equiv_T B\}$ is called the *Turing degree* of B. An oracle A is said to be *Peano-complete*, if every disjoint set of recursively enumerable sets can be separated by an A-recursive function. In the sequel, we assume familiarity with formal language theory (cf. [10]). For more details about sets and Turing-Reducibility, we refer the reader to Odifreddi or Soare (cf. [22] or [26]).

Let Σ be any fixed finite alphabet of symbols and let Σ^* be the free monoid over Σ. Any subset $L \subseteq \Sigma^*$ is called a language. Let L be a language, and let $s = s_0, s_1, \ldots$ be a finite or infinite sequence of strings from Σ^*. Define $\mathrm{rng}(s) := \{s_k|k \in \mathbb{N}\}$. An infinite sequence $\tau = s_0, s_1, \ldots$ of strings from Σ^* with $\mathrm{rng}(\tau) = L$ is called a *text* for L. For a text τ and a number x, let τ_x be the initial segment of τ of length $x + 1$. Following Angluin [1], and Lange, Zeugmann and others (cf., e.g., [31]), we exclusively deal with the learnability of indexed families of uniformly recursive languages defined as follows. A sequence

$\mathcal{L} = (L_j)_{j \in \mathbb{N}}$ is said to be an *indexed family of uniformly recursive languages* provided $L_j \neq \emptyset$ for all $j \in \mathbb{N}$, and there is a recursive function F such that for all $j \in \mathbb{N}$ and $s \in \Sigma^*$:

$$F(j, s) := \begin{cases} 1, & \text{if } s \in L_j, \\ 0, & \text{otherwise.} \end{cases}$$

In the following, we refer to indexed families of uniformly recursive languages as *indexed families* for short.

Now we will precise the learning models considered in this paper. Let $\mathcal{L}$ be an indexed family. An *inductive inference machine* (abbr. IIM) is an algorithmic device that takes as its input a text for a language $L \in \mathcal{L}$. When fed a text for L, it outputs a sequence of grammars. The hypotheses the IIM outputs have to be members of an admissible set of hypotheses; every such set is called *hypothesis space*. In this paper, we do not allow arbitrary sets of hypothesis as a hypothesis space but only enumerable families of grammars $G_0, G_1, G_2, \ldots$ over the terminal alphabet Σ such that $\text{rng}(\mathcal{L}) \subseteq \{L(G_j) | j \in \mathbb{N}\}$, and membership in $L(G_j)$ is uniformly decidable for all $j \in \mathbb{N}$, and all strings $s \in \Sigma^*$. If an IIM M outputs a number j, then we are interpreting this number to be the index of the grammar G_j, i.e., M guesses the language $L(G_j)$. For a hypothesis space $\mathcal{G} = (L(G_j))_{j \in \mathbb{N}}$, we use $\text{rng}(\mathcal{G})$ to denote $\{L(G_j) | j \in \mathbb{N}\}$. $\mathcal{G}$ is called *class comprising*, if $\text{rng}(\mathcal{L}) \subseteq \text{rng}(\mathcal{G})$, and *class preserving*, if $\text{rng}(\mathcal{L}) = \text{rng}(\mathcal{G})$.

If, for any text for L, M outputs a sequence of grammars that converges to a grammar correctly describing L, then M is said to *identify the language in the limit from text*. This learning paradigm is called *identification in the limit* and was introduced by Gold [9]. By LIM, we denote the collection of all indexed families $\mathcal{L}$ that can be identified in the limit with respect to a class comprising hypothesis space $\mathcal{G}$. For more information about inductive inference and inductive learning of indexed families, we refer the reader to [23] and [31] for an overview.

In this paper, we consider a probabilistic modification of this concept, namely *probabilistic inductive inference* (cf., e.g., [5], [24], [29]). A *probabilistic inductive inference machine* (abbr. PIM) is an *algorithmic device equipped with a t-sided coin*. A PIM P takes as its input larger and larger initial segments of a text τ and it either takes the next input string, or it first outputs a hypothesis, i.e., a number encoding a certain computer program, and then requests the next input string. Each time, P requests a new input string, it flips the t-sided coin. The hypotheses produced by P, when fed a text τ, depend on the text seen so far and on the outcome of the coin flips.

Let P be a PIM equipped with a t-sided coin. An *coin-oracle* c is an infinite sequence $c_0, c_1, \ldots$ where $c_i \in \{0, \ldots, t-1\}$. By c^n, we denote the initial segment $c_0, \ldots, c_n$ of c for all $n \in \mathcal{N}$. Let c be an coin-oracle. We denote the deterministic algorithmic device defined by running P with coin-oracle c by P^c. By $P^{c^x}(\tau_x)$, we denote the last hypothesis P outputs, when fed τ_x, under the condition that the first $x + 1$ flips of the t-sided coin were c^x. If there is no such hypothesis, then $P^{c^x}(\tau_x)$ is said to be $\bot$. The sequence $(P^{c^x}(\tau_x))_{x \in \mathbb{N}}$

is said to be a *converging path*. We say that $(P^{c^x}(\tau_x))_{x \in \mathbb{N}}$ *converges in the limit* to the number j iff either there exists some $n \in \mathbb{N}$ with $P^{c^x}(\tau_x) = j$ for all $x \geq n$, or $(P^{c^x}(\tau_x))_{x \in \mathbb{N}}$ is finite and its last member is j. Let $\mathcal{G}$ be a hypothesis space. $(P^{c^x}(\tau_x))_{x \in \mathbb{N}}$ is said to *converge correctly with respect to* $\mathcal{G}$ iff $(P^{c^x}(\tau_x))_{x \in \mathbb{N}}$ converges in the limit to a number j and $L(G_j) = L$. Now let Pr denote the canonical Borel-measure on the Borel-σ-algebra on $\{0, \ldots, t-1\}^\infty$. For more details about PIMs, measurability and infinite computation trees we refer the reader to Pitt (cf. [24]).

In the following, we define *probabilistic inference under monotonicity constraints*. In general, this notion is defined for inductive inference machines. Due to the lack of space, we directly give the definitions for probabilistic inductive inference machines and refer the reader to [1], and [31] for more information about deterministic learning under monotonicity constraints.

Let c be an coin-oracle, let τ be a text for a recursive language L, and let P be a PIM. Then the path $(P^{c^x}(\tau_x))_{x \in \mathbb{N}}$ is said to be *strong-monotonic* if and only if for all $x, k \in \mathbb{N}$, $k \geq 1$ with $P^{c^x}(\tau_x) \neq \bot$, $L(G_{P^{c^x}(\tau_x)}) \subseteq L(G_{P^{c^{x+k}}(\tau_{x+k})})$. It is called *monotonic* if $L(G_{P^{c^x}(\tau_x)}) \cap L \subseteq L(G_{P^{c^{x+k}}(\tau_{x+k})}) \cap L$. Moreover, it is called *weak-monotonic* if the following holds: if $\mathrm{rng}(\tau_{x+k}) \subseteq L(G_{P^{c^x}(\tau_x)})$, then $L(G_{P^{c^x}(\tau_x)}) \subseteq L(G_{P^{c^{x+k}}(\tau_{x+k})})$ Notice that in the settings of probabilistic learning and oracle identification of indexed families, weak-monotonicity is equivalent to conservative learning as defined in [1]. Thereby, a path $(P^{c^x}(\tau_x))_{x \in \mathbb{N}}$ is said to be *conservative* if and only if for all $x, k \in \mathbb{N}$, $k \geq 1$ with $P^{c^x}(\tau_x) \neq \bot$, holds: $P^{c^x}(\tau_x) \neq P^{c^{x+k}}(\tau_{x+k})$, then $\mathrm{rng}(\tau_{x+k}) \not\subseteq L(G_{P^{c^x}(\tau_x)})$. In the sequel, we only deal with *conservative learning* (cf. [1]).

Let $\mu \in \{SMON, MON, COV\}$. $(P^{c^x}(\tau_x))_{x \in \mathbb{N}}$ is said to $C\mu$-*converge correctly with respect to* $\mathcal{G}$ iff $(P^{c^x}(\tau_x))_{x \in \mathbb{N}}$ fulfils the condition μ, and converges correctly with respect to $\mathcal{G}$. Now we are ready to define probabilistic learning under monotonicity constraints.

Definition 1. *Let $\mathcal{L}$ be an indexed family, let L be a language, let $\mathcal{G}$ be a class comprising hypothesis space, and let $p \in [0, 1]$. Let $\mu \in \{SMON, MON, COV\}$. Let P be a PIM equipped with a t-sided coin. Set*

$$S_\tau := \{ c \mid (P^{c^x}(\tau_x))_{x \in \mathbb{N}} \; C\mu - converges \; correctly \; w.r.t. \; \mathcal{G} \}.$$

$P \; C\mu_{prob}(p)$-*identifies L from text with probability p with respect to $\mathcal{G}$ if and only if $Pr(S_\tau) \geq p$ for every text τ for L. $P \; C\mu_{prob}(p)$-identifies $\mathcal{L}$ with probability p with respect to $\mathcal{G}$ iff $P \; C\mu_{(p)prob}$-identifies each $L \in \mathrm{rng}(\mathcal{L})$ with probability p.*

Let $\mu \in \{SMON, MON, COV\}$. By $C\mu_{prob}(p)$, we denote the collection of all indexed families $\mathcal{L}$ that can be $C\mu_{prob}(p)$-identified with probability p with respect to a class comprising hypothesis space $\mathcal{G}$. $\mu_{prob}(p)$ is the collection of all indexed families $\mathcal{L}$ that can be $C\mu_{prob}(p)$-identified with probability p with respect to a class preserving hypothesis space $\mathcal{G}$. Furthermore, $E\mu_{prob}(p)$ denotes the collection of all indexed families that can be learned properly with probability p. More exactly, $\mathcal{L} \in E\mu_{prob}(p)$ iff $\mathcal{L}$ is $C\mu_{prob}(p)$-identifiable with probability p

with respect to $\mathcal{L}$ itself. The corresponding *deterministic learning classes* are denoted by $C\mu$, μ and $E\mu$.

Finally, we have to define *oracle identification*. Let A be an oracle. An oracle inference machine (abbr. OIM) is an inductive inference machine M which has access to an oracle A. We denote an OIM M having access to A by $M[A]$.

Definition 2. *Let $\mathcal{L}$ be an indexed family, let L be a language, and let $\mathcal{G}$ be a class comprising hypothesis space. Let $\mu \in \{SMON, MON, COV\}$. Let A be an oracle, and let $M[A]$ be an OIM. Then $M[A]$ $C\mu$-identifies L from text with respect to $\mathcal{G}$ if, for every text τ for L, the sequence $(L_{G_{M[A](\tau_x)}})_{x\in\mathbb{N}}$ $C\mu$-converges correctly with respect to $\mathcal{G}$. $M[A]$ $C\mu$-identifies $\mathcal{L}$ with respect to $\mathcal{G}$ iff $M[A]$ $C\mu$-identifies each $L \in \mathrm{rng}(\mathcal{L})$.*

By $C\mu[A]$, we denote the collection of all indexed families $\mathcal{L}$ that can be $C\mu$-identified by an OIM $M[A]$ with respect to a class comprising hypothesis space. $\mu[A]$, and $E\mu[A]$ are defined analogously.

In the following sections, we often need a special set of recursive languages which encodes the halting problem (cf., e.g., [17]). Let $k \in \mathbb{N}$. Define $L_k := \{a^k b^m | m \in \mathbb{N}\}$, and

$$L'_k := \begin{cases} L_k, & \text{if } \varphi_k(k) \uparrow, \\ \{a^k b^m | m \leq \Phi_k(k)\}, & \text{if } \varphi_k(k) \downarrow. \end{cases}$$

3 Comparing the Power

3.1 The power of oracle identification

In [19], we showed that $CCOV_{prob}(p) = CCOV$, and $CSMON_{prob}(p) = CSMON$ for all $p > 1/2$. Furthermore, $CMON_{prob}(p) = CMON$ for all $p > 2/3$. Consequently, in the case of class comprising learning, the learning capabilities of $\mathcal{K}$-oracle machines working under monotonicity constraints are larger than the learning capabilities of their probabilistic counterparts, provided the probabilistic learners are claimed to learn with probability $p > 1/2$ ($p > 2/3$ in the monotonic case). The following theorem yields the same result holds for proper and class preserving probabilistic learning.

Theorem 1. *Let $p > \frac{1}{2}$, let $\mu \in \{SMON, COV\}$ be a monotonicity constraint and let $\mathcal{L}$ be an indexed family such that $\mathcal{L}$ is $\mu_{prob}(p)$-identifiable with probability p with respect to a class preserving hypothesis space $\mathcal{G}$. Then $\mathcal{L}$ is μ-identifiable with respect to $\mathcal{G}$ by an oracle machine which has access to $\mathcal{K}$. Moreover, every indexed family $\mathcal{L}$ which is $MON_{prob}(p)$-identifiable with respect to a class preserving hypothesis space $\mathcal{G}$ with probability $p > \frac{2}{3}$ is MON-identifiable with respect to $\mathcal{G}$ by an oracle machine which has access to $\mathcal{K}$.*

Proof. Due to the lack of space, we omit the proof. For details see [21]. ∎

Next, we show that for every recursively enumerable oracle A, there exists an indexed family $\mathcal{L}^A$ which is strong-monotonically identifiable by an oracle machine having access to A, but not conservatively or monotonically identifiable with any probability $p > 0$ with respect to any class comprising hypothesis space $\mathcal{G}$.

Theorem 2. *Let A be a recursively enumerable oracle, A not recursive. There exists an indexed family $\mathcal{L}$ with*

a. $\mathcal{L}^A \in ESMON[A]$,

b. $\mathcal{L}^A \notin CCOV_{prob}(p)$ for all $p \in [0,1]$,

c. $\mathcal{L}^A \notin CMON_{prob}(p)$ for all $p \in [0,1]$.

Before proving Theorem 2, we note a technical result.

Lemma 1. *Let $\mu \in \{SMON, MON, COV\}$. Let $\mathcal{L}$ be an indexed family, let A be an oracle, and let $\mathcal{L} \in SMON[A] \setminus C\mu_{prob}(p)$ for some probability $p < 1$. Then there exists an indexed family $\mathcal{L}'$ such that $\mathcal{L}' \in SMON[A] \setminus C\mu(q)$ for every $q \in [0,1]$.*

Proof. Due to the lack of space, we omit the proof.

Proof. (of Theorem 2)

It is sufficient to prove the claim for $p > 1/2$ (in b.), and $p > 2/3$ (in c.), since Lemma 1 yields the result for arbitrary $p \in [0,1]$.

Let A be recursively enumerable, A not recursive. Let E_A be an algorithm which enumerates A. By $E_A(n)$, we denote the $n+1$-th element of A generated by E_A. Define an indexed family $\mathcal{L}$ as follows. Let $\langle\ ,\ \rangle: \mathbb{N} \times \mathbb{N} \to \mathbb{N}$ be an effective encoding of $\mathbb{N} \times \mathbb{N}$. Then set $L_{\langle k,j \rangle} := L_k$ iff $k \notin \{E_A(0), \ldots, E_A(j)\}$. If $k \in A$, then add all subsets of $\{a^k b^i | i \leq E_A^{-1}(k) + 1\}$. A similar construction for $A = \mathcal{K}$ can be found in [17] or [19]. By applying the proof techniques developed therein, we can easily show that $\mathcal{L}^A := (L_{\langle k,j \rangle})_{k,j \in \mathbb{N}}$ witnesses the desired separation.

Notice, that the indexed family defined in the proof of Theorem 2 is in every oracle learning class $\lambda\mu[A]$, $\lambda \in \{E, \epsilon, C\}$, $\mu \in \{SMON, MON, COV\}$, but not in the probabilistic learning classes $\lambda\mu_{prob}(p)$, $\lambda \in \{E, \epsilon, C\}$, $\mu \in \{SMON, COV\}$, $p > 1/2$, and $\lambda MON_{prob}(p)$, $\lambda \in \{E, \epsilon, C\}$, $p > 2/3$. In particular, $C\mu[A] \setminus C\mu \neq \emptyset$ for all $\mu \in \{SMON, MON, COV\}$, and A recursively enumerable.

Let $\mu \in \{SMON, MON, COV\}$, and let A be a recursively enumerable oracle. In the following, we show that, for $p > 1/2$, $p \in \mathcal{Q}$, ($p > 2/3$ in the monotonic case), it is possible to separate $E\mu_{prob}(p)$ and $E\mu[A]$ simultaneously from $E\mu_{prob}(q)$, $q > p$. Thereby, $\mathcal{Q}$ denotes the set of *rational numbers*. Moreover, the proof of the following theorem yields an analogous result for Peano-complete oracles.

Theorem 3. *Let A be a recursively enumerable oracle, A not recursive. Let $c, d \in \mathbb{N}$, $gcd(c, d) = 1$. Then there exists an indexed family $\mathcal{L} \in ESMON[A]$ with*

$\mathcal{L} \in ESMON_{prob}(\frac{c}{d}) \setminus \bigcup_{p < q \leq 1} ECOV_{prob}(q)$, *and*

$\mathcal{L} \in EMON_{prob}(\frac{2c}{c+d}) \setminus \bigcup_{p < q \leq 1} EMON_{prob}(q)$.

Proof. Let A be a recursively enumerable oracle, A not recursive, and let E_A be an algorithm which enumerates A. Let $p > 1/2$. Let $c, d \in \mathbb{N}$ with $gcd(c,d) = 1$. Let $\langle \ , \ \rangle : \mathbb{N} \times \mathbb{N} \to \mathbb{N}$ be an effective encoding of $\mathbb{N} \times \mathbb{N}$. Let $k, k_1, k_2 \in \mathbb{N}$, $k = \langle k_1, k_2 \rangle$, and let $j \in \mathbb{N}$, $j \le c - 1$. Finally, we set $M_{2c-d}^c = \{S | S \subset \{0, \ldots, c-1\}, |S| = 2c - d\}$. Let $cod_{2c-d}^c : M_{2c-d}^c \to \{0, \ldots, \binom{c}{2c-d} - 1\}$ be an effective encoding of M_{2c-d}^c. Then define $mod_{2c-d}^c : \mathbb{N} \to \{0, \ldots, \binom{c}{2c-d} - 1\}$ by setting $mod_{2c-d}^c(y) := x$ iff $x \in \{0, \ldots, \binom{c}{2c-d} - 1\} \ \wedge \ y \equiv x \ mod \ \binom{c}{2c-d}$ for all $y \in \mathbb{N}$. In order to define the family witnessing the desired separation, we define a recursive relation R_k uniformly for $k \in \mathbb{N}$ as follows. Let $k, n \in \mathbb{N}$. $R_k(n)$ if and only if there exists an $m < n$ with $E_A(n) = k_1$ and $\Phi_{k_2}(k) = m$. Let $k, j \in \mathbb{N}$. Define $L_{\langle k,j \rangle}$ as follows. Let $n \in \mathbb{N}$.

If $\neg R_k(n)$, then $a^k b^n \in L_{\langle k,j \rangle}$.

If $R_k(n)$, then $a^k b^n \in L_{\langle k,j \rangle}$ if and only if $j \notin (cod_{2c-d}^c)^{-1}(mod_{2c-d}^c(\varphi_{k_2}(k)))$.

Obviously, $\mathcal{L}_{c/d} := (L_{\langle k,j \rangle})_{k,j \in \mathbb{N}, \ j \le c-1}$ is an indexed family. It immediately follows that $\mathcal{L}_{c/d} \in ESMON[A]$, and hence in $EMON[A]$ and $ECOV[A]$. Moreover, $\mathcal{L}_{c/d} \in ESMON_{prob}(c/d)$. By using the proof technique developed in [19], we can show that $\mathcal{L}_{c/d}$ is not $ECOV_{prob}(p0$-learnable with probability $p > c/d$.

Let B be a Peano-complete oracle. Since the sets $\{j \in \mathbb{N} | j \ mod \ n = i \ mod \ n\})$, $i \le n - 1$, are separable for all $n \in \mathbb{N}$ by any Peano-complete oracle, the indexed families constructed in the proof of Theorem 3 are properly strong-monotonically identifiable by an oracle machine having access to B. By applying Lemma 1, we can draw the following corollary from Theorem 3.

Corollary 1. *Let B be a Peano-complete oracle. Then $ESMON[B] \setminus ECOV_{prob}(p) \ne \emptyset$ for every $p \in [0,1]$, and $EMON[B] \setminus EMON_{prob}(p) \ne \emptyset$ for every $p \in [0,1]$.*

3.2 Characterizing recursively enumerable oracles

In this section, we investigate the relation between the probabilistic learning classes $\mu_{prob}(p)$ and $\mu[A]$ for $A \le_T \mathcal{K}$. Let A be an oracle, $A \le_T \mathcal{K}$. For $p > 2/3$, $SMON_{prob}(p) \subset SMON[A]$, since $SMON_{prob}(p) = SMON$ for every $p > 2/3$ (cf. [19]). However, the probabilistic learning class $SMON_{prob}(2/3)$ is able to encode every recursively enumerable oracle.

Let A be recursively enumerable, A not recursive, and let E_A be an algorithm which enumerates A. Let $\langle \ , \ \rangle : \mathbb{N} \times \{0,1\} \to \mathbb{N}$ be an effective encoding of $\mathbb{N} \times \{0,1\}$, and let $k, j \in \mathbb{N}$, $j \le 1$. Set

$$L_{\langle k,j \rangle} := \begin{cases} L_k' \cup \{a^k b^{E_A^{-1}(k)+1}\}, & \text{if } j = 0, \\ L_k' \cup \{a^k b^{E_A^{-1}(k)+2}\}, & \text{if } j = 1. \end{cases}$$

Obviously, $\mathcal{L}_A = (L_{\langle k,j \rangle})_{k,j \in \mathbb{N}, j \le 1}$ is an indexed family. Let B be an oracle. By using a known argument from [19], we can show that $\mathcal{L}_A \in SMON[B]$ if and only if $A \le_T B$. Consequently, $SMON_{prob}(2/3)$ and $SMON[B]$ are not comparable for every $B <_T \mathcal{K}$.

In the case of monotonic (conservative) class preserving learning, we are able to show an analogous result for every $p > 2/3$ ($p > 1/2$). Thus, the probabilistic learning classes $MON_{prob}(p)$, $p > 2/3$, and $COV_{prob}(p)$, $p > 1/2$, are "rich" enough to encode every recursively enumerable set.

Theorem 4. *Let A be a recursively enumerable oracle, A not recursive. Let $n, s \in \mathbb{N}$ such that $s + 1$ is a factor of n. Then there exists an indexed family $\mathcal{L}_{n,s} \in EMON_{prob}(\frac{2n}{2n+s})$ such that every OIM $M[B]$ which monotonically identifies $\mathcal{L}_{n,s}$ with respect to a class preserving hypothesis space may be transformed into a decision procedure for A.*

Proof. Let E_A be an algorithm enumerating A. Let $z \in \mathbb{N}$ with $n = z(s+1)$. Let $\langle , \rangle : \mathbb{N} \times \{0, \ldots, (n + z\binom{s+1}{2}) - 1\} \to \mathbb{N}$ be an effective encoding of $\mathbb{N} \times \{0, \ldots, (n + z\binom{s+1}{2}) - 1\}$. Let $D^r = \{j \in \mathbb{N} | r(s+1) \le j < (r+1)(s+1)\}$. Let $(D_i^r)_{i \le \binom{s+1}{2} - 1}$ be an effective enumeration of all subsets of D_r with cardinality 2. Let $k, j \in \mathbb{N}$, $j \le (n + z\binom{s+1}{2}) - 1$. If $x \notin A$, then set $L_{\langle k,j \rangle} := L_k$ for all $j \le (n + z\binom{s+1}{2}) - 1$. If $x \in A$, and $j \le n - 1$, then set $L_{\langle k,j \rangle} := L'_k \cup \{a^k b^{(E_A)^{-1}(k) + (j+1)}\}$. If $x \in A$, and $j \ge n$, then let $r \in \mathbb{N}$, $0 \le r \le z - 1$ with $n + r\binom{s+1}{2}) \le j < (n + (r+1)\binom{s+1}{2})$. Set $L_{\langle k,j \rangle} := L'_k \cup \{a^k b^{(E_A)^{-1}(k) + (m+1)} | m \in D_j^r\}$. It follows that $(L_{\langle k,j \rangle})_{k, j \in \mathbb{N}, j \le (n + z\binom{s+1}{2}) - 1}$ witnesses the desired separation.

By using some arguments from [19], we may even show that an oracle machine $M[B]$ already decides A in case it is claimed to identify $\mathcal{L}_{n,s}$ with a probability $p > 2n/(2n + s)$.

Theorem 5. *Let A be a recursively enumerable oracle, A not recursive. Let $n, s \in \mathbb{N}$ such that $s + 1$ is a factor of n. Then there exists an indexed family $\mathcal{L}_{n,s} \in EMON_{prob}(\frac{2n}{2n+s})$ such that every probabilistic OIM $M[B]$ which monotonically identifies $\mathcal{L}_{n,s}$ with a probability $p > \frac{2n}{2n+s}$ with respect to a class preserving hypothesis space may be transformed into a decision procedure for A.*

In particular, we can follow that every probabilistic learning class contains maximal complicated problems.

Corollary 2. *For $p > \frac{2}{3}$, there exists an indexed family $\mathcal{L}_K^p \in MON_{prob}(p)$ such that every oracle machine $M[A]$ identifying $\mathcal{L}_K^p$ can be transformed into a decision procedure for K. In particular, $EMON_{prob}(p) \setminus MON[A] \ne \emptyset$ for all $A <_T K$.*

From Theorem 2 and Corollary 2 follows that probabilistic monotonic learning with probability $p > 2/3$ cannot be characterized in terms of oracle identification.

Corollary 3. *Let $A <_T K$, and let $p \in [0, 1]$. Then $EMON_{prob}(p)$ and $MON[A]$ are not comparable. The same result holds for $ECOV_{prob}(p)$ and $ECOV[A]$.*

Since the set $D = \{m \in [2/3, 1] \mid \exists\, n, s \in \mathbb{N}\ 1 \le s \le n \text{ with } m = 2n/(2n + s)\}$ is dense in the interval $[2/3, 1]$, it follows from Theorem 5 that the probabilistic hierarchy in the case of class preserving monotonic probabilistic learning is dense.

Corollary 4. $\langle MON_{prob}(p)\rangle_{p\in[0,1]}$ *is dense in the interval* $[\frac{2}{3},1]$.

For conservative probabilistic learning with probability $p > 1/2$, the analogous results follow from the results proved in [20].

Remark 1. Let $\mu = COV$ or $\mu = MON$. In the last theorems we defined for every recursively enumerable oracle A a learning problem which encodes A. This technique can be used to define an indexed family encoding an uniformly recursively enumerable set of recursively enumerable sets $(A_i)_{i\in\mathbb{N}}$, i.e., there is an indexed family $\mathcal{L}$ such that for every oracle machine $M[B]$ μ-identifying this family holds: $A_i \leq_T B$ for all $i \in \mathbb{N}$.

In [27], Stephan proved that $LIM[A] = COV[\mathcal{K}]$ for every low r.e. oracle. Thus, $LIM[A] = LIM[B]$ for any two low r.e. enumerable oracles A, B. In the case of inductive inference under monotonicity constraints, we can conclude that $\mu[A] \neq \mu[B]$ for all low r.e. oracles A, B with $A \not\equiv_T B$. Furthermore, we can draw the following corollary.

Corollary 5. *Let* $\mu \in \{SMON, MON, COV\}$. *Let* A, B *be oracles. If* A *is r.e.,* *then* $\mu[A] \subseteq \mu[B]$ *if and only if* $A \leq_T B$.

3.3 Peano-complete oracles revisited

Let $\mu \in \{MON, COV\}$. By modifying the indexed families defined in Theorem 4, we can immediately follow that in every probabilistic learning class $\mu_{prob}(p)$, there are learning problems which separate $\mu_{prob}(p)$ from $\mu_{prob}(q)$, $q > p$, and which are conservatively identifiable by an oracle having access to a Peano-complete oracle.

Theorem 6. *Let* $n, s \in \mathbb{N}$, $1 \leq s \leq n$. *Then there exists an indexed family* $\mathcal{L}_{n,s} \in ECOV_{prob}(\frac{n}{n+s}) \setminus \bigcup_{q>n/(n+s)} COV_{prob}(q)$, *and* $\mathcal{L}_{n,s} \in ECOV[B]$ *for all oracles* B, B *Peano-complete.*

Let $n, s \in \mathbb{N}$, *where* $s+1$ *is a factor of* n. *Then there exists an indexed family* $\mathcal{L}_{n,s} \in EMON_{prob}(\frac{2n}{2n+s}) \setminus \bigcup_{q>2n/(2n+s)} MON_{prob}(q)$, *and* $\mathcal{L}_{n,s} \in EMON[B]$ *for all oracles* B, B *Peano-complete.*

Proof. Let $n, s \in \mathbb{N}$, $s \leq n$. Let $\langle \ , \ \rangle$ be an effective encoding of $\mathbb{N} \times \mathbb{N}$, and let $k, j \in \mathbb{N}$. Let $z \in \mathbb{N}$, and let $r \in \{0, \ldots, \binom{n}{s} - 1\}$ with $j = \binom{n}{s}z + r$. Let $(D_i)_{i\in\mathbb{N}, i\leq\binom{n}{s}-1}$ be an enumeration of all subsets of the set $\{0, \ldots, n-1\}$ of cardinality s.

If $\Phi_k(k) \downarrow$, $\varphi_k(k) = 0 \mod 2$ and $z < \Phi_k(k) - 1$, then set
$L_{\langle k,j\rangle} = \{a^k b^m | m \leq \Phi_k(k)\} \cup \{a^k b^{\langle\Phi_k(k)+(r+1),i\rangle} \mid i \in D_r \}$,
if $\Phi_k(k) \downarrow$, $\varphi_k(k) = 0 \mod 2$, $\Phi_k(k) \leq z \leq 2\Phi_k(k) - 1$, and $r < n$ then set
$L_{\langle k,j\rangle} = \{a^k b^m | m \leq \Phi_k(k) - z\} \cup \{a^k b^{\langle\Phi_k(k)+(r+1),j\rangle}\}$,
if $\Phi_k(k) \downarrow$, $\varphi_k(k) = 0 \mod 2$, $\Phi_k(k) \leq z \leq 2\Phi_k(k) - 1$, and $r \geq n$, then set
$L_{\langle k,j\rangle} = L_k$, if $\Phi_k(k) \downarrow$ and $z \geq 2\Phi_k(k)$, or $\Phi_k(k) \downarrow$ and $\varphi_k(k) = 1 \mod 2$, or $\Phi_k(k) \uparrow$, then set $L_{\langle k,j\rangle} = L_k$. $\mathcal{L}_n = (L_{\langle k,j\rangle})_{k,j\in\mathbb{N}}$ is an indexed family which fulfils the desired conditions. The second part of the theorem can be proved by combining the proof of the first part and the proof of Theorem 4.

Remark 2. We suggest that it is possible to characterize the class of Peano-complete oracles by a problem $\mathcal{L}_{PA}$, i.e., $\mathcal{L}_{PA}$ is μ-identifiable by an oracle machine $M[A]$ if and only if A is Peano-complete.

4 Verifying the Bounds

In the section, we show that $\mathcal{K}$ is *not sufficient to compensate the power of probabilistic learning under monotonicity constraints.*

Theorem 7. *Let A be an oracle with $\mathcal{K} \leq_T A$.*
There exist an indexed family $\mathcal{L}^{1/2} \in ECOV_{prob}(1/2) \cap ECOV[\mathcal{TOT}]$ with

$$\mathcal{L}^{1/2} \in ECOV[A] \quad \text{if and only if} \quad \mathcal{TOT} \leq_T A,$$

and an indexed family $\mathcal{L}^{2/3} \in EMON_{prob}(2/3) \cap EMON[\mathcal{TOT}]$ with

$$\mathcal{L}^{2/3} \in EMON[A] \quad \text{if and only if} \quad \mathcal{TOT} \leq_T A.$$

Proof. In order to prove the first part of the theorem, we define an indexed family as follows. Let $\langle\ ,\ \rangle : \mathbb{N} \times \mathbb{N} \to \mathbb{N}$ be an effective encoding of $\mathbb{N} \times \mathbb{N}$. We define for each $k \in \mathbb{N}$ a chain of languages $(L_{\langle k,i \rangle})_{i \in \mathbb{N}}$ in dependence from $\varphi_k(j)$, $j \in \mathbb{N}$. Let $\Sigma := \{a, b, d\}$. Let $\langle\ ,\ \rangle : \mathbb{N} \times \mathbb{N} \to \mathbb{N}$ be an effective encoding of $\mathbb{N} \times \mathbb{N}$. Define the indexed family $(L_{\langle k,j \rangle})_{k,j \in \mathbb{N}}$ as follows. Let $k, n \in \mathbb{N}$.
If $\Phi_k(0) \geq n$, then $a^k b^n \in L_{\langle k,j \rangle}$ for all $j \in \mathbb{N}$.
Assume $\Phi_k(0) < n$. Let $j \in \mathbb{N}$, $j > n$. In case $\Phi_k(0) + 1 + \Phi_k(1) > j$, add $a^k b^n$ to $L_{\langle k,0 \rangle}$ but not to $L_{\langle k,u \rangle}$, $1 \leq u \leq j$. If $\Phi_k(0) + 1 + \Phi_k(1) \leq j$, compute the least $s \in \mathbb{N}$, $s \geq 1$, such that $\sum_{i=0}^{s}(\Phi_k(i)+1) \leq j$ and $\sum_{i=0}^{s}(\Phi_k(i)+1)+\Phi_k(s+1) > j$. Remark that in this case $\varphi_k(i) \downarrow$ for all $i \in \{0, \ldots, s\}$. We define whether $a^k b^n$, d^m belong to $L_{\langle k,u \rangle}$ for $n, u \leq j$, $m \in \mathbb{N}$.

- $a^k b^n \in L_{\langle k,0 \rangle}$.
- If $\sum_{i=0}^{m-1}(\Phi_k(i)+1) \leq n < \sum_{i=0}^{m-1}(\Phi_k(i)+1) + \Phi_k(m)$ for an $m \leq s$, then $a^k b^n \in L_{\langle k,u \rangle}$ for all $\sum_{i=0}^{m}(\Phi_k(i)+1) \leq u \leq j$.
- If $\sum_{i=0}^{s}(\Phi_k(i)+1) \leq n$, then $a^k b^n \notin L_{\langle k,u \rangle}$ for all $1 \leq u \leq j$.
- $d^{\sum_{i=0}^{s}\Phi_k(i)} \in L_{\langle k,u \rangle}$ for all $\sum_{i=0}^{s-1}(\Phi_k(i)+1) \leq u \leq \sum_{i=0}^{s-1}(\Phi_k(i)+1)+\Phi_k(s)$.

Set $\mathcal{L}^{1/2} = (L_{\langle k,j \rangle})_{k,j \in \mathbb{N}}$. Obviously, $\mathcal{L}^{1/2}$ is an indexed family, and $\mathcal{L}^{1/2} \in ECOV_{prob}(1/2)$. Now let $M[A]$ be an oracle machine which conservatively identifies $\mathcal{L}^{1/2}$. Let $k \in \mathbb{N}$, and let $\tau = (a^k b^i)_{i \in \mathbb{N}}$ be a text for $L_{\langle k,0 \rangle}$. Then $L_{\langle k,0 \rangle} = L_k$ independently from φ_k being total or not. Moreover, no other language equals L_k, since in both cases, every language $L_{\langle k,j \rangle}$, $j > 0$, is finite. Since $M[A]$ identifies L_k, there must be an $n_0 \in \mathbb{N}$ such that $M[A](\tau_{n_0}) = 0$. Let ℓ be the least natural number such that $\sum_{i=1}^{\ell} \Phi_k(i) + 1 > n_0$. Then either φ_k is total or $min\{r \in \mathbb{N} | \varphi_k(r) \uparrow\} \leq \ell$. Since $\mathcal{K} \leq_T A$, it follows that $\mathcal{TOT} \leq_T A$.

In order to prove the second part of the theorem, define $(L_{\langle k,j,v \rangle})_{k,j,v \in \mathbb{N}, v \in \{0,1\}}$ as follows. Let $k, j, v, n \in \mathbb{N}$, $v \in \{0,1\}$. If $\Phi_k(0) > n$, then $a^k b^m \in L_{\langle k,j,v \rangle}$ for all $m, j \leq n$, $v \in \{0,1\}$. Assume $\Phi_k(0) \leq n$. Let $j \in \mathbb{N}$, $n \leq j$. In case $\Phi_k(0) + 2 + \Phi_k(1) > j$, add $a^k b^{\Phi_k(0)+1}$ to $L_{\langle k,u,0 \rangle}$ but not to $L_{\langle k,u,1 \rangle}$, add $a^k b^{\Phi_k(0)+2}$ to $L_{\langle k,u,1 \rangle}$ but not to $L_{\langle k,u,0 \rangle}$, for $1 \leq u \leq \Phi_k(0)$. If $n > \Phi_k(0) + 2$, we add $a^k b^n$ to every $L_{\langle k,u,v \rangle}$ for $1 \leq u \leq j$, $v \in \{0,1\}$. Add no other elements to any language. In case $\Phi_k(0) + 2 + \Phi_k(1) \leq j$, compute the least $s \in \mathbb{N}$, $s \geq 1$ such that $\sum_{i=0}^{s-1}(\Phi_k(i) + 2) + \Phi_k(s) \leq j$ and $\sum_{i=0}^{s}(\Phi_k(i) + 2) + \Phi_k(s+1) > j$. We define whether $a^k b^n$, d^m belongs to $L_{\langle k,u \rangle}$ for $n, u \leq j$.

- $a^k b^n \in L_{\langle k,0 \rangle}$.
- If $\sum_{i=0}^{m-1}(\Phi_k(i) + 2) + \Phi_k(m) < n \leq \sum_{i=0}^{m-1}(\Phi_k(i) + 2) + \Phi_k(m)$ for an $m \leq s$, then $a^k b^n \in L_{\langle k,u \rangle}$ for all $\sum_{i=0}^{m-1}(\Phi_k(i) + 2) + \Phi_k(m) < u \leq \sum_{i=0}^{m}(\Phi_k(i) + 2) + \Phi_k(m+1)$.
- If $n = \sum_{i=0}^{s-1}(\Phi_k(i) + 2) + \Phi_k(s) + 1$, then $a^k b^n \in L_{\langle k,u,0 \rangle}$, $a^k b^n \notin L_{\langle k,u,0 \rangle}$, if $n = \sum_{i=0}^{s-1}(\Phi_k(i) + 2) + \Phi_k(s) + 2$, then $a^k b^n \notin L_{\langle k,u,1 \rangle}$, and $a^k b^n \in L_{\langle k,u,1 \rangle}$ for all $\sum_{i=0}^{s-2}(\Phi_k(i) + 2) + \Phi_k(s-1) < u \leq \sum_{i=0}^{s-1}(\Phi_k(i) + 2) + \Phi_k(s)$.
  In both cases, $a^k b^n \in L_{\langle k,u,v \rangle}$ for all $u \leq \sum_{i=0}^{s-2}(\Phi_k(i) + 2) + \Phi_k(s-1)$, $v \in \{0,1\}$.
  If $n > \sum_{i=0}^{s}(\Phi_k(i) + 2)$, then $a^k b^n \in L_{\langle k,u,v \rangle}$ for all $u \leq j$, $v \in \{0,1\}$.
- $d^{\sum_{i=0}^{s} \Phi_k(i)} \in L_{\langle k,u,0 \rangle}$, and $d^{\sum_{i=0}^{s} \Phi_k(i)+1} \in L_{\langle k,u,1 \rangle}$ for all $\sum_{i=0}^{s-3}(\Phi_k(i) + 2) + \Phi_k(s-2) < u \leq \sum_{i=0}^{s-2}(\Phi_k(i) + 2) + \Phi_k(s-1)$. In case $s = 2$, we interpret $s - 3$ as 0. Add not other elements to any language.

Set $\mathcal{L}^{2/3} = (L_{\langle k,j,v \rangle})_{k,j,v \in \mathbb{N}, v \in \{0,1\}}$. As in the first part of the proof, we can show that $\mathcal{L}^{2/3}$ witnesses the desired separation.

In the case of conservative learning, Stephan [27] proved that $LIM[A] \subseteq LIM[\mathcal{K}]$, and $COV[A'] = LIM[A]$ for every oracle A. Thus, for every oracle A, $COV[A]$ is contained in $LIM[A]$ which is contained in $LIM[\mathcal{K}] = COV[\mathcal{TOT}]$. Moreover, we can draw the following corollary.

Corollary 6. *There exists $\mathcal{L} \in EMON[\mathcal{TOT}]$ with $\mathcal{L} \in LIM \setminus EMON[A] \neq \emptyset$ for every oracle A with $\mathcal{TOT} \not\leq_T A$.*

Proof. The indexed family $\mathcal{L}^{2/3}$ defined in Theorem 7 is not in $EMON[A]$ for any $\mathcal{K} \leq_T A <_T \mathcal{TOT}$. However, $\mathcal{L}^{2/3} \in LIM$, since $LIM_{prob}(2/3) = LIM$ (cf. [19]). From Corollary 2 follows that $\mathcal{L}_\mathcal{K}$ is LIM-identifiable but not monotonically identifiable by any OIM $M[B]$ where $\mathcal{K} \not\leq_T B$. Now we can easily define a "join" of $\mathcal{L}^{2/3}$ and $\mathcal{L}_\mathcal{K}$ which is LIM-identifiable, but not identifiable by an oracle machine having access to any oracle A with $\mathcal{TOT} \not\leq_T A$.

The indexed families defined in Theorem 7 are not properly strong-monotonically identifiable with $p = 1/2$. The next theorem shows that there is an indexed family which is strong-monotonically identifiable with $p = 1/2$ but not conservatively or monotonically identifiable by any A-oracle machine where $\mathcal{TOT} \not\leq_T A$.

Theorem 8. *There exists an indexed family $\mathcal{L} \in ESMON_{prob}(1/2)$ with $\mathcal{L} \in ECOV[\mathcal{TOT}] \cap EMON[\mathcal{TOT}]$.*
$\mathcal{L} \notin CCOV[A] \cup CMON[A]$ for every oracle A with $\mathcal{TOT} \not\leq_T A$.

Proof. Due to the lack of space we only give a sketch of the proof. Let $\Sigma :=$ $\{a, b, d\}$. Let $\langle \ , \ \rangle : \mathbb{N} \times \mathbb{N} \to \mathbb{N}$ an effective encoding of $\mathbb{N} \times \mathbb{N}$. We define $(L_{\langle k,j \rangle})_{k,j \in \mathbb{N}}$ in dependence of $\varphi_k(j)$, $k, j \in \mathbb{N}$. Let $k \in \mathbb{N}$. In Step 0 of the construction, we add $a^k b^0$ to every language. In the n-th step of the construction, compute the least $s \in \mathbb{N}$, $s \geq 1$, such that $\sum_{i=0}^{s-1}(\Phi_k(i) + 1) + \Phi_k(s) \leq n$ and $\sum_{i=0}^{s}(\Phi_k(i) + 1) + \Phi_k(s + 1) > n$. In case $n \neq \sum_{i=0}^{s} \Phi_k(i)$, add every subset of $\{a^k b^i | i \leq n\}$ to $\mathcal{L}$. In case $n = \sum_{i=0}^{s} \Phi_k(i)$, add $a^k b^{\sum_{i=0}^{s-1}(\Phi_k(i)+1)+\Phi_k(s)}$ to $L_{\langle k,0 \rangle}$. Moreover, add $\{d^{\sum_{i=0}^{j} \Phi_k(i)} | j \leq s\}$, to every language $L_{\langle k,j \rangle}$, $j \neq 0$, with $L_{\langle k,j \rangle} \subset \{a^k b^{\sum_{j=0}^{y} \Phi_k(j)} | y \leq s\}$. Then $\mathcal{L} := (L_{\langle k,j \rangle})_{k,j \in \mathbb{N}}$ fulfils the desired conditions. Notice that $\mathcal{L} \notin EMON_{prob}(2/3)$, since $EMON_{prob}(2/3) \subset LIM$, and $LIM = COV[\mathcal{K}]$.

5 Acknowledgements

The author wishes to thank Thomas Zeugmann for suggesting the topic and for helpful discussion, and Britta Schinzel for encouragement and helpful comments. Especially, I would like to thank the program committee and the referees who gave me a lot of useful hints to enhance the quality of the paper.

References

1. D. Angluin, Inductive Inference of formal languages from positive data, *Information and Control* **45** (1980) 117 – 135.
2. D. Angluin, C. Smith, Inductive inference: theory and methods, *Comp. Survey* **15**, **3** (1983) 237 – 269.
3. M. Blum, Machine independent theory of complexity of recursive functions, *Journal of the ACM* **14** (1967) 322 – 336.
4. J. Case, C. Smith, Comparison of Identification Criteria for Machine Inductive Inference, *Theoretical Computer Science* **25**, **2** (1983) 193 – 220.
5. R. Freivalds, Finite identification of general recursive functions by probabilistic strategies, in: *Proc. of the Conf. on Fundamentals of Computation Theory* (Akademie-Verlag, Berlin, 1979) 138 – 145.
6. L. Fortnow, M. Gasarch, S. Jain, E. B. Kinber, M. Kummer, S. Kurtz, M. Pleszkoch, T. Slaman, R. Solovay, F. Stephan, Extremes in the degrees in inferability, *Ann. Pure Appl. Logic* **66** (1994) 231 – 276.
7. Gasarch, W., Plezkoch, M., Learning via Queries to an oracle, in: *Proc. 2th ACM Conf. on Comp. Learning Theory* (ACM Press, Santa Cruz, July 1989) 175 – 188.
8. Gasarch, W., Smith, C., Learning via queries, *Journal of the ACM* **39** 1 (1992), 649 – 675.
9. E.M. Gold, Language identification in the limit, *Information and Control* **10** (1967) 447 – 474.
10. J. Hopcroft, J. Ullman, *Introduction to Automata Theory Languages and Computation* (Addison-Wesley Publ. Company, 1979).
11. S. Jain, A. Sharma, Probability is more powerful than team for language identification, in: *Proc. 6th ACM Conf. on Comp. Learning Theory* (ACM Press, Santa Cruz, July 1993) 192 – 198.

320

12. S. Jain, A. Sharma, On monotonic strategies for learning r.e. languages, *Annals of Mathematics and Artificial Intelligence* (1994)
13. K.P. Jantke, Monotonic and non-monotonic inductive inference, *New Generation Computing* **8** 349 – 360.
14. K.P. Jantke, Monotonic and non-monotonic inductive inference of functions an patterns, in: J. Dix, K.P. Jantke, P.H. Schmitt, eds., *Proc. 1nd Int. Workshop on Nonmonotonic and Inductive Logics*, Lecture Notes in AI **543** (Springer, Berlin, 1991) 161 – 177.
15. M. Kummer, F. Stephan, On the structure of degrees of inferability, in: *Journal of Computer and System Sciences* **52** (1996) 214 – 238.
16. S. Lange, T. Zeugmann, Monotonic versus non-monotonic language learning, in: G. Brewka, K.P. Jantke, P.H. Schmitt, eds., *Proc. 2nd Int. Workshop on Nonmonotonic and Inductive Logics*, Lecture Notes in AI **659** (Springer, Berlin, 1993) 254 – 269.
17. S. Lange, T. Zeugmann, Language learning in the dependence on the space of hypotheses, in: *Proc. of the 6th ACM Conf. on Comp. Learning Theory* (ACM Press, Santa Cruz, July 1993) 127 – 136.
18. L. Meyer, Probabilistic language learning under monotonicity constraints, in: K.P. Jantke, T. Shinohara, T. Zeugmann, eds., *Proc. of ALT'95*, Lect. notes in AI **997** (Springer, Berlin, 1995) 169 – 185.
19. L. Meyer, Probabilistic language learning under monotonicity constraints, in: *TCS* **185** (1997) 81 – 128.
20. L. Meyer, Aspects of complexity of conservative probabilistic learning, to appear (COLT'98).
21. L. Meyer, Aspects of complexity of probabilistic language learning (Institutsbericht, IIG, Freiburg, to appear).
22. P. Odifreddi, *Classical Recursion Theory* (North Holland, 1989).
23. D. Osherson, M. Stob, S. Weinstein, *Systems that Learn, An Introduction to Learning Theory for Cognitive and Computer Scientists* (MIT Press, Cambridge MA, 1986).
24. L. Pitt, Probabilistic Inductive Inference, *J. of the ACM* **36, 2** (1989) 383 – 433.
25. T. Slaman, R. Solovay, When oracles do not help, *Proc. of the 4th ACM Conf. on Comp. Learning Theory* (ACM Press, Santa Cruz, July 1991), 379 – 383.
26. R. Soare, *Recursively Enumerable Sets and Degrees* (Springer, 1987)
27. F. Stephan, Noisy inference and oracles, in: *TCS* **185** (1997) 129 – 157.
28. R. Wiehagen, A Thesis in Inductive Inference, in: J. Dix, K.P. Jantke, P.H. Schmitt, eds., *Proc. First International Workshop on Nonmonotonic and Inductive Logic*, Lecture Notes in Artificial Intelligence **534** (Springer, Berlin, 1990) 184 – 207.
29. R. Wiehagen, R. Freivalds, E.B. Kinber, On the Power of Probabilistic Strategies in Inductive Inference, *Theoretical Computer Science* **28** (1984), 111 – 133.
30. R. Wiehagen, R. Freivalds, E.B. Kinber, Probabilistic versus Deterministic Inductive Inference in Nonstandard Numberings, *Zeitschr. f. math. Logik und Grundlagen d. Math.* **34** (1988) 531 – 539.
31. T. Zeugmann, S. Lange, A Guided Tour Across the Boundaries of Learning Recursive Languages, in: K.P. Jantke and S. Lange, eds., *Algorithmic Learning for Knowledge-Based Systems*, Lecture Notes in Artificial Intelligence **961** (Springer, Berlin, 1995) 193 – 262.

Learning Algebraic Structures from Text Using Semantical Knowledge*

Frank Stephan[1] and Yuri Ventsov[2]

[1] Mathematisches Institut, Im Neuenheimer Feld 294, Universität Heidelberg, 69120 Heidelberg, Germany, fstephan@math.uni-heidelberg.de.
[2] School of Computer Science and Engineering, The University of New South Wales, Sydney, NSW, 2052, Australia, ventsov@cse.unsw.edu.au.

Abstract. The present work investigates to which extent semantical knowledge can support the learning of basic mathematical concepts. The considered learning criteria are learning characteristic or enumerable indices for languages from positive data where the learner has to converge either syntactically (Ex) or semantically (BC). The considered classes are the classes of all monoids of a given group, all ideals of a given ring or all subspaces of a given vector space. The following is shown:

(a) Learnability depends much on the amount of semantic knowledge given at the synthesis of the learner where this knowledge is represented by programs for the algebraic operations, codes for prominent elements of the algebraic structure (like 0 and 1 in fields) and certain parameters (like the dimension of finite dimensional vector spaces). For several natural examples good knowledge of the semantics may enable to keep ordinal mind change bounds while restricted knowledge may either allow only BC-convergence or even not permit learnability at all.

(b) A recursive commutative ring is Noetherian iff the class of its ideals is BC-learnable. Such a BC-learner can be synthesized from programs for addition and multiplication. In many Noetherian rings, one can Ex-learn characteristic indices for the ideals with an ordinal bound on the number of mind changes. But there are also some Noetherian rings where it is impossible to Ex-learn the ideals or to learn characteristic indices for them.

1 Introduction

The topic of the present work is to study the learnability of mathematical structures, in particular the learnability of the classes of all ideals, monoids or similar subsets within a ring, group or field. A special emphasis is placed on the influence of semantic knowledge, that is, which kinds of knowledge about the algebraic

---

* A more comprehensive version of this paper is available as Forschungsbericht Mathematische Logik 34 of the Mathematisches Insitut at the Universität Heidelberg (same authors and title). This paper was written when Frank Stephan was visiting Arun Sharma at the School of Computer Science and Engineering, UNSW. The first author is supported by the Deutsche Forschungsgemeinschaft (DFG) grant Am 60/9-2. The second author is supported by the Australian Research Council grant A49600456 to Arun Sharma. The latter grant also supported the first author's visit to UNSW.

structure (for example, programs to compute the algebraic operations or codes for prominent elements) are necessary to synthesize the learning algorithm.

The modelling of semantic knowledge is one major problem in many applications of artificial intelligence. An automatic translator searching for the Japanese translation of the English word "brother" has four choices: "otōto" (my younger brother), "otōtosan" (your younger brother), "ani" (my older brother) and "onīsan" (your older brother). For finding the correct choice, the translator might have to hunt in the whole text for hints, for example, the author himself is visiting a secondary school while his brother is studying at the university so that the word "ani" is correct. This semantical knowledge is the main difficulty for automatic translation, syntactic grammatical rules are easier to deal with.

In mathematics, semantical properties of structures are given by the operations on a group or ring. Also the dimension of a vector space or a basis for it may serve as such semantical knowledge. The underlying mathematical structures interplay with the learnability with respect to the three aspects: the existence of a learning algorithm, the quality of the best possible learning algorithm in terms of convergence and the amount of knowledge necessary to synthesize a learner.

All learnable classes considered in this paper satisfy the analogue of Noether's chain condition as well as the fact that the intersection of two sets is again a set in the class to be learned. So it is possible to learn every such class having a uniform decision procedure [3, 19] in contrast to the general case, where such classes are sometimes not learnable and, if one considers only the learnable classes, then it is impossible to synthesize a learner from a program for the uniform decision procedure [16]. Also the class of ideals in a Noetherian ring has either limited learning quality (BC) or a learner which converges on every sequence of data, even if it does not belong to a set within the given class — so the semantical constraints imply that there are no rings of intermediate learning quality like for example the class of all finite sets. This class is learnable with finitely many syntactical mind changes but not by a learner which also converges on the illegal data sequences. Furthermore, the general learning algorithm for Noetherian rings outputs only guesses which enumerate the elements of the ideal to be learned. Although Baur [5] showed that every ideal of a Noetherian ring is recursive, there are still Noetherian rings where it is impossible to learn decision procedures.

Basic Algebraic Definitions. Before defining the algebraic structures, the reader should note, that within the present work, the operations $+$ and $\cdot$ are always taken to be commutative, that is $a + b = b + a$ and $a \cdot b = b \cdot a$ for all a, b. This is not essential for many theorems, but it makes proof and argumentation easier and helps also the reader to follow the theorems and proofs. Also the operations $+$ and $\cdot$ are always associative: $a + (b + c) = (a + b) + c$. Now further restrictions have to be introduced in order to define groups, rings and fields within this framework of structures with commutative and associative operations.

A group $(\mathbf{G}, +)$ has a neutral element, always denoted by 0, such that $a + 0 = a$ for all $a \in \mathbf{G}$. This element is unique. Furthermore there is for every element a the element $-a$ such that their sum equals 0. Quite prominent groups are the group $(\mathbf{Z}, +)$ of integers and $(\mathbf{Q}, +)$ of rationals. A monoid A is a subset of a group which contains 0 and is closed under $+$: whenever $a, b \in A$ then also $a + b \in A$. The natural numbers $(\mathbf{N}, +)$ form a monoid where $\mathbf{N} = \{0, 1, 2, \ldots\}$. A subgroup $(A, +)$ is a set which is closed under $+$ and contains for every a also the inverse $-a$. For example, $(\{\ldots, -4, -2, 0, 2, 4, \ldots\}, +)$ is a subgroup of the integers.

In a ring $(\mathbf{R}, +, \cdot)$, the substructure $(\mathbf{R}, +)$ is a group with a neutral additive element 0. Furthermore there is a multiplicative neutral element 1 and the distributive law has to be satisfied: $a(b + c) = ab + ac$ for all a, b, c. An ideal is a subset A of a ring such that $a + b \in A$ for all $a, b \in A$, $-a \in A$ for all $a \in A$ and $a \cdot b \in A$ for all $a \in \mathbf{R}$ and $b \in A$. Adding the multiplication, the integers $(\mathbf{Z}, +, \cdot)$ and rationals $(\mathbf{Q}, +, \cdot)$ are rings. The ideals and the subgroups coincide in the case of the integers, so every ideal there has the form $\{\ldots, -2a, -a, 0, a, 2a, \ldots\}$ for some a.

A field $(\mathbf{F}, +, \cdot)$ is a ring with the additional property, that every $a \neq 0$ has a multiplicative inverse b such that $ab = 1$. So a field is a ring where $(\mathbf{F} - \{0\}, \cdot)$ is a group. The rationals and also the reals are examples for fields, but the integers are not a field since there is no integer b such that $2 \cdot b = 1$. Note that fields have only the two trivial ideals: $\{0\}$ and the whole set. But subfields and subrings may be nontrivial structures.

A vector space $(\mathbf{V}, +, \cdot)$ over some field, say $(\mathbf{Q}, +, \cdot)$, is a group $(\mathbf{V}, +)$ which in addition has a multiplicative operation. For all elements $a, a' \in \mathbf{V}$ and $b, b' \in \mathbf{Q}$ it holds that $a \cdot (b \cdot b') = (a \cdot b) \cdot b'$, $a \cdot (b + b') = a \cdot b + a \cdot b'$ and $(a + a') \cdot b = a \cdot b + a' \cdot b$.

Further information on on algebraic definitions can be found in textbooks like those of Cohen [8], Eisenbud [9] and Kaplansky [15].

Recursion Theoretic Notation. A set A can be represented in two ways in recursion theory: by (a) a grammar or a program which generates every element in A but which does not give any information on the non-elements of the set and (b) a program which computes the characteristic function $x \to A(x)$ of a set — $A(x) = 1$ if x is in the set and $A(x) = 0$ otherwise. A program e which generates the elements of A is called an enumerable index for A, a program which computes the characteristic function of A is called a characteristic index for A.

Within this paper, the coding of the mathematical structures is always done by indexing them with natural numbers. So the additive and multiplicative operations $+$ and $\cdot$ within the structures are always also operations on the codes in $\mathbf{N}$. The coding is furthermore 1-1 except in the last chapter which deals with coding where the equality is enumerable or the domain is not a proper non-recursive subset of $\mathbf{N}$. Since the operations inside the mathematical objects are given by programs and not as abstract operations which one builds into the programs as oracle calls, one might expect that the information obtained is a bit more than in the model of Blum, Shub and Smale [7]. Nevertheless the results of the present work could also be executed by a machine doing these ring operations as oracle calls; much more information can be exploited from the knowledge of the semantic structure of the underlying objects than from the syntactic structure of the given programs. But presenting them as programs has the advantage that all operations within this work can be dealt within the uniform framework of recursive functions, although complexity theoretic aspects with respect to computation time or space (where oracle calls would have the cost 1) are lost since the learners have to deal with every, sometimes very inefficient, program for the algebraic operations.

More information on the theory of recursive and enumerable sets can be found in the books of Odifreddi [23] and Soare [26].

Learning Theoretic Notation. Learning in the present work follows Gold style learning of languages in the limit [6, 12, 24]. A language is generally an enumerable set, within this paper it is mostly a recursive set. The learning procedure receives a text which is an arbitrary sequence containing all elements of the set but no non-element. For each such text T and each finite prefix $\sigma \preceq T$ of the text, the learner produces an output $M(\sigma)$ which is a guess for a program to compute the characteristic function of the set to be learned. The most general notion of convergence is BC ("behaviourally correct"): it just requires that M learns a language L iff M outputs for every text T of L and almost every $\sigma \preceq T$ an index $M(\sigma)$ of L. A whole class S is learnable under a given criterion like BC iff there is a recursive learner which learns every $L \in S$ from every text under this criterion.

The programs output by a BC-learner may all be different and since it is impossible to check the equality of programs, one cannot see whether momentary changes of the hypothesis give really some improved program or just rephrases the previous program. So one favours a learner, which identifies the languages syntactically. The underlying criterion is called Ex ("explanatory") and most natural BC-learnable classes, but not all, are also Ex-learnable. Formally, a machine M Ex-learns a language L iff M outputs on every text T of L for almost all $\sigma \preceq T$ the same program e_T for L. Note that every such algorithm can translated into an equivalent one which learns the same languages and in addition converges on every text to the same program e_L for L.

A more restrictive variant is learning with a bounded number of mind changes when the learner may output only a constant number of different hypotheses among which the last one is correct. Freivalds and Smith [10] introduced the more general notion of bounding mind changes by ordinals: Here the learner has to count down an ordinal at every mind change and when the ordinal reaches 0, no further mind change is possible. For practical purposes it is often sufficient to consider ordinals which can be expressed as polynomials in ω with positive integer coefficients. For example, the numbers $1, 3, \omega + 2, \omega + 5, 2\omega + 3, \omega^2 + 4$ and ω^3 are such ordinals. The class containing $\emptyset$ and all sets $L_n = \{n, n+1, \ldots\}$ is a quite natural example of a class learnable with the ordinal mind change bound ω but not with any constant mind change bound.

Since there is no infinite descending sequence of ordinals, it is clear, that a learner with an ordinal bound on the number of mind changes converges on every input text — even if the language generated by it is not enumerable and therefore definitely not learnable. Ambainis, Jain and Sharma [2] showed that also the converse holds: If a machine M learns a class S of languages and converges on every text whatever it comes from, then there is a recursive ordinal α such that S can be learned with an α bound on mind changes.

Learning with Semantic Knowledge. Adleman and Blum [1] showed that the semantic knowledge which programs are total and which not allowed to learn all recursive functions in the limit. In their approach it is even sufficient to get this information in the limit. Formally this is done by using high oracles: Adleman and Blum [1] showed that exactly the high oracles allow to learn the class REC of all recursive functions in the limit.

Semantic knowledge is in the present work mainly knowledge on some mathematical structures linked to the languages to be learned. For example, if ideals within a ring are learned, the semantic knowledge might consist in programs which compute the ring operations. These programs may be i for the addition and j for the multiplication. Of course the learning algorithm depends on i and j: so given i and j, one has first to synthesize the learner which then learns the ideal using some semantic knowledge also derived from i and j. Osherson, Stob and Weinstein [25] showed that synthesis can be quite difficult: there is no effective procedure which synthesizes an Ex-learner for the finite class $\{W_e, W_{e'}\}$ from grammars e and e' generating these sets. In the case of learning uniformly recursive families of languages or functions, synthesis is quite more powerful [14, 25, 28]. Note that synthesizing a learner via a recursive function and having a learner with parameters, which is correct for every fixed legal value of these parameters, is the same concept — both can be transformed into each other. This holds in an abstract manner for all parameterized recursion theoretic procedures and recursion theorists deal with it as "substitution" or an application of the "S_n^m-Theorem" [23, Proposition II.1.7].

In the setting of learning uniformly recursive (or indexed) families of languages, the (quite restricted) semantics are present in form of a program [3, 28]. In the case of learning functions by enumeration, it is quite obvious how to synthesize a learner from this information. On the other hand, this is not possible in the case of language learning from positive data. Here one exploits semantic knowledge about the family which cannot be obtained algorithmically from the decision procedure. Kobayashi and Yokomori [19, 20, 21] obtained for these families results parallel to those obtained for BC-learning within the present work. Since for uniformly recursive families, the notions of syntactic and behavioural convergence coincide, Kobayashi and Yokomori [19] state there results for Ex-learning. Later, they [21] investigated the learnability of certain classes of regular languages and to which degree this learnability is preserved under the formation of subclasses and the application of homomorphisms.

The topic of the present work is to find connections between the ability to learn or to synthesize learners on one hand and the access to semantic knowledge on the class to be learned on the other hand. The classes to be learned are mainly substructures (ideals, subgroups, subrings, subspaces) of prominent mathematical objects.

2   The Ring of Integers

Within this section it is investigated to which extent it is possible to learn subsets of the integers which satisfy certain natural requirements. These subsets are either ideals within the ring $(\mathbf{Z}, +, \cdot)$ or at least monoids, that is, closed under $+$. It is shown that learnability depends very much on the fact to which extent semantical information is accessible on the present coding of the natural numbers.

There are direct encodings of the integers into the natural numbers such that all operations (addition, negation and multiplication) are easily computable and codes for prominent numbers like 0 and 1 are known to the learner. The next theorem shows how one can learn in this standard model the classes of all ideals and monoids and gives optimal bounds on the mind change complexity which can be achieved. Later variants are considered where less information is present and therefore some of the specific semantic of the integers is lost. It is then shown that either the complexity of the learning process goes up or learning becomes impossible at all. This loss of semantics makes it necessary to distinguish between a number x and the code a_x representing it. Nevertheless relations and operations can also be carried out on the codes, so $x + y$ stands just for the z which satisfies $a_z = a_x + a_y$.

Theorem 2.1 *For the standard model, the class of the ideals of $(\mathbf{Z}, +, \cdot)$ can be learned from positive data with mind change complexity ω and the class of the monoids of $(\mathbf{Z}, +)$ with mind change complexity ω^2. These bounds are optimal.*

The next theorem analyzes under which circumstances one can still recover all necessary informations on $\mathbf{Z}$ in order to learn with optimal mind change bounds.

Theorem 2.2 *Using the below information on $(\mathbf{Z}, +, \cdot)$ one can synthesize a machine which Ex-learns characteristic indices from positive data and satisfies the ordinal mind change bounds ω for ideals and ω^2 for monoids:*
(a)   *a program for a 1-1 mapping to the standard model;*
(b)   *a program for the addition, the code for 0 and the code for 1;*
(c)   *a program for the addition and a program for the multiplication.*

A uniform decision procedure for a class of sets is a mapping $i, x \to U_i(x)$ such that the sets U_i cover all sets in the class and such that every U_i is in the given class. Such a class has the characteristic sample property, if for every set U_i there is a finite subset E_i such that $E_i \subseteq U_j - U_i \subseteq U_j$ for all j. Kobayashi and Yokomori [19, 20, 21] showed that classes which have a uniform decision procedure and the characteristic sample property are Ex-learnable. The proof is effective in the sense that a program for the mapping $i, x \to U_i(x)$ can be uniformly translated into a program for the learner.

Fact 2.3 [3, 19] *Assume that for a uniformly recursive family U_i there is a family E_i of finite sets such that, for all j, $E_i \subseteq U_j - U_i \subseteq U_j$. Then it is possible to synthesize an Ex-learner which converges on every text of some U_j to the least i with $U_i = U_j$.*

A notation of ordinals assigns to every code one fixed ordinal such that there ordering is computable. An easy way to represent notations of ordinals is to identify them with enumerable and well-ordered set $O \subseteq \mathbf{Q}$. Recall that a set is well-ordered iff there is no infinite descending sequence $q_0 > q_1 > \ldots$ of elements of this set. Usually notations of ordinals are also equipped with further operations to detect limit ordinals, successors and so on — but the negative result of the next theorem is obtained by diagonalizing against all well-ordered enumerable sets of rationals and therefore, these additional structures can just be ignored.

Theorem 2.4 *It is possible to synthesize learners for the class of all ideals or all monoids in $(\mathbf{Z}, +, \cdot)$ from the following data:*
(a) *a program for an uniform decision procedure for the class;*
(b) *a program for the addition.*
The obtained machines learn the given class from positive data and satisfy some ordinal mind change bound. But there is no fixed notation of ordinals such that the synthesized learner can succeed by bounding its mind changes with respect to this notation.

The loss of the concrete ordinal bound is mainly due to the fact, that knowing the addition alone does not enable to identify the code for 1. The next result shows that it is even worse not to know the 0: then learning is impossible at all. Let $\mathbf{G}$ be a copy of $\mathbf{Z}$ on which a translation $f : \mathbf{G} \times \mathbf{Z} \to \mathbf{G}$ which assigns to every code a and every integer n the "n-th neighbour" of a. Such an operation is still near to the addition, but it covers every incidence which number is 0. Therefore the learner has not only to learn the monoids but also to learn every structure which cannot be distinguished from a monoid like for example the set corresponding to $\{-2, -1, 0, 1, 2, \ldots\}$ in $\mathbf{G}$. This makes it impossible to learn monoids.

Theorem 2.5 *Let $f : \mathbf{G} \times \mathbf{Z} \to \mathbf{G}$ be a translation on the copy $\mathbf{G} = g(\mathbf{Z})$ of the integers via some unknown bijection g, that is, $f(g(x), y) = g(x + y)$ for all $x, y \in \mathbf{Z}$. Then it is impossible to synthesize any machine which BC-learns the class of monoids in $\mathbf{G}$ from positive data where the monoids in $\mathbf{G}$ are just the sets of the form $g(A)$ for monoids A in $\mathbf{Z}$.*

3 Noetherian Rings

Noether [22] studied rings without infinite ascending chains of ideals. She characterized these rings as those where all ideals are generated by a finite subset of their elements. Due to this and further results, these rings were named after her. The next result gives a further characterization of the recursive Noetherian rings among all rings with recursive ring-operations: they are the rings whose class of ideals is learnable.

Theorem 3.1 *Let* $(\mathbf{R}, +, \cdot)$ *be a ring with recursive ring operations and let S be the class of all ideals in this ring. Then the following statements are equivalent:*
(a) $(\mathbf{R}, +, \cdot)$ *is Noetherian;*
(b)   *Enumerable indices for S can be BC-learned from positive data;*
(c)   *A machine, which BC-learns enumerable indices for S from positive data, can be synthesized from programs for $+$ and $\cdot$.*

Proof For (a $\Rightarrow$ c), let $M_{i,j}$ assign to every string σ the ideal generated by $range(\sigma)$ using the additive operation $+$ given by the index i and the multiplicative operation $\cdot$ given by the index j. For every σ and every ideal I containing all elements of $range(\sigma)$ it holds that $M_{i,j}(\sigma)$ outputs some set enumerating some ideal J such that $range(\sigma) \subseteq J \subseteq I$. If the learner has enough seen of some text for I, then all elements of a finite set generating I have already shown up in the text and $J = I$. So $M_{i,j}$ BC-learns enumerable indices for ideals in $(\mathbf{R}, +, \cdot)$.

For (c $\Rightarrow$ b), observe that (c) requires effective synthesis of a learner while (b) requires only its existence.

For (b $\Rightarrow$ a) and let M be an BC-learner for S. For every ideal I, M has a locking sequence σ such that $range(\sigma) \subseteq I$. Now let J be the ideal generated by the finite set $range(\sigma)$, clearly $J \subseteq I$. For every $\tau \in J^*$ it follows that $M(\sigma\tau)$ outputs an index for I. Since M also learns J it follows that $I = J$ and so I is finitely generated. The ring $(\mathbf{R}, +, \cdot)$ is Noetherian. $\blacksquare$

Applications Baur [5] obtained some of his results in a very general setting where he did not consider concrete ideals generated by finite sets E but only an abstract hull operation in a countable universe which assigns to every E the hull $I(E)$ in the sense that $I(I(E)) = I(E)$, $I(E) \subseteq I(E')$ whenever $E \subseteq E'$ and $I(E) = \cup_n I(\{x_1, x_2, \ldots, x_n\})$ if $E = \{x_1, x_2, \ldots\}$ is infinite. Within such a setting, he defined Noetherian hull operations as those where every set E has a finite subset E' such that $I(E) = I(E')$. For these structures one can show that corresponding versions of the Theorems 3.1 and 3.3 hold; so they hold in particular for learning subgroups or monoids within a basic group $(\mathbf{G}, +)$.

Considering Angluin's model of uniformly computable families [3], Kobayashi and Yokomori [19, Theorems 11 and 12] obtained a general result which implies a parallel theorem for rings whose ideals are uniformly recursive. They used only the abstract property of the monoids and ideals that they are closed under infinite unions. Note, that in the world of uniformly recursive families there is no difference between BC-learning and Ex-learning.

Theorem 3.2 [19] *Let S be a uniformly recursive family closed under infinite union. Then S is Ex-learnable from text iff S is Noetherian (in the sense that there are no infinite ascending chains of sets in S).*

So there are rings where BC-learning can be improved to Ex-learning, namely those where S is uniformly recursive. The next result states that whenever there is an improvement then this improvement is a major one: Given any algorithm which can either Ex-learn enumerable indices or BC-learn characteristic indices, one can find effectively a better an Ex-learner which outputs characteristic indices and which has some ordinal mind change bound. So Noetherian rings have either bad or good learning qualities, but nothing in between. The intuitive reason is, that all Noetherian rings are "almost good" learnable and any ring whose structure is a bit helpful for learning, has already a good learning algorithm. So it takes a quite involved construction for getting a Noetherian ring which has only bad learning quality.

Theorem 3.3 *Let S be the class of all ideals of $(\mathbf{R}, +, \cdot)$ with recursive ring operations $+$ and $\cdot$. Then S can be Ex-learned with an ordinal bound on the number of mind changes if one of the following conditions is satisfied:*
(a)   *Enumerable indices for S are Ex-learnable;*
(b)   *Characteristic indices for S are BC-learnable.*

Proof (a): Fulk [11] showed that every Ex-learner for a class of languages can be modified such that the learner on every text for every language on the class ends up in a locking sequence. Given such a learner M, it will be transformed within two stages to a learner N satisfying the desired requirements.

First characteristic indices $f(\sigma)$ based on the information σ already seen is computed. f may be faulty on some strings σ but is defined such that it is total and correct on sufficient long prefixes $\sigma \preceq T$ for texts T of languages $L \in S$. Note that there is an effective way to generate for every enumerable set W_e the ideal $I(W_e)$ generated by W_e. Now one defines the following program associated to σ by interpreting the behaviour of the recursive learner M:

$$\varphi_{f(\sigma)}(x) = \begin{cases} 1 & \text{if } x \text{ is enumerated into } I(W_{M(\sigma)}); \\ 0 & \text{if there is } \tau \in I(W_{M(\sigma)} \cup \{x\})^* \text{ such that } M(\sigma\tau) \neq M(\sigma). \end{cases}$$

If both conditions are satisfied, then the output is an arbitrary one, if none are defined, then the function is undefined at x. Given some ideal L, some text T for L and some locking sequence $\sigma \preceq T$ then $f(\sigma)$ is a total index for L: If $x \in L$ then x will be enumerated into $W_{M(\sigma)}$ and thus also into $I(W_{M(\sigma)})$, so the 1-case above is defined. Also the 0-case does not occur since also $I(W_{M(\sigma)} \cup \{x\})$ equals to L and σ is a locking sequence for L. If $x \notin L$, then x will not be enumerated into $I(W_{M(\sigma)})$ which equals L since σ is a locking sequence. Furthermore, the ideal $I(W_{M(\sigma)} \cup \{x\})$ is different from L and since M infers it, there is some $\tau \in I(W_{M(\sigma)} \cup \{x\})^*$ such that M makes a mind change to $M(\sigma\tau)$. So $\varphi_{f(\sigma)}(x) = 0$ in this case.

Furthermore one can transform any text T into a text $g(T)$ for the ideal $I(T)$ generated by $range(T)$. This transformation only uses the build-in operations $+$ and $\cdot$ of the ring and is independent of the learner M. One can realize the transformation such that the elements at the even positions of $g(T)$ are — just a bit delayed — those of T while those at the odd positions are generated from some enumeration of all elements contained in the ideal of T and pasted between the original elements. The procedure to find these elements to be pasted in is just to check at every stage s which is the first number which on one hand had not occurred within the first $s - 1$ elements of $g(T)$ and which on the other hand is enumerated into the ideal generated by T within s steps. Thus one obtains that every text T is translated into some text $g(T)$ for the ideal generated by the elements of T. The translation is effective and the function g is also defined on strings by assigning to every σ the first $2|\sigma|$ elements of $g(T)$ which depend only on σ. Now both functions f and g are combined to give the desired learner N.

$N(\sigma) = f(\tau)$ for the first $\tau \preceq g(\sigma)$ with $M(\tau\eta) = M(\tau)$ for all $\eta \in range(g(\sigma))^*$ of length up to $2|\sigma| - |\tau|$.

It is easy to see that N picks up in the limit the value $f(\tau)$ for some locking sequence τ of $g(T)$. Furthermore since M converges on every $g(T)$, N converges on every text T, for whatever set it is, and thus N satisfies some ordinal mind change bound [2].

(b): Again one takes a learner which has on every text a locking-sequence; this time M BC-learns characteristic indices and for each text T of some $L \in S$ there is a $\sigma \preceq T$ such that $M(\sigma\tau)$ is an index of the characteristic function of L for all $\tau \in L^*$. The function g to translate the texts is the same as in part (a) but the function f has to be adapted:

$$\varphi_{f(\sigma)}(x) = \begin{cases} 1 & \text{if } x \in I(range(\sigma)); \\ 0 & \text{if } \varphi_{M(\sigma\tau)}(x) = 0 \text{ for some } \tau \in I(range(\sigma))^*. \end{cases}$$

If both cases are defined, then the program $f(\tau)$ takes just the first one to occur. Now the new learner N combines f and g such that

$N(\sigma) = f(\tau)$ for the first $\tau \preceq g(\sigma)$ such that there is no $x \in range(g(\sigma))$ with $\varphi_{f(\tau),|\sigma|}(x)\downarrow = 0$.

The verification is similar to the previous case, with the main difference, that $f(\sigma)$ is total for every σ since the whole behaviour of M on texts beginning with $g(\sigma)$ on the ideal $I(range(\sigma))$ is analized. Note that by definition, N translates any text T into the text $g(T)$ on which M has to converge and that thus N converges on every text, so some ordinal mind change bound is kept. ∎

A ring is Artinian if every descending chain of ideals is finite. Artinian rings are also Noetherian. Baur [5, Theorem 3.8] showed that the class of all ideals of an Artinian ring with recursive operations $+$ and $\cdot$ is a uniformly recursive family.

Given a ring $(\mathbf{R}, +, \cdot)$ and a symbol x, one can define the ring $(\mathbf{R}[x], +, \cdot)$ of all polynomials in the variable x over $(\mathbf{R}, +, \cdot)$ where $+$ and $\cdot$ are extended to this new domain by the well-known algorithms to add and multiply polynomials. By the Hilbert Basis Theorem, the ring of the polynomials in one variable x is also Noetherian if the given original ring is Noetherian. Therefore, whenever it is possible to BC-learn enumerable indices for the ideals of some ring $(\mathbf{R}, +, \cdot)$, then the same can be done for $(\mathbf{R}[x_1, x_2, \ldots, x_n], +, \cdot)$. Furthermore, Hermann [5, 13] showed that for every recursive field $(\mathbf{F}, +, \cdot)$ the class of ideals in the ring $(\mathbf{F}[x_1, x_2, \ldots, x_n], +, \cdot)$ is a uniformly recursive family. So by Theorem 3.3 (c), the class of ideals of both rings can be Ex-learned.

Corollary 3.4 *The class S of all ideals in a given ring can be Ex-learned from positive data, if the ring is Artinian or of the form $(\mathbf{F}[x_1, x_2, \ldots, x_n], +, \cdot)$ for some recursive field $(\mathbf{F}, +, \cdot)$.*

While in Theorem 3.3 conditions (a) and (b) are also necessary, this is not longer for condition (c). Baur [5] showed that every ideal in a Noetherian ring is recursive, but also gives an example of a recursive Noetherian ring, whose ideals are not uniformly recursive in the sense, that every uniformly recursive family containing all ideals also contains some other sets. Therefore the algorithm from Fact 2.3 does not work here.

The next two constructions use localization [15, Section 1–4]. If a set $H \subseteq \mathbf{R}$ is closed under multiplication and contains 1 but not contain 0 then the ring $(\mathbf{R}_H, +, \cdot)$ is given by $\mathbf{R}_H = \{\frac{n}{m} : n \in H, m \in \mathbf{R}\}$ where $\frac{m}{n} = \frac{m'}{n'}$ iff $k(mn' - m'n) = 0$ for some $k \in H$, $\frac{m}{n} \cdot \frac{m'}{n'} = \frac{mm'}{nn'}$ and $\frac{m}{n} + \frac{m'}{n'} = \frac{mn' + m'n}{nn'}$.

It easy to see that by operating on pairs and taking an enumerable set H, one obtains again a ring with an representation on which the ring operations are recursive. The definition of the equality gives that the equality is enumerable in the sense that the set $\{(a, b) \in \mathbf{R}_H \times \mathbf{R}_H : a = b\}$ is enumerable. But Baur [5, Satz 3.4] showed that, for every Noetherian ring with enumerable equality, the equality is in fact already recursive.

Example 3.5 *Let P be an enumerable but not recursive set of prime numbers and let H be the multiplicative closure of P. Then the ring $(\mathbf{Z}_H, +, \cdot)$ has a recursive representation, the class of its ideals are not uniformly recursive in any of its recursive representations and an Ex-learner with mind change bound ω can be synthesized from programs for $+$ and $\cdot$.*

While BC-learners outputting enumerable indices can be synthesized from programs for $+$ and $\cdot$, this is not longer possible for Ex-learners or BC-learners outputting characteristic indices, even in rings of the form $(\mathbf{Q}[x_1, x_2, \ldots, x_n], +, \cdot)$. Since the constructions in Theorem 3.3 are effective, it is sufficient to show that it is impossible to synthesize an Ex-learner outputting characteristic indices.

Theorem 3.6 *Let i and j be indices for the operations $+$ and $\cdot$ such that they define a ring either isomorphic to $(\mathbf{Q}[x], +, \cdot)$ or to $(\mathbf{Q}[x, y], +, \cdot)$. Then it is impossible to synthesize from given i and j a machine, which Ex-learns the characteristic function for some default ideal of this ring from positive data.*

The method to construct this example can be adapted to construct a Noetherian ring such that its ideals cannot be learned from text under the criterion Ex. Recall that any Ex-learner outputting enumerable indices for the ideals can be transformed into learners outputting characteristic indices so that one can without loss of generality consider Ex-learner of the latter type.

Theorem 3.7 *There is a Noetherian ring such that the class of its ideals is not Ex-learnable.*

No algebraic characterization of the Ex-learnable rings is known and it is quite probable that there is no nice one. Nevertheless, one can give a recursion-theoretic characterization: The class S of all ideals of a Noetherian ring is Ex-learnable iff there is a K-recursive set B containing characteristic indices of exactly the sets in S.

The omitted proof of Theorem 3.7 showed that whenever M is a Ex-learner for S then M has high Turing degree, that is, K' can be computed in the limit using M as an oracle. The following theorem shows that this complexity is also sufficient to establish an Ex-learner for the ideals of all Noetherian rings which gets programs for $+$ and $\cdot$ as parameters. Stated in the terminology of Stephan and Terwijn [27] one has that, for learning the ideals of Noetherian rings, there exist universal BC-learners in all and universal Ex-learners exactly in the high Turing degrees.

Theorem 3.8 *Exactly the high Turing degrees allow to compute an Ex-learner for every Noetherian ring, this Ex-learner can be synthesized from programs for the ring operations $+$ and $\cdot$.*

The next theorem looks at the concrete class of all ideals within the Noetherian ring $(\mathbf{Q}[x_1, x_2, \ldots, x_n], +, \cdot)$. Note that by Hermann's result [13] already the class of all ideals is learnable since it is uniformly recursive; so the accent lies more on the complexity of the learning process. The learner knows the dimension n, programs for $+$ and $\cdot$ as well as codes for the important elements $0, 1, x_1, x_2, \ldots, x_n$ in advance. It is shown that ω^n is the optimal ordinal mind change bound under these circumstances.

Theorem 3.9 *The class S of all ideals in $(\mathbf{Q}[x_1, x_2, \ldots, x_n], +, \cdot)$ can be learned with mind change bound ω^n from positive data but not with any mind change bound $\alpha < \omega^n$.*

4 The Field of Rational Numbers

Learning suitable classes of subsets of fields exploit two operations, the addition $+$ and the multiplication $\cdot$ in the field. There may be learning situations, where only one operation is given. So the next two theorems deal with the situation, where the semantic knowhow of the learner is a program for one operation and the other one should be learned from data. The next result shows that the multiplication can be learned if the addition is known.

Theorem 4.1 *It is possible to synthesize a finite learner from an index e of the addition in the field $(\mathbf{Q}, +, \cdot)$ which learns a program for the multiplication from a stream of data consisting of exactly the tuples (x, y, z) with $z = x \cdot y$.*

The converse direction to learn the addition from the multiplication is not possible, in particular because there are too many ways to define a recursive additive operation compatible with the given multiplication.

Theorem 4.2 *Given the standard encoding of the rationals and the multiplication $\cdot$, the standard addition is not the only additive operation which is compatible with $\cdot$. Indeed there are uncountably many additive operations, each of them defining an isomorphic copy of the field $(\mathbf{Q}, +, \cdot)$. It is impossible to learn the recursive ones among these additive operations in the limit from the data provided by all tuples $(a_x, a_y, a_x + a_y)$.*

So one has for the field of rationals (and also for the ring of integers $\mathbf{Z}$ and the monoid of natural numbers $\mathbf{N}$), that it is easy to learn the multiplication if the addition is known while the opposite direction is impossible. This result has in the real world the parallel, that pupils learn in school first how to add natural numbers and then how to multiply them since they would face much more difficulties to do it the other way round — the abstract "non-learnability" does of course not hold in such a strict sense in the real world but "difficult" is an appropriate term to describe the situation.

The (omitted) proof of Theorem 4.1 highly depends on the semantic knowledge over the field of the rationals. Already for the ring $(\mathbf{Q}[x], +, \cdot)$ it is impossible to learn the multiplication from the addition.

Finite dimensional vector spaces of the rational numbers are quite common in mathematics, in particular in number theory. The next result deals with the question, which semantic information is necessary to learn the subspaces of finite dimensional vector spaces over the rational numbers from positive data.

Theorem 4.3 *Let $(\mathbf{V}, +, \cdot)$ be a k-dimensional rational vector space and k be finite. It is possible to synthesize a machine Ex-learning all linear subspaces from a program for the addition $+$ and the dimension k but it is impossible to do this from a program for $+$ alone without having any information on the dimension k.*

One can even show that for some family of the vector spaces with dimension at most 2 it is impossible to synthesize an Ex-learner for the class of the subspaces of this vector space from an index of the addition. So if it would be possible to generate learners which satisfy an ordinal bound on the mind changes via some fixed notation of ordinals, one could effectively produce the union of the learners $M_{e,0}$ and $M_{e,1}$ in the construction and obtain an Ex-learner for both cases. However such a learner does not exist and it is impossible to synthesize a learner from an index of the addition and the dimension of the space which respects ordinal mind change bounds with respect to a fixed notation of ordinals.

A typical example for finite dimensional vector spaces over the rational numbers is the superfield generated by adding a variable x which represents $\sqrt{2}$. Such finite dimensional superfields are called number fields of finite degree and have an additional structure, namely the multiplication. The next results shows, that in number fields of finite degree, programs for the addition and multiplication are sufficient to generated a learner for the class of their vector subspaces.

Theorem 4.4 *It is possible to synthesize, from programs for addition and multiplication, a learner which Ex-learns from positive data the characteristic function of any subspace of a number field of finite degree.*

5 Models Without Decidable Equality

Within the previous sections, there was always a 1–1 coding of the objects represented. This assumption is not so natural as one thinks of: in an acceptable numbering, every function has infinitely many codes (programs) and furthermore, it is undecidable which programs are equal and which not. In model theory, mathematicians study many models for·whose representation the equality is undecidable. The next theorem provides also an example of this type and shows, that the learnability for the two most natural representations is different. In such a model, an learner M learns a set L iff it converges to enumerable indices of the set of all codes of elements of L.

Theorem 5.1 *There is a group* $(\mathbf{G}, +)$ *having two representations:*
(a)   *The addition* $+$ *is recursive but the equality* $=$ *only enumerable and not recursive;*
(b)   *The equality is recursive but the addition not.*
Now in case (a) *there is a BC-learner but no Ex-learner for the class* S *of all finitely generated monoids in* $\mathbf{G}$, *in case* (b) S *can be Ex-learned.*

So this example showed that learnability depends much on the representation. The further dichotomy that the first representation has only enumerable indices while the second can give characteristic ones is more due to the model itself than to learning theory since none of the non-empty sets in S in the first representation is recursive. It is not possible to have an equivalent example for Noetherian rings since whenever the ring operations are recursive and the set $\{(a, a') : a = a'\}$ is enumerable, then the equality is also recursive [5, Satz 3.4].

References

1. Leonard Adleman and Manuel Blum: Inductive Inference and Unsolvability. *Journal of Symbolic Logic*, 56:891–900, 1991.
2. Andris Ambainis, Sanjay Jain and Arun Sharma: Ordinal mind change complexity of language identification. *Submitted for publication.*
3. Dana Angluin: Inductive Inference of Formal Languages from Positive Data. *Information and Control*, 45:117–135, 1980.
4. Ganesh Baliga and John Case: Learning with Higher Order Additional Information. *Proceedings of the Fifth International Workshop on Algorithmic Learning Theory, Reinhardsbrunn*, 64–75, 1994.
5. Walter Baur: Rekursive Algebren mit Kettenbedingungen. *Zeitschrift für mathematische Logik und Grundlagen der Mathematik*, 20:37–46, 1974.
6. Lenore Blum and Manuel Blum: Toward a mathematical theory of inductive inference. *Information and Control*, 28:125–155, 1975.
7. Leonore Blum, Micheal Shub and Steve Smale: On a theory of computation and complexity over the real numbers: NP-completeness, recursive functions and universal machines. *Bulletin of the American Mathematical Society*, 21:1–46, 1989.
8. Henri Cohen: *A Course in Computational Algebraic Number Theory.* Springer, Heidelberg, 1993.

9. David Eisenbud: *Commutative Algebra with a View Toward Algebraic Geometry.* Springer, Heidelberg, 1995.

10. Rūsiņš Freivalds and Carl H. Smith: On the Role of Procrastination for Machine Learning. *Information and Computation,* 107:237–271, 1993.

11. Mark A. Fulk: Saving the Phenomena: Requirements that Inductive Inference Machines Not Contradict Known Data. *Information and Computation,* 79:193–209, 1988.

12. E. Mark Gold: Language Identification in the Limit. *Information and Control,* 10:447–474, 1967.

13. Grete Hermann: Die Frage der endlich vielen Schritte in der Theorie der Polynomideale. *Mathematische Annalen,* 95:736–788, 1926.

14. Klaus Peter Jantke: Automatic synthesis of programs and inductive inference of functions. *Proceedings of the International Conference on Fundamentals of Computations Theory,* 219–225, 1979.

15. Irving Kaplansky: *Commutative Rings.* Allyn and Bacon, Inc., Boston, 1970.

16. Shyam Kapur and Gianfranco Bilardi: On uniform learnability of language families. *Information Processing Letters,* 44:35–38, 1992.

17. N. Kh. Kasymov: Logical programming without equality and constructive representations. *Vychisl. Sist.* 122:3–18, 1987.

18. Susanne Kaufmann and Frank Stephan: Robust Learning with Infinite Additional Information. *Proceedings of the Third European Conference on Computational Learning Theory* – EuroCOLT'97, Springer LNCS 1208, 316-330, 1997.

19. Satoshi Kobayashi and Takashi Yokomori: On approximately identifying concept classes in the limit. *Proceedings of the Sixth International Workshop on Algorithmic Learning Theory* – ALT'95, Springer LNCS 997, 298–312, 1995.

20. Satoshi Kobayashi: Approximate identification, finite elasticity and lattice structure of hypothesis space. *Technical Report* CSIM 96-04, Department of Computer Science and Information Mathematics, University of Electro-Communications, 1996.

21. Satoshi Kobayashi and Takashi Yokomori: Identifiability of subspaces and homomorphic images of zero-reversible languages. *Proceedings of the Eighth International Workshop on Algorithmic Learning Theory* – ALT'97, Springer LNCS 1316, 48–61, 1997.

22. Emmy Noether: Idealtheorie in Ringbereichen. *Mathematische Annalen,* 83:24–66, 1921.

23. Piergiorgio Odifreddi: *Classical recursion theory.* North-Holland, Amsterdam, 1989.

24. Daniel N. Osherson, Michael Stob and Scott Weinstein: *Systems that learn.* Bradford / MIT Press, London, 1986.

25. Daniel N. Osherson, Michael Stob and Scott Weinstein: Synthesizing inductive expertise. *Information and Computation,* 77:138–161, 1988.

26. Robert Soare: *Recursively enumerable sets and degrees.* Springer-Verlag, Heidelberg, 1987.

27. Frank Stephan and Sebastiaan Terwijn: The complexity of universal text-learners. *Proceedings of the Eleventh International Symposium on Fundamentals of Computation Theory* – FCT '97, Springer LNCS 1279, 441–451, 1997.

28. Thomas Zeugmann and Steffen Lange: A Guided Tour Across the Boundaries of Learning Recursive Languages. *Algorithmic Learning for Knowledge-Based Systems,* Springer LNCS 961, 193–262, 1995.

LIME: A System for Learning Relations

Eric McCreath,* and Arun Sharma,**

Department of Artificial Intelligence, School of Computer Science and Engineering,
The University of New South Wales, Sydney NSW 2052, Australia,
Email : {ericm,arun}@cse.unsw.edu.au

Abstract. This paper describes the design of the inductive logic programming system LIME. Instead of employing a greedy covering approach to constructing clauses, LIME employs a Bayesian heuristic to evaluate logic programs as hypotheses.

The notion of a *simple clause* is introduced. These sets of literals may be viewed as subparts of clauses that are effectively independent in terms of variables used. Instead of growing a clause one literal at a time, LIME efficiently combines simple clauses to construct a set of gainful candidate clauses. Subsets of these candidate clauses are evaluated via the Bayesian heuristic to find the final hypothesis.

Details of the algorithms and data structures of LIME are discussed. LIME's handling of recursive logic programs is also described.

Experimental results to illustrate how LIME achieves its design goals of better noise handling, learning from fixed set of examples (and from only positive data), and of learning recursive logic programs are provided. Experimental results comparing LIME with FOIL and PROGOL in the KRK domain in the presence of noise are presented. It is also shown that the already good noise handling performance of LIME further improves when learning recursive definitions in the presence of noise.

1 Introduction

This paper is a progress report on LIME—an inductive logic programming (ILP) system that induces logic programs as hypotheses from ground facts.[1] Unlike many systems (e.g., Quinlan's FOIL [23], Muggleton and Feng's GOLEM [19], and Muggleton's Progol [21]) that employ a greedy covering approach to constructing the hypothesis one clause at a time, LIME employs a Bayesian framework that evaluates logic programs as candidate hypotheses. This framework, introduced in [14] and incorporated in the LIME system, has been shown to have the following features:

– better noise handling,

* Supported by an Australian Postgraduate Award and by the Australian Research Council grant A49703068 to Ross Quinlan.
** Supported by the Australian Research Council grant A49530274.
[1] This is a preliminary report of work in progress; updated versions of the report on LIME can be obtained from http://www.cse.unsw.edu.au/~ericm/lime .

- ability to learn from fixed example size (i.e., there is no implicit assumption that the distribution of examples received by the learner matches the true "proportion" of the underlying concept to the instance space),
- capability of learning from only positive data[2], and
- improved ability to learn predicates with recursive definitions.

Empirical evidence was provided for the effectiveness of this framework with respect to the above four criteria in [14]. The present paper describes the design of the LIME system. Since the Bayesian heuristic employed in LIME requires evaluation of entire logic programs as hypotheses, the search space is naturally huge. This paper explains how LIME exploits the structure in the hypothesis space to tame the combinatorial explosion in the search space.

The main idea of the design of LIME is that instead of growing a clause one literal at a time, it builds candidate clauses from "groups of literals" referred to as "simple clauses". These simple clauses can be very efficiently combined to form new clauses in such a way that the coverage of a clause is the intersection of the coverage of the simple clauses from which it is formed. Once a list of candidate clauses has been constructed, the Bayesian heuristic is used to evaluate its subsets as potential hypotheses.

Structurally, LIME has four distinct stages:

- structural decomposition (preprocessing of the background knowledge),
- construction of simple clauses,
- construction of clauses, and
- search for the final hypothesis.

Within each stage care is taken that no redundant information is passed to the next stage. A diagrammatic outline of the various phases of LIME is given in Figure 1.

1.1 Related Work

We refer the reader for preliminaries and notation about ILP to the book by Nienhuys-Cheng and de Wolf [22] or the article by Muggleton and De Raedt [18]. Other source books for ILP are Bergadano and Gunetti [3], Lavrač and Džeroski [12], and Muggleton [17]. Below, we briefly touch upon work that is related to ours.

The design of LIME is somewhat reminiscent of the approach of translating an ILP problem into a propositional one. Džeroski, Muggleton, and Russell [10] describe the transformation of determinate ILP problems into propositional form. The systems LINUS and DINUS by Lavrač and Džeroski [12] employ attribute value learners after transforming restricted versions of the ILP problem.

Kietz and Lübe [11] introduced the notion of k-local clauses which is somewhat similar to simple clauses. They divided a clause into determinate and nondeterminate part and further subdivided the nondeterminate part into k-local

---

[2] The system can also learn from only negative data, but this capability is diminished when the concept requires a recursive definition.

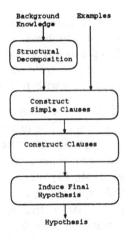

Fig. 1. The partitioning of LIME's stages.

parts. They were motivated by a desire to find efficient algorithms for subsumption.

As already noted LIME considers entire logic programs as hypotheses instead of building the hypothesis one clause at a time. Another system that follows this approach is TRACY by Bergadano and Gunetti [2]. During the preprocessing phase of the background knowledge, LIME automatically extracts type and mode information. Similar issues are addressed by Morik et al [16] in their system MOBAL.

1.2 Outline of the Paper

The outline of the paper is as follows. In Section 2, we introduce the noise model and the Bayesian framework employed in LIME. In Section 3, we describe the hypothesis language of LIME and discuss the notion of simple clauses in some detail. Sections 4–9 are devoted to a detailed discussion of the system design of LIME. Preprocessing of the background knowledge is discussed in Section 4. Section 5 describes the construction of simple clauses. Later sections describe the construction of clauses and the search for the final hypothesis. Finally, in Section 10 we report on experiments with LIME.

2 Noise Model and the Bayesian Heuristic

In this section we describe our framework for modeling learning from data of fixed example size with noise. Within this framework, we derive a Bayesian heuristic for the optimal hypothesis.

Let X denote a countable class of instances. Let D_X be a distribution on the instance space X. Let $C \subseteq 2^X$ be a countable concept class. Let D_C represent

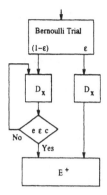

Fig. 2. Model of positive example generation

the distribution on $\mathcal{C}$. Let H be a hypothesis space and P be the distribution (prior) over H. The concept represented by a hypothesis $h \in H$ is referred to as the extension of h (written: ext(h)). Further, let $\mathcal{C}$ and H be such that:

- for each $C \in \mathcal{C}$, there is an $h \in H$ such that $C = \text{ext}(h)$; and
- for each $C \in \mathcal{C}$, $D_{\mathcal{C}}(C) = \sum_{\{\ h \in \mathcal{H} | C = \text{ext}(h)\ \}} P(h)$.

Let $\theta(C)$ denote the "proportion" of the concept C with respect to the instance space X, that is, $\theta(C) = \sum_{x \in C} D_X(x)$.

We assume that a concept C is chosen with the distribution $D_{\mathcal{C}}$. Let $\epsilon \in [0, 1]$ be the level of noise. Suppose we want to generate m positive examples and n negative examples (the reader should note that in the fixed example model, m and n are independent of the concept C).

Each of the m positive examples are generated as follows: With probability ϵ, a instance is randomly choose from X and made a positive example (this could possibly introduce noise). With probability $1 - \epsilon$, an instance is repeatedly selected randomly from X until the instance is an element of the concept. This instance is the positive example generated. Figure 2 illustrates this process. The generation of negative examples is done similarly[3].

A fixed example size framework allows learning to take place from only positive data (and from only negative data) in addition to the usual combination of positive and negative data. Additionally, the choice of such a framework can be motivated as follows. Many learning systems have an implicit expectation that the distribution of examples received by the learner matches the true "proportion" of the underlying concept to the instance space. However, in many situations such an assumption is unjustified. Usually the size of positive and negative examples is fixed and independent of the concept being learned. As an example, consider a learner presented with a set of 100 positive and 100 negative examples of cancer patients. It is very unlikely that this set of examples is representative of the population from where the examples are drawn.

---

[3] The level of noise ϵ can be made different for the positive and negative examples, but for simplicity we take it to be the same.

We now derive a Bayesian heuristic for finding the most probable hypothesis h given the example set E.[4] This induction can be formally expressed as follows.[5]

$$h_{\text{induced}} = \max_{h \in H} P(h|E) \qquad (1)$$

Using Bayes' formula, $P(h|E)$ can be expressed as follows.

$$P(h|E) = \frac{P(h)P(E|h)}{P(E)} \qquad (2)$$

We will apply Occam's razor in computation of $P(h)$, the prior probability of the hypothesis h, thereby assigning higher probabilities to simpler hypotheses. $P(E|h)$, probability of examples E given that hypothesis h represents the target concept, can be calculated by taking the product of the conditional probabilities of the positive and negative example sets. As each positive example is generated independently, $P(E^+|h)$ may be calculated by taking the product of the conditional probabilities of each positive example. $P^+(e|h)$, the conditional probability of a positive example e given hypothesis h, is computed as follows.

$$P^+(e|h) = \begin{cases} \frac{D_X(e)(1-\epsilon)}{\theta(\text{ext}(h))} + D_X(e)\epsilon, & \text{if } e \in \text{ext}(h); \\ D_X(e)\epsilon, & \text{if } e \notin \text{ext}(h). \end{cases} \qquad (3)$$

A few words about the above equation are in order. Given that h represents the target concept, the only way in which $e \notin \text{ext}(h)$ is if the right hand path in Figure 2 was chosen. Hence, in this case the conditional probability of e given h is $D_X(e)\epsilon$. On the other hand, if $e \in \text{ext}(h)$ then either the left or right hand paths in Figure 2 could have been chosen. The contribution of the right hand path to $P^+(e|h)$ is then $D_X(e)\epsilon$. If the left hand path is taken, then the instance drawn is guaranteed to be from the target concept; hence $D_X(e)(1-\epsilon)$ is divided by $\theta(\text{ext}(h))$—the proportion of the target concept to the instance space. By a similar reasoning we compute $P^-(e|h)$, the conditional probability of a negative example e given hypothesis h.

$$P^-(e|h) = \begin{cases} \frac{D_X(e)(1-\epsilon)}{1-\theta(\text{ext}(h))} + D_X(e)\epsilon, & \text{if } e \notin \text{ext}(h); \\ D_X(e)\epsilon, & \text{if } e \in \text{ext}(h). \end{cases} \qquad (4)$$

Now, $P(E|h)$ can be computed as follows.

$$P(E|h) = \prod_{e \in E^+} P^+(e|h) \prod_{e \in E^-} P^-(e|h) \qquad (5)$$

We let TP denote the set of true positives $\{ e \in E^+ \mid e \in \text{ext}(h) \}$; TN denote the set of true negatives $\{ e \in E^- \mid e \notin \text{ext}(h) \}$; FPN denote the set of false positives and false negatives, $\{ e \in E^+ \mid e \notin \text{ext}(h) \} \cup \{ e \in E^- \mid e \in \text{ext}(h) \}$.

---

[4] All references to example sets are actually references to *example multisets*. E is the union of positive (E^+) and negative (E^-) examples.

[5] The notation $\max_{h \in H} P(h|E)$ denotes a hypothesis $h \in H$ such that $(\forall h' \in H)[P(h|E) \geq P(h'|E)]$.

Substituting 3 and 4 into 5 and using TP, TN, and FPN, we get the following.

$$P(E|h) = \left(\prod_{e \in E^+ \cup E^-} D_X(e) \right) \left(\frac{1-\epsilon}{\theta(\text{ext}(h))} + \epsilon \right)^{|TP|}$$
$$\left(\frac{1-\epsilon}{1-\theta(\text{ext}(h))} + \epsilon \right)^{|TN|} \epsilon^{|FPN|} \tag{6}$$

Now substituting 6 into 2 and 2 into 1 and performing additional arithmetic manipulation, we obtain the final h_{induced} as $\max_{h \in H} Q(h)$, where $Q(h)$ is defined as follows.

$$Q(h) = \lg(P(h)) + |TP| \lg \left(\frac{1-\epsilon}{\theta(\text{ext}(h))} + \epsilon \right) +$$
$$|TN| \lg \left(\frac{1-\epsilon}{1-\theta(ext(h))} + \epsilon \right) + |FPN| \lg(\epsilon) \tag{7}$$

Hence, in our inductive framework, a learning system attempts to maximize $Q(h)$ (referred to as the *quality* of the hypothesis h). LIME evaluates logic programs as candidate hypotheses by computing their Q values. The details of how LIME computes $P(h)$ and $\theta(ext(h))$ are provided in Sections 8 and 9, respectively.

Finally, we would like to note that the treatment of noise in our framework has some similarities to that of Angluin and Laird [1]. Their noise level parameter measures the percentage of data with the incorrect sign, that is, elements of the concept being mislabeled as negative data and vice versa. In their model 50% noise level means the data is truly random, whereas in our model truly random data is at noise level of 100%. Thus, in their model it is not useful to consider noise levels of greater than 50%. Our current model requires that the noise level be provided to the system. Although this may appear to be a weakness, in practice, a reasonable estimate suffices, and it can be shown that with increase in the example size, the impact of an inaccurate noise estimate diminishes. It should be noted that experiments reported in this paper always used a noise parameter of 10% in computing $Q(h)$ even if the actual noise in the data was considerably higher.

3 Hypothesis Space and Simple Clauses

The hypothesis space of LIME is chosen not only to reduce the size of the search but to also simplify the structure of the search space. The hypothesis space of LIME consists of definite ordered logic programs whose clauses are:

- *function free*: this simplifies the structure of each clause without seriously affecting expressiveness,

- *determinate*[6]: although this restricts expressiveness, clause handling is simplified as each variable may only be bound in a unique way, and
- terms in the head of the target clause are required to be distinct variables, and terms in literals of the body can only be variables (this restriction can be overcome by introducing predicates that define a constant and the equality relation in the background knowledge).

We next motivate the notion of simple clauses.

Each clause consists of a head literal and a list of body literals. In general, a literal within the body of a clause may use a variable that has been introduced and bound by a previous literal in the body. Since variables within the clause overlap, this literal can't be considered independent. However, the list of literals in the body may be broken down into lists of literals that are effectively independent in terms of variables used. We refer to such lists as *simple clauses*. This notion is best illustrated with the help of an example. Consider the predicate teen_age_boy where the background knowledge consists of each person's age, each person's sex, and the greater than relation. Now a clause[7] for teen_age_boy is:

$$\text{teen\_age\_boy}(A) \leftarrow \text{male}(A), \text{age}(A, B), B > 12, 20 > B.$$

The above clause can be "constructed" from the following three simple clauses by "combining" their bodies.

$$\text{teen\_age\_boy}(A) \leftarrow \text{male}(A).$$
$$\text{teen\_age\_boy}(A) \leftarrow \text{age}(A, B), B > 12.$$
$$\text{teen\_age\_boy}(A) \leftarrow \text{age}(A, B), 20 > B.$$

To see how the above works and to formally define a simple clause, we introduce the notion of a directed graph associated with an ordered clause. For any two literals l_1 and l_2 in a clause, we say that l_2 is *directly dependent* on l_1 just in case there exists a variable in l_2 that is bound in l_1. Hence, a directed graph may be associated with a clause by associating each literal to a node in the graph and by forming a directed edge from the node associated with literal l_1 to l_2 just in case l_2 is directly dependent on l_1. A literal l_2 is said to be *dependent* on literal l_1 just in case there is a path in the graph from l_1 to l_2.

Clearly, graphs associated with determinate clauses are acyclic. A literal in a clause is said to be a *source* literal just in case there are no literals in the clause on which it depends. A literal in a clause is said to be a *sink* literal just in case there are no literals in the clause that depend on it. Clearly, the head of a clause is always a source literal.

---

[6] Intuitively, a clause is *determinate* if each of its literals are determinate; a literal is *determinate* if each of its variables that do not occur in previous literals has only one possible binding given the bindings of its variables that appear in previous literals. See Džeroski, Muggleton, and Russell [10] for a more formal definition.

[7] LIME will of course use a slightly different representation as it does not allow constants; this example has been chosen to illustrate the notion of a simple clause.

Definition 1. A clause is said to be *simple* just in case it contains at most one sink literal.

The directed graph for the clause defining `teen_age_boy` is show in Figure 3. Since it has three sink nodes, it is not a simple clause. However, the directed graph for the clause describing `over12`, shown in Figure 4, has exactly one sink node and hence is a simple clause.

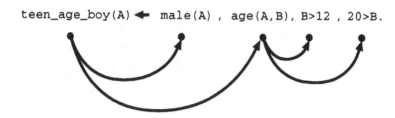

Fig. 3. Directed graph corresponding to the example clause

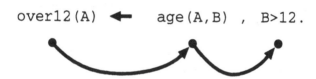

Fig. 4. Directed graph corresponding to the over twelve clauses

We next discuss some properties of simple clauses which makes them suitable for our needs. Since we are considering determinate clauses, the ordering of the literals in the body is important; the body of a clause is considered a list, not a set. Although there is some flexibility in the ordering, the constraint that "if l_1 depends on l_2 then l_1 is to the right of l_2" must be respected. This constraint yields an equivalence class over the set of clauses. If C is the set of all clauses, then we define $[c]$ to denote the set of all clauses in C that are equivalent to c. As these partitions are finite, and there is a lexicographic ordering over the clauses, a unique clause may be used to represent the equivalence partition, which we take to be the clause in $[c]$ with the least lexicographic ordering.

Let b_1 and b_2 be the bodies of two clauses with the same head. Then $b_1 \uplus b_2$ denotes the concatenation of b_1 with b_3, where b_3 is b_2 with all the b_1 literals removed. Consistency in variable naming is carefully maintained as follows:

- variables in the heads of the two clauses are the same;

– if there is a literal in b_1 and another in b_2 with the same predicate symbol and the same variables that have been bound in previous literals, then the new variables in these two literals have the same variable names. A simple way of maintaining this consistency in variable naming is to name variables by the simple clauses that created them.

We also adopt the notation $\uplus$ for clauses. Let $c_1 = h_1 \leftarrow b_1$ and $c_2 = h \leftarrow b_2$. Then $c_1 \uplus c_2$ is $h_1 \leftarrow b_1 \uplus b_2$ if $h_1 = h_2$ and undefined otherwise.

Simple clauses have three useful properties. First, any clause may be constructed from a finite set of simple clauses. Second, the intersection of the coverage of a set of simple clauses is the coverage of the clause formed by combining the set of simple clauses. The third property is about the completeness of the method of constructing simple clauses; i.e., there is an algorithm that enumerates the complete set of simple clauses for a given hypothesis language.

The next three propositions formalize these properties. Let C be the set of all clauses in the hypothesis space and let S be the set of all simple clauses. Clearly $S \subset C$.

Proposition 1. *For all $c \in C$, there exists a finite set of simple clauses S such that $c \in [\uplus_{s \in S} s]$.*

Proof. Let $c = h \leftarrow b$ and let g be the graph associated with c. Then for each sink literal in g we construct a simple clause by including all the literals that this sink literal is dependent on. Let $\{h \leftarrow b_1, h \leftarrow b_2, \ldots, h \leftarrow b_n\}$ be the set of simple clauses thus formed.

We claim that $c \in [h \leftarrow b_1 \uplus b_2 \uplus \cdots \uplus b_n]$. Clearly, $b_1 \uplus b_2 \uplus \cdots \uplus b_n$ will not contain any literal not in c as each literal in the body of the simple clauses is from c. Also, the combined clause, $h \leftarrow b_1 \uplus b_2 \uplus \cdots \uplus b_n$, will not be missing any literal from c because each literal in c is either a sink literal or has at least one sink literal dependent on it. In the former case the literal will be found in the simple clause formed by the sink literal; in the latter case the literal will be found in the corresponding simple clause. Λ

We next show that the coverage of a clause can be calculated by taking the intersection of the coverage of its simple clauses. This is because in the case of determinate clauses, the variable bindings for the simple clauses and the corresponding combined clause match. Hence, given the same interpretation prescribed by the background knowledge, if all the literals in the combined clause are true then all the literals in the simple clauses will also be true, and vice versa.

Proposition 2. *Let $c \in C$ be given. Let the set of simple clauses $\{s_1, s_2, \ldots, s_n\}$ be such that $c = s_1 \uplus s_2 \uplus \cdots \uplus s_n$. Then the coverage of c is the intersection of the coverage of each simple clause in $\{s_1, s_2, \ldots, s_n\}$.*

The above property yields a very efficient method of calculating coverage of a clause — by taking the conjunction of coverage bit vectors associated with the simple clauses that are combined to form the clause.

Proof. Suppose $c \in C$ covers an instance e. When e is resolved with c, each variable in c is uniquely bound (since c is determinate) in such a way that each literal in the body of c is true in the interpretation implied by the background knowledge. As each simple clause contains both a sink literal and all the literals that this sink literal depends on, the binding for each variable in the simple clause will be the same as the binding in c. Hence, each literal in the body of the simple clause will also be true in the intended interpretation. Thus, each simple clause also covers the instance e.

Suppose an instance e is covered by each simple clause in the $\{s_1, s_2, \ldots, s_n\}$. Then for each s_i there is a unique variable binding (since each s_i is also determinate) σ_i that witnesses coverage of e by s_i. Moreover, each literal in the body of $s_i \sigma_i$ is true in the intended interpretation. Now, the same variables may appear in different simple clauses. It is easy to argue that when e is resolved with different simple clauses the binding for a variable appearing in these simple clauses is the same (if this was not the case then we will have a contradiction to the assumption that c is determinate). Hence, when the bodies of the simple clauses are combined the bindings for variables across all the simple clauses will be the same. Therefore, each literal in c will also be true in the interpretation. Hence, c covers e. Λ

Proposition 3. *There exists an algorithm that enumerates the complete set of simple clauses.*

Proof. We first discuss the idea behind such an algorithm. The graph associated with a simple clause contains one sink literal which directly or indirectly depends on all other literals in the clause. Now if this sink literal is removed from the simple clause, we get a clause that has one or more sink literals. For each sink literal in this new clause, a new simple clause may be created by including the sink literal and all the literals that the sink literal depends on. Each new clause thus formed is simple and is smaller than the original simple clause. Reversing this process, it is easy to see that any simple clause may be created by combining a set of smaller simple clauses with a new literal l in such a way that the newly formed clause has l as the only sink literal. The one exception to this property is the simple clause with empty body. A complete algorithm for enumerating the simple clauses follows directly from this property, and such an algorithm forms the basis of LIME's simple clause table construction.

Algorithm 1 *Simple Clause Enumeration.*

begin
   current_simple_clause := $\{h \leftarrow .\}$
   output $h \leftarrow .$
   loop do
     $N := \{\}$
     foreach $S \subset current\_simple\_clause$ **do**
       foreach $l \in possible\_literals$ **do**
         $sc :=$ combine l with S

```
        if sc is a new simple clause then
           output sc
           N := N ∪ {sc}
        fi
     od
  od
  current_simple_clause := current_simple_clause ∪ N
od
end
```

We now show that Algorithm 1 enumerates the complete set of simple clauses. The proof is by induction: we show that after the i'th iteration of the loop all simple clauses with up to i literals in their bodies have been enumerated.

Clearly this is the case for $i = 0$ as the only simple clause with 0 literals in its body is the clause with empty body.

Now suppose the inductive hypothesis is true for $i = k$. Then all simple clauses with k or fewer literals in their bodies will be in '*curent_simple_clause*'. After the next iteration of the loop all simple clauses with $k + 1$ literals in their bodies will have been enumerated. This is because any simple clause with $k + 1$ literals can be formed by a set of simple clauses with at most k literals in their bodies, and a new literal. Hence, the inductive proposition is true for $i = k + 1$. Also note that the number of new simple clauses in each iteration of the loop is finite, as the number of both possible subsets and new literals are finite. Λ

The above algorithm is clearly very inefficient in the way it forms simple clauses — in each iteration it repeatedly considers simple clauses that have already been formed, and it also must detect and remove clauses that are not simple. By requiring new simple clauses to contain a variable from the previous level, repetition in the algorithm is removed; and by maintaining the literal dependency information, the non-simple clauses may be avoided. These techniques are employed by LIME.

4 Preprocessing the Background Knowledge

The first stage in LIME's inductive process involves the preprocessing of the background knowledge. This phase has three goals:

- automatic extraction of information from the background knowledge to enable the system to dynamically direct the search,
- removal of any redundancy within the background knowledge, and
- encoding of the background knowledge so that it may be efficiently indexed for the search.

We briefly discuss these aspects of the preprocessing phase.

4.1 Extracting Type and Mode Information

Each term in a predicate has an implicit type. A clause in which the type associated with a variable is inconsistent will not form part of a good hypothesis. Hence, by learning the type information from the examples and the background knowledge, inconsistent clauses may be skipped in the search. LIME uses a flat type hierarchy. Integer and floating point types are inferred simply from the syntax. Other types are induced from the example and the background knowledge. This process is thoroughly examined in [13].

Also, since the search space is restricted to determinate clauses, it is useful to know the mode restrictions for each predicate prior to the search. In the absence of such information each time a literal is added to a clause the system would need to assert that unbound variables are uniquely bound. As this check is essentially the same each time it is conducted, considerable improvement in performance can be achieved if mode information was available. LIME extracts mode information from the data which enables it to skip clauses that are not determinate. This process is also detailed in [13]. Another system that addresses these issues is MOBAL [16].

4.2 Removing Redundancy

There are three ways in which redundancy is removed from the background knowledge. First, if a set of relations are equivalent then only one needs to be considered in the inductive process. For this purpose two relations are said to be equivalent if they consist of identical ground facts in such a way that the predicate name and the ordering of the terms in the predicate are ignored. Second, if there exists symmetry within the terms in a relation then it is only necessary to consider one ordering of the terms. Consider the add relation which is symmetric in the first two terms. If the variables in the first two terms of an add literal in the body of a clause are flipped the new clause will be equivalent with respect to its coverage and size. Hence, only one of the clauses need be considered. This is illustrated in the two mult clauses shown below. Although, they are different syntactically, they may be considered equivalent, and hence only one needs to be considered in the search space.

$$\text{mult}(A, B, C) \leftarrow \text{inc}(D, A), \text{mult}(D, B, E), \text{add}(E, B, C).$$
$$\text{mult}(A, B, C) \leftarrow \text{inc}(D, A), \text{mult}(D, B, E), \text{add}(B, E, C).$$

Third, as only determinate logic programs are considered, any background relations that do not produce a determinate clause are not considered in the search space.

4.3 Improving Indexing

Once the background knowledge is preprocessed it is used either to determine a ground query or a query that uniquely binds new variables. Due to the large number of queries to be performed, this operation must be efficient. Hence, hash tables are use to store the background knowledge. The time complexity of a query operation is $O(1)$ with respect to the number of ground facts defining the background predicate.

5 Simple Clause Table Construction

After the background knowledge is preprocessed, a table of candidate simple clauses is constructed. The simple clause table is the central data structure in LIME. Care is taken that there are no repetitions in this table. Also, as the table is constructed a record is maintained of both the instances each clause covers and the binding of each variable for different instances. This makes the process more efficient as the variable bindings need not be recalculated each time a simple clause is extended to form a new simple clause. The simple clause table of LIME may be viewed as consisting of two tables:

- *Simple Clause Coverage Table*: The first part of the table contains information about the coverage of instances by candidate simple clauses. This part of the table is stored as a bit vector: 1 indicating that the simple clause covers the instance and 0 indicating that the simple clause does not cover the instance.[8] The advantage of this storage scheme is that the coverage of a clause formed by combination of two simple clauses can be very efficiently determined by taking the conjunction of the bit-vectors describing the coverage of the two simple clauses.
- *Variable Binding Table*: The second part of the table consists of the binding information for each variable introduced in the simple clauses. Since we are concerned here with only determinate clauses, these bindings are unique. We use X to represent the fact that a variable does not have a binding for the instance.

An example of LIME's simple clause table is shown in Figure 5. This table captures the snapshot when LIME is in the process of learning the add relation. The two tables, *Simple Clause Coverage Table* and the *Variable Binding Table*, are shown side by side. It can be seen that the base clause for the add relation may be formed by combining the simple clauses 30 and 33. The conjunction of the bit-vectors for the these clauses will give the coverage of the following definite clause:

$$\text{add}(V0, V1, V2) : -\text{zero}(V0), \text{equal}(V0, V2).$$

The above clause once formed can be disjuncted with the clause consisting of just one simple clause (no. 500) to form the complete definition of the add

---

[8] In addition to 0 and 1, we also use the *don't care* state, denoted here as X, to indicate that a better simple clause exists (hence, the coverage information is not tabulated, although the simple clause possibly produces a useful new variable, and hence is kept).

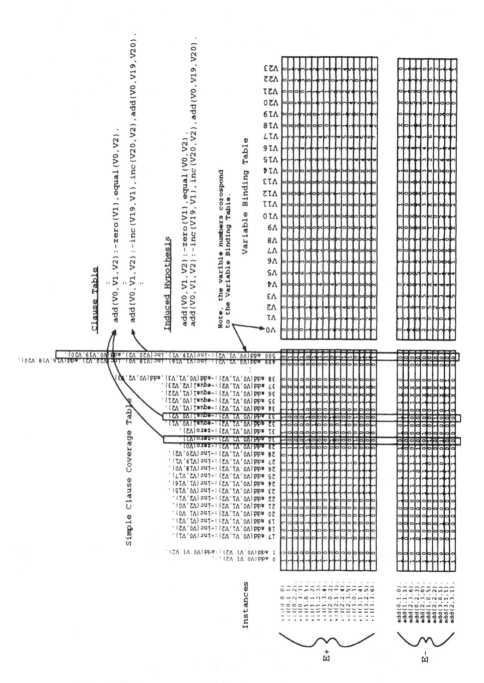

Fig. 5. Tables constructed in the simple clause stage for *add*

relation. The reader should note that disjunction of the bit vectors for the simple clause 500 with the conjunction of the bit vectors for 30 and 33 covers all the positive instances and none of the negative instances.

The simple clause table acts as an intermediate stage between the enhanced background knowledge and the candidate clauses. In many respects this intermediate stage is redundant, as the system could generate the candidate clauses directly from the preprocessed background knowledge. However, there are at least four efficiency reasons for doing so: removal of redundancy, introduction of memorization, removal of paths from search space that are not fruitful, and consolidating the construction of new variables in a clause at an initial stage.

First, we discuss the reduction of redundancy. Suppose a clause $c_1 = h \leftarrow l_1, l_2, l_3, l_4$. consists of three simple clauses:

$$h \leftarrow l_1, l_2.$$
$$h \leftarrow l_3.$$
$$h \leftarrow l_4.$$

By constructing the simple clauses first and then forming c_1 by combining them, c_1 is only considered only once. However, if the system constructed c_1 literal by literal, the same clause c_1 many be considered many times as outlined below.

$$h \leftarrow l_1. \Rightarrow h \leftarrow l_1, l_2. \Rightarrow h \leftarrow l_1, l_2, l_3. \Rightarrow h \leftarrow l_1, l_2, l_3, l_4.$$
$$h \leftarrow l_2. \Rightarrow h \leftarrow l_2, l_3. \Rightarrow h \leftarrow l_2, l_3, l_1. \Rightarrow h \leftarrow l_2, l_3, l_1, l_4.$$
$$h \leftarrow l_4. \Rightarrow h \leftarrow l_4, l_3. \Rightarrow h \leftarrow l_4, l_3, l_2. \Rightarrow h \leftarrow l_4, l_3, l_2, l_1.$$
$$\vdots \qquad \qquad \vdots \qquad \qquad \vdots \qquad \qquad \vdots$$

However, the above redundancy could be eliminated without the intermediate stage. One way to do this would be to place a syntactic ordering on the literals, and adhering to this ordering in considering clauses. However, this introduces its own problem: the syntactic ordering may not be the most gainful path in constructing a clause thereby making the use of a gain heuristic in the search less effective.

Second, the simple clause table introduces memorization in the system. LIME records the coverage of simple clauses, hence each time the literals of a simple clause are considered within a clause, the coverage does not need to be recalculated, it is simply looked up in the simple clause table. This is also the case for the variable bindings.

Third, the simple clause table provides a mechanism for removing entire branches of the search space. LIME only records simple clauses that are not dead-ends, thus eliminating the search of clauses that are not potentially useful in the final hypothesis. This is best illustrated with an example. Consider two literals l_1 and l_2. When these literals are combined in a clause, the clause covers no positive or negative examples[9] Any clause that contained these literal would

---

[9] The clause should also cover no examples used in the theta estimation (see Section 9). Otherwise, this constraint would fail when the system is learning from only negative

be a dead-end. Hence, by identifying l_1 and l_2, and not considering them, a whole series of 'dead-ends' are removed.

Fourth, by separating the clause generation into two stages, induction of simple clauses followed by induction of candidate clauses, all aspects of generating new variables in a clause are assigned to the first stage. This makes the latter stage more efficient as it is not concerned with generating new variables and maintaining their bindings.

5.1 Algorithm for Simple Clause Coverage Table and Variable Binding Table

We now present the algorithm for constructing the two tables. The algorithm maintains three data structures: a list of simple clauses, a list of bit vectors representing coverage of the simple clauses, and a table of variable bindings for the variables used in the simple clauses. These structures are initialized to contain just the simple clause with an empty body. Then candidate literals are created by considering each predicate symbol in the preprocessed background knowledge with all possible variable bindings generated until now and some new variable provided certain conditions are satisfied. A syntactic ordering is used to label variables to avoid considering literals which are equivalent to the ones already considered. If the coverage of a clause is different from the coverage of clauses generated until now or if the clause introduces a new variable, then it is incorporated into the data structure. To ensure that no simple clauses are repeated, the new literal must contain at least one variable from the previous cycle through the background relations. Note, some simple clauses produce new variables that are of use, but their instance coverage is of no value, in which case the new variables are recorded, but not the bit vector. The variable binding table not only maintains the variable binding of each variable for each instance, it also maintains an index of the simple clause the variable was generated in, and also maintains the level at which the variable was created. The task is complete if no new simple clauses are added in a given iteration, or if one of the tables is full. The detailed algorithm follows:

Algorithm 2 *Simple Clause Table Construction.*

Input :
  BG – preprocessed background knowledge
Output :
  C – A list of simple clauses
  BV – A bit vector table that stores coverage information for simple clauses
  VT – A variable binding table for each variable used in a simple clause
begin
  $C := h \leftarrow \{\}$ /* h is the head of the target predicatedefinition */

---

examples, as the target hypothesis would in general cover no negative examples and clearly no positive examples. Hence, the system would consider the target hypothesis a dead-end.

Add to BV the bit vector for the empty body clause
Add to VT the variable bindings for the empty body clause
$added := \text{true}$
$level := 0$
while $added$ **do**
  $added := \text{false}$
  foreach predicate symbol P in BG **do**
    foreach $\left[\begin{array}{l}\text{possible variable assignment } \sigma \text{ for } P \\ \text{with at least one variable from the previous level}\end{array}\right]$ **do**
    $lit := \text{literal formed by } P \text{ and } \sigma$
    $clause := \text{simple clause formed by adding } lit \text{ to simple clauses}$
                      $\text{from } C \text{ that originate variables from } \sigma$
    $vector := \text{generate bit vector from } clause$
    $binding\_vectors := \text{compute the binding vector for}$
                      $\text{each new variable in } literal$
    if $vector$ not in BV **then**
      /* This simple clause is not equivalent to a previous one */
      Add $clause$ to C
      Add $vector$ to BV
      Add $(binding\_vectors, level)$ to VT
      $added := \text{true}$
    else if $binding\_vectors$ may be useful **then**
      Add $clause$ to C
      Add $(binding\_vectors, level)$ to VT
      $added := \text{true}$
    fi
    if any table full **then**
      break while loop
    fi
    od
  od
  $level := level + 1$
  od
  output C, BV, VT
end

6   Clause Table Construction

The simple clauses may now be combined to form a table of candidate clauses. Clearly, this has to be done efficiently as there are 2^k candidate clauses to consider for any k simple clauses. To this end LIME takes advantage of the following.

- Simple clauses may be combined efficiently by conjunction of bit vectors.
- When combining simple clauses, large branches of the search tree may be pruned without explicit search.

– The selection heuristic feeds back clear bounds on the required search.

We next shed some light on the crucial aspects of the clause table construction algorithm, followed by the details of the actual algorithm.

The algorithm is essentially depth-first search in nature.[10] At each node in the search tree the clause associated with the node is considered in conjunction with every simple clause. A gain heuristic is employed to direct which portion of the search space to consider. The resulting clauses are added to the best candidate clause list. There is a restriction on the number of candidate clauses maintained at any given time; only the best candidates added to the list are saved. Also, at each node in the search tree a list of the most gainful clauses are generated. Size of this list is also restricted and is dependent on the level in the search tree — deeper one goes in the search tree, smaller is the list of gainful clauses. This is because the heuristic is less accurate high up the search tree. Overlap is eliminated in the search by placing an ordering on the simple clauses, and requiring that they be considered in that order. This ensures that each simple clause is only considered once.

Figure 6 shows a search tree with $gain\_list\_length = 100$, which is the default value. It should be noted how the branching decreases as the tree depth increases. Suppose the depth of the tree is 5, then if there was no restriction of the branching factor, there will be 10101010101 nodes[11]. However, by reducing the branching factor as the tree is descended, the number of nodes is reduced to 10101 nodes, thereby making the search feasible without significantly affecting the chance of finding optimal clauses.

There are two stopping criteria for the search to bound the depth of each branch in the search tree. As simple clauses are combined the new clauses cover fewer examples. Thus, an obvious stopping criterion is when the clause covers no example. The other stopping criterion is when a node is reached such that the best possible clause that can be derived from descendents of this node are not good enough to make it to the candidate clause list.

Finally, a few words on the gain heuristic employed to guide the search for simple clauses and the Bayesian heuristic employed to determine the most gainful clauses. Suppose old_clause and new_clause are two clauses with the obvious meaning. Then the gain heuristic for going from old_clause to new_clause is calculated as $(n\_old - n\_new) \times (\lg(p\_new + 2))$, where n_old denotes the size of the negative coverage of old_clause, n_new denotes the size of the negative coverage of new_clause, and p_new is the size of the positive coverage of new_clause. The calculation of the Bayesian heuristic for the most gainful clause is based on the idea of Q-heuristic from Section 2.

The algorithm is given below. It is a standard implementation of the depth-first algorithm using the program stack recursively calling **probe_simple_clause**. Note that **calc_gain_list_size** calculates the number of branches in the search tree at a certain depth in the tree. Also, **gain** estimates the gain when a simple

---

[10] Earlier implementations have looked at best-first [5, 24] and depth-bounded discrepancy search [25], but depth-first was found to be the most effective.

[11] This is a decimal number

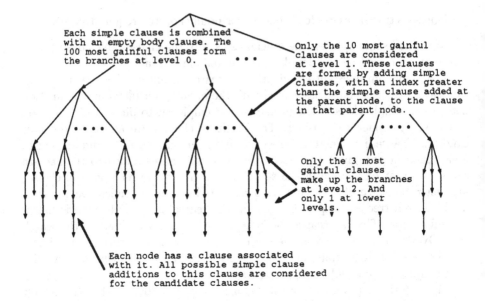

Fig. 6. The search tree where gain_list_length = 100

clause is combined with a clause to form a new clause. And **best_bay** estimates the best possible value for the Q-heuristic given this clause forms part of the final hypothesis. This best estimate is achieved by assuming the other clauses that make up the final hypothesis, which is a set of clauses, is as good as this clause in terms of positive cover, accuracy, and prior probability.

A list of clauses' data structure and associated functions has been created for this algorithm. This list is sorted by a value associated with each clause. Also, the cover of each clause is maintained in the form of a bit vector. For the gain list, the index of the last simple clause added to the clause is kept with each clause in the list. When a new list is created it is given a maximum size. If a list has reached its maximum size and a clause is added which has a value worse than the worst clause in the list, then the clause is ignored and the list is not altered. If a clause is added which has a value better than the worst clause in the list, then the worst clause is removed and the added clause is inserted in its appropriate place.

Algorithm 3 *Clause Construction from Simple Clauses.*

Input :

    S – Array of simple clauses and their coverage bit vectors

        /* Each element in S consists of the clause body */

        /* and a bit vector giving the coverage of the simple clause */

Output :

    C – A set of candidate clauses.

Parameters :

num_candidate_clauses /* The maximum number of candidate */
                      /* clauses to generate */
gain_list_length /* The length of the gain list used at level 0 */
begin
  foreach simple clause $c \in S$ **do**
    compute **gain**(simple clause with empty body, c)
  od
  Sort S in descending order of gain computed above
  Let C be a list of size *num_candidate_clauses*
  Let E be a record representing a new clause
  Initialize E as follows
  $E.body := \{\}$
  $E.bitvector :=$ all bits set to 1
  $E.last\_index := -1$
      /* *last_index* is the index of the last */
      /* simple clause in S used to form the new clause */
  probe_simple_clause$(S, C, E, 0)$
  output C
end

probe_simple_clause(S, C, R, L)
  Let GL be a new list of size **calc_gain_list_size**$(L, gain\_list\_length)$
  foreach $i \in \{R.last\_index + 1, R.last\_index + 2, \ldots, |S| - 1\}$ **do**
    Let NC be a record representing a new clause
    Initialize NC as follows
    $NC.body := S[i].body \uplus R.body$
    $NC.bitvector := S[i].bitvector \wedge R.bitvector$
    $NC.last\_index := i$
    if $(NC$ covers some elements$) \wedge (NC.bitvector \neq R.bitvector)$ **then**
      $gain :=$ **gain**(R, NC)
      if $\begin{bmatrix} (\text{extensions to } NC \text{ could prove better than} \\ \text{the worst clause in } C) \vee (C \text{ list not full}) \end{bmatrix}$ **then**
        Add $(NC, gain)$ to the list GL
      fi
      $value :=$ bay_best(NC)
      Add $(NC, value)$ to the list C
      /* Of course, the above addition only takes place if there is */
      /* space in C or the Bayesian estimate for NC */
      /* is better than the clause with the worst estimate in C */
    fi
  od
  foreach $GE \in GL$ **do**
    probe_simple_clause$(S, C, GE, L + 1)$
  od

calc_gain_list_size(*level*, *length*)

return $\lfloor length^{(2^{-level})} \rfloor$

gain(old_clause, new_clause)
    n_old := negative_cover(old_clause)
    n_new := negative_cover(new_clause)
    p_new := positive_cover(new_clause)
    return $(n\_old - n\_new) \times (\lg(p\_new + 2))$

best_bay(clause)
    NN := number of negatives
    NP := number of positives
    TP := NP
    TN := NN − negative_cover(clause)
    FP := 0
    FN := negative_cover(clause)
    $S := \frac{NP}{positive\_cover(clause)}$
    $theta$:= estimate_theta_cover(clause)
    return $TP \times (\lg(\frac{1-noise}{theta} + noise)) +$
        $(NN - FN \times S) \times (\lg(\frac{1-noise}{1-theta} + noise)) +$
        $(FN \times S) \times (\lg(noise)) +$
        $prob(clause) \times S$

6.1 Other Approaches

Earlier versions of LIME employed two other search strategies. However, they turned out to be less effective than depth-first search. The first of these was the best-first search. While this approach combines the advantages of both depth-first and breadth-first by extending the search tree at the node that appears to be the most promising, it also retains the main drawback of breadth-first search — excessive storage requirement. This may partly be overcome by maintaining a bounded set of nodes for exploration in the search tree. However, such an implementation tends to either not search deep enough, or to only search a small portion of the possible branches at the top of the search tree depending on the heuristic used for determining the most promising nodes. In either case the algorithm does not perform very well in many situations. For similar reasons a beam search like the one employed by Clark and Niblett [8] in CN2 is not as effective as depth search.

The other approach attempted was a depth-bounded discrepancy search [25]. This simply re-orders a depth-first search, examining more probable clauses first. Hence, the search space is restricted earlier in the search as "good" clauses are found earlier. However, because this technique required either revisiting nodes or storing the search tree, the efficiency gain did not overcome the overhead of either revisiting nodes or storage.

6.2 Efficiency

It is difficult to determine the exact actual size of the search tree as it is dynamically pruned. However, there is an upper bound on the size of the search tree. The number of nodes in the search tree depends on the *gain_list_size*.

Let $l = \lceil -\lg \frac{1}{\lg gain\_list\_size} \rceil$ and let $b = gain\_list\_size$. Then the maximum number of nodes in a tree of depth d will be

$$1 + b + b \times b^{2^{-1}} + b \times b^{2^{-1}} \times b^{2^{-2}} + \cdots +$$
$$b \times b^{2^{-1}} \times \cdots \times b^{2^{-(l-1)}} + (d - l) \times b \times b^{2^{-1}} \times \cdots \times b^{2^{-l}}$$

The number of operations required at each node is dependent linearly on the number of examples for the bit vector operation times the number of simple clauses considered at the node. It should be noted that the bit vector operations can be performed efficiently using the system level bitwise operations provided by most architectures. The memory requirement is minimal as it is a depth search algorithm.

7 Inducing the Final Hypothesis

The final stage in LIME's inductive process is similar to the previous stage, though with some crucial differences. First, the search is for a logic program from a set of candidate clauses. Second, instead of using conjunction of the coverage vectors of simple clauses, we use disjunction of the coverage vectors of clauses, as an instance may be covered by any one of the clauses. Third, as there may not always be independence between clauses (due to recursion), a Prolog interpreter is used to accurately evaluate the hypothesis cover. Fourth, as the Prolog interpreter used has no backtracking, order is important in the list of clauses induced. The details are given in the following algorithm.

Algorithm 4 *Induction of Final Hypotheses from Candidate Clauses.*
Input :
  C – array of clauses. /* Each element in the array consists of the clause */
                    /* and a bit vector giving the coverage of the clause. */
Output :
  H – A set of induced hypotheses.
Parameters :
  num_final_hypothesis /* The maximum number of hypotheses induced */
  gain_list_length /* The length of the gain list used at level 0 */
begin
  Let H be a list of size *num_final_hypothesis*
  Let L be a record representing a new logic program
  Initialize L as follows
  L.clauses := {}
  L.bitvector := all bits set to 0
  probe_clause$(C, H, L, 0)$
  output C
end

probe_clause(C, H, R, L)
   Let GL be a new list of size **calc_gain_list_size**$(L, gain\_list\_length)$
       /* **calc_gain_list_size** is defined in Algorithm 3 */
  foreach $i \in \{0 \ldots |C| - 1\}$ **do**
    Let NL be a record representing a new logic program
    Initialize NL as follows
    $NL.\text{clauses} := \{C[i].clause\} \cup R.clauses$
    $NL.\text{bitvector} := C[i].bitvector \vee R.bitvector$
    if (NL covers some elements) $\wedge$ ($NL.\text{bitvector} \neq R.bitvector$) **then**
      $gain := \textbf{gain\_lp}(R, NL)$
      if $\left[\begin{array}{l}(\text{ extensions to } NL \text{ could prove better} \\ \text{than the worst clause in } H) \vee (H \text{ list not full})\end{array}\right]$ **then**
        Add $(NL, gain)$ to the list GL
      fi
      $value := \textbf{bay}(NL)$
      if $value$ better than worst value in H **then**
        Update $NL.\text{bitvector}$ using Prolog interpreter and $NL.clauses$
          /* If $NL.clauses$ is recursive then $NL.\text{bitvector}$ (and $value$) */
          /* are only estimates; therefore, the Prolog interpreter is used */
          /* to compute the actual coverage and $value$. */
        $value := \textbf{bay}(NL)$
        Add $(NC, value)$ to the list H
      fi
    fi
  od
  foreach $GE \in GL$ **do**
    probe_clause$(C, H, GE, L + 1)$
  od

gain_lp(old_clause, new_clause)
  $n\_old := \text{negative\_cover}(old\_clause)$
  $p\_old := \text{positive\_cover}(old\_clause)$
  $n\_new := \text{negative\_cover}(new\_clause)$
  $p\_new := \text{positive\_cover}(new\_clause)$
  return $(\lg(p\_new + 2)) \times (2 \times (n\_old - n\_new) + (p\_new - p\_old))$

bay$(logic\_program)$
  $NN := \text{number of negatives}$
  $NP := \text{number of positives}$
  $TP := \text{positive\_cover}(logic\_program)$
  $TN := NN - \text{negative\_cover}(clause)$
  $FP := NP - \text{positive\_cover}(logic\_program)$
  $FN := \text{negative\_cover}(logic\_program)$
  $theta := \text{estimate\_theta\_cover}(logic\_program)$
  return $TP \times (\lg(\frac{1 - noise}{theta} + noise)) +$
        $TN \times (\lg(\frac{1 - noise}{1 - theta} + noise)) +$
        $(FP + FN) \times (\lg(noise)) +$
        $\text{prob}(logic\_program)$

7.1 Recursive Logic Programs

In most cases each clause in a hypothesis may be considered independently. This allows the clauses to be be induced individually and then combined to form the final hypothesis. This is the approach taken in ILP systems employing a greedy covering strategy (e.g., [19, 7]). Unfortunately, the independence of each clause breaks down when recursion is involved because a recursive clause by itself will not cover any examples.

The common approach in learning recursive clauses is to include all the positive examples into the background knowledge. This allows the algorithm to determine coverage by using these facts to unify with the recursive literals in the body of the clause. However, this introduces many problems, different systems handle them in a variety of ways. For example, FOIL[6] induces a partial ordering on the constants, and then requires at least one term in the recursive literal to descend or ascend this ordering. This ensures that there are no loops in the recursive call. CHILLIN[27], on the other hand, requires that at least one term in the recursive literal be a proper sub-term of the corresponding term in the head of this clause. This ensures that the clause induced does not lead to infinite recursion.

Since, in the induction of the final hypothesis LIME considers entire logic programs, a Prolog interpreter is used to accurately determine the coverage of potential hypotheses. This step, without including the positive examples into the background knowledge, weeds out any poorly constructed recursive hypotheses. For example, if a recursive logic program is missing its base case, it will quickly be shown to cover no examples, and hence give a poor posterior probability. However, it should be noted that when LIME needs to evaluate coverage of simple clauses or clauses in previous stages, it behaves like other ILP systems and estimates the coverage of an individual recursive clause by including the positive examples in the background knowledge. However, to address the problem of infinite recursion, it does not directly restrict undesirable clauses, rather it constructs a graph of how the positive examples recursively use each other. This approach enables a better estimate of a clause's final coverage as part of a complete logic program.

This process is best explained with an example. Consider the recursive clause $add(A, B, C) \leftarrow add(B, A, C)$. We wish to estimate its coverage when it forms part of a complete hypothesis, of which we do not know the other clauses. Also suppose the positive examples consist of three instances: $add(1, 2, 3)$, $add(1, 1, 2)$, and $add(2, 1, 3)$. Now if we naively include the positive examples into the background knowledge, then resolve the clause with each instance, the clause would cover all three instances. This clearly misrepresents the quality of the clause. So as each instance is resolved a graph is maintained of the instances an instance uses for its resolution. If a loop in the graph is detected by resolving an instance, then the recursive clause has an infinite recursive loop. Hence, one of the examples should be a base case to solve this dilemma so that the current instance is considered not covered by the recursive clause and the dependence is kept loop free. This will give a better estimate of the coverage of the recursive clauses.

Figure 7 illustrates this process for our example. At stage 1 the first instance add(1, 2, 3) is tested by resolving it with the recursive clause which uses the third instance add(2, 1, 3). Since no loops are created in the graph the first example is considered covered by the clause and the edge is added to the graph. At stage 2 the second instance add(1, 1, 2) when resolved requires itself and would form a circuit in the graph, so the clause is considered not to cover the instance, and the graph is left unchanged. At stage 3 the third instance add(2, 1, 3) would, when resolved, require the first instance add(1, 2, 3). This would form a circuit in the graph so the recursive clause could not cover both instances. One instance needs to be covered by another clause, hence, we estimate the recursive clause to still cover the first instance but not the third. Finally, the recursive clause is estimated to cover only the first of three instances. A naive approach would have it covering all three instance, which is a poor estimator of the recursive clause. Figure 7 shows the stages LIME undertakens in this process.

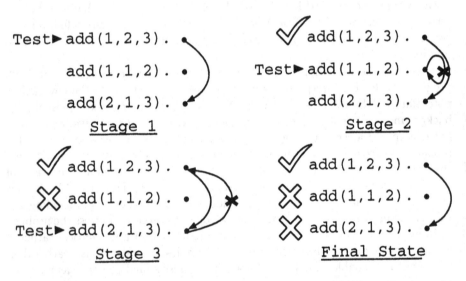

Fig. 7. Example of estimating coverage of a individual recursive clause

Also this approach directs the search toward the base cases by attempting to cover examples the recursive clause will finally cover in the logic program.

Another problem that is encountered when learning recursive logic programs is a sparse set of positive examples. That is, if many of the examples are separated by more than one resolution step then the strategy of including the positive examples in the background knowledge will not help in determining coverage. LIME partly handles this problem by the use of a Prolog interpreter in the final stage of induction. Although, a recursive clause must show some potential when evaluated by itself to form part of the candidate clauses; this will not be the case when the example set is sparse.

8   Prior Probability

To generate priors over the hypothesis space a probabilistic context-free grammar is used. A probabilistic context-free grammar $\langle G, \mathcal{P} \rangle$ is a context-free grammar G where each production rule is assigned a probability p_i. Note, $0 \leq p_i \leq 1$ and the sum of the probabilities with the same nonterminal left-hand side is 1. The probability of a derivation is given by the product of the probabilities of the productions used in the derivation. The probability of a sentence, generated by the grammar, is the sum over all possible distinct derivations from the start non-terminal to the sentence.

In many respects the way priors are attached is arbitrary. As the number of examples increases the prior becomes irrelevant. Basically, the probabilistic context-free grammar forms a mapping between sentences of the grammar, which are logic programs, and a probability value for the sentence, which is then defined to be the prior for this logic program.

Another way of attaching priors would be to encode the hypothesis into a bit string, then calculate the prior from its length. In this approach care must be taken when encoding the logic program, as it requires a prefix code. This still forms a mapping between the logic program and its probability via a bit string. By using probabilistic context-free grammars the intermediate stage is removed, simplifying the task and allowing more flexibility in the formation of the mapping.

The probabilistic context-free grammar [26] used by LIME for calculating priors of logic programs is given in table 1. The non-terminals LP, C, B, L,

P_1	$p_1 = \frac{1}{\mu_C + 1}$	$LP \longrightarrow \epsilon$
P_2	$p_2 = 1 - \frac{1}{\mu_C + 1}$	$LP \longrightarrow C\,LP$
P_3	$p_3 = 1$	$C \longrightarrow \text{head} \leftarrow B$
P_4	$p_4 = \frac{1}{\mu_L + 1}$	$B \longrightarrow \epsilon$
P_5	$p_5 = 1 - \frac{1}{\mu_L + 1}$	$B \longrightarrow L, B$
P_6	$p_6 = \frac{1}{n_L}$	$L \longrightarrow \text{name}_1 \overbrace{(T, T, \cdots, T)}^{arity_1}$
P_7	$p_7 = \frac{1}{n_L}$	$L \longrightarrow \text{name}_2 \overbrace{(T, T, \cdots, T)}^{arity_2}$
$\vdots$	$\vdots$	$\vdots$
P_{5+n_L}	$p_{5+n_L} = \frac{1}{n_L}$	$L \longrightarrow \text{name}_{n_L} \overbrace{(T, T, \cdots, T)}^{arity_{n_L}}$
P_{5+n_L+1}	$p_{5+n_L+1} = \frac{1}{\mu_V + 1}$	$T \longrightarrow v$
P_{5+n_L+2}	$p_{5+n_L+2} = 1 - \frac{1}{\mu_V + 1}$	$T \longrightarrow T'$

Table 1. Grammar use by LIME for calculating prior of hypothesis.

and T correspond respectively to a logic program, clause, the body of a clause, literal, and term. μ_C is a parameter which sets the expected number of clauses in a logic program. Similarly μ_L is the expected number of literals in the body of clauses. And μ_V is the expected variable number for any term in a logic program. Details such as "commas" and "periods" are ignored as they only have cosmetic effects.

From this grammar the stochastic expectation matrix M many be calculated, given in table 2, where an element at the row corresponding to non-terminal X and the column corresponding to non-terminal Y is the expected number of times X will be replaced by Y in exactly one production rule. As the spectral radius $\rho(M)$, which is the modulus of the largest eigenvalue, is always less then 1 the probabilistic grammar is consistent [4]. That is, the sum over all the sentences generated from this grammar is 1.

$$
M = \begin{array}{c} LP \\ C \\ B \\ L \\ T \end{array}
\begin{array}{c} LP \\ \hline \end{array}
\left[\begin{array}{ccccc}
1 - \frac{1}{\mu_C+1} & 1 - \frac{1}{\mu_C+1} & 0 & 0 & 0 \\
0 & 0 & 1 & 0 & 0 \\
0 & 0 & 1 - \frac{1}{\mu_L+1} & 1 - \frac{1}{\mu_L+1} & 0 \\
0 & 0 & 0 & 0 & \frac{1}{n_L}\sum_{i=1}^{n_L} arity_i \\
0 & 0 & 0 & 0 & 1 - \frac{1}{\mu_V+1}
\end{array} \right]
$$

with column headers $LP \quad C \quad B \quad L \quad T$.

Table 2. Stochastic expectation matrix M for the logic program probabilistic context-free grammar.

The calculation of $P(h)$ in LIME is trivial, as there is a unique derivation from the start non-terminal LP to any logic program h. This derivation is simply obtained by parsing h and calculating the product of the probabilities assigned to the production rules. As LIME requires $\lg(P(h))$ rather than $P(h)$, $\lg(P(h))$ is calculated directly. This moves the lg into the calculation, changing multiplication to addition. Also, the numbers used are manageable — they do not become exponentially small.

Note, if any clause is added to a hypothesis then the prior must decrease, hence, for all h and c $P(h) > P(h \cup \{c\})$. This gives a simple way of calculating a bound on the maximum prior for any partly completed hypothesis. Although obvious, this bound is useful in restricting the search space.

9 θ Estimation

An estimate of $\theta(ext(h))$ is required for computing the Q heuristic for a hypothesis h. In general, LIME considers many candidate hypotheses, so an efficient method of estimating the θ value for a hypothesis is essential to make LIME viable. Recall from Section 2 that the θ value is a measure of the proportion of the instance space a hypothesis covers.

It may be calculated exactly by taking the sum over the probability of each instance that is in the extension of the hypothesis as shown in equation 8. However, this is impossible for three reasons: the extension of the hypothesis is usually infinite; the instance space distribution is unknown; and as the instance space distribution is a mapping to the reals, the result given by a θ evaluation is not, in general, representable by a Turing machine, let alone computable by one. Hence, an approximate estimation of this value must be found.

$$\theta = \sum_{e \in \text{ext}(h)} D_X(e) \tag{8}$$

LIME estimates θ by taking a random sample of n instances, then calculating the number c of these instances the hypothesis covers. Next, a Laplacian estimate, $\frac{c+1}{n+2}$, is used. Note, the random sample of instances is generated at the start of LIME's execution, and the same sample is used for all θ estimations in simple clause construction, clause construction, and the induction of the final hypotheses. This is for reasons of efficiency, and it keeps the estimation consistent across different hypotheses. A more general hypothesis, therefore, will always have the same or a higher θ estimation.

To generate a single random instance, each term in the instance is randomly selected by a uniform distribution over the constants that constitute the term's type. This implicitly assumes a uniform distribution over a finite restriction of the instance space, as prescribed by the ground terms given in the examples and background knowledge given to LIME. Although, this uniform distribution is in general different from the unknown distribution that generated the examples, it will still produce useful estimates of θ, as the θ estimate is used mainly to compare different hypotheses. The comparison by the θ estimate does not change greatly under transformations in the instance space distribution. That is, if $\text{ext}(h_1) \subset \text{ext}(h_2)$ then $\theta(h_1) \leq \theta(h_2)$ for any instance space distribution. This process is repeated until the required number of samples is generated. By default LIME uses 500 instances to make up the random sample.

10 Empirical Results

In this section we present experimental results to illustrate how LIME achieves its design goals of better noise handling, learning from fixed set of examples, and of learning recursive logic programs.

10.1 Recursive Logic Programs

Bratko's Logic Programs Examples A set of logic programs based on Ivan Bratko's book *PROLOG Programming for Artificial Intelligence* [5] have been generated to assess ILP systems. These were obtained from UCI Machine Learning Repository [15] and given to LIME without changing the examples or background knowledge (some cosmetic changes are required to the file format to make it understandable to LIME). The examples consist of all the positive and negative examples restricted to lists of maximum length 3; also, the constant symbols are restricted to the numbers 1, 2, and 3. Table 3 shows the logic programs in question. The table also shows the background knowledge that is provided to the learner. As there is no noise in the examples the noise parameter is set to 0 for LIME. Table 4 gives the results of both LIME and FOIL on these data sets. Note, that LIME successfully induces the target hypothesis for 11 out of the 16 logic programs whereas FOIL was successful on 8 out of the 16 logic programs.

Quick Sort The relation quick sort is used as a bench mark to test the ability of an ILP system. Quick sort is a difficult recursive relation to learn as the key recursive clause is complex. The complexity is due to the presence of two recursive literals in the body, and the size of this clause. Another, difficulty, especially with regard to LIME, is that the recursive clause is one big simple clause which has a depth of 3, hence, LIME must explore the space of simple clauses deep enough to discover this clause. However, LIME successfully induced the following logic program for quick sort:

$$\text{qsort}(A, B) \leftarrow \text{partition1}(A, C), \text{partition2}(A, D),$$
$$\text{concat}(C, D, B), \text{partition2}(B, D).$$
$$\text{qsort}(A, B) \leftarrow \text{partition1}(A, C), \text{partition2}(A, D),$$
$$\text{qsort}(D, E), \text{qsort}(D, F), \text{concat}(E, F, B).$$

LIME took 393.57 seconds for inducing the above program.

10.2 Noise

We present results from three sets of representative experiments that compare LIME with FOIL and PROGOL. The first experiment considers learning the recursive predicate add with different levels of noise. The second experiment is performed on the complex *krk* domain, also with different noise levels. Third, we randomly generate a domain and consider how the number of clauses in the target concept affects predictive accuracy.

Plus Two We first demonstrate LIME's superior noise handling ability for the simple concept plus2, which may be represented by the following logic program:
$$\text{plus2}(A, B) \leftarrow \text{inc}(A, C), \text{inc}(C, B).$$
In the above inc denotes the increment predicate available as background knowledge. A random selection of 50 positive and 50 negative examples are given to LIME. These examples include noise. The predictive error of the induced hypothesis is measured against a noise-free test set that is generated by taking the

Name	Logic Program	Background Knowledge
Concatenation	$conc(A, B, C) \leftarrow empty(A), equal(B, C).$ $conc(A, B, C) \leftarrow components(A, D, E),$ $\quad\quad components(C, D, F),$ $\quad\quad conc(E, B, F).$	components, member, empty, equal
Delete	$del(A, B, C) \leftarrow components(B, A, C).$ $del(A, B, C) \leftarrow components(B, D, E), del(A, E, F),$ $\quad\quad components(C, D, F).$	components, member, conc, last
Dividelist	$dividelist(A, B, C) \leftarrow empty(A), empty(B), empty(C).$ $dividelist(A, B, C) \leftarrow odd(A), components(A, D, E),$ $\quad\quad dividelist(E, F, C)$ $\quad\quad components(B, D, F).$ $dividelist(A, B, C) \leftarrow even(A), components(A, D, E),$ $\quad\quad dividelist(E, B, F),$ $\quad\quad components(C, D, F).$	components, member, conc, last, del, insert, sublist, permutation, even, odd, reverse, palindrome, shift, subset
Evenlength	$even(A) \leftarrow empty(A).$ $even(A) \leftarrow components(A, B, C),$ $\quad\quad components(C, D, E), even(E).$	components, member, conc, last, del, insert, sublist, permutation
Insert	$insert(A, B, C) \leftarrow del(A, C, B).$	components, member, conc, last, del
Last	$last(A, B) \leftarrow components(B, A, C), empty(C).$ $last(A.B) \leftarrow components(B, C, D), last(A, D).$	components, member
Member	$member(A, B) \leftarrow components(B, A, C).$ $member(A.B) \leftarrow components(B, C, D), member(A, D).$	components, conc
Oddlength	$odd(A) \leftarrow components(A, B, C), empty(C).$ $odd(A) \leftarrow components(A, B, C), components(C, D, E),$ $\quad\quad odd(E).$	components, member, conc, last, del, insert, sublist, permutation
Palindrome1	$palindrome(A) \leftarrow reverse(A, B), equal(A, B).$	components, member, conc, last, del, insert, sublist, permutation, even, odd
Palindrome2	$palindrome(A) \leftarrow empty(A).$ $palindrome(A) \leftarrow components(A, B, C), empty(C).$ $palindrome(A) \leftarrow components(A, B, C), last(B, A),$ $\quad\quad front(C, D), palindrome(C, D).$	components, member, conc, last, del, insert, sublist, permutation, even, odd, reverse
Permutation	$permutation(A, B) \leftarrow empty(A), empty(B).$ $permutation(A, B) \leftarrow components(A, C, D),$ $\quad\quad permutation(D, E),$ $\quad\quad insert(C, E, B).$	components, member, conc, last, del, insert, sublist, permutation
Reverse	$reverse(A, B) \leftarrow empty(A), empty(B).$ $reverse(A, B) \leftarrow components(A, C, D),$ $\quad\quad empty(D), equal(B, A).$ $reverse(A, B) \leftarrow components(A, C, D),$ $\quad\quad components(B, E, F),$ $\quad\quad last(C, B), last(E, A), front(D, G),$ $\quad\quad front(F, H), reverse(G, H).$	components, member, conc, last, del, insert, sublist, permutation, even, odd, reverse
Shift	$shift(A, B) \leftarrow components(A, C, D),$ $\quad\quad front(B, D), last(C, B).$	components, member, conc, last, del, insert, sublist, permutation, even, odd, reverse, palindrome
Sublist	$sublist(A, B) \leftarrow conc(A, C, B).$ $sublist(A, B) \leftarrow components(B, C, D), sublist(A, D).$	components, member, conc, last, del, insertshift
Subset	$subset(A, B) \leftarrow empty(A).$ $subset(A, B) \leftarrow components(A, C, D),$ $\quad\quad member(C, B), subset(D, B).$	components, member, conc, last, del, insert, sublist, permutation, even, odd, reverse, palindrome, shift
Translate	$translate(A, B) \leftarrow empty(A), empty(B), empty(C).$ $translate(A, B) \leftarrow components(A, C, D), means(C, E),$ $\quad\quad components(B, E, F),$ $\quad\quad translate(D, F).$	components, member, conc, last, del, insert, sublist, permutation, even, odd, reverse, palindrome, shift, means

Table 3. Bratko's recursive logic programs

Name	LIME	Foil
Concatenation	Unsuccessful	Successful
Delete	Successful	Successful
Dividelist	Unsuccessful	Unsuccessful
Evenlength	Successful	Unsuccessful
Insert	Successful	Successful
Last	Successful	Successful
Member	Successful	Successful
Oddlength	Successful	Unsuccessful
Palindrome1	Successful	Successful
Palindrome2	Successful	Unsuccessful
Permutation	Unsuccessful	Unsuccessful
Reverse	Unsuccessful	Unsuccessful
Shift	Successful	Unsuccessful
Sublist	Successful	Successful
Subset	Successful	Unsuccessful
Translate	Unsuccessful	Successful

Table 4. Bratko's recursive logic programs - empirical results of LIME and Foil.

"first" 20 positive examples and a random selection of 20 negative examples. This process is repeated 100 times to calculate the average predictive error. This is repeated with different noise levels and the results are shown in Figure 8. The error bars in the figure indicate the sample standard deviation. The results show that LIME is able to correctly learn the concept with noise levels of up to approximately 70%. The same test is carried out with FOIL and PROGOL.[12]

LIME performs better than FOIL and PROGOL for noise levels of up to approximately 70%. Here, FOIL over-generalizes inducing a less predictive hypothesis. This is mainly due to the covering approach which introduces unnecessary clauses. However, for noise levels greater than 70%, all three systems perform poorly.

Addition LIME's noise handling ability is demonstrated in the context of add (the addition relation)—a target predicate that requires a recursive definition. The target concept may be represented by the hypothesis:

$$\text{add}(A, B, C) \leftarrow \text{equal}(A, C), \text{zero}(B).$$
$$\text{add}(A, B, C) \leftarrow \text{inc}(D, B), \text{add}(A, D, E), \text{inc}(E, C).$$

We take a random selection of 200 positive and 200 negative examples but perform only 20 repetitions at each noise level. Figure 9 shows the relationship between noise and predictive error measured against a noise-free test set of the "first" 25 positive examples and a random set of 25 negative examples. The results show that the gap between LIME and other systems widens further when the target concept requires a recursive definition. Experiments with FOIL and PROGOL were limited to 40% and 15% noise levels respectively because the quality of the programs output by these systems beyond these noise levels were difficult to assess.

---

[12] All our experiments are with FOIL, version 6.3 and with PROGOL, version 4.1.

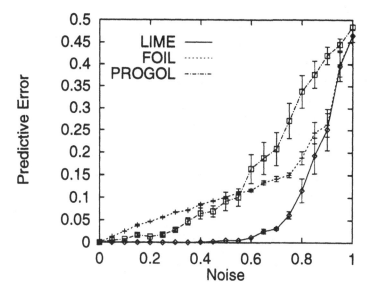

Fig. 8. Predictive Error vs Noise for `plus2`

KRK Domain The KRK domain has been well studied especially with respect to noise [20, 9]. This concept is exactly representable in first order logic, though the representation requires several clauses. The relation *illegal* checks if an end game position is an illegal chess position.

In each trial the training example set is constructed from 300 examples of which a proportion are noisy. Examples that are not noisy are chosen by randomly selecting the rank and file of each piece, where the distribution is uniform over both rank and file, then determining if the state is illegal and labeling it appropriately. A noisy example is constructed by again randomly positioning each piece, then randomly labeling it as either illegal or not-illegal. Note, a noisy example may be correctly classified. The accuracy of a hypothesis produced by the learning system is estimated by creating 10000 random examples and calculating the proportion of these the hypothesis correctly classifies. Each trial is repeated 20 times and the mean and sample standard deviation of the accuracy is calculated.

Quinlan's decision tree learner *c4.5* is also considered in this domain. The attribute giving the rank and file distance between pieces is included to help *c4.5* represent the concept. The results of these experiments are shown in Figure 10. The error bars show the sample standard deviation.

The diagram shows that PROGOL induces a more accurate hypothesis for low levels of noise, however LIME performs better at higher levels of noise. The predictive error shown by FOIL appears to be linearly dependent on the noise in the the training set. The poorer result shown by *c4.5* is partly due to its inadequacy in representing the concept.

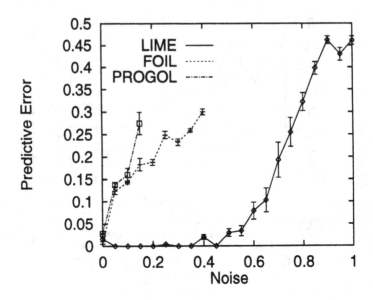

Fig. 9. Predictive error vs Noise for **add**

Randomly Generated Domain A randomly generated domain is created to examine how the ILP systems perform as the concept becomes more complex. A simple approach to introducing complexity into a concept is to include more clauses. So our measure of complexity here is the number of clauses in the target hypothesis.

Each target predicate consists of two terms, which when grounded are integers from 0 to 29. This yields an instance space of size 900. The background knowledge consists of 10 unary randomly generated predicates. Each clause consists of exactly 2 literals which are randomly selected from the background knowledge. Training and test sets are constructed by first randomly generating a target hypothesis, with the set number of clause, then this hypothesis is used to classify the 900 training instances. These are divided into training and test sets with a 90%/10% split, respectively. Before the training set is given to the learner it is corrupted by 10% noise. This process is repeated 10 times and the average error and sample standard deviation is calculated. Figure 11 shows these results for 1 to 10 clauses.

Interestingly FOIL shows the same predictive error independent of the number of clauses considered, whereas both PROGOL and LIME become less accurate as the number of clauses and hence the complexity, increases.

10.3 Learning from Positive Examples and from Negative Examples

Plus two This set of experiments gives empirical evidence that positive examples are more useful than negative examples for a target concept that is "small" with respect to the instance space distribution. The experiments also give evidence for the converse that negative examples are more useful than positive

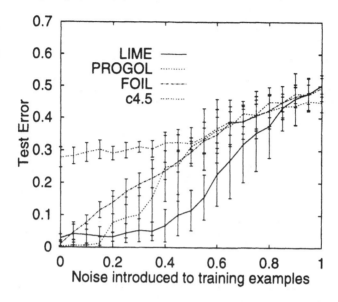

Fig. 10. The predictive error as noise is introduced into the training examples in the KRK domain.

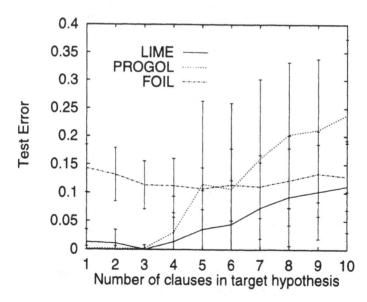

Fig. 11. The predictive error vs number of clauses in the randomly generated domain.

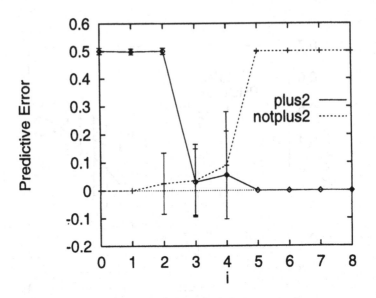

Fig. 12. Error vs i (i = number of positive examples & 8-i = number of negative examples) for the **plus2** and **notplus2** logic programs

examples for a target concept that is "large" with respect to the instance space distribution. These experiments also establish that LIME is capable of learning from only positive data and from only negative data.

We consider two concepts, the **plus2** and **notplus2** (the complement of **plus2**—that is, **notplus2**(A, B) holds if $B \neq A + 2$). It is easy to see that under reasonable assumptions, **plus2** is a "small" concept and **notplus2** is a "large" concept. Assuming the instance space $X = \{\ 1..n\ \}^2$ then under a uniform distribution the concept covers $\frac{n-2}{n^2}$ of the instance space. In the experiment $n = 50$ and hence the **plus2** concept covers 0.0192 of the instance space. The background knowledge is identical for both **plus2** and **notplus2** consisting of the increment relation and its complement, and a constant relations for each number in the range. LIME is run on examples of **plus2** and **notplus2**. The total number of examples is invariant over each test, however, the number of positive examples is increased as the number of negative examples is decreased. Each test is repeated 100 times and the results for both **plus2** and **notplus2** are shown in Figure 12. In all experiments the test set consists of 100 randomly selected positive examples and 100 randomly selected negative examples. The error bars show the sample standard deviation.

These experiments are also repeated at different levels of noise used in generating the training examples. The graph for **plus2** and **notplus2** are shown in Figure 13.

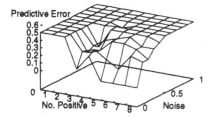 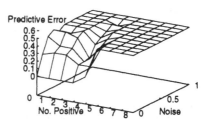

Fig. 13. Error vs i (i = number of positive examples & 8-i = number of negative examples) for the `plus2` relation shown on the left and the `notplus2` relation shown on the right. These trails are conduced with different levels of noise used in generating the training examples.

Addition In this set of experiments we examine the number of examples required for LIME to induce the *addition* relation from only positive examples. Note, as there is only positive examples the empty bodied clause is complete and consistent with respect to these examples. However, with enough positive examples the Q heuristic favors the *addition* relation over the empty body clause, as, the θ estimate for *addition* is smaller, this outweights the effect of the larger prior probability for the empty body clause.

The positive examples are randomly generated using a distribution over the instance space. Rather than restricting the instance space to a finite domain and using a uniform distribution over this space, a distribution over all three term predicates is used. The advantage of this approach is small numbers are given higher probabilities and hence occur more frequently in the example set. This aids the induction of the base case in the recursive *addition* relation. The background knowledge consists of the *inc, zero,* and *equal* relations these are necessary and sufficient to learn *addition*. Initially 10 positive examples are randomly generated and given to LIME, once LIME has run, the induced hypothesis is tested on the "first" 25 positive examples and a random selection of 25 negative examples. We also note if the hypothesis exactly expresses the *addition* relation. This is repeated 10 time and the mean and sample standard deviation is tabulated, also, the number of times the correct relation is induced is counted. This is repeated for different number of positive examples in increments of 10. The graph in figure 14 shows average error decreasing as the number of positive examples increases and the number of tests LIME takes to induce the exact *addition* relation.

Learning the addition relation from only negative examples is not investigated as positive examples are used in estimating the preliminary cover of recursive clauses and since these are absent in negative only data LIME will not learn recursive logic programs from only negative data.

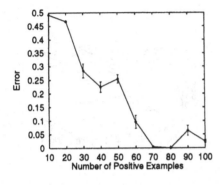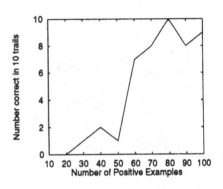

Fig. 14. LIME inducing *addition* from only positive examples. With error vs number of training examples on the left and number correctly induced hyptheses, out of 10 trials, vs number of training examples on the right.

11 Conclusion

The design of the ILP system LIME was described. The notion of simple clause was introduced and its use in the design of LIME was discussed. It was shown that combining simple clauses to form candidate clauses provides an effective alternative to growing clauses one literal at a time. Detailed algorithms for simple clause construction, clause construction, and logic program construction were given. Empirical results were presented that reinforce the superior noise handling ability of LIME. The performance of LIME is particularly good when it is learning recursive definitions in the presence of noise.

Work in progress involves application of LIME on real world domains and experiments with a boosted version of LIME.

Acknowledgements

Preliminary versions of parts of this work have had the benefit of being reviewed for earlier conferences [13, 14]. We are grateful to several anonymous reviewers for their comments.

Eric McCreath has been supported by an Australian Postgraduate Award and by the Australian Research Council grant A49703068 to Ross Quinlan. Arun Sharma has been supported by the Australian Research Council grant A49530274.

References

1. D. Angluin and P. Laird. Learning from noisy examples. *Machine Learning*, 2:343–370, 1987.
2. F. Bergadano and D. Gunetti. An interactive system to learn functional logic programs. In *Machine Learning*, 1994.

3. F. Bergadano and G. Gunetti. *Inductive Logic Programming: from Machine Learning to Software Engineering.* MIT Press, 1996.
4. T. L. Booth and R. A. Thompson. Applying probability measures to abstract languages. *IEEE Trans. Comput.*, C-22:442–450, 1973.
5. I. Bratko. *Prolog Programming for Artificial Intelligence.* Addison-Wesley, Workingham, 1990. second edition.
6. M. Cameron-Jones and J. Quinlan. Avoiding pitfalls when learning recursive theories. In *Proceedings of the Thirteenth International Joint Conference on Artificial Intelligence.* Morgan Kauffmann, San Mateo, CA, 1993.
7. R.M. Cameron-Jones and J.R. Quinlan. Efficient top-down induction of logic programs. *SIGART Bulletin*, 5(1):33–42, 1994.
8. P. Clark and T. Niblett. The CN2 induction algorithm. *Machine Learning*, 3(4):261–283, 1989.
9. S. Dzeroski and I. Bratko. Handling noise in inductive logic programming. In *Proceedings of the Second International Workshop on Inductive Logic Programming*, 1992. Tokyo, Japan. ICOT TM-1182.
10. S. Dzeroski, S. Muggleton, and S. Russell. PAC-Learnability of determinate logic programs. In *Proceedings of the Fifth Annual Workshop on Computational Learning Theory, Pittsburgh, Pennsylvania*, pages 128–135. ACM Press, July 1992.
11. J-U. Kietz and M. Lube. An efficient subsumption algorithm for inductive logic programming. In *Proceedings of the Eleventh International Conference on Machine Learning.* Morgan Kaufmann, San Mateo, CA, 1994.
12. N. Lavrač and S. Džeroski. *Inductive Logic Programming: Techniques and Applications.* Ellis Horwood (Simon and Schuster), 1994.
13. E. McCreath and A. Sharma. Extraction of meta-knowledge to restrict the hypothesis space for ILP systems. In X. Yao, editor, *Proceedings of the Eighth Australian Joint Conference on Artificial Intelligence*, pages 75–82. World Scientific, November 1995.
14. E. McCreath and A. Sharma. ILP with noise and fixed example size: A Bayesian approach. In *Fifteenth International Joint Conference on Artificial Intelligence*, volume 2, pages 1310–1315, 1997.
15. C.J. Merz and P.M. Murphy. UCI repository of machine learning databases, 1996.
16. K. Morik, S. Wrobel, J-U. Kietz, and W. Emde. *Knowledge Acquisition and Machine Learning: Theory, Methods and Applications.* Academic Press, 1993.
17. S. Muggleton, editor. *Inductive Logic Programming.* Academic Press, 1992.
18. S. Muggleton and L. De Raedt. Inductive Logic Programming: Theory and Methods. *Journal of Logic Programming*, 19(20):629–679, 1994.
19. S. Muggleton and C. Feng. Efficient induction of logic programs. In *Proceedings of the First Conference on Algorithmic Learning Theory, Tokyo*, pages 368–381. Ohmsa Publishers, 1990. Reprinted by Ohmsa Springer-Verlag.
20. S. Muggleton, A. Srinivasan, and M. Bain. Compression, significance and accuracy. In *Proceedings of the Ninth International Conference on Machine Learning*, pages 338–347. Morgan Kaufmann, San Mateo, CA, 1992.
21. Stephen Muggleton. Inverse entailment and progol. *New Generation Computing Journal*, 13, May 1995.
22. S.H. Nienhuys-Cheng and R. de Wolf. *Foundations of Inductive Logic Programming.* LNAI Tutorial 1228. Springer-Verlag, 1997.
23. J.R. Quinlan. Learning logical definitions from relations. *Machine Learning*, 5(3):239–266, 1990.
24. Elaine Rich. *Artificial Intelligence.* McGraw Hill, 1983.

25. Toby Walsh. Depth-boundid discrepancy search. In *Fifteenth International Joint Conference on Artificial Intelligence*, volume 2, pages 1388–1393, 1997.

26. C. S. Wetherall. Probabilistic languages a review and some open questions. *ACM Computing Surveys*, 12(4):361–377, 1980.

27. J Zelle, R Mooney, and J Konvisser. Combining top-down and bottom-up techniques in iductive logic programming. In *Proceedings of the Eleventh International Conference on Machine Learning*, pages 343–351, 1994.

On the Sample Complexity for Neural Trees

Michael Schmitt*

Lehrstuhl Mathematik und Informatik
Fakultät für Mathematik
Ruhr-Universität Bochum
D–44780 Bochum
Germany
mschmitt@lmi.ruhr-uni-bochum.de

Abstract. A neural tree is a feedforward neural network with at most one edge outgoing from each node. We investigate the number of examples that a learning algorithm needs when using neural trees as hypothesis class. We give bounds for this sample complexity in terms of the VC dimension. We consider trees consisting of threshold, sigmoidal and linear gates. In particular, we show that the class of threshold trees and the class of sigmoidal trees on n inputs both have VC dimension $\Omega(n \log n)$. This bound is asymptotically tight for the class of threshold trees. We also present an upper bound for this class where the constants involved are considerably smaller than in a previous calculation. Finally, we argue that the VC dimension of threshold or sigmoidal trees cannot become larger by allowing the nodes to compute linear functions. This sheds some light on a recent result that exhibited neural networks with quadratic VC dimension.

1 Introduction

The sample complexity, that is, the number of examples required for a learning algorithm to create hypotheses that generalize well, is a central issue in the theory of machine learning. In this paper we study the sample complexity for hypothesis classes consisting of neural trees. These are feedforward neural networks where each node, except the output node, has exactly one outgoing connection. Since these networks have less degrees of freedom, they are expected to be learnable more efficiently than unrestricted neural networks.

The computational complexity of learning using trees has been extensively studied in the literature. Angluin et al. [1], for instance, investigated the existence of efficient algorithms that use queries to learn Boolean trees, also known as read-once formulas. Research on trees employing neural gates has been initiated by Golea et al. [8]. They designed algorithms for learning so-called μ-Perceptron networks with binary weights. (A μ-Perceptron network is a disjunction of threshold gates where each input node is connected to exactly one threshold gate.) They

---

* Part of this work was done while the author was with the Institute for Theoretical Computer Science at the Technische Universität Graz, A-8010 Graz, Austria.

also considered tree structures in the form of μ-Perceptron decision lists [9] and nonoverlapping Perceptron networks [10].

We investigate the sample complexity for neural trees in terms of their Vapnik-Chervonenkis (VC) dimension. It is well known that the VC dimension of a function class gives asymptotically tight bounds on the number of training examples needed for probably approximately correct (PAC) learning this class. For detailed definitions we refer the reader to [2, 4, 22]. Moreover, these estimates the sample complexity in terms of the VC dimension hold even for agnostic PAC learning, that is, in the case when the training examples are generated by some arbitrary probability distribution [11]. Furthermore, the VC dimension is known to yield bounds for the complexity of learning in various on-line learning models [14, 18].

Results on the VC dimension for neural networks abound. See, for instance, the survey by Maass [16]. We briefly mention the most relevant ones for this paper. A feedforward network of threshold gates is known to have VC dimension at most $O(w \log w)$ where w is the number of weights [3]. Networks using piecewise polynomial functions for their gates have VC dimension $O(w^2)$ [7] whereas for sigmoidal networks the bound $O(w^4)$ is known [12]. With respect to lower bounds it has been shown that there are threshold networks with VC dimension $\Omega(w \log w)$ [15]. Furthermore, networks with VC dimension $\Omega(w^2)$ have been exhibited [13]. Among these are networks that consist of both threshold and linear gates, and sigmoidal networks.

Bounds on the VC dimension for neural networks are usually given in terms of the number of programmable parameters, that are, most commonly, the weights, of these networks. In contrast to the majority of the results in the literature, however, we are not looking at the VC dimension of a single network with a fixed underlying graph, but of the entire class of trees employing a specified activation function. This must be taken into account when comparing our results with other ones.

Hancock et al. [10] have shown that the VC dimension of the class of trees having threshold gates as nodes—they called them nonoverlapping Perceptron networks—is $O(n \log n)$ where n is the number of inputs.[1] We take this result as a starting line for our work. The basic definitions are introduced in Section 2. In Section 3 we show that the class of threshold trees has VC dimension $\Omega(n \log n)$, which is asymptotically tight. Moreover, we show that this bound remains valid even when all trees are required to have depth two and the output gate computes a disjunction. This lower bound is then easily transferred to trees with sigmoidal gates. In Section 4 we provide a new calculation for an upper bound that considerably improves the constants of [10]. Section 5 is a short note on how to derive the upper bound $O(n^4)$ for the class of sigmoidal trees. Finally, in Section 6 we show that adding linear gates to threshold or sigmoidal trees cannot increase their VC dimension. Interestingly, it was this use of linear gates that lead to

---

[1] Since a neural tree on n inputs has $O(n)$ weights, it is convenient to formulate the bounds in terms of the number of inputs. We follow this convention throughout the paper.

a quadratic lower bound for sigmoidal neural networks in the work by Koiran and Sontag [13]. Consequently, if the lower bound $\Omega(n \log n)$ is not tight for sigmoidal trees one has to look for new techniques in search for asymptotically better bounds.

2 Basic Definitions

A *neural tree* is a feedforward neural network where the connectivity, or architecture, of the network is a tree, that is, there is at most one edge outgoing from each node. Further, there is exactly one node, the root of the tree or *output node*, that has no edge outgoing. A *neural tree on n inputs* has n leaves, also called *input nodes*. The *depth* of a tree is the length of the longest path from an input node to the output node. The nodes that are not leaves are also known as *computation nodes*. Each computation node has associated with itself a set of $k + 1$ real-valued parameters where k is the in-degree of the node: the weights $w_1, \ldots, w_k$ and the threshold t.

We use trees for computations over the reals by assigning functions to its computation nodes and values to their parameters. We consider three types of functions that the nodes may use. All types can be obtained by applying a so-called activation function to the weighted sum $w_1 x_1 + \cdots + w_k x_k - t$ where $x_1, \ldots, x_k$ are the input values for the node computed by its predecessors. (The values computed by the input nodes are the input values for the tree.) A node becomes a *threshold gate* when it uses the signum function with $\text{sign}(y) = 1$ if $y \geq 0$, and $\text{sign}(y) = 0$ otherwise. A *sigmoidal gate* is a node that uses the sigmoidal function $1/(1 + e^{-y})$. Finally, a *linear gate* applies the identity function, that is, it simply outputs the weighted sum.

We say that a neural tree is a *threshold tree* if all its computation nodes are threshold gates. Correspondingly, we speak of *sigmoidal trees* and *linear trees*. If we allow more than one type of activation function for a tree then we shall assume that each of its computation nodes may use all types specified. Since we restrict our investigations to trees that compute $\{0, 1\}$-valued functions, we assume the output of a tree to be thresholded at $1/2$ if the output node is a linear or sigmoidal gate. Thus we can associate with each tree on n inputs a set of functions from $\mathbb{R}^n$ to $\{0, 1\}$ which are obtained by choosing activation functions for its nodes and varying its parameters over the reals. In a *class of trees* all members have the same number of inputs, denoted by n, and choose gate functions for their nodes from a specified set, which can be of the three types introduced above. The set of functions computed by a class of trees is then defined straightforward as the union of the sets computed by its members.

A *dichotomy* of a set $S \subseteq \mathbb{R}^n$ is a partition of S into two disjoint subsets S_0, S_1 such that $S_0 \cup S_1 = S$. Given a set $\mathcal{F}$ of functions from $\mathbb{R}^n$ to $\{0, 1\}$ and a dichotomy S_0, S_1 of S, we say that $\mathcal{F}$ *induces* the dichotomy S_0, S_1 *on* S if there is a function $f \in \mathcal{F}$ such that $f(S_0) \subseteq \{0\}$ and $f(S_1) \subseteq \{1\}$. We say further that $\mathcal{F}$ *shatters* S if $\mathcal{F}$ induces all dichotomies on S. The *Vapnik-Chervonenkis (VC) dimension* of $\mathcal{F}$, VCdim($\mathcal{F}$), is defined as the largest number m such that there is a set of m elements that is shattered by $\mathcal{F}$.

3 Lower Bounds on the VC Dimension for Threshold and Sigmoidal Trees

In this section we consider neural trees consisting of threshold and sigmoidal gates. We first establish a lower bound for the VC dimension for a class of threshold trees with certain restrictions: We assume that each tree has only one layer of hidden nodes and that the output node computes a disjunction.

Theorem 1. *For each* $m, k \geq 1$ *there exists a set* $S \subseteq \{0,1\}^{m+k \cdot 2^{k-1}}$ *of cardinality* $|S| = m \cdot k$ *that is shattered by the class of depth-two threshold trees with disjunctions as output gates.*

Proof. Let the set $S \subseteq \{0,1\}^{m+k \cdot 2^{k-1}}$ be defined as

$$S = \{e_i : i = 1, \ldots, m\} \times \{d_j : j = 1, \ldots, k\}$$

where $e_i \in \{0,1\}^m$ is the i-th unit vector and $d_j \in \{0,1\}^{k \cdot 2^{k-1}}$ is specified as follows: Let $A_1, \ldots, A_{2^k}$ be an enumeration of all subsets of $\{1, \ldots, k\}$. We arrange the $k \cdot 2^{k-1}$ components of d_j in 2^k blocks $b_1, \ldots, b_{2^k}$ such that block b_l has length $|A_l|$ for $l = 1, \ldots, 2^k$. (Hence the block corresponding to the empty set has length 0.) Thus all blocks together comprise exactly $k \cdot 2^{k-1}$ components.

Fix $j \in \{1, \ldots, k\}$, $l \in \{1, \ldots, 2^k\}$ and consider the components of block b_l in d_j. Each of these components is assumed to represent one specific element of A_l. For such an element $a \in A_l$ let $d_j(b_l, a)$ denote the value of this component. We define

$$d_j(b_l, a) = \begin{cases} 1 & \text{if } a = j \\ 0 & \text{otherwise} \end{cases}.$$

Thus we proceed for $j = 1, \ldots, k$ and $l = 1, \ldots, 2^k$. Observe that due to this construction, each block b_l contains at most one 1. (Furthermore, the number of 1s in d_j is equal to 2^{k-1} since j occurs in exactly half of all subsets A_l.)

Obviously, S consists of $m \cdot k$ elements. We claim that S is shattered by the class of depth-two threshold trees having a disjunction as output gate. In order to prove this we show that for each $S' \subseteq S$ there are weights and thresholds for such a tree such that this network outputs 1 for elements in S', and 0 for elements in $S \backslash S'$. Fix $S' \subseteq S$. For $i = 1, \ldots, m$ let $\alpha(i)$ be the (unique) element in $\{1, \ldots, 2^k\}$ such that

$$A_{\alpha(i)} = \{j : e_i d_j \in S'\} .$$

For convenience we call the input nodes $1, \ldots, m$ the e-inputs, and the input nodes $m+1, \ldots, m+k \cdot 2^{k-1}$ the d-inputs. We employ for each element in the range of α a threshold gate $G_{\alpha(i)}$ that has connections from all d-inputs in block $b_{\alpha(i)}$ and from none of the other blocks b_l where $l \neq \alpha(i)$. Further, we connect e-input i to gate $G_{\alpha(i)}$ for $i = 1,\ldots,m$. (Notice that this may result in gates that have connections from more than one e-input.) The weights of all connections are fixed to 1 and the thresholds are set to 2. Obviously, there is at most one connection outgoing from each input node, so that the disjunction of these threshold gates is a tree.

Finally, we verify that the network computes the desired function on S. Suppose that $x \in S'$ where $x = e_i d_j$. The definition of α implies that $j \in A_{\alpha(i)}$. Hence $d_j(b_{\alpha(i)}, j)$ is defined and has value $d_j(b_{\alpha(i)}, j) = 1$. Since gate $G_{\alpha(i)}$ receives two 1s—one from e-input i and one from block $b_{\alpha(i)}$—the output of the network for $e_i d_j$ is 1.

Assume on the other hand that $e_i d_j \in S \backslash S'$. Then $j \notin A_{\alpha(i)}$ and gate $G_{\alpha(i)}$, which is the only gate that receives a 1 from an e-input, receives only 0s from block $b_{\alpha(i)}$. All other gates G_l, where $l \neq \alpha(i)$, receive at most one 1, which is then from block b_l only. Hence, the output of the network for $e_i d_j$ is 0. $\quad\square$

Choosing $m = n/2$ and $k = (\log(n/2))/2 + 1$ in Theorem 1, we have $m + k \cdot 2^{k-1} \leq n/2 + 2^{2(k-1)} = n$. Hence there is a set $S \subseteq \{0,1\}^n$ of cardinality $m \cdot k = \Omega(n \log n)$ that is shattered by the class of trees considered.

Corollary 2. *The VC dimension of the class of threshold trees on n inputs is $\Omega(n \log n)$. This even holds if all input values are binary and the class is restricted to trees of depth two with a disjunction as output gate.*

It is well known that in a network that computes a Boolean function, a threshold gate can be replaced by a sigmoidal gate without changing the function of the network. (If necessary, the weights have to be scaled appropriately. See, for instance, Maass et al. [17] for a treatment in the context of circuit complexity). Thus, the lower bound $\Omega(n \log n)$ also holds for depth-two trees that may consist of threshold or sigmoidal gates.

Corollary 3. *The class of depth-two trees on n inputs with threshold or sigmoidal gates has VC dimension $\Omega(n \log n)$. This even holds if the inputs are restricted to binary values.*

We note that depth two is minimal for this lower bound since a threshold gate and a sigmoidal gate both have VC dimension $n + 1$: This follows for the threshold gate from a bound on the number of regions generated by a certain number of hyperplanes in $\mathbb{R}^n$ which is due to Schläfli [20] (see also [5]). For the sigmoidal gate this follows from the fact that its pseudo dimension is $n + 1$ [11].

Together with the upper bound $O(n \log n)$ due to Hancock et al. [10] we get asymptotically tight bounds for the class of threshold trees.

Corollary 4. *The VC dimension of the class of threshold trees on n inputs is $\Theta(n \log n)$. This holds also for the class of depth-two threshold trees. Moreover, this bound is valid for both classes if the inputs are restricted to binary values.*

4 Improved Upper Bounds for Threshold Trees

In this section we establish upper bounds for the VC dimension of the class of threshold trees. Regarding the constants they are better than a previous bound derived by Hancock et al. [10] which is $13n\log(2en) + 4n\log\log(4n)$.

Theorem 5. *The class of threshold trees on n inputs, where $n \geq 16e$, has VC dimension at most $6n\log(\sqrt{3}n)$.*

Proof. We estimate the number of dichotomies that are induced by the class of threshold trees on an arbitrary set of cardinality m. First we bound the number of these trees, then we calculate an upper bound on the number of dichotomies that a single tree induces when all its weights and thresholds are varied.

For the number of trees on n inputs we use the upper bound $(4n)^{n-1}$, which was derived in [10, Lemma 3]. We assume without loss of generality that the computation nodes at the lowest level (i.e., those nodes that have input nodes as predecessors) have in-degree 1 and that all other computation nodes have in-degree at least 2. Each of the computation nodes at the lowest level induces at most $2m$ dichotomies on a set of cardinality m. The whole level induces therefore at most $(2m)^n$ different functions. The computation nodes with in-degree at least 2 form a tree that consists of at most $n - 1$ nodes and has at most $2n - 2$ edges leading to one of these nodes.

According to a result by Shawe-Taylor[2] [21] the number of dichotomies that a threshold network with N computation nodes, partitioned into ν equivalence classes, and W edges induces on a set of cardinality m is at most

$$2^\nu \left(\frac{emN}{W - \nu}\right)^{W-\nu} .$$

Using $N = n - 1$, $\nu = n - 1$, and $W = 2n - 2$ we get that the number of dichotomies induced by a threshold tree consisting of $n - 1$ computation nodes and $2n - 2$ edges is at most $2^{n-1}(em)^{n-1}$.

Putting the bounds together, the total number of dichotomies induced on a set of cardinality m by the class of threshold trees on n inputs is at most

$$(4n)^{n-1} \cdot (2m)^n \cdot 2^{n-1}(em)^{n-1} .$$

Assume now that a set of cardinality m is shattered. Then

$$2^m \leq (4n)^{n-1} \cdot (2m)^n \cdot 2^{n-1}(em)^{n-1}$$
$$= 2(16en)^{n-1} \cdot m^{2n-1}$$
$$\leq 2(mn)^{2n-1} .$$

For the last inequality we have used the assumption $n \geq 16e$. Taking logarithms on both sides we obtain

$$m \leq (2n - 1)\log(mn) + 1 .$$

---

[2] We do not make use of the equivalence relations involved in this result but of the improvement that it achieves compared to [3].

We weaken this to

$$m \leq 2n \log(mn) . \tag{1}$$

Assume without loss of generality that $m \geq \log n$. Then it is easy to see that for each such m there is a real number $r \geq 1$ such that m can be written as $m = r \log(rn)$. Substituting this in (1) yields

$$r \log(rn) \leq 2n(\log(rn \log(rn)))$$
$$= 2n(\log(rn) + \log \log(rn)) \tag{2}$$
$$\leq 3n \log(rn) . \tag{3}$$

The last inequality follows from $\log(rn) \leq \sqrt{rn}$ which holds since $rn \geq 16e$. We divide both sides by $\log(rn)$ and get

$$r \leq 3n . \tag{4}$$

This implies

$$r \log(rn) \leq 3n \log(3n^2) .$$

Resubstituting $m = r \log(rn)$ for the left hand side and rearranging the right hand side yields

$$m \leq 6n \log(\sqrt{3}n)$$

as claimed. $\qquad\qquad\qquad\qquad\qquad\qquad\qquad\qquad\qquad\qquad\qquad\qquad\square$

In the statement of Theorem 5 the number n of inputs is required to satisfy $n \geq 16e$. We shall show now that we can get the upper bound as close to $4n \log(\sqrt{2}n)$ as we want provided that n is large enough.

Theorem 6. *For each $\varepsilon > 0$, the class of threshold trees on n inputs has VC dimension at most $4(1 + \varepsilon)n \log(\sqrt{2(1 + \varepsilon)}n)$ for all sufficiently large n.*

Proof. (Sketch) Fix $\varepsilon > 0$. For n sufficiently large we have $\log(rn) \leq (rn)^{\varepsilon}$. Using this in the inequality from (2) to (3) we can infer $r \leq 2(1 + \varepsilon)n$ in place of (4). This leads then to the claimed result. $\qquad\qquad\qquad\qquad\square$

5 A Note on the Upper Bound for Sigmoidal Trees

Using known results on the VC dimension it is straightforward to derive the upper bound $O(n^4)$ for sigmoidal trees. We give a brief account.

Proposition 7. *The class of sigmoidal trees on n inputs has VC dimension $O(n^4)$.*

Proof. The VC dimension of a sigmoidal neural network with w weights is $O(w^4)$. This has been shown by Karpinski and Macintyre [12]. By Sauer's Lemma (see e.g. [2]) the number of dichotomies induced by a class of functions with VC dimension $d \geq 2$ on a set of cardinality $m \geq 2$ can be bounded by m^d. Thus a sigmoidal tree on n inputs induces at most $m^{O(n^4)}$ dichotomies on such a set. Combining this with the bound $(4n)^{n-1}$ employed in the proof of Theorem 5 and using similar arguments we obtain the bound as claimed. $\qquad\qquad\square$

6   Trees with Linear Gates

By the work of Goldberg and Jerrum [7] it has been known that neural networks employing piecewise polynomial activation functions have VC dimension $O(w^2)$, where w is the number of weights. The question whether this bound is tight for such networks has been settled by Koiran and Sontag [13]. They have shown that networks consisting of threshold and linear gates can have VC dimension $\Omega(w^2)$. This result was somewhat unexpected since networks consisting of linear gates only compute linear functions and have therefore VC dimension $O(w)$. On the other hand, networks consisting of threshold gates only have VC dimension $O(w \log w)$. This follows from work by Cover [6] and has also been shown by Baum and Haussler [3]. Results that this bound is tight for threshold networks are due to Sakurai [19] and Maass [15].

Therefore, the question arises whether a similar increase of the VC dimension is possible for threshold or sigmoidal trees by allowing some of the nodes to compute linear functions. We show now that this cannot happen.

Theorem 8. *Let T be a class of neural trees consisting of threshold or sigmoidal gates and let T^{lin} be a class of trees obtained from T by replacing some of the gates by linear gates. Then $\mathrm{VCdim}(T) \geq \mathrm{VCdim}(T^{\mathrm{lin}})$.*

Proof. We show that nodes computing linear functions can be replaced or eliminated without changing the function of the tree. Assume T is a tree and y is a node in T computing a linear function. If y is the output node then y can be replaced by a threshold gate or a sigmoidal gate, where weights and threshold are modified if necessary. (Note that the output of the tree is thresholded at $1/2$ for linear and sigmoidal output gates.)

If y is a hidden node then there is a unique edge e outgoing from y to its successor z. Denote the weight of e by w. Assume that y computes the function $u_1 x_1 + \cdots + u_k x_k - t$ where $x_1, \ldots, x_k$ are the predecessors of y, and $u_1, \ldots, u_k, t$ are its weights and threshold. We delete node y and edge e, and introduce k edges from $x_1, \ldots, x_k$ respectively to z. We assign weight $w u_i$ to the edge from x_i for $i = 1, \ldots, n$ and decrease the threshold of z by wt. It can readily be seen that the resulting network is still a tree and computes the same function as T. $\square$

Combining Theorems 5 and 6 with Theorem 8 we obtain an upper bound for the class of trees with threshold or linear gates.

Corollary 9. *The class of neural trees on n inputs with threshold or linear gates has VC dimension at most $6n \log(\sqrt{3}n)$ for $n \geq 16e$. Furthermore, for each $\varepsilon > 0$, this class has VC dimension at most $4(1+\varepsilon)n \log(\sqrt{2(1+\varepsilon)}n)$ for all sufficiently large n.*

The technique used in the proof can also be applied to neural trees employing a much wider class of gates. If the function computed by a gate can be decomposed into a linear and a non-linear part then the method of deleting a hidden linear node works the same way. Only if the node to be treated is the output node there have to be some further demands on its function. For instance, if the non-linear part of this function is monotonous then a linear output node can be replaced by such a gate without decreasing the VC dimension of the tree.

7 Conclusions

Finding methods that incorporate prior knowledge into learning algorithms is an active research area in theoretical and applied machine learning. In the case of neural learning algorithms such knowledge might be reflected in a restricted connectivity of the network generated by the algorithm. We have studied the impact of a particular kind of such a restriction on the sample complexity for neural networks. Results were given in terms of bounds for the VC dimension.

We have established the asymptotically tight bound $\Omega(n \log n)$ for the class of threshold trees. We have also derived an improved upper bound for this class. Due to our result demonstrating that the use of linear gates in threshold trees cannot increase their VC dimension, a known technique to construct networks with quadratic VC dimension does not work for trees. As a consequence of this, the gap between the currently best known lower and upper bounds for the class of sigmoidal trees, which are $\Omega(n \log n)$ and $O(n^4)$, is larger than it is for sigmoidal networks. To reduce this gap and to extend these investigations to other frequently used types of gates are challenging open problems for future research.

Acknowledgement. I thank an anonymous referee for helpful comments leading to a clarification in the proof of Theorem 1.

References

1. D. Angluin, L. Hellerstein, and M. Karpinski. Learning read-once formulas with queries. *Journal of the Association for Computing Machinery*, 40:185–210, 1993.
2. M. Anthony and N. Biggs. *Computational Learning Theory*. Cambridge Tracts in Theoretical Computer Science. Cambridge University Press, Cambridge, 1992.
3. E. B. Baum and D. Haussler. What size net gives valid generalization? *Neural Computation*, 1:151–160, 1989.
4. A. Blumer, A. Ehrenfeucht, D. Haussler, and M. K. Warmuth. Learnability and the Vapnik-Chervonenkis dimension. *Journal of the Association for Computing Machinery*, 36:929–965, 1989.
5. T. M. Cover. Geometrical and statistical properties of systems of linear inequalities with applications in pattern recognition. *IEEE Transactions on Electronic Computers*, 14:326–334, 1965.
6. T. M. Cover. Capacity problems for linear machines. In L. N. Kanal, editor, *Pattern Recognition*, pages 283–289, Thompson Book Co., Washington, 1968.
7. P. W. Goldberg and M. R. Jerrum. Bounding the Vapnik-Chervonenkis dimension of concept classes parameterized by real numbers. *Machine Learning*, 18:131–148, 1995.

8. M. Golea, M. Marchand, and T. R. Hancock. On learning μ-Perceptron networks with binary weights. In S. J. Hanson, J. D. Cowan, and C. L. Giles, editors, *Advances in Neural Information Processing Systems 5*, pages 591–598. Morgan Kaufmann, San Mateo, CA, 1993.

9. M. Golea, M. Marchand, and T. R. Hancock. On learning μ-Perceptron networks on the uniform distribution. *Neural Networks*, 9:67–82, 1996.

10. T. R. Hancock, M. Golea, and M. Marchand. Learning nonoverlapping Perceptron networks from examples and membership queries. *Machine Learning*, 16:161–183, 1994.

11. D. Haussler. Decision theoretic generalizations of the PAC model for neural net and other learning applications. *Information and Computation*, 100:78–150, 1992.

12. M. Karpinski and A. Macintyre. Polynomial bounds for VC dimension of sigmoidal and general pfaffian neural networks. *Journal of Computer and System Sciences*, 54:169–176, 1997.

13. P. Koiran and E. D. Sontag. Neural networks with quadratic VC dimension. *Journal of Computer and System Sciences*, 54:190–198, 1997.

14. N. Littlestone. Learning quickly when irrelevant attributes abound: A new linear-threshold algorithm. *Machine Learning*, 2:285–318, 1988.

15. W. Maass. Neural nets with superlinear VC-dimension. *Neural Computation*, 6:877–884, 1994.

16. W. Maass. Vapnik-Chervonenkis dimension of neural nets. In M. A. Arbib, editor, *The Handbook of Brain Theory and Neural Networks*, pages 1000–1003. MIT Press, Cambridge, Mass., 1995.

17. W. Maass, G. Schnitger, and E. D. Sontag. A comparison of the computational power of sigmoid and Boolean threshold circuits. In V. Roychowdhury, K.-Y. Siu, and A. Orlitsky, editors, *Theoretical Advances in Neural Computation and Learning*, pages 127–151. Kluwer, Boston, 1994.

18. W. Maass and G. Turán. Lower bound methods and separation results for on-line learning models. *Machine Learning*, 9:107–145, 1992.

19. A. Sakurai. Tighter bounds of the VC-dimension of three-layer networks. In *Proceedings of the World Congress on Neural Networks WCNN'93*, volume 3, pages 540–543, 1993.

20. L. Schläfli. *Theorie der vielfachen Kontinuität*. Zürcher & Furrer, Zürich, 1901. Reprinted in: L. Schläfli, Gesammelte Mathematische Abhandlungen, Band I, Birkhäuser, Basel, 1950.

21. J. Shawe-Taylor. Sample sizes for threshold networks with equivalences. *Information and Computation*, 118:65–72, 1995.

22. L. G. Valiant. A theory of the learnable. *Communications of the ACM*, 27:1134–1142, 1984.

Learning Sub-classes of Monotone DNF on the Uniform Distribution

Karsten A. Verbeurgt[1]

Department of Computer Science, University of Waterloo
Waterloo, Ontario, N2L 3G1, Canada
kaverbeu@neumann.uwaterloo.ca

Abstract. In this paper, we give learning algorithms for two new sub-class of DNF formulas: poly-disjoint One-read-once Monotone DNF; and Read-once Factorable Monotone DNF, which is a generalization of Read-once Monotone DNF formulas. Our result uses Fourier analysis to construct the terms of the target formula based on the Fourier coefficients corresponding to these terms. To facilitate this result, we give a novel theorem on the approximation of Read-once Factorable Monotone DNF formulas, in which we show that if a set of terms of the target formula have polynomially small mutually disjoint satisfying sets, then the set of terms can be approximated with small error by the greatest common factor of the set of terms. This approximation theorem may be of independent interest.

1 Introduction and Previous Work

Since the inception of computational learning theory in the PAC (Probably Approximately Correct) learning model due to Valiant [Val 84], the problem of the learnability of DNF has received much attention. One of the reasons for this is the potential of DNF as a form of knowledge representation, with applications in expert systems and data mining. DNF is also interesting in that it appears to be near the boundary of learnability. Learning general Boolean formulas and log-depth circuits is known to be as hard as factoring [KV 88]. The results of Lund and Yannakakis [LY 93] on the hardness of approximating the k-coloring problem and the results of Pitt and Valiant [PV 86] reducing the coloring problem to the DNF learning problem show that s-term DNF formulas are not learnable by $n^\epsilon s$-term DNF hypotheses for some ϵ, unless NP = RP. In contrast, several sub-classes of DNF formulas are known to be learnable. For an excellent survey of the DNF learning problem, we refer the reader to [AP 95].

Due to the apparent difficulty of learning DNF for arbitrary distributions, research efforts have focused on learning this class for specific distributions, in particular for the uniform distribution. The first distribution-specific results were given by Kearns, Li, Pitt and Valiant [KLPV 87,KLV 94] for learning μ-DNF formulas, in which every attribute occurs at most once in the formula, on the uniform distribution. Hancock [H 92] further studied restricted-read DNF, and gave polynomial time algorithms for learning kμ-DNF, where each attribute occurs at most k times in the formula, on the uniform distribution.

There have been several positive results for the learnability of DNF on the uniform distribution, although no polynomial time algorithms are known. Linial, Mansour and Nisan [LMN 89] show how to learn AC^0 circuits on the uniform distribution by learning the Fourier coefficients in $O(n^{\log n})$ time. In [Ver 90a], we show that DNF is learnable under the uniform distribution with a similar time bound, but for which the output hypothesis is a DNF formula.

In the membership query learning model, Mansour [Man 95] showed that DNF can be learned on the uniform distribution in $O(n^{\log \log n})$ time. A polynomial time algorithm is given by Khardon [Khar 94] for learning Disjoint-DNF, where every example satisfies at most one term. In a break-through result, Jackson [J 94] showed that DNF is learnable in polynomial time on the uniform distribution when membership queries are allowed. It remains an open question whether Monotone DNF is learnable on the uniform distribution in polynomial time using only examples.

The learnability of Read-once Boolean formulas has been studied by several authors in the membership query and equivalence query models. Angluin, Hellerstein and Karpinski [AHK 93] show that Monotone Read-once formulas can be learned from membership queries alone, and that Read-once formulas can be learned using membership and equivalence queries. In the PAC-learning model, Goldman, Kearns and Schapire show in [GKS 90] that Read-once formulas can be learned on the uniform distribution in time $O(\frac{n^9}{\epsilon^6})$, using $O(\frac{n^6}{\epsilon^6})$ examples. This result is generalized to product distributions in [S 92], giving an algorithm with time complexity $O(\frac{n^{14}}{\epsilon^6})$ and sample complexity $O(\frac{n^{12}}{\epsilon^6})$.

In this paper, we introduce the classes of One-read-once Monotone DNF formulas, and Read-once Factorable Monotone DNF formulas. We give a positive learnability results for poly-disjoint One-read-once Monotone DNF, and for Read-once Factorable Monotone DNF on the uniform distribution. The class of Read-once Factorable Monotone DNF is a superclass of Read-once Monotone DNF, but a sub-class of Read-once Monotone Boolean formulas. Thus, the learnability of this class is implied by [GKS 90] and [S 92]; however, the complexity of our algorithm is of a lower order: time and sample complexity $\tilde{O}(n\frac{s^5}{\epsilon^4})$. This complexity is not directly comparable to the algorithms of [GKS 90], since the complexity of their algorithm is in terms of n, and ours is in terms of s. However, our results give a lower complexity for small formulas. The class of One-read-once Monotone DNF is also generalization of Read-once Monotone DNF, but since the algorithms we give here work only for poly-disjoint formulas from this class, this result is incomparable to the results for Read-once formulas discussed above.

For the results of this paper, we use spectral analysis to show the correspondence between the Fourier coefficients of terms of a One-read-once Monotone DNF formula and the probability weight of the set of vectors that satisfy exactly one term of the formula.

2 Definitions and Terminology

2.1 Functions and Classes

Let $X = \{x_1, x_2, \ldots x_n\}$ be the set of Boolean attributes in the learning domain. A Boolean function is a function $f : \{0,1\}^n \rightarrow \{-1,1\}$, where -1 represents "false", and $+1$ represents "true". A (monotone) *term* t_i is a conjunction of attributes in X, none of which appear negated. Let m_i denote the set of indices of attributes in t_i, and let function t map the sets of indices onto terms; thus $t_i = t(m_i)$. Let function m be the inverse of t, mapping a term onto the set of indices of attributes in the term. Thus $m(t_i) = m_i$. We use set notation for terms where the context is clear; for example, $x_i \in t_i$ to imply that $i \in m_i$. For $x \in \{0,1\}^n$, and a term t_i, we use $x \Rightarrow t_i$ to indicate that vector x satisfies t_i. A *cross-term* of a formula f is a term that contains attributes from more than one term of f. Let $S(t_i) = \{x | x \Rightarrow t_i\}$, the *satisfying set* of t_i, be the set of vectors that satisfy term t_i. We also refer to the satisfying set of a formula f, $S(f)$, as the set of vectors that satisfy f. Let $\mathcal{DS}(t_i)$, the *disjoint satisfying set* of t_i, denote the set of vectors that satisfy term t_i, but do not satisfy any other term t_j, $i \neq j$.

A Boolean formula f is a Monotone DNF (hereafter MDNF) formula if f is of the form $f = t_1 + t_2 + \ldots + t_s$, where each t_i is a monotone term. The size of the formula is s, the number of terms in the formula. A formula f is *read-once* if no variable appears more than once in f. An attribute x_i is *read-once* if it occurs exactly once in f. A formula f is *one-read-once* if for every term of f, at least one attribute is read-once.

For a term t and a formula $f = t_1 + \ldots + t_s$, we define the restriction of f to t, f_t, by $f_t = t \cdot t_1 + \ldots + t \cdot t_s$. For a set of terms T we define the greatest common factor of T to be the largest term t that is contained in every term in T.

We define the factorization of an MDNF formula recursively. As the base case, a read-once formula is a factorization (with the trivial factor of the empty set of attributes). Any formula that is formed as the sum of products of terms (factors) and a factorization of an MDNF formula is also a factorization. A Monotone DNF formula is said to be *read-once factorable* if there exists a factorization of f such that no attribute occurs more than once in the factorization. For example, for the formula $f = x_1 x_2 + x_1 x_3 + x_2 x_3$, a factorization of f is $f = x_1(x_2 + x_3) + x_2(x_1 + x_3) + x_3(x_1 + x_2)$. Such a representation is called a factored form of f. This formula is not, however, a read-once factorization of f, and indeed, no read-once factorization exists for f. However, the formula $g = x_1 x_2 x_3 + x_1 x_2 x_4 + x_1 x_5 x_6$ is read-once factorable, and $g = x_1(x_2(x_3 + x_4) + x_5 x_6)$ is a factorization. The *set of maximal factors* of a formula f is the set of maximal greatest common factors over all subsets of terms in f (i.e., the set of terms t such that for some subset T of the terms in f, t is contained in all terms in T, and t is the largest such factor.) Formula g above has maximal factor set $\{x_1, x_1 x_2\}$.

Each of Monotone DNF, Read-once MDNF, One-read-once MDNF and Read-once Factorable MDNF is referred to as a *class* of formulas. For each of the classes discussed above, we may use the qualifier "poly-disjoint" to refer to the set of all formulas in the class for which every term t_i in the formula has $Pr_D[\mathcal{DS}(t_i)] \geq \frac{1}{p(s, \frac{1}{\epsilon})}$, where p is a polynomial, s is the size of the formula, $0 \leq \epsilon \leq 1$, and D is a probability distribution.

2.2 Learnability

We use the standard definitions for PAC-learnability in this paper. We assume that the reader is familiar with these (see [HKLW 88] for an excellent description). Here, we give only the following definitions. Let D^+ denote the uniform distribution over the positive examples of the target formula f, D^- be the uniform distribution over the negative examples, and D be the uniform distribution over the entire example space, $\{0,1\}^n$. Let the positive error, $e^+(h)$ of hypothesis h with respect to the target formula f be the probability that h miss-classifies a positive example drawn according to distribution D, and similarly for $e^-(h)$. Let $e(h) = e^+(h) + e^-(h)$. For a hypothesis h, and for $0 \leq \alpha \leq \frac{1}{2}$, we say that h is an α-good hypothesis, or α-approximate hypothesis, if $e(h) \leq \alpha$. Let $\Pr[f \triangle g]$ denote the probability that $f \neq g$.

Let $\mathbf{C}$ and $\mathbf{H}$ be classes of formulas; let $C_{n,s}$ be the formulas is class $\mathbf{C}$ with domain size n and size s, and H_n be the formulas in class $\mathbf{H}$ with domain size n. $\mathbf{C}$ is polynomially learnable by $\mathbf{H}$ on the uniform distribution if and only if there exists an algorithm A with inputs ϵ, δ, s, and n, which $\forall \epsilon, \delta \leq 1$, $\forall s, n \geq 1$, and all target formulas $f \in C_{n,s}$, outputs a representation of a hypothesis $h \in H_n$ that with probability $\geq 1 - \delta$ has $e^+(h) \leq \epsilon$ and $e^-(h) \leq \epsilon$, and the run-time of A is bounded by a polynomial in $\frac{1}{\epsilon}$, $\frac{1}{\delta}$, s, and n.

2.3 Fourier Transform

We use the definitions of the Fourier transform given in [LMN 89] and [J 94]. For every subset $A \subseteq \{1, \ldots, n\}$ and for $x \in \{0,1\}^n$, we define the function $\chi_A : \{0,1\}^n \rightarrow \{-1, +1\}$, by: $\chi_A(x) = (-1)^{\sum_{i \in A} x_i}$. The function $\chi_A(x)$ is 1 if the parity of the bits in x indexed by A is even, and -1 if the parity is odd. As is shown in [LMN 89], the set of functions $\chi_A(x)$ form an orthonormal basis for the vector space of real-valued functions on the Boolean cube $\mathbb{Z}_2^n$. Thus, every function $f : \{0,1\}^n \rightarrow \mathbb{R}$ can be uniquely expressed as a linear combination of parity functions, by $f = \sum_A \hat{f}(A) \chi_A$, where $\hat{f}(A) = E[f \chi_A]$. The vector of coefficients $\hat{f}$ is called the *Fourier transform* of f. For Boolean f, $\hat{f}$ represents the correlation of f and χ_A with respect to the uniform distribution. For the results of this paper, we define the *Positive Fourier Coefficient* (PFC), which we denote by $\hat{f}^p(A)$, as $\hat{f}^p(A) = (-1)^{|A|} E_{D^+}[\chi_A f]$. Note that since $f = 1$ on all positive examples, this reduces to $\hat{f}^p(A) = (-1)^{|A|} E_{D^+}[\chi_A]$. We use $(-1)^{|A|} \hat{E}_{D^+}[\chi_A]$ to denote the estimate of $\hat{f}^p(A)$.

3 Approximation Results for Monotone DNF

Before giving our learnability results, we need some preliminary results on the approximation of MDNF formulas. The main result of this section, the Diffraction Lemma, applies to Read-once Factorable MDNF formulas.

The first fact we give states that every MDNF formula can be approximated with error bounded by $\frac{\epsilon}{2}$ by an MDNF formula with terms of size $\log \frac{2s}{\epsilon}$. In the statement of the results of this section, we will use superscript f to denote a term from formula f, and similarly for g.

Fact 1 *Let* $f = t_1^f + \ldots + t_s^f$ *be an MDNF formula. There exists an MDNF formula* $g = t_1^g + \ldots + t_s^g$ *for which* $|t_i^g| \leq \lg \frac{2s}{\epsilon}$, $t_i^g \subseteq t_i^f$, *and* $e^-(t_i^g) \leq \frac{\epsilon}{2s}$.

The proof of this fact is given in [Ver 90a]. By Fact 1, for every MDNF formula f, there exists a formula g with log-sized terms that approximates f well. In this section, we give a lemma that shows how to approximate the formula g.

Recall that the greatest common factor of a set T of terms is defined to be the largest term t that is contained in every term $t_i^g \in T$. We refer to the set of examples satisfying t as the subspace defined by t. Note that the subspace defined by t may contain both positive and negative examples.

The technique we will develop in the proofs of the following lemmas is to project a set of positive examples, or a formula, onto a larger subspace. For a term v, let $PS(v)$ be the set of vectors that are zero on all $x_i \not\subseteq v$, and that range over all possible combinations of assignments to the attributes in v. We call the set $PS(v)$ the projection set for v. We can then define the projection of a set of examples. For a set X of examples and a term v, let the projection function $P_v : 2^{\{0,1\}^n} \rightarrow 2^{\{0,1\}^n}$ be defined as: $P_v(X) = \{x \oplus y | x \in X, y \in PS(v)\}$, where $\oplus$ denotes bitwise exclusive or. Thus, the projection function $P_v(X)$ takes each example in X and maps it onto each of the $2^{|v|}$ possible combinations of assignments to the attributes in v, and leaves all other attributes unchanged. We will refer to such a projection of examples as the projection of X over v.

We will also use the projection function $P_v(g)$ with a formula g as an argument to mean the projection of the satisfying set of g onto all possible combinations of assignments to the attributes of v. Note that this is equivalent to deleting all attributes from g that occur in v. For example, $P_{x_1}(x_1 x_2 + x_1 x_3) = x_2 + x_3$.

Let g_i be the Boolean function consisting of all terms of g except t_i^g. Thus, $g_i = t_1^g + \ldots + t_{i-1}^g + t_{i+1}^g + \ldots + t_s^g$. As an example, consider the formula

$$g = x_1 x_2 x_3 + x_1 x_2 x_4 + x_1 x_5 x_6 \qquad (1)$$

We then have: $g_1 = x_1 x_2 x_4 + x_1 x_5 x_6$, $g_2 = x_1 x_2 x_3 + x_1 x_5 x_6$, and $g_3 = x_1 x_2 x_3 + x_1 x_2 x_4$.

In the following proofs, we will consider various properties of the product $\prod_{1 \leq i \leq s} g_i$. First, note that by the above definition,

$$\prod_{1 \leq i \leq s} g_i = \prod_{1 \leq i \leq s} \sum_{j \neq i} t_j^g = (t_2^g + t_3^g + \ldots + t_s^g) \cdot (t_1^g + t_3^g + \ldots + t_s^g) \cdot \ldots \ . \qquad (2)$$

We prove the following properties showing the relationship between the functions g_i and projections over factors of g.

Claim 2 *For an MDNF formula* $g = t_1^g + \ldots + t_s^g$, *let* $g_i = \sum_{j \neq i} t_j^g$. *Then* $\prod_{1 \leq i \leq s} g_i = \sum_{1 \leq i < j \leq s} t_i^g \cdot t_j^g$.

Proof. First, we show that each term in $\sum_{1 \leq i < j \leq s} t_i^g \cdot t_j^g$ is generated by $\prod_{1 \leq i \leq s} g_i$. Suppose that term t_i^g is satisfied. All formulas g_j, $j \neq i$ contain t_i^g; hence $\prod_{1 \leq i \leq s} g_i$ is satisfied if g_i is. Arguing in this manner for each i, we get the formula $t_1^g \cdot g_1 + t_2^g \cdot g_2 + \ldots + t_s^g \cdot g_s$. Expanding each g_i gives $t_1^g \cdot (t_2^g + t_3^g + \ldots t_s^g) + t_2^g \cdot (t_1^g + t_3^g + \ldots t_s^g) + \ldots + t_s^g \cdot (t_1^g + t_2^g + \ldots t_{s-1}^g)$, which is $\sum_{1 \leq i < j \leq s} t_i^g \cdot t_j^g$. We have thus shown that every term in $\sum_{1 \leq i < j \leq s} t_i^g \cdot t_j^g$ is generated by $\prod_{1 \leq i \leq s} g_i$, and it follows that

$$\prod_{1 \leq i \leq s} g_i = t_1^g \cdot g_1 + t_2^g \cdot g_2 + \ldots + t_s^g \cdot g_s = \sum_{1 \leq i < j \leq s} t_i^g \cdot t_j^g \ . \tag{3}$$

$\square$

As an illustration of Claim 2, we continue with the example from (1). We then get

$$\prod_{1 \leq i \leq s} g_i = g_1 \cdot g_2 \cdot g_3$$

$$= (x_1 x_2 x_4 + x_1 x_5 x_6) \cdot (x_1 x_2 x_3 + x_1 x_5 x_6) \cdot (x_1 x_2 x_3 + x_1 x_2 x_4)$$

$$= x_1 x_2 x_4 \cdot x_1 x_2 x_3 + x_1 x_5 x_6 \cdot x_1 x_2 x_3 + x_1 x_5 x_6 \cdot x_1 x_2 x_4 \ . \tag{4}$$

Claim 3 *For an MDNF formula* $g = t_1^g + \ldots + t_s^g$ *let* $g_i = \sum_{j \neq i} t_j^g$. *Then for any term* t, $\prod_{1 \leq i \leq s} P_t(g_i) = P_t(\prod_{1 \leq i \leq s} g_i)$.

Claim 3 follows from Claim 2 and the definition of the projection function. The proof is not given in this extended abstract.

We continue our example above to illustrate Claim 3. Consider the example from (1), and let $t = x_1$. In (4), we have $\prod_{1 \leq i \leq s} g_i = x_1 x_2 x_4 \cdot x_1 x_2 x_3 + x_1 x_5 x_6 \cdot x_1 x_2 x_3 + x_1 x_5 x_6 \cdot x_1 x_2 x_4 = x_1 x_2 x_3 x_4 + x_1 x_2 x_3 x_5 x_6 + x_1 x_2 x_4 x_5 x_6$. Now, taking the projection over t, we get $P_t \left(\prod_{1 \leq i \leq s} g_i \right) = x_2 x_3 x_4 + x_2 x_3 x_5 x_6 + x_2 x_4 x_5 x_6$. Taking the projection over each g_i before taking their product, we get $P_t(g_1) = x_2 x_4 + x_5 x_6$, $P_t(g_2) = x_2 x_3 + x_5 x_6$, and $P_t(g_3) = x_2 x_3 + x_2 x_4$, and taking their product gives $\prod_{1 \leq i \leq s} P_t(g_i) = (x_2 x_4 + x_5 x_6) \cdot (x_2 x_3 + x_5 x_6) \cdot (x_2 x_3 + x_2 x_4) = x_2 x_3 x_4 + x_2 x_3 x_5 x_6 + x_2 x_4 x_5 x_6$. Thus, we have $\prod_{1 \leq i \leq s} P_t(g_i) = P_t(\prod_{1 \leq i \leq s} g_i)$ for our example, as in Claim 3.

Lemma 4 (Projection Lemma). *For a Read-once Factorable MDNF formula* $g = t_1^g + \ldots + t_s^g$ *with maximal factor set* F, *let* $g_i = \sum_{j \neq i} t_j^g$. *Then for any maximal factor* $t \in F$, $\prod_{\{t_i^g | t \subseteq t_i^g\}} P_{t_i^g}(g_i) = \prod_{\{t_i^g | t \subseteq t_i^g\}} P_t(g_i)$.

The proof of this lemma is given in Appendix A.

We finish with our example from (1) by demonstrating Lemma 4. Note that the formula of (1) is a Read-once Factorable MDNF, with factorization $g = x_1(x_2(x_3 + x_4) + x_5x_6)$. Thus, x_1 is a factor of g. Taking the projection of each g_i over t_i^g, we get $P_{t_1^g}(g_1) = x_4 + x_5x_6$, $P_{t_2^g}(g_2) = x_3 + x_5x_6$ and $P_{t_3^g}(g_3) = x_2x_3 + x_2x_4$. Now, taking the product of these projections over all i gives us $\prod_{1 \le i \le s} P_{t_i^g}(g_i) = (x_4 + x_5x_6) \cdot (x_3 + x_5x_6) \cdot (x_2x_3 + x_2x_4) = x_2x_3x_4 + x_2x_3x_5x_6 + x_2x_4x_5x_6$. We thus have that $\prod_{1 \le i \le s} P_{t_i^g}(g_i) = \prod_{1 \le i \le s} P_t(g_i)$.

We now state the main result of this section, which will be instrumental in proving the learnability of Read-once Factorable MDNF.

Lemma 5 (Diffraction Lemma). *For a Read-once Factorable MDNF formula* $g = t_1^g + \ldots + t_s^g$ *with terms of size at most* $\lg \frac{2s}{\epsilon}$ *and with maximal factor set* F, *and for the uniform distribution* D *on examples of* g, *let* $F' = \{t \in F \mid$ *every* $t \subseteq t_i^g$ *has* $\Pr_D[\mathcal{DS}(t_i^g)] \le \frac{\epsilon^2}{4s^2}\}$ *be the set of maximal factors such than every term* t_i^g *containing a factor in* F' *has* $\Pr_D[\mathcal{DS}(t_i^g)] \le \frac{\epsilon^2}{4s^2}$. *Then* $\Pr_D[(\sum_{t \in F'} t) \Delta (\sum_{t \in F'} (\sum_{\{t_i^g \mid t \subseteq t_i^g\}} t_i^g))] \le \frac{\epsilon}{2}$.

Lemma 5 states that the terms in formula g that all have small disjoint probability weight can be approximated by a factor from the factor set F, with error bounded by $\frac{\epsilon}{2}$. We call this lemma the diffraction lemma because it shows that if the "power" of the formula is concentrated in the subspaces of the common factors, and then it "diffracts" over orthogonal sub-spaces, then these subspaces cannot capture much of the negative example space.

Proof. Recall that $\mathcal{DS}(t_i^g)$ is the set of vectors that satisfy term t_i^g but no other term. The idea of the proof is to take each vector that satisfies exactly one term (i.e., is in $\mathcal{DS}(t_i^g)$) and to project it onto a polynomial number of negative examples. We show that if we restrict the space to vectors satisfying one or more of the common factors of formula g, then the projection covers all negative examples in the restricted space. More specifically, we show that all negative examples in the subspace restricted to satisfying one of more of the common factors of g are in $\cup_{1 \le i \le s} P_{t_i^g}(\mathcal{DS}(t_i^g))$.

The set of vectors $\mathcal{DS}(t_i^g)$ (i.e., the set satisfying t_i^g, but not satisfying any other term) is the satisfying set of the formula $t_i^g \cdot \overline{g_i}$. The projection $P_{t_i^g}(\mathcal{DS}(t_i^g))$ is the mapping of vectors in $\mathcal{DS}(t_i^g)$ onto all possible combinations of values over the attributes in t_i^g. Let g_i' be the formula obtained from g_i by deleting all attributes that occur in t_i^g. It is easy to verify that the projection $P_{t_i^g}(\mathcal{DS}(t_i^g))$ is the set of examples satisfying formula $\overline{g_i'}$. Thus, $\cup_{1 \le i \le s} P_{t_i^g}(\mathcal{DS}(t_i^g))$ is the set of examples satisfying formula $\overline{g_1'} + \overline{g_2'} + \ldots + \overline{g_s'}$. Now, any negative example of g does not satisfy g, by definition. We can thus construct a formula that is satisfied by the set of negative examples not in the set $\cup_{1 \le i \le s} P_{t_i^g}(\mathcal{DS}(t_i^g))$ as follows:

$$\overline{\overline{g_1'} + \overline{g_2'} + \ldots + \overline{g_s'} + g} = g_1' \cdot g_2' \cdot \ldots \cdot g_s' \cdot \overline{g} = g_1' \cdot g_2' \cdot \ldots \cdot g_s' \cdot \overline{t_1^g} \cdot \ldots \cdot \overline{t_s^g} . \quad (5)$$

Since $g_i' = P_{t_i^g}(g_i)$, by Lemma 4, (5) gives $\prod_{1 \le i \le s} g_i' = \prod_{1 \le i \le s} P_{t_i^g}(g_i) = \prod_{t \in F} \prod_{\{t_i^g | t \subseteq t_i^g\}} P_{t_i^g}(g_i) = \prod_{t \in F} \prod_{\{t_i^g | t \subseteq t_i^g\}} P_t(g_i)$. Restricting this product to the space $\sum_{t \in F} t$, we get $(\sum_{t \in F} t) \cdot \prod_{t \in F} \prod_{\{t_i^g | t \subseteq t_i^g\}} P_t(g_i)$. But this means that at least one of the $P_t(g_i)$ must be restricted to t, giving $\prod_{\{t_i^g | t \subseteq t_i^g\}} g_i$. From (5), this would require that $\prod_{\{t_i^g | t \subseteq t_i^g\}} g_i \cdot \prod_{1 \le i \le s} \overline{t_i^g}$ be satisfiable, which is not possible. Since this formula represents all negative examples in the subspace defined by $\sum_{t \in F} t$ that are not in the set $\cup_{1 \le i \le s} P_{t_i^g}(\mathcal{DS}(t_i^g))$, this implies that there is no negative example on this subspace that is not covered by the set $\cup_{1 \le i \le s} P_{t_i^g}(\mathcal{DS}(t_i^g))$.

We have now established that every negative example that satisfies $\sum_{t \in F} t$ must belong to the set $\cup_{1 \le i \le s} P_{t_i^g}(\mathcal{DS}(t_i^g))$. Now, we take the subset F' of F such that $F' = \{t \in F | \Pr_D[\mathcal{DS}(t_i^g)] \le \frac{\epsilon^2}{4s^2} \text{ for all } t \subseteq t_i^g\}$. The probability weight of each set $P_{t_i^g}(\mathcal{DS}(t_i^g))$ is bounded by $\frac{\epsilon^2}{4s^2} \cdot 2^{\log \frac{2s}{\epsilon}} = \frac{\epsilon}{2s}$, since by assumption $\Pr_D[\mathcal{DS}(t_i^g)] \le \frac{\epsilon^2}{4s^2}$, and the size of the projection set $PS(t_i^g)$ is at most $2^{\log \frac{2s}{\epsilon}}$. Thus, the probability weight of the set $\cup_{1 \le i \le s} P_{t_i^g}(\mathcal{DS}(t_i^g))$ is at most $\frac{\epsilon}{2}$. Since all negative examples satisfying $\sum_{t \in F'} t$ are contained in $\cup_{1 \le i \le s} P_{t_i^g}(\mathcal{DS}(t_i^g))$, we have that $\Pr_D[(\sum_{t \in F'} t) \Delta (\sum_{t \in F'} (\sum_{\{t_i^g | t \subseteq t_i^g\}} t_i^g))] \le \frac{\epsilon}{2}$.

□

In Sect. 5, we apply Lemma 5 in the analysis of Read-once Factorable MDNF formulas to develop an algorithm for learning this class. First, however, we give a learnability result for the class of poly-disjoint One-read-once MDNF. The algorithm we develop for this class will be used also in Sect. 5.

4 Learning Poly-disjoint One-read-once MDNF

For this result, we show that for One-read-once MDNF formulas, the Positive Fourier Coefficient, $\hat{f}^p(t)$ (defined in Sect. 2.3), of a term t is related to the probability of the disjoint set of examples, $\mathcal{DS}(t)$; thus by finding all terms with $\hat{f}^p(t) \ge \frac{\epsilon^2}{4s^2}$, we find the terms with $\Pr_D[\mathcal{DS}(t)] \ge \frac{\epsilon^2}{4s^2}$. By doing so, we obtain a learning algorithm for poly-disjoint One-read-once MDNF, for polynomial $p = \frac{\epsilon^2}{4s^2}$.

The algorithm we give in this section for learning poly-disjoint One-read-once MDNF begins by drawing examples of the formula from the uniform distribution, which we will refer to as D_0. After having learned a term of the target formula on D_0, the algorithm will then filter examples on distribution D_0 to produce a new distribution, D_1. In general, the algorithm will learn the ith term of the target formula on distribution D_{i-1}.

Let D_0 be the initial (uniform) distribution on the examples. After each term of the formula is found, it is added to the hypothesis h. Let h_i denote the hypothesis h after the ith term has been added. Let D_i be the uniform distribution on examples not satisfying any term of h_i.

The algorithm for learning a term of a poly-disjoint One-read-once MDNF formula on distribution D_{i-1} is given in Fig. 1. The idea of the algorithm is as follows. We begin with an empty set m. For each attribute x_i such that index i is not already in m, we estimate the Positive Fourier Coefficient on $\{i\} \cup m$ [1] We add the attribute with the minimal Positive Fourier Coefficient that is of magnitude at least $\frac{\epsilon^2}{8s^2}$. We continue choosing attributes according to this statistic until either the error of the term is small enough, or no attribute x_i has a Positive Fourier Coefficient statistic larger than $\frac{\epsilon^2}{8s^2}$. We use Algorithm 1-Read-1$(D_{i-1}, \epsilon, \delta, s)$ as a subroutine to find each term of the target formula in Algorithm Learn-1-Read-1(ϵ, δ, s), given in Fig. 1.

Algorithm **1-Read-1**$(D_{i-1}, \epsilon, \delta, s)$
1.   Set $m = \emptyset$
2.   While $e^-(m) \geq \frac{\epsilon}{2s}$
3.   Choose the $\ell \notin m$ with the minimal
        $\hat{E}_{D_{i-1}^+}[(-1)^{|m \cup \{\ell\}|} \chi_{m \cup \{\ell\}}] \geq \frac{\epsilon^2}{8s^2}$
4.   Set $m = \{\ell\} \cup m$
5.   return $t(m)$

Algorithm **Learn-1-Read-1**(ϵ, δ, s)
1.   If $e^-(1) \leq \frac{\epsilon}{2}$ then
2.   Set $h = 1$
3.   Else
4.   Set $h = 0$
5.   While $e^+(h) \geq \frac{\epsilon}{2}$
6. $h = h + $ 1-Read-1$(D_{i-1}, \epsilon, \delta, s)$
7.   return h

Fig. 1. Algorithm for Learning a Poly-disjoint One-read-once MDNF Formula

In the following lemma, we show that every term of a One-read-once MDNF formula has a positive PFC statistic. We show this result for the uniform distribution, D_0, and will generalize it later to all distributions D_i. Let $\{x_{j_1} \ldots x_{j_s}\}$ be the read-once attributes in terms $t_1, \ldots, t_s$ respectively.

Lemma 6. *If $g = t_1 + \ldots + t_s$ is a One-read-once MDNF formula with read-once attributes $\{x_{j_1} \ldots x_{j_s}\}$ in terms $t_1, \ldots, t_s$ respectively, then for every $1 \leq i \leq s$ and every $m \subset m(t_i)$ such that $j_i \in m$, $E_{D_0^+}[(-1)^{|m|} \chi_m] = \Pr_{D^+}[\mathcal{DS}(t_i)]$.*

---

[1] See the proof of Theorem 9 for the sample complexity required to estimate this statistic.

Proof. Note that $E_{D_0^+}[(-1)^{|m|}\chi_m] = \sum_{x \Rightarrow g}(-1)^{|m|}\chi_m(x)D_0^+(x)$, where $D_0^+(x)$ is the probability that distribution D_0^+ assigns to x. Let g_i be the formula consisting of all terms in g except t_i. We show that for any i, and for any set m containing j_i, $\sum_{x \Rightarrow g_i}\chi_m(x) = 0$. This holds since attribute x_{j_i} does not occur in g_i, hence any vector satisfying g_i with $x_{j_i} = 0$ also satisfies g_i if $x_{j_i} = 1$. Thus, $\sum_{x \Rightarrow g_i}(-1)^{|m|}\chi_m(x)D_0^+(x) = 0$. Note that $\mathcal{DS}(t_i)$ is the set of positive examples x such that $x \not\Rightarrow g_i$. Since by definition, $E_{D_0^+}[(-1)^{|m|}\chi_m] = \sum_{x \Rightarrow g}(-1)^{|m|}\chi_m(x)D_0^+(x)$, the Positive Fourier Coefficient of m is given by $E_{D_0^+}[(-1)^{|m|}\chi_m g] = \sum_{x \in \mathcal{DS}(t_i)}(-1)^{|m|}\chi_m(x)D_0^+(x)$. Now, $(-1)^{|m|}\chi_m(x) = 1$ for every vector in $\mathcal{DS}(t_i)$, and it follows that $E_{D_0^+}[(-1)^{|m|}\chi_m g]$, the Positive Fourier Coefficient of m, is equal to $\Pr_{D_0^+}[\mathcal{DS}(t_i)]$. □

By the above lemma, we have shown that for all subterms of a term of the target formula, the PFC statistic is equal to the size of the disjoint satisfying set of the term. We now show that for all cross-terms, this statistic is negative.

Lemma 7. *If $g = t_1 + \ldots + t_s$ is a One-read-once MDNF formula with read-once attributes $\{x_{j_1} \ldots x_{j_s}\}$ in terms $t_1, \ldots, t_s$ respectively, then for every $1 \le i \le s$, every $m \subset m(t_i)$ such that $j_i \in m$, and any $\ell \notin m(t_i)$, $E_{D_0^+}[(-1)^{|m \cup \{\ell\}|}\chi_{m \cup \{\ell\}}] \le 0$.*

Proof. Let $D_{\mathcal{DS}(t_i)}$ be the uniform distribution on the set of vectors in $\mathcal{DS}(t_i)$. Since the vectors in $\mathcal{DS}(t_i)$ do not satisfy any term t_j for $j \ne i$, $\Pr_{D_{\mathcal{DS}(t_i)}}[x_\ell = 0] \ge \frac{1}{2}$. It follows that $\sum_{x \in \mathcal{DS}(t_i)}(-1)^{|(m \cup \{\ell\})|}\chi_{(m \cup \{\ell\})}(x)D_0(x) \le 0$. □

We have proved Lemmas 6 and 7 above for the uniform distribution. In our algorithm for learning One-read-once MDNF, we will learn only the first term on the uniform distribution, and then skew the distribution by filtering in order to find subsequent terms. Recall that distribution D_i is formed by filtering examples out that satisfy the hypothesis h_{i-1}. In the following lemma, we show that the bounds shown in the above lemmas apply to all distributions D_i. In fact, they improve on each D_i by magnifying the Positive Fourier Coefficient statistic. We assume here that term i is learned on the ith call of Algorithm 1-Read-1.

Lemma 8. *Let $\{x_{i_1} \ldots x_{i_s}\}$ be the read-once attributes in terms $t_1, \ldots, t_s$ respectively. For $j \ge i$, and any m containing some attribute in $\{x_{i_j}, \ldots, x_{i_s}\}$, we have $E_{D_{i-1}^+}[(-1)^{|m|}\chi_m] = cE_{D_0^+}[(-1)^{|m|}\chi_m]$ for some $c \ge 1$.*

Proof. Distribution D_i is formed by filtering out all examples that satisfy the hypothesis h_{i-1}. Since no term in h_{i-1} contains any attribute in $\{x_{i_j}, \ldots, x_{i_s}\}$, $\sum_{x \Rightarrow h_{i-1}}\chi_m(x) = 0$ for any m containing an attribute in $\{x_{i_j}, \ldots, x_{i_s}\}$; thus $\sum_{x \Rightarrow h_{i-1}}(-1)^{|m|}\chi_m(x) = 0$ and it follows that $\sum_{x \Rightarrow g, x \not\Rightarrow h_{i-1}}(-1)^{|m|}\chi_m(x) = \sum_{x \Rightarrow g}(-1)^{|m|}\chi_m(x)$. Now, the Positive Fourier Coefficient is $E_{D_0^+}[(-1)^{|m|}\chi_m] = \frac{1}{|S(g)|}\sum_{x \Rightarrow g}(-1)^{|m|}\chi_m(x)$, where $|S(g)|$ is the number of examples satisfying g. The expectation on distribution D_i is then given by $E_{D_{i-1}^+}[(-1)^{|m|}\chi_m] =$

$\frac{1}{|S(g)|-|S(h_{i-1})|}\sum_{x\Rightarrow g}(-1)^{|m|}\chi_m(x)$, where $S(h_{i-1})$ is the set of examples satisfying h_{i-1}. We then have the result of the lemma, that $E_{D_{i-1}^+}[(-1)^{|m|}\chi_m] = cE_{D_0^+}[(-1)^{|m|}\chi_m]$ for $c = \frac{|S(g)|}{|S(g)|-|S(h_{i-1})|}$. $\qquad\square$

We can now state the following theorem.

Theorem 9. *The class of poly-disjoint One-read-once MDNF formulas is learnable on the uniform distribution.*

Proof. By Fact 1, any MDNF formula f can be approximated by a formula g with terms of size at most $\lg\frac{2s}{\epsilon}$, with error bounded by $\frac{\epsilon}{2}$. Thus, we assume hereafter without loss of generality that the target formula is such a g, and show in the remainder of the proof that g can be approximated with error $\frac{\epsilon}{2}$.

Consider the index ℓ chosen at the first execution of step 3 of Algorithm 1-Read-1 (see Fig. 1). ℓ is chosen to be the index of the attribute with the minimal estimated PFC, $\hat{E}_{D_{i-1}^+}[(-1)^{|m\cup\{\ell\}|}\chi_{m\cup\{\ell\}}]$, that is at least $\frac{\epsilon^2}{8s^2}$ in magnitude.

We first argue that the first attribute chosen will, with high probability, be a read-once attribute. By definition of poly-disjoint, each term t_i^g in the formula g has $\Pr[\mathcal{DS}(t_i^g)] \geq \frac{\epsilon^2}{4s^2}$. In particular, the read-once attribute x_{j_i} must have $E_{D_{i-1}^+}[(-1)^{|\{j_i\}|}\chi_{\{j_i\}}] \geq \frac{\epsilon^2}{4s^2}$. Any attribute x_ℓ that is not a read-once attribute must either occur in no term of the formula, or else occur in two or more terms. If x_ℓ is not in any term of the formula, then $E_{D_{i-1}^+}[(-1)^{|\{\ell\}|}\chi_{\{\ell\}}] = 0$. Furthermore, if ℓ occurs in two or more terms, then since all terms are poly disjoint, its probability must be at least $\frac{\epsilon^2}{4s^2}$ greater than that of the read-once attributes of those terms. Using Chernoff bounds [C 52,AV 79], a sample of size $O(\frac{s^4}{\epsilon^4}(\log\frac{sn}{\delta} + \log\log\frac{s}{\epsilon}))$ is sufficient to ensure with probability at least $1-\frac{\delta}{sn\log\frac{s}{\epsilon}}$ that x_ℓ occurs in exactly one term.

By Lemma 6, once we have a read-once attribute from term t_i^g, on each subsequent execution of step 3, $E_{D_{i-1}^+}[(-1)^{|m\cup\{\ell\}|}\chi_{m\cup\{\ell\}}] \geq \frac{\epsilon^2}{4s^2}$ if attribute ℓ is in the same term as m. If ℓ is not in the same term as m, by Lemma 7, $E_{D_{i-1}^+}[(-1)^{|m\cup\{\ell\}|}\chi_{m\cup\{\ell\}}] < 0$. By the Chernoff bound argument above, a sample of size $O(\frac{s^4}{\epsilon^4}(\log\frac{sn}{\delta} + \log\log\frac{s}{\epsilon}))$ is sufficient to ensure with probability at least $1 - \frac{\delta}{sn\log\frac{s}{\epsilon}}$, that ℓ is in the same term as m.

Estimating the PFC requires $O(\frac{s^4}{\epsilon^4}(\log\frac{sn}{\delta} + \log\log\frac{s}{\epsilon}))$ examples for each attribute x_ℓ. Since there are s terms in the target formula each with $\log\frac{s}{\epsilon}$ attributes, and we measure this statistic on all attributes each time we choose an attribute, the overall time and sample complexities are $O(n\frac{s^5}{\epsilon^4}\log\frac{s}{\epsilon}(\log\frac{sn}{\delta} + \log\log\frac{s}{\epsilon}))$. The probability that any attribute is chosen incorrectly is bounded by δ. $\qquad\square$

5 Learning Read-once Factorable MDNF

We now apply the Diffraction Lemma of Sect. 3 to show that the learning algorithm of the previous section is also a learning algorithm for the class of Read-once Factorable MDNF.

Theorem 10. *The class of Read-once Factorable MDNF formulas is learnable on the uniform distribution.*

Proof. As in the proof of the previous section, by Fact 1, the MDNF formula f can be approximated by a formula g with terms of size at most $\lg \frac{2s}{\epsilon}$, with error bounded by $\frac{\epsilon}{2}$, so we assume hereafter without loss of generality that the target formula is such a g, and show in the remainder of the proof that g can be approximated with error $\frac{\epsilon}{2}$.

We use Algorithm 1-Read-1 of Fig. 1 to learn a term of the Read-once Factorable MDNF formula g. Consider the index ℓ chosen at step 3 of the algorithm. Either x_ℓ is a read-once attribute, or else it is an attribute from the factor of two or more terms that all have $\Pr_{D+}[\mathcal{DS}(t_i)] < \frac{\epsilon^2}{4s^2}$.

If x_ℓ is a read-once attribute, then by the same argument as in the proof of the previous theorem, Algorithm 1-Read-1 will return term t_i. If x_ℓ is not a read-once attribute in term t_i, then it is an attribute from the factor of two or more terms that all have $\Pr_{D+}[\mathcal{DS}(t_i)] < \frac{\epsilon^2}{4s^2}$. By Lemma 5, all terms t_i with factor t can be approximated by t. Since the factored form is read-once, attribute x_ℓ does not occur in any other term; thus, x_ℓ is a read-once attribute in term t. Applying Lemmas 6 and 7 as in the proof of the previous theorem, Algorithm 1-Read-1 will return the greatest common factor t. The total error incurred by all such approximations by common factors is bounded by $\frac{\epsilon}{2}$, by Lemma 5.

The time and sample complexities are as shown in the proof of Theorem 9: $O(n \frac{s^5}{\epsilon^4} \log \frac{s}{\epsilon} (\log \frac{sn}{\delta} + \log \log \frac{s}{\epsilon}))$. $\qquad \square$

6 Conclusions and Open Problems

In this paper, we have given learning algorithms for two new sub-classes of MDNF formulas on the uniform distribution: poly-disjoint One-read-once MDNF formulas; and Read-once Factorable MDNF formulas. The class of Read-once Factorable MDNF formulas is a generalization of Read-once MDNF. Since the same algorithm is used for both classes, we in fact have a learning algorithm for the union of these two classes.

The worst case time complexity of the algorithm is a fifth order polynomial, a time complexity which would be impractical for large instances. The worst case scenario occurs if the probability weight of the set of vectors satisfying each term is very small (i.e., $\frac{\epsilon^2}{4s^2}$). This will not be the case for most formulas; a more typical case would be when each term has disjoint probability near $\frac{1}{s}$, since for a formula with s terms, at least one term must have probability weight at least $\frac{1}{s}$. The threshold in Algorithm 1-Read-1 could be adjusted for such cases to yield an improved complexity. Cubic complexity would result for formulas where the disjoint probability is $\frac{1}{s}$, for example. Extending this idea, a rigorous average case analysis for the algorithm presented in this paper would be an interesting area of future research.

References

[AP 95]   Aizenstein, H., Pitt, L.: On the Learnability of Disjunctive Normal Form Formulas. Machine Learning **19** (1995) 183–208

[AV 79]   Angluin, D., Valiant, L.: Fast Probabilistic Algorithms for Hamiltonian Circuits and Matchings. Journal of Computer and Systems Sciences **18** (1979) 155–193

[AHK 93]   Angluin, D., Hellerstein, L., Karpinski, M.: Learning Read-Once Formulas with Queries. Journal of the ACM **40** (1993) 185–210

[C 52]   Chernoff, H.: A measure of Asymptotic Efficiency for Tests of a Hypothesis Based on the Sum of Observations. Annals of Mathematical Statistics **23** (1952) 493–509

[GKS 90]   Goldman, S., Kearns, M., Schapire, R.: Exact Identification of Circuits Using Fixed Points of Amplification Functions. Proceedings of the 31st Annual Symposium on Foundations of Computer Science (1990) 193–202

[H 92]   Hancock, T.R.: The Complexity of Learning Formulas and Decision Trees that have Restricted Reads. PhD Thesis, Department of Computer Science, Harvard University, Technical Report TR-15-92 (1992)

[HKLW 88]   Haussler, D., Kearns, M., Littlestone, N., Warmuth, M.K.: Equivalence of Models for Polynomial Learnability. Proceedings of the 1988 Workshop on Computational Learning Theory (1988)

[J 94]   Jackson, J.: An Efficient Membership-Query Algorithm for Learning DNF with Respect to the Uniform Distribution. Proceedings of the 35th Annual Symposium on Foundations of Computer Science (1994) 42–53

[KLPV 87]   Kearns, M., Li, M., Pitt, L., Valiant, L.: On the Learnability of Boolean Formulae. Proceedings of the 19th Annual ACM Symposium on the Theory of Computing (1987) 285–295

[KLV 94]   Kearns, M., Li, M., Valiant, L.: Learning Boolean Formulas. Journal of the ACM **41-6** (1994) 1298–1328

[KV 88]   Kearns, M., Valiant, L.G.: Learning Boolean Formulae or Finite Automata is As Hard as Factoring. Tech Report TR- 14-88, Aiken Computer Laboratory, Harvard University (1988)

[Khar 94]   Khardon, R.: On using the Fourier transform to learn Disjoint DNF. Information Processing Letters, **49** (1994) 219–222

[LMN 89]   Linial, N., Mansour, Y., Nisan, N.: Constant Depth Circuits, Fourier Transform, and Learnability. Proceedings of the 30th Annual IEEE Symposium on Foundations of Computer Science (1989) 574–579

[LY 93]   Lund, C., Yannakakis, Y.: On the Hardness of Approximating Minimization Problems. Proceedings of the 25th Annual ACM Symposium on the Theory of Computing (1993) 286–293

[Man 95]   Mansour, Y.: An $O(n^{\log \log n})$ Learning Algorithm for DNF under the Uniform Distribution. Proceedings of the 5th Annual Workshop on Computational Learning Theory (1992) 53–61

[PV 86]   Pitt, L., Valiant, L.: Computational Limits on Learning from Examples.
           Tech. Rep. TR-05-86, Aiken Computer Laboratory, Harvard University
           (1986)
[S 92]   Schapire, R.: The Design and Analysis of Efficient Learning Algorithms.
           Doctoral Dissertation, MIT, The MIT Press (1992)
[Val 84]   Valiant, L.: A Theory of the Learnable. Communications of the ACM
           27-11 (1984) 1134–1142
[Ver 90]   Verbeurgt, K.: On the Learnability of DNF Formulae. Master's Thesis,
           University of Toronto (1990)
[Ver 90a] Verbeurgt, K.: Learning DNF Under the Uniform Distribution in Quasi-
           polynomial Time. Proceedings of the 3rd Annual Workshop on Computa-
           tional Learning Theory (1990) 314–326

A   Appendix

In this appendix, we give the proof of Lemma 4. For this proof, we require the
following additional terminology.

Let $R_i = \{j | 1 \leq j \leq s \text{ and } j \neq i\}$ denote the set of all integers from 1 to s
except i. We can then denote (2) by

$$\prod_{1 \leq i \leq s} g_i = \sum_{(j_1, j_2, \ldots, j_s) \in R_1 \times R_2 \times \ldots \times R_s} \prod_{1 \leq i \leq s} t^g_{j_i} . \tag{6}$$

Proof (of Lemma 4). We will first show that every term in $\prod_{\{t^g_i | t \subseteq t^g_i\}} P_t(g_i)$
is also contained in $\prod_{\{t^g_i | t \subseteq t^g_i\}} P_{t^g_i}(g_i)$. Taking the projection of (3) over t, and
applying Claim 3, $\prod_{\{t^g_i | t \subseteq t^g_i\}} P_t(g_i)$ can be expressed as:

$$\prod_{\{t^g_i | t \subseteq t^g_i\}} P_t(g_i) = \sum_{\{t^g_i | t \subseteq t^g_i\}} P_t(t^g_i) \cdot P_t(g_i) .$$

We will show that each $P_t(t^g_i) \cdot P_t(g_i)$ is generated by $\prod_{\{t^g_i | t \subseteq t^g_i\}} P_{t^g_i}(g_i)$.

Taking the projection of (6) over t^g_i, we get

$$\prod_{\{t^g_i | t \subseteq t^g_i\}} P_{t^g_i}(g_i) = \sum_{(j_1, j_2, \ldots, j_s) \in R_1 \times R_2 \times \ldots \times R_s} \prod_{\{t^g_i | t \subseteq t^g_i\}} P_{t^g_i}(t^g_{j_i}) . \tag{7}$$

For any k such that factor $t \subseteq t^g_k$, consider $P_{t^g_k}(g_k) \cdot \prod_{\{j | t \subseteq t^g_j, j \neq k\}} P_{t^g_j}(t^g_k)$. This
is the term of (7) in which j_k varies over R_k, and all other j_i are equal.

We claim that $\prod_{\{j | t \subseteq t^g_j, j \neq k\}} P_{t^g_j}(t^g_k) = P_t(t^g_k)$. This follows from the maximal-
ity of t: since t is a factor of t^g_j, and for every attribute x in $t^g_j - t$, there exists some
term not containing x. Thus, if $x \in t$, x does not occur in $\prod_{\{j | t \subseteq t^g_j, j \neq k\}} P_{t^g_j}(t^g_k)$,
but if x occurs in t^g_k but not in t^g_j for $j \neq k$, then x will occur in $\prod_{\{t^g_i | t \subseteq t^g_i\}} P_{t^g_j}(t^g_k)$.
Thus, $\prod_{\{t^g_i | t \subseteq t^g_i\}} P_{t^g_j}(t^g_k) = P_t(t^g_k)$.

Now, we have $P_{t^g_k}(g_k) \cdot \prod_{\{t^g_i | t \subseteq t^g_i\}} P_{t^g_j}(t^g_k) = P_{t^g_k}(g_k) \cdot P_t(t^g_k)$. But this is equiv-
alent to $P_t(g_k) \cdot P_t(t^g_k)$, and we have completed the proof that every term of
$P_t(t^g_i) \cdot P_t(g_i)$ is generated by $\prod_{\{t^g_i | t \subseteq t^g_i\}} P_{t^g_i}(g_i)$.

We now show that $\prod_{\{t_i^g \mid t \subseteq t_i^g\}} P_{t_i^q}(g_i)$ does not generate any term not in $P_t(t_i^g) \cdot P_t(g_i)$. In the above, we considered only the terms generated by $P_{t_k^q}(g_k) \cdot \prod_{\{j \mid t \subseteq t_j^q, j \neq k\}} P_{t_j^q}(t_k^g)$, which are terms in (7) where j_k varies over R_k, and all other j_i are equal. But $\prod_{\{t_i^q \mid t \subseteq t_i^q\}} P_{t_i^q}(g_i)$ also contains terms of the form $P_{t_k^q}(g_k) \cdot (\prod_{\{j \mid t \subseteq t_j^q, j \neq k, \ell \neq k\}} P_{t_j^q}(t_k^g)) P_{t_\ell^q}(t_{\ell'}^g)$ where ℓ' may be any value such that $t \subseteq t_{\ell'}^g$, except k or ℓ. (i.e., terms in (7) where all j_i are not equal, for $i \neq k$.) We show here that all of the attributes in $\prod_{\{j \mid t \subseteq t_j^q, j \neq k\}} P_{t_j^q}(t_k^g)$ must be contained in $\prod_{\{j \mid t \subseteq t_j^q, j \neq k, \ell \neq k\}} P_{t_j^q}(t_k^g) P_{t_\ell^q}(t_{\ell'}^g)$. Suppose that there exists some attribute x in t_k^g such that x is contained in all terms except t_ℓ^g. If there is no such attribute, then $\prod_{\{j \mid t \subseteq t_j^q, j \neq k, \ell \neq k\}} P_{t_j^q}(t_k^g) = P_t(t_k^g)$. Now, since x occurs in every term except t_ℓ^g, it follows that for any ℓ', $P_{t_\ell^q}(t_{\ell'}^g)$ contains x; hence for any choice of ℓ and ℓ', $\prod_{\{j \mid t \subseteq t_j^q, j \neq k, \ell \neq k\}} P_{t_j^q}(t_k^g) P_{t_\ell^q}(t_{\ell'}^g) = P_t(t_k^g)$. This completes the proof that the terms of $P_t(t_i^g) \cdot P_t(g_i)$ are the only terms generated by $\prod_{\{t_i^q \mid t \subseteq t_i^q\}} P_{t_i^q}(g_i)$.

$\square$

Using Attribute Grammars for Description of Inductive Inference Search Space

Uģis Sarkans*, Jānis Bārzdiņš**

Institute of Mathematics and Computer Science,
University of Latvia,
Raiņa bulvāris 29, LV-1459, Riga, Latvia

Abstract. The problem of practically feasible inductive inference of functions or other objects that can be described by means of an attribute grammar is studied in this paper. In our approach based on attribute grammars various kinds of knowledge about the object to be found can be encoded, ranging from usual input/output examples to assumptions about unknown object's syntactic structure to some dynamic object's properties. We present theoretical results as well as describe the architecture of a practical inductive synthesis system based on theoretical findings.

1 Introduction

The problem of discovering new proofs, formulas, algorithms etc. usually is solved by some kind of exhaustive search. One of the main issues here is how to minimize the extent of search by using our hypothetical knowledge about the object to be discovered. In this article we will concentrate our attention to synthesis of syntactic objects using various kinds of knowledge about them. If the objects we are trying to synthesize are, e. g., expressions in some fixed signature, then in the simplest case that knowledge will be (after assigning some interpretation to the signature) function values computed on some sample argument values, i.e., usual input/output examples. However, we want to be able to describe also some other properties of the unknown expression (function), i.e., treat the unknown function not as a black box function but as a "gray box" function. These other properties could be either some entirely syntactical properties of the expression we are looking for, or, taking into account also some interpretation, dynamical properties of the function evaluation process.

The question we are seeking answers to in this paper is, how we should present our knowledge so that it would be possible to rapidly examine those and only those objects that match our knowledge? Roughly speaking, the aim of this article is to show that in some sense it is possible to perform such search efficiently enough.

---
* usarkans@cclu.lv
** jbarzdin@cclu.lv

Our central aim is synthesis of syntactic objects, i.e., expressions over some fixed signature or programs in some fixed programming language, that can be supplemented by semantic interpretation.

It was understood already long ago that it is convenient to describe such syntactic objects by means of context-free grammars. Then a grammar generates a language with strings belonging to this language being our syntactic objects.

The well-known notion of attribute grammars is linked with the notion of context-free grammars. Our central observation that our approach is based on is that various kinds of hypothetical knowledge about the unknown object usually can be described by means of an attribute grammar that is based on the context-free grammar defining the description space.

As an example, suppose that our description space is defined by a context-free grammar describing the language of simple arithmetic expressions. Then, by supplementing each nonterminal with just a single attribute, we can make an attribute grammar that, for example, counts the number of multiplication operations in expressions, or that can be used to calculate the value of the expression when variable values are fixed, or that limits the values of intermediate expressions. See [3] for more details.

The main problem we will solve is the following: if some attribute grammar is given, is it possible to efficiently enumerate the corresponding language without considering strings that do not belong to it? The aim of this article is to show that, if some conditions hold, it is possible.

The results discussed in this article generalize the results presented in [3], which in turn was generalization of results presented in [1] and [2]. In [3] we considered only attribute grammars with synthesized attributes, and these attributes had to be independent, i.e., equations for computing one attribute could involve only the same attribute of the production right-hand side symbols. In this article we show that a more general class of attribute grammars can be considered, having possibly also inherited attributes and dependencies between different attributes. In some sense the presented article can be regarded as the concluding article in the series that started with [1].

Other approaches to synthesis of expressions include discovery systems BACON ([7], [8]), genetic programming ([4], [5], [6]).

2 Definitions and the Main Result

We suppose that an attribute grammar associates constant values with terminal symbols. For nonterminals attribute values are evaluated by means of corresponding functions. Every production of the grammar has one function for each synthesized attribute of the left-hand side nonterminal and one function for each inherited attribute of each of the right-hand side nonterminal and terminal symbols. If there is a production with several instances of the same nonterminal on the right-hand side, we would write the expression defining the function for computing attributes like this:

$$S \leftarrow AA \ / \ a_S \leftarrow a_{A_1} - a_{A_2}$$

In article [3] we used conditions — binary predicates that could be attached to every production —, and only inference trees with every predicate being true for every tree node were acceptable. Here predicates will be modeled by partially defined functions, and only inference trees with all attributes defined will be acceptable; see below for more detailed explanation.

By language that is defined by such a grammar we will understand the set of all strings that can be inferred by means of acceptable inference trees.

There is some domain associated with every attribute. From now on we will consider only attributes with finite domains D (for the sake of simplicity we will assume that these domains are subsets of $\mathbb{N}$). That means that arguments of functions for computing attributes, as well as their results belong to D. As we already mentioned, these functions can be partially defined as well. We will say that a grammar is finite if its attributes are of finite domain.

In the following discussion, in order to avoid talking about complexity of attribute evaluation functions, we will assume that each function value, given function arguments, can be computed in constant time.

We will say that an algorithm enumerates a language in setup time T and ith step time T_i, if this algorithm outputs the first string w_1 in time $T + T_1$, and the ith string w_i $(i = 2, 3, \ldots)$ in time T_i from the moment when outputting the previous string w_{i-1} was finished. In this paper by *algorithm* we mean a RAM-machine.

Now let us repeat some definitions in a more formal manner that would be convenient for presenting our results.

Let $G = \langle T, N, P, S \rangle$ is a context-free grammar, where:

- T — finite terminal symbol set;
- N — finite nonterminal symbol set;
- $S \in N$ — start symbol;
- P — a finite production set, where each production $(1 \leq k \leq |P|)$ is in form

$$A_k \leftarrow B_{k,1} B_{k,2} \ldots B_{k,s(k)}, \text{ where } A_k \in N \text{ and } B_{k,i} \in N \cup T$$

By trees we will denote structures of the form

- $\langle T_i \rangle$, where $T_i \in T$, or
- $\langle N_i, K_1, K_2, \ldots, K_n \rangle$, where $N_i \in N$ and K_j are trees.

We will say that a tree K corresponds to a terminal symbol T_i, if $K = \langle T_i \rangle$. We will say that a tree K corresponds to a production $N_i \leftarrow B_{k,1} B_{k,2} \ldots B_{k,s(k)}$, if $K = \langle N_i, K_{k,1}, K_{k,2} \ldots K_{k,s(k)} \rangle$, where trees $K_{k,i}$ correspond to symbols $B_{k,i}$. We will say that a tree K corresponds to a nonterminal N_i, if it corresponds to some of productions $N_i \leftarrow B_{k,1} B_{k,2} \ldots B_{k,s(k)}$.

Now we will define the terminal string $w(K)$ corresponding to a tree K:

$$w(\langle T_i \rangle) = T_i$$
$$w(\langle N_i, K_1, K_2, \ldots, K_n \rangle) = w(K_1) w(K_2) \ldots w(K_n)$$

A string $w \in T^*$ can be inferred in grammar G, if there exists a finite tree K_w corresponding to start symbol S such that $w = w(K_w)$; such tree will be called an inference tree of w. The set of all strings that can be inferred in G will be called language $L(G)$. The grammar G is unambiguous, if for every string $w \in L(G)$ there exists only one inference tree K_w. By depth of a string $w \in L(G)$ we will denote the depth of the corresponding inference tree.

Each of the elements $C_k \in N \cup T$ may have several attributes $c_{k,i}$, domains of all attributes are finite subsets of natural numbers. Values of attributes assigned to T elements (terminals) are constants, while values of N (nonterminals) are computed, using attribute evaluation functions. We will denote by $\bar{c}_k$ the tuple of all attributes of C_k, i.e., $(c_{k,0}, \ldots, c_{k,j})$.

There will be two kinds of attributes: synthesized and inherited attributes. We will denote synthesized attributes by c^{syn} and inherited attributes by c^{inh}.

Every production has several attribute evaluation functions assigned to it: if the production is in form $C_{i_0} \leftarrow C_{i_1} C_{i_2} \ldots C_{i_j}$, then there is a corresponding function for each synthesized attribute of C_{i_0} and for each inherited attribute of $C_{i_1} C_{i_2} \ldots C_{i_j}$. For a synthesized attribute $c^{syn}_{i_0,k}$ the evaluation function is $f(\bar{c}_{i_0}, \ldots, \bar{c}_{i_j})$, for an inherited attribute $c^{inh}_{i_m,k}$ the evaluation function is $f(\bar{c}_{i_0}, \bar{c}_{i_m})$, i.e., synthesized attributes can depend on all other attributes in the production, while inherited attributes can depend only on other attributes of the same symbol as well as on attributes of the left hand side symbol of the production.

Although there could be the same function used as the attribute evaluation function for several attributes (e.g., the identity function), we will assume that each attribute has its own, separate evaluation function (possibly partially defined). If we regard some evaluation function as defined by means of a table where there is a separate row for each possible argument tuple together with the corresponding function value, then by function volume we will understand the number of rows in this table. By production volume we will understand the sum of volumes of all attribute evaluation functions attached to this production. By volume of the grammar we will call the sum of all grammar production volumes.

A context-free grammar G that is supplemented with attributes and attribute evaluation functions will be called attribute grammar and denoted by G^+.

A tree $\langle T_i \rangle$ has the same attributes as the terminal symbol T_i, and attribute values are the same constants. A tree $\langle C_{i_0}, K_{i_1}, K_{i_2} \ldots K_{i_j} \rangle$ that corresponds to the production $P_i = (C_{i_0} \leftarrow C_{i_1} C_{i_2} \ldots C_{i_j})$ has the same synthesized attributes as nonterminal C_{i_0}, and attributes are evaluated by first evaluating the values of attributes $\bar{c}_{i_1}, \ldots, \bar{c}_{i_j}$ that are assigned to $K_{i_1}, \ldots, K_{i_j}$ and then by using the corresponding functions attached to production P_i. Similarly, subtrees K_j have the same inherited attributes as nonterminals C_j.

We will say that a string w can be inferred in grammar G^+, if

- it can be inferred in G, and
- it is possible to compute the values of all attributes assigned to the inference tree and each of its subtrees (it is not always possible, because attribute evaluation functions are partially defined).

By language $L(G^+)$ generated by an attribute grammar G^+ we will understand the set of all strings that can be inferred in G^+.

Theorem 1. *There exists an algorithm which, having received an arbitrary finite unambiguous noncircular attribute grammar, enumerates without repeating the corresponding language in setup time $O(|G^+|^k)$, where $|G^+|$ is the volume of the grammar and k is the maximal number of attributes belonging in the grammar to a single symbol, and ith step time $O(|w_i|)$, where w_i is the string output in the ith step.*

3 Sketch of Proof

We will define the grammar graph $\mathcal{G}_{G^+}$ corresponding to the grammar G^+. It will contain two kinds of nodes: terminal and nonterminal symbol nodes and production nodes.

There will be a symbol node in $\mathcal{G}_{G^+}$ corresponding to each triple $\langle C, a, v \rangle$, where $C \in N \cup T$, a is some attribute belonging to C and v is some value of this attribute. Production nodes will correspond to table rows (equalities) that define G^+ attribute evaluation functions: if the function f that is defined for computing attribute c of production $C_{i_0} \leftarrow C_{i_1} C_{i_2} \ldots C_{i_j}$ is defined by n rows of the form $f(\bar{c}_{i_0}, \bar{c}_{i_1}, \ldots, \bar{c}_{i_j}) = c$, each of these rows will have a corresponding production node p. For each p there will be the following arcs in $\mathcal{G}_{G^+}$ as well. There will be an arc from p to symbol nodes $\langle C_{i_0}, c_{i_{0.k}}, v \rangle$, where $c_{i_{0.k}}$ is an attribute present in the definition of the attribute evaluation function corresponding to p and v is some value of this attribute that is used in the specific table row for p. These symbol nodes will be called upper nodes of the production node p. There will also be arcs from every node $\langle C_{i_m}, c_{i_{m.k}}, v \rangle$ $(m > 0)$ to p where $c_{i_{m.k}}$ is some attribute present in the definition of the attribute evaluation function corresponding to p and v is some value of this attribute that is used in the specific table row for p; these symbol nodes will be called lower nodes of p.

Now we will define the compressed grammar graph $\mathcal{C}_{G^+}$ that corresponds to the grammar graph $\mathcal{G}_{G^+}$. It will also contain symbol nodes and production nodes. In this graph symbol nodes will contain pointers to symbol nodes in grammar graph $\mathcal{G}_{G^+}$, and similarly production nodes will contain pointers to production nodes in the grammar graph $\mathcal{G}_{G^+}$. For each symbol node in $\mathcal{C}_{G^+}$ there will be as many pointers to symbol nodes in $\mathcal{G}_{G^+}$ as there are attributes attached to the corresponding symbol in G^+, and for each production node in $\mathcal{C}_{G^+}$ the number of pointers to symbol nodes in $\mathcal{G}_{G^+}$ will equal the number of attribute evaluation functions attached to the corresponding production in G^+.

The compressed grammar graph $\mathcal{C}_{G^+}$ will contain the following nodes:

- For each terminal symbol in G^+ there will be a single terminal symbol node in $\mathcal{C}_{G^+}$ with pointers to corresponding terminal nodes in $\mathcal{G}_{G^+}$ (for each attribute c of $C \in T$ there is only one node $\langle C, c, v \rangle$ in $\mathcal{G}_{G^+}$).
- If, for some production P with k attached attribute evaluation functions, there are k production nodes p_i in $\mathcal{G}_{G^+}$ such that for every attribute c of the right hand side of P and for all lower nodes of p_i corresponding to c there is a symbol node s_i in $\mathcal{C}_{G^+}$ with pointers to all these nodes, than there is a

production node in C_{G^+} with pointers to all nodes p_i, and there are arcs in C_{G^+} from all s_i to this production node.

- If there is a set of symbol nodes S_i in $\mathcal{G}_{G^+}$ such that there is a production node p in C_{G^+} containing pointers to all lower nodes of s_i, then there is a symbol node in C_{G^+} containing pointers to all s_i nodes, and there is an arc from p to this symbol node.

For nodes of C_{G^+} (not necessarily for each of them) we will define weights:

- the weight of terminal symbol nodes is 0;
- if a production node p has lower nodes $s_1, \ldots, s_k$, the weight of this node equals $\max(w_{s_1}, \ldots, w_{s_k}) + 1$, where w_{s_i} are weights of p lower nodes;
- if $p_1, \ldots, p_k$ are production nodes with a common upper node s whose weights are defined and are equal to $w_{p_1}, \ldots, w_{p_k}$, then the weight of s equals $\min(w_1, \ldots, w_k)$, otherwise the weight of s is not defined (i. e., if there is no such production node).

Graph C_{G^+} will be augmented by dotted arcs according to the following rule. Assume that s is some symbol node and $p_1, \ldots, p_k$ are production nodes with defined weights $w(p_i)$ such that their upper node is s, and they are ordered so that $w(p_1) \leq w(p_2) \leq \cdots \leq w(p_k)$. Then dotted arcs go from s to p_1, from p_1 to $p_2, \ldots$, from p_{k-1} to p_k.

By C we will denote some symbol of G, and by $\bar{v} = (v_1, \ldots, v_k)$ — some vector of its attributes' values. It is easy to see that the weight of the symbol node in C_{G^+} that corresponds to C and has pointers to nodes $\langle C, c_j, v_j \rangle$ in $\mathcal{G}_{G^+}$ equals the depth of the most shallow inference tree that corresponds to C whose attributes' value vector is $\bar{v}$.

Grammar graph $\mathcal{G}_{G^+}$ construction. Can be performed in time $O(|G^+|)$, because in $\mathcal{G}_{G^+}$ the number of production nodes equals $|G^+|$ and each production node can be added in constant time.

Graph compression. The compressed graph C_{G^+} will be constructed in several stages. During the first stage for each grammar symbol two attributes will be compressed, obtaining a partial C_{G^+} with every node containing no more than two pointers to nodes of $\mathcal{G}_{G^+}$. In the consequtive stages other attributes will be added, until the full C_{G^+} is obtained. For the sake of simplicity here we will briefly consider only how the first stage is carried out. The algorithm will consist of the initial step and iterative step.

Initial step. Terminal symbol nodes of C_{G^+} are constructed. Weights 0 are assigned to these nodes.

Iterative step. Consider all pairs of production nodes p_1 and p_2 in $\mathcal{G}_{G^+}$ such that no corresponding node in C_{G^+} is constructed yet, but for all lower nodes in $\mathcal{G}_{G^+}$ there are matching nodes in C_{G^+}. Then a production node p in C_{G^+} with pointers to p_1 and p_2 can be constructed and its weight can be computed. If there is a symbol node s in C_{G^+} with pointers to upper nodes of p_1 and p_2, a dotted arc is added in C_{G^+} from the last production node on the path formed by dotted arcs leaving s to p. Otherwise such s is constructed, and a dotted arc is added from s to p.

The j-th stage of graph compression can be performed in time $O(|G^+|^{j+1})$, hence we get the time complexity estimation of $O(|G^+|^k)$ where k is the maximum number of attributes attached to a single symbol in G^+.

In the terms of Theorem 1 grammar graph construction and graph compression comprise the setup stage, therefore we have shown that time complexity of the setup stage is $O(|G^+|^k)$.

String output. The inference tree K of a string $w \in L(G^+)$ will be called annotated if there is a node of graph C_{G^+} associated with every K subtree K_i according to the rule that, if K_i is in form $\langle S \rangle$, where $S \in T$, or $\langle S, K_{i,1}, \ldots, K_{i,n} \rangle$, where $S \in N$, and the value of its attribute vector is $\bar{v}$, the associated graph node is $\langle S, \bar{v} \rangle$.

We will define the minimal subtree of a symbol node s in C_{G^+} that corresponds to symbol S. If $S \in T$, then the minimal subtree is $\langle S \rangle$. If $S \in N$ and there is no dotted arc leaving s, the minimal subtree is not defined for this node. If $S \in N$ and there is a dotted arc leaving s, then we have to consider the production node p that this arc enters. If this production node corresponds to the production $P \leftarrow S_1 \ldots S_n$, then the minimal subtree of s is $\langle S, K_1, \ldots, K_n \rangle$, where K_i are minimal subtrees of p lower nodes. If for some node the minimal subtree is defined, it is a finite object with depth equal to the weight of this node.

Similarly we define the minimal subtree of a production node of C_{G^+}. It will be defined only for production nodes with defined weights. The minimal subtree of a production node will be equal to the minimal subtree of its upper node. The depth of minimal subtrees of production nodes are equal to their weights as well. The number of steps necessary for outputting the terminal string $w(K)$ that corresponds to the minimal subtree K of some node is $O(|w(K)|)$, where $|w(K)|$ is the length of this string.

We will say that for an annotated inference tree K there exists an alternative inference tree, if there is a dotted arc leaving the production node p corresponding to K and entering some production node p'. Then the minimal subtree of node p' will be called alternative inference tree for tree K.

The language $L(G^+)$ that the presented algorithm enumerates can be infinite, therefore enumeration will be performed in a breadth-first manner. A potentially infinite queue will be used for storing marked inference trees. By marked inference trees we will understand annotated inference trees with (possibly) marked subtrees for which there exist alternative inference subtrees.

Assuming that C_{G^+} contains only one node s corresponding to the start symbol S of grammar G^+, the algorithm for enumerating will be as follows.

Initial step.

- The terminal string $w(K)$ that corresponds to the minimal subtree of the node s is output.
- K is entered into the queue, marking all subtrees for which alternative subtrees exist.

Iterative step. While the queue is not empty:

- Take the first inference tree K from the queue.
- If at least two subtrees of K are marked, enter K at the end of the queue, removing the first marker from the left-hand side.
- Replace the first marked subtree of K by its alternative inference subtree, obtaining inference tree K'.
- Output $w(K')$.
- If in K' there is a subtree to the right of the changed point with an alternative, put K' at the end of the queue, marking all alternative points from the changed point (including) to the right.

In the general case when graph C_{G^+} contains n nodes s_j corresponding to the grammar start symbol S, n separate queues are set up. The words for which the value of their inference tree corresponds to s_1 are output on the first, $n + 1$-st, $2n + 1$-st etc. steps of the algorithm, the words for which that value corresponds to s_2 are output on the second, $n + 2$-nd, $2n + 2$-nd etc. steps, etc.

4 Notes on implementation details

The described algorithms are being implemented in a practical inductive inference system. Here we will shortly describe its architecture. For purposes of practical implementation some deviations were made compared to the theoretically "clean" algorithms.

There is a separate module of grammar graph construction and a separate module of graph compression in the system. According to the theoretical algorithms these two modules have to work sequentially in the order that they were just mentioned in. However, we have noticed that for some search spaces it is more efficient to start compressing the graph before it is fully constructed. To be able to organize synthesis process in such manner we implemented a control module which acts as a dispatcher between graph constructor and graph compressor, that can be easily customized for different dispatching strategies.

For real world examples domain node and production node sets become quite large, and we have experimented with several strategies of compressing these sets. In the compression process several domain nodes are merged into a single node. When such compression takes place, the graph loses precision in the sense that it encodes some strings that do not belong to the language. However, if we add to the grammar some more information, e.g., additional input/output examples, incorrect paths through the graph are filtered out. In the case of input/output examples graph nodes can be compressed more safely if they have values further from zero. For experimentation purposes we have implemented a separate domain node writer module that can be easily changed to support different node compression strategies.

A separate module implements graph cleaning procedure. According to our theoretical algorithms graphs are constructed and compressed in a bottom-up manner, and language strings are output in a top-down manner. Compressed graphs can be made smaller by traversing noncompressed graphs in a top-down manner and registering which nodes are reachable; then during compression only reachable nodes are considered. We call this process graph cleaning.

At present inductive inference system implementation is in progress.

5 Conclusion

There were successful computer experiments carried out that employed methods developed in [1] and [2]. In these experiments algebraic expressions were synthesized from input/output examples. In the most successful experiments the formula for the volume of a frustum of a square pyramid and the formula for finding roots of a quadratic equation were synthesized in reasonable time. Algorithms and the synthesis system described in this paper are general and flexible enough to permit easier setup of computer experiments. We believe that computer experiments can bring new insights into inductive synthesis process in our framework and help in obtaining new theoretical results.

References

1. J.M.Barzdin and G.J.Barzdin. Rapid construction of algebraic axioms from samples. Theoretical Computer Science 90. – 1991. – pp. 199–208.
2. J.Barzdins, G.Barzdins, K.Apsitis, U.Sarkans. Towards Efficient Inductive Synthesis of Expressions from input/output Examples. Lecture Notes in Artificial Intelligence, vol.744. – 1993. – pp. 59–72.
3. J.Barzdins, U.Sarkans. Incorporating Hypothetical Knowledge into the Process of Inductive Synthesis. Lecture Notes in Artificial Intelligence, vol.1160. – 1996. – pp. 156–168.
4. J.H.Holland. Adaptation in Natural and Artificial Systems: An Introductory Analysis with Applications to Biology, Control, and Artificial Intelligence. MIT Press, 1992.
5. J.R.Koza. Genetic Programming: On the Programming of Computers by Means of Natural Selection. MIT Press, 1992.
6. J.R.Koza. Genetic Programming II: Automatic Discovery of Reusable Programs. MIT Press, 1994.
7. P.Langley, G.Bradshaw, H.A.Simon. Rediscovering chemistry with the BACON system. In Machine Learning: An Artificial Intelligence Approach, R.S.Michalski, J.G.Carbonell, T.M.Mitchell (eds.), Tioga Press, Palo Alto, CA, 1983.
8. P.Langley, H.A.Simon, G.Bradshaw. Heuristics for Empirical Discovery. In Computational Models of Learning, L.Bolc (ed.), Springer-Verlag, 1987.

Towards the Validation of Inductive Learning Systems

Gunter Grieser[1], Klaus P. Jantke[2], and Steffen Lange[3]

[1] Technische Universität Darmstadt, Fachbereich Informatik
Alexanderstraße 10, 64283 Darmstadt, Germany
gunter@intellektik.informatik.tu-darmstadt.de

[2] Meme Media Laboratory, Hokkaido University
Kita-13, Nishi-8, Kita-ku, Sapporo 060-8628, Japan
jantke@meme.hokudai.ac.jp

[3] Universität Leipzig, Institut für Informatik
Augustusplatz 10-11, 04109 Leipzig, Germany
slange@informatik.uni-leipzig.de

Abstract. The present paper deals with inductive inference of recursive functions, in general, and with the problem of validating inductive learning devices, in particular.

Thus, the paper aims at a contribution to the research and development area of intelligent systems validation. As those systems are typically interactive and, therefore, utilized in open loops of human–machine interactions, the problem of their validity is substantially complicated. A certain family of validation scenarios is adopted. Within this framework, we ask for the power and the limitations of these validation approaches. The expertise necessary and sufficient to accomplish successful validation is of some particular interest. One of the key questions is for the comparison of domain expertise and validation expertise.

The area of inductive inference of recursive functions is taken as a case for complex interactive systems validation.

Computability theory is providing a rich source of theoretical concepts and results suitable for the focused investigations. Emphasis is put on explicating the importance of abstract computational complexity, limiting computability, and relativized computability. These concepts are exploited for characterizing the expertise necessary and sufficient in the validation of inductive inference systems. Particular emphasis is put on relating validation expertise and domain expertise by means of relativized computability concepts. One of the key results on validation of inductive learning systems exhibits that validation expertise necessarily implies the expertise for solving the focused learning problems.

1 Motivation

The focus of the present paper is on inductive inference systems, but we draw a particular motivation from another area: complex interactive systems validation. u There is an obvious necessity to validate and verify complex systems, respectively. It might easily happen that ...*the inability to adequately evaluate systems may become the limiting factor in our ability to employ systems that our technology and knowledge will allow us to design.* (cf. [12])

Unfortunately, there are numerous severe accidents bearing abundant evidence for the truly urgent need for complex systems validation. Besides spectacular cases, daily experience with more or less invalid systems is providing paramount illustrative examples. Progress in the area of validation and verification of complex systems requires both disciplinary results and solutions in the humanities including cognitive psychology, e.g. Even social and political aspects come into play. The authors refrain from an in-depth discussion.

Following [4] and [10], validation is distinguished from verification by the illustrative circumscription of dealing with *building the right system*, whereas verification deals with *building the system right*. The prototypical application area considered in the present paper is systems *validation*, which – according to the perspective cited above – is less constrained and less formalized than verification.

Assume computer systems which are designed and implemented for an interactive use to assist human beings in open loops of human–machine interactions of a usually unforeseeable length. The validation task is substantially complicated, if it is intermediately undecidable whether or not some human–machine co-operation will eventually succeed.

Nontrivial learning problems, for instance, are quite typical representatives of such a class of problems attacked through complex and usually time consuming sequences of human–machine interactions. Knowledge discovery in data bases, for instance, is a practically relevant application domain for those learning approaches.

For assessing those systems' validity, there have been proposed validation scenarios of several types (cf. [9], e.g.). As soon as human experts are involved in the implementation of validation scenarios, there arises the problem of the experts' competence. An in-depth investigation of validation scenarios, of their appropriateness for certain classes of target systems, and of their power and limitations involves inevitably reasoning about the experts' competence.

Still informally speaking, the key question is *how to characterize the human expertise necessary or sufficient for validating certain AI systems.*

The issue of human expertise is usually understood a problem of cognitive sciences (cf. [5]). This is complicating a thorough computer science investigation of validation scenarios mostly based on formal concepts and methodologies.

Therefore, the present papers is focusing on approaches to characterize human expertise in formal terms. This is deemed a substantial step towards a better understanding of the power and limitations of interactive validation scenarios.

2 Learning Systems Validation - Basic Concepts

We adopt validation scenarios according to [9], e.g. Validation is performed through the essential stages of test case generation, experimentation, evaluation, and assessment.

Test cases are generated in dependence on some intended target behaviour and, possibly, with respect to peculiarities of the system under validation. Interactive validation is performed by feeding test data into the system and, hopefully, receiving system's response. The results of such an experimentation are subject to evaluation. The ultimate validity assessment is synthesized upon the totality of evaluation outcomes.

Human experts who are invoked for learning systems validation within the framework of those scenarios need to have some topical competence. It is one of the key problems of validation approaches based on human expertise how to characterize the experts' potentials which allow them to do their job sufficiently well. Even more exciting, it is usually unknown whether or not the humans engaged in those interactive scenarios can be replaced by computer programs without any substantial loss of validation power. This problem is of a great philosophical interest and of a tremendous practical importance.

For the validation of inductive inference systems, we will be able to characterize the human expertise *sufficient* for trustable systems validation. Some characterizations are even both *sufficient* and *necessary*. Thus, this paper is understood a contribution to the theory of inductive inference.

2.1 Preliminaries

For most of the notions and notations of this section, [11] is a standard reference. Let $I\!N$ denote the set of natural numbers, and let $I\!N_\perp = I\!N \cup \{\perp\}$. For any $M \subseteq I\!N$ we denote the power set of M by $\wp(M)$. For any $k \geq 1$, $\mathcal{F}_p^k$ ($\mathcal{F}_t^k$) denotes the set of all partial (total) function from $I\!N^k$ into $I\!N$. For some function f, $dom(f)$ denotes the domain of f.

Computable functions are defined over $I\!N$. $\mathcal{P}$ is the class of all partial recursive functions. The class of total recursive functions is denoted by $\mathcal{R}$.

By $cod: I\!N^2 \to I\!N$ let us denote CANTOR's pairing function, i.e. a particularly simple primitive recursive function that is bijective (injective and surjective).

For a GÖDEL numbering φ, each number $j \in I\!N$ is specifying a particular function denoted by φ_j. For the rest of this paper, a GÖDEL numbering φ and a corresponding BLUM complexity measure ϕ are fixed (cf. [3]). For any $j, x \in I\!N$, $\varphi_j(x)\downarrow$ indicates that $\varphi_j(x)$ is defined. For some set $F \subseteq \mathcal{P}$, the index set I_F contains exactly all programs for functions from F, i.e. $I_F = \{i \in I\!N \,|\, \varphi_i \in F\}$.

Let $U \subseteq \mathcal{R}$. Then, U is said to be enumerable provided there is a $g \in \mathcal{R}$ such that $U \subseteq \{\varphi_{g(n)} \,|\, n \in I\!N\} \subseteq \mathcal{R}$. If $U = \{\varphi_{g(n)} \,|\, n \in I\!N\}$ for some $g \in \mathcal{R}$, then U is called exactly enumerable. By NUM (NUM!) we denote the collection of all enumerable (exactly enumerable) subsets of $\mathcal{R}$.

A sequence $(n_t)_{t \in I\!N}$ of natural numbers is said to converge to some ultimately final value n, if past some point t' all numbers n_t ($t \geq t'$) are identical to n. This so-called discrete limit is denoted by $\lim(n_t)_{t \in I\!N} = n$.

A function f is said to be limiting computable, if there is some $g \in \mathcal{R}^2$ meeting (i) for all $x \in dom(f)$, there is some $t' \in I\!N$ such that, for all $t \in I\!N$ with $t > t'$, $g(x, t) = f(x)$, and meeting (ii) for all $x \notin dom(f)$ and all $t \in I\!N$, there exists some $t' \in I\!N$ such that $t' > t$, and $g(x, t') \neq g(x, t)$.

Any $M \subseteq I\!N$ is said to be limiting decidable, if M's characteristic function χ_M is limiting computable. Similarly, $M \subseteq I\!N$ is said to be limiting enumerable, if 'half' of M's characteristic function χ_M^+ is limiting computable, where $\chi_M^+(x) = 1$ if and only if $x \in M$.

We use the abbreviation f^A to indicate that f is computable relative to some oracle A, i.e. there is an algorithm computing f that is allowed to ask, from time to time, question of the type '$n \in A$?', and that may use the answers supplied to determine how to continue.

We use the abbreviation $[M\, l.r.e.]^A$ to indicate that there is some function computable relative to some oracle A (A-computable, for short) limiting enumerating some set $M \subseteq \mathbb{N}$.

2.2 Inductive Inference – Notions and Notations

Induction constitutes an important feature of learning. The corresponding theory is called *inductive inference*. Inductive inference may be characterized as the study of systems that map evidence on a target concept into hypotheses about it. The investigation of scenarios in which the sequence of hypotheses *stabilizes* to an *accurate* and *finite* description of the target concept is of some particular interest. The precise definitions of the notions evidence, stabilization, and accuracy go back to GOLD (cf. [6]) who introduced the model of learning in the limit.

This section is focused on essential features of inductive learning which complicate the validation task, and it introduces a few basic formalisms. For both conceptual simplicity and expressive generality, the focus of the present investigations is on learning of total recursive functions from finite sets of input/output examples (cf. [2]).

When learning any total recursive function f, the input/output examples $\langle 0, f(0)\rangle, \langle 1, f(1)\rangle, \langle 2, f(2)\rangle, \ldots$ are subsequently presented. Learning devices are computable procedures generating hypotheses upon natural numbers $f[t]$ encoding finite samples $\langle 0, f(0)\rangle, \langle 1, f(1)\rangle, \ldots, \langle t, f(t)\rangle$. Note that, for every $x \in \mathbb{N}$, there is the one and only finite sample encoded by x.

For notational convenience, hypotheses are just natural numbers which are to be interpreted via the underlying GÖDEL numbering φ.

Note that learning will usually take place over time. Thus, hypotheses are generated subsequently.

An individual learning problem is always understood to be a class of target functions. A corresponding learning device has to learn each of these functions individually when fed with appropriate samples.

Definition 1 (LIM). $U \in LIM$ iff there is an $S \in \mathcal{P}$ satisfying for any $f \in U$: (1) for all $t \in \mathbb{N}$, $h_t = S(f[t])$ is defined and (2) $\lim(h_t)_{t \in \mathbb{N}} = h$ with $\varphi_h = f$ exists.

Thus, LIM is a collection of function classes U for which some recursive learning device S as indicated exists. As usual, by $LIM(S)$ we denote the function class learned by S. For some $\mathcal{S} \subseteq \mathcal{P}$, we set $LIM(\mathcal{S}) = \{LIM(S) \mid S \in \mathcal{S}\}$. If the learning device S exclusively outputs indices for total recursive functions then U belongs to the learning type $TOTAL$.

Definition 2 (TOTAL). $U \in TOTAL$ iff there exists some $S \in \mathcal{P}$ satisfying for any $f \in U$: (1) for all $t \in \mathbb{N}$, $h_t = S(f[t])$ is defined, (2) $\lim(h_t)_{t \in \mathbb{N}} = h$ with $\varphi_h = f$ exists, and (3) for all $t \in \mathbb{N}$, $h_t \in I_{\mathcal{R}}$.

Alternatively, if it is decidable whether or not S, when learning any $f \in U$, has reached the ultimate learning goal then S witnesses that U belongs to the special learning type FIN. This approach is easily formalized as well:

Definition 3 (FIN). $U \in FIN$ iff there exist some $S \in P$ and some related decision procedure $d \in P$ which satisfy for any $f \in U$: (1) for all $t \in I\!N$, $h_t = S(f[t])$ is defined, (2) $\lim(h_t)_{t \in I\!N} = h$ with $\varphi_h = f$ exists, (3) for all $t \in I\!N$, $d(f[t])$ is defined, and (4) for all $t \in I\!N$, $d(f[t]) = 1$ iff $S(f[t]) = h$.

The relation between the learning types introduced above is as follows:

$$FIN \subset TOTAL \subset LIM \subset \wp(\mathcal{R}).$$

To sum up, although inductive learning succeeds after finitely many steps, in its right perspective, it is appropriately understood as a limiting process. This fact is causing unavoidable difficulties to validation attempts based on local information, only.

2.3 Interactive Scenarios for Learning Systems Validation

A validation problem for inductive inference systems is given as a triple of (1) some function class $U \subseteq \mathcal{R}$, (2) some learning function $S \in P$, and (3) an inductive inference type like LIM, $TOTAL$, or FIN, e.g. The precise question is whether S is able to learn all functions f from U with respect to the considered inductive inference type.

There are two substantial difficulties. First, function classes U under consideration are usually infinite. Second, every individual function is an infinite object in its own right. In contrast, every human attempt to validate some learning system by a series of *systematic tests* is essentially finite. Thus, validity statements are necessarily approximate.

When some process of (hopefully) learning some target function $f \in U$ by some device $S \in P$ with respect to some inductive inference type is under progress, one may inspect snapshots determined by any point t in time.

Any pair of an index of a recursive function and a time point is called *test data*. Those pairs represent initial segments of functions. Certain data are chosen for testing by a *test data selection*.

Definition 4 (Test Data, Test Data Selection). Any pair $\langle j, t \rangle$ that meets $\varphi_j(x) \downarrow$, for all $x \leq t$, is called test data. TD denotes the set of all potential test data. Furthermore, a function $Ds: I\!N \to \wp(TD)$ defines a test data selection provided that, for all $n \in I\!N$, $Ds(n) \subset Ds(n+1)$.

In practice, the selection of test data is frequently done by hand. So, there is no need to consider the test data selection to be recursive.

Intuitively, the two numbers refer to a program and an intensity, with which the behaviour of the system is tested for this program. Test data $\langle j, t \rangle$ are interpreted as $\varphi_j[t]$. Therefore, the second parameter is called a time stamp.

In order to verify whether or not a learning system is valid with respect to some function class U, enough relevant test data have to be selected.

Definition 5 (Completeness). Let $U \subseteq \mathcal{R}$ and let Ds be a test data selection. Ds is said to be complete for U iff the set $T = \bigcup_{n \in I\!N} Ds(n)$ satisfies conditions (1) for all $f \in U$, there is a φ-index j for f such that $\langle j, t \rangle \in T$ for every $t \in I\!N$, (2) there are only finitely many test data $\langle j, t \rangle \in T$ with $j \notin I_U$, and (3) there are only finitely many test data $\langle j, t \rangle \in T$ with $\langle j, t+1 \rangle \notin T$.

When testing some learning system S on test data $\langle j,t \rangle$, one is interested in knowing how S behaves on input $\varphi_j[t]$. *Experimentation* means feeding test data to the system under investigation and, if possible, receiving system's response.

Definition 6 (Experimentation). Any total mapping $Expmt : I\!N \to I\!N_\perp$ is said to be an experimentation. The mapping $Expmt$ is an experimentation for $S \in \mathcal{P}$ iff, for all $\langle j,t \rangle \in TD$, either $Expmt(\varphi_j[t]) = \perp$ or $Expmt(\varphi_j[t]) = S(\varphi_j[t])$.

Because experimentation is a human activity, the mapping $Expmt$ is not necessarily computable.

Intuitively, the result $\perp$ means that no proper system's response has been received. This may be due to some time out, e.g. Clearly, if it frequently happens that $Expmt(\varphi_j[t]) = \perp$, but $S(\varphi_j[t])$ terminates, then this particular experimentation does not reflect the learning system's behaviour sufficiently well.

Insistency characterizes a manner of interactively validating a system where the human interrogator does never give up too early.

Definition 7 (Insistency). Let $Expmt$ be an experimentation for $S \in \mathcal{P}$. $Expmt$ is said to be insistent for S iff $Expmt(\varphi_j[t]) = S(\varphi_j[t])$ for exactly all $\langle j,t \rangle \in TD$, where $S(\varphi_j[t]) \downarrow$.

These formalisms are aimed at the description of an expert's interactive validation of any given learning system S. An expert is performing experiments with some target object φ_j in mind resulting in *protocols*. A protocol is a triple $\langle j,t,h \rangle$ with $\langle j,t \rangle \in TD$ and $h = Expmt(\varphi_j[t])$.

Those protocols are subject to the expert's evaluation marked 1 or 0, respectively, expressing the opinion whether or not the experiment witnesses the system's ability to learn the target function φ_j. This realizes a certain mapping $Eval : TD \times I\!N \to \{0,1\}$, a so-called expert's evaluation function. As before, this might be not computable. The tuple consisting of a protocol and the expert's evaluation is a *report*.

Validation statements are synthesized upon reports which reflect interactive systems validation to some extent. In dependence on the underlying validation scenario, there are concepts of different sophistication. We adopt the most simple approach, and consider any finite set of reports to be a *validation statement*.

For interactive systems, in general, and for learning systems, in particular, any one-shot validation does not seem to be appropriate. Thus, one is led to validation scenarios in open loops which result in sequences of validation statements. Hence, a *validation dialogue* arises, constituted by any test data selection, experimentation, and the expert's evaluation function.

Definition 8 (Validation Dialogue). Assume any test data selection Ds, any experimentation $Expmt$, and any expert's evaluation function $Eval$. The triple $VD = \langle Ds, Expmt, Eval \rangle$ defines a sequence of validation statements $(VS_n)_{n \in I\!N}$ called a validation dialogue, where, for all $n \in I\!N$, VS_n is the collection of all reports $\langle \langle j,t,h \rangle, b \rangle$ with $\langle j,t \rangle \in Ds(n)$, $h = Expmt(\varphi_j[t])$, and $b = Eval(j,t,h)$.

Such a validation dialogue is said to be *successful* for U and S if and only if the underlying data selection is complete for U, the experimentation is insistent for S, and the experts' evaluation is converging to the success value 1, for every program which is subject to unbounded experimentation.

Definition 9 (Successful Validation Dialogue). Let $U \subseteq \mathcal{R}$ and $S \in \mathcal{P}$. Furthermore, assume any test data selection Ds, any experimentation $Expmt$, and any expert's evaluation function $Eval$. The validation dialogue $(VS_n)_{n \in \mathbb{N}}$ defined by $VD = \langle Ds, Expmt, Eval \rangle$ is successful for U and S iff (1) Ds is complete for U, (2) $Expmt$ is insistent for S, and (3) for every $j \in \mathbb{N}$, there are only finitely many reports $\langle\langle j,t,h\rangle, b\rangle \in \bigcup_{n \in \mathbb{N}} VS_n$ with $b = 0$.

The formal concepts introduced will suffice for systematically investigating the possibilities of interactive learning systems validation.

3 Learning Systems Validation - Results

Within the preceding section, a formalization of a general scenario for learning systems validation has been presented. It mainly consists of the following three phases: test case generation, experimentation, and evaluation. Based on this formalization, we are systematically addressing the following questions separately for each phase of the validation process:

- *Which level of expertise is necessary and sufficient to supervise the corresponding phase of the validation process?*
- *For which problem classes a module can be implemented that realizes the required functionality?*
- *What are relevant criteria to measure the effort needed to supervise resp. automate parts of the validation process? Do those criteria allow for a stratification of problem classes?*

3.1 Test Data Selection

We go only very briefly into the details of test data selection. There are several areas of more traditional computer science and of AI where the generation of test cases or test sets plays an important role. The methodologies invoked range from sophisticated mathematical considerations to comprehensive investigations taking aspects of cognitive psychology into account. We are aware of the narrowness of our present approach, but we had to trade generality for precision.

First, we introduce a notion for the collection of all those learning problems for which some complete data selection exists.

Definition 10 (CDS). Let $U \subseteq \mathcal{R}$. $U \in CDS$ iff there is a test data selection $Ds \in \mathcal{F}_p$ which is complete for U.

Let A be an oracle and let $U \subseteq \mathcal{R}$. We use the notation $[U \in CDS]^A$ to indicate that there is an A-computable data selection Ds which is complete for U.

In most investigations, it is of a particular interest to find out whether or not sets of test cases can be generated automatically. Within the technical terms of the present approach, this is the question for the computability and relativized computability of the data selection function Ds, respectively.

Theorem 11. *Let* $U \subseteq \mathcal{R}$. *Then, for any oracle* A, $[U \in CDS]^A \Longleftrightarrow [U \in NUM!]^A$.

416

Theorem 11 yields the following corollary which exhibits the restrictiveness of areas in which the selection of relevant test data can be fully automated.

Corollary 12. $CDS = NUM!$

Finally, let us point to the following result stating that there is no level of expertise that allows to generate complete test data for all learning problems.

Theorem 13. *For any oracle A, there is some $U \in LIM$ such that $[U \notin CDS]^A$.*

3.2 Experimentation

Recall that an experimentation is called insistent, exactly if it always guarantees to take system outputs into account, in case those are eventually generated.

The question considered in the present section is how to implement any form of control to accomplish insistent experimentation. Conceptually, one needs any module supervising experimentation and 'telling' the validator whether or not (s)he should wait a little longer for some system's response.

Any given learning function S under validation is effectively computable and, therefore, when being subject to experimentation, may be understood as some particular φ_s with $\varphi_s = S$. Note that this does not mean that the validator is necessarily aware of the particular program s under inspection. However, the actual experimentation process is characterized by the computation time of φ_s which can be suitably formalized by any related BLUM complexity measure.

In order to formalize control concepts of insistent experimentation, it is necessary to distinguish between so-called 'white box' validation and 'black box' validation (cf. [8], e.g.). In the first case, one has access to the program under validation, whereas one is restricted to only the program's behaviour, in the latter case. This is formally reflected by a control function c which depends either on both the information $\varphi_j[t]$ presented and the program s inspected or exclusively on the recent information $\varphi_j[t]$.

Definition 14 (Control). Let $c \in \mathcal{F}_t^2$ and let $s \in \mathbb{N}$. Then, control c allows for an insistent white box experimentation with φ-program s iff, for any $\varphi_j[t] \in \mathbb{N}$, $\varphi_s(\varphi_j[t]) \downarrow$ implies $c(\varphi_j[t], s) \geq \phi_s(\varphi_j[t])$.

Let $c \in \mathcal{F}_t$ and let $s \in \mathbb{N}$. Then, control c allows for an insistent black box experimentation with φ-program s iff, for any $\varphi_j[t] \in \mathbb{N}$, $\varphi_s(\varphi_j[t]) \downarrow$ implies $c(\varphi_j[t]) \geq \phi_s(\varphi_j[t])$.

Let $c \in \mathcal{F}_t^2$. Then, $COP^w(c)$ is the set of all φ-programs controlled by c, accordingly. Furthermore, $COF^w(c)$ is the set of all computable functions for which there is a φ-program controlled by c, i.e. $COF^w(c) = \{\varphi_s \mid s \in COP^w(c)\}$. Concerning insistent black box experimentation via some control $c \in \mathcal{F}_t$, the sets $COP^b(c)$ and $COF^b(c)$ are defined analogously.

The following lemma justifies the focus of the investigations on control functions. As it turns out, insistent experimentation can be replaced by control functions. So from now on, instead of investigating some abstract experimentation, insistent control functions will be analyzed.

Lemma 15. *For any learning device S, the following statements are equivalent:*
(1) There exists an insistent experimentation for S.
(2) There is a $c \in \mathcal{F}_t^2$ with $S \in COF^w(c)$.
(3) There is a $c \in \mathcal{F}_t$ with $S \in COF^b(c)$.

Subsequently, we study to what extent insistent experimentation can be implemented.

It is well known that there are arbitrary complex programs. In other words, for each recursive bound, there are infinitely many total recursive functions that have a program which exceeds this bound (cf. [3]). Thus, one may expect that insistent experimentation for larger classes of inductive learning devices requires some non-recursive expertise.

A prominent example for non-recursive expertise is the halting set $H = \{\langle i, x \rangle \mid i, x \in I\!N, \; \varphi_i(x) \downarrow\}$. As we will see, the halting set H exactly characterizes the level of non-recursive expertise which is both necessary and sufficient to accomplish white box experimentation for all learning devices. In order to verify the correctness of this statement, some additional notation is needed.

Let A be an oracle, $Q \subseteq I\!N$, and $S \subseteq \mathcal{P}$. Then, the notation $[Q \in COP^w]^A$ and $[S \in COF^w]^A$ indicates that there is an A-computable control c allowing for an insistent white box experimentation with all programs in Q and all learning devices in S, respectively. We adopt these notations for black box experimentation.

Theorem 16. *Let A be any oracle. Then, $[I_\mathcal{P} \in COP^w]^A \Longleftrightarrow [H \text{ is recursive}]^A$.*

In the black box approach, the situation changes drastically. In this setting, the control c does not receive any information about the program it is supposed to control. Thus, the result from [3] already mentioned at the beginning of this subsection immediately allows for the following insight.

Theorem 17. *There is no oracle A such that $[\mathcal{P} \in COF^b]^A$.*

From the above result, we may easily conclude that, in the black box setting, the analogue of Theorem 16 does not hold.

Corollary 18. *There is no oracle A such that $[I_\mathcal{P} \in COP^b]^A$.*

Next, we investigate the power and limitations of computable control. As we shall see, it is still impossible to control all programs for any given total recursive learning device.

Corollary 19. *Let $S \in \mathcal{R}$ be any learning device and let $c \in \mathcal{R}$ be any control. Then, there is a program s for S with $s \notin COP^b(c)$.*

In the white box case, the same insight can be achieved. However, the justification is a little bit more complex.

Theorem 20. *Let $S \in \mathcal{R}$ be any learning device and let $c \in \mathcal{R}^2$ be any control. Then, there is a program s for S with $s \notin COP^w(c)$.*

Naturally, the question arose to characterize the class of programs a single control can handle. Our next theorem gives an answer to this question.

Corollary 21. *Let* $c \in \mathcal{R}^2$ *and let* $S = COF^w(c)$. *Then, there is some* $S' \in NUM$ *such that* $LIM(S) \subseteq LIM(S')$.

Proof. Let S and c be given. First, we define an appropriate class of learning devices $S' \in NUM$. Let $s \in I\!N$. For all $f[n] \in I\!N$, we set:

$$\psi_s(f[n]) = \begin{cases} \varphi_s(f[n]) & : \langle s, f[n]\rangle \text{ is } c\text{-bounded} \\ n & : \text{otherwise} \end{cases}$$

A pair $\langle s, f[n]\rangle$ is said to be c-bounded if $\phi_s(f[x]) \leq c(f[x], s)$ for all $x \leq n$.

Clearly, the function class $S' = \{\psi_s \mid s \in I\!N\}$ is enumerable. Thus, it remains to verify that $LIM(S) \subseteq LIM(S')$. This can be done as follows.

Let s be any program controlled by c. Clearly, it suffices to verify that $LIM(\psi_s) = LIM(\varphi_s)$.

First, let $f \in LIM(\varphi_s)$. Therefore, for all $n \in I\!N$, the pair $\langle s, f[n]\rangle$ is c-bounded, and thus $\psi_s(f[n]) = \varphi_s(f[n])$. Hence, $f \in LIM(\psi_s)$, too.

Second, let $g \in LIM(\psi_s)$. Then, we know that the sequence $(\psi_s(g[n]))_{n \in I\!N}$ of hypotheses generated by ψ_s, when successively fed information about g, must converge. By definition of ψ_s, this implies that, for all $n \in I\!N$, the pair $\langle s, g[n]\rangle$ has to be c-bounded. Therefore, $\varphi_s(g[n]) = \psi_s(g[n])$ for all $n \in I\!N$, and, since $g \in LIM(\psi_s)$, $g \in LIM(\varphi_s)$ as well. $\qquad\square$

3.3 Evaluation Expertise

Within the last two subsections, we have investigated the problem of automating the data selection and the experimentation. Now, we focus our attention on the evaluation phase. The next definition provides the formal framework for an appropriate investigation.

Definition 22 (EVAL). Let ID be an identification type, let $S \subseteq \mathcal{P}$ be a collection of learning devices, and let $\mathcal{U} \subseteq$ ID be a collection of learning problems. Then, the learning devices in S are said to be ID–evaluable with respect to all learning problems in $\mathcal{U}$ ($\langle$ID$, S, \mathcal{U}\rangle \in$ EVAL, for short) iff there is an evaluation $Eval \in \mathcal{F}_p^3$ such that, for all $S \in S$, all $U \in \mathcal{U}$, all data selections Ds complete for U, and all experimentations $Expmt$ insistent for S, the resulting validation dialogue $VD = \langle Ds, Expmt, Eval\rangle$ is successful for U and S iff $U \subseteq$ ID(S).

In case that there is an evaluation $Eval$ that witnesses that the overall collection of all learning devices $\mathcal{P}$ is ID–evaluable with respect to all possible learning problems in ID, we use the shorthand ID $\in$ EVAL instead of $\langle$ID$, \mathcal{P},$ID$\rangle \in$ EVAL.

Let A be any oracle. Then, if there is an A-computable evaluation $Eval$ witnessing $\langle$ID$, S, \mathcal{U}\rangle \in$ EVAL for an identification type ID, some class of learning devices S, and some collection $\mathcal{U}$ of learning problems, this is expressed as $[\langle$ID$, S, \mathcal{U}\rangle \in$ EVAL$]^A$.

The key question considered next is, given some learning type ID, how powerful an expert must be to ID-evaluate *all* computable learning devices with respect to all learning problems in ID.

Formal concepts can be invoked to implement the following program:

(i) Choose the requirements an acceptable learning device should meet. For instance, it should learn in the limit or should finitely learn.

(ii) Find some characterization of expertise.

(iii) Prove a theorem that any expert who is competent according to the conditions of (ii) is, therefore, able to truly evaluate whether or not any given learning device meets the requirements focused under (i) when being confronted with such a learning problem.

(iv) Prove a theorem that an expert's ability to evaluate all devices with respect to the requirements fixed within (i) necessarily needs some skill as formalized within (ii).

The problem of determining in the limit, whether or not an arbitrary computable function is total, seems to play a key role in validating learning systems.

Proposition 23. *Let A be any oracle. Then, $[LIM \in EVAL]^A \iff [I_{\mathcal{R}} \ l.r.e.]^A$.*

Proof. We start with the following claim.

Claim 1. $[I_{\mathcal{R}} \ l.r.e.]^A \Rightarrow [LIM \in EVAL]^A$.

Let S be any learner and let U be any learning problem in LIM. Furthermore, we assume an insistent experimentation $Expmt$ for S and a complete data selection Ds for U.

In the sequel, we are going to illustrate the way in which an expert might exploit the assumed expertise for systematic validation. Let d be a function that limiting enumerates $I_{\mathcal{R}}$. For each $n \in I\!N$, let P_n be the set of all protocols for $Ds(n)$, that is $P_n = \{\langle j,t,h \rangle \mid \langle j,t \rangle \in Ds(n), Expmt(\varphi_j[t]) = h\}$.

For any report $\langle j,t,h \rangle \in P_n$, let $P_n(j,t)$ denote the set of protocols for program j having a time stamp smaller than t, i.e. $P_n(j,t) = \{\langle j,t',h' \rangle \in P_n \mid t' < t\}$. Furthermore, we say that $P_n(j,t)$ is nice, provided that $P_n(j,t)$ is non-empty and $\hat{h} = h$, where $\hat{h}$ is the hypothesis documented in the report with the maximal time stamp in $P_n(j,t)$.

The evaluation of any particular protocol $p = \langle j,t,h \rangle \in P_n$ is done as follows. We distinguish the following cases:

(i) If (A), (B), and (C) are satisfied, then set $Eval(\langle j,t,h \rangle) = 1$.
    (A) For all $\langle j,t',h' \rangle \in P_n(j,t)$, $h' \neq \perp$.
    (B) $P_n(j,t)$ is nice.
    (C) $d(h,t) = 1$ and, for all $x \leq t$,
        $\phi_h(x) \leq t$ implies $\varphi_h(x) = \varphi_j(x)$.

(ii) Otherwise, set $Eval(\langle j,t,h \rangle) = 0$.

First, assume that S is learning some target function f in the limit. By assumption, there is some program for f, say j, such that, for all $t \in I\!N$, the report $\langle j,t,h \rangle$ will be presented. Moreover, since the underlying experimentation $Expmt$ is insistent, we know that h equals $S(\varphi_j[t])$. By Definition 1, S is defined for all initial segments of f. Thus, (A) is always true. Since S, when learning f, performs at most finitely many mind changes, (B) is almost always true. Furthermore, S converges to some correct φ-index for f, say h', and therefore h' is almost always the input for the test performed in (C). Since $\varphi_{h'} = f$, and therefore $\varphi_{h'} \in \mathcal{R}$, (C) is almost always true, too. Hence, $Eval(j,t,h)$ equals 1 for almost all time stamps t, and we are done.

In contrast, if S fails on some function f, then one of the following three events must happen. (i) S does not return a hypothesis, for at least one test data input. (ii) S does not converge. (iii) S does converge, but to some final hypothesis h'' not correctly reflecting the target function f. In case that (i) happens, the validation dialogue does not succeed because of (A). In case (ii) happens, (B) prevents $Eval$ from successfully converging to 1. Finally, if (iii) happens, it will be recognized that at least one of the following cases occurs: $\varphi_{h''}(x) \neq f(x)$, for some $x \in I\!N$, or $\varphi_{h''} \notin \mathcal{R}$. In any of both cases, the validation dialogue will not converge. Hence, the claim follows.

Claim 2. $[LIM \in EVAL]^A \Rightarrow [I_\mathcal{R} \ l.r.e.]^A$.

Fix any non-empty $U \in LIM$, any learning device S with $U \subseteq LIM(S)$, any target function $g \in U$, and any $k \in I\!N$ with $\varphi_k = g$. For every $j \in I\!N$, let $\varphi_{\hat{j}}$ be the following function. For all $x \in I\!N$, it holds:

$$\varphi_{\hat{j}}(x) = \begin{cases} g(x) & : \varphi_j(x) \downarrow \\ \text{undefined} & : \text{otherwise} \end{cases}$$

Clearly, for all $j \in I\!N$, $\varphi_{\hat{j}}$ equals g if and only if $\varphi_j \in \mathcal{R}$.

Furthermore, for all $j \in I\!N$, let S_j be a learning device which is defined as follows. For all $f[n] \in I\!N$, we let:

$$S_j(f[n]) = \begin{cases} \hat{j} & : f[n] = g[n] \\ S(f[n]) & : \text{otherwise} \end{cases}$$

Obviously, for all $j \in I\!N$, we have $LIM(S_j) = LIM(S)$, and thus S_j learns g, if and only if $\varphi_{\hat{j}}$ equals g if and only if $\varphi_j \in \mathcal{R}$.

Now, we are ready to show that the evaluation $Eval$ can be used to limiting enumerate $I_\mathcal{R}$. Recall, that $\varphi_k = g$. For all $j, n \in I\!N$, we specify $d(j,n) = Eval(k,n,\hat{j})$.

We claim that d limiting enumerates $I_\mathcal{R}$.

Suppose any $j \in I\!N$. We have to show that the subsequence $(Eval(k,n,\hat{j}))_{n \in I\!N}$ converges to 1 if and only if $\varphi_j \in \mathcal{R}$. Since, by construction, $\varphi_j \in \mathcal{R}$ if and only if S_j learns g, it suffices to show that $\lim(Eval(k,n,\hat{j}))_{n \in I\!N} = 1$ if and only if S_j learns g. This can be seen as follows.

First, suppose that S_j learns g. Then, $LIM(S_j) = LIM(S)$. Now, since $Eval$ is witnessing $[LIM \in EVAL]$, by assumption, the subsequence $(Eval(k,n,\hat{j}))_{n \in I\!N}$ has to converge to 1.

Second, suppose that S_j does not learn g. Now, fix any validation dialogue VD for S and U. Clearly, this dialogue contains at most finitely many reports with the evaluation 0. Now, delete all reports $\langle\langle k',t,h\rangle,b\rangle$ with $\varphi_{k'} = g$. Obviously, the remaining dialogue VD' also contains at most finitely many reports with the evaluation 0. Now, consider the dialogue $VD'' = VD' \cup \{\langle\langle k,n,\hat{j}\rangle, Eval(k,n,\hat{j})\rangle \mid n \in I\!N\}$. (Note that one can easily fix some test data selection complete for U and some experimentation insistent for S_j that, together with $Eval$, result exactly in this particular validation dialogue.) Clearly, the dialogue VD'' must contain infinitely many reports with the evaluation 0, since S_j fails to learn g. Obviously, this can only happen, if there are infinitely many n with $Eval(k,n,\hat{j}) = 0$. This finishes the proof of the claim, and the theorem follows. $\qquad\square$

Proposition 23 characterizes validation expertise. Next, we attack the general problem to relate validation expertise to domain expertise, i.e. the ability to solve learning problems in the required sense. The following result is due to ADLEMANN and BLUM (cf. [1]).

Proposition 24. *Let A be any oracle. Then, $[I_{\mathcal{R}} \; l.r.e.]^A \iff [\mathcal{R} \in LIM]^A$.*

Putting the last two results together, we arrive at the following insight.

Theorem 25. *Let A be any oracle. Then, $[LIM \in EVAL]^A \iff [\mathcal{R} \in LIM]^A$.*

Consequently, an expert who has the ability to LIM-evaluate all learning devices has a level of expertise which is sufficient to solve every possible learning task, i.e. to learn in the limit every total recursive function from input/output examples.

The ideas underlying the proof of Proposition 23 apply *mutatis mutandis* to elaborate the following result.

Proposition 26. *Let A be any oracle. Then,*
(1) $[TOTAL \in EVAL]^A \iff [I_{\mathcal{R}} \; l.r.e.]^A$.
(2) $[FIN \in EVAL]^A \iff [I_{\mathcal{R}} \; l.r.e.]^A$.

Our final result in this subsection summarizes the insights obtained so far.

Theorem 27. *Let A be any oracle. Then, the following statements are equivalent: $[LIM \in EVAL]^A$, $[TOTAL \in EVAL]^A$, $[FIN \in EVAL]^A$, and $[\mathcal{R} \in LIM]^A$.*

Although different types of learning behaviour may require different validation approaches, the needed level of expertise turns out to be the same.

Subsequently, we would like to direct the reader's attention to the following problems:

(A) Imagine one has to solve a particular learning problem. Characterize the level of expertise that is necessary and sufficient to figure out which learning devices are able to solve the learning problem on hand.

(B) Imagine someone is the provider of a particular learning system. Characterize the level of expertise that is necessary and sufficient to evaluate whether or not the system provided is able to solve the learning problems of some potential costumer.

In investigating these problems, we confine ourselves to study LIM–type evaluation, only.

Note that most of the results may be easily adapted to handle the $TOTAL$– and FIN–case, as well.

Having a closer look at the demonstration of Proposition 23, one might easily recognize that the verification of Claim 2 is supporting the following considerably stronger result.

Proposition 28. *For any oracle A and any $U \in LIM$, $[\langle LIM, \mathcal{P}, \{U\}\rangle \in EVAL]^A$ implies $[I_{\mathcal{R}} \; l.r.e.]^A$.*

Concerning question (B), the situation is much more involved. As it turns out, the answer to this question heavily depends on the properties of the favoured learning device.

Proposition 29. *Let $S \in \mathcal{P}$ such that $LIM(S) \in NUM!$. Then, there is some evaluation $Eval \in \mathcal{P}^3$ witnessing $\langle LIM, \{S\}, LIM \rangle \in EVAL$.*

As we have seen, there are learning devices that can be *LIM*-evaluated by an expert without any additional non-computable expertise. Interestingly, the opposite extreme can be observed, as well. In order to evaluate a particular learning device, expertise is needed that allows to *LIM*-evaluate every learning strategy with respect to all learning problems.

Proposition 30. *There is some learning device $S \in \mathcal{P}$ such that, for any oracle A, $[\langle LIM, \{S\}, LIM \rangle \in EVAL]^A$ implies $[I_{\mathcal{R}} \ l.r.e.]^A$.*

4 Conclusions

Let us very briefly sum up the technical contents of the present paper. We know about *sufficient* and *necessary expertise* to accomplish some validation tasks. Interestingly, this expertise *can not be automated*. The strength of the expertise is illustrated by the following informal statement: *Who is able to validate certain learning devices, is also able to replace them in solving learning problems.*

Evidence for this thesis is provided by several of our results above. There are some results illuminating the necessity to have an expertise formally expressed by the oracle H, i.e. by the power to decide the halting problem. In case this power is available, it is immediately possible to learn in the limit any recursive function: $[\mathcal{R} \in LIM]^H$.

However, these remarks refer only to the technical perspective of our present paper. Our starting point was more general.

The validation of complex systems is a remarkably urgent problem area. Several validation approaches and scenarios are recently under development, under theoretical investigation, and also under experimental exploration.

As soon as human experts are becoming involved, the question for the experts' competence is becoming crucial. Most problems, even some very fundamental one, are still open. A quite typical question is how the validation experts' expertise relates to the domain experts' skills. Is it necessary that anybody involved in systems validation needs to be qualified for doing the systems' job, at least in principle? Or does a substantially lower degree of qualification suffice for validating a system's behaviour?

There might be no generally valid answers to those questions. Despite this, any clear answer derived under certain more specific circumstances might be discussed controversially. Therefore, a firm justification is both theoretically and practically relevant. The present paper is intended to provide an example, only. There is evidence for the thesis that validation is not simpler than doing the job itself.

Acknowledgement

We thank the anonymous referees for many valuable comments. One referee pointed to the following interesting generalization of Proposition 29: For any reliable[4] learning device S, there is some computable evaluation $Eval$ that allows to LIM-evaluate S with respect to all learning problems in LIM.

This work was mainly performed while the first and third author were visiting the Meme Media Laboratory at Hokkaido University. Both are gratefully acknowledging the excellent working conditions provided and the stimulating atmosphere in the Meme Media Laboratory. The first author has been partially supported by the German Research Fund (DFG) under contract number Ja 566/10-1.

A full version of this paper [7] that includes all proofs is available via the following URL: http://www.meme.hokudai.ac.jp/~jantke/select_rep.html.

References

1. Adleman, L. M. and Blum, M. (1991) Inductive inference and unsolvability. *The Journal of Symbolic Logic*, **56**:891–900.
2. Angluin, D. and Smith, C.H. (1983) A survey of inductive inference: Theory and methods. *Computing Surveys*, **15**:237–269.
3. Blum, M. (1967) A machine-independent theory of the complexity of recursive functions. *Journal of the ACM*, **14**:322–336.
4. Boehm, B.W. (1984) Verifying and validating software requirements and design specifications. *IEEE Trans. Software*, 1:75–88.
5. Cooke, N.J. (1992) Modeling human expertise in expert systems. In R.R. Hoffman (ed.), *The Psychology of Expertise. Cognitive Research of Empirical AI* (Berlin: Springer-Verlag), pp. 29–60.
6. Gold, E M. (1967) Language identification in the limit. *Information and Control*, 14:447–474.
7. Grieser, G., Jantke, K.P., and Lange, S. (1998) Validation of inductive learning systems: A case for characterizing expertise in complex interactive systems validation. Technical Report MEME-MMM-98-1, Meme Media Laboratory (Sapporo: Hokkaido University).
8. Gupta, U.G. (1993) *Validation and Verification of Expert Systems*. (Los Alamitos, CA: IEEE Press).
9. Knauf, R., Jantke, K.P., Abel, T., and Philippow, I. (1997) Fundamentals of a TURING test approach to validation of AI systems. In W. Gens (ed.), *Proceedings 42nd International Scientific Colloquium, Ilmenau University of Technology Vol. 2* (TU Ilmenau), pp. 59–64.
10. O'Keefe, R.M. and O'Leary, D.E. (1993) Expert system verification and validation: A survey and tutorial. *Artificial Intelligence Review*, 7:3–42.
11. Rogers, H. (1967) *The Theory of Recursive Functions and Effective Computability* (McGraw-Hill).
12. Wise, J.A. and Wise, M.A. (1993) Basic considerations in verification and validation. In J.A. Wise, V.D. Hopkin, and P. Stager (eds.), *Verification and Validation of Complex Systems: Human Factors Issues*, NATO ASI Series, Series F: Computer and Systems Sciences, Vol. 110 (Berlin: Springer–Verlag), pp. 87–95.

---

[4] A learning device S is said to be reliable provided that S converges on information sequences for functions in $LIM(S)$, only.

Consistent Polynomial Identification in the Limit

Werner Stein

University of Kaiserslautern
Postfach 30 49,
D-67653 Kaiserslautern, Germany
Stein@Informatik.Uni-KL.de
http://www-agrw.informatik.uni-kl.de/home/stein/index.html

Abstract. This paper aims to extend well known results about polynomial update-time bounded learning strategies in a recursion theoretic setting.
We generalize the update-time complexity using the approach of Blum's computational complexity measures.
It will turn out, that consistency is the first natural condition having a narrowing effect for arbitrary update boundaries. We show the existence of arbitrary hard, as well as an infinite chain of harder and harder consistent learnable sets. The complexity gap between consistent und inconsistent strategies solving the same problem can be arbitrary large. We prove an exact characterization for polynomial consistent learnability, giving a deeper insight in the problem of hard consistent learnability.

1 Introduction

Since Gold's definition of identification in the limit [Gol65], there has been extensive research on the problem of what can be learned and what cannot. A huge number of learning classes were defined, applying more or less natural constraints to the basic LIM definition. The resulting classes as well as their relationships are well explored. On the other hand very few results about the complexity of identification in the limit are known. There seem to be two types of complexity theoretic results. A) General approaches which apply to sets of learning problems [DS86,FKS93,FKS95,JS95] and B) specific approaches, which only apply to specific problems in specific hypotheses spaces or for specific strategies [WL76,WZ94,Pit89,Ish90,Wat94,Fla94,PW90,Kin94,LZ95,BDGW94]

From the computational complexity theory it is well known, that a polynomial complexity bound naturally means a good or fast solution. All general approaches for learning complexities do not have this "natural" property. Their complexity upper bounds are at least polynomials. On the other hand, most of the specific approaches satisfy the above "natural" condition.

Pitt in [Pit89] reviews some definitions of identification in the limit and discusses the problem of augmenting the definitions in order to incorporate a notion of computational efficiency. He summerized his discussion: "finding a natural formal definition that captures the notion of (polynomial) efficient inference ... is not at all straightforward". Comparing his results for learning DFA with those of Lange, Wiehagen and Zeugmann [LW91,WZ92] (learning pattern languages) and Valiant [Val84] (PAC learning), we found one common constraint for their polynomial learning strategies: consistency.

In this paper we examine polynomial limiting consistent identification in the Gold-style learning model of recursive functions. Coming from the above results and based on Blum's axiomatic computational complexity theory, we explore the update complexity of consistent learning strategies. We will give different degrees of hard learnability and show the existence of an infinite complexity hierarchy. We will prove that the demand for consistency can require any amount of resources. Our main result is a characterization of polynomial consistent learnability. We will show the relationships between the polynomial learnable sets and different non-complexity-bounded learning classes. We will outline, that the above results also apply to other learning conditions.

2 Preliminaries

$\mathbf{N} = \{0, 1, 2, \ldots\}$ denotes the set of all natural numbers. The set of finite sequences of natural numbers is denoted by $\mathbf{N}^*$. The set of all partial recursive and recursive functions of one, and two arguments over $\mathbf{N}$ are denoted by $\mathcal{P}, \mathcal{P}^2, \mathcal{R}$, and $\mathcal{R}^2$, respectively. From time to time, we equate a recursive function with the sequence of its values. For arbitrary $f \in \mathcal{P}$ and $x \in \mathbf{N}$, we write $f(x) \downarrow$, to denote that $f(x)$ is defined. Let $f \in \mathcal{P}$ and $\alpha \in \mathbf{N}^*$; we write $\alpha \sqsubseteq f$ iff α is a prefix of the sequence of values associated with f. By $\alpha(x)$ we denote the x-th element in the sequence α. Let $f, g \in \mathcal{P}, n \in \mathbf{N}$, we write $f =_n g$ iff for all $x \leq n$ $f(x) = g(x)$. Any function $\psi \in \mathcal{P}^2$ is called a numbering, or a programming system. ψ_i abbreviates $\lambda x.\psi(i, x)$. $\mathcal{P}_\psi$ is the set of all ψ_i. A numbering $\varphi \in \mathcal{P}^2$ is called a Gödelnumbering iff $\mathcal{P}_\varphi = \mathcal{P}$ and for any numbering $\psi \in \mathcal{P}^2$, there is a $c \in \mathcal{R}$ such that $\psi_i = \varphi_{c(i)}$ for all $i \in \mathbf{N}$. The tuple (φ, Φ) is a Blum complexity measure [Blu67] iff φ is a Gödelnumbering, $\Phi_i(x) \downarrow \iff \varphi_i(x) \downarrow$, and $\Phi_i(x) = y$ is recursive in i, x, and y. For any $S \in \mathcal{P}$ we write Φ_S to denote Φ_i for an i providing $\varphi_i = S$. Time and memory complexity will be called natural complexities. Poly^Φ is the set of all φ_i such that Φ_i is a polynomial. We write Poly, as a placeholder for any polynomial. For any function $f \in \mathcal{R}$, f is said to be unbounded monotone increasing iff for all $x \in \mathbf{N}$ $f(x) \leq f(x+1)$ and $lim_{x \to \infty} f(x) = \infty$. Using a fixed 1-1-coding $d(\ldots)$ of $\mathbf{N}^*$ onto $\mathbf{N}$, we write f^n instead of $d(f(0), \ldots, f(n))$. f^{-1} is defined to be the empty sequence. We also write f^n, to abbreviate the sequence $(f(0), \ldots, f(n))$. The usage will be clear from the context. Proper subset, subset, superset, and proper superset will be denoted by $\subset, \subseteq, \supset$, and $\supseteq$, respectively. min, max, and $length$ are functions for the minimum, maximum and the length of a sequence. For the empty sequence $()$, we define $max() = 0, min() = \infty$, and $length() = 0$. By $\forall, \exists, \forall^\infty$, and $\exists^\infty$ we denote the quantifiers for all, exists a, for all but finitely many, and exists infinitely many, respectively.

3   Definitions and Basic Properties

Following Gold [Gol65] and Solmonoff [Sol64], we define an identification in the limit process as follows: A strategy is presented with some total recursive function f by feeding successively growing parts of its graph $f^0, f^1, \ldots, f^n$. At each time n, the strategy has to make a guess, i, as to the identity of f. The guess i is interpreted as a program for f in an underlying programming system ψ, called the hypothesis space. A strategy learns f, iff the hypotheses generated on f^n converge to an i satisfying $\psi_i = f$. A set of recursive functions U is called to be learnable in the limit with respect to a strategy $S \in \mathcal{P}$ and a hypothesis space $\psi \in \mathcal{P}^2$ (write $U \in \text{LIM}_\psi(S)$) iff the strategy can learn all functions in the set. The set of all sets of recursive function learnable in the limit will be denoted by LIM ($:= \{U \subseteq \mathcal{R} | \exists S \in \mathcal{P}, \exists \psi \in \mathcal{P}^2 : U \in \text{LIM}_\psi(S)\}$).

Learning takes place, if, after reaching the (unknown) point of convergence, the strategy outputs the correct function inferred from the knowledge about a finite part of the infinite object. A main problem in LIM learning is, that every temporary hypothesis can fool the user as much as it wants. Scientists tried to solve this problem, by applying more or less natural constraints to the LIM-definition, exploring the narrowing effect of learnability. The resulting learning classes (e.g. FIN, CONS, NUM, ...) as well as there relationships are all well explored [JB84]. One of those "natural" learning classes is CONS. A set of recursive functions, U, is consistent learnable with respect to a strategy $S \in \mathcal{P}$ and a hypothesis space $\psi \in \mathcal{P}^2$ ($U \in \text{CONS}_\psi(S)$) iff a) $U \in \text{LIM}_\psi(S)$ and b) every hypothesis produced during the learning process of one of the functions in U, is consistent with the graph seen so far, formally $\forall f \in U \; \forall n \in \mathbf{N} : [f^n \subseteq \psi_{S(f^n)}]$. Again, we define CONS to be the set of all consistent learnable sets of recursive functions.

Consistency has a practical aspect: the user of a consistent learning system can be sure that the hypothesis is of good quality, that is, it has a total recall of the presented examples. This seems to be a quite natural condition for learning strategies. At the first glance, there seems no reason to produce inconsistent hypothesis. Nevertheless, Barzdin first [Bar74] announced that there are classes of recursive functions that can be learned in the limit but only by strategies working inconsistently. There are two characterizations known for consistent learnability, giving a deeper insight in this phenomenon.

Theorem 1. $U \in CONS \iff$
$\exists \psi \in \mathcal{P}^2 \exists g \in \mathcal{R}^3 : $ (a) $U \subseteq \mathcal{P}_\psi$ and
$\qquad\qquad\qquad$ (b) $\forall i, j, n \in \mathbf{N} : [g(i, j, n) = 1 \iff \psi_i =_n \psi_j]$

Theorem 2. $U \in CONS \iff$
$\exists \psi \in \mathcal{P}^2 : U\text{-consistency is decidable in } \psi \iff$
$\exists \psi \in \mathcal{P}^2 \exists g \in \mathcal{P}^2 : $ (a) $U \subseteq \mathcal{P}_\psi$ and
$\qquad\qquad\qquad$ (b) $\forall f \in U, \forall i, n \in \mathbf{N} : g(f^n, i) \downarrow$ and
$\qquad\qquad\qquad\qquad [g(f^n, i) = 1 \iff f^n \subseteq \psi_i]$

We still mentioned another phenomenon about consistent strategies: To the best of our knowledge, consistency is the only condition having a narrowing effect for polynomial update-time bounds.

The following will investigate the problem of defining resource bounded consistent learnability and finding a characterization for fast consistent learnability in Gold's model of learning in the limit.

The learning complexity measure we use, is based on the amound of resources needed by a strategy to update an hypothesis between two successive inputs. This inference complexity is well known as update complexity. It was shown [DS86] that a polynomial update-space boundary does not effect the learning power of learning in the limit. On the other side, Wiehagen and Zeugmann [WZ92] provided a learning problem such that using a fixed hypothesis space, every **consistent** learner must exceed any polynomial time bound for its updates on at least one object to be learned, unless $P = NP$. Pitt [Pit89] proofs a similar result for learning DFA: using the hypothesis space of DFA's, there is no consistent strategy learning DFA's fast.

We will generalize the above results in two ways: First, we allow the strategy to use arbitrary hypothesis spaces, and second, we use the general approach of Blum's axiomatic complexity theory to define the update complexity.

Let (φ, Φ) be an arbitrary Blum complexity measure, $\mathcal{I}$ a learning class (e.g. FIN, CONS, LIM, ...) and p a recursive function. A set U of recursive functions is said to be $\mathcal{I}$-learnable within a bound p of Φ-resources via strategy $S \in \mathcal{P}$ and programming system $\psi \in \mathcal{P}^2$ ($U \in p$-Φ-$\mathcal{I}_\psi(S)$) iff a) U is $\mathcal{I}$-learnable via S and ψ, and b) for all n, S fed with some $f^n \subset f \in U$ consumes less than $p(f^n)$ Φ-resources.

In most cases we will restrict ourselves to special **natural** Blum complexity measures, such as time and memory resources. Those have the nice propertie, that the amount of resources used to run two programs successively, can be estimated by the sum of resources needed to run each program seperatly. Note that this is not true for arbitrary Blum complexity measures.

Definition 1 (p-Φ-$\mathcal{I}$).

Let $p \in \mathcal{R}$ be a recursive function (called complexity bound), (φ, Φ) a Blum complexity measure, $\mathcal{I}$ a learning class from $\{FIN, CONS, LIM, \ldots\}$, and U a set of recursive functions.

$$U \in p\text{-}\Phi\text{-}\mathcal{I} \iff$$
$$\exists S = \varphi_i \in \mathcal{R}, \psi \in \mathcal{P}^2 : (a)\ U \in \mathcal{I}_\psi(S)$$
$$(b)\ \forall f \in U, n \in \mathbb{N} : [\Phi_i(f^n) \le p(f^n)]$$

Showing that a set of functions is **not** p-Φ-$\mathcal{I}$ learnable, it is sufficient to show that every $\mathcal{I}$-learner must exceed the p bound for its update Φ-complexity on at least one object to be learned. To prove much harder non-learnability results, we need the following definitions.

Definition 2 (Φ-insufficient, Φ-hard).

Let $p \in \mathcal{R}$ be a recursive function, (φ, Φ) a Blum complexity measure, $\mathcal{I}$ a learning class from $\{FIN, CONS, LIM, \ldots\}$, and U a set of recursive functions.

p is Φ-insufficient for U wrt $\mathcal{I}$, iff for all strategies $S = \varphi_i$ and all programming systems ψ:

$$U \in \mathcal{I}_\psi(\varphi_i) \Rightarrow \forall f \in U \exists^\infty n : [\Phi_i(f^n) \geq p(f^n)]$$

p ist Φ-hard for U wrt $\mathcal{I}$, iff for all strategies $S = \varphi_i$ and all programming systems ψ:

$$U \in \mathcal{I}_\psi(\varphi_i) \Rightarrow \forall f \in U \forall^\infty n : [\Phi_i(f^n) \geq p(f^n)]$$

The following corollary follows immediatly:

Corollary 1. *For arbitrary* $(\varphi, \Phi), \mathcal{I}, U, p$:

$$p \text{ is } \Phi\text{-hard for } U \text{ wrt } \mathcal{I} \Rightarrow p \text{ is } \Phi\text{-insufficient for } U \text{ wrt } \mathcal{I} \Rightarrow U \notin p\text{-}\Phi\text{-}\mathcal{I}$$

For **natural** Blum complexity measures (φ, Φ) it is well known [DS86], that any unbounded monotone increasing update boundary does not reduce the learning power of learning in the limit:

Theorem 3. *For any unbounded monotone increasing recursive function p:*

$$p\text{-}\Phi\text{-}LIM = LIM.$$

The proof is based on a simulation of the strategy S (which is known to do the learning task), but only consuming resources within the p-complexity-bound, during this simulation. In the following we abbreviate this simulation with $Poly_S^p$, or simply with $Poly_S$, if p is not important. Note, that it is necessary to demand p to be an **unbounded monotone increasing** function, since Daley and Smith [DS86] exhibited a hierarchy for LIM learning classes bounded by total limiting recursive functionals.

Also note that this proof cannot be taken over for arbitrary Blum complexity measures, since there is no possibility to estimate the complexity of the simulation task. Even the well known result, that for any two complexity measures there is a two-valued recursive compiler, cannot save Theorem 3 for non-natural Blum complexities.

Likewise, for most other learning classes, learning with few resources does not have a narrowing effect on the learning power of this class.

Corollary 2. *Let $\mathcal{I} \in \{FIN, LIM\}$:*

$$Poly\text{-}\Phi\text{-}\mathcal{I} = \mathcal{I}$$

4 Consistent Polynomial Learning

While polynomial update bounds does not effect the learning power of most learning classes, this is not true for consistent learnability.

For any **natural** complexity measure (φ, Φ) and recursive unbounded monotone increasing function p, it is not hard to give an example for a class, that can be learned consistently, but is no member of p-Φ-CONS.

Theorem 4. *Let p an unbounded monotone increasing function:*

$$p\text{-}\Phi\text{-}CONS \subset CONS.$$

Proof. Choose an arbitrary $f \in \mathcal{R}_{\{0,1\}}$. Let $U_f = \{\alpha 0^\infty | \alpha \in \{0,1\}^\star\} \cup \{f\}$. Since for all f, $U_f \in CONS$, it remains to prove that there is an f, such that $U_f \notin p\text{-}\Phi\text{-}CONS$ for some arbitrary f.

Suppose there is a strategy $S \in \mathcal{P}$ and a numbering $\psi \in \mathcal{P}^2$, such that $U_f \in CONS_\psi(S)$. Let c be the point of convergence for strategy S on input f, and let $S(f^c) = j$. Let $Table[f]$ be a list for the values of f up to argument c. Now, we define a procedure computing f as follows:

Procedure f: Input: x
  1. if $x < c$ return $Table[f](x)$;
  2. for $i = 0$ to $x - 1$ do compute $f(i)$;
  3. Do (A) and (B) in parallel until (A) or (B) returns j:
      (A) evaluate $S(f^{x-1}1)$;
      (B) evaluate $S(f^{x-1}0)$;
  4. if (A) evaluates to j return 1;
  5. if (B) evaluates to j return 0;

It is easy to see that procedure f really computes the function f. The amount of resources needed for evaluating the values of f for arguments 1 to $c - 1$ is a constant, say g. Since Φ is **natural** we can estimate the amount of resources for all values $x \geq c$:

$$\Phi_f(x) \leq g + \sum_{i=c}^{x} 2\Phi_S(f^i)$$

Since f is choosen arbitrarily, we can assume $\Phi_f(x) > g + \sum_{i=c}^{x} 2p(f^i)$ for infinitely many x.

$$\Rightarrow \exists^\infty x : g + \sum_{i=c}^{x} 2p(f^i) \leq \Phi_f(x) \leq \Phi_f(x) < g + \sum_{i=c}^{x} 2\Phi_S(f^i)$$

$$\Rightarrow \exists^\infty x : \sum_{i=c}^{x} p(f^i) < \sum_{i=c}^{x} \Phi_S(f^i)$$

$$\Rightarrow \exists^\infty x : p(f^x) < \Phi_S(f^x)$$

$$\Rightarrow U \notin p\text{-}\Phi\text{-}CONS_\psi(S)$$

♮

Repeating the arguments of Theroem 3, we can point out that the above techniques to prove Theorem 4 cannot be used for arbitrary Blum complexity measures.

A simple modification of Theorem 4 can be used to prove the existence of arbitrarily Φ-insufficient, as well as, arbitrarily Φ-hard consistent learnable sets.

Corollary 3. *For any unbounded increasing recursive function p, there is a $U \subseteq \mathcal{R}$, such that p is Φ-insufficient for U wrt CONS.*

Proof. Choose $f \in \mathcal{R}_{0,1}$ such that $\Phi_f(x) > g + \sum_{i=c}^{x} 2p(f^i)$ for infintly many x. Set $U = \{g \in \mathcal{R}_{0,1} | \forall^{\infty} x : f(x) = g(x)\}$. The corollary follows immediately from Theorem 4. ♮

Corollary 4. *For any unbounded increasing recursive function p, there is a $U \subseteq \mathcal{R}$, such that p is Φ-hard for U wrt CONS.*

Proof. Suppose $f \in \mathcal{R}_{\{0,1\}}$ is a function, such that for all but finitely many x, $\Phi_f(x) > q(f^x)$, for some $q \in \mathcal{R}$. Let $U = \{g \in \mathcal{R}_{0,1} | \forall^{\infty} x : f(x) = g(x)\}$. Using the simulation-technique of Theorem 4, we can show that for any strategy S and any programming system ψ, if $U \in \mathrm{CONS}_{\psi}(S)$, then for all but finitely many x, $\Phi_S(f^x) > \frac{q(f^x) - q(f^{x-1} - 1)}{2}$. Since for any $p \in \mathcal{R}$, there is a corresponding $q \in \mathcal{R}$, such that for all $n > 1$: $p(n) \leq \frac{q(f^x) - q(f^{x-1} - 1)}{2}$, the corollary follows immediately. ♮

Now we are ready to prove an infinite chain for resource bounded consistent learning classes.

Theorem 5.
There is an infinite chain of recursive functions $(p_i)_{i \in \mathbb{N}}$ such that for all i:

$$p_i\text{-}\Phi\text{-}CONS \subset p_{i+1}\text{-}\Phi\text{-}CONS$$

Proof. Start with some recursive function p_0. Use Theorem 4 to prove the existence of a set U_0 such that $U_0 \in p\text{-}\Phi\text{-}CONS \setminus CONS$. Since $U_0 \in CONS$, there is a strategy S_0 (for example the enumeration strategy) learning U_0. Choosing $p_1 = \Phi_{S_0}$, it is clear that $p_0\text{-}\Phi\text{-}CONS \subset p_1\text{-}\Phi\text{-}CONS$. Repeat the above construction using p_1 to find p_2 and so on. ♮

Corollary 5.

$$Poly\text{-}\Phi\text{-}CONS \subset CONS$$

Up to now, the proofs of all theorems and corollaries are based on a simple simulation-technique to estimate the resources needed to compute a function. We already mentioned, that this technique is not available for arbitrary Blum complexities. Anyhow, we are able to prove Theorems 4 and 5, as well as Corollaries 3 and 5, if we do not restrict ourselves to natural Blum complexities.

The proof is an extention of Blums computational theoretic counterpart [Blu67]: Given any total recursive function p, and any Blum complexity measure (φ, Φ), there is a subset, M, of the natural numbers, whose characteristic function has at least a fixed Φ-complexity. But while Blum could use a simple diagonalization technique to prove the existence for arbitrary hard functions, we need something like a limiting diagonalization technique, that is, the diagonalization is also a limiting process.

In the following we use **any** Blum complexity measure (φ, Φ) and recursive function p. We will construct an **infinite** set of functions, for which **every** consistent strategy using **any** hypothesis space, and needing **everywhere few** resources, fails **infinitely many times** to converge to a (correct) hypothesis, for at least one function to be learned. First, we will show, how the general limiting diagonalization process will work for a fixed strategy. Note, that it is useful to demand the strategy to be consistent on all possible sequences of natural numbers. This forces the strategy to be a recursive function and to produce different hypothesis for different sequences. To abbreviate the notation, we define a predicate $F_j^t(f^n)$ to hold iff $t \in \{0, 1\}$ and strategy φ_j on input $f^n t$ consumes not more than $p(f^n t)$ Φ-resources. $F_j(f^n)$ holds iff $F_j^t(f^n)$ holds, either for $t = 0$ or $t = 1$. Now, fix an arbitrary strategy $S = \varphi_j$. Suppose function f is defined up to argument n. The value for the next argument $n+1$ will be either 1 or 0. If $F_j(f^n)$ does not hold, that is, if we cannot extend f^n, such that strategy S produced a hypothesis within the given complexity bounds, the value of $f(n + 1)$ can be set to whatever we want, say 1. On the other hand assume wlog $F_j^1(n)$ holds and the strategy is able to produce a hypothesis, say $S(f^n 1) = h'$. The first time (and all odd times, if h equals $\star$) this happens, we allow the strategy to produce this hypothesis, setting $f(n+1) = 1$, but we save the hypothesis, in a global variable h. The second time (and all even times, if h is a natural number) this happens, we remember the last hypothesis (h) and compare it with the new hypothesis (h'). If $h' \neq h$, we simply extend f^n by 1. In the other case, if $h' = h$, we set $f(n + 1) = 0$, forcing the strategy which is consistent on both sequences, $f^n 0$ and $f^n 1$, to produce a hypothesis different from h'. In both cases the strategy must change the hypothesis.

The above construction for $f(n + 1)$ is well defined for arbitrary strategies. Moreover, assuming S to be a strategy, which is consistent on arbitrary sequences and using few resources on almost all parts of the graph of f, leads to non learnability of f for strategy S. The formal definition for procedure $g(f^n, j, h)$ $(:= f(n + 1))$ is as follows:

Procedure g:

    0. Case: $F_j(f^n)$ does not hold: set $f(n + 1) = 1$

    1. Case: h is $\star$ (the initial value of h):

        a. if $F_j^1(f^n)$ holds **then** set $f(n + 1) = 1$

                        else set $f(n + 1) = 0$.

        b. set h to be $\varphi_j(f^{n+1})$.

    2. Case: the value of h is natural number:

        a. if $F_j^1(f^n)$ holds

            i. if $\varphi_j(f^n 1) = h$ then set $f(n + 1) = 0$.

            ii. if $\varphi_j(f^n 1) \neq h$ then set $f(n + 1) = 1$.

        b. else if $F_j^0(\alpha, i, n)$ holds

            i. if $\varphi(f^n 1) = h$ then set $f(n + 1) = 1$.

            ii. if $\varphi_j(f^n)1) \neq h$ then set $f(n + 1) = 0$.

        c. set h to $\star$.

    3. return $f(n + 1)$.

Now we are ready to prove the next theorem

Theorem 6. *For all Blum complexity measures* (φ, Φ) *and recursive functions* p:

$$p\text{-}\Phi\text{-}CONS \subset CONS$$

Proof. It is sufficient to show $\exists U \in CONS$:

$$\forall S \in P, \psi \in P^2, \exists f \in U, \exists^\infty n : [U \in CONS_\psi(S) \Rightarrow \Phi_S(f^n) \geq p(f^n)]$$

For each $i \in \mathbf{N}$ define f_i: if $\alpha \in \mathbf{N}^*$ satisfies $d(\alpha) = i$, then initialize f_i with α and continue to define f_i using procedure g. Let $U = \{f_i | i \in \mathbf{N}\}$. U is enumerable, hence in CONS, but no resource bounded learner φ_i, which is consistent on U (hence on $\mathcal{R}$) can learn f_i. ♮

We even can show the existence of a single recursive function, such that all strategies learning this function and being consistent on all initial sequences of recursive functions[1] must waste resources for infinitely many inputs from f.

Theorem 7. *For all Blum complexity measures* (φ, Φ) *and recursive functions* p, *there is a single recursive function* f:

$$\{f\} \notin p\text{-}\Phi\text{-}\mathcal{R}CONS$$

Proof. It is sufficient to show:

$$\exists f \in \mathcal{R}, \exists^\infty n, \forall S \in P, \psi \in P^2 : [\{f\} \in \mathcal{R}CONS_\psi(S) \Rightarrow \Phi_S(f^n) \geq p(f^n)]$$

The difficulty is to do the diagonalization used in Theorem 6 for all strategies within the definition of a single function. To do so, we must give any strategy, which seems to learn the function using few resources, the chance to define the next value of f infinitely often.

We give all natural number two marks: a priority mark $(pmark(x))$ and an hypothesis mark $(hmark(x))$, all initially set to $\star$. $pmark(x)$ is the priority of strategie φ_x ($\star$ means unused up till now), to be the next candidate to define the next value of f. $hmark$ is used to remember the hypothesis used in the diagonaliziation process.

Suppose f is definied until argument n. The next value $f(n+1)$ is defined using procedure $g'(f^n)$:

Procedure g':

0. Set $hmark(n) := \star$ and set $pmark(n)$ to a priority lower than all priorities used up to now.

1. Choose j with highest priority, such that $F_j(f^n)$ holds. If no such j exists, set j to 0.

2. Set $h := hmark(j)$.

---

[1] Those strategies are called $\mathcal{R}$-consistent. The corresponding learning class is written $\mathcal{R}CONS$.

3. Set $f(n+1) = g(f^n, j, h)$ (taken from Theorem 6)
4. Give $pmark(j)$ a priority lower than all priorities used up till now.
5. Set $hmark(j)$ to the new value of h coming from procedure g.
6. Return $f(n+1)$.

$pmark$ implements a fair selection rule, such that each strategy φ_j satisfying $F_j(f^n)$ infinitely often, will be selected infinitely often. Thus, $\{f\}$ is $\mathcal{R}$-consistent learnable, but only via strategies wasting too much resources. ♮

The next theorem proves the existence of arbitrary insufficient consistent learning classes, that is:
There is a set of functions, such that no consistent learner, can learn even a single function from this set using few resources. In other words: For all functions p, exists a $U \in CONS$, such that p is Φ-insufficient for consistent U learning.

Theorem 8. *For all $p \in \mathcal{R}$, there exists a $U \in CONS$ such that:*

$$\forall S \in \mathcal{P}, \psi \in \mathcal{P}^2 : [U \in CONS_\psi(S) \Rightarrow \forall f \in U, \exists^\infty n : \Phi_S(f^n) \geq p(f^n)]$$

Proof. For each $i \in \mathbf{N}$, if $\alpha \in \mathbf{N}^*$ satisfies $d(\alpha) = i$, we initialize f_i with α and continue to define f_i using the techniques in Lemma 7. The set $U = \{f_i | i \in \mathbf{N}\}$ proves the Theorem. ♮

Coding a self reference in each function allows us to show, that the speed-up between consistent and "intelligent"[2] inconsistent learners, can be arbitrary large.

Corollary 6. *There is a function $q \in \mathcal{R}$, such that for all functions $p \in \mathcal{R}$, a $U \subseteq \mathcal{R}$ can be found, such that:*
  (a) $U \in CONS$ (even $U \in NUM!$) and
  (b) $U \in q\text{-}\Phi\text{-}LIM$ and
  (c) $U \notin (p+q)\text{-}\Phi\text{-}CONS$.

Proof. Let $S(f^n) = f(max(\{0\} \cup \{x \leq n | f(x) > 1\}))$ and set $q = \Phi_S$. Take U from Theorem 8 using $\lambda x : p(x) + q(x)$ as the monotone increasing function. The conditions follow immediately from Theorem 8. ♮

Now let us return to an arbitrary fixed **natural** complexity measure (φ, Φ), and let us try to find a characterization for polynomial consistent identification in the limit. This will give us a deeper insight in the nature of hard learnability. Until now we always used, a computationally hard function in a set, such that consistent learnability also gets hard. But using $U = \{f | \varphi_{f(0)} = f \wedge f \notin Poly_\Phi\}$ and $V = Poly_\Phi$, we can prove, that computational hardness of the functions to be learned must not lead to hard learnability of the functions ($U \in Poly\text{-}CONS$) and vice versa ($V \notin Poly\text{-}CONS$).

---

[2] intelligent means that we do not use the $Poly$-Strategie of Theorem 3, which only slows down the normal learning process.

Since we already know two characterizations for consistent learnability (Theorem 1 and 2), one could try to modify them for polynomial consistent learnability. We will see that only one of them (Theorem 1) is a good choice to give a new characterization. The proof of Theorem 9 is the same as it is for the non-complexity counterpart.

Theorem 9. $U \in Poly\text{-}\Phi\text{-}CONS \iff$
$$\exists \psi \in \mathcal{P}^2 : U\text{-consistency is } \Phi\text{-polynomial in } \psi \text{ decidable} \iff$$
$$\exists \psi, g \in \mathcal{P}^2, p \in Poly_\Phi : (a) \ U \subseteq \mathcal{P}_\psi$$
$$(b) \ \forall f \in U, \forall i, n \in \mathbf{N} : \Phi_g(f^n, i) \leq p(f^n, i) \wedge$$
$$[g(f^n, i) = 1 \iff f^n \subseteq \psi_i]$$

Nevertheless, the other characterization (Theorem 2) gave us a sufficient condition to test polynomial consistent learnability.

Theorem 10. $U \in Poly\text{-}\Phi\text{-}CONS \Rightarrow$
$$\exists \psi \in \mathcal{P}^2, \exists g \in Poly^\Phi : (a) \ U \in \mathcal{P}_\psi$$
$$(b) \ \forall i, j, n \in \mathbf{N} : [g(i, j, n) = 1 \iff \psi_i =_n \psi_j]$$

Proof. Choose $U \subseteq \mathcal{R}, p \in Poly, \psi \in \mathcal{P}^2$, and $S \in \mathcal{P}$, such that $U \in p\text{-}\Phi\text{-}CONS_\psi(S)$. To prove Theorem 10 we need some auxiliary functions:

$ct: ct(\alpha, S) = 1 \iff \alpha \subseteq \psi_{S(\alpha)}$
For arbitrary $\alpha \in \mathbf{N}^*$ and strategies $S \in \mathcal{P}$, ct computes the hypothesis $S(\alpha)$ and, if defined, tests consistency. ct is undefined if either $S(\alpha)$ or $\psi_{S(\alpha)}$ is undefined for some $x \leq length(\alpha)$.

$\lambda: \lambda(n, \alpha, S) = max\{k | \sum_{i=0}^{k} \Phi_{ct}(\alpha^i, S) \leq n\}$
λ computes for n steps the results of $S(\alpha^0), S(\alpha^1), \ldots, S(\alpha)$, and outputs the maximal length of α, for which S computes a consistent hypothesis. Note, that $\lambda(n, \alpha, S)$ does not need more than n Φ-resources.

$conv: conv(\alpha, S) = min\{n | S(\alpha^n) = S(\alpha^{n+1}) = \ldots = S(\alpha) = i\}$
$conv$ is the (temporary) point of convergence for strategy S on input α.

$conv^*: conv^*(n, \alpha, S) = conv(\alpha^{\lambda(n, \alpha, S)}, S)$
$conv^*$ searches the (temporary) point of convergence for strategy S on inputs $\alpha^0, \alpha^1, \ldots, \alpha^{\lambda(n, \alpha, S)}$. It is easy to see that not much more than n Φ-resources are needed to do so.

Now we are ready to define a new numbering ψ'. For arbitrary j choose $\alpha \in \mathbf{N}^*, i, n \in \mathbf{N}$ such that $j = d(\alpha, d(i, n))$, and define:

$$\psi'_j(x) = \begin{cases} \alpha(x) & \text{if } x \leq conv^*(n, \alpha, S) \\ \psi_i(x) & \text{if } x > conv^*(n, \alpha, S) \wedge i = S(\psi'^{x-1}_j) = S(\psi^x_i) \\ \uparrow & \text{otherwise} \end{cases}$$

$\psi' \in \mathcal{P}^2$ and $U \subseteq \mathcal{P}_\psi$ is easy to see, if we know that for all $x \leq conv^*(n, \alpha, S)$, $\alpha^x \subseteq \psi'_j$ holds, and $\psi'_j \in \mathcal{R}$ if and only if $\psi'_j = \psi_i$.

We define the test g as follows: For arbitrary i', j', k, choose the other variables, such that $i' = d(\alpha, i, n), j' = d(\beta, j, m), l = conv^*(n, \alpha, S), l' = conv^*(m, \beta, S)$. Wlog assume $l \leq l'$.

$$g(i', j', k) = 1 \iff \begin{cases} k \leq l \wedge \quad \alpha^k = \beta^k \\ \text{or} \\ l < k \leq l' \wedge \alpha^l \subseteq \beta \wedge S(\beta^l) = \ldots = S(\beta^k) = i \\ \text{or} \\ l' < k \wedge \quad \alpha^l \subseteq \beta \wedge S(\beta^l) = \ldots = S(\beta^{l'}) = i \end{cases}$$

Note, that using $k = l'$, we even can test equivalence for all functions in ψ'.

Remember the notes we made while defining ct, λ and $conv^*$, to see that g is in Poly^Φ. Moreover, we can give an upper bound for Φ_g without taking the third argument into account.

The last thing is to prove: $p(i', j', k) = 1 \iff \psi'_{i'} =_k \psi'_{j'}$. It is useful do name the first, second and third condition in the definition of g, $^{(*)}, ^{(**)}$, and $^{(***)}$ respectively. We distinguish several cases: First we assume $p(i', j', k) = 1$

- Suppose $^{(*)}$ holds. Then, by definition of ψ', $\psi'_{i'} =_k \psi'_{j'}$.
- Suppose $^{(**)}$ holds. Then for all x, such that $l \leq x \leq k : S(\beta^x) = i$ and $\beta^x \subseteq \psi_i$. But then $\beta^k \subseteq \psi'_{i'}$ must hold, and therefore $\psi'_{i'} =_k \psi'_{j'}$.
- Suppose $^{(***)}$ holds. Then $S(\alpha^l) = i = S(\beta^l) = \ldots = S(\beta^{l'}) = j$ and $\beta^{l'} \subseteq \psi'_{i'}$. With a look at the definition of ψ', we can see that in this case $\psi_{i'} = \psi_{j'}$ and so $\psi'_{i'} =_k \psi'_{j'}$ also holds.

For the rest we assume $p(i', j', k) = 0$

- Suppose $k \leq l$ and $\alpha^k \neq \beta^k$. Then by definition of ψ, $\psi'_{i'} \neq_k \psi'_{j'}$.
- Suppose $l < k$ and $\alpha^l \not\subseteq \beta$. Then again by definition of ψ, $\psi'_{i'} \neq_k \psi'_{j'}$.
- Suppose $l < k \leq l'$ and $\alpha^l \subseteq \beta$ and there is an x between l and k such that $S(\beta^x) \neq i$. Choose x to be minimal, than $\psi'_{i'} =_{x-1} \psi'_{j'}$. If $y = \beta(x)$, than $\psi'_{i'}(x) \neq y$, since $S(\beta^x) = S(\psi')_{i'}^{x-1}y) \neq i$. It follows that $\psi'_{i'} \neq_k \psi'_{j'}$.
- The case when $l' < k$, $\alpha^l \subseteq \beta$ and there is an x between l and l' such that $S(\beta^x) \neq i$, is similar to the last case.

The above list of cases is complete and proves $p(i', j', k) = 1 \iff \psi'_{i'} =_k \psi'_{j'}$.

♮

Note that Theorem 10 is only sufficient but not necessary, that is:

Theorem 11. *There are $U \in NUM \setminus \text{Poly-}\Phi\text{-CONS}, \psi \in P^2$, and $g \in \text{Poly}_\Phi$, such that $U \subseteq P_\psi$ and for all $i, j, n \in \mathbf{N}: g(i, j, n) = 1 \iff \psi_i =_n \psi_j$.*

Proof. Choose an arbitrary $f \notin \text{Poly}_\Phi$. Let $U = \{h | \exists \alpha \in \mathbf{N}^* : [h = \alpha 0^\infty]\}$. We already proved that $U \not\subseteq \text{Poly-}\Phi\text{-CONS}$. It is left to show the existence of a numbering ψ such that for all $i, j, n \in \mathbf{N}$, $\psi_i =_n \psi_j$ is decidable. For any $k \in \mathbf{N}$ and $\alpha \in \mathbf{N}^*$ compute f until m Φ-resources are used. Suppose we can compute

f^h. Now, if $f^h \subseteq \alpha 0^\infty$, define $\psi_{d(\alpha,m)} = f$. In the other case $\psi_{d(\alpha,m)}$ is set to $\alpha 0^\infty$. In other words: $\psi_{d(\alpha,m)}$ equals $\alpha 0^\infty$ if and only if after computing the graph of f for less than m Φ-resources, no difference between f and α^∞ can be found.

We have to show two things: First $U \subseteq \mathcal{P}_\psi$ and second $\psi_i =_n \psi_j$ polynomial decidable.

First note, that for all $\alpha \in \mathbf{N}^*$, $f \neq \alpha 0^\infty$ holds. Now fixing $\alpha \in \mathbf{N}^*$, we can find $h \in \mathbf{N}$ such that $f^h \not\subseteq \alpha 0^\infty$. Suppose f^h can be computed with less then m Φ resources, then $\psi_{d(\alpha,m)} = \alpha 0^\infty$. On the other hand we can easily verify that $\psi_{d(\alpha,0)} = f$. An easy proof of $\psi_i =_n \psi_j$, for arbitrary $i,j,n \in \mathbf{N}^*$ is the following: Let $i = d(\alpha,m)$ and $j = d(\beta,k)$. First try to find whether $\psi_i = f$ or $\psi_i = \alpha 0^\infty$ holds, and do the same for ψ_j. This can be done polynomial in i and j.

- If both ψ_i and ψ_j equal f then of course $\psi_i =_n \psi_j$ for all n.
- If $\psi_i = \alpha 0^\infty$ and $\psi_j = \beta 0^\infty$, then $\psi_i =_n \psi_j$ can be tested via α and β.
- If (wlog) $\psi_i = f$ and $\psi_j = \beta 0^\infty$, then by definition of ψ_j we know that we can find a difference between f and $\beta 0^\infty$ using less then k Φ-resources. Say h is the smallest number such that $f^h \not\subseteq \beta 0^\infty$. Then $\psi_i =_n \psi_j \iff n < h$.

All cases can be verified polynomial in i and j. ♮

Last, but not least, we will insert Poly-Φ-CONS in the well known hierarchy of learning classes.

Theorem 12. *FIN $\subset$ Poly-Φ-CONS $\subset$ CONS*

5 Conclusions

As we have seen, a natural formal definition that captures the notion of polynomial efficient inference is not at all straightforward. We proved that consistency is a natural condition having a narrowing effect for polynomial update boundaries. At this point we will outline, that conform strategies (hypothesis must be consistent or can be undefined on the graph seen so far) as well as some definitions for monoton strategies have the same effect. It is an **open problem** to find a general condition that satisfies this narrowing effect for polynomial efficiency.

The update inference complexity is based on the general approach of Blum's computational complexities and thus covers a huge set of different specific complexities. Theorem 6 and 8 extend and strengthen well known results about the update-time and update-space of consistent strategies. Corollary 6 encourages programmers not only to look for consistent learning strategies, but also to involve inconsistent ones, since this can save arbitrary resources. Moreover Theorem 9 is an exact characterization for polynomial consistent learnability, giving a deep view inside the problem of resource bounded consistent learnability.

We were not able to take over Corollary 2 for arbitrary Blum complexity measures and it is **still open** if there are arbitrary Φ-hard consistent learnable sets. The last Theorem (12) joins complexity and non-complexity learning theoretic problems.

References

[Bar74]   J. Barzdin. Inductive inference of automata, functions and programs. In *Proceedings International Congress of Math.*, pages 455–460, Vancouver, 1974.

[BDGW94] Balcazar, Diaz, Gavalda, and Watanabe. The query complexity of learning DFA. *NEWGEN: New Generation Computing*, 12, 1994.

[Blu67]   M. Blum. A machine-independent theory of the complexity of recursive functions. In *Journal of Association for Computing Machinery*, volume 11, pages 322–336, April 1967.

[DS86]   R. P. Daley and C. H. Smith. On the complexity of inductive inference. In *Information and Control*, volume 69, pages 12–30, March 1986.

[FKS93]   R. Freivalds, E. Kinber, and C.H. Smith. On the impact of forgetting on learning machines. Computer Science Technical Report Series CS-TR-3072, University of Maryland, College Park, MD, 20742, May 1993.

[FKS95]   Rūsiņš Freivalds, Efim B. Kinber, and Carl H. Smith. On the intrinsic complexity of learning. *Information and Computation*, 123(1):64–71, 15 November 1995.

[Fla94]   Michele Flammini. On the learnability of monotone $k\mu$-DNF formulae. *Information Processing Letters*, 52(3):167–173, 11 November 1994.

[Gol65]   M. E. Gold. Limiting recursion. In *Journal of Symbolic Logic*, volume 30, pages 28–48, March 1965.

[Ish90]   H. Ishizaka. Polynomial time learnability of simple deterministic languages. *Machine Learning*, 5(2):151–164, 1990. Special Issue on Computational Learning Theory; first appeared in 2nd COLT conference (1989).

[JB84]   K.P. Jantke and H.-R. Beick. Combining postulates of naturalness in inductive inference. In *Elektronische Informationsverarbeitung und Kybernetik*, volume 17, pages 465–484, 1984.

[JS95]   S. Jain and A. Sharma. The structure of intrinsic complexity of learning. *Lecture Notes in Computer Science*, 904, 1995.

[Kin94]   E. Kinber. Monotonicity versus efficiency for learning languages from texts. *Lecture Notes in Computer Science*, 872, 1994.

[LW91]   S. Lange and R. Wiehagen. Polynomial-time inference of arbitrary pattern languages. In *New Generation Computing*, volume 8, pages 361–370, 1991.

[LZ95]   S. Lange and T. Zeugmann. Trading monotonicity demands versus efficiency. *Bulletin of Informatics and Cybernetics*, 27:53–83, 1995.

[Pit89]   L. Pitt. Inductive inference, DFAs and computational complexity. In *Proceedings of the Workshop Analogical and Inductive Inference*, volume 397 of *LNAI*, pages 18–44, 1989.

[PW90]   L. Pitt and M. K. Warmuth. Prediction preserving reducibility. *J. of Comput. Syst. Sci.*, 41(3):430–467, December 1990. Special issue of the for the *Third Annual Conference of Structure in Complexity Theory* (Washington, DC., June 88).

[Sol64]   R. Solomonoff. A formal theory of inductive inference. In *Information and Control*, volume 7, pages 1–22, 234–254, 1964.

[Val84]   L.G. Valiant. A theory of the learnable. In *Comm. Assoc. Comp. Math.*, volume 27(11), pages 1134–1142, 1984.

[Wat94]   Osamu Watanabe. A framework for polynomial-time query learnability. *Mathematical Systems Theory*, 27(3):211–229, May/June 1994.

438

[WL76]   R. Wiehagen and W. Liepe.   Charakteristische Eigenschaften von erkennbaren Klassen rekursiver Funktionen. In *Elektronische Informationsverarbeitung und Kybernetik*, volume 12, pages 421–436, 1976.

[WZ92]   R. Wiehagen and T. Zeugmann. Too much information can be too much for learning efficiently. In *3.rd Int. Workshop on Analogical and Inductive Inference*, volume 642 of *Lecture Notes in Artificial Intelligence*, pages 72–86, 1992.

[WZ94]   R. Wiehagen and T. Zeugamnn. Ignoring data may be the only way to learn efficiently. In *Journal of Experimental and Theoretic Artifical Intelligence*, volume 6, pages 131–144, 1994.

Author Index

Springer
and the
environment

At Springer we firmly believe that an
international science publisher has a
special obligation to the environment,
and our corporate policies consistently
reflect this conviction.
We also expect our business partners –
paper mills, printers, packaging
manufacturers, etc. – to commit
themselves to using materials and
production processes that do not harm
the environment. The paper in this
book is made from low- or no-chlorine
pulp and is acid free, in conformance
with international standards for paper
permanency.

Springer

Lecture Notes in Artificial Intelligence (LNAI)

Lecture Notes in Computer Science